THE RICH AND POOR ARE *BOTH* BEING VICTIMIZED BY THE PROBLEM OF WORLD HUNGER!

THE SOLUTION TO THE PROBLEM WOULD MAKE ALLIES OF ALL THE HUNGRY MULTITUDES WE HAVE LEARNED TO FEAR!

THE SOLUTION IS AT HAND—IF WE HAVE THE COURAGE AND WISDOM TO USE IT!

"Full of intriguing perceptions . . . lively and easy to read . . . THE CONTROVERSY IT WILL SET OFF CAN ONLY BE VALUABLE."   —*New York Times Book Review*

"A CLEAR-HEADED EXPLANATION OF A COMPLEX AND IMPORTANT SUBJECT."   —*Los Angeles Times*

"A lucid and comprehensive account of a much-neglected problem. It not only illuminates the agricultural aspects of the situation, but also the political, social and economic factors . . . AN EXCELLENT ANALYSIS OF WHY STARVATION EXISTS IN THE WORLD." —*Colorado Sun*

FOOD FIRST
Beyond the Myth of Scarcity

Also by Frances Moore Lappé
Published by Ballantine Books:

DIET FOR A SMALL PLANET

FOOD FIRST

Beyond the Myth of Scarcity

**Frances Moore Lappé and Joseph Collins
with Cary Fowler**

Revised & Updated

BALLANTINE BOOKS • NEW YORK

Library of Congress Catalog Card Number: 77-3733

ISBN 0-345-25150-4

This edition published by arrangement with
Houghton Mifflin Company

Manufactured in the United States of America

First Ballantine Books Edition: September 1979

Acknowledgments

DURING THE YEARS devoted to this book, one of our greatest satisfactions has been the discovery of a diverse network of people throughout the world, working hard on these difficult problems and willing to share their information and insights. We thank all of them. The very existence of this growing network is significant: It suggests that for more and more people the paradox of hunger in a world of plenty is catalyzing both deeper probing and a greater commitment to action.

We especially wish to thank three people whose contribution was so varied that it is impossible to detail but so invaluable that the book would have been impossible without them—Deborah Hepworth, Sue Kanor, and Judy Warneck.

The book benefited greatly from the research assistance of Henry Frundt, Robert Olorenshaw, David Kinley, Erica Byrd, Connie Phillips, Clark Fisher, Sandra Callier, Peter Mann, and Tonia Heinrichs.

We are grateful to Kathe Flinker, Ann Nicols-Jones, Irene Rusnak, and Sonia Senkiwsky, who helped organize a library of thousands of documents from around the world on which this book draws. We are also grateful for the secretarial assistance of Jo Ann Isaacs, Ellen McAvoy, Jan Martin, Ina Moore, and Diane Spatz.

We also appreciate the help of Ruth Bua, John Callahan, Irene Fleming, Irene Gifford, Joan and Doreen Pietropaulo and Paul and Jeanette Lappé, who lovingly cared for Frances's children, Anthony and Anna, while this book was in progress.

We want to acknowledge those whose work we

found especially useful and whose advice we valued
highly—Keith Abercrombie, Peter Adamson, Cynthia
Hewitt de Alcántara, Silvio Almeida, George Anthan,
Gonzalo Arroyo, Jun Atienza, George Baker, Solon
Barraclough, David Baytleman, Fred Beck, Joe Bel-
den, Alan Berg, Thierry Brun, Roger Burbach, The
Center for Rural Affairs, Jacques Chonchol, Harry
Cleaver, Robert Cohen, Barry Commoner, Kim Con-
roy, Kenneth Dahlberg, Susan DeMarco, Erik Eck-
holm, Richard Edwards, Richard Elsner, Ron Erickson,
M. Taghi Farvar, Ernest Feder, Pat Flynn, Gil Friend,
Isao Fujimoto, Johan Galtung, Susan George, Richard
Gilmore, Ole Gjerstad, Harris Gleckman, Jerry Gold-
stein, Marcel Ganzin, Keith Griffin, Ross Hall, Merle
Hansen, Jim Hightower, Anne-Marie Holenstein, An-
gus Hone, Michael Jacobson, Erich Jacoby, Brennon
Jones, Jacques Kozub, Al Krebs, Ken Laidlaw, Robert
Ledogar, Al Levinson, Cassio Luiselli, Arthur Mac-
Ewan, James McQuigg, Larry Minear, David Morris,
Ingrid Palmer, Cheryl Payer, Andrew Pearse, Marco
Quiñones, Christopher Robbins, Clodomir Santos de
Morais, Susan Sechler, David Stohlberg, Colin Tudge,
Liszt Aragon Vieira, Peter de Vries, Jean-Marc von de
Weid, H. Garrison Wilkes, and Ben Wisner.

We want to express here our gratitude to all those
who read all or part of the rough drafts, offering help-
ful comment—Ann Barnet, Richard Barnet, Erna Ben-
nett, Richard Berliner, Roger Blobaum, Stephen
Bossi, Michael Carder, Arthur Domike, Marion Gallis,
Michael Gertler, Grace Goodell, Michael Henry, Marc
Lappé, William Luttrell, Maureen MacKintosh, Harry
Magdoff, Ali Manwar, Leah Margulies, John Moore,
Fatemah Moyhadam, Vahid Nowshirvani, Ted Owens,
Pascal de Pury, Marcus Raskin, Idrian Resnick, Mark
Ritchie, Plinio Sampaio, Paul Sweezy in addition to
many of those previously mentioned.

There are many whose general support and encour-
agement have been valuable to one or both of us—
Eqbal Ahmad, Angus Archer, Sherry Barnes, Victoria
Bawtree, Clifflyn Bromling, Diana Calafati, Dick
Clark, William Sloane Coffin, Bettina Connor, Rusty
Davenport, John Dillon, Frank Dobyns, Norman Fara-

melli, Edmundo Flores, Ramon Garcia, Nathan Gray, Ted Greiner, Joan Gussow, Steve Hayes, Jack Healey, B. Henderson, Nick Herman, Fred Just, Rich Killmer, Arthur Lincoln, Michael Locker, Ellen McAvoy, Brian MacCall, Julie Marshall, Eleanor McCallie, Mike McCoy, Dan McCurry, Michael Moffitt, Bill Moyer, Charles Paolillo, Elliott Postol, Jim Ridgeway, Doug Ross, Emma Rothschild, Jacobo Schatan, Nevin Scrimshaw, Jay Steptoe, Milo Thornberry, Erica Thorne, Mark Vermillion, Stanley Weiss, Edie Wilson, and Debbie Wright.

We want to take this opportunity to thank our friends at World Hunger Year—Bill Ayres, Jeri Barr, Rory Bedell, Harry Chapin, Lyn Dobrin, Diane Feyler, and Wray MacKay.

We are grateful to Harry Chapin, Samuel Rubin (through the Transnational Institute), and Stanley Weiss for their much-needed financial assistance for parts of this project.

We want to thank Joan Raines, our literary agent, and Ronald Busch and George Walsh at Ballantine Books for their unwavering faith in this project and Robert Cowley at Houghton Mifflin for his supportive editorial contributions with the assistance of Dale Conway and Mandira Sen.

Finally, our thanks to Frances's brother, John Moore, Jr., for hitting upon *Food First* as just the right name for our book.

Acknowledgments for the Revised Edition

OUR FIRST THANKS must go to our associates here at the Institute—to David Kinley who contributed valuable research assistance, and to Adele Beccar-Varela, Toby Stewart, Rodney Freeland, Robert Gabriner, Terry McClain, and Bruce Johnson. Their contributions have been manifold and are deeply appreciated. In addition, we wish to thank Wendy Tanowitz and Patty Neel for their assistance. The revised edition, just as was the first edition, is truly the product of a dedicated team.

In addition, the revised edition especially benefits from the work of Charles Avila, Lasse and Lisa Berg, James Boyce, Steve Commins, Richard Franke, Jo Froman, Robert Gersony, Kathleen Gough, Guy Gran, Betsy Hartmann, Tony Jackson, Grace and William Liu, Mitch Meisner, Jim Newcomer, Bill Shurtleff, Yash Tandon, and Henry Weinstein.

The revised edition could not have gone forward without the financial support of funders who, like us, see the critical nature of the issues we discuss in this book. For the support of this and all the projects of the Institute, we are grateful to the Samuel Rubin Foundation, Stern Fund, United Presbyterian Church USA, Church of the Brethren, Jesuit Council for Theological Reflection, Tides Foundation, Episcopal Church USA, and First United Church of Oak Park, Illinois.

Contents

Introduction to the Revised Edition   xv

Why This Book?   3

Part I
THE SCARCITY SCARE

1. Too Many People?   13
2. But What About the Real "Basketcases"?   17
3. Are People a Liability or a Resource?   24
4. Does Ignorance Breed Babies?   30
5. Sophisticated Fatalism?   33
6. Controlling Births or Controlling the Population?   36
7. Population Pressure on the Environment?   40
8. The Price Scare?   54
9. The Food vs. Poison Trade-off?   59

Part II
BLAMING NATURE

10. Haven't There Always Been Famines?   79
11. Can We Hold Back the Desert?   84

Part III
COLONIAL INHERITANCE

12. Why Can't People Feed Themselves?   99
13. Isn't Colonialism Dead?   112

xi

Part IV
MODERNIZING HUNGER

14. Shouldn't Production Be the Priority?   121
15. But Isn't Nature Neutral?   129
16. Hasn't the Green Revolution "Bought
    us Time"?   134
17. Wasn't the Green Revolution a Vital
    Scientific Breakthrough?   148
18. Hasn't the Green Revolution Strengthened
    Food Security?   154
19. Where Has All the Production Gone?   165
20. Don't They Need Our Machines?   168

Part V
THE INEFFICIENCY OF INEQUALITY

21. Isn't the Backwardness of Small Farmers
    to Blame?   183
22. Why Don't Small Farmers Produce More?   185
23. Isn't Bigger Better?   188
24. Is Small Always Beautiful?   195
25. But Hasn't Land Reform Sacrificed
    Production?   196

Part VI
THE TRADE TRAP

26. What About Their Natural Advantage?   209
27. Don't They Have Cartels Now?   216
28. Doesn't Export Income Help the Hungry?   220
29. If It's So Bad, Why Does It Continue?   225
30. Is Export Agriculture the Enemy?   229

Part VII
THE MYTH OF FOOD POWER

31. Don't They Need Our Food? 237
32. Food Power to Save the Economy? 239
33. At Least Food Power Works? 250
34. Who Gains and Who Loses? 255

Part VIII
WORLD HUNGER AS BIG BUSINESS

35. Don't They Need American Corporate Know-How? 277
36. Still, Don't the People Benefit? 299
37. Better Than Beans and Rice? 320
38. Do They Really Kill Babies? 336
39. Agribusiness Abroad: A Boon for Americans? 348

Part IX
THE HELPING HANDOUT: AID FOR WHOM?

40. Triage? 359
41. Debt for Development? 361
42. Doesn't Our Food Aid Help? 363
43. What About the World Bank's "Assault on Poverty"? 388
44. And AID's New Directions? 412
45. Can Voluntary Aid Agencies Help? 444

Part X
FOOD SELF-RELIANCE

46. What is Food Self-Reliance? 457
47. But Where Would Funds for Development Come from? 476

48. Aren't Poor Peasants Too Oppressed Ever
    to Change?   485

49. Food Versus Freedom?   488

50. What Can We Do?   491

Appendix A.   Organizing for Change   505

              Action Groups and Their
              Publications by Issue   506

Appendix B.   Recommended Books, Periodicals,
              and Films   514

Notes   525

Index   581

Introduction to the Revised Edition

THIS BALLANTINE EDITION of *Food First* is being published over three years after we finished the manuscript for the hardcover edition. During the intervening time at the Institute for Food and Development Policy we have continued to study, investigate, travel abroad, write and speak—often with people throughout the world, many of whom have vast experience in the problems we write about in *Food First*.

As we had expected and hoped, our book has stirred controversy. In debating the issues, we feel our grasp of the problems has become ever firmer. We have also come to see why some of our ideas have been misunderstood or misconstrued by some.

Our phrase "Food First" has been reduced at times to mean that the pat solution to hunger is simply to replace luxury export crops with local food crops. Export agriculture is said to be *the* enemy. In this edition, we counter this misrepresentation in several ways. In Question 1, we now introduce the book by pointing to the ways in which inequality in control over productive resources is the primary constraint—both on food production and on equitable distribution. Thus, until the question of who controls the production process is confronted, no shift from one crop to another, even to a nutritious food, will solve the problem of hunger.

Moreover, we have excerpted and developed some critical material subsumed in other chapters in order to create a new part, titled "The Inefficiency of Inequality" (Part V). Here we explore in some depth the constraints on production built into anti-democratic structures that we mention in our response to

Question 1. In this new Part V we also have added an entirely new question (25), in which we address the impact of land reform on agricultural output.

A closely related misreading of our book concerns trade. Is *Food First* advocating autarky and isolationism? In a word, no. We explicitly summarize our position in Question 30, "Is Export Agriculture the Enemy?" Moreover, in Question 46 we contrast trade from a self-reliant base with the vulnerability resulting when survival desperately depends on trade.

In this edition, the positive guidelines for food self-reliance called "Food First Fundamentals" are more fully developed. Again in Question 46 we devote more space to reflecting on the rich historical experience that indicates the elements necessary to create food security for all.

Furthermore, a principal benefit of returning to the book after two years is that our own field investigations and communications with others working here and in the Third World have provided us with a clearer understanding and more concrete cases with which to analyze the role of development aid and powerful institutions, such as the World Bank and A.I.D., the United States Agency for International Development. Questions 42 through 45 in this edition include some of what we have been learning. Besides adding such clarifications and fresh material, this new edition affords the opportunity to update information where pertinent.

Finally, since we hope our book will awaken in many readers a desire toward deeper involvement, we have labored over the "What Can We Do?" chapter with which the book concludes. In addition, Appendix A provides, we hope, a yet more useful presentation of the many action groups working in this country and Canada on these issues. Through these groups, many are learning that their lives can have new meaning and greater purpose as they ever more consciously and concretely confront our society's deepest problems.

We hope that this revised edition also will elicit comment, criticism, and controversy. Only then will this book be of service to all of us—honing our critical awareness and igniting our passion to confront the arduous task of constructing forms of social organization capable of ending hunger and deprivation.

Frances Moore Lappé
Joseph Collins
Institute for Food and Development Policy
San Francisco, 1978

Why This Book?

WRITING A POSITIVE BOOK about world hunger sounds to most people like trying to make a joke about death —it just isn't in the material! This attitude comes home to us every time we are introduced to someone and attempt to describe what we are doing. A typical response is a sigh of sympathy overlaid with a look of bewilderment: "Why would any normal person choose to think all day and every day about starving people?" Sometimes we sense latent feelings of guilt because we inevitably appear as individuals who are "making a sacrifice."

We, too, feel uncomfortable. How can we explain in a few sentences that we are not dwelling only on the tragedy of hunger and deprivation? Instead, we are learning for the first time where our own self-interest lies. Rather than being a depressing subject to be avoided, the world food problem has become for us the most useful tool in making sense out of our complex world. But how can we explain that in a few sentences? We cannot—and that is why we decided to write a book.

To discover the positive message hidden in the apparent "hopelessness" of the world food problem we must first face the forces now pushing Americans into positions of guilt, fear, and ultimate despair. Given the threatening way that the global food problem is interpreted for us, is it surprising that most of us wish to shut it out most of the time? Everywhere newspaper headlines carry a clear message:

POPULATION BOMB AND FOOD SHORTAGE: WORLD LOSING FIGHT FOR VITAL BALANCE

New York Times, August 14, 1974

3

WORLD FOOD CRISIS: BASIC WAYS OF LIFE FACE UP-
HEAVAL FROM CHRONIC SHORTAGES
New York Times, November 5, 1974

We are all in a life-and-death contest, we are told,
between growing numbers of people and limited
amounts of food. We are in a race and some must
inevitably lose. The implicit message is that not everyone will have enough to eat. And how will we come
out? According to C. W. Cook, retired chairman of
General Foods, if we have "to compete with . . . an
increasingly crowded and hungry world, providing
adequate nutrition to millions of lower-income Americans could become an impossible dream." In *This
Hungry World,* Ray Vicker warns: "If food shortages
lead to starvation in Asia, Latin America or Africa,
we may be affected directly too in inflation, in disease,
in shortages and in forced changes in our American
way of life."

Since there are *already* so many hungry people in
the world, many think it obvious that even now we
do not have sufficient food to go around. "Malthus
has already been proved correct," declares the president of the Rockefeller Foundation, Dr. John Knowles.
Another officer of the Rockefeller Foundation has
likened the growth of the world's population to our
most dreaded disease, cancer. Population growth was
pronounced a "bomb" in the 1960s and a "human
tidal wave" in the 1970s.

It is not, however, mere numbers that we are made
to fear by these frightening images; the real issue we
are supposed to take to heart is that of *whose* numbers are increasing. While describing the "race against
hunger," President Nixon told us that "the frightening fact is that the poor are multiplying twice as fast
as the rich."

Some writers threaten complete "catastrophe." They
refer not just to starvation but to the amorphous specter of the submersion of our "civilized values" and
the emergence of "thousands of desperadoes for every
one now terrorizing the rich today." Thus not only
our diet appears to be at stake, but the very fabric

of our civilization is threatened by the hungry seeking our food.

To this dual threat our new, and potentially valuable, environmental awareness adds its own version of the apocalypse. Lester Brown warns that "new signs of agricultural stress on the earth's ecosystem appear almost daily as the exponentially rising food demand, fueled by population growth and rising incomes, presses the ecosystem's finite capacities. . . . There is no way to calculate the trade-off between increases in population and improvements in the quality of life —a choice we must now make as we press against the finite limits of our ecosystem." Such warnings lead people to believe that increases in food production will necessarily damage the environment and thereby threaten our future food supply. We are made to fear that there is no way out of scarcity without making our children pay the price.

These threats are sometimes accompanied by a more subtle but just as pervasive message. Americans, we are told, have a special role to play in staving off the apocalypse. We are made to feel that world hunger is our cross to bear. Again and again we read and we hear that the United States is the world's only remaining buffer against starvation. We see world food security defined strictly in terms of how much grain the United States can produce or hold as grain reserves. Inevitably the American consumer believes that food exports to the hungry are to blame for our rising food prices.

One intuitive response to such a burden on our national shoulders is to toughen up, to feel we are being unfairly put upon, to resist. "The United States is not under any moral obligation to feed the world. . . . The responsibility of America's leadership is to America's people," declared Anthony Harrigan of the United States Industrial Council.

Such a reaction to the frightening story of scarcity would be typical of even more Americans, if it were not for an equally deceptive and ultimately negative message pulling us in the opposite direction. Well-intended attempts to stir public action have shifted the world food crisis out of the political-economic arena onto the ground of individual morality. Our consumption is tirelessly contrasted with deprivation elsewhere; the message being that *our* consumption causes *their* suffering. We are told, for example, that the amount of fertilizer used on our lawns, golf courses, and cemeteries equals all of what India uses to grow food. We inevitably experience some shame, feeling our wastefulness must reflect a moral failing. Some find protection by pointing out, quite rightly, that eating one less hamburger a week will not mean that the grain saved will necessarily get to a hungry mouth.

With no understanding of how hunger is actually created, we are defenseless against a diffuse but powerful sense of guilt—guilt for just being American. The hungry are made into a powerful threat and, at the same time, a burdensome responsibility. We are torn.

To resolve our conflict, one appealing answer has emerged: "lifeboat ethics"—the simple notion, popularized by scientist Garrett Hardin, that the earth now constitutes a lifeboat in which there is not enough food to go around. Isn't it then only logical that food should go to those most likely to survive, that you do not risk the safety of all by bringing new passengers on board? "What happens if you share space in a lifeboat?" asks Dr. Hardin. "The boat is swamped, and everyone drowns. Complete justice, complete catastrophe."

The remedy offered to ease the pain of our conflict is simple: *Stop feeling.* We are told that the Judeo-Christian ethic is outmoded in this new era of scarcity; that compassion is a luxury we can no longer afford. A letter from a sociologist in *Science* magazine (March 21, 1975) tells us that our Judeo-Christian do-gooderism is the true root of the world's present predicament. "We Westerners brought it on ourselves, by saving lives through medical skill and humanitarian generosity. . . . The millions of lives saved by our medical help became the hundreds of millions of lives that are due to be lost in famines. . . ." In the same issue a letter from a group of scientists continues in a similar vein: "The time is now to stop responding emotionally to what all evidence indicates is an impending disaster. The Judeo-Christian ethic cannot offer long-term solutions." We are told we must learn a *new ethic,* the ethic of detached reason; we must learn to let people die for the ultimate survival of the human race.

Such voices do offer one resolution of our conflicting feelings. In the words of writer Peter Collier, they offer us "novocaine for the uneasy soul." But must we take the novocaine? Do we have to deaden our sensibilities in order to find some surcease for our anxieties? Or can we transform what appears to be the most impossible problem of our generation—the world food crisis—into the most useful and constructive tool for understanding the complex forces that limit our own lives? Can we, moreover, on the strength of that new insight, gain a sense of personal power over those forces—forces that increasingly diminish our own freedom of choice and our own well-being?

Why *Food First?* We met each other on the first national Food Day in the spring of 1975 at Ann Arbor, Michigan. Frances had been invited as the author of *Diet for a Small Planet* and Joe because of his work on *Global Reach,* a book on multinational corporations, and his coauthorship of *World Hunger: Causes and Remedies,* a work countering establishment wisdom at the time of the 1974 World Food Conference. Following our talks, the students asked us the same urgent questions we each had been asked many times before, and we tried to answer them. Yes, we did have some answers. But we were not satisfied. So afterward we talked and talked. Finally, we concluded that together we would throw all our energy into a search for answers to all the toughest questions that we ourselves had ever asked or that we had ever been asked by others about the causes of hunger. We would then put those answers together in a way we could share with others.

As you read this book you will find that our title *Food First* takes on more than one meaning. Most fundamentally, it means that whether or not people are hungry appears to us as the primary test of a just and effective social and economic system. The security of any people has historically rested in meeting its own basic food needs. Thus every country should mobilize its own food resources to meet its own needs first. Only then can trade serve to expand choices rather than to deprive people of the benefits from the resources that are rightfully theirs.

As we studied, read, traveled, and interviewed, we found that the media-repeated themes of scarcity, guilt, and fear are all based on myths. We had to learn that in fact:

• *No country in the world is a hopeless "basket-case."*

There may indeed be *no* country lacking ample food-producing resources. But inequities in control over these resources thwart both food production and equitable distribution.

• *Food redistribution is not the solution to hunger.*

The solution lies rather in a redistribution of control over food-producing resources.

• *The hungry are not our enemies.*

It is not they who threaten our well-being. Rather we and they are victims of the same economic system, undercutting their food security as well as ours.

The task of Americans is clear. We need to build a movement—a movement that lays bare the truth that it is a single system, supported by governments, corporations, and landed elites, that is undermining food security both in our country and abroad. The forces in the Third World that cut people out of the production process, and therefore out of consumption, turn out to be the same forces that have converted our food system into one of the most tightly controlled sectors of our own economy. Ever fewer land operators and food companies control a larger and larger portion of our food. We wind up with increased and needless processing, exposure to dangerous chemicals, less nutrition, and consistently higher prices, resulting in hunger for some and malnourishment for many. In fighting the forces tightening their hold over our food economy, we are directly fighting some of the very forces that promote hunger in other countries.

Many have been misled to believe that if justice were made a priority, production would be sacrificed. We have come to learn that the opposite is true. The unjust monopoly of the land both by traditional landed elites and by agribusiness corporations has demonstrated that they are the most inefficient, unreliable, and destructive users of food-producing resources. Democratizing the control over food-producing resources is the only road to long-term agricultural productivity for others and for us.

The greatest reward of our work has been the discovery of realistic and liberating answers to *the* most urgent question: What can we do? To find an answer, we first had to grasp that hungry people can free themselves from hunger once they have overthrown the obstacles in their way. Indeed, wherever people now are not feeding themselves, you can be sure that powerful obstacles have been placed in their way. So now, instead of asking, "How can we feed the world?" we ask an entirely different question: "What are we doing, and what is being done in our name, with our tax money and by corporations based in our economy, to create those obstacles? How can we put ourselves on the side of the hungry struggling to remove them?"

The first step in putting Food First is demystifying the problem of hunger. Perhaps this is where our work can help most. We did not start out as experts. We began just as you might: We became interested. Hunger loomed as the greatest problem of our lifetime. What could be more compelling? As we learned more and more, read what the "experts" read, traveled through our own country and abroad, we found that the solution to world hunger is no mystery. It is not locked inside the germ plasm of a seed waiting for a brilliant young agricultural scientist to discover it. It is not spelled out in econometric studies of development planners. No. The real block to the solution to world hunger is the sense of powerlessness we are made to feel: that the enormity of

the problem is outside our control and that it should
be entrusted to others. In truth, however, the solution
to hunger is firmly in all of our hands.

As you read the questions and answers that follow,
please remember that many of these questions are, or
once were, our own. All are questions we have been
asked over and over again by concerned persons
everywhere.

Part I

The Scarcity Scare

1. Too Many People?

Question: Doesn't the fact that there are now at least 500 million undernourished and starving people prove that there isn't enough food or land for everyone to be adequately fed?

Our Response: To diagnose the cause of hunger as a scarcity of food and land is to blame nature for people-made problems. In doing the research for this book, we have learned that the earth's natural limits are not to blame. Hunger exists in the face of abundance; therein lies the outrage.

One way to demonstrate that land and food scarcity is not the true cause of hunger is to show that there is no scarcity of either. The second is to explain what really does cause hunger. In this book, we will seek to do both. But we will begin where this question begins: Haven't we run out of food and land?

Measured globally, there is enough food for everyone now. The world is producing each day two pounds of grain—more than 3000 calories and ample protein —for every man, woman and child on earth.[1] A third of this grain now goes to feed livestock. This 3000-calorie estimate, about what the average American consumes, does not include the many other nutritious foods people eat—beans, nuts, fruits, vegetables, root crops, and grass-fed meat. Thus, on a global scale, the idea that there is not enough food to go around simply does not hold up.

But global figures mean little, except to dispel the widespread notion that we have reached the earth's limits. What counts is whether adequate food-producing resources exist in countries where so many people go hungry. The resources *do* exist, we have found, but they are invariably underused or misused, creating hunger for many and surfeit for a few.

How can we measure this untapped potential? One way is to note the gaps between current production and possible production. According to United Nations Food and Agricultural Organization (FAO) less than 60 percent of the world's cultivable land is now being cropped.[2] In both Africa and South America less than 20 percent of the potentially arable land is cultivated.[3] Grain yields in the underdeveloped countries could more than double before reaching the average yields of the industrial countries. And there is no physical reason why production per acre in most underdeveloped countries could not *exceed* that of the industrial countries. In many underdeveloped countries, land presently harvested only once yearly could provide two or even more harvests.

Barriers to unleashing this productive capacity are, in most cases, not physical; rather, they are economic: Wherever there is unjust, undemocratic control over productive resources, their development is thwarted.

In most countries where people are hungry, large landholders control most of the land. A study of 83 countries showed that slightly more than 3 percent of all landholders, those with 114 acres or more, control a staggering 79 percent of all farmland.[4] But these large landholders are the *least* productive. Studies in seemingly diverse countries reveal that large landholders consistently harvest lower yields per acre than the smallest farmers, as we detail in a later response. Furthermore, many who hold large amounts of land for prestige or as an investment, not as a source of food, leave considerable acreage unplanted. A 1960 study of Colombia, for instance, found that the largest landholders, in control of 70 percent of the land, planted only 6 percent of their land.[5] Land monopolized by a few is inevitably underused. Moreover, the wealth produced is invariably not reinvested for rural development but drained off for conspicuous consumption and for investment in industries catering to the fancies of urban and foreign well-to-do.

In addition, low productivity results from economic and social injustices that obstruct agricultural improvements by small, poor farmers. The larger, more influential landholders monopolize access to extension services, markets, and, perhaps most critically, non-usurious credit (moneylenders commonly charge the poor 50-200 percent interest). With no individual or shared ownership of the land, how can tenants, sharecroppers, and landless laborers either be motivated or have the wherewithal to conserve and improve the land for better crops? They realize any improvement will overwhelmingly go to advance the landowners, not themselves.

Finally, cooperation is the most essential ingredient of development. We discuss this point, with examples from Bangladesh, in our next response. To build and maintain irrigation and drainage systems, for instance, it is essential that everyone in a village work *together* in order to be effective. The same is true for controlling pests. But cooperation is unlikely where there is such grossly unequal ownership of the land and other productive resources. Large landholders do not want their poor neighbors to progress; then the poor might become less exploitable by them. And poor peasant families are likely to feel they must compete against each other for survival.

In measuring the untapped potential of the earth to nourish those who now are hungry, we should assess not only the underused potential, as we have just done, but also the *mis*use of resources. Food-producing resources are misused when they are diverted, as they increasingly are, away from meeting basic food needs and toward the satisfaction of those already fed. Even though the majority of a country's population may be in grave need of food, if they have too little money to make that need felt in the marketplace, agricultural resources will be made to serve those who can pay—the domestic upper strata and high-paying markets abroad. Luxury crops expand, therefore, while basic food crops are neglected.

In Central America and the Caribbean, where as many as 80 percent of the children are undernourished, approximately half of the agricultural land, invariably the best land, is made to produce crops and cattle for a domestic elite and for export—instead of basic food for the people.[6] In 1973, 36 out of 40 of the world's poorest countries—those classified by the United Nations as being most seriously affected (MSA's) by inflated world food prices—exported agricultural commodities to the United States.[7]

The pattern of diverting food-producing resources to the already well-fed continues, even in the face of famine. Agricultural exports from the Sahelian countries actually increased during the late 1960s and early 1970s, in the face of worsening drought and widespread hunger. During the drought in Mali, the area devoted to the two most important *export* crops, peanuts and cotton, was expanded by almost 50 percent and over 100 percent respectively between 1965 and 1972.[8]

Many crops long considered basic staples have recently come to be used as luxury or export crops. Corn, sorghum, vegetables, cassava, and rice turn out to be increasingly grown for export, for fattening livestock for export, or for the local elite.

In Mexico, more basic grains are consumed by livestock than by the country's peasants.[9] In Brazil, the most widely planted crop is corn, accounting for about one-fourth of Brazil's total crop area. But in 1977, well over one-third of this traditional crop went to fatten livestock, either in Brazil or Europe.[10] Several South American countries have been rapidly expanding soybean acreage (largely with foreign investment); yet almost all of this highly nutritious food is for export to fatten livestock.

Or consider cassava. In many countries, cassava has become the belly-filler of last resort for the poor. But now, this poor folks' food is being "discovered" by European firms as a low-priced feed for European cattle. On a 1978 research trip to Thailand, we found that urban elites are buying up large tracts of land to plant cassava. Continuous planting so rapidly depletes the soil that ever greater acreage is needed to get the same production from season to season. Cassava now takes up well over 2 million acres and has overnight become Thailand's second most important export.[11]

When the earth's tremendous productive capacity is underused and when its bounty is increasingly siphoned off to feed the already well-fed, scarcity can hardly be considered the cause of hunger.

While hunger is real, scarcity is an illusion. Throughout *Food First* we will see that the illusion of scarcity is a product of extreme inequalities in control over food-producing resources that thwart development and distort utilization.

2. But What About the Real "Basketcases"?

Question: Don't we find the greatest hunger in the heavily populated countries? And aren't there "basketcase" countries like Bangladesh that can't possibly feed themselves?

Our Response: One sees so many maps with the "hungry countries" colored in a darker shade and reads so many references to the "hungry world" that it is hard to escape thinking of hunger as a place—usually a place "over there."

But think for a minute. Hungry people are living in a country with the greatest food surpluses in history. Over 15 percent of all Americans are eligible for food stamps. Yet nutritionists have testified that even with food stamps it would be impossible for these people to buy a nutritionally adequate diet. Stanislaus

County, California, in the heart of some of America's most productive farmland, was nevertheless designated an official Hunger Disaster Area in 1969. Thousands of jobless and underpaid residents went hungry because they did not have money to buy the food they could actually see growing in the fields.

Is it true that the most densely populated countries are also the hungriest countries? Surveys around the world show no such pattern. Some nations very dense in people per acre also have adequately nourished populations. France has just about the same number of people for each cultivated acre as India.[1] China, where starvation has been eradicated in only twenty-five years, has twice as many people for each cropped acre as India.[2]

On the other hand, countries with relatively few people per cultivated acre nevertheless are often ones where most of the people are malnourished. In Africa, south of the Sahara, one of the worst famine areas in the world, there are almost two and one-half *cultivated* acres per inhabitant, more than in the United States or the Soviet Union and six to eight times more than in China. And this estimate for Africa may represent as little as 12 percent of the region's potentially cultivable land.[3] (In Questions 7 and 11 we will discuss the real causes of the famine in the Sahelian countries in the early 1970s.)

Moreover, the population in many parts of Africa is probably less dense than it was in the sixteenth century before the slave trade. Indeed some economists have argued that certain African countries are *under*-populated in terms of the labor force needed for agricultural development.

At the other extreme, a few African countries such as Ghana and Kenya have population-to-cultivated acre ratios approaching or greater than that of India. Yet these two countries do not hold the worst nutrition record in Africa. At present, that record is held by Zaire, a country with a smaller population per cultivated acre than most European and many Latin American countries. Zaire has the lowest protein per person intake in the world.[4]

Latin America, like Africa, is a region of overall low population density. With 16 percent of the world's cultivable land it has only 6 percent of the world's population yet proportionately more hungry people than India, Pakistan, and Bangladesh. Here again there is no apparent relationship between the amount of agricultural land available per person and the extent of hunger. In a country like Bolivia, severe undernourishment is a daily reality for most of the population; yet Bolivia has well over one-half acre of cultivated land per person, significantly more than France (and a potential of over ten cultivable acres per person). Mexico, where most of the rural population is poorly fed, has more cultivated land per person than Cuba,[5] where now virtually no one is underfed.

Certainly there are countries in Latin America with both relatively high population density and widespread hunger—countries like Haiti and the Dominican Republic. But they are the exceptions. Haiti and the Dominican Republic, nonetheless, have just slightly less cultivated land per person, and a much longer growing season, than Italy.[6] This calculation does not even include the considerable additional area in Haiti and the Dominican Republic that many observers agree is good agricultural land. This land is officially classified as "permanent pasture" simply because the owners choose to graze livestock on it.

As long as food is something bought and sold in a society with great income differences, hunger is not related to the number of people per cultivated acre.

Bangladesh—A "Basketcase"?

Bangladesh for many is the archetype of a country whose population has simply overwhelmed its food-producing resources. Eighty million people live in an area the size of Wisconsin. So, even when our studies of countries around the world revealed in case after case that sheer physical limits are not the cause of hunger, we thought that Bangladesh might be an exception. It isn't.

Even now, with resources grossly underused, Bangladesh grows enough in grain alone to provide everyone in the country with at least 2600 calories a day. Yet, according to nutrition surveys,[7] over half of the families in Bangladesh daily consume less than 1500 calories per person, the minimum survival level. Two-thirds of the population suffer from protein and vitamin deficiencies.

If enough is produced, then why don't the hungry in Bangladesh eat? Ironically, the hungry grow much of the country's rice. At harvest time, when prices are at their lowest, many are forced to sell so much of what they produce that they do not have enough to cover their own needs until the next harvest. They are forced to do so in great part in order to pay back, with considerable interest, the moneylender-merchants, from whom they needed to borrow food at much higher prices before the harvest. Many of those trapped in this vicious circle are tenant farmers who must pay for all the agricultural inputs and still give over half of their harvest to the landlord. Not surprisingly, many landlords have become moneylender-merchants. The moneylender-merchants' hoarding of grain is a prime cause of the very "scarcity" on which they speculate.

Landless laborers, dependent on meager wages, are particularly vulnerable. Precisely when floods and droughts deprive them of work altogether, speculative food prices due to hoarding shoot up 200 to 500 percent. Once we became aware of these realities, we were not surprised to learn that, while many starved after the 1974 floods, hoarders stacked up an estimated 4 million tons of rice because "the vast majority . . . were too poor to buy it."[8]

Not only is there no legitimate scarcity now, but Bangladesh has what it takes to grow much more food. Traveling about the country we were struck by its stunning fertility. For Bangladesh is blessed not only with a luxuriant tropical climate (abundant sun and water) but also with deep, rich alluvial soils annually deposited by three great rivers and their countless tributaries. (In the dry winter season we found vegetables larger and more succulent than those we knew in California.)

Yet, despite very favorable conditions for agriculture, the current rice yield is only half the world average and a mere sixth of what has been demonstrated possible in Bangladesh. Sizing up Bangladesh's food potential, a 1976 report for Congress concluded, "The country is rich enough in fertile land, water, manpower and natural gas for fertilizer, not only to be self-sufficient in food, but a food exporter, even with its rapidly increasing population size."[9]

So what is the problem?

Bangladesh's food potential is nowhere near to being realized. Inequalities in control over the country's productive resources thwart their development.

A 1977 A.I.D.-commissioned study found that about 90 percent of all land in Bangladesh is worked in whole or part by sharecroppers and laborers.[10] How does this reality stifle productivity?

One of Bangladesh's chief assets, for instance, is rainfall—50 to 250 inches of it annually—but mostly during the 3- to 4-month monsoon season. The trick then is to control water, otherwise you first have flooding and then drought. But what incentives are there for sharecroppers and laborers to build and maintain drainage and irrigation canals and embankments when such investments would primarily benefit the landowners? And the small landholders rightfully fear that any improvement in the land might heighten the desire of the larger landholder to take it over.

The sharecropper saves any extra effort for what little piece of land he might own himself. Hired laborers concern themselves with their wages, not the landlord's yields. And since the landlord pays for their labor, he uses it sparingly. Moreover, the landlord is increasingly likely to be absentee, perhaps a military officer or petty government official, living and investing in urban real estate or even abroad. In Bangladesh we were repeatedly told that it is not uncommon for a landlord to sabotage irrigation and other improvements simply because he does not wish his tenants to prosper and become less dependent.

Not surprisingly, only about 7 percent of the country's cultivated land is irrigated. Simple irrigation, making the "dry season" no longer dry, would amount to doubling the country's food base. And in much of Bangladesh an extra crop each year could result from reinstituting precolonial practices for collecting the monsoon rains.

Cooperation in digging and maintaining ponds was common before 1793, when the British instituted the individual ownership of land. Today in villages throughout Bangladesh we sadly noted many silted ponds and canals hardly capable of holding much water. And they are no longer *village* ponds but private ponds.

Village-wide cooperative work is impossible when less than 10 percent of the rural households own 51 percent of the cultivated land (not even considering the significant number of urban owners of rural land) and when almost half the families are, for all practical purposes, deprived of land.[11] The poor feel forced to compete against each other for sheer survival. Poor small farmers face the large landholders who scheme daily to further impoverish them, in order to foreclose on them. During the 1974 famine, rich landholders stood in line all night at land registry offices in order to buy land that hungry, mortgaged small farmers were selling as a last resort.

Consider also Bangladesh's inland fishing resources, which according to one FAO (the United Nations Food and Agriculture Organization) report are "possibly the richest in the world."[12] At present, most of the fishing waters are controlled by absentee owners who are satisfied to sell a small quantity of fish at high prices to a few well-off consumers. With profits already so inflated, why should they invest in improving fishing methods? The fishermen, as mere hired hands, see no point in improving their fishing skills or the fish resources: They know they themselves would not benefit. The fishermen are, according to a confidential United Nations report,[13] severely exploited by the absentee owners, for the urban consumers pay about 500 to 600 percent more than what the fishermen receive—prices that moreover keep fish out of the reach of millions.

So in Bangladesh, as in many countries which we are made to perceive as hopelessly poor, it is the extreme inequality in the control over productive resources that makes cooperative work difficult and thwarts production. For this reason, a 1975 FAO report on Bangladesh concludes, "A policy of really drastic land redistribution might promote both production and equity."[14]

Cooperative farming structures could overcome the danger that redistribution would break up the land into units too fragmented to make efficient use of irrigation and drainage networks. Likewise, cooperative fishing could provide employment to hundreds of thousands of landless families. The fish would be an excellent protein source for millions of farming people who, under the new order, would be productive enough to buy it. Greater production would result because, for the first time, the *entire* rural population would sense that in working together they could master the forces of nature and become the beneficiaries, not the landlords and moneylenders. And an active, decision-making rural population would be the best foundation for democracy.

The obstacles in the way of these constructive developments are not the natural limits of the country. The key obstacle to development for the people of Bangladesh is the present power of a few that prevents the majority from realizing their common interests and the strength of their unified effort. Bangladesh is by no means a hopeless basketcase.

3. Are People a Liability or a Resource?

Question: In theory there may not be too many people in relation to the land. But what about in relation to jobs?

Economist Barbara Ward has likened the urban migration resulting from rural unemployment in underdeveloped countries to a "tidal wave, a hurricane Camille of country people." For her, "it is not so much immigration as inundation." Robert McNamara, President of the World Bank, has described the growing number of unemployed as " 'marginal men,' the wretched strugglers for survival on the fringes of farm and city."

Isn't the tragedy of unemployment-related hunger simply that a long-needed technological revolution in agriculture is inevitably leaving behind an increasing number of unskilled, illiterate people? Haven't their numbers long surpassed what agriculture can constructively absorb? Aren't these modernizing countries condemned to growing numbers of surplus people left behind without jobs and thus without income for food?

Our Response: Terms like "tidal wave" and "inundation" can readily lead us to believe that we are witnessing a natural and inevitable process. Dramatic metaphors can jolt us by the very power of their imagery, but they can also lead us away from real understanding.

This question reflects several widely held beliefs that we have found to be myths.

24

MYTH ONE: *Agriculture in underdeveloped countries is held back because there are just too many people in the countryside to be productively put to work.*

If too many workers per acre really stood in the way of production, wouldn't countries that have a *more* productive agriculture have *fewer* workers per acre than their less successful neighbors? Yet, what do we find? Japan and Taiwan, both thought of as agriculturally successful, have more than twice as many agricultural workers per acre than the Philippines and India. The value of production per acre in Japan is seven times that of the Philippines and ten times that of India.[1] The overall trend, in fact, seems to show a *positive* relationship between the number of workers on a unit of land and the level of agricultural output. This may be hard for Americans to accept because we are taught to measure productivity in terms of how *few* people it takes to grow food. Such a measure makes no sense at all in underdeveloped countries with vast, untapped human labor resources.

Countries we think of as heavily overpopulated—countries that we assume could not use even one more farmer—are not necessarily overcrowded agriculturally. When China attempted to increase production utilizing its human labor potential, it found that it could gainfully triple or even quadruple the labor input per acre. According to the World Bank, if countries like India could attain Japan's level of labor intensity—two workers per hectare (2.5 acres)—their agriculture could absorb all the labor force expected by 1985.[2] The significant difference, of course, is that countries like Japan and China have developed labor-intensive farming that *productively* employs the additional labor; India and the Philippines have not. Clearly, a large rural population is far from the handicap it is often perceived to be.

MYTH TWO: *Since agriculture cannot absorb any more people, the overflow from rural areas must go to the cities where new jobs in industry must be created for them.*

It was exactly this analysis of the problem that prompted both the neglect of agriculture and the promotion of industrialization by development planners during the 1950s and 1960s. The result? A lot of capital investment but remarkably few new industrial jobs.

The percentage of the total workforce employed in manufacturing dropped from 8.5 percent to 7.6 percent between 1900 and 1950 in underdeveloped countries.[8] This pattern holds even in countries like Brazil touted as "miracles" of industrial development. In India, between, 1950 and 1964, the government increased the capital invested in large-scale manufacturing fifteenfold. Yet during the same period, the number of workers employed by such manufacturing only slightly more than doubled.[4] Foreign corporations with their labor-saving technologies from countries with high labor costs like the United States have aggravated the chronic "job crisis." Two hundred fifty-seven multinational corporations studied in Latin America employ less than one-half the number of people per unit of sales as do local companies.[5]

A corporation invariably claims its investment "created" so many hundred jobs. Many economists have come to recognize, however, that a new modern factory employing a couple hundred persons might well put thousands of local craftsmen out of business. Moreover, local savings borrowed by a foreign corporation to create a factory could have been used in entirely different ways that would have created many more jobs.

Efforts to solve the unemployment problem by creating jobs in centralized, urban areas are misplaced in any case. In underdeveloped countries agriculture and small-scale decentralized workshops serving the needs of local agriculture have the greater potential to absorb workers. China has been able to reduce the percentage of its workforce in full-time agricultural jobs to about 54 percent in contrast to the 70 to 85 percent in most underdeveloped countries. This was accomplished not by creating urban industries but by developing small factories and workshops throughout the countryside to make farm implements and basic consumer goods. China's large *rural,* but nonagricultural, population also represents a sizable reserve labor force for agriculture. Nonagricultural workers are on hand to deal with peak season farm labor "bottlenecks" that in many countries are the common excuse for mechanization that both squanders scarce financial resources and takes away jobs when there are no others.

MYTH THREE: *Population growth is a tremendous burden to Third World economies since it means having to scare up more jobs when 15 to 30 percent of the population is already without work and much of the so-called employed are really underemployed. The result is increasing numbers of half-starved, marginal people living outside the economy.*

Researching this book helped us to understand that "marginal" people are not born. They are not caused by the *inevitable* overflow of a limited land base or by the fixed capacity of an economy to absorb workers. What, then, makes people appear marginal and superfluous?

In sixteenth-century England and nineteenth-century Scotland a shift in land use led directly to the appearance of "too many people." The landed gentry had decided that sheep would be more profitable than farming. Sheep, however, need a lot of land and only a few shepherds. Land, therefore, was "enclosed" and thousands of farming peasants were shut out. Many contemporary commentators saw in the growing number of landless vagabonds sure evidence of "too many people"—a view that helped to motivate overseas colonizations. The overpopulation existed, of course, only in relation to a sheep-based agricultural economy. The total population of England in the sixteenth century was less than in any one of several present-day English cities.[6]

Colonial powers similarly created such marginal people by reducing highly diversified agricultural systems to single crops—monocultures on which the most profit could be made in foreign markets. Converting whole countries into production sites for one or two crops meant that planting and harvests were no longer staggered throughout the year. Employment opportunities were therefore limited to the cycle of the one or two main export crops. Thus, in the predominantly sugar-plantation economy of Cuba during the mid-fifties a half million sugar workers were employed only for four months a year—at the time of the sugar harvest.[7]

Indeed, people are being made to appear marginal today by the further transformation of agriculture taking place in most underdeveloped countries. Agriculture, once the livelihood of millions of self-provisioning farmers, is becoming the profit base of influential commercial entrepreneurs—traditional landed elites, city-based agricultural speculators, and foreign corporations. These new agricultural entrepreneurs use profits both to enlarge their landholdings at the expense of the small farmer and the landless and to mechanize production at the expense of the laborer's job. Some examples:

- Pakistan: A Pakistan Planning Commission official states that full mechanization on farms of twenty-five acres or more could displace 600,000 to 700,000 workers in fifteen years. The number of tractors in Pakistan has gone up from 3000 in 1960 to 20,000 in 1969.[8]
- Latin America: Each tractor displaces about three workers in Chile and about four in Colombia and Guatemala. A conservative estimate is that two and a half million laborers have been already displaced by tractor mechanization in Latin America. And less than a third of these will find other rural employment.[9]
- Central America: Coffee growers in Guatemala and Costa Rica have roughly halved their labor requirements by mechanization. The number of laborers needed per acre for banana production is now one quarter of what it was in 1930.[10] Sugar is a similar story.

- India: In the Punjab it is expected that by 1980 the demand for hired labor in field crop production will all but disappear.[11]

Displacing tenants and laborers with machines means a larger marketable harvest and more profit for the commercial cultivator—in addition to freedom from the "management problem" of a sizable underpaid labor force. Replacing people with machines in countries with immense untapped labor resources is not, of course, of social value. The value accrues only to the individual operator who can use machines to maximize the profit made on each laborer. As this process proceeds, however, all the outsider sees is more unemployment and therefore concludes that there are just too many people.

This question reveals a lot about how we all are conditioned to regard people. We are made to think of people as an economic liability when, in reality, all the wealth of any country begins with people—*with human labor*. The economic success of a nation does not depend so much on rich natural resources as on how effectively its people can be motivated and their labor utilized. People appear as a liability *only* in a certain type of economic system: one in which economic success is not measured by the well-being of all the people; one in which production is increasingly monopolized by a few; and one in which technology is used to exclude people from the production process so as to maximize the profit the landlord makes on each worker. People are not born marginal.

4. Does Ignorance Breed Babies?

Question: Many people throughout the Third World do not perceive that having fewer children would be in their own best interest. If they could be helped to see that the more children they have, the poorer and hungrier they will be, then perhaps they would not want more children. An urgent and prodigious educational task faces us—perhaps the greatest of all time —to convince so many of our planet's citizens of the folly of not having small families. Don't you agree?

Our Response: The question suggests that people in underdeveloped countries desire large families out of ignorance of their own interests. We have found, however, that while their reasons are complex, they reflect powerlessness more than ignorance.

Most Third World families are rural. Survival for them often depends on having children to bring in extra food or money for the family and to provide minimal old-age security for the parents. At the age of 45, people in underdeveloped countries may be depleted and old. And with nutrition, sanitation, and health services poor or nonexistent, parents know all too well that their children often die. Giving birth to "extra" is therefore the only way to increase the likelihood that enough will survive.

Those of us in urban industrial societies might disbelieve that any child can earn more than he or she consumes. But demographers working around the world have calculated that a rural child at the age of 10 or even 8 can bring a net food or income benefit to the family.[1] Children, for example, herd animals, fetch water, firewood and dung, transplant rice, glean fields, and cut stubble. Young children can free parents and older children for other productive work. All of this we also have seen in our field investigations.

We might see such children—and certainly the mothers who bear the burden of so many pregnancies and childbearings—as exploited. But as long as the social order keeps isolated family units—often competing against each other—as the only basis of productive work and security, there is little hope for change. This is plainly the case, given that the usurpation of resources by the powerful few leaves the majority of families with little or no land and but a few miserably paying jobs.

For each such family, the number of children determines the number of workers it can field to support itself. If the family has little or no land, its income might depend on the number of children that can be hired out as laborers in the fields of others. If the family survives by sharecropping a rich family's land, then the more children it has, the more land it can try to contract to work. And a poor family with some land of its own sees children as an asset too. As one Indian farmer explained to a population researcher: "Just look around. No one, without sons or brothers to help him, farms his land. He rents it out to others with large families. Without sons, there is no living off the land. The more sons you have, the less labor you need to hire, and the more saving you can have." Another peasant in northern India summed it up this way: "A rich man invests in his machines. We must invest in our children."[2]

Parents may also need many children simply because they have no alternative old-age security. In the African Sahel there are "no pension funds, no welfare benefits, no homes for the aged," observes demographer Helen Ware.[3] Milkha Singh, a farmer in Manupur, a village in the Indian Punjab, put it this way: "You think I am poor because I have too many children." He laughed, "If I didn't have my sons . . . God knows what would happen to me and their mother when we are too old to work and earn."[4]

In such societies, how can a family be sure to meet

its need for a family labor force and for old-age security by having just one or two sons? The belief of peasants in India that many births are necessary to ensure that some sons survive is apparently valid. According to a computer simulation, an Indian couple would have to bear an average of 6.3 children to be confident (at a 95 percent level of probability) of the survival of one son.[5]

Powerlessness of Women

Even given the economic victimization of the majority of rural families, the question of family size is not an uncomplicated one of "the more, the better." For many mothers, so often undernourished, the burden of yet another pregnancy and child outweighs any prospective gain from an additional laborer in the family. But with no life options outside the context of a husband's approval, many women are powerless to make reproductive decisions. Having no personal autonomy, they find it unthinkable even to ask a husband if he would allow the use of contraceptives. In a survey for the United Nations Fund for Population Activities, social worker Perdita Huston, interviewing rural women in Tunisia, the Sudan, Kenya, Sri Lanka, Mexico, and Egypt, found that it is not women who need to be convinced to have fewer children. In each of the six very different cultures, she repeatedly heard variations of "I am tired. Look at me. I am nothing but a beast working in the fields and bearing all the children. I don't want any more but my husband says I must have as many as come."[6] (We would note, however, that two researchers living for nine months in a Bangladesh village found that men, too, particularly young men, thought that after a certain number, additional children were no longer an economic asset.[7])

So lowering birth rates is not, as the questioner suggests, so much a matter of overcoming ignorance. The poor more often than not know their own best interests. Birth rates cannot decrease until the poor overcome their powerlessness, including the special powerlessness of women vis-à-vis men. Then, giving birth to fewer children will be in the best interests of the poor, and they themselves can control the programs to control births.

5. Sophisticated Fatalism?

Question: It seems to me that people in the hungry countries are multiplying at higher rates than ever. If rapid population growth is at root caused by so many people being kept poor, is there really any hope for limiting population growth before it's too late? Poverty, after all, is not about to be eliminated everywhere in the world. Frankly, don't your arguments boil down to sophisticated fatalism?

Our Response: Because of the way the "population bomb" has been thrown into the public's consciousness, most people are convinced that the poor are multiplying faster than ever. In reality, at least 11 underdeveloped countries are undergoing an even more precipitous decline in their birth rates than did any of the now-industrial countries, including the United States, during their "demographic transition" of the nineteenth and early twentieth centuries.[1] Dr. Parker Maudlin of the Population Council observes that not only has fertility declined much more significantly than most people realize, but that the rate of decline is accelerating. The drop in birth rates between 1970 and 1977 in underdeveloped countries was three times as great as the drop between 1950 and 1970, he notes.[2]

These trends, added to the slowing rate of population growth in certain industrial countries, mean that the annual increment in world population has dropped in the last few years. In 1970 the growth in world population, that is, the excess of births over deaths, was 70 million. By 1977 the increase was probably closer to 68.7 million. When one considers that the *number* of people of reproductive age is still getting larger each year, any such drop in annual increment indicates a significant lowering of birth rates. The rate of world population growth appears to have reached an all-time high around 1970 and has since begun to subside.[3]

Such generalizations do not tell us a great deal. More useful is to look at which countries have declining birth rates and to contrast them with countries that do not. The lowering of the population growth rate is apparently *not* related to the growth rate of the Gross National Product (GNP) or even to the *level* of per capita income but to a trend toward *equal distribution* of income and services such as health care.[4]

In countries where birth rates are declining such as Sri Lanka, Singapore, Hong Kong, Taiwan, Egypt, Argentina, Uruguay, Costa Rica, and Cuba, most have, or once had, some national policies favoring the low-income groups, whereas in countries such as Brazil, Venezuela, the Philippines, and Mexico, the well-being of low-income groups is diminishing and birth rates are not declining significantly. In countries where the decline in birth rate has been significant, the causal factors do not appear to be direct birth control programs so much as a shift in resources toward the poorest groups.

Well-being is not measured in income alone. Other factors besides income distribution per se seem to correlate with declining birth rates. Two Asian examples of declining birth rates—the state of Kerala in India and China—illustrate this. In Kerala, statistics show that the population is poorer than in many other Indian states, but there are critical social and political differences that may well contribute to Kerala's declining birth rate. Alan Berg, a World Bank nutritionist, has noted that of all the states of India, Kerala has the highest literacy rate (it is the only state where the majority of women are educated); the highest per capita consumption of nutritionally important foods; the lowest infant mortality rate; and a death rate lower than that of West Germany or Great Britain.[5]

The average Indian birth rate has fallen from 41 to 37.2 per 1000 over the last twenty years. By contrast, Kerala's birth rate has dropped from 37 to 27 per 1000 during only a ten-year period.

China has the most comprehensive approach to providing what seem to be social and economic prerequisites to population limitation. After retirement, workers receive 50 to 75 percent of their earnings while most other benefits, notably health care, continue. In the countryside, the commune maintains a welfare fund to provide for those unable to work. In both city and countryside the collective working group ensures that no family's income falls below a certain minimal level.[6] Women are encouraged to join the workforce; liberal maternity leave and convenient nurseries are provided.

In addition, you will recall from our previous response that families competing against other families must have their own labor supply for survival. But when labor and production are shared beyond the family through group ownership and work, as it is in China, then the need to give birth to one's own family workforce disappears.

China demonstrates the capacity of people to change their rate of reproduction with impressive rapidity once basic security needs have been met. China's birth rate has declined at perhaps unprecedented speed— down from 32 per 1000 in 1970 to between 20 and 25 per 1000 five years later.[7] Since the Chinese people constitute one fifth of humanity, their efforts to lower their birth rate have significantly lowered world figures.

To those of us in the industrial West, the people in the countries experiencing real declines in their birth rates may still seem "poor"—some with per capita incomes not much over $200 per year—but in most of these countries the lives of the poor are changing in critical ways. Viable income and old-age security needs that had previously been met only by bearing many children are beginning to be met by social and political reform: by more secure land tenure, by more reliable food supply, by better health care, and by retirement security. Do we need still more studies to prove that people will limit the number of their off-spring only when the social and economic context makes such a decision rational and feasible?

6. Controlling Births or Controlling the Population?

Question: Certainly basic security through economic justice appears to be the prerequisite for bringing down growth rates. But isn't this only half the story? Even if the economic prerequisites exist that make it in the people's interest to choose smaller families, aren't birth control programs needed? You are not saying, are you, that when there is more equitable distribution of control over resources, the problem of rapid population growth will automatically take care of itself?

Our Response: The questioner is right. Reconstruction of the social order, providing all the people with basic material security, is necessary to make birth control a *rational* option. Then, birth control programs are essential to make having fewer children a *feasible* option as well.

But birth control programs that simply aim to shower rural areas with contraceptives will never work. Moreover, they run the risk of actually harming the poor. Without regular supervision by trained health care personnel, women can suffer both physical and psychological damage. Reports from Bangladesh stress that symptoms caused by irregular supply of oral contraceptives and bleeding from IUD's have caused severe personal suffering. In the Moslem cultures a woman too weak to do her household tasks can simply be rejected in favor of another wife.

Moreover, without improved health care having already reduced child mortality rates, families run the risk of severe loss. Sterilization programs are becoming a major part of birth control programs in the underdeveloped countries. But if child mortality rates are still high, parents who become sterilized run the risk of great economic loss if their children die and they are unable to replace them.

Thus birth control programs can only be effective and serve the interests of the poor when they

—are integrated into a total health care system that reduces child mortality rates.

—include both men and women.

—are village-based, training people from the village in which they will serve. (Dacca-based health workers in fine silk saris were perceived by the rural Bangladesh women as Americans.)

—can become self-supporting and therefore permanent through, for example, a health insurance program. (One such effort in rural Bangladesh requires 13¢ a month per family.)

—are part of an educational program in which people become conscious of the economic forces limiting their lives. Without this, the poor are unable to build effective organizations to protect their own interests, so necessary when the village elite tries to sabotage their efforts.

China's extensive and successful birth control programs illustrate that rapid population growth does not "automatically take care of itself" once the social prerequisites are met. China's programs also illustrate many of the above features that would need to be integrated into truly effective and beneficial programs.

In China population planning activities are not limited to separate "birth control programs."[1] Rather, population planning activities—discussion of the rationale behind limiting births and the means to achieve it —permeate the many different organizations, from trade unions to residential committees, to which almost everyone belongs. As part of the public health system, including neighborhood health centers and mobile family planning units, birth control information and devices reach virtually every community. The health centers almost never close and are operated not by aloof, outsider professionals but by local residents who maintain ongoing contact with families. China is self-sufficient in all contraceptive devices. They are free and readily available.

Clearly we support the goals of lowered population growth rates and a stabilized global population. And we do not underestimate the need for positive action in providing family planning programs once the social prerequisites are being met. We stand firmly against, however, family planning programs that *purport to alleviate the problem of hunger*. They carry the message that the poor themselves are to blame for their own hunger, masking the true economic and political roots of their suffering.

As they implement such programs, claiming all the while to address social problems, elite-controlled governments in more and more underdeveloped countries will increasingly call for laws that would fine or imprison those not limiting the size of their families —selectively penalizing the poor who can least afford to restrict their families—as we have seen in several states in India. This approach brings to mind Barry Commoner's words in *The Closing Circle:* "War is . . . a means of solving a social issue, not by social means but by a biological process—death. The same is true, I believe, of enforced population control."[2]

The specter of overpopulation arises as more and more people are severed from control over and participation in the production process. They appear as superfluous. And often the very people who prefer to blame the poor themselves—and their breeding—for deplorable social conditions are those who stand to lose by the redistribution of power over productive resources that, for the first time, would give people the real option of limiting their family size.

Because some might misinterpret our words, suggesting that we discount the problem of rapid population growth, we must be absolutely clear. Population density and rapid growth can, of course, be grave problems. These problems are, as we have seen, symptoms of the powerlessness of so many to choose fewer children. Population factors also can exacerbate the difficult tasks of social and economic restructuring necessary to eliminate hunger. The error, however, is in transforming the problem of population—a symptom and exacerbating factor—into the cause of hunger. And this is no semantic squabble. Getting at the solution to a problem hinges entirely on how well one can pinpoint its cause. The root cause of hunger has to do with the relationships of people to each other and to the control over basic resources. As long as people think the fundamental causes are elsewhere, this root cause will go neglected and people will in fact become hungrier.

Continued population growth at current rates will certainly undercut the future well-being of all of us. This is self-evident. But this self-evident truth adds, for us, even *greater urgency* to the task of identifying clearly the root causes of rapid population growth.

7. Population Pressure on the Environment?

Question: You have talked about the population problem in terms of the economic system. But what about the impact of increasing numbers of people on the ecosystem? The present high rates of population growth are putting tremendous pressures on the global environment that could have irreparable consequences for future food production. Perhaps *we* will not suffer but what about our children and their children?

Overgrazing, large-scale erosion, and encroaching deserts provide evidence of strain on the ecosystem, as the number of livestock and people increase. Increasing numbers of people are forcing agriculture onto marginal and vulnerable land. According to Lester Brown's *By Bread Alone:* "One consequence of the continuous growth in population is the spread of agriculture to land with thin mantles of topsoil that will not sustain continuous and intensive cultivation."[1] Surely you must recognize population pressures as the crucial factor in these ominous trends toward environmental decay.

Our Response: We share this concern about the long-term consequences of our present path. We, too, see signs of ecological destruction. The deterioration of our global ecosystem and its agricultural resources does coincide with an increase in the population of human beings and livestock. Yet is there a *necessary* causal link? We have had to conclude there is not.

Much of the current destruction of the ecosystem in

underdeveloped countries began with colonialism.*
The plantations established by the colonial powers put
a double burden on the land. First, they expropriated
the best land for continuous cultivation of crops for
export. Second, they usually pushed the local farmers
onto marginal, often hilly, land not at all suitable for
intensive farming. Land that otherwise might have
served for grazing, forestry, or recreation soon became
ravaged by erosion.

This double burden—cash cropping for export and
squeezing the majority of farmers onto erosion-prone
lands—is being reinforced today. Take a Central
American country like El Salvador. The country is
mostly steep hills and mountains. The most fertile and
productive lands are the middle volcanic slopes, some
scattered interior river basins, and the coastal plain.
Beginning with the Spanish conquest, these prime lands
have been owned by large estates devoted to exports:
cotton, sugar, coffee crops, and cattle ranches. Less
than one in a hundred farms in El Salvador has more
than 250 acres; but those few that do together take up
half of the total farming area of the country, including
all of the prime land.[2]

The land left over, now mainly barren hills, is all
that some 350,000 *campesinos* have on which to
scratch out a subsistence living for their families. Much
of the land they are forced to cultivate is so steep, it
has to be planted with a stick. The erosion can be so
devastating—one study concluded 77 percent of the
nation's land is suffering from accelerated erosion[3]
—that the *campesinos* must abandon a slope after a
single year's meager yield. Where they will go in the
future is not at all clear. Already the rapid soil depletion
has set off a heavy migration of Salvadorians into neighboring Honduras. This land search by desperate Salvadorians helped precipitate a war between the two
countries in 1969. And we were told that this was the
first war in history caused by the population explosion.

It is tempting to look at an area such as the Carib-

---

* For a discussion of the impact of colonialism, see Questions 12 and 13.

bean, where semitropical forests have been destroyed
and soil badly eroded, and simply diagnose the problem as too many people. Currently, local farms feed
only one third of the Caribbean population and 70
percent of the children are malnourished.[4]

But before accepting "too many people" as the
cause, consider some figures on Caribbean land use.
Over half of all the arable land is made to produce
crops and cattle for export. In individual countries
the usurpation of the best land for export crops is
even more dramatic. In Guadeloupe over 66 percent of
the arable land produces sugar cane, cocoa, and
bananas. In Martinique over 70 percent is planted
with sugar cane, cocoa, bananas, and coffee. In Barbados, 77 percent of the arable land grows sugar cane
alone.[5]

"Haiti," comments environmental writer Erik Eckholm, "is among the few countries that already rival
or perhaps surpass El Salvador in nationwide environmental destruction."[6] Not coincidentally, only a few
people own the country's farmland. The best valley
lands belong to a handful of elites and their foreign
partners, who produce endless vistas of sugar cane,
coffee trees, and cattle—all for export. We were particularly struck to see the miserable shacks of the landless along the edge of fertile irrigated fields growing
feed for thousands of pigs that wind up as sausages
for Chicago's Servbest Foods. Meanwhile the majority
of Haitians are left to ravage the once-green mountain
slopes in near futile efforts to grow food. In desperation
thousands have fled to the United States, where they
compete with the poorest paid Americans for minimum
wage jobs.

The same pattern holds in South America. In
Colombia the good level land, according to a World
Bank study,[7] belongs to absentee landlords who frequently use it only for grazing cattle. We already noted
that in 1960 rich landowners controlling 70 percent
of all the country's agricultural land actually cultivated
only 6 percent. Moreover, much of their land that once
did grow staples like corn and wheat is now producing

feed grain as well as carnations and other "ornamental crops" for export. The same World Bank study found that at the same time "large numbers of farm families . . . try to eke out an existence on too little land, often on slopes of . . . 45 degrees or more. As a result, they exploit the land very severely, adding to erosion and other problems, and even so are not able to make a decent living."[8]

In Africa it is colonialism's cash crops and their continuing legacy, not the pressure of its population, that are destroying soil resources. Vast tracts of geologically old sediments perfectly suitable for permanent crops such as grazing grasses or trees have instead been torn up for planting cotton and peanuts. The soil becomes rapidly poor in humus and loses its cohesiveness. The wind, quite strong in the dry season, then easily erodes the soils. Soil deterioration leads to declining crop yields[9] and consequently to an expansion of cultivated land, often onto marginal soils.

In dramatic contrast to cash-cropping monoculture, the traditional self-provisioning agriculture that it replaces is often quite sound ecologically. It is a long-evolved adaptation to tropical soil and climate. It reflects a sophisticated understanding of the complex rhythms of the local ecosystem. The mixing of crops, sometimes of more than twenty different species, means harvests are staggered and provides maximum security against wholesale losses due to unseasonable weather, pests, or disease. Moreover, mixed cropping provides the soil with year-round protection from the sun and rain.

The problem of soil erosion *is* serious. We have discovered, however, that soil erosion occurs largely because fertile land is monopolized by a few, forcing the majority of farmers to overuse vulnerable soils. Moreover, soil impoverishment results, not from an effort to meet the basic food needs of expanding populations, but increasingly from the pressure to grow continuously nonfood and luxury export crops over large areas to the neglect of traditional techniques that once protected the soil.

Overgrazing: A Case Study in Land Misuse

Overgrazing is another sure way to ruin marginal lands. But to get at the cause one must ask, Who is overgrazing and why? And does it follow that marginal lands can never be suitable for livestock? Finally, since overgrazing means too many cattle on the land, must we conclude this reflects too many people?

Some outsiders see Africa's nomadic pastoralists as the culprits. We have come to learn, however, that nomadic pastoralists have traditionally made efficient use of vast stretches of semiarid land that otherwise would remain unproductive. While their migrations might look random to the outsider, they are, in reality, patterned to take advantage of variations in rainfall and vegetation. The nomads may herd their livestock over hundreds of miles from rainy season pastures to oases of perennial grasses in dry seasons. Pastoral nomadism, then, is a rational response to an environment characterized by the scarcity of water, seasonal drought, and widely scattered seasonal fodder resources. The nomads' tactics make use of resources that others would not even consider as resources.[10]

Another adaptation technique of traditional pastoralists is keeping a herd that consists of different types of livestock: camels, sheep, goats, donkeys, as well as cattle. A mixed herd can exploit a variety of ecological niches. Cattle and sheep graze on grasslands; camels graze but also browse on shrubs and high parts of trees; and goats browse on shrubs and low parts of trees. Valuable protein for human consumption is thus produced by plants that humans cannot eat. Different species also have different reproductive cycles; staggered breeding seasons ensure some type of milk throughout the year. The hardiness of goats and camels makes them good animals to fall back on in times of drought when cattle die off. A varied herd also acts as a walking storehouse for food, either directly or in exchange for grain, during annual dry spells and periodic droughts.

Pastoralists traditionally produced enough meat and

dairy products to exchange with farmers for grain. In addition, the pastoralists' herds annually manured the fallow fields of the farmers. The animals thus gained good grazing land and the fertility of the farmers' soil improved. This symbiotic relationship allowed for remarkably dense populations to comfortably inhabit seemingly inhospitable lands.[11]

If raising livestock has been and can be such an excellent way to make marginal lands productive, what has gone wrong? What is behind the many reports of overgrazing in regions, like the African Sahel, that vast stretch of semiarid land along the southern border of the Sahara?

To answer such questions we have to go back to the beginning of this century. The French colonial administration created arbitrary "national" borders (today enforced by the newly independent governments) without regard to the need of the nomads to migrate. Endless restrictions have made it increasingly difficult for the nomads to shift their herds in response to the short- and long-term cycles of nature.

The French also slapped a head tax on each nomad. The tax had to be paid in French francs even though most nomads lived within a barter economy. The nomads needed, therefore, to raise more livestock, so that some could be sold for cash. Over the years, their need for money has been compounded by the growing lure of imported consumer goods. Higher market prices also prompted pastoralists to build up their herds beyond the carrying capacity of the lands.

The expansion of lands for peanut and cotton production (see Question 11) sharply decreased the amount of pasture available to herders. Farmers also began to keep small herds near their houses. These herds, kept in such a confined space, resulted in localized overgrazing.[12] Moreover, the urban and export demand for beef induced the pastoralists to upset the natural balance of a diversified herd in favor of cattle. Modern inoculations against disease also facilitated the build-up of herds beyond the carrying capacity of the grazing lands. Medicine that was meant to save these herds ultimately contributed to the death by starvation of tens of thousands of animals.

Aid agencies, including the United States Agency for International Development (A.I.D.), drilled deep water wells in the late 1950s and early 1960s. They ignored the reality that the only grazing pattern that would not overtax semiarid land is one relying on free migration over a wide area and that a year-round watering hole is an inadequate substitute, as experience would show. When the rains began to fail, the nomads started to move their cattle en masse to these wells. A well, however, acts as a false signal in the traditional culture's communication system. A well *appears* to be a good substitute for rain. Unlike rain, however, it does not make pasture grow. A seemingly continuous supply of water, usually the most fickle and limiting factor in their economy, convinced the nomads to keep on increasing the size of their herds.

Before long on average in the Sahel 6000 head of cattle were milling about wells surrounded by grazing lands that at best could feed 600. After the cattle ate out the areas around the wells and trampled down the soil, the caked earth could no longer even absorb the scarce rains. One eyewitness reported that each well "quickly became the center of its own little desert forty or fifty miles square."[13]

From 1955 to 1960, the number of cattle, goats, and sheep in Mali alone increased by 800,000. After 1960, when more boreholes were drilled, the total number of livestock shot up from five million to sixteen million, or more than three animals for every Malien. In the recent drought a large number of animals, crowded on the rapidly exhausted grazing lands around the wells, died, not of thirst, but of hunger.[14]

You probably have read that the plight of the pastoralists proves that these countries are overpopulated and have exhausted their resources. Does more cattle mean there are too many people? We think the answer is by now obvious: not necessarily. But there is no need to romanticize nomads. Undoubtedly they must come into a new ecological balance within the context of the rest of society. This will require some changes, such as regulation of herd composition and size. But it will also require even more fundamental changes in the larger society, for instance, the integration of agriculture and pastoralism, in part through equitable and *stable* values for the exchange of livestock and grain.

Outsiders, especially urban-based government elites who have pronounced pastoralism an anachronism and an ecological disaster (perhaps principally because they cannot control the nomads), invariably advocate ranching as the "modern way." Commercial ranching with fenced-in grazing and grain feeding that squanders precious grain—geared largely to exporting beef —stands in dramatic contrast to the ecological sanity of traditional pastoralism that utilizes a full range of resources otherwise not available for human consumption. Ranching looms as a grave threat to Africa's semiarid lands and their traditional inhabitants.[15]

Moreover, commercial cattle ranching overlooks the vast potential of game animals in Africa. Game, unlike cattle, are not affected by the tsetse fly that inhabits large areas of central and southern Africa. As strange as it may sound, some scientists suggest the tsetse fly may be a blessing in disguise.[16] If the flies were eradicated cattle ranching would probably lead to the extinction of game animals, which, properly "cropped," represent an enormous meat potential for Africans. The noted ecologist Dr. Raymond F. Dasmann argues that game cropping "has the capacity in Africa, in many areas, of producing more meat per acre than can be obtained from the traditional domestic animals on the same land."

There is certainly a critical choice ahead for Africa. Commercial ranching would mean expensive, imported inputs with serious environmental risks, the extinction of many species of animals, and increased vulnerability to widely fluctuating foreign beef markets. The other alternative, the restoration of a balanced pastoral system and well-planned game cropping, could realize Africa's enormous natural protein potential through the optimum utilization of vegetation.

The choice would seem obvious. But are the lure of foreign exchange, foreign loans for cattle projects, the foreign demand for beef, and the beef mystique of African urban elites all too irresistible to oppose before it's too late?

The Amazon

Like the wildlife of Africa, the Amazon River basin has long been seen as one of the world's few remaining great natural preserves. Recently the public has become vaguely aware that it too is being threatened. The Amazon basin *is* being "ravaged," but is the cause overpopulation?

Since the mid-1960s Brazil's largest government project is the "colonization" of this extraordinary region. The plans call for sweeping clean tens of millions of acres of tropical forest. Already legions of Caterpillar Tractors' gargantuan 35-ton D-9s, mounted with angle plows weighing 2500 pounds each, are bulldozing the forest at 2700 yards an hour, up-rooting everything in sight. In some areas the job calls for two D-9s with a heavy chain between them rolling a huge hollow steel ball eight feet in diameter and weighing 6000 pounds. As the tractors move forward, the chain jerks out the trees, destroying the extensive matted root system and exposing the thin tropical soil. Fires visible for miles devour the debris.[17] Such massive deforestation is, according to the President of the Brazilian Academy of Science, Warwick Kerr, "taking place at a faster pace than Brazil and perhaps the world has ever known before. The Amazon forest will disappear in 35 years if it continues to be destroyed at the present rate."[18]

Is it really Brazil's expanding population behind those unrelenting D-9 "jungle crushers?" No, the truth is that Brazil with 2.3 acres of already cropped land per person hardly needs to invade its tropical forests in order to feed its people. The ratio of cultivated land to people is slightly better than what we enjoy in the United States. The Amazon forest is earmarked for destruction for two entirely different reasons.

Settlement or "colonization" schemes historically

have been safety valves—primarily a way to sidestep the urgent need for land redistribution. In Brazil, a mere 1 percent of the farms take up over 43 percent of the country's total farmland, and the best land at that. In brutal contrast, 50 percent of the farms are left with less than 3 percent of the land. In addition, at least 7 million rural families own no land at all— in a country where, even without taking the Amazon region into consideration, there are potentially ten cultivable acres for every family. Four out of five rural families, even if they do find work on a large estate, earn less than $33 a month. Yet a family of three needs at least $65 a month to buy food alone. It all translates into a massive waste of human life. Almost 200 of every 1000 babies born in rural northeast Brazil die in their first year of life.[19]

To avoid provoking Brazil's most powerful families by dividing up the large, generally export-oriented estates, the military government announced an absurd solution: move the rural poor to the Amazon basin, a tropical region totally unsuited for intensive and continuous farming.[20] Thus the pressure on the Amazon forest comes *not* from Brazil's population growth but from a government's effort to diffuse pressures for a just redistribution of land.

Ten years after much self-serving fanfare, the government has resettled a mere 10,000 small farmers. Even then, despite enormous bureaucratic expenditures, many of these farms have soon been abandoned, in part since their tropical soils cannot support intensive cultivation. Far from being concerned, the government has added insult to injury. Only a few years after trumpeting that prosperity for the rural poor was just a thousand or so miles down a not yet completed road, the government opted for a different type of pioneer. Kingdom-sized concessions, none smaller than 125,000 acres, were the new order of the day—mainly for export-oriented ranching and pulpwood production.

The "pioneers" are some of Brazil's richest families, already among the country's largest landholders, a number of Brazilian corporations, and, for good measure, a few television stars. Also quick to find out what

Brazil can do for them are many of the world's largest multinational corporations. These corporations include Anderson Clayton, Goodyear, Volkswagen, Nestlé, Liquigas, Borden, Mitsubishi, and Universe Tank Ship (a low-profile giant chartered in Liberia for tax reasons but in fact belonging to the aged American multi-billionaire, D. K. Ludwig). The "homesteads" of these pioneers run as large as 3.7 million acres, half the size of Holland.[21]

Never has a government given so much to so few for so little. A seemingly endless list of "fiscal encouragements" is offered. One such incentive allows a corporation to invest in the Amazon half the taxes it owes on its earnings in Brazil.

Additional special incentives are offered to beef export operations. The goal is to make Brazil a major supplier of beef to Europe and the United States. Belem, at the mouth of the Amazon, is virtually as close to Miami as it is to the most populous cities of Brazil and five days closer by ship to Europe than are the Argentine slaughter houses.

In 1975 a United States reconnaissance satellite's heat sensor detected a sudden and intense warming of the earth in the Amazon basin usually associated with an imminent volcanic eruption. A special alert mission was dispatched. And what did they find? A German multinational corporation burning down one million acres of tropical forest for a cattle ranch. Unlike the slash and burn of a few acres here and there by Cayapó tribes, the corporation's burning a million acres means the death of most local wildlife.

Several corporations like Ludwig's Universe Tank Ship, Georgia-Pacific, and Bruyznell are actively stripping the forest (which contains over a sixth of the world's remaining timberland) of its valuable lumber resources. They are in reality mining the forests. The plan is to sweep clean the unwanted trees with more D-9 Caterpillars backed up by power saws and voracious fires. The next stage calls for planting a "homogeneous forest" of hundreds of thousands of gmelina trees uprooted from West Africa (who knows what environmental havoc this will cause?). The companies are betting the topsoil will hold long enough for these fast-growing trees to be ready to be made into paper pulp for export. All this with government incentives and multimillions in profits, of course.

If you are wondering whether at least all this devastation will provide employment, the answer is that it won't. You could go out and do a head count of the total number to be employed. Like most mega-money corporations, the money invested goes mainly for machines, not to people. On his 3.7 million acres, Ludwig's cattle, pulp, and export-oriented rice operations expect to employ 1200 permanent workers and a relative handful of seasonal hired hands.[22]

Some justify the whole Amazon scheme as necessitated by Brazil's or the world's population problem. In reality the scheme is a public relations fraud by the Brazilian government at the expense of the landless, a devastation of the country's natural resources to provide a fleeting profit for the rich. It is also, in the opinion of many noted environmental scientists, an ecological disaster in the making not only for Brazil but for the entire world. Many ecologists warn that such grand-scale tampering with the soil structure, drainage, and water evaporation rates might well set off chain reactions that could alter climates on a worldwide basis.

You may find yourself asking how it can be so utterly disastrous to clear a forest. After all, weren't the North American forests cleared to grow food? All forests, however, are not the same. In a temperate forest leaves decay relatively slowly, thereby creating an ever deeper accumulation of nutrient-rich topsoil. In a tropical forest, by contrast, the heat and humidity promote a rapid decomposition of vegetation. A leaf that may take eighteen *months* to fully decompose in England could be broken down in a matter of *hours* in the Amazon. Given such rapid decay, the organic matter for the most part is directly assimilated into new plant life. Tropical plant life, then, is virtually a closed cycle of growth and decay. The minute fraction that escapes this cycle becomes a thin, nutrient-poor topsoil that acts more as a mechanical support for plant life than a source of nutrients. If the multicanopied vegetation is stripped away, torrential rains, sometimes dumping six to eight inches in a single day, wash away the unshielded topsoil, and the equatorial sun bakes what remains into a bricklike wasteland.[23]

You might ask why such bleak prospects could ever attract a profit-oriented organization. Just consider that if the soil erodes on one holding of 100,000 acres, a corporation can always slash and burn a few more million trees nearby. But the heart of the matter is that, in part due to the government's "fiscal encouragements," the anticipated return on the little capital invested is extremely attractive. Investors, therefore, do not have to think beyond a five- to ten-year framework, let alone worry about future generations. They call it "making a killing."

It is not, then, growing population that threatens to destroy the environment, either here or abroad, but a system that promotes utilization of food-producing resources according to narrow profit-seeking criteria. Taking advantage of this system are land monopolizers growing nonfood and luxury crops, and colonial patterns of taxation and cash cropping that force the rural majority to abuse marginal land. Moreover, even well-intentioned outside intervention, some of it couched as "aid," has disrupted traditionally adapted systems.

Of course there are areas where population density exacerbates environmental deterioration. But, just as we said in our discussion of the cause of hunger, what is most critical is to distinguish exacerbating factors from the root cause. Where environmental destruction is most severe, would halving the population solve the problem? Or do basic changes in the control of resources remain the only path to ecologically sane use of the land?

While taking credit for our tenacity and our considerable experience gained in manufacturing in 42 plants in 12 countries, Massey-Ferguson's success in Brazil certainly could not have been achieved without the enlightened policies of the Government since 1964 toward stability and development.

> "Massey-Ferguson in Brazil," statement by
> Albert A. Thornbrough, President, 1975

I first visited Brazil over a decade ago. I was struck by the unbounded confidence and breadth of vision of the people I met. These reminded me of the moral strengths that marked the earlier generations that built the United States. And I could only conclude that your nation, like mine, was destined for greatness.

> Henry Kissinger in Brazil,
> February 1976

You can buy the land out there now for the same price as a couple of bottles of beer per acre. When you've got half a million acres and twenty thousand head of cattle, you can leave the lousy place and go live in Paris, Hawaii, Switzerland, or anywhere you choose.

> An American rancher who owns land in the
> Mato Grosso, as quoted in Robin Hanbury-
> Tenison, *A Question of Survival for
> the Indians of Brazil,* London, 1973

Mr. Ludwig doesn't want to waste time with research. He just wants to begin. Naturally we make mistakes, but we also get things done a lot faster.

> An American manager of Ludwig's
> Brazilian operation, quoted in *Time,*
> November 15, 1976

8. The Price Scare?

Question: Perhaps in specific countries you can make the case that the misappropriation of the land generates hunger. But how can you avoid seeing the *global* trend? Is not the rising price of food throughout the world proof that we have entered an age of scarcity? The time of cheap food appears to be over for good. The poor countries are placing greater demands on our food resources than ever before, not to mention the Russians. How can you say that these global trends are not, at least in large part, a reflection of a growing number of people on a limited agricultural base?

Our Response: As strange as it may sound, what we are taught to view as scarcity is actually a product of efforts to cope with the problem of *over*production in a world where most hungry people cannot buy the food that is produced.

This crisis of overproduction spawns scarcity-creating solutions: production cutbacks, the planting of nonfood and animal feed instead of food crops, and built-in inefficiencies in the use of what is produced. There *is* scarcity, but it is not a scarcity of food. The scarcity is of people who have either access to the means to grow their own food or the money to buy it.

Agricultural legislation in the United States going back to the 1930s reveals that historically the major farm problem has been overproduction. After the scourge of overproduction during the Depression toppled farm prices, the Agricultural Adjustment Act of 1933 established guaranteed minimum prices for crops. The allotment system (establishing limits to the acreage a farmer could plant with a particular crop), the Soil Bank (paying farmers to hold a certain number of acres out of production), and various other programs are some of the methods employed over the years to regulate and curtail the production capacity of America's farmers.

Approaching the 1970s, who would have thought that scarcity was around the corner? 1969 was called the year of the "Great Wheat Glut." An article in *Nation's Business,* in September 1969, entitled "Too Much of a Good Thing" and subtitled "America's Farm Problem Is Not How to Grow More Food but How to Grow Less" pictured a farmer standing on a tractor in the middle of a "field of plenty" waving the white flag of surrender. The article's conclusion: "There are too many farmers, working too many farms, with too vast a capacity to produce."

What Americans know as the "food crisis of rising prices," starting in 1972–1973, was largely the direct and intentional result of United States "Food Power" policies that hit upon scarcity as a way to increase both the volume and price of agricultural exports. As we will show in Part VII, Food Power was a strategy to create demand and raise prices so as to increase the foreign exchange earnings of the United States. The stage had already been set by acreage cutbacks in the late sixties and early seventies to deal with the mounting surplus of grain. The acreage allotment figure for 1970 was only 75 percent of that of 1967; less land was cultivated in 1970 than in 1948–1952.[1] In both 1969 and 1970 the amount of grain that could have been grown, but was not, on land held out of production amounted to over seventy million metric tons[2] —about double all the grain imported annually in the early seventies by the underdeveloped countries.

Against this backdrop, United States officials started to maneuver. By devaluing the dollar (thus making our grain cheaper abroad), by rescinding a law requiring that half of our grain going to the Soviet Union and Eastern Europe be carried by American ships, and by offering the Soviet Union financing for its grain purchases, the United States set the food bait. Other countries began to bite. The notorious Soviet grain deal was the first catch.

Nature cooperated, too, with a late monsoon in India, drought conditions in West Africa, China, Australia, and Argentina and a precipitous drop in the anchovy fish catch (used for feeding livestock). But United States strategists could not depend on the weather to create scarcity. Although they must have been aware of these adverse weather conditions in many parts of the world, President Nixon and Secretary of Agriculture Earl Butz took another five million acres of wheat land *out* of production in September 1972. This act marked the largest holdout of cropland in several years—equal in size to all the farmland in the United Kingdom. Then in early 1973, when export sales had started to cool down, the United States devalued the dollar for a second time—suddenly making American grain 15 percent cheaper for the Japanese. The Japanese jumped at the bait. A new cycle of scarcity was generated by the decisions of a few government policy makers.

The result was that world grain stocks that had stood at ninety five days worth of grain in 1961 were now down below thirty days. This planned and rapid depletion of grain reserves, more than any other single factor, contributed to the unprecedented increase and volatility in food prices. Scarcity, however, was *not* the problem; the world produced more grain per capita in the so-called scarcity year 1972–1973— about 632 pounds—than it had in the year 1960, not considered a crisis year.

Yo-Yo Prices

The market system has built-in commodity cycles in which "years of glut" follow "years of want." The result? Yo-yo prices.

Do you remember that in 1973–1974 we were experiencing a rice "shortage"? By 1975 a Louisiana rice producer assessed the situation in this manner: "In my opinion there is just too much rice."[3] In the market system, a period of glut is the consequence of the previous period of scarcity. In the 1960s there was overproduction in relation to what people could buy. Prices fell as rice bags piled up. With low prices by 1970, investment in rice dropped and planting was cut back. The result: By 1973 the price of rice had doubled compared to the early 1960s. We then heard cries of scarcity. With prices up, of course, investment flowed in and production soared. By 1975, then, the rice growers grumbled about "the glut."

Chemical fertilizer is another dramatic example. New plants were constructed in the 1960s. Profits dipped as supply outdistanced buyers because most of the world's farmers are too poor to afford chemical fertilizer. The companies then cut back production in hopes of increasing profits. As the world price of fertilizer climbed, the return on investment by the fertilizer industry jumped from 1.1 percent in 1971 to 39.6 percent in 1974.[4] Then, in less than a year, prices had soared so high that purchases again slowed down. In June, 1975, *Business Week* was covering the "fertilizer glut."

These alternating periods of glut and shortage occur because we have a food production system in which investment decisions are basically made only on assessments of *current* profitability. If prices are good now, farmers and livestock producers will plant or breed to take advantage of the prices. But since all other producers are following exactly the same cue, when the time comes to reap the harvest or slaughter the animal (in the case of cattle this may be thirty-two months from the initial decision to breed), there may well be a surplus, causing prices to drop. With prices down, farmers and cattlemen will be reluctant to plant or breed heavily; thus, there will be a future shortage, causing high prices. So the cycle begins anew.

When all farmers are planting at the same time in response to high prices, the result can be not simply a drop in prices at harvest time, but the waste of a tremendous amount of food. Farmers will decide it is less costly to let their crop rot in the ground than to harvest it at a loss. According to the Department of

Agriculture, the amount of fruit not harvested or discarded "for economic reasons" amounted to over one *billion* pounds during the period 1959 through 1973.[5]

Americans are told that price cycles represent the healthy balancing mechanism at the heart of a market system. The catch is that in a food processing and marketing system tightly controlled by a few corporations, consumer prices climb up in response to basic commodity cycles but often never come back down to where they were when the cycle began. Commodity price cycles then become a handy smoke screen for profit margin increases.

Chronic Surplus

The American people are being asked to believe that the age of scarcity is upon us. Yet, as long as food is bought and sold like any other commodity and as long as a large portion of people are too poor to buy the food they need, the major problem of agricultural economists will continue to be the threat of surplus, not scarcity.

Feeding over a third of the world's grain production to animals is one way enterprising profit-seekers have devised to reduce a price-deflating surplus and simultaneously to create a product for which the consumer will be willing to pay a high price. (Such a way of dealing with a chronic surplus situation makes it easy to forget that livestock *can* be produced with virtually no grain, as are the 250 million pigs in China!)

But feeding grain to livestock does not always so easily take care of the surplus. In 1975–1976 we were in the midst of a chronic world dairy surplus with stocks in Western markets heading toward an all-time peak—at least double those in most recent years. One way to deal with the surplus produced by livestock is to feed it right back to livestock. The European Common Market recently introduced a plan to get rid of its 400,000 tons of surplus powdered skim milk by requiring livestock producers to incorporate the milk into their feed rations.[6] This practice is nothing new. In 1973 the Common Market countries used one million tons of skim milk powder as calf feed to produce high-cost veal.

The theory that we are now entering the age of inevitable scarcity because our numbers have surpassed some supposed threshold cannot be substantiated. In a world where food stocks are deliberately depleted so that United States grain exports might earn the greatest foreign exchange and where the major headache of hundreds of agricultural specialists around the world is how to *reduce* mountains of so-called surplus, the notion of scarcity is worse than a distortion. It shifts the blame for scarcity onto nameless masses of people and onto the "natural limits" of the earth. Seen this way, scarcity becomes a scare word before which we all feel powerless.

9. The Food vs. Poison Trade-Off?

Question: We have all read and seen on television frightening accounts of the dangers of manufacturing and using pesticides to increase food production. But won't we have to live with these dangers, since the application of pesticides is one of the big reasons the United States can produce so much food?

Perhaps U.S. food surpluses might allow for a slight cutback in pesticides used in this country—such as the ban on DDT. But what can you say about the underdeveloped countries where every bushel counts for survival? Won't they need to use massive amounts of pesticides? Shouldn't food for starving people take precedence over all else? I feel trapped: the choice seems to be between mass starvation and mass poisoning.

Our Response: In trying to decide how necessary pesticides are, the first eye-openers for us came from uncovering a few basic facts about pesticide use in the United States. A great deal of pesticides are used in this country—about 1.1 billion pounds annually[1]—five pounds of toxic chemicals for every American and over 30 percent of the world's total consumption. Such heavy use of pesticides might lead us to assume that the chemicals are applied to most of the nation's farmland and that our food growing productivity is in no small way thanks to liberal doses of pesticides. Wrong and wrong again.

- Fact one: About one-third of the pesticides used in the United States goes not to farmland but to industry, golf courses, parks, and lawns.[2]
- Fact two: Only 5 percent of the nation's crop and pasture land is treated with insecticides, 15 percent with weedkillers, and 0.5 percent with fungicides.[3]
- Fact three: Nonfood crops account for over half of all insecticides used in United States agriculture. Cotton alone receives almost half (47 percent) of all insecticides used. It should be noted that even then half of the total cotton acreage receives no insecticide treatment at all.[4]
- Fact four: Despite a tenfold increase in the use of pesticides between 1947 and 1974, crop losses due to pests have not declined but have remained at an estimated 33 percent. Losses due to insects alone have nearly doubled, increasing from about 7 percent in the 1942–51 period to about 13 percent in 1974.[5]
- Fact five: Even if all pesticides were eliminated, crop loss due to all pests (insects, pathogens, weeds, mammals, and birds) would rise only about seven percentage points, from 33.6 to 40.7 percent.[6]

Even before we could investigate possible alternatives to heavy and increasing pesticide use, these straightforward facts totally undermined our assumptions about the role of pesticides in U.S. agricultural production.

Do Pesticides Help the Hungry to Produce Food?

We put this question to the chief of the Plant Protection Service of the U.N.'s Food and Agriculture Organization. He estimates that annually 800 million pounds of pesticides are used in underdeveloped countries. The "vast majority," however, are for export crops, principally cotton and to a lesser extent "fruits and vegetables grown under plantation conditions for export."[7]

An underdeveloped country, moreover, easily gets locked into producing more and more export crops, in part to earn foreign exchange to pay for more and more imported pesticides. Pesticides lead to an agricultural environment requiring more pesticides, as we will explain. The diminishing financial returns per acre that result often step up the pressure to devote even more land to export crops. The entire process bypasses the need of local people for food.

Nor should we overlook the monetary cost to the individual farmer. Pesticides, in economic terms, are often just one more factor taking farming out of the hands of small, self-provisioning farmers.

Pesticide usage in underdeveloped countries is concentrated in little export-oriented enclaves that are functionally mere extensions of the agricultural systems of the industrial countries. In these enclaves pesticides are commonly applied so intensively that environmental scientists are given the "opportunity" to study the effects of extreme chemical farming.

One such opportunity came with the introduction of pesticides into the cotton fields of the Cañete Valley of Peru after World War II. By 1956, pests so overran the fields that cultivation had to be suspended. Dr.

Boza Barducci, the director of the region's agricultural experiment station notes, "In 1956 we concluded that it was nearly impossible, in practice, to obtain successful control of cotton pests by chemical methods, including the most efficient pesticides presently known." He further comments, "Such drastic losses as in the Cañete Valley disprove the worldwide belief in the theoretical efficiency of chemical products, an illusion created by the chemical industry."[8]

Insecticides introduced into Egyptian cotton fields in the mid-1950s were hailed as "a major triumph over nature." By 1961 yields began dropping by 35 percent a year. A similar pattern in northeastern Mexico brought a near halt to cotton production. In Malaysia and elsewhere, cocoa, palm oil, rubber, and other export crops have been devastated by pest attacks unleashed, ironically, by the introduction of pesticides.[9]

In Nicaragua cotton acreage was increased tenfold between 1950 and 1964. By the late 1950s the large growers acting on the advice of U.S. Agency for International Development (AID) technicians scheduled insecticide applications an average of eight times per season as well as liberal fertilizer treatments. Yields increased. But by 1966 the growers found it necessary to apply insecticides thirty times per season. Even then cotton yields began to drop: from 821 pounds per acre in 1965 to 621 pounds in 1968. Along the fertile Pacific coastal plain of Central America large cotton estates by the late 1960s had to schedule so many (45 to 50 a season) aerial sprays of a "cocktail" of pesticides (including DDT) that cotton production ceased to be profitable. By 1968 Nicaragua had the dubious distinction of holding the world's record for the number of applications of insecticides on a single crop.[10]

In spite of (or because of?) heavy pesticide doses, food crops such as corn and beans, not themselves sprayed but merely located near the cotton fields, were for the first time heavily damaged by insects. Very little food could be harvested, according to an AID report.

In regions where pesticides have been intensively used, mosquitoes have developed resistance. Malaria, once thought to have been "eradicated" by DDT, has broken out again in Central America and South Asia. In the Danli area of Honduras (population 32,000), only three years after the start of large-scale cotton production and pesticide sprayings, over one fourth of the population contracted malaria.[11] Similar outbreaks near cotton plantations using insecticides have been occurring throughout Central America.

What is happening? Why has everything seemingly gone wrong?

In country after country there is a regular progression of events. For the first few years insects are controlled at reasonable cost and yields are higher than ever before. The growers, seeing the bugs literally drop from plants, feel the pesticides give them power over forces that have always been beyond their control. Gradually, however, the pest species develop resistant strains through a survival-of-the-fittest selection.

It is not true that the only good bug is a dead bug. Some bugs are parasites or flesh-eating predators that live off the insect species doing the plant damage. Some eat only very specific parts of the crop plant. Studies show that the vast majority of insect species never cause sufficient damage to justify the cost of insecticide treatment. Their numbers are restricted below economic injury levels by the action of parasites and predators. But, when an insecticide kills some of these parasites and predators, many ordinarily insignificant insects are able to multiply faster.

Because plant-eating pests generally are present in larger numbers than their predators, they statistically are more likely than their predators to contain a few individuals with inheritable resistance to the insecticide. As the few resistant pests gradually multiply, every application of the insecticide will kill more predators and fewer pests, compounding the damage to the crops. With this understanding we should not be surprised that twenty-four of the twenty-five most serious pests in California agriculture—those responsible for a million dollars or more in losses in 1970—are either insecticide-aggravated or actually insecticide-induced pests.[12]

Only twenty-five years ago the spider mite was a minor pest. Repeated use of pesticides supposedly aimed at other pests has decimated the natural enemies and competitors of the mite. Today the mite is the pest most seriously threatening agriculture worldwide.

Already by 1971 fifteen major pest species had developed resistance to the insecticides applied. The time taken to overcome susceptibility to an insecticide has ranged from four to fourteen years. The irony of nature is that the more effective an insecticide is in killing susceptible individuals of a pest population, the faster resistant individuals will evolve. Such is the case of several pest species (including the rice water weevil, the cabbage looper, the soybean looper, the banded cucumber beetle, the two-spotted spider mite, and the banded-wing whitefly) for which no new insecticide has been developed to buy a few more years' grace. Ecologist Dr. M. Taghi Farvar notes the alarming possibility that the present pest control strategy in Central America may be leading to resistant populations of pests on a hemispheric scale.[13]

Exporting Hazard

Half of the pesticides now exported from the United States go to the Third World. And pressure to expand the market for pesticides in the underdeveloped countries will undoubtedly step up if the introduction of alternative pest control strategies (which we will discuss later) actually begins to undercut the domestic pesticide market.

The question implies that these pesticide exports might well be a boon to the hungry who need food. But as we already pointed out, most pesticides used in the Third World are not applied to basic food crops. Just as important, it is often the hungry—the landless laborers working on export estates—who are jeopardized precisely by the heavy exposure to pesticides, many of which have been deemed too hazardous to be used in the United States. According to the Environmental Protection Agency data, nineteen U.S.-produced pesticides now being exported have either never been cleared by U.S. authorities or have been restricted or banned in the United States.[14]

Even after the insecticide Phosvel had been linked to fatal human and water buffalo poisoning in Egypt, the Velsicol Chemical Corporation in Texas continued to manufacture it for export. Phosvel was designed to attack the central nervous system of insects. Apparently it can do the same thing to humans. Raymond David, a former supervisor at a Velsicol Corporation plant, reported that workers in the Phosvel section were dubbed "the Phosvel zombies" because of their obvious nervous disorders. "The company knew people were getting sick," claimed David. But the management tried to dismiss the problem. "They told me all those guys smoked marijuana. They said the guys were acid freaks," recalled David. In 1975 David quit, feeling that he could no longer take responsibility for the hazards his subordinates faced. Former employees of Velsicol have brought a suit against the company for damage to their health, including muscle paralysis, nervous system disorders, blurred vision, and speech and memory blocks. As a result, Phosvel production has been stopped. But sales in the Third world continue. Some vegetables imported from Mexico were recently found to be contaminated.[15]

With low levels of literacy, meager extension services, and heavy company propaganda about the chemicals' benefits, farmers in the Third World cannot be expected to appreciate the hazards of an apparently innocuous white powder. A research team in Pakistan in 1974 reported that "one customer, lacking a suitable container, unwrapped his turban, poured a granular pesticide therein, and replaced it on his head for transport."[16]

Most critically, people in underdeveloped countries, just like many farmworkers here who handle pesticides, have no voice in the conditions of their exposure. On Del Monte-controlled banana plantations in the Philippines, we saw workers exposed to pesticides in three ways. Twice each month, airplanes blanket everything below with deadly chemicals. Neither water sources nor people are protected. Second, workers carrying tanks of pesticides on their backs into the fields spray the plants directly. Third, in the packing house, women workers spray every bunch of bananas before loading them into boxes for export. None of the women are provided with protective clothing or masks. One woman showed us a large lesion on her leg caused, she said, when a fellow employee accidentally sprayed her.

"In Central America, thousands of highland Indians who annually emigrate to the estates on the Pacific Coast to pick the cotton crop are poisoned by insecticides," reports Dr. Farvar. "Hundreds of documented cases of death are recorded per year."[17] In 1967–1968 in Nicaragua there were over 500 reported cases of human poisoning by insecticides with eighty deaths.[18] The United States Embassy in Mexico in 1974 reported 689 poisonings and seven deaths of agricultural workers due to insecticides manufactured by Shell and duPont.[19] The National Academy of Sciences Special Commission on Pesticides found that severe occupational injuries "might be seriously underestimated."[20]

In Asia pesticides are destroying an important protein source of the rural population—fish. In the flooded rice paddies peasants have traditionally cultivated fish as a cash crop as well as an excellent low-cost source of protein to fall back on in times of declining rice prices. But today the widespread use of pesticides is sharply reducing fish production on rice farms in the Philippines, Malaysia, and Indonesia. In Indonesia in 1969–1970, German and Japanese multinational corporations began spraying over two million acres of paddy with the same chemical that allegedly only a few years before had killed millions of fish in the Rhine. Water buffalo, an important source of labor and food to the peasant population of Indonesia, reportedly have died.[21]

The Human Toll at Home

United States pesticide safety regulations are much more lenient than those of most other industrial countries, largely due to lobbying by the powerful chemical corporations.[22] According to a comprehensive study of international standards, if the United States applied Japan's standards governing toxicity levels, we would have to "do away with about half the organophosphate pesticides [the common substitute for DDT]."[23]

In 1974 the Environmental Protection Agency estimated that "as many as 14,000 individuals may be non-fatally poisoned by pesticides in a given year, 6000 seriously enough to require hospitalization."[24] Other investigators estimate that 200 die annually.[25] In 1977, 14 of 27 men handling the soil fumigant, DBCP, were found to be sterile or to have low sperm counts. In addition to causing sterility, this pesticide, widely used on crops like carrots, peanuts, and tomatoes, has been shown to cause stomach and mammary cancer in rats. Health officials in Arkansas reported workers developing such cancer after two years' exposure.[26]

Although most of these ill effects are suffered by farmers and farmworkers, all of us are exposed through what we eat. Neither can we escape the poisons injected into the environment abroad. Our planet's ecosystem does not allow for the convenient quarantining of the underdeveloped countries. Despite the ban in most industrial countries, more DDT (over 150,000 metric tons) is annually deposited in the environment now than ten years ago.[27] One reason is that chemical corporation lobbyists have succeeded in persuading Congress to exempt exports from every ban or restriction on the domestic use of DDT and other pesticides. And DDT, like all pesticides, does not stay just where it is put. Once applied to crops, it works its way into lakes, streams, rivers, and oceans. Over one-fourth of all DDT ever produced has wound up in our oceans. Fish are now almost universally contaminated.[28] DDT applied to cotton in Nicaragua showed up in beef carcasses imported through Miami.

Pesticides easily enter into the food chain and wind up in human tissue. About 50 percent of the food samples tested in a 1973 study contained detectable insecticide residues. Each young American adult already carries at least .003 ounce (0.085 gram) of pesticides permanently in his or her body fat.[29] Although, at this level, pesticide residue now presents no measurable health hazard, little is known about the effects of long-term pesticide dosages and residues.

The Poison Business

In light of the self-defeating cycle set off by heavy doses of pesticides and the documented, life-endangering hazards, why are pesticide sales still increasing? The simple answer is that a pesticide corporation receives low marks from Wall Street analysts unless they maximize profits and expand, at a steady clip, sales that now are well over $2.5 billion a year.

Basic environmental security, not to mention truly effective pest control, clearly points both to the need to develop pesticides that are as *target-specific* as possible and the need to study fully the effects of each new pesticide on nontarget insects, other wildlife, and people; but a chemical corporation's interests propel us in exactly the opposite direction. In order to maximize profit margins and expand sales, a chemical company seeks to minimize research and marketing costs and to come up with pesticides that kill the broadest spectrum of pests.

Pesticide sales are further expanded by promoting "100 percent" pest elimination. Aiming for 100 percent eradication, however, is extremely expensive, unnecessary, often fails, is likely to be dangerous, and can result in costly "overkills."

Also, to maximize profits, the companies promote *scheduled* spraying, instead of spraying in response to a need. Scheduled spraying means greater and more predictable sales. It is easier for a chemical company manager to judge how much pesticide to produce and distribute to different outlets if he can simply multiply the number of acres his customers own by a given quantity per acre. That way he does not have to take into account predictions about how bad a particular pest really is going to be in a given year.

Poison for Beauty

What we gain from pesticides turns out in many cases not to be higher yields or better eating quality. We pay a heavy price in pesticides for skin-deep beauty. Our notion of what an orange or apple should look like is largely the creation of tens of millions of dollars spent on full-color ads depicting "perfect" fruit. In several Latin American countries the sharply increased use of dangerous and costly fungicides has nothing to do with efforts to grow more food for local people, but with making sure that fruits and vegetables grown for export can meet the inflated beauty standards of the United States.

In California citrus fields, tons of pesticides are applied several times each year in the war against the humble thrips.[30] The thrips is a minute pest that does not reduce yields, harm trees, or lower the nutritional value or eating quality of citrus fruits. Its only crime is that it can lightly scar the citrus skin. The intensive pesticide treatments backfire as usual. The thrips develops resistance. The growers pour on more and more deadly pesticides, significantly raising costs. Worse yet, other once-innocuous pests, such as the red mite, become real pests in the unnatural absence of their natural enemies.

Why do growers continue to release such deadly poisons into the environment and risk their own long-term welfare? One reason is that advertising by giant grower associations such as Sunkist, Inc., have conditioned the buying public to expect their fresh fruit to be blemish-free. Growers get premium prices only for such fruit. For example, in 1965 California growers received an average of $2.61 a box for navel oranges that passed the beauty standards. Navel oranges that were equally good inside yet destined for processing into juice due to small skin blemishes brought only 12¢ a box. Tomato processors demand a visually perfect fruit, even when the tomatoes are destined to be smashed for paste, sauce, or puree. About two-thirds of the insecticide used on tomatoes grown for processing is to control the tomato fruit worm—an "essentially cosmetic pest."[31]

No plant-eating insects presently found in fruits and vegetables are harmful to people. Yet the United States Food and Drug Administration (FDA) has regularly lowered, over the last 40 years, the amount of insect residue that it will permit—in some cases, three- to fivefold. In part to meet such standards, insecticide use on vegetables and fruits has jumped by 100–300 percent.[32]

Thus, an investigative team headed by Cornell University's David Pimentel concluded that, due to the heightened emphasis on cosmetic appearance by food processors, wholesalers, retailers and also the FDA's tightened insect residue standards, 10 to 20 percent of insecticides used on fruits and vegetables serve only to improve the appearance. They in no way serve our health. In fact, this team points out the multi-layered price we are paying for blemish-free food: greater insecticide residues in our produce, more factory and farmworker pesticide poisoning, environmental pollution, increased energy consumption, and higher food costs.

Pesticides Versus Pest Management

In the last five years the potential for pest control sanity has taken form in what is now called "integrated pest management." "Integrated" suggests that chemical control alone is not the answer. Chemicals are judiciously integrated into a total strategy that includes the manipulation of the natural environment to control pests: rotating crops to deprive a pest of its host plant; developing resistant varieties through genetic breeding; skillfully manipulating the predators and parasites that attack pests; and disrupting the reproductive behavior of the pests themselves. "Management" suggests that the goal is not necessarily the total obliteration of the pest but simply keeping the pest population below harmful levels.

"Integrated pest management," in perhaps a less

sophisticated form, is the way pests were always dealt with before the pesticide blitz of the last 40 years. In the 1880's, for example, the cottony cushion scale, brought by accident to this country 20 years earlier, threatened the California citrus groves. The answer? Import the scale's predator too, the vedalia beetle. Only one and a half years later this hungry beetle had brought the entire scale threat under control. (And everything was fine until the 1950's, when the vedalia beetle succumbed to the growing applications of DDT.[33])

For decades crop rotation proved effective in managing pests. The corn rootworm, for example, will not eat the soybean plant, so that when soybeans alternate with corn, the rootworm has nothing to survive on.[34] But some weedkillers now commonly used on corn in the United States preclude this type of crop rotation. They remain in the soil and kill non-corn plants. Farmers who rely on pesticides thus must plant corn crop after corn crop, a practice that in itself tends to increase insects, disease, and weed problems. (Given such a vicious cycle, it is not surprising that corn accounts for almost half the weedkillers in U.S. agriculture.) By now the corn rootworm has developed almost total resistance to major pesticides.[35]

In some areas crop rotation is mandated by the state authorities to control pests. To control the yellowing virus on sugar beets, a number of beet-free periods are enforced in California's several beet growing districts.

Mixed cropping patterns have been found to reduce the pest problem, as compared to monoculture. Small cotton plots in Costa Rica, scattered among those growing other crops, have less severe pest problems than cotton fields in Guatemala, where cotton grows in solid blocks covering as much as 50,000 acres.[36]

In underdeveloped countries with abundant rural labor, hoeing and corn knifing to control weeds require no machinery and create opportunities for productive employment. (In the United States most weed control is still accomplished by tillage.) Mulching, simply covering the soil around the plants, can reduce weeds without using herbicides. A study in Nigeria showed that mulching reduced the competition from weeds to such an extent that corn yields doubled.[37]

The good news is that effective pest management methods minimize what underdeveloped countries and small farmers have least of—money for imported pesticides. Moreover, they create a demand for what is most available—labor power—and thereby involve more people in the production process.

Pest management can also include the selective use of pesticides. While agribusiness corporations are trying to promote "blind" scheduled spraying in underdeveloped countries such as India,[38] some farmers in the United States have realized that on top of environmental and health damage they were being just plain swindled. In Graham County, Arizona, cotton growers, working with scientists from the University of Arizona, proved they could save a lot of money by eliminating blind sprayings. Instead, they sent trained scouts out into the fields to measure pest levels. Pesticide expenditures dropped tenfold and so did pest damage. Even adding on fees paid to the "pest scouts," the total pest control costs were less than a fifth of what they had been with the scheduled approach. The chemical companies brought enormous pressure on the highest level of the university's administration to force the withdrawal of the scientists from the program.[39]

Similar experiments on forty-two cotton and thirty-nine citrus farms in California reduced pesticide expenditures by more than 60 percent.[40] A conservative estimate is that United States farmers could reduce insecticide use 35 to 50 percent with no effect on crop production, simply by treating only when necessary rather than by schedule.[41]

Integrated pest management has achieved some marked successes in the United States in recent years. In the state of Washington, such integrated pest management programs have reduced by 50 percent the pesticide use on apples—the crop using the largest amount of pesticides per acre in the United States. Integrated programs in New Jersey have reduced the percentage of alfalfa cropland treated with insecticides from 94 percent in 1966 to 8 percent in 1975.[42]

In China integrated pest management is carried out through the large-scale participation of the rural communities. Pests are controlled before they become a serious problem. With the guidance of experienced agronomists, young members of the production brigades organize themselves into a pest early-warning system. In Shao-tung county in Honan Province 10,000 youths patrol the fields and report any sign of pathogenic change. These youth teams are appropriately called the "barefoot doctors of agriculture." Their efforts have reduced the damage caused by wheat rust and the riceborer to less than 1 percent and have brought under control the recurrent locust invasions. Such a people-intensive technique has greatly reduced the need for pesticides.[43]

The Knowledge Monopoly

Partly because of integrated pest strategies and the banning of certain dangerous chemicals, the use of insecticides in the United States has dropped somewhat in the last four years. But the use of chemical weedkillers—accounting for two-thirds of total pesticide sales—is climbing. Nonchemical weed control strategies are harder to come by. But even where integrated pest management has proven itself effective and less risky, farmers hesitate to switch from chemicals. Why is this? A recent study in California revealed that "in 70 percent of the cases, insect problem solving decisions originate with chemical company fieldmen." And even so-called impartial sources—state and federal experiment stations—are dominated by research primarily on how to kill insects with chemicals. Even now, relatively little research is being done, for example, to pinpoint the economic injury level for a pest—a prerequisite for being able to apply pesticides only to manage pests below that level rather than having to go for the total obliteration of the pest.[44]

Thus farmers (and many government officials

throughout the Third World) continue to fall into the chemical trap in part because they lack information and advice about alternatives. In the United States, the USDA and land grant colleges, many of whose trustees are connected to agrichemical corporations, have not taken the lead in exploring integrated pest management alternatives.

On the international level, the United Nations Food and Agriculture Organization (FAO) was founded to provide a pool of independent experts discovering and disseminating plant protection information, including the proper uses of chemical pesticides and alternatives. But more and more FAO technicians have come to see themselves as "brokers" linking up a multinational agribusiness firm and an underdeveloped country. Institutionalized *within* the FAO structure has been a direct collaboration with agribusiness corporations whose profits are directly threatened by any nonchemical alternatives. A key part of this Industry Cooperative Program, until recently within the FAO, has been the Pesticide Working Group, whose roster includes BASF, Bayer, Borden, British Petroleum, Ciba-Geigy, Cyanamid, FMC, Hoechst, Hoffman-La-Roche, Imperial Chemical, Liquigas, Merck, Phillips, Sandoz, Shell, Stauffer, and something called the Wellcome Foundation.

An example of the thrust of the Pesticide Working Group is its action paper printed on United Nations letterhead at the official "Consultation with Agro-Industrial Leaders" organized before the 1974 World Food Conference. Corporate executives stress how chemical pesticides are "necessary" to solve the hunger problem in underdeveloped countries. They argue for *shorter* delays in approval of new pesticides. Publicly funded international agencies should, according to them, carry out a long-range study of how much pesticides will be needed (read "marketed") in each region. Public funds should establish an international stockpile of "essential pesticides" (DDT included). Corporations should work more closely in training government technical staffs in pesticide use. (Some pesticide firms already work so closely with governments that the two must be indistinguishable to most peasants. In Tanzania, for example, Hoechst became an advisor to the government on insecticides and spraying equipment. Hoechst even used government agricultural extension officers to supervise the spraying, for which they got a salary over and above the one they received from the government. Hoechst had the power to fire a government extension officer who does not supervise "properly."[45])

Pressure to get the Industry Cooperative Program out of the FAO because of the obvious conflict of interest succeeded in 1978. But the multinational firms and their allies have not given up. At this writing, Secretary General Kurt Waldheim is proposing that the U.N. set up new technical assistance machinery (duplicating the existing FAO function) within the U.N. to be financed by a trust fund whose contributors are—who else but multinational corporations?

We hope you now see through the false threat that poisoning our environment will be necessary if the hungry are to eat. The massive increase in pesticide use is not because of the pressure of hungry people's need for food. And, as will be abundantly clear from this book, lack of pesticides is not what is keeping them hungry. The real threat is that pesticide technology is in the hands of a few corporations that will profit only if they can continue to make farmers and "concerned" people everywhere believe that our very survival depends on the indiscriminate use of their products.

The threat is even more ominous since some supposedly impartial bodies that could form a counter force to the power of multinational agribusiness have become, instead, their agents. Organizations such as the FAO, far from developing and disseminating suitable alternatives or even the knowledge of the appropriate use of pesticides, are becoming partners in promotion for the chemical corporations.

If possible sterility is the main problem [in handling

pesticide DCBP], couldn't workers who were old enough that they no longer wanted to have children accept such positions voluntarily? Or . . . some might volunteer for such work posts as an alternative to . . . a vasectomy or tubal ligation, or as a means of getting around religious bans on birth control . . . We do believe in safety in the workplace but there can be good as well as bad sides to a situation.

Robert K. Phillips
Executive Secretary
National Peach Council (U.S.)

Part II

Blaming Nature

10. Haven't There Always Been Famines?

Question: Haven't there always been famines due to droughts and floods? Wouldn't we now be somewhat immodest to expect that we can eliminate all famines everywhere in the world? After all, we cannot control the weather.

Our Response: No, we cannot control the weather. And since everyone associates famines with weather disasters, we too once felt the world must resign itself to periodic famine. What we have learned, however, is that famine is a social fact, not a natural one; the result of human arrangements, not an act of God. Invariably the problem is *not* the weather. The problem is *not* a drought or a flood. The problem is the failure of a social system to meet the challenges of nature.

This is true not only today but perhaps throughout much more of history than we ever realized. We were struck by the words of a French historian: "The great French famines and food shortages of the Middle Ages occurred during periods when foodstuffs were not lacking; they were indeed produced in great quantity and exported. The social system and structure were largely responsible for these deficiencies."[1]

Most people believe famines in India have been constant phenomena related to a poor climate. But the frequency of famine in India has not been constant. Famine intensified under colonialism, especially during the second half of the nineteenth century, even though food production kept pace with population growth. After the opening of the Suez Canal in 1870, India became a major exporter of wheat to England, other Western countries, and Egypt. As Sir George Watt wrote in 1908, ". . . the better classes of the community were exporting the surplus stocks that formerly were stored against times of scarcity and famine."[2]

Let us take a closer look at one of the most "famous" famines of this century, that of Bengal, India, in the 1940s. By 1944, an official government report conservatively estimated that one and a half million lives had been lost by famine.

What caused such loss of life?

The immediate food crisis was precipitated by the exigencies of war. In 1943, Churchill ordered the Indians and the thousands of British military in India to "live off their own stocks" when the Japanese conquest of Burma had cut off a main outside source of rice for Bengal and all of India. A drought in 1942 translated into a poor winter rice harvest. But despite all this, the colonial government allowed rice to flow out of Bengal (185,000 tons was exported in the first seven months of 1942).[3] The food went where the money was and great profits were registered along the way. Similarly in a severe famine of 1876–1877 India exported record quantities of food grains. In 1943, The Royal Famine Commission—the twelfth such commission during the two centuries of British rule —commented:

> We have referred to the atmosphere of fear and greed which, in the absence of controls, was one of the causes of the rapid rise in the price level. Enormous profits were made out of this calamity, and in the circumstances, profits for some meant death for others. A large part of the community lived in plenty while others starved, and there was much indifference in the face of suffering. Corruption was widespread throughout the province. . . .[4]

The failure was one of the social and economic system, not merely of the rains.

The underlying causes of the Bengal famine are rooted in the long-term stagnation of Indian agricultural production under the two centuries of British rule. What few investments in agriculture the British did make were for nonfood crops. From the mid-1890s to the time of the Bengal famine, production of nonfood commercial crops (such as cotton and rape seed) increased by 85 percent, while food production declined by 7 percent. During the same period in eastern India, including Bengal, food (rice) production declined even more markedly, by 38 percent per capita between 1901 and 1941.[5] The result was that by the early 1940s nonfood production equaled almost one third of total production.[6]

How should we react, then, the next time we see the Bengal famine referred to by writers such as Lester Brown as "the last great famine due to the vicissitudes of weather?"[7]

Land of Famine?

As a child were you admonished not to leave any food on your plate because people were starving in China? Even if the connection wasn't clear, there was good reason for your parents to associate China and famine. According to Walter Mallory's 1928 book, *China: Land of Famine*,[8] China experienced famine in some province nearly every year and had done so for over a thousand years. A 1929 American Red Cross report estimated that 3 million deaths a year could be attributed to starvation. The same report commented on the affluence of the elite.[9]

Official dynastic histories going back over 2000 years record a total of 1621 floods and 1392 droughts —confirming Mallory's estimate of more than one disaster a year![10] Certainly, the "vicissitudes of weather" in China have not changed. The North Plain, potentially the most productive area of the country, has undergone a drought, a flood, or both every year, for the past several years.

If the weather has not changed, what has? The *effect*

of the weather on both the land and the people of China has changed and changed dramatically. In 1972–1973 when eighteen nations, containing one third of the world's people, were being hit by droughts, when western India was facing famine and herds of cattle were dying in the Sahel in Africa, China was also facing its third year of drought, the worst in three decades. But China had no famine. In fact the provinces *most affected* reaped three years of record harvests.[11] What made the difference?

In China food now comes first. The focus has not been simply on production and distribution but on the creation of an agricultural system that is less vulnerable to weather change. Traditionally, areas devastated by drought are just as likely to be vulnerable to floods next season, as is the case in Bangladesh. But a system of water control can make one season's flood into a blessing for the next.

The harnessing of the Hai River in Hopei province near Peking was one major effort at water control. In just eight years several hundred thousand men and women improved 1700 miles of the riverbed, digging 200 new tributaries and 12,000 channels and building 50,000 bridges and tunnels, in addition to over 800 other major and medium construction works. In all, thirty-five large and medium-sized reservoirs in the mountains were built to store over 106 billion cubic meters of water.[12]

Complementing the water control projects were mobilizations to tap underground water resources. Under the slogan, "We'll exchange sweat for water and water for grain," the people of Hopei, Honan, and Shantung provinces organized themselves to sink hundreds of wells, sometimes working with picks and shovels or with labor-saving rigs they devised themselves. These three provinces now benefit from some 700,000 pump wells. During one year of the drought in Peking's Hopei province alone, this work expanded the irrigated land by over 850,000 acres.[13]

Just as important, all these projects were carried out with low capital expenditures. Instead of the usual huge sums spent on machinery, it was possible to mobilize the work power of millions of peasants because they knew *they* would be the beneficiaries—never again to experience famine. China, without a single World Bank or a U.S. Agency for International Development (AID) loan, has become the country with one third of the world's irrigated cropland.[14] Wind destruction and erosion have been controlled by widespread tree planting programs. In the area around Peking alone, eleven million trees are being planted each year.[15]

The Chinese people have prepared not only the land but also themselves. Each family in the Tachai commune in Hopei has two below-ground rooms, one of which is commonly used as a storeroom for stockpiling ground maize, millet, and some wheat flour.[16]

We human beings have been on this planet long enough to know that adverse weather changes are to be *expected*. The evolution of human civilization can largely be defined as the process of working out many ingenious ways of protecting ourselves against the vagaries of nature. Therefore, when we hear of a widespread famine the first question we should ask is not "What terrible natural event caused it?" but "Why wasn't that society able to cope with the bad fortune? Why is it that one country can suffer natural disasters and have no deaths and another have a million deaths?"

China quite literally cannot feed more people . . . the greatest tragedy that China could suffer at the present time would be a reduction in her death rate . . . millions are going to die. There can be no way out. These men and women, boys and girls, must starve as tragic sacrifices, on the twin altars of uncontrolled reproduction and uncontrolled abuse of the land and resources.

William Vogt, *Road to Survival,* 1948

11. Can We Hold Back the Desert?

Question: Are there not important exceptions? What can we really do, for example, about the expansion of deserts? We have all seen pictures of the barren, parched land of the Sahel, that vast tract cutting through several countries bordering the Sahara. Obviously, it cannot support life. Do you really believe that in this case the deteriorating climate and encroaching desert have not been the cause of hunger?

Our Response: We have seen many references to an AID study[1] in which the Sahara is supposedly taking giant steps south at rates of up to thirty miles a year. On examination, however, it turns out to be merely based on hearsay collections of travelers' impressions. More scientific attempts to measure desert movements have reached different conclusions. Although there is evidence of some southward "movement," the rate appears to be more like one-half mile a year (or 100 miles over the last two centuries)—hardly thirty miles per year![2] We do not wish, however, to argue over how fast or how slow the desert is supposedly advancing and thus reinforce the notion of the desert as an independent, unstoppable force. Such debates only cloud the *social origins* of the problem.

Many falsely assume that the Sahelian drought beginning in 1969 was *the* Sahelian drought. But climatologists consider drought to be an "integral part" of the climate of the region.[3] Most of the older inhabitants of the Sahel believe that the drought years of 1910–1913 were more severe than the recent, much more publicized ones and the figures bear them out.[4] Rainfall, lake, and river levels were not as low in

1969–1973 as they were during the earlier drought. By studying the retardation in the growth of tree-rings scientists have detected that there have been severe droughts several times over the past three centuries and numerous dry spells from time to time. The most recent study we know of concluded "there is no indication of any long continued upward or downward trend in rainfall nor is there any obvious cycle." Thus the expansion of the desert cannot be attributed to any long-term climatic change.[5]

In any case, desertification is not a one-way process. Deserts *can* be reclaimed—and without great financial expense—if great reserves of labor power are invested. For example, Algeria is today the site of a massive and successful reforestation program. The goal over the next twenty years is to plant six million trees in a 1000-mile belt across the northern fringe of the Sahara.[6] Between 1965 and 1970, 160 acres were reclaimed at the Saharan village of Bou Saadu in Algeria, through planting acacia and eucalyptus trees. These gave protection from sandstorms and increased surface humidity. According to one report, "Soon grasses and shrubs sprang up and later [farmers cultivated] citrus fruits, olives, figs and pomegranates, grain, tomatoes, potatoes, peas, beans and onions."

The experience of China further confirms that deserts can be reclaimed. More than one tenth of China is made up of deserts. Thirty years ago Western observers wrote of "encroaching sand covering fertile fields forcing the people to flee." Since the Revolution the Chinese people have transformed the deserts by planting trees and grasses, building wind-and-sand breaks, and developing water conservation projects. Tens of thousands of acres of desert have been brought under cultivation and many more have become pastures.[7]

The Sahel

In an earlier response, we discussed the many adaptive techniques of the pastoral nomads to the climate of the Sahel, showing how colonial intervention and commercial interests led to the breakdown of the traditional system of the nomads, making them vulnerable to drought.

But what about the small farmers who inhabit the southern region of the Sahel? Over the centuries they also had developed a profound understanding of their environment. They knew the necessity of letting land lie fallow for up to twenty years and they cultivated a wide variety of crops, each adapted to a different microenvironment and yet together offering nutritional complementarity. Nomads and cultivators often developed a mutually beneficial relationship. The cultivators offered the nomads lands for pasture in the dry season and grain in exchange for milk, manure for the fields, and donkeys for plowing.

Sahelian Mali was once known as the breadbasket of Africa. It could always be counted upon to trade grain in times of neighbors' needs. The Sahelian precolonial custom was to construct small farming and village granaries for storing millet for flour and in some cases for even more years of consumption, knowing full well that small-harvest years should be expected. One United Nations study arguing against the idea that the Sahel is overpopulated noted that, if the traditional storage practices were followed, the "carrying capacity" of the land in people and animals would be that of the average years and not that of the poorest years.[8]

What happened to a system that was adapted over centuries to deal with periodic drought? First, even before the French conquest in the late nineteenth and early twentieth centuries these civilizations had already been severely undermined by two centuries of forced depopulation as millions of the youngest and strongest were taken as slaves to the New World. Then came the French and years of bloody fighting. Having established a permanent presence, the French looked for ways to make their new subjects pay for the administrative costs of occupation. As Thurston Clarke poignantly writes of Niger at this period, "The Nigerian people were self-sufficient; the colonial administration was not."[9] The French solution to this problem of their own making was to force the peasants to cultivate crops for export, particularly peanuts and cotton. Cotton was needed for France's textile mills since England controlled most other sources. Peanuts were to provide a cheap substitute for walnut oil then commonly used in France.

Where previously complementary crops such as millet and legumes were rotated, crop after crop of peanuts or of cotton were cultivated until the soils were exhausted. To maintain cotton exports for the French, given the resulting decline in cotton yields, farmers were forced to expand the acreage in cotton in part by reducing the planting of millet and sorghum. Clarke also notes that before the French pushed cash crops, Nigerian farmers planted several different strains of sorghum, each requiring a different amount of rainfall. Thus some strains were likely to survive even when rains were poor. But when farmers had to sacrifice so much food acreage to peanuts and cotton, they shifted to only one strain of sorghum—the one yielding the greatest quantity. This strain, however, required the most moisture. Thus farmers had increased their risk that all their sorghum would fail.

The techniques of colonialism and their devastating impact on the land and its people are hardly realities only of the past. While the Sahelian countries achieved formal independence in 1960, the successor governments have often outdone the French in forcing export crop production. Taxes that farmers can pay only by producing crops for export have been increased. In Mali in 1929 the French levied a tax that required each adult over fifteen to grow between five and ten kilos of cotton to pay it. By 1960, the last year of French rule, the tax had risen to the equivalent of forty kilos. By 1970, during the drought, the successor government forced each adult peasant to grow at least forty-eight kilos of cotton just to pay taxes.[10]

Higher taxes, as well as falling export prices, force the peasants to increase the production of export crops. But since colonial times, up to and including the recent drought years, these increases are mainly achieved by destructive methods of cultivation. Ever deeper plowing for planting cotton has eroded vast areas. With even less humus to retain water, it appears as though there is less rain. Larger and larger tracts are cultivated (more accurately, "mined") against the norms of traditional wisdom on soil maintenance. Expanding export crop production means that lands, once allowed to lie fallow for a number of years and manured by the pastoralists' herds, are forced into virtually uninterrupted cultivation.[11]

The circle is vicious. Continual cultivation rapidly depletes the soil, necessitating still further expansion of export cropping at the expense of food crops and pasture land. Chemical fertilizers that once raised yields of some export crops, making the expansion of cultivation less pressing, are now so costly that the peasants in the end are obliged to bring still more land under cash cropping. Moreover, as the farmers grow less grain, they have had little or none to exchange for milk with the pastoralists. With less grain being produced, speculators force up prices. The pastoralists then must raise ever more cattle just to obtain the same amount of grain. In southern Niger before World War II, one cow was worth 30 sacks of millet. Just before the drought of the 1970s, it was worth only one. The result, as you can imagine, is hunger for farmers and pastoralists alike, starvation for thousands of animals—and an "encroaching desert."

Studies confirm the hunger impact of export. The Yatenga villagers of Upper Volta have found that the soil that once grew cotton is impoverished as now evidenced by the low yield of food crops. The villagers doubly complained, for they found their cotton earnings could not buy enough millet (at inflated drought prices) to cover their grain shortfall.[12] A detailed study in Niger concluded that the peasant families in villages that emphasized peanut production earned a smaller income and ate less well than those in villages in the same province where farmers gave priority to food crops rather than peanuts.[13]

Exports from Famine

How do those who blame drought and an encroaching desert for famine in the Sahel explain the vast amounts of agricultural goods sent out of the region, even during the worst years of drought? Ships in the Dakar port bringing in "relief" food departed with stores of peanuts, cotton, vegetables, and meat. Of the hundreds of millions of dollars' worth of agricultural goods the Sahel exported during the drought, over 60 percent went to consumers in Europe and North America and the rest to the elites in other African countries, principally in the Ivory Coast and Nigeria.[14] Marketing control—and profits—are still by and large in the hands of foreign, primarily French, corporations.

During the drought many exports from the Sahelian countries increased, some attaining record levels. Cattle exports during 1971, the first year of full drought, totaled over 200 million pounds, up 41 percent compared to 1968. The annual export of chilled or frozen beef tripled compared with a typical year before the drought. In addition, 56 million pounds of fish and 32 million pounds of vegetables were exported from the famine-stricken Sahel in 1971 alone.[15] During the drought years 1970–1974, the total value of agricultural exports from the Sahelian countries—a startling $1.5 *billion* dollars—was three times that of all cereals imported into the region.[16]

Mali was one of the countries most affected by the drought, and a principal recipient of emergency shipments of food. During the five years before the drought, there had been a significant decline in the total area dedicated to food grain production. During this same period, the acreage devoted to cotton more than doubled. Raw cotton exports during the drought years reached record levels (approximately 50 million pounds or 10 pounds for every man, woman and child)—three to four times the levels of the years preceding the drought.[17] The fact that cotton yields during the drought averaged considerably higher than during the years before the drought suggests that cotton was being planted on the best soils—those least vulnerable to the drought.

In 1934 peanuts occupied 182,000 acres in Niger. By 1954 the area had doubled, and by 1961 it had increased five times. On the "eve of the famine" in 1968, the area planted in peanuts covered a record 1,080,000 acres, six times the peanut area of 1934. Government campaigns, taxation, and "gifts" from peanut companies that had to be repaid at harvest as well as extensive research on new varieties of peanuts were some key forces behind this extraordinary expansion. The expansion was at the expense of fallow zones of "green belts" critical especially during drought years. The cutback on fallow land only compounded the soil depletion caused by the planting of peanuts year after year on the same soil. Peanut cultivation in the 1960s began to spread north, usurping lands traditionally used by pastoralists. This encroachment made the pastoralists and their animals more vulnerable to drought. Moreover, the farmers' crops were less likely to benefit from animal fertilizers, leading to still greater expansion due to declining yields.

In the five years immediately before and during the drought, Chad carried out a major program (with fertilizer subsidized by the European Common Market countries) to increase cotton production. Two thirds of a million acres of the best of Chad's scarce resources are devoted not to food but to cotton. This increase in cotton production throughout the Sahel prompted one French nutritionist to observe, "If people were starving, it was not for want of cotton."[18]

More important than the sheer number of acres in the Sahel producing for export (as great as that number might be) is that the governments have pressured farmers and skewed every conceivable program to favor export production (irrigation, fertilizers, credit, new land development, research to develop drought-resistant varieties, extension services, and marketing facilities). And all this they do with the support of foreign aid agencies! A major 1974 U.N. proposal to "aid the hungry" in the Sahel—and one with strong

U.S. government backing—is a quarter-billion-dollar Trans-Sahelian highway, a construction boondoggle, useful only to get production out to the principal ports. With such support for exports, it comes as no surprise that even *before the drought* food production was seriously deteriorating, while export crops were booming.[19]

How are the peasant farmers reacting? Abba Sidick, Secretary General of the National Liberation Front of Chad, a peasant-based movement that has seized control of large areas of Chad, told us in an interview that growing food crops before cotton is a goal of the liberation movement. In certain regions of Senegal peasants have refused to plant more peanuts.[20] In the face of the resistance of the peasants and a drop in world market prices, the Senegalese Government is taking—in the words of the World Bank—"drastic measures" to "stimulate" peanut output. Promoting "modern, labor-saving production methods on the biggest farms" means less dependence on peasants who might always decide they prefer the security of food in the ground.[21]

Why is it that the Sahelian governments push export crops?

To earn foreign exchange. That is the answer everyone gives. But for what is the foreign exchange used? Much of it is used to enable government bureaucrats and other better-off urban workers to live an imported life-style—refrigerators, air conditioners, refined sugar, alcoholic beverages, tobacco, and so on. In 1974, about 30 percent of the foreign exchange earned by Senegal went for just such items.[22] The peanut exports annually account for one-third of the national budget of Senegal—but 47.2 percent of the budget goes for the salaries of the government bureaucrats.[23] Between 1961 and the worst drought year, 1971, Niger, a country with marked malnutrition and a life expectancy of only thirty-eight years, quadrupled its cotton production and tripled that of peanuts. Together these two exports in 1971 earned about $18 million. But $20 million in foreign exchange was then used up importing clothing, over nine times the amount earned by exporting raw cotton. Over $1 million went for private cars and over $4 million for gasoline and tires. In only three years, 1967–1970, the number of private cars increased by over 50 percent, most of them driven by the miniscule elite in the capital. Over $1 million was spent to import alcoholic beverages and tobacco products.[24] On a visit to the capital city, Niamey, we found that the local elites were shopping in a well-stocked supermarket right out of Paris—complete with frozen ice cream cones from a shop on the Champs-Elysées.

Even when part of the export earnings is used to import food, it generally does not reach the poor, whose labor produces the cotton, peanuts, and livestock, but is consumed by the better-off of those living in the cities and towns. More than half of the foreign exchange Senegal earned exporting peanuts in 1974 was spent to import wheat for French-owned mills that turn out flour to make French bread for urban dwellers.[25]

Fattening on Famine

Even more shocking than the pushing of export crops in the face of declining food production is the fact that *every Sahelian country, with the possible exception of mineral-rich Mauritania, actually produced enough grain to feed its total population, even during the worst drought year.*[26] Why then did so many go hungry?

Most farmers who grow cash crops find themselves without enough money or food reserves to meet their families' needs from one marketing season to the next, In order to survive what they call the "hungry" season —the months of particularly arduous work right before harvest—they are forced to take out loans in cash or millet at usurious interest rates from the local merchants. Local merchants have the grain because they buy it from farmers during harvest time when abundant supply makes for low prices and when farmers must sell to pay their debts and taxes. When we

visited the Tensobentenga region of Upper Volta, we
found that even during the normal rainfall year of 1976
the price of grain virtually doubled between the time
of harvest and only seven months later. The merchants
can sell the hoarded grain during the hungry season
at two or three times the price originally paid and even
export it to higher income markets in neighboring
countries. An AID officer in Ouagadougou, Upper
Volta, shocked us with his "conservative estimate"
that two thirds of the grain that merchants obtain
from peasants in payment of debts gets exported to the
Ivory Coast and Ghana. In such societies where speculation in food is "normal," adequate production can
still result in scarcity for many—even for the producers.

For farmers made vulnerable by the vicious cycle
of indebtedness, drought *does* precipitate famine.
Victimized by profiteers, farmers cannot afford to improve the quality of their land and are often forced to
exhaust the soil and even to forfeit their land altogether. But clearly, hunger and the seeming expansion
of the desert are the products not of drought but of a
parasitic class of usurers and grain-hoarding speculators.

The recent hard times actually were good times for
the already better-off minority. An FAO report concludes that the overall collective structure that helped
the people to adapt to crises is rapidly disappearing.
Once this process of individual gain-seeking had begun, a few years of scarce rain greatly increased the
polarization of ownership of resources. As a recent
United Nations report on the Sahel states, "All it now
takes is a year or two of short rains and what is left
lands in the hands of a few individuals."[27] This process
has already driven many pastoralists and peasants off
the land.

The Sahel: A Future Breadbasket?

Far from being a forsaken waste land, there are
those who see the Sahel as a potential breadbasket.

They point to the region's exceptionally large underground lake basin and three major river systems, including the Niger, the world's twelfth largest river. With this potential for irrigation and the region's gift of a tropical sun, they estimate the Sahel could produce at least six times more grain than at present, as well as startling quantities of meat, vegetables, and fruit for the lucrative European and Middle Eastern markets.

A special correspondent for *The Economist* (Oct. 6, 1973) wrote glowingly that big profits could be made with boats "fitted as floating feedlots" bringing young feeder cattle from places like the Sahel to Western Europe, North America and Japan. He estimated that such "golden calves" are worth 20 to 40 times more in the industrial countries than in the Sahel. On a recent visit to Upper Volta we found a German agribusiness firm experimenting with the use of a blimp to "lift" vegetables and fruits from outlying villages to the Ouagadougou airport so that they could be airfreighted to Frankfurt.

A French research team even suggests that the drought has acted as a modern enclosure movement, paving the way for large-scale, mechanized, irrigated agricultural enterprises.[28] The now landless peasants would at best be available for seasonal, low-wage work on the commercial complexes. The rural majority's impoverishment in the midst of an agricultural boom would ensure that the bulk of production would be exported to the continued enrichment of the same old elites and their foreign partners. We will examine an example of an agribusiness corporation already "rolling back the desert" in Senegal on pages 286ff.

Anyone who knows the Sahel knows that there is no doubt that much more could be produced. But if the government elites and multinational corporations control that production, what chance is there that the majority of the people will benefit?

An analysis of famine that puts the blame on an "encroaching desert" will never come to grips with the inequalities in power at the root of the problem. Solutions proposed will inevitably be limited to the technical and administrative aspects—irrigation programs, modern mechanization, new seed varieties, foreign investment, grain reserve banks, and so on. Such an analysis allows no reflection upon the political and economic arrangements that, far more than changes in rainfall or even climate, are at the root of low productivity and human deprivation. Until all the people in a country control their nation's resources, such "solutions" can only work against the interest of the majority.

We have seen that drought cannot be considered the cause of famine. Drought is a natural phenomenon. Famine is a human phenomenon. Any link that does exist is precisely through the economic and political order of a society that can either minimize the human consequences of drought or exacerbate them. While a people cannot change the weather, they can change the political and economic order.

The recurrent drought of the past few years has made clear that the desert is encroaching on a large scale and that food production capacity in western Africa is seriously threatened. . . . What is now needed is a comprehensive international program that, rather than ease the effects of the drought, will help roll back the desert.

Henry Kissinger, 1976

Above all, the Sahelian situation calls for the immediate launching of a major effort to slow and stabilize population growth in the region. Such a long-term cooperative international program will have to be comparable in scope to the program that launched the Green Revolution in the late sixties.

Lester R. Brown, *By Bread Alone,* 1975

Space-age farms, modern cattle ranches and lush market gardens in the middle of the Sahara. . . . This is no mirage. It is what experts from six of the world's most backward nations have conjured up for the future. Their idea is to roll back the desert

and turn their drought-ravaged countries into a
fertile green belt of productive crop land and
pasture.

The plan calls for giant dams to harness the Senegal
and Niger rivers and provide power; advanced irrigation systems to water the dust bowls; and forest
walls to check the southern march of the Sahara.

It could eventually turn the rural subsistence economies of the west African nations of Chad, Mali,
Mauritania, Niger, Senegal and Upper Volta into a
vegetable garden for Europe and a vast beef belt.

To the Point International,
"The Sahel: Today's Disaster Area . . .
Tomorrow's Glorious Garden?"
(October 5, 1974)

Part III

Colonial Inheritance

12. Why Can't People Feed Themselves?

Question: You have said that the hunger problem is not the result of overpopulation. But you have not yet answered the most basic and simple question of all: Why can't people feed themselves? As Senator Daniel P. Moynihan put it bluntly, when addressing himself to the Third World, "Food growing is the first thing you do when you come down out of the trees. The question is, how come the United States can grow food and you can't?"

Our Response: In the very first speech I, Frances, ever gave after writing *Diet for a Small Planet*, I tried to take my audience along the path that I had taken in attempting to understand why so many are hungry in this world. Here is the gist of that talk that was a turning point in my life.

When I started, I saw a world divided into two parts: a *minority* of nations that had "taken off" through their agricultural and industrial revolutions to reach a level of unparalleled material abundance and a *majority* that remained behind in a primitive, traditional, undeveloped state. This lagging behind of the majority of the world's peoples must be due, I thought, to some internal deficiency or even to several of them. It seemed obvious that the under-developed countries must be deficient in natural resources—particularly good land and climate—and in cultural development, including modern attitudes conducive to work and progress.

But when looking for the historical roots of the predicament, I learned that my picture of these two separate worlds was quite false. My "two separate worlds" were really just different sides of the same coin. One side was on top largely because the other side was on the bottom. Could this be true? How were these separate worlds related?

Colonialism appeared to me to be the link. Colonialism destroyed the cultural patterns of production and exchange by which traditional societies in "underdeveloped" countries previously had met the needs of the people. Many precolonial social structures, while dominated by exploitative elites, had evolved a system of mutual obligations among the classes that helped to ensure at least a minimal diet for all. A friend of mine once said, "Precolonial village existence in subsistence agriculture was a limited life indeed, but it's certainly not Calcutta." The misery of starvation in the streets of Calcutta can only be understood as the end-point of a long historical process—one that has destroyed a traditional social system.

"Underdeveloped," instead of being an adjective that evokes the picture of a static society, became for me a verb (to "underdevelop") meaning the *process* by which the minority of the world has transformed—indeed often robbed and degraded—the majority.

That was 1972. I clearly recall my thoughts on my return home. I had stated publicly for the first time a world view that had taken me years of study to grasp. The sense of relief was tremendous. For me the breakthrough lay in realizing that today's "hunger crisis" could not be described in static, descriptive terms. Hunger and underdevelopment must always be thought of as a *process*.

To answer the question "why hunger?" it is counterproductive to simply *describe* the conditions in an underdeveloped country today. For these conditions, whether they be the degree of malnutrition, the levels of agricultural production, or even the country's ecological endowment, are not static facts—they are not "givens." They are rather the *results* of an ongoing historical process. As we dug ever deeper into that historical process for the preparation of this book, we began to discover the existence of scarcity-creating mechanisms that we had only vaguely intuited before.

We have gotten great satisfaction from probing into the past since we recognized it is the only way to approach a solution to hunger today. We have come to see that it is the *force* creating the condition, not the condition itself, that must be the target of change. Otherwise we might change the condition today, only to find tomorrow that it has been recreated—with a vengeance.

Asking the question "Why can't people feed themselves?" carries a sense of bewilderment that there are so many people in the world not able to feed themselves adequately. What astonished us, however, is that there are not *more* people in the world who are hungry—considering the weight of the centuries of effort by the few to undermine the capacity of the majority to feed themselves. No, we are not crying "conspiracy!" If these forces were entirely conspiratorial, they would be easier to detect and many more people would by now have risen up to resist. We are talking about something more subtle and insidious; a heritage of a colonial order in which people with the advantage of considerable power sought their own self-interest, often arrogantly believing they were acting in the interest of the people whose lives they were destroying.

The Colonial Mind

The colonizer viewed agriculture in the subjugated lands as primitive and backward. Yet such a view contrasts sharply with documents from the colonial period now coming to light. For example, A. J. Voelker, a British agricultural scientist assigned to India during the 1890s, wrote:

Nowhere would one find better instances of keeping land scrupulously clean from weeds, of ingenuity in device of water-raising appliances, of knowledge of soils and their capabilities, as well as of the exact time to sow and reap, as one would find in Indian agriculture. It is wonderful, too, how much is known of rotation, the system of "mixed crops" and of fallowing. . . . I, at least, have never seen a more perfect picture of cultivation.[1]

Nonetheless, viewing the agriculture of the vanquished as primitive and backward reinforced the colonizer's rationale for destroying it. To the colonizers of Africa, Asia, and Latin America, agriculture became merely a means to extract wealth—much as gold from a mine—on behalf of the colonizing power. Agriculture was no longer seen as a source of food for the local population, nor even as their livelihood. Indeed the English economist John Stuart Mill reasoned that colonies should not be thought of as civilizations or countries at all but as "agricultural establishments" whose sole purpose was to supply the "larger community to which they belong." The colonized society's agriculture was only a subdivision of the agricultural system of the metropolitan country. As Mill acknowledged, "Our West India colonies, for example, cannot be regarded as countries. . . . The West Indies are the place where England *finds it convenient* to carry on the production of sugar, coffee and a few other tropical commodities."[2]

Prior to European intervention, Africans practiced a diversified agriculture that included the introduction of new food plants of Asian or American origin. But colonial rule simplified this diversified production to single cash crops—often to the exclusion of staple foods—and in the process sowed the seeds of famine.[3] Rice farming once had been common in Gambia. But with colonial rule so much of the best land was taken over by peanuts (grown for the European market) that rice had to be imported to counter the mounting prospect of famine. Central Ghana, once famous for its yams and other foodstuffs, was forced to concentrate solely on cocoa. Most of the Gold Coast thus became dependent on cocoa. Liberia was turned into a virtual plantation subsidiary of Firestone Tire and Rubber. Food production in Dahomey and southeast Nigeria was all but abandoned in favor of palm oil; Tanganyika (now Tanzania) was forced to focus on sisal and Uganda on cotton.

The same happened in Indochina. About the time of the American Civil War the French decided that the Mekong Delta in Vietnam would be ideal for producing rice for export. Through a production system based on enriching the large landowners, Vietnam became the world's third largest exporter of rice by the 1930s; yet many landless Vietnamese went hungry.[4]

Rather than helping the peasants, colonialism's public works programs only reinforced export crop production. British irrigation works built in nineteenth-century India did help increase production, but the expansion was for spring export crops at the expense of millets and legumes grown in the fall as the basic local food crops.

Because people living on the land do not easily go against their natural and adaptive drive to grow food for themselves, colonial powers had to force the production of cash crops. The first strategy was to use physical or economic force to get the local population to grow cash crops instead of food on their own plots and then turn them over to the colonizer, generally for export. The second strategy was the direct takeover of the land by large-scale plantations growing crops for export.

Forced Peasant Production

As Walter Rodney recounts in *How Europe Underdeveloped Africa,* cash crops were often grown literally under threat of guns and whips.[5] One visitor to the Sahel commented in 1928: "Cotton is an artificial crop and one the value of which is not entirely clear to the natives . . ." He wryly noted the "enforced enthusiasm with which the natives . . . have thrown themselves into . . . planting cotton."[6] The forced cultivation of cotton was a major grievance leading to the Maji Maji wars in Tanganyika and behind the nationalist revolt in Angola as late as 1960.[7]

Although raw force was used, taxation was the preferred colonial technique to force Africans to grow cash crops. The colonial administrations simply levied taxes on cattle, land, houses, and even the people themselves. Since the tax had to be paid in the coin of the realm, the peasants had either to grow crops to sell or to work on the plantations or in the mines of the Europeans.[8] Taxation was both an effective tool to "stimulate" cash cropping and a source of revenue that the colonial bureaucracy needed to enforce the system. To expand their production of export crops to pay the mounting taxes, peasant producers were forced to neglect the farming of food crops. In 1830, the Dutch administration in Java (Indonesia) made the peasants an offer they could not refuse; if they would grow government-owned export crops on one fifth of their land, the Dutch would remit their land taxes.[9] If they refused and thus could not pay the taxes, they lost their land.

Marketing boards emerged in Africa in the 1930s as another technique for getting the profit from cash-crop production by native producers into the hands of the colonial government and international firms. Purchases by the marketing boards were well below the world market price. Peanuts bought by the boards from peasant cultivators in West Africa were sold in Britain for more than *seven times* what the peasants received.[10]

The marketing board concept was born with the "cocoa hold-up" in the Gold Coast in 1937. Small cocoa farmers refused to sell to the large cocoa concerns like United Africa Company (a subsidiary of the Anglo-Dutch firm Unilever—which we know as Lever Brothers) and Cadbury until they got a higher price. When the British government stepped in and agreed to buy the cocoa directly in place of the big business concerns, the smallholders must have thought they had scored at least a minor victory. But had they really? The following year the British formally set up the West African Cocoa Control Board. Theoretically, its purpose was to pay the peasants a reasonable price for their crops. In practice, however, the board, as sole purchaser, was able to hold down the prices paid the peasants for their crops when the world prices were rising. Rodney sums up the real "victory":

> None of the benefits went to Africans, but rather to the British government itself and to the private companies . . . Big companies like the United Africa Company and John Holt were given . . . quotas to fulfill on behalf of the boards. As agents of the government, they were no longer exposed to direct attack, and their profits were secure.[11]

These marketing boards, set up for most export crops, were actually controlled by the companies. The chairman of the Cocoa Board was none other than John Cadbury of Cadbury Brothers (ever had a Cadbury chocolate bar?) who was part of a buying pool exploiting West African cocoa farmers.

The marketing boards funneled part of the profits from the exploitation of peasant producers indirectly into the royal treasury. While the Cocoa Board sold to the British Food Ministry at low prices, the ministry upped the price for British manufacturers, thus netting a profit as high as 11 million pounds in some years.[12]

These marketing boards of Africa were only the institutionalized rendition of what is the essence of colonialism—the extraction of wealth. While profits continued to accrue to foreign interests and local elites, prices received by those actually growing the commodities remained low.

Plantations

A second approach was direct takeover of the land either by the colonizing government or by private foreign interests. Previously self-provisioning farmers were forced to cultivate the plantation fields through either enslavement or economic coercion.

After the conquest of the Kandyan Kingdom (in present-day Sri Lanka), in 1815, the British designated all the vast central part of the island as crown land. When it was determined that coffee, a profitable export crop, could be grown there, the Kandyan lands were sold off to British investors and planters at a mere five shillings per acre, the government even defraying the cost of surveying and road building.[13]

Java is also a prime example of a colonial government seizing territory and then putting it into private foreign hands. In 1870, the Dutch declared all uncultivated land—called waste land—property of the state for lease to Dutch plantation enterprises. In addition, the Agrarian Land Law of 1870 authorized foreign companies to lease village-owned land. The peasants, in chronic need of cash for taxes and tempted by foreign consumer goods, were only too willing to lease their land to the foreign companies for very modest sums and under terms dictated by the firms. Where land was still held communally, the village headman was tempted by high cash commissions offered by plantation companies. He would lease the village land even more cheaply than would the individual peasant or, as was frequently the case, sell out the entire village to the company.[14]

The introduction of the plantation meant the divorce of agriculture from nourishment, as the notion of food value was lost to the overriding claim of "market value" in international trade. Crops such as sugar, tobacco, and coffee were selected, not on the basis of how well they feed people, but for their high price value relative to their weight and bulk so that profit margins could be maintained even after the costs of shipping to Europe.

Suppressing Peasant Farming

The stagnation and impoverishment of the peasant food-producing sector was not the mere by-product of benign neglect, that is, the unintended consequence of an overemphasis on export production. Plantations— just like modern "agroindustrial complexes"—needed an abundant and readily available supply of low-wage agricultural workers. Colonial administrations thus devised a variety of tactics, all to undercut self-provisioning agriculture and thus make rural populations dependent on plantation wages. Government services and even the most minimal infrastructure (access to water, roads, seeds, credit, pest and disease control information, and so on) were systematically denied. Plantations usurped most of the good land, either making much of the rural population landless or pushing them onto marginal soils. (Yet the plantations have often held much of their land idle simply to prevent the peasants from using it—even to this day. Del Monte owns 57,000 acres of Guatemala but plants only 9000. The rest lies idle except for a few thousand head of grazing cattle.)[15]

In some cases a colonial administration would go even further to guarantee itself a labor supply. In at least twelve countries in the eastern and southern parts of Africa the exploitation of mineral wealth (gold, diamonds, and copper) and the establishment of cash-crop plantations demanded a continuous supply of low-cost labor. To assure this labor supply, colonial administrations simply expropriated the land of the African communities by violence and drove the people into small reserves.[16] With neither adequate land for their traditional slash-and-burn methods nor access to the means—tools, water, and fertilizer—to make continuous farming of such limited areas viable, the indigenous population could scarcely meet subsistence needs, much less produce surplus to sell in order to cover the colonial taxes. Hundreds of thousands of Africans were forced to become the cheap labor source so "needed" by the colonial enterprises. Only by laboring on plantations and in the mines could they hope to pay the colonial taxes.

The tax scheme to produce reserves of cheap plantation and mining labor was particularly effective when the Great Depression hit and the bottom dropped out of cash-crop economies. In 1929 the cotton market collapsed, leaving peasant cotton producers, such as those in Upper Volta, unable to pay their colonial taxes. More and more young people, in some years as many as 80,000, were thus forced to migrate to the Gold Coast to compete with each other for low-wage jobs on cocoa plantations.[17]

The forced migration of Africa's most able-bodied workers—stripping village food farming of needed hands—was a recurring feature of colonialism. As late as 1973 the Portuguese "exported" 400,000 Mozambican peasants to work in South Africa in exchange for gold deposited in the Lisbon treasury.

The many techniques of colonialism to undercut self-provisioning agriculture in order to ensure a cheap labor supply are no better illustrated than by the story of how, in the mid-nineteenth century, sugar plantation owners in British Guiana coped with the double blow of the emancipation of slaves and the crash in the world sugar market. The story is graphically recounted by Alan Adamson in *Sugar without Slaves*.[18]

Would the ex-slaves be allowed to take over the plantation land and grow the food they needed? The planters, many ruined by the sugar slump, were determined they would not. The planter-dominated government devised several schemes for thwarting food self-sufficiency. The price of crown land was kept artificially high, and the purchase of land in parcels smaller than 100 acres was outlawed—two measures guaranteeing that newly organized ex-slave cooperatives could not hope to gain access to much land. The government also prohibited cultivation on as much as 400,000 acres—on the grounds of "uncertain property titles." Moreover, although many planters held part of their land out of sugar production due to the depressed world price, they would not allow any alternative production on it. They feared that once the ex-slaves started growing food it would be difficult to return them to sugar production when world market prices began to recover. In addition, the government taxed peasant production, then turned around and used the funds to subsidize the immigration of laborers from India and Malaysia to replace the freed slaves, thereby making sugar production again profitable for the planters. Finally, the government neglected the infrastructure for subsistence agriculture and denied credit for small farmers.

Perhaps the most insidious tactic to "lure" the peasant away from food production—and the one with profound historical consequences—was a policy of keeping the price of imported food low through the removal of tariffs and subsidies. The policy was double-edged: first, peasants were told they need not grow food because they could always buy it cheaply with their plantation wages; second, cheap food imports destroyed the market for domestic food and thereby impoverished local food producers.

Adamson relates how both the Governor of British Guiana and the Secretary for the Colonies Earl Grey favored low duties on imports in order to erode local food production and thereby release labor for the plantations. In 1851 the governor rushed through a reduction of the duty on cereals in order to "divert" labor to the sugar estates. As Adamson comments, "Without realizing it, he [the governor] had put his finger on the most mordant feature of monoculture: . . . its convulsive need to destroy any other sector of the economy which might compete for 'its' labor."[19]

Many colonial governments succeeded in establishing dependence on imported foodstuffs. In 1647 an observer in the West Indies wrote to Governor Winthrop of Massachusetts: "Men are so intent upon planting sugar that they had rather buy foode at very deare rates than produce it by labour, so infinite is the profitt of sugar workes. . . ."[20] By 1770, the West Indies were importing most of the continental colonies' exports of dried fish, grain, beans, and vegetables. A dependence on imported food made the West Indian colonies vulnerable to any disruption in supply. This dependence on imported foodstuffs spelled disaster when the thirteen continental colonies gained independence and food exports from the continent to the West Indies were interrupted. With no diversified food system to fall back on, 15,000 plantation workers died of famine between 1780 and 1787 in Jamaica alone.[21] The dependence of the West Indies on imported food persists to this day.

Suppressing Peasant Competition

We have talked about the techniques by which indigenous populations were forced to cultivate cash crops. In some countries with large plantations, however, colonial governments found it necessary to *prevent* peasants from independently growing cash crops not out of concern for their welfare, but so that they would not compete with colonial interests growing the same crop. For peasant farmers, given a modicum of opportunity, proved themselves capable of outproducing the large plantations not only in terms of output per unit of land but, more important, in terms of capital cost per unit produced.

In the Dutch East Indies (Indonesia and Dutch New Guinea) colonial policy in the middle of the nineteenth century forbade the sugar refineries to buy sugar cane from indigenous growers and imposed a discriminatory tax on rubber produced by native smallholders.[22] A recent unpublished United Nations study of agricultural development in Africa concluded that large-scale agricultural operations owned and controlled by foreign commercial interests (such as the rubber plantations of Liberia, the sisal estates of Tanganyika, and the coffee estates of Angola) only survived the competition of peasant producers because "the authorities actively supported them by suppressing indigenous rural development."[23]

The suppression of indigenous agricultural development served the interests of the colonizing powers in two ways. Not only did it prevent direct competition from more efficient native producers of the same crops, but it also guaranteed a labor force to work on the foreign-owned estates. Planters and foreign investors were not unaware that peasants who could survive economically by their own production would be under less pressure to sell their labor cheaply to the large estates.

The answer to the question, then, "Why can't people feed themselves?" must begin with an understanding of how colonialism actively prevented people from doing just that. Colonialism

- forced peasants to replace food crops with cash crops that were then expropriated at very low rates;
- took over the best agricultural land for export-crop plantations and then forced the most able-bodied workers to leave the village fields to work as slaves or for very low wages on plantations;
- encouraged a dependence on imported food;
- blocked native peasant cash-crop production from competing with cash crops produced by settlers or foreign firms.

These are concrete examples of the development of underdevelopment that we should have perceived as such even as we read our history schoolbooks. Why didn't we? Somehow our schoolbooks always seemed to make the flow of history appear to have its own logic—as if it could not have been any other way. I, Frances, recall, in particular, a grade-school, social studies pamphlet on the idyllic life of Pedro, a nine-year-old boy on a coffee plantation in South America. The drawings of lush vegetation and "exotic" huts made his life seem romantic indeed. Wasn't it natural and proper that South America should have plantations to supply my mother and father with coffee? Isn't that the way it was *meant* to be?

13. Isn't Colonialism Dead?

Question: It may be true that colonialism impaired people's ability to feed themselves. But most of the underdeveloped countries have been independent for ten to twenty years, or even longer. If colonialism is dead, why can't people now feed themselves?

Our Response: First of all we must grasp the breadth of colonialism's reach: As late as 1914 seventy percent of the entire world's population lived in colonies, semi-colonies or dominions. Secondly we must grasp the depth of its reach. While formal colonialism may be dead, it left an indelible imprint on every society it touched. The effects of colonialism could not be wiped clean simply by a proclamation of independence.

The colonial enforcement of export agriculture handicapped future development by orienting indigenous production and trade patterns to serve narrow export interests. Internal trade that might have served as the means for autonomous development was disrupted or even destroyed in the wake of all-encompassing colonial cash-crop systems geared to the needs of foreign interests. Thriving industries serving indigenous markets were destroyed. The onslaught of low-priced textiles from the mills of the colonizing countries ruined skilled village spinners and weavers in India and Africa.

Whole countries became synonymous with only one city—the capital—or, if it was inland, the capital and its port. Internal communications and trade never developed. Latin American Eduardo Galeano writes poignantly:

Brazil has no permanent land connections with three of its neighbors; Colombia, Peru and Venezuela. . . . Each Latin American country still identifies itself with its own port—a negation of its roots and real identity—to such an extent that almost all intra-regional trade goes by sea: Inland transport is virtually nonexistent.[1]

Colonialism stunted indigenous agriculture by directing agricultural research only to export crops. Moreover, slavery severely limited the impetus for improved agricultural techniques. As Rodney points out: "People can be forced to perform simple manual labor, but very little else. This was proven when Africans were used as slaves in the West Indies and America. Slaves damaged tools and carried out sabotage, which could only be controlled by extra supervision and by keeping tools and productive processes very elementary."[2] As another writer observed, the African peasant "went into colonialism with a hoe and came out with a hoe."[3]

The most ignored but perhaps pervasive effects of colonial plantation culture are these: A narrowing of the experience of agriculture to plantation work, especially with tree crops, has over generations robbed entire populations of basic peasant farming skills. Moreover, it is more difficult today for people to return to growing the food they need because farming has come to be associated in their minds with misery and degradation.

From 1650 to 1850, when the populations of other continents increased many times, greatly stimulating development, the slave trade caused Africa's population to stagnate.[4] Moreover, the slave trade depleted Africa of its most able-bodied workers.

The transfer of people of one race and culture to work plantations in a foreign land was a basic strategy of colonialism in all parts of the world. People of different racial and cultural backgrounds were thrown together in conditions of extreme hardship. Racial differences and antagonisms among laborers were ways for colonizers to control the labor force.[5] Is it at all surprising that this forced mixing of races and cultures has left a legacy of social tensions that make cooperation and economic unity almost impossible? By the forced migration of people, the pitting of race against race for the crumbs from the colonial table, colonialism undermined development based on mutual cooperation.

Colonialism also undercut the moral substratum of traditional societies. Traditional societies appear to many as totally autocratic, with the chief, the warlord, or the village headman having unlimited power. But while the peasants were obliged to serve their rulers in most traditional societies, the privileged elite were also under obligation to protect and provide for the welfare of the peasant majority. Because of this principle of reciprocity, such societies did have a degree of trust and compassion in human relationships. Hard times were shared to some degree.[6] In Vietnam before the French, for example, the rulers allowed communal land to be used to ensure that each family had at least a minimal food supply.

But colonialism destroyed the basis for this traditional moral system. First, the traditional rulers lost much of their authority in the eyes of the peasants when they proved unable to defend their territory against the colonial invader. With the introduction of a commercialized production system, traditional obligations were replaced by money-based ties. The belief that ruler and ruled were responsible for each other was replaced by the notion that a growing GNP would provide for all. Most important, while colonialism undermined the traditional respect for the elite class, it invested that class with greater real power. In eighteenth-century Bengal, India, for example, the British made the traditional elites—previously responsible only for fiscal and administrative duties—into landed proprietors, now responsible for collecting revenue from the tenant-cultivators for the crown. These *zamindars,* as they were called, used their power to acquire vast holdings of land for themselves.[7]

Before the British ruled India, debt was commonplace but the moneylender was not powerful. Part of the reason was that land was not owned privately.

Without private ownership it was impossible to lose land through indebtedness. But once the British had established private ownership to facilitate tax collection, the position of the smallholders, as most were, became precarious. Rain or drought, good harvest or bad—the taxes had to be paid in cash. With private ownership, land became the collateral for loans with which to pay one's taxes in bad times. If hard times continued, cultivators lost their land as the colonial legal system put its weight behind foreclosures.

When colonial policy tried to stem this transfer of land to nonagriculturalist moneylenders, many moneylenders simply became landlords themselves. Also larger landholders took on the role of moneylending. They were hardly sorry to see their debtors fail since foreclosure meant they could add to their property. Here we find some of the origins of present-day India's mushrooming landless laborer class.[8]

In Java, before the Dutch, the peasants had substantial economic strength. But the Dutch introduced a system similar to the British one of indirect rule through an existing elite. Peasants unable to pay their taxes to the Dutch could only turn to the local Chinese moneylenders. When the peasants could not repay a loan, they in effect became tenants on their own land, forced to grow crops chosen by the creditors for a below-market price determined by the creditors.[9]

In these two examples we see how colonialism, in its need to extract wealth from the colony, introduced a money economy and put its power behind the already well-placed. Colonialism thus promoted the increasing concentration of landholding by the few and the increasing landlessness of the many. It is this force, set in motion centuries ago, that forms such a great obstacle to true agricultural development today.

But colonialism did more than simply reinforce the emergence of one class over another. Colonialism exacerbated regional inequalities. And, as colonial policy focused on the rapid development of the most potentially profitable regions, the less obviously well endowed were left behind. A few urban areas became the seats of colonial power. These imbalances still plague development efforts.

We have seen how colonialism stifled and distorted traditional agriculture to extract wealth in the form of luxury cash crops; how colonialism enslaved or forced the migration of the agriculturally productive population in search of wage labor to pay colonial taxes; how colonialism laid the foundation for racial and social strife as disparate cultures were thrown together in competition for survival; and how colonialism exacerbated inequalities in the countryside, ending land-tenure security, a security that is now recognized as the first prerequisite of agricultural progress.

Our knowledge of the past is fundamental to our understanding of the present. The history of the colonial period should be familiar to any of us, its outcome predictable by any of us: declining food production and greater food imports, increasing impoverishment, growing vulnerability to the constant fluctuations in the international market, and internally uneven growth.

But it has not been so familiar. In the 1960s as college students we read the latest textbooks on "international development" that described these economies as "dualistic"—meaning that one sector, the commercial export sector, had potential for dynamic growth as part of an expanding international economy while the other sector, the traditional sector, was hopelessly mired in the past. According to this analysis, the task of development was to give the subsistence sector a big shove into the modern world, into the international market economy.

But dualism describes a condition while ignoring a process. If, however, we describe underdevelopment as a *process* and understand its colonial roots, we know that the traditional and the modern sectors do not stand side by side by mere chance. The history of underdevelopment shows that the economic decline of the backward sector was the direct product of the formation of the other, commercial sector, tied into the international economy. Once colonialism has raked over a country, there is no such thing as a "traditional" culture left for economic planners to push into the present.

The irony is that development "experts" see the answer to underdevelopment in making Third World economies ever more dependent on the international market system that was originally structured to keep them in submission (see Part IV).

Part IV

Modernizing Hunger

14. Shouldn't Production Be the Priority?

Question: The Third World countries clearly lag far behind in food production. Only four decades ago the average grain yields in both the industrial countries and the underdeveloped countries were about the same. Now the grain yields in the industrial countries are more than double those of the underdeveloped countries.

By 1985 it is estimated that the underdeveloped countries will fall short of the food they require by 85 million tons annually. Don't all other questions fade before the most urgent one of how to produce more food?

Our Response: Who wouldn't agree? If people are hungry, everyone assumes there must not be enough food. Indeed, for at least thirty years the central question of every War on Hunger has been: How can more food be produced? We learn of supposed answers almost daily in what we call the "news release" approach to hunger, one new breakthrough after another—protein from petroleum, harvests of kelp, extracts from alfalfa—all to expand the food supply.

In the view of many, the production approach is working. Today more food is, in fact, being produced. The "Green Revolution" now adds an estimated 20 million tons annually to the grain larders of Asia (not including China). In Mexico wheat yields tripled in only two decades.

Yet in country after country where a narrow production focus has resulted in more food than ever before there are also more hungry people than ever before.

We can draw two alternative conclusions:

Either the production focus was correct but soaring numbers of people simply overran even the dramatic production gains;

or the diagnosis was incorrect. Scarcity is not the cause of hunger. A production increase, no matter how great, can never in itself solve the problem.

The simple facts of world food production make clear that the overpopulation-scarcity diagnosis is, in fact, incorrect. Present world grain production alone could provide every person on earth with more than 3000 calories a day. Even more to the point, between 1952 and 1972, 86 percent of the total population living in underdeveloped countries lived where food production kept pace with or exceeded the rate of population growth.[1]

Indeed, as ironic as it may sound, the narrow focus on increasing production has actually *compounded* the problem of hunger. Because this startling conclusion goes against the popular wisdom, we have found ourselves wanting to verify and re-verify it in country after country.

Most useful to us in understanding just why and how a narrow focus on production undercuts the welfare of the poor majority has been to examine the Mexican origins of the Green Revolution, the most highly publicized attempt to increase production. Before we began our research we assumed that the Green Revolution (the campaign to breed "miracle seeds" and to provide the "ideal conditions"—the fertilizers, irrigation, insect-and-weed killers they depend on) was introduced into countries like Mexico in order to bring new hope to people trapped by backward, stagnating agricultures. We found we were wrong.

Agrarian Reconstruction under Lázaro Cárdenas

In 1910, 2 percent of the Mexican population owned 97 percent of the land while in most states 95 percent of the rural population had no land at all. During the bloody revolutionary war between 1910 and 1917, well over one million peasants died fighting for land. But for seventeen years the country's peasant majority saw less than revolutionary changes. Then, in 1934, Lázaro Cárdenas, a rural-born general in the revolutionary army, was elected president. His administration immediately enacted the country's most sweeping agrarian reform law. For the first time much of the country's better land was appropriated for distribution to the landless, some to be farmed individually and some cooperatively. By 1940, near the end of Cárdenas's term, 42 percent of the entire agricultural population benefited from the distribution of over 78 million acres.[2] Together these small farmers owned 47 percent of all farmland and produced an impressive 52 percent of the value of the nation's farm output.[3]

One reason for such productivity was that a newly created national bank channeled credit and technical assistance specifically to the now numerous land-reform beneficiaries. The provision of peasant-oriented services—literacy programs, health services, farm-relevant schooling, and modest rural communications—injected new life into the countryside. Often the results were immediate. In the Laguna area, to cite but one example, the real income of land-reform beneficiaries quadrupled between 1935 and 1938.[4]

The Cárdenas administration also invested in scientific research. The purpose, however, was not to "modernize" agriculture in imitation of United States agriculture but to improve on traditional farming methods. Researchers began to develop improved varieties of wheat and especially corn, the main staple of the rural population, always concentrating on what could be utilized by small farmers who had little money and less than ideal farm conditions.

Social and economic progress was being achieved not through dependence on foreign expertise or costly imported agricultural inputs but rather with the abundant, underutilized resources of local peasants. While production increases were seen as important, the goal was to achieve them through helping every peasant to be productive, for only then would the rural majority benefit from the production increases. Freed from the fear of landlords, bosses, and moneylenders, peasants were motivated to produce, knowing that at last they would benefit from their own labor. Power was perceptibly shifting to agrarian reform organizations controlled by those who worked the fields.

The Green Revolution as Counter Revolution: Agriculture to Serve Industrialists

Not surprisingly, by the end of his administration in 1940, Cárdenas had made powerful enemies. First were those who had seen their haciendas expropriated. Next were the urban-based monied groups, alarmed by the Cárdenas model of cooperative ownership of land and public ownership of certain industries. Instead of investing in rural services and collective enterprises, they wanted the state to pay for electric power, highways, dams, airports, telecommunications, and urban services that would serve privately owned, commercial agriculture and urban industrialization—from which they would profit.

Not the least of the enemies of Cárdenas was the United States foreign policy establishment. Land redistribution with cooperative ownership, as well as Cárdenas's nationalization of the Rockefeller Standard Oil subsidiary and foreign-owned railroads, caused "concern" in Washington and on Wall Street. United States corporate investment dropped by about 40 percent between the mid-thirties and the early 1940s.[5]

By 1942, these enemies of Cárdenas's rural reconstruction succeeded in seizing the balance of power within the administration of Cárdenas's successor Avila Camacho. The significance of this shift for the future of Mexican agriculture was immediately clear. President Avila Camacho's first agricultural plan stated that agriculture was now to serve as the basis for the "founding of industrial greatness."[6] Agricultural progress was no longer to be measured first and foremost in terms of the well-being of the rural majority but in how well it served growth elsewhere in the economy.

The United States only reinforced this fundamental shift. United States policy makers identified American interests with the stability of the Avila Camacho administration, with Mexico's ability to produce manufactured goods to support the war effort, and with private control over resources. Getting more food out of the rural areas and into the cities was seen as critical. More food in the urban areas meant lower food prices, an essential ingredient for quieting urban unrest and keeping industrial wages low. Low wages would ensure industrial profits high enough to attract investors, both local and foreign.

It was in this historical context that the Green Revolution was born. The Avila Camacho administration welcomed the Rockefeller Foundation to Mexico, and in 1943 the Foundation joined with the new administration to initiate an agricultural research program. The result on one level was in the much-heralded technical package later to be publicized as the Green Revolution. On another level, it served to reverse the entire thrust of the Cárdenas rural reconstruction.

The field director of the Rockefeller Foundation in Mexico became head of a new office *within* the Mexican Ministry of Agriculture. His job was to oversee a technical revolution in Mexican agriculture. Policy choices systematically discarded research alternatives oriented toward the nonirrigated, subsistence sector of Mexican agriculture. Instead, all effort went to the development of a capital-intensive technology applicable only to the relatively best-endowed areas or those that could be created by massive irrigation projects. The focus was on how to make seeds, not people, more productive. Agricultural modernization came to substitute for rural development.

Rapid urban-centered industrialization, so profitable for a few, simply could not coexist with the type of rural development promoted by the Cárdenas administration. First, true rural development based on making each rural family productive and better-off would have meant that the rural majority itself would have eaten much of the increment in food production. This increment was exactly what the ascendant urban interests counted on taking *out* of the countryside to feed an industrial workforce. Second, genuine improvement in rural life would have sharply diminished the steady exodus to the towns and cities. But it was just this ongoing influx of rural refugees that was so "needed" to perpetuate low industrial wages.

Thus, only one type of agricultural policy would serve the ends of the urban and industrial interests— one that willfully neglected the problems of the land-reform communities created by Cárdenas while lavishing public funds on increasing the production of a few large commercial growers, marketing outside the rural areas. In the words of a United Nations study:

> The burden of transforming the frontier of Sonora into a vast agricultural emporium was . . . borne to a great extent by the federal treasury; but most of the fruits of the effort remained firmly under the control of the private landowning elite. . . .[7]

The Mexican government subsidized imports of agricultural machinery. In addition, between 1941 and 1952, 18 percent of Mexico's federal budget and 92 percent of its agricultural budget was spent on large irrigation projects to create vast new stretches of rich farmland in the north. This valuable land was then sold at low prices, not primarily to the landless poor, but to politically powerful families of businessmen and bureaucrats. Although by law no one in Mexico can own more than 250 irrigated acres, today the average farm in the Mexican Green Revolution area of Hermosillo has grown to 2000 irrigated acres[8] with some holdings running much larger.[9] Not surprisingly, about 3 percent of all farms accounted for 80 percent of the production increase during the 1950s.

Here we have the model of agricultural development that has been actively exported to virtually all the underdeveloped countries within the sphere of influence of the United States.

Betting on a Winner

Ignoring overwhelming evidence from around the world* that small, carefully farmed plots are more productive per acre than large estates and use fewer costly inputs, governments, international lending agencies and foreign assistance programs have invariably passed over small farmers (not to mention the landless). The French agronomist René Dumont describes a Ford Foundation mission of thirteen North American agronomists to India in 1959. The mission argued that it was practically impossible to make simultaneous headway in all of India's 550,000 villages. So they advised subsidization of technical inputs in those areas that were well irrigated—thereby leaving over half of the nation's farms totally out of the national agricultural development program. It appeared easier to help a small number of large farmers increase wheat production by 50 percent within just a few years than to mobilize the productive potential of 50 to 60 million farm families. Thus in the mid-sixties, India's New Agricultural Strategy to promote the improved seed varieties ended up concentrating on merely one-tenth of the cultivable land and to a great extent on only one crop, wheat.[10]

Everywhere the large farmer has been directly favored. A study of Gapan, Nueva Ecija, in the Philippines, in 1966, showed that the first seeds produced by the Rockefeller-funded International Rice Research

* See Question 21.

Institute were distributed only to landholders owning 25 acres of rice paddy or more.[11] No seeds were sold directly to sharecroppers or tenants.

The Tunisian agriculture program provided credit only to those owning a certain minimum acreage— usually 125 acres, a largeholding indeed in that country. Moreover, subsidies to dairy farmers went only to those producing more than 525 quarts of milk a day. Subsidies for purchasing combine harvesters benefited only the largeholder, the only one in a position to even consider such a purchase.

Once selected as the focus of government help, the large farmers have taken full advantage of their head start. Frequently the wealthiest landowning families have reaped additional profits by monopolizing distribution of fertilizers, pesticides, and machinery needed to make the new seeds respond. Associations of large commercial farmers like those in Mexico have been able to make considerable extra earnings by exporting the Green Revolution, selling thousands of tons of the new seeds annually to Asia and Africa.

Focusing narrowly on production totals transforms rural development into a technical problem—one of getting the "right," usually foreign-made, inputs to the "progressive," invariably well-placed farmers. We refer to this production focus as *narrow* precisely because it ignores the social reality of hunger—that the hungry are those with control over little or no food-producing resources. Until control over productive resources is democratized such "agricultural modernization" will remain but a mirage of rural development —a mirage that undermines the interests of the majority of the rural population in order to serve those of a few—large landholders, moneylenders, industrialists, bureaucrats, and foreign investors.

The influx of public funds for the purpose of increasing production has turned farming into a place for profiteering and speculative investment. But to take part, one has needed some combination of land, money, access to credit, and political influence. That alone has eliminated most of the world's rural majority.

15. But Isn't Nature Neutral?

Question: You see the Green Revolution as a prime example of a narrow production approach that has given the upper hand to the larger landholders. But isn't the essence of the Green Revolution the new, high-yielding seeds? Why shouldn't they grow as well for the poor farmer as for the rich? Nature, after all, is less partial than are governments beholden to the vested interests of the wealthy. Once the poor obtain the high-yielding varieties, can't they improve their positions too? Even though the gap between rich and poor may still exist, won't all farmers eventually improve their yields, their livelihood, and their nutritional status?

Our Response: The term "high-yielding varieties"—HYV's as they are called in the Green Revolution literature—is, in fact, a misnomer. Understanding why the term is a misnomer is the key to grasping why the new seeds might not be as neutral as the question suggests.

As part of a fifteen-nation study of the impact of the new seeds conducted by the United Nations Research Institute for Social Development, Dr. Ingrid Palmer concludes that the term "high-yielding varieties" is a misnomer because it implies that the new seeds are high-yielding *in and of themselves.*[1] The distinguishing feature of the seeds, however, is that they are highly *responsive* to certain key inputs such as irrigation and fertilizer. Following Palmer's lead we have chosen to use the term "high-response varieties" (HRV's) as much more revealing of the true character of the seeds. The Green Revolution is obviously more complicated than just sticking new varieties of seeds into the ground. Unless the poor farmers can afford to ensure the ideal conditions that will make these new seeds respond (in which case they wouldn't be poor!), their new seeds are just not going to grow as well as the ones planted by better-off farmers. The new seeds prefer the "better neighborhoods."

Just as significant for the majority of the world's farmers is that the new seeds show a greater yield variation than the seeds they displace.[2] The HRV's are more sensitive to drought and flood than their traditional predecessors. They are particularly prone to water stress—the inability to assimilate nutrients when not enough water is getting to the plant roots, especially at certain stages in their growth cycles. Under these conditions it is often no more profitable to apply fertilizers to the new seeds than to the previous ones.[3] In 1968–1969 in Pakistan, for example, yields of Mexican dwarf wheat declined by about 20 percent because of a two-thirds reduction in average rainfall and higher than normal temperatures. The locally adapted varieties, however, were not adversely affected by the weather changes. Instead their yields increased 11 percent.[4] The new sorghums now being planted in Upper Volta in Africa are also less drought-resistant than their local cousins.[5] The HRV's can also be more vulnerable to too much water. Being shorter, the HRV's of rice cannot tolerate the higher flood levels that indigenous varieties can endure.

Since the HRV's are more sensitive to both too much and too little water, they need, not mere irrigation, but sophisticated water management. The significance of this need becomes clear in India's Punjab. Higher yields from the new seeds depend on a tubewell for a controlled water supply. But a tubewell is well beyond the means of the small farmer.

Taking advantage of the HRV's has required farmers to double or even triple their indebtedness. Since small farmers are already in debt for preharvest consumption and for other family needs—often at very high rates of interest—most will not be able to take on this heavy new burden.

HRV's are often less resistant to disease and pests. Vulnerability results from transplanting a variety that "evolved" over a short period in one climate (with a little help from agronomists) to an entirely different climate, thus supplanting varieties that had evolved over centuries in response to natural threats in that environment. A small farmer, whose family's very survival depends on each and every harvest, cannot afford to risk crop failure. For the large farmer that risk is minimized. The difference is not just that the large farmer can better withstand a crop failure. Large farmers have also managed in many instances to protect themselves against disease-prone seeds. In Mexico, for example, associations of large farmers have, since the early days of the Green Revolution, kept in constant touch with government seed agencies and have, therefore, been warned of any disease likely to attack a particular new plant variety. By way of contrast, when the agency to which the land-reform beneficiaries were tied was notified that its seeds had become susceptible to disease, it was reluctant to throw them out and often continued to sell them. To a large extent this accounts for the disastrous yields in the Mexican land-reform sector during the late 1950s and early 1960s.[6]

In addition, the new seeds have been restricted to well rain-fed and irrigated regions. It is not coincidental that these favored regions are inhabited by the more affluent farmers. Almost all of the HRV increases in wheat cultivation in India have taken place in the states of Punjab and Haryana, largely because the soil is alluvial and a canal system assures a year-round water supply.[7]

Nyle C. Brady, Director of the International Rice Research Institute, where many of the new strains have been developed, estimates that the "new rice varieties may be suitable for only 25 percent of the world's acreage, largely those areas with water for irrigation."[8] Because the new varieties are less resistant to flooding, there are many parts of Thailand, Bangladesh, and South Vietnam in which they cannot be used.[9] None of the new seeds are successful in areas of constant high temperatures and rainfall, limited sun, and thin, badly leached soils.

Knowing the biological requirements of the seeds, we should not be surprised that as late as 1972–1973 the HRV's covered a very small percentage—only about 15 percent of the total world area excluding the socialist countries.[10] Furthermore, they are highly concentrated: 81 percent of the HRV wheat grows in a small area in India and in Pakistan; and four countries (India, the Philippines, Indonesia, and Bangladesh) account for 83 percent of the HRV rice.[11]

The seeds, due to their need for ideal conditions, are restricted to certain favored areas. They therefore have reinforced income disparities between geographic regions, just as they have exacerbated the inequalities between social classes.

Two other factors contribute to making the new seeds less than neutral. First, hybrids of corn and sorghum do not remain genetically pure year after year. To maintain high yields new hybrid seeds must be purchased each year. This requirement alone gives the edge to the wealthier farmer and to the farmer more closely linked to seed distributors and other credit sources. The many farmers with only enough land to grow the food their families need will never have the cash to purchase hybrid seeds.

Second, the new seeds, because they require special knowledge to be used effectively, are inherently biased in favor of those who have access to government agricultural extension agents and instruction literature. In many countries the large landowners have been able to monopolize the services of the extension agencies. They have also been able, as in the Mexican state of Sonora, to hire private agricultural and pest experts to solve their technical problems.[12] A study in Uttar Pradesh, India, showed that, since 70 percent of the family heads were completely illiterate, "access to literature is thus primarily the prerogative of the better educated, wealthier landowners." Nonwritten material was no more successful in overcoming the problem: the village headman regarded the radio as his private property and invited only his friends to listen.[13]

The bias can be quite subtle. As one student of the Green Revolution so aptly describes it: "The new technology puts a relative handicap on those whose assets include traditional knowledge of the local idiosyncrasies of soil and climate and whose energies are absorbed by the labors of husbandry. . . . It gives the advantage to those skilled in manipulating influence."[14]

Still the idea that a seed, the product of impartial scientific research, must be neutral, without built-in bias, is deeply rooted in most of us. Most assume it will just be a matter of time before the new seeds spread out to the poor and bring the standard of living up for all farmers. But the dependence of HRV's on *optimal* conditions makes that impossible in most areas today. Both the rich and the poor farmer certainly can plant the seed, but who can feed the plants the optimal diet of nutrients and water and protect them from disease and pests? Can the family who depends for their food on what they grow afford to gamble with the less dependable seeds?

The only way that such seeds can be neutral is if the society prepares the way—giving equal access to the necessary inputs to all farmers. If this means redistribution of control over all food-producing resources, including land redistribution, it can work. In Cuba, for example, between 75 and 90 percent of the rice acreage is planted with the high-response seeds.[15] In Taiwan, also a country that has undergone land redistribution, the use of improved seeds is over 90 percent. But where "equalizing access" has merely meant credit programs it has rarely worked.

Any notion of equalizing access to a new technology without altering the basic social structure overlooks the only truly workable approach—the farmers themselves becoming the innovators. Then the issue of dissemination of new seeds or new skills evaporates as a problem. And, as you might guess, the kinds of seeds developed are not those demanding ideal conditions.

In China, production of the new seeds does not take place in central experimental stations but is handled by ordinary families themselves.[16] Most communes have their own laboratories for locally developing new varieties. Spreading the new technology is therefore not a problem. As early as 1961 the Chinese were breeding seeds for less favorable climes. Chinese farmers have successfully developed seeds that are both higher yielding and *more* able to withstand bad weather and other dangers, such as barley strains adapted to high altitudes and cold-resistant strains of wheat.[17]

Once manipulated by people, nature loses its neutrality. Elite research institutes will produce new seeds that work—at least in the short term—for a privileged class of commercial farmers. Genetic research that involves ordinary farmers themselves will produce seeds that are useful to them. A new seed, then, is like any other technological development; its contribution to social progress depends entirely on who develops it and who controls it.

16. Hasn't the Green Revolution "Bought Us Time"?

Question: You say that the narrow focus on increased production has benefited the already well-off farmer. But at least more food has been produced. How could this hurt the poor? They need food more than anything else. You seem to expect the strategies that increase production, such as the Green Revolution, to also solve *social* problems. How could they? Increasing production is a scientific and a technological problem. Norman Borlaug, father of the Green Revolution, has said that the most the Green Revolution could do is to "buy us time" while we slow population growth and work on economic problems. Hasn't the Green Revolution meant progress, in at least this sense?

Our Response: To answer this question we had to examine systematically just what happens once the solution to hunger is sought in a single-minded technological push to increase production. This investigation has uncovered the dynamics by which the better-off have "progressed" *at the expense* of the majority. Around the world we find a strikingly consistent pattern. And although the question implies that the impact of the Green Revolution is limited to underdeveloped countries, it is not. Part VII will reveal a similar pattern at work in the United States.

More Grain: Who Gains?

For many outsiders looking at hunger in underdeveloped countries, the fact that greater production can bring cheaper grain appears as part of the solution. The mistake is in forgetting two points: First, many of the poor are also producers whose livelihood in part depends on selling their grain. Second, for those unable to take part in the new technology, yields have often *not* increased. With overall greater availability, however, and the failure of government policies to maintain prices, the poor farmers with the unimproved yields are in a worse plight than ever.

In Greece the agricultural credit corporations pressured farmers to sow foreign-bred HRV wheats. In the lowland areas occupied by large farms the result has been higher yields, thus increasing total Greek output. But in the mountains the HRV seeds yielded less than the varieties that had been grown for generations by the mountain people. As the national (and world) yields increased, wheat prices fell. The large commercial farms in the plains could withstand the price drop because their volume of production was large and increasing. But for the poorer farm on the mountain slopes the fall in income resulting from lower yields was often the final blow leading to the desertion of many mountain villages, as well as the loss to the world of wheat varieties unconsciously selected, over centuries, to thrive in more difficult conditions.[1]

Rents Go Up

Landlords in many countries have found they can transfer part of the burden of increased production costs onto the tenants or sharecroppers, in effect, forcing the tenants to pay for the new technology. For instance, with the introduction of the new technology, the cash rents tenants must pay have gone up by about one-third to one-half. Crop share rents are changing from the traditional 50-50 division between the landlord and the tenant to 70-30 in favor of the landlord,[2] effectively cutting the tenant out of the production gains. In one area of India where the sharecropper used to get half the harvest, he now gets only one-third; another third goes to the landlord and the remaining third goes to pay off the debt for the tubewell the landlord purchased (it will, of course, go to the landlord once the tubewell is paid for).[3] In one area of Malaysia tenants now have to provide 100 percent of the fertilizer costs.[4]

Traditional landlords once had very clearcut, reciprocal obligations to tenants or sharecroppers. The landlord would have never considered passing on his obligations to the tenants. But now that more and more landlords are absentee city dwellers, traditional face-to-face dealings are being replaced by impersonal, money-based relationships. Landlords increasingly demand cash payment of rent instead of payment in kind. In the northern states of Malaysia cash payments are required at the *beginning* of the season. The tenant has to come up with rent at just the time he is least likely to have it. He therefore has to borrow at high rates of interest—thus reducing his total income. Moreover, if the crops fail, the tenant still has to come up with the rent.

By the same token, many landlords now prefer to pay in money wages rather than in farm produce. In times of inflating food prices, however, it would be much better for the tenant-farmer to have part of the harvest than money. We learned of one district in India where landlords now pay only money wages, preferring to hoard and sell the rice later for enormous profit. In 1974, India's *Economic and Political Weekly* reported that in Thanjavur, Tamil Nadu, "hordes of the police were stationed in the paddy fields to quell disturbances arising out of the landlords' refusal to pay even a part of the wages in kind."[5]

Land Values Soar

In countries where food resources are still allowed to be held exclusively for private gain, government funds in the form of irrigation works and subsidies for fertilizers and machinery have combined with the higher potential yields of the new seeds to turn farming into the world's hottest growth industry. Instead of a way of livelihood for millions of small, self-provisioning farmers, agriculture is increasingly seen as a lucrative opportunity by a new class of "farmers" with the money or influence to get in on the action—moneylenders, military officers, bureaucrats, city-based speculators, and foreign corporations. In those areas targeted by the "production strategy" land values have gone up three-, four-, or even fivefold as these so-called farmers compete for the land that they believe, often rightly, will make them a fortune.[6]

Here is development economist Wolf Ladejinsky's well-known account of how nonfarmers in India buy up land for speculation:

The buyers are a motley group: some connected with land through family ties, some altogether new to agriculture. A few have unemployed rupees acquired through undeclared earnings, and most of them look upon farming as a tax-haven, which it is, and as a source of earning tax-free supplementary income. The medical doctor from Jullundur who turned part-time farmer is sitting pretty. The 15 acres purchased four years ago have tripled in value. To listen to him, he is in farming "for the good of the country." . . . His only vexation is whether or not he will succeed in buying another 10 acres he has his eyes on—and what a disappointed man he will be if they escape him! As we watched him supervise the threshing, he was anything but a "gentleman farmer."[7]

Nonfarmers are taking over agriculture not only because governments have made investments attractive, but because increasingly only the wealthier urban dwellers can obtain credit or afford to buy the higher-priced land and the necessary inputs. As the price of land rises, purchase by the smallholder or tenant, if unlikely before, becomes completely out of the question. In countries where security of tenure is legally guaranteed after the tenant has continuously cultivated a given plot for a certain number of years, some landlords maneuver to ensure that their tenants are never given legal title to the land, now that land is more valuable. In Tanjore, India, landlords shift sharecroppers from one plot to another each year to successfully dodge such tenure regulations.[8]

Moreover, as the market value of land increases, taxes increase. In Colombia wealthy potential buyers of small plots persuade tax authorities to revalue the land in order to put pressure on the small farmers. Peasants who cannot afford to plant the new varieties of coffee find that they cannot pay the higher tax bill and are forced to sell to larger landholders who usually can evade the tax by paying a bribe.[9]

Fewer People Control More Land

Fewer and fewer people control more and more of farm production. A pattern of increasing monopolization of agricultural land moves ahead in India, Bangladesh, Mexico, the Philippines, Colombia—in virtually all countries where officially subsidized "modernization" now means that high returns stem from the sheer amount of land one can control, not from how well one farms.

In the area of Tamesis, Colombia, the better-off coffee growers able to adopt the new seed varieties increased the average size of their holdings by 76 percent between 1963 and 1970.[10] Similarly, in the government-subsidized irrigated zones of Morocco land concentration is increasing. In just five years, from 1965 to 1970, the average size of modern, Moroccan-owned farms in one irrigated area increased 30 percent.[11] In the Indian Punjab, between the fifties and the mid-sixties, the amount of land owned by the largest farmers (those with 100–150 acres) increased at a rate four to ten times greater than that of the smaller-sized farms.[12]

Another sign of increasing concentration of land ownership is that the smallest farmers are selling their land. In Bangladesh, in both 1969–1970 and 1972–1973, well over half the land belonging to farmers owning less than one acre (about one-fourth of all farmers) was sold.[13]

To some, the decline of the small farmer appears unfortunate, but, alas, inevitable. But the tightening of control over agricultural production is not inevitable. It results from the actions and even the planning of people. In the early 1950s, large farmers in the Mexican state of Sonora saw that land values were about to go up because of massive government irrigation plans for the area. They began to contrive to take over cheaply the land owned by thousands of smallholders. They turned to their friends within the National Agricultural Credit Bank—the government agency on which smallholders in the area depended for survival. The bank began to delay crop credit for smallholders. In some cases they received credit so late that their wheat, to take but one example, had to be planted out of season and thus failed during several years. The bank also began to provide sacks of wheat seed that some say turned to dust between their fingers and fertilizer which they are sure was nothing more than white powder. The smallholders' expenses soared. They had several disastrous years. Then came the final

blow: The government foreclosed on all properties
with outstanding debts to federal agencies. The large
farmers had succeeded. The majority of the smallholders in one devastated settlement ended up selling
their land for about one ninth of the market price to
two of the largest and most politically influential
landowners in the state.[14]

Where much land has traditionally been communally worked, as in Africa, the new agricultural entrepreneurs might have an even easier time expanding
commercial operations. Without a tradition of private
property and small farms that exists in Asia, little if
anything stands in the way of tribal chieftains and
foreign corporations who want to appropriate communal land for their private gain.

The Making of the Landless

In certain areas landlords are moving to push their
tenants off the land. The landlords see several advantages. For instance, they are freed from tenants who
might conceivably claim land under a land-to-the-tiller
reform movement. Moreover, the large landowner
finds it more profitable to mechanize production or
take advantage of part-time laborers who have no
claim on the land or on the harvest. A study for the
World Bank on the size of farms in the Indian Punjab
during the 1960s concluded that farms that had been
mechanized grew by an average of 240 percent over a
three-year period, primarily because the landlords decided to cultivate land they had previously rented out.[15]
The landlord's gain—higher cash income—was society's loss, as a substantial number of tenants could
no longer rent the land they needed to support themselves. In India, in 1969, there were 40,000 eviction
suits against sharecroppers in Bihar alone and 80,000
in Karnatika (Mysore).[16]

As the control of land tightens and more tenants are
evicted, the number of landless laborers mounts. In
all nonsocialist underdeveloped countries 30 to 60
percent of rural adult males are now landless. In

Mexico between 1950 and 1960 the number of landless laborers increased much faster than the general population, from 2.3 to 3.3 million.[17] In the state of Sonora, where Mexico first concentrated its Green Revolution production push in the 1940s, landless laborers represented 57 percent of the agricultural work force. By 1960, the proportion had grown to 62 percent and by 1970, it was roughly 75 percent.[18] Between 1964 and 1970 the number of landless families in Colombia more than doubled.[19] During the fifteen years beginning in 1951, the number of landless laborers in Bangladesh has increased by two and a quarter times.[20] In India, between 1961 and 1971, the number of agricultural laborers increased by over 20 million (by 75 percent). In the same period the number of cultivators decreased by 15 million (by 16 percent). None of these startling figures includes the millions of landless refugees who, finding no farm work, join an often hopeless search for work in the urban areas.

So the number of landless mounts while the number of rural jobs shrinks. Traditionally in many countries even the poorest landless peasant had access to part of the harvest. In India, Bangladesh, Pakistan, and Indonesia the large landowner once felt obligated to permit all who wished to participate in the harvest to retain one sixth of what they harvested. Even the most impoverished were assured of work for a few bags of grain. Now, with the increased likelihood of profitable sales, the new agricultural entrepreneurs are rejecting the traditional obligations of the landowner to the poor. It is now common for landowners to sell the standing crop to an outside contractor before harvest. The outsider, with no local obligations, can seek the cheapest labor, even bringing in workers from neighboring areas.[21]

In Java, landless laborers were once permitted to squat on dry land in the off-season to grow cassava and vegetables. With the new rice seeds, landlords are now interested in irrigating the land for year-round production for commercial markets. Squatters are no longer welcome.[22]

In addition, the introduction of large-scale mechanization is a double-edged sword for the rural poor. Large landowners say that the only way they can make their new machines pay off is to reduce per acre cost by expanding their acreage. As we have already seen, expansion by the largeholders forces more and more tenants and small farmers off the land, thereby creating greater numbers of landless in search of farm work. Simultaneously, however, the machines drastically decrease the number and length of jobs available. A tractor cuts to a fifth the number of workers needed to prepare the same field with a bullock-drawn plow. The same is true of a mechanical reaper compared to a hand scythe.[23]

The net result in the Pakistani Punjab, for example, is that the amount of human labor required in the fields is 50 percent less than in the premechanization period only a few years ago. An analysis of the trend in India concluded that "the introduction of mechanical harvesting will eventually result in an overall decrease of about 90 million man-days of employment in the Punjab, most of it for day laborers."[24]

During Mexico's rapid mechanization, when the number of landless laborers rapidly rose, the average number of days worked by each laborer fell from 190 to 100. The larger the number looking for work, the easier it is for the large landholders to keep wages low and thereby, ironically, to offset the operating costs of machinery (often already heavily subsidized). The incomes of landless laborers around the world, incredibly low to begin with, are steadily declining. In the same period in Mexico, the decade of the 1950s, the *annual* income of landless rural workers declined from $68 to $56, while per capita national income increased from $308 to $405.[25]

The production strategy we have been describing often offers the poor the illusion of rural employment. One of the best-documented cases is the Mexican state of Sonora. There, the clearing of new land and vast irrigation projects executed with public funds attracted workers to Sonora during the fifties and sixties. By 1971, when these projects had been completed, the laborers still needed jobs but, with the land now run as large highly mechanized operations, they could at best hope for six months' work a year.[26] Thus those who actually had labored to make it possible for Sonora to become Mexico's production showcase were largely cut out of its bounty.

"Landless laborer" is a term used to refer to rural people without land only in underdeveloped countries. But the industrial countries also have millions of landless agricultural laborers—over two million in the United States alone. Their already meager livelihood, too, is being undercut by mechanization. From 1964 to 1972, the tomato harvester has replaced 23,000 jobs just in California. Since the harvester has been fitted with an electronic sorter using infrared light and color sensors to distinguish red from green tomatoes, another 5,000 farm jobs have disappeared. And the lettuce harvester is threatening an additional 13,500 jobs.[27] Just as in the underdeveloped countries, the mechanization of agriculture contributes directly to the concentration of control over the land. Since the introduction of the mechanized harvester—uneconomical for farmers with fewer than 350 acres—about 85 percent of the original 4000 cannery tomato growers have been driven out of business in California.[28]

We have seen that with the introduction of new technologies into societies where small groups can monopolize agricultural resources, the price of land and therefore land rents go up and tenants are displaced from the land and laborers from their jobs. It is not surprising, therefore, to find peasants in these countries invariably sinking deeper into debt to stay alive. Cheap credit schemes often only worsen the predicament of the poor. In Malaysia, for example, landlords commonly obtain loans from rural banks by using their land as collateral. (The banks are reluctant to issue low-interest loans to tenants because they have no collateral.) The money obtained by the landlord is then re-lent to tenants at interest rates left to the landlord's own discretion. The result is the reinforcement of debt bondage, making the peasant permanently so indebted that he is obliged to accept wages for his labor at a rate 30 to 50 percent below the going market rate.

Women Undercut

In the severing of rural people from control over food-producing resources we have just described, women are often doubly hurt: Work demands on women increase while their effective control over family resources erodes.[29] The family now has less or no land; the men are more and more often forced to seek wage labor away from the home. Women who have traditionally labored to grow a variety of crops near the home as the mainstay of the family's diet now must take sole responsibility, often with less land and fewer cash resources.

In some areas of the world women are also involved in wage labor away from home and yet still shoulder the responsibility of the family plot. This double load inevitably leads to the substitution of a less labor-demanding but less nutritious crop like cassava for a more labor-demanding and nutritious crop like corn. The whole family suffers.

With the spread of commercialized agriculture, moreover, government extension services, credit, and membership in marketing cooperatives are now overwhelmingly geared to the men, not the women. And income is largely under the control of the men, also. With women in less control of the family's resources, the new cash income often goes for what one rural sociologist has called "bachelor-type goods"—radios, wristwatches, or bicycles. And even if the cash income gained from selling the commercial crop is used for the family's food, it is unlikely to be the nutritional equivalent of the home-grown diet.

When More Food Means More Hunger

In country after country, where agricultural resources are allowed to be sources of private wealth, the drive to increase food production has made even worse the lives of the poor majority, despite per capita production increases. We have seen how:

- Land values go up, forcing tenants and small farmers off the land.
- Rents increase.
- Payments in money become the rule, yet money buys less food.
- The control over farmland becomes concentrated in fewer landowners, many of whom are speculative entrepreneurs, not farmers.
- Even communal lands (as in many African villages or land-reform areas) are appropriated by powerful individuals such as chieftains or caciques for their private gain at the expense of the welfare of the community.
- Corporate control, often foreign, extends further into production.
- Peasants are trapped into debt bondage.
- Poverty and inequality deepen.
- The position of women is even further undercut.
- Production totals, not the participation of the rural population in the production process (livelihood and nourishment), become the measure of success for agricultural planners.
- Quantity and market value, not nutritive value, become the goal of agricultural planning.

The net result? Hunger tightens its hold on the rural majority.

A series of major studies now being completed for the International Labor Organization (ILO) documents that in the seven South Asian countries comprising 70 percent of the rural population of the nonsocialist underdeveloped world, the rural poor have become worse off than they were ten or twenty years ago.

The summary study notes that ironically *"the increase in poverty has been associated not with a fall but with a rise in cereal production per head, the main component of the diet of the poor."* Here are typical examples:

- The Philippines: Despite the fact that agricultural production increased by 3 to 4 percent per year during the last fifteen to twenty years, about one fifth of the rural households experienced a dramatic and *absolute* decline in living standards, which accelerated during the early seventies. By 1974 daily real wages in agriculture fell to almost one third of what they were in 1965.[30]
- Bangladesh: Between 1963 and 1975, the proportion of rural households classified as absolutely poor increased by more than a third and that of those classified as extremely poor increased five times. Yet about 15 percent of the rural households in Bangladesh had significantly higher real incomes in 1975.[31]
- West Malaysia: By 1970 the bottom 20 percent of rural households had experienced a fall of over 40 percent in their average income since 1957, while the average income of the next 20 percent fell 16 percent. By contrast, the top 20 percent of rural households increased their mean income 21 percent.[32]
- Sri Lanka: Despite a rise in per capita income between 1963 and 1973, actual rice consumption *fell* for all except the highest income class. All workers experienced a fall in real wages, except for those in industry and commerce whose real wages remained static.[33]

Part of the reason that most people have not been able to perceive this tragic retrogression is what we have come to call the "language of deception"—terms that obfuscate reality. One such term is "per capita." In Indonesia, for example, we discovered that the country's per capita GNP is $220 but, for the bottom

40 percent, it is $95. Of what use is the per capita figure?

It is precisely the kind of development policy that measures itself in per capita terms that results in the absolute decline of the majority. As the above examples show, per capita production and income have been going up in the very countries where often the majority of the people have become worse off with each succeeding year.

Bought Us Time?

Many view the Green Revolution as a technical innovation and feel that, as such, it should not be expected to solve social problems. But what we have found is that there can be no separation between technical innovation and social change. Whether promotion of the wealthier class of farmers is deliberate government policy or not, inserting any profitable technology into a society shot through with power inequalities (money, landownership, privilege, access to credit) sets off the disastrous retrogression of the less powerful majority. The better-off and powerful in a society further enrich themselves at the expense of the national treasury and the rural poor. As those initially better-off gain even greater control over the production process, the majority of people are made marginal, in fact, totally irrelevant, to the process of agricultural production. In such societies the reserves of landless and jobless function only to keep wages down for those who do find jobs. Excluded from contributing to the agricultural economy, the poor majority are no longer its beneficiaries, for being excluded from production means being excluded from consumption. A thirty-six-cents-a-day laborer in Bihar, India, knows this truth well: "If you don't own any land, you never get enough to eat," he says, "even if the land is producing well."[34]

The Green Revolution has *not* "bought us time" as the question suggests. "Modernization" overlaid on oppressive social structures entrenches the ownership classes who are now even better positioned and less

willing to part with their new-found wealth. Thus, to
focus only on raising production, without first confronting the issue of who controls and who participates
in the production process, actually compounds the
problem. It leaves the majority of people worse off
than before. In a very real sense the idea that we are
progressing is our greatest handicap. We cannot move
forward—we cannot take the first step toward helping
improve the welfare of the vast majority of the world's
people—until we can see clearly that we are now
moving backward.

―――――――――

In most of the developing nations, rural people have
traditionally had little faith in the national governments. Governments' policies were usually regarded
with suspicion and perhaps with good reason. . . .
The rural people are beginning to regard this government with more trust and confidence, to feel to some
degree at least, that it is their government. In this
way, the Green Revolution can also be said to be
contributing constructively towards political stability.

George Harrar, President of the Rockefeller
Foundation, in his *Review and
Annual Report,* 1970

17. Wasn't the Green Revolution a Vital Scientific Breakthrough?

Question: You may criticize the impact of the Green
Revolution, but didn't the Green Revolution at least
provide us with critical knowledge that we wouldn't have

gotten any other way? Now that farmland can't be expanded in many parts of the world, what could be more important than plant research to improve yields?

Our Response: To assume, as this question does, that breakthroughs in knowledge of plant genetics would never have been made without the Rockefeller Foundation's research institutes is an acute form of cultural myopia. The attempt to improve yields genetically is hardly a new departure. Since the early 1950s, improved indigenous rice seeds, referred to now as "locally improved varieties," have been independently produced in several Asian countries—specifically Japan, Taiwan, Malaysia, Indonesia, Sri Lanka, and China. Such efforts in India and Egypt go back at least half a century.

Even before the introduction of the new seeds from the International Rice Research Institute during the 1960s, locally improved varieties occupied 34 percent of the rice area in India.[1] The portion of Sri Lanka's croplands growing improved seeds from foreign sources, only 4.4 percent in 1970–1971, was cut in half by 1972–1973.[2] Sri Lanka decided to concentrate on its own improved seeds when the imported variety, pushed for years by international agencies, was virtually wiped out one year by disease.[3]

Several other countries have significantly large areas planted with locally improved varieties. In the 1969–1970 season 69 percent of Brazil's rain-fed wheatlands was planted with seeds selected and improved locally. Egypt uses local varieties suitable for rain-fed conditions on 45 percent of its wheatlands. Significantly, the locally improved varieties are grown without irrigation, a condition that the more sensitive foreign-bred seeds, as discussed earlier, cannot tolerate.[4] United Nations researcher Dr. Ingrid Palmer reports that in Iran and Iraq improved local types may do better than imported seeds. This is also true of wheat in Tunisia and of rice in Brazil and Sri Lanka.[5]

During a recent trip to China, American agricultural scientists were surprised to find high-response dwarf rice varieties similar to the "miracle" rice developed by the International Rice Research Institute in the Philippines.[6] Between 1952 and 1964, 1200 major kinds of improved-grain seeds were developed and put into general use in China. Indeed, if, as reported by the Chinese Academy of Science, one half of China's cultivated land was planted with improved seeds in 1965, then China was far ahead of the rest of the agrarian countries in the world.[7]

Now that the initial flurry of attention to *the* Green Revolution has begun to wane, some areas are returning to the locally improved varieties, better suited to both the local ecology and the local taste.

A Little Better Farming

The question also suggests that *genetic* research is the most important contribution to improving agricultural production now that land area is limited. But higher yields do not come only from seeds better able to utilize the sun and water and resist pest infestation. Higher yields have historically come from that old-fashioned idea—better farming practices: how the seeds are planted, how the land is plowed, how the plants are protected and how the fields weeded. An American wheat expert who helped farmers in Turkey double their wheat yields admits, "There are no miracle seeds involved. . . . It is just farming a little better." The key element was the retention of moisture in the soil during the fallow period achieved by using careful plowing and harrowing techniques and eliminating weeds.[8]

In some areas of the world, improved seeds are hardly the appropriate place to start when the soil structure is the limiting factor. In her work on Africa, Dr. Palmer concluded that ". . . the main problem in the foreseeable future is not raising responses or yields of plants, but improving the soil." Until this is accomplished, she feels the local seed varieties would probably do better than the imported varieties.[9] In parts of Africa the soil structure is so poor that it cannot even absorb the nitrogen fertilizer on which the new seeds depend. The first step would not be introducing new seeds, but crop rotation, including grasses and legumes, and adding organic matter to rebuild the soil structure.

In areas of Africa such as Togo and Upper Volta improved farming techniques could certainly increase yields without "miracle" seeds. Sowing in lines could enable about 80 percent more seed to be sown. Foot-high dykes in shallow valleys would be enough to hold rain so that flood rice could be grown, which in itself could double production. In Sri Lanka in 1966–1970, a national weeding program (mainly schoolchildren and students, working during the few weeks most crucial for rice production) resulted in a production increase of more than a third.

Turning worldwide attention via Nobel prizes and newspaper coverage to the miracles occurring under the ideal conditions of research test fields makes it easy to ignore proven traditional practices that could still be improved upon to use the soil better. For example, a proper cropping sequence can restore nutrients taken out by one crop with those put in by another—thus providing one alternative to imported chemical fertilizers.

Why is crop sequence so important? Some crops (like corn and wheat) are heavy consumers of nitrogen, while crops of the legume family (peas, beans, and lentils), because they house nitrogen-fixing bacteria, actually take nitrogen from the air and put it back into the depleted soil. Even now with the heavy emphasis on chemical fertilizers, pulses contribute about as much nitrogen to the soil of India as manufactured fertilizers. Moreover, the contribution of pulses could probably be increased. For example, the large area of irrigated wheatlands left fallow in India during the off-season could be replenishing its nitrogen by being planted with pulses. Besides, pulses are excellent foods.

We have already noted how the Green Revolution's focus on monoculture displaces interest in the advantages of the opposite approach—mixed cropping. It has become fashionable to view mixed cropping, the planting of several crops in one field, as primitive and less scientific. When local farmers suggested planting beans and corn in the same field, the technical advisors to the United States AID-sponsored Puebla project in Mexico dismissed the idea. Finally, after a number of years, the "experts" discovered that the mixed-field approach gave better yields. Putting the two crops in one field had the same effect as alternating legume crops with grains. Mixed cropping can have multiple advantages including the maximum use of the land and the most efficient use of labor because of staggered planting and harvesting times. It is a technique that is profitable and suitable to local labor and land conditions. In an area of northern Nigeria over three quarters of the cropland is planted with more than one crop and sometimes as many as six, including pulses, starchy roots, tubers, and vegetables. Such sensible farming is threatened by the Green Revolution's introduction of single-stand crops, best suited to large-scale mechanized commercial operations, not the peasant farmer.

Divorcing Agriculture and Nutrition

Concentrating narrowly on yields makes it easy to forget to ask *what* is being produced. In Mexico, 60 percent of the people eat corn as a staple. Yet corn has been the neglected stepchild of the Green Revolution. Between 1940 and 1960, Mexico's large entrepreneur farmers often shifted out of corn to plant more lucrative commercial crops such as wheat, cotton, and feedgrains.[10]

The focus on a few cereal grains has shifted the traditional diet of several Third World countries away from the balanced consumption of grains (like corn or rice) in combination with legumes (like beans or lentils). The wisdom of the traditional mix has only recently been appreciated by nutritionists in "developed" countries.

When I, Frances, first started the work that eventually became *Diet for a Small Planet,* I was fascinated by the discovery that diets evolving independently in different parts of the world had a common, nutritionally sound base. Combining corn and beans in Mexico, or rice and lentils in India, or rice and soybean products in Japan, was no accident. These combinations created more biologically usable protein than if the diet centered on only one food. When eaten together, the two foods, because of contrasting amino acid patterns (the building blocks of protein), make up for each other's weaknesses. Thus, if Green Revolution grain displaces legumes in the traditional diet, not only does the overall protein intake fall, since legumes have two to four times the protein content of grain, but just as critical, the *balanced combination* of grains and legumes that improves the biological usability of protein is also undercut.

Yet cropland planted in legumes continues to shrink. Since the early 1960s the legume acreage in India alone has declined by two and a half million acres.[11] This drop is reflected in the Indian diet. Between 1956 and 1971 the average daily consumption in India of legumes declined by about 31 percent. On Java the cultivation of soybeans, virtually the highest protein plant food in the world, is giving way to the government's promotion of Green Revolution rice and its enforcement of mandatory sugar quotas.[12]

The Green Revolution Imperative

Historically, the Green Revolution represented a choice to breed seed varieties that produce high yields under optimum conditions. It was a choice *not* to start by developing seeds better able to withstand drought or pests. It was a choice *not* to concentrate first on improving traditional methods of increasing yields, such as mixed cropping. It was a choice *not* to develop technology that was productive, labor-intensive, and independent of foreign input supply. It was a choice *not* to concentrate on reinforcing the balanced, traditional diets of grains plus legumes.

Moreover, in light of all these "paths not taken," we must ask ourselves: In our eagerness to embrace the new, in our rush to extend the scope of human knowledge and control, do we forget to work on *applying* the collected wisdom already handed down to us? Has our fascination with science prevented us from tackling the incomparably more difficult problems of social organization and the agricultural practices of real farmers? For the majority who are hungry, "miracle" seeds are meaningless without control over land, water, tools, storage, and marketing.

18. Hasn't the Green Revolution Strengthened Food Security?

Question: You choose to see only failure. You fail to recognize the real contribution of the Green Revolution. The *New York Times* has reported that the improved seed varieties are adding 20 million tons of grain annually to production in Asia and Southeast Asia.

You are undoubtedly right that certain groups have benefited more than others. But just where would we be today if the new seeds had not been introduced? In the early 1970s we were faced with unusually bad weather. International reserves dropped dramatically, but somehow we squeezed by. At least the situation was not as desperate as it would have been if the Green Revolution had not increased world grain output in the previous decade. Hasn't the Green Revolution at least provided some level of global food security?

Our Response: There is no food security, no matter how much is produced, if the food-producing resources are controlled by a small minority and used only to profit them. In such a system the greater profit will always be found in catering to those who can pay the most—not the hungry.

Here is what we mean: If farm businessmen in Colombia find they can make more money growing livestock feed for processors like Ralston Purina than a staple like beans, they will grow feed. When a Mexican commercial grower in Sinaloa discovers he can make almost twenty times more raising tomatoes of export quality than raising wheat, he is likely to switch to tomatoes. If large operators in Central and South America find they can make more money growing flowers for export rather than corn for local people, they will plant flowers.

On a research trip to northwest Mexico, we came upon several distilleries newly built to produce brandy from grapes to be grown on thousands of irrigated acres, land on which local people could grow nutritious food. The next day the head of cereal research at a nearby government-sponsored research center explained to us that a farmer in the area makes a profit of almost $500 per acre growing grapes—four times more than with wheat.

In a country like Mexico, where early childhood death due to malnutrition has gone up 10 percent over the last ten years, acreage devoted to basic food crops —corn, wheat, beans and rice—actually declined 25 percent over the same period. Not surprisingly, between 1973 and 1976, Mexico had to import 15 percent of its corn, 25 percent of its wheat, and 45 percent of its soybeans.

Mexico is a prime example of a country that has gone far down the path of entrusting its agricultural resources to large commercial growers. The result? The government has had to practically bribe the "modernized" growers to keep them producing basic staples for the national market; the Mexican government had to hike price guarantees by 112 percent between 1970 and 1975 and even then the proportion of land growing basic foods has declined. Because of the tight control of the commercial farming sector over production, the large commercial growers have been able to use threats of production cutbacks to get higher government-supported prices. At times they have carried out the threats—switching to feedgrains or export crops—until the support offered by the government for growing a basic food was raised high enough. The food security of a country in which large commercial growers virtually control food production is forever in jeopardy for yet another reason: The large growers can withhold food from the market in periods of rising prices in expectation of higher profits later. Entrusting a country's food supply to a pampered elite turns out to be a dangerous and costly choice indeed.

How Vulnerable Is an Agricultural System to Natural Hazards?

Can we measure food security in production totals if the agricultural base that produced the gains is itself threatened?

Consider these apparently isolated events:

- Indonesia, 1974–1975: At least 500,000 acres of riceland planted with the new variety was devastated by a viral disease spread by plagues of brown leaf hoppers.[1] (Indonesia has since inaugurated a program aimed at replacing HRV rice with its own locally improved varieties.)
- Philippines, 1970–1972: Tungro rice virus reached epidemic levels in the Green Revolution rice fields.[2]
- Zambia, 1970s: Disaster in the form of a newly identified mold called *fusarium* has struck new hybrid corn strains grown by the commercial farmers while the traditional corn crops of the villagers appear free from attack.[3]

What do these examples of crop loss from disease and pests reveal?

Green Revolution fields are often more vulnerable to attack than fields planted in traditional ways with locally evolved seeds. Why? Part of the reason is simply that the denser stands in Green Revolution fields provide a more abundant diet for pests. Multiple cropping allowed by the faster-maturing new seeds also provides pests with a more even year-round food supply. Moreover, the new seeds were bred with the highest priority on the greatest yield possible, not on resistance to disease or pests.

The danger of crop loss is compounded because, while the new seeds present novel opportunities for disease and pests, effective traditional practices for dealing with these problems are becoming casualties of the Green Revolution. Historically, wet-rice farming involved flooding the fields for several weeks each year, thus drowning many pests. Unfortunately, the rigorous timing of the new seeds often does not accommodate this practice. Alternating the cultivation of a food crop with a soil-building crop (called green manuring) is a proven traditional way to control pests by eliminating their hosts for a season. This practice was widespread even in the United States until recently. But with increasing use of chemical fertilizers, green manuring has become passé. Puddling is yet another practice on the way out. (In case you are wondering, puddling means using water buffaloes to plod through the fields in order to aerate the soil, increase water retention, trample the weeds, and eliminate insects.)[4]

Finally, the genetic uniformity of the new seeds planted over large areas means that they are more vulnerable to epidemics. A few years ago, the United States had a glimpse of what this could mean. In 1970, the great southern corn leaf blight wiped out 50 percent or more of the crop in many of the Gulf Coast states (15 to 20 percent of the total domestic corn crop). A more tragic example is the Irish potato blight in which over 1 million people died during the 1840s. Scientists now believe that the underlying problem was the lack of genetic diversity of the potato crop.

Today all the Green Revolution dwarf wheats* (now 20 percent of all wheat grown) trace themselves to a

---

* "Dwarf" refers to characteristic shortness of the plants that prevents their tipping over even when more abundant yields make their tops heavier.

single parent plant. The same is true of dwarf-rice varieties. Should the genes that those parents have for dwarfness ever be linked to one conferring susceptibility to a plant disease such as glume botch, root rot, or Karnal smut (real names!), the Green Revolution could turn black overnight.

Because of their denser stands, multiple cropping, and genetic uniformity, the new seeds can be more vulnerable to attack. Current plant research is therefore placing greater emphasis on breeding for resistance. But the issue is much more complex than simply finding a seed that is resistant to today's diseases. Nature is not static. Pests and diseases are constantly adapting.

Scientists such as Dr. H. Garrison Wilkes, a specialist in corn genetics at the University of Massachusetts, believe that it is only a matter of time before a mutation of an existing disease will take place, permitting it to attack a new seed strain. Wilkes states that "In their wilderness state, both plants and diseases which attack them are forever adapting to each other through the evolutionary process. The diseases mutate new forms of attack, the plants new forms of resistance." But, he warns, "Under modern agriculture plants no longer mutate but are grown from new seeds each year for continuous high yields. *The mutation of diseases, however, cannot be stopped.*"[5]

This inevitability would not be so serious if we could always rush back to the lab to produce a new strain—keeping one step ahead of nature and losing at most one crop. But it takes time to develop a resistant strain. Could the world wait as many as ten to twenty generations of seeds, that is, four to five years, for a resistant hybrid?[6] Clearly the answer is no.

Moreover, this scenario presumes that the material will continue to exist from which plant breeders can always come up with a new resistant strain. But will it? We have talked here in Part IV about the social and economic transformation of agriculture. But what of the transformation of world agriculture in terms of the plants themselves? What happens when commercialized, standardized agriculture permeates almost every corner of the globe?

The human race historically cultivated over 3000 species of plants for food, about half of them in sufficient quantity to enter into commerce. Today, in stark contrast, only fifteen species including rice, corn, wheat, sorghum, barley, sugar cane, sugar beets, potato, sweet potato, cassava, the common bean, soybean, peanut, coconut, and banana actually feed the entire world, providing 85–90 percent of all human energy. Of these, only *three* plants, wheat, rice, and corn, now supply 66 percent of the world's seed crop.[7]

Especially since there are now so *few* plants on which we all depend, the maintenance of genetic diversity within these species is absolutely critical. Genetic diversity, as we have already seen, is necessary to prevent the wholesale wiping out of a crop in which all the plants are vulnerable to the same pathogen and it is also crucial as the storehouse of material from which to breed new resistant strains. The heritage of genetic diversity has not been evenly spread over the earth. In the 1920s, the Russian plant geneticist N. I. Vavilov discovered eight major and three minor centers of extreme plant gene diversity, all located in underdeveloped countries (along the Tropic of Cancer and the Tropic of Capricorn), in mountainous regions isolated by steep terrain or other natural barriers. These centers represent only one fortieth of the world's land area but have been the source of almost all our food plants. From these reservoirs have come many of the most valuable strains and genes used by plant geneticists in the last fifty years.[8]

Until now scientists have returned to these areas of diversity for new germ plasm with which to breed resistance. But this diversity has never been adequately protected. Collections of genetic material were often lost when scientists discarded them after hitting upon the genes that would serve their immediate purpose. Suddenly in the 1970s the problem worsened dramatically. As plant geneticist Wilkes puts it: "We are discovering Mexican farmers are planting hybrid corn seed from a Midwestern seed firm, that Tibetan farmers are planting barley from a Scandinavian plant breeding station, and that Turkish farmers are planting wheat from the Mexican Wheat Program." He concludes, "Each of these classic areas of genetic diversity is rapidly becoming an area of seed uniformity."[9]

Once foreign strains are introduced, the native varieties can become extinct in a single year if their seeds are consumed and not kept. Dr. Wilkes states, "Quite literally, the genetic heritage of a millennium in a particular valley can disappear in a single bowl of porridge."[10]

Some argue that our security against genetic "wipe outs" will lie in establishing seed banks that would be treasuries of genetic diversity. Unfortunately, seed banks, too, are vulnerable. A major Peruvian collection of corn germ plasm, one of South America's largest, was irretrievably lost when the compressors for the refrigerators in which it was stored failed! And the corn research center in Mexico that produced the original Green Revolution seeds inadvertently lost some of its irreplaceable corn germ plasm collected during the 1940s.[11] Bangladesh still has some 1200 different traditional varieties of rice and Indonesia has 600. How effectively can that genetic diversity be protected once it is removed from the field for cold storage in a seed bank? One alternative to seed banks proposed by many scientists is carefully selected natural preserves throughout the world that could maintain living collections in the field.

As long as such research is primarily the domain of a few corporations one wonders what protective measures will be taken. Already Pioneer Hy-Bred International, Inc., and DeKalb Ag Research supply 55 percent of the hybrid corn market. These two, plus six others, dominate virtually all hybrid development and marketing.[12] Can such firms be expected to help maintain living treasuries of genetic diversity in which all countries might participate? Or will they guard their genetic research against competitors and promote only the currently most salable variety?

How Self-Contained Is the Agricultural System?

This is the third measure of true food security. To measure how self-contained an agricultural system is one must first know who controls the farm inputs necessary to make the land productive. Take, for example, the new hybrid corn seeds. Since these seeds do not reproduce themselves perfectly, farmers who save seeds from one crop for the next planting find their yields and quality greatly diminished. The farmer—once he is hooked into the hybrid seed system—is dependent, therefore, on a new supply of seeds season after season. These seeds now come primarily from private companies able to produce them through controlled pollination. The USDA has just developed seeds called "apomictic" hybrids that the farmers would be able to use year after year without new purchases from seed companies.[13] It is unlikely, we are told, that this development will be pursued by the big seed companies since their whole sales system would be threatened.

Reliance on imported chemical fertilizers also runs counter to the maintenance of a secure, self-contained agricultural system. Nevertheless, corporations and institutions based in the industrial countries are exporting the myth that chemical fertilizers are the best way to achieve production gains. This road to increased yields is a model most Americans take for granted. From 1942 to 1967 chemical fertilizer use in the United States expanded tenfold—not because it was the only path to production gains but for other reasons. For one thing, chemical fertilizers became dirt-cheap. The cost of nitrogen fertilizer dropped to one half and in some cases one quarter of what it was immediately after World War II. The greater demand for nitrogen fertilizer can also be linked to the rapid promotion of meat consumption. (It takes about sixteen times more nitrogen to produce grain-fed meat than it does to produce plant protein.)

Even more significantly, chemical fertilizer use is accelerating in order to compensate for soil nutrient depletion due to the nitrogen lost by bad cultivation practices and resultant erosion. One estimate places the loss of soil nitrogen in rich Midwest soils at 40 percent in the last century.[14] It is estimated that fifteen to twenty years of returning organic matter—manure, crop residues, sewage sludge, and so on—would be necessary to restore the organic content and the nitrogen of American soils. Such soil depletion reveals much about American agriculture. Careful husbandry necessary to maintain fragile soils or enrich poor soils never evolved here because until now it simply did not seem necessary.

The critical importance of careful land husbandry came home to us recently. A Soil Conservation Service official in Iowa explained how, depending on the way the land is cared for, topsoil might last only thirty-six years or for an indefinite period. If the soil is plowed up and downhill in the fall and corn is planted year after year with no crop residue left, the entire six to eight remaining inches of Iowa's top soil will be lost from land with even a very slight slope. If, by contrast, no-till farming and contour terracing are practiced and crop residue is left on all year, the eight inches of top soil could last indefinitely since new top soil would always be in formation. Yet, as of today, only one third of Iowa's agricultural land is protected by the kind of conservation practices needed to protect the top soil.[15]

Is this American record—neglect of soil maintenance and reliance on chemical fertilizers—a useful model for underdeveloped countries today?

Underdeveloped countries now import 55 percent of their nitrogen fertilizer,[16] making them highly vulnerable to skyrocketing fertilizer prices. World fertilizer prices jumped threefold between 1970 and 1974. Crop production fell in many underdeveloped countries simply because they had become hooked on chemical fertilizers and yet could no longer afford to import them. But even if it *were* possible to rely on imported chemical fertilizer to increase food production, is this the place for underdeveloped countries to start?

Chemical fertilizers can increase yields but they cannot maintain or enhance the soil's organic matter. Organic matter, however, is the ultimate key to fertility; it maintains the porous soil structure, providing superior waterholding capacity (critical during droughts) and allowing oxygen to penetrate for use by soil organisms that break down manure, crop residues, and other organic matter. Relying primarily on chemical fertilizers can be self-defeating in the long term. The more one relies on chemical fertilizers instead of manure, compost, crop rotation, and green manure, the more the organic matter declines, the less able plants are to absorb inorganic nitrogen in chemical fertilizers. This helps to explain why U.S. agriculture, according to biologist Dr. Barry Commoner, now uses about five times as much fertilizer as it did in 1947 to produce the *same amount of crop.*

Chemical fertilizer must, therefore, never be thought of as a *substitute* for organic sources. First, all sources of organic matter should be mobilized and returned to the soil. Then, for countries like China and Algeria with petroleum available to produce chemical fertilizer, developing and using that potential can make sense. (Furthermore, even though China is making a big push to utilize its petroleum for fertilizer, 70 percent of its fertilizer is still from organic sources, enough to guarantee sufficient food production.)

Even if there are no local resources for chemical fertilizer production (and this is the case for most underdeveloped countries), yield gains can be achieved by mobilizing the now wasted potential of organic matter. Conservatively estimated, waste material from animals, plants, and humans in underdeveloped countries could supply *six to eight times* more nutrients than these countries obtained during 1970-1971 from the use of chemical fertilizers. In 1973, the economic value of such organic wastes in underdeveloped countries was estimated at over \$16 billion. Using labor-intensive methods, urban waste in India could be processed into fertilizers at one-third the cost of imported chemical fertilizers.[17] Yet virtually none of this potential has been tapped.

What Is Food Security?

Most measures of food security fixate on global statistics of agricultural production. But food security simply cannot exist in a market system where there is no democratic control over resource use. Commercial growers will not grow food for hungry people when they can make more money growing luxury crops for the minority who can always pay more. Moreover, we have seen that much of the increased production has been at the price of increased vulnerability, *and unnecessarily so*. Increased production approached as a mere technical problem has completely re-shaped agriculture itself, reducing a very complex, self-contained system into a highly simplified and dependent one. The Green Revolution approach converts a recycling, self-contained system into a linear production formula: pick the "best" seeds, plant uniformly over the largest area possible, and dose with chemical fertilizer. The reduction of agriculture to this simple formula leaves crops open to attack and soils highly vulnerable to deterioration.

Such reductionist agriculture turns chemical fertilizers and pesticides into necessities to cover for its built-in vulnerabilities. True food security is further undermined as production is made increasingly dependent on external sources of supply over which there is no local control. We are all exposed repeatedly to catchy corporate ads that attempt to scare us into believing that the corporate-marketed inputs are the only safeguards against hunger. Yet the increasing capital costs of this way of producing food exclude ever larger numbers of rural people abroad as well as in the United States from a livelihood and push the price of food beyond the means of those who most need it.

This system of agriculture has been in operation no more than twenty-five years in the industrial countries, yet it is being exported as the sure, indeed, the only, answer for the entire world. That is an incredibly risky proposition, however you look at it.

We have learned that real food security simply cannot be measured in production figures. Production figures may well go up while the majority are getting less of the food they need. Food security must be measured by how close a country is to achieving sound nutrition for all. It must also be measured in how reliable, how resilient, and how self-contained the agricultural system is. On each of those counts the Green Revolution approach means less food security for us all.

19. Where Has All the Production Gone?

Question: You said that in many countries huge capital investments made in the modernization approach to production did boost the yields of many better-off farmers. So at least there is more food. Yet if people are still hungry, in fact hungrier than before, what has happened to that extra production? Certainly the increased production is helping somebody. Whom has it helped? Where has it gone?

Our Response: Through livestock feeding, greater food processing and switching from staples to luxuries, a larger volume of food can be made to feed fewer people at a higher profit.

So here is what we have discovered is happening to much of the increased production:

- Some of it goes to urban middle- and upper-income groups.

In countries like the Philippines and Mexico increased production has benefited emerging industrialists and their foreign partners who want to have cheap food for workers in urban industries in order to keep wage demands low. Total production increases have also helped government elites who fear urban unrest —such as the food riots in Mexican cities during the 1940s—if not enough food could be extracted from the rural areas.

- Some of it gets reduced into luxury products the poor cannot afford.

The governments of the United States and Pakistan collaborated with the New Jersey-based Corn Products Corporation to improve yields of Pakistani corn—traditionally a staple food grown by the rural poor. Hybrid seeds and other inputs did increase yields. The corn, however, is now a cash crop grown by relatively few large farmers for manufacturing a corn-based sweetener used in such things as soft drinks.

- Some of it gets fed to livestock to create meat that the majority of the local population cannot afford.

In 1971, an FAO report advised Third World countries on the problem of how to dispose of "surplus" grain resulting from the success of the Green Revolution production campaigns. The FAO suggested using a greater proportion of wheat for animal feed or shifting to cultivation of coarse grains more suitable for livestock than wheat and rice. Could they be serious? FAO was advising countries with the most serious undernutrition problems in the world to deal with the so-called surplus problem by stepped up livestock feeding!

In 1973 two-thirds of Colombia's Green Revolution rice was being fed to livestock or going into the production of beer. Increased yields of corn provided the raw material for starting up a chicken feed industry. Did this mean Colombia's undernourished would be eating chicken? For over a quarter of the country's families, buying just two pounds of chicken or a dozen eggs would require an entire week's earnings or more. Much of the increased egg production goes into processed foods such as snacks and mayonnaise sold by multinational food companies to elite urban groups.[1]

Even though in many countries per capita grain production totals are higher, they do not result, as one would think, in a decline in prices. The "demand" for grain by cattle and chickens keeps grain prices up.

And what has happened to the fruits of our own Green Revolution? Although the United States succeeded in increasing corn yields almost three times over, it has not meant the elimination of hunger in America. The increased corn production has gone to livestock—doubling the meat consumption of many Americans who already were taking in more protein than their bodies could use.

With a good deal of help, then, from food processors and animals, food for many can be converted—and sold for higher profits—into food for a few.

- Some of the increased production gets exported.

Where the majority of people are kept too poor to constitute a domestic market and agriculture is made to rely on imported inputs like fertilizers and machines, the colonial pattern of production for export is reinforced in the search for a paying market and the foreign exchange needed to pay for imported inputs. India exports such excellent staples as potatoes to countries like Sweden and the Soviet Union yet the amount of potatoes available to the Indian people has been reduced by 12 percent between 1972 and 1974.[2] Central America exports between one third and one half of its beef to the United States alone.

- Some of the increased production simply gets dumped.

Fruits and vegetables produced in Central America for export to the United States frequently either are shut out from an oversupplied market or fail to meet

United States "quality" standards—size, color, smoothness. Since the local population, mostly landless, is too poor to buy anything, fully 65 percent of the fruits and vegetables produced, according to one study, "must be literally dumped or, where possible, fed to livestock" (which in turn are exported).[3]

Neglect of rural reform and concentration instead on the production advances of commercial growers have determined where the production goes. Since any increase in production is not met by a similarly enlarged buying public, no matter how much food is produced it will end up going to an urban elite, to an export market, or to make livestock products that can only be purchased by the well-off.

Mexico exported 10 percent of its grain crop between 1965 and 1969, but the production gains were overwhelmed by one of the world's fastest population growth rates. . . . By the mid-seventies, Mexico was importing one-fifth of its grain needs. . . . The problem is not that agriculture did not advance in Mexico and the Philippines, but rather that the advances were simply eaten up by the relentless growth in population.

Lester R. Brown, *The Global Politics of Food: Role and Responsibility of North America*, 1975

20. Don't They Need Our Machines?

Question: In your discussion of the Green Revolution you always seem to include mechanization as one of the problems. But isn't mechanization part of the solution to hunger? Are you sure that in your eagerness to empathize with the poor peasant in underdeveloped countries, you are not running the risk of romanticizing misery? Wouldn't a poor agricultural laborer in India be glad to be relieved of backbreaking work by a more efficient machine?

Our Response: In countries with an abundant potential labor supply but limited land, productivity per *acre* is what counts. And increasing productivity per acre is often not a matter of a "modern" machine but of intensive and careful farming by people who have a living stake in the production. According to an International Rice Research Institute (IRRI) study of lowland rice farming, there is no significant difference in yields between farms using a tractor and those using a water buffalo. Even more striking was the conclusion that in Japan, in 1960, highly mechanized farms had no higher yields than those farmed with a hoe. (And no one has ever accused the IRRI of romanticizing the hoe!) The striking rise in rice yields in agrarian-reform Japan before 1960 was not due to mechanization but in part to the small farmers' use of improved seeds, fertilizer, water pumps, better animal-drawn plows and harrows, and simple revolving weeders and pedal threshers. This is hardly high technology—but it worked.[1]

Proponents of large-scale mechanization have one case, however, that they feel is airtight. The faster growing seeds of the Green Revolution make it possible for two and sometimes more crops to be grown successively in the same field in one year. Those promoting tractors and harvesters claim there is often a labor bottleneck during planting and harvesting time due to the extra work required to get each crop harvested quickly so that the next one can be planted.

But, we must ask, who is defining the term "bottleneck"? A bottleneck to a landlord may mean that time of year when he has to pay higher wages because the greater demand for labor gives laborers some bargaining power. The same period the landlord calls a bottleneck may be the time of year the laborer depends on to earn the extra rupees or pesos to survive throughout the rest of the year, when jobs are scarce and wages even lower.

In any case, large-scale mechanization is not the only solution to the problem of peak periods of labor needs. Small-scale improved techniques can help, as we will show below. Moreover, the need for labor can be spread more evenly throughout the year by, for instance, improving irrigation facilities to make planting less dependent on weather and staggering harvests by using seed varieties and crops of varying maturation periods.[2]

There is still another aspect that rarely (never) enters the heads of planners in industrial countries for whom city and country are distant and unrelated. Light industry and services can be integrated into the life of the countryside, an approach that has been successful in countries as different as Egypt and China. In many Chinese rural communes as much as 30 percent of the population is not directly employed in agriculture but in local, small-scale industry. This group represents a critical reserve labor force to help plant or harvest a crop. On the other hand, once the peak work is over, these workers are not unemployed but return to their factories and service industries. Such a plan works in China because most people no longer look down on farming and nearly everyone has practical experience in the fields.

What must be kept in mind in all discussions of mechanization is that "labor-saving" to the rural entrepreneur means displacing laborers from their jobs, thereby saving on his labor costs. Labor-saving mechanization, however, is good for the society at large only when it means saving workers from unnecessarily arduous labor and when a genuine economic evolution ensures employment in other sectors of the economy for anyone displaced.

Finally, we Americans assume large-scale mechanization is necessary to increase production in underdeveloped countries because that is exactly what we have been taught about the introduction of mechanization in the United States. But has this been true in every case? At least two cases—the mechanization of

tobacco and of cotton—show that it has not. One thing
is obvious to anyone who has ever seen a mechanical
harvester sweep through a cotton or tobacco field.
The machines were certainly not invented to increase
yields. A harvester actually reduces the amount taken
out of the fields by picking less cotton or tobacco
than a human being. One estimate is that mechanical
tobacco harvesters reduce the harvest per acre by 15
percent.[3] Moreover, the tobacco harvester lowers the
grade and quality of the harvest because it cannot
discriminate in picking the leaves. The attraction is
that they cut down on the wages per bushel as well
as the need to deal with workers. The tobacco harvester certainly is "labor-saving"; a recent Department
of Agriculture estimate is that the introduction of tobacco harvesters will eliminate 350,000 jobs in the
Carolinas and Virginia.[4]

If Not American-Style Machines, Then What?

Clearly large-scale mechanization is not necessary
to increase production. On the other hand, technological improvements are possible that can increase
production per acre, make work easier, and yet do
not displace laborers as do U.S.-style machines. Contrast, for example, a 100 horsepower tractor and a 10
horsepower rotary cultivator. A rotary cultivator is
affordable and usable by small farmers; a tractor is
not. While a 100 horsepower tractor *replaces* human
labor, a rotary cultivator *complements* human labor.

In the response to Question 3, we pointed out that
agriculture in most underdeveloped countries could
use many more workers than are presently employed.
Indeed, the more successful agricultural systems were
shown to have a *greater* number of workers per cultivated acre. What is needed, then, are machines that
both make work less arduous and increase the need
for human labor instead of replacing it.

What is needed in agrarian countries today is not
a different level of technology but a different kind of
technology. One with a different purpose. One that

raises production while usefully involving *more* people in the production process.

The irony is that the Green Revolution seeds could have been part of such an approach. The new seeds and their need for greater care and greater application of fertilizer have the potential to create more jobs. But in most countries the forces that started the Green Revolution also initiated a process of mechanization that reduced employment. In Colombia an estimate was made of the labor requirements of modernization using high response seeds, more fertilizer, greater care in planting, and so on. *Without* mechanization these improvements would require 45 percent more human labor per acre. With mechanization, 34 percent *less* labor would be required.[5]

The potential for greater employment with the High Response Varieties (HRVs) is due to several factors. We have already noted that the generally faster-maturing varieties allow farmers to plant more than one crop each year—thereby increasing the need for human labor and the need to speed up all operations. But speeding up operations would not have to mean large-scale mechanization. Reducing seed bed preparation time can be accomplished by a moldboard plow (a simple wedge-shaped instrument) and a modern harrow (an implement for breaking up the earth resembling a giant comb) that do the job in one-fifteenth the time needed using the traditional plow and plank method.[6] Threshing by hand may take too long to accommodate multiple cropping. Large-scale machines, however, are not required. A simple thresher can reduce the job from a month to only several days, making double cropping possible. (Machines do not always speed things up. On some rice fields, Chinese farmers have discovered they can squeeze in three crops if an entire team joins in to plant intensively by hand rather than relying on the slower-going rice-planting machines.)

Moreover, the introduction of certain simple machines can actually increase labor input. The rotary weeder is one example. The new seeds, with their high-response potential, make weeding even more worthwhile. And, precisely because the rotary weeder is more efficient, it makes more sense to put more labor into weeding with it.[7]

We do not want to give you the impression that we are talking only of techniques recently dreamed up in some alternative technology research center. Pascal de Pury, an indefatigable agronomist with years of experience in Africa and now working with the World Council of Churches on appropriate technology, told us that often such technology turns out to be rediscoveries of a people's traditional practices that Western arrogance caused them to be ashamed of. Over and over again he finds peasant cultures that had refined and adapted techniques over centuries to be losing them in our time. What stands to be irretrievably lost is not the quaintness of "cultural diversity" but successful, productive techniques uniquely suited to local conditions and, by definition, controllable by the people. They will be lost if elites in these countries continue, indeed encouraged by foreign aid, to import machines in order to increase their profit margins.

The hallmark of techniques that grow out of the experience of the people is that they can be made by the people themselves. There is simply no need to depend on costly and imported technologies. Basic agricultural techniques are not of complicated design. Tubewells, simple diesel engines, animal-powered plows and seed drills can all be manufactured at the local level by workers without the need for heavy capital equipment. For example, in the city of Daska, in the Pakistani Punjab, more than 100 small factories produce diesel engines principally from local materials.[8] In Pakistan, as in most other underdeveloped countries, this is the exception. In China it is the rule. As mentioned earlier, each commune houses some light industry, often more like a workshop than a factory, to service agriculture. One example is the low cost pump, locally invented in 1962 through the stimulus of the *withdrawal* of Soviet technicians. It costs one-eighth as much as the Russian equipment previously used and is manufactured in thousands of rural communes.

In China, most significantly, designs for new machines come from those who work in the fields. Agricultural researcher and China visitor Roger Blobaum tells of a new Chinese tractor that "isn't much to look at." But he adds, "the factory manager emphasized that it was designed by engineers who spend their summers out on the communes, is just what the peasants ordered, and will be redesigned anytime they decide they want something else."[9]

What Are the Forces Behind Large-Scale Mechanization?

If large-scale foreign technology is not necessary to increase production, why is it being increasingly imported into underdeveloped countries? To answer that question we first have to understand who is introducing the machines. Mechanization is fully the business of the large landholders. The 4 percent of Indian farmers with holdings of more than 25 acres make up 96 percent of tractor owners in India.[10] With the breakdown of the traditional ties that have held agrarian societies together, large landholders are eager to be rid of all tenants so that they might retain a greater share of the profits. Mechanization gives them the way. Rhetoric about the efficiency of mechanization gives them the rationale.

Large landholders have seen mechanization as a way to escape minimum wage requirements, such as the Agricultural Minimum Wages Act in Kerala, India. Studies of agricultural modernization in India reveal a major reason for rapid "tractorization" in the late 1960s was not increased efficiency but the opportunity to get rid of tenants. Getting rid of tenants is attractive to a landlord threatened by land-reform legislation that would give land to those who till it, that is, to his tenants.

Mechanization makes it possible for wealthier farmers to increase further their cultivated holdings. As long as a farm relies on laborers, there are limits to the size of the holding that a landowner can efficiently oversee. But machines can make it possible to farm land of virtually any size. Moreover, machines are more easily controlled than human beings. Landlords do not have to worry about rice being taken out of the fields to feed the hungry family of a tractor.

Who else gains from the spread of large-scale technology around the world? The people who manufacture it, of course. As Green Revolution commentator Lester Brown put it in *Seeds of Change,* "the multinational corporation has a vested interest in the agricultural revolution along with the poor countries themselves."[11] The thought has not been wasted on multinational agribusiness, as we found on our visits to such Green Revolution areas as northwest Mexico.

The giant agribusiness firms, their markets at home becoming saturated, began to push in the 1960s for new markets, especially in the underdeveloped countries. During the period 1968 to 1975, International Harvester built up its sales outside North America from less than one fifth to almost one third of total sales and John Deere's sales overseas jumped from 16 percent to 23 percent of its total. Massey-Ferguson, a farm machinery giant with headquarters in Canada, was first to see the real growth potential abroad; 70 percent of its sales are now outside North America.[12]

This rapid expansion has not been without the help of powerful friends. The governments of industrial countries, directly and through international lending agencies such as the World Bank, provide foreign agricultural assistance in the form of credits to import machinery.

Both the United States Agency for International Development (AID) and the World Bank have given large loans to Pakistan for farm mechanization. The Bank has given similar loans to India, the Philippines, and Sri Lanka. In 1966, when a World Bank loan to the Philippines made cheap credit available for farm mechanization, tractor sales soared.[13] Although the Bank, observes development economist Keith Griffin, claims to be "having second thoughts about this policy . . . the Agricultural Projects Department of the Bank remains firmly pro-tractor."[14]

As with the problems of protecting plants from pests, the United Nations Food and Agriculture Organization, rather than help develop appropriate alternatives, is becoming a broker between underdeveloped countries and multinational farm machinery firms. Its advisory Farm Mechanization Working Group includes Caterpillar Tractor, John Deere, Fiat, FMC, Massey-Ferguson, Mitsui, British Petroleum, and Shell. The FAO has joined with Massey-Ferguson to set up in Colombia the School of Agricultural Mechanization for all of Spanish-speaking Latin America. Such a prestigious institution would easily lead to an overdose of machines for Latin America's rural societies.

In many underdeveloped countries the value of domestic currency in relation to foreign currency is kept artificially high to promote certain imports. Agricultural machinery brought from abroad is thus often "cheaper" than it otherwise might be. This policy and other forms of subsidization in countries like Pakistan ended up making the same tractor cost one half of what it would in Iowa, calculated in terms of wheat. In the late 1960s, the Indian government subsidized mechanization so heavily through cheap credit that in the Ludhiana district of the Punjab farmers with even less than 15 acres were encouraged to buy tractors. This was in spite of the fact that even the principal suppliers of farm machinery thought that at least 25 to 30 acres were needed to make the tractors economical.[15] The government of Iran encouraged large, mechanized farming by exempting those farms that mechanized from the Land Reform Act.[16]

Those who promote large-scale mechanization as the answer for underdeveloped countries like to throw out this challenge: "Look at China," they say. "Chinese agriculture is now starting to mechanize in a big way. Isn't this a lesson for the rest of the Third World?"

This view is correct in one sense: There is an important lesson here. It is not, however, that large-scale mechanization is the answer for agriculture in the underdeveloped countries. The lesson is that mechanization is itself not the issue at all. The issue is *who* owns the machines.

Where the workers themselves own the machines, as in China, mechanization will proceed because the workers naturally wish to lighten the backbreaking toil of field labor. In China the goal is to eliminate the "three bendings"—pulling weeds, transplanting seedlings, and harvesting. The result of mechanization will likely be a better life for farmers, not unemployment. In China farm mechanization is a high priority in part because labor is needed to expand the cultivated area and to upgrade and expand the irrigation system. Farm mechanization that frees labor for such other vital work contributes to Chinese society as a whole, not to private gain. Moreover, the goal of farm mechanization must be understood in the Chinese context. By 1980, the Chinese plan to have a tractor density of one per 125 acres compared, for example, to one tractor for every 2.5 acres in Japan.[17]

Cuba now has the greatest tractor density of any country in Latin America. Yet no one is unemployed. The story of loading sugar freighters in Cuba is instructive. Traditionally Cuban raw sugar was loaded into freighters by laborers lugging a sack at a time on their backs up a gangplank and into the hold. It took over a month to fill a ship. The sugar companies tried to mechanize the operation (with conveyor belts) but they were continually thwarted by organized workers who knew that their very lives depended on keeping the machines out. But once the Cuban government expanded other sectors of the economy and guaranteed everyone a productive job, the sugar terminals were quickly mechanized. Now a ship is loaded in a little over 24 hours! Nobody objected when the conveyor belts came in; no one ever *wanted* a life of carrying sugar sacks up and down a gangplank. Cuba is also rapidly mechanizing the cutting of sugar cane, one of the most grueling of all agricultural jobs. Rather than creating masses of unemployed, it will speed the development of Cuba by releasing workers for other jobs important to the economy.

Isn't Appropriate Technology the Answer?

Just as we cannot say that all large-scale mechanization is necessarily bad, neither can we say that appropriate technology is necessarily the answer. Even the "right" technology cannot be imposed nor is it likely to do much good in the "wrong" society.

Contrast, for example, the impact of biogas technology in India and China. Biogasification is a relatively simple method of fermenting organic raw materials such as crop residues and manure to produce both fuel and fertilizer. A small-scale biogas plant can be built from local materials. Since the 1940s India has been developing cow-dung biogas plants, acclaimed widely as a truly "appropriate technology." But, in the highly stratified economic reality of rural India, this apparently beneficial technology has created even greater problems for the poorer groups, according to *New Scientist* writer Joseph Hanlon.[18]

First, even the smallest plants require a significant investment and the dung from two cows. Thus only well-off farmers who have at least two cows and some capital to invest now control the biogas. Furthermore, the dung, which once was free, now has cash value. In areas where biogas plants operate, landless laborers can no longer pick it off the road and use it for fuel. And since the landless and other poor villagers are in no position to buy biogas, they end up with no fuel at all. In other words, their position is worsened by the introduction of biogas plants, according to A. K. N. Reddy, governor of the appropriate technology unit at the Indian Institute of Science, Bangladore.

What about biogas in China? Many visitors to China have noted the growing use of biogas in the countryside, now providing fuel and lighting for 17 million commune peasants in Szechwan, China's most populated province. In China, the biogas benefits all members of the community because plants are owned and operated cooperatively.

The largely methane gas produced by China's more

than 4 million biogas pits is used for cooking, lighting and running farm machinery. A member of one commune noted, "It takes only 20 minutes to cook a meal for my family of seven using marsh gas [the Chinese term for biogas[19]]. Unlike firewood or coal, marsh gas does not make the kitchen walls grimy and it has no smoke or smell." The Chinese also note that the sealed biogas pits have helped to significantly reduce the incidence of parasitic diseases and eliminated breeding grounds for flies and mosquitoes.

The contrast between biogas technology in these two countries suggests that even technology theoretically appropriate to the needs of the people will *not* necessarily serve their needs. It can even exacerbate social inequalities unless a prior redistribution of social power has created structures in which all share in the control over and the use of the new technology.

Nevertheless, many people might be taken in by the claim of multinational firms that they now have converted to "appropriate technology." Firestone-India provides a good example of what we mean. In 1976 the company announced a solid rubber tire and steel wheel that they said would increase the carrying capacity of India's 13 million bullock carts by 50 percent. Sounds great. But there are two snags. At a price of 60 percent more than the conventional wooden wheel, Firestone-India's wheel is beyond the means of the poor peasant. Moreover, the new wheel will put traditional wheel makers out of business. When asked why the company was introducing the new wheel, the factory director explained that the motivation was the current glut in the natural rubber market. "Rubber tired wheels on bullock carts will provide a large outlet for this surplus rubber."

The source of this account, Joseph Hanlon, noted as he traveled across India: "There is no shortage of technology, nor even of 'appropriate' technology . . . [But] the power and profits remain with those who have always had them and who have been able to exploit the new technologies as they did the old."[20]

We need redistribution not of wealth but of the technology possessed by the industrial world. . . . The receiver of technology must be willing to change his way of life, and like it or not, he may have to cooperate closely with the donor of that technology during a transition training period of years. Some Third Worlders may term this "neocolonialism," and they are welcome to their opinions. Others might call it "mutually beneficial cooperation."

Ray Vicker, *Wall Street Journal* bureau chief,
in *This Hungry World*

In Telukpinang, 60 miles south of Jakarta, as in other parts of Indonesia, the mill has taken over work traditionally done by women by hand—the threshing and hulling of rice stalks. Rice mills are estimated to have eliminated a million or more jobs in the fields of Java alone, the principal Indonesian island.

He [the landlord] recalled that he used to employ two women, sometimes three or four, giving them two liters of rice for every 10 they produced. But now, he said, he keeps the entire crop, paying those who help him the equivalent of about 60 cents a day plus lunch.

The mill is owned by a major general in the Indonesian army who lives in a Jakarta suburb. The villagers asked that his name not be disclosed since they fear his power.

New York Times, November 30, 1975

Some past attempts to apply mechanization have also found resistance in less developed countries— especially in areas with high unemployment and a seemingly unlimited supply of low-cost labor. . . . These have been temporary setbacks.

Arthur J. Olsen, Vice-President, FMC Corporation,
speech at "Feeding the World's Hungry"
Conference, 1974

Part V

The Inefficiency of Inequality

21. Isn't the Backwardness of Small Farmers to Blame?

Question: You seem to think the small farmer is the savior of the hungry world. But isn't one basic reason for low production levels in the poor countries that so much land is in farms too small to be efficient? Aren't most small farmers just too backward and tradition-bound to respond to development programs?

Our Response: Whether a small farm is necessarily less efficient and less productive than a large operation is of critical importance in assessing the production potential of the underdeveloped countries, since about 80 percent of all farms are of less than 12 acres of land.

So we asked: Does smallness equal low levels of production? To answer that question we looked at studies from all over the world and everywhere the verdict is the same: Contrary to our previous assumption, the small farmer in most cases produces more per unit of land than the large farmer. Here are just a few examples:

- The value of output per acre in India is more than one-third higher on the smallest farms than on the larger farms.[1]
- In Thailand plots of two to four acres produce almost 60 percent more rice per acre than farms of 140 acres and more.[2]
- In Taiwan net income per acre of farms with less than one and a quarter acres is nearly twice that of farms over five acres.[3]

- The World Bank has reported on an analysis of the differences in the value of output on large and small farms in Argentina, Brazil, Chile, Colombia, Ecuador, and Guatemala. The conclusion? The small farms were three to fourteen times more productive per acre than the large farms.[4]

Such comparisons go a long way toward explaining the low productivity of agriculture in underdeveloped countries when you bear in mind that, according to a study of 83 countries, only 3 percent of all the landowners control a staggering 80 percent of all farmland.[5] The point is that the largest landholders control most of the farmland, yet studies from all over the world show that they are the least productive.

To explain the higher productivity of the small farmer, one need not romanticize the peasant. Peasant farmers get more out of their land precisely because they need to survive on the meager resources allowed to them. Studies show that small landholders plant more carefully than a machine would, mix and rotate complementary crops, choose a combination of cultivation and livestock that is labor-intensive and, above all, work their perceptibly limited resources (especially themselves) to the fullest. Farming for the peasant family is not an abstract calculation of profit to be weighed against other investments. It is a matter of life and death.

What About Small Farmer Efficiency in the United States?

Every single study ever made by the United States Department of Agriculture (USDA) has found that the most efficient farm, measured in terms of cost per unit of output, is the mechanized one- or two-farmer unit, not the largest operations. Any savings associated with sheer size (and there are remarkably few) are quickly offset by the higher management, supervisory, and labor costs of large farms.[6]

To test this finding we looked at net income per acre by farm size in the United States from 1960 through 1973. We found that in all those fourteen years there were only two in which the biggest farms realized a net income per acre greater than the family farm.[7] The very pattern of greater productivity by small farmers that struck us in our study of underdeveloped countries is found right here in America.

22. Why Don't Small Farmers Produce More?

Question: You say that small landholders produce more per acre than the large landholders. But are not the yields of small peasant holdings in the Third World only a fraction of the yields of the farms in the industrial countries? Why don't they produce more?

Our Response: Compared to large landholders, small peasant producers do not have equal access to credit and agricultural inputs, such as water, fertilizer, and tools. As Green Revolution pioneer Norman Borlaug himself expressed it:

I have a lot of respect for the small farmer. . . . Almost invariably when you look at what he's doing with his land, you find he's producing the maximum under the situation he has to work with. The thing is that he usually doesn't have much to work with.[1]

The Small Pay More

As we showed in focusing on Bangladesh early in the book, small farmers often cannot get ahead because their initiatives are actively obstructed by the landed elite, who are threatened by any advance that would make the village's small farmers less dependent on them.

Moreover, necessities such as fertilizer and water do not reach small farmers because they have neither the cash nor the credit to buy them. Quite often loans from government agencies stipulate a minimum holding that cuts out the small farmer. In Pakistan, for example, to get a loan for a tubewell from the Agricultural Development Bank, a peasant must have at least 12.5 acres. This single stipulation excludes over 80 percent of Pakistan's farmers.[2] One estimate is that only about 5 percent of Africa's farmers have access to institutional credit—and it is not hard to guess which 5 percent![3]

Sudhir Sen, Indian economist and commentator on the Green Revolution, has estimated that roughly one-half of India's small farmers lack any recorded right to the land, without which they are unable to obtain crop loans from credit institutions.[4] (Even where there are exceptions, the tenant is still penalized. In Tamil Nadu, India, the tenant is allowed only 60 percent of the amount of credit per acre advanced to landowners.[5]) Perhaps, even more important, small farmers are reluctant to use their land for loan collateral anyway. Poor farmers quite sensibly decide that they do not want to risk losing their land.

Largely excluded from institutional credit, small landholders are left dependent on private moneylenders and merchants who charge usurious rates of interest. We have seen estimates of interest rates ranging from 50 percent to 200 percent! In one area of the Philippines 15 percent of the borrowers paid an interest rate of over 200 percent while 20 percent of the borrowers paid only 16 percent. Moreover, merchant-creditors can increase the interest by underpricing farm products used to repay loans and overpricing the goods that debtors buy from them.[6] By contrast, the large operator may pay no interest, or even come out ahead by borrowing money. When the nominal rates of interest on credit available to large operators from commercial institutions are adjusted for inflation, the real rate of interest is often negative.[7]

Obligations to Moneylenders and Landlords

Earlier we described the debt bondage that keeps so many peasant farmers in a form of perpetual vassalage. As agricultural economist Keith Griffin so aptly puts it, "The *campesinos* of Latin America have suffered not from insecurity of tenure but from excessively secure tenure." Debt bondage, he points out, has been used to tie peasants to the land to assure landowners that labor would be available, particularly in labor-scarce economies in Latin America.[8] What is the impact on production? Inevitably, motivation to increase production is stifled because the trapped peasants know that higher yields will never benefit them, only the landowner or moneylender. "The constantly indebted peasant is virtually bound by contract to sell his produce at prices set by the private moneylender-cum-trader, as no effective marketing cooperatives exist to safeguard his interests," explain Erich and Charlotte Jacoby in their classic *Man and Land*.[9]

Debt bondage can mean that the peasant farmer must work off the debt by tending the fields of the creditor. The peasant's own plot then suffers neglect. Unable to work his land adequately, the peasant farmer often has no choice but to give it up.

Consider sharecroppers who represent a significant portion of the rural population in many underdeveloped countries. Although in many cases they must provide all of the inputs, they get only a portion of the crop. Why then make the investments necessary to increase production? In Bangladesh, we learned that while owner-cultivators need the prospect of a 2-to-1 advantage in order to take the risk of adopting a new technology, sharecroppers need the prospect of a 4-to-1 advantage since they get only half the crop.[10]

Insecure tenancies result in soil depletion. Tenants, in constant indebtedness and unsure of whether or not they will be on the same plot next year, can hardly be expected to protect the soil fertility by rotating crops and leaving fields fallow.

Without a certain minimum landholding, security of tenure, credit at a reasonable rate, and control over what is produced, farmers make the realistic assessment that it is not in their best interest to invest to increase production or to take steps to preserve the soil fertility. Thus it is not the alleged "backwardness" of the peasant farmers that keeps them from buying fertilizer and other modern inputs, but hard economic sense.

23. Isn't Bigger Better?

Question: But haven't big farmers proved themselves to be more efficient and resourceful than small ones? How else could they have gotten on top? As Ray Vicker put it in his book *This Hungry World,* ". . . the big farmer may be big because he has the intelligence, the capital, and the management talent to stay big." Moreover, big farmers are more willing to take risks. Isn't this the kind of farmer we need now more than ever? Maybe we have just reached the point where we cannot afford equality—if we are also going to eat.

Our Response: The notion that those at the top are there because they are better at whatever they are doing is deeply imbedded in most of us. But it is a false assumption. Erich and Charlotte Jacoby, like so many other agricultural researchers, have come to a different conclusion:

> Landlords, moneylenders and traders, the chief components of any rural hierarchy, did not attain their strong economic position because they increased agricultural production through improved farm management or reasonable investment, but merely because they were able to take advantage of the economic opportunities arising from the weak bargaining power and social helplessness of the peasants.[1]

We have already seen how largeholders gain preferential access to credit and government-subsidized technology, not because of a proven record of efficient production, but because they have the assets and the influence to be creditworthy. Having this access to credit makes it possible to finance farm improvements that can generate still more income. As of 1968 a small minority of Pakistani farmers, those with more than 13 acres, had installed 96 percent of the tubewells in Pakistan. Studies suggest that a tubewell alone, even without improved seeds and fertilizer, can increase net farm revenue by 35 percent. Now, all the outsider sees is that the production of the larger farmer increases and that perhaps his farm grows too. But is this due to the individual farmer's intelligence and talent or to a social factor: the unequal access of the larger landowner to credit that enabled him to buy the tubewell?[2]

Large farmers also benefit because of the inability of small peasant producers to meet institutional credit terms. Large commercial farmers in Mexico were only too happy to buy, at a discount on the black market, the inputs (seeds, fertilizer, or pesticides) that poor farmers had received as government loans. The poor farmers had been forced to sell these inputs on the black market because they were too poor to make them productive enough to pay back the loans which originally purchased the inputs.[3] The same process was reported in Tunisia during the Green Revolution campaign of 1970–1971.

In addition, large landowners are able to obtain higher prices than small farmers through devices that in no way reflect greater efficiency in their farming operation. In Mexico during the late 1940s and early 1950s the large landlords formed exclusive producer associations. Often with the help of government credit these associations invested in warehouses and silos that enabled them to bargain collectively, thus freeing them from dependence on the official price of grain. The small farmers who had received land through the earlier land reform could not, however, follow the same path. They were bound by the terms of the official credit on which they were dependent. They had to sell their crops to the government credit banks that kept prices paid to these small farmers low in order to keep food prices down for the urban population.[4]

The Risk-Taking Large Farmer?

The question suggests that large landowners are more willing than small ones to take risks. But if this is accurate, how can one explain the slowness with which large landowners in Mexico adopted the new varieties of wheat? The reason is that powerful large landowners found they could continue to increase their profit *without* increasing yields. After 1954 they bargained successfully to keep the guaranteed price of wheat so high that they could reap fortunes without making use of the new Green Revolution inputs. Green Revolution analyst Cynthia Hewitt de Alcántara tersely comments: "If one felt it necessary to make more money from wheat, the logical path to follow was to lobby in Mexico City for a still-higher wheat price, and only secondarily to master the subtler requirements of the new technology."[5] Furthermore, large commercial Mexican growers during the 1950s and early 1960s found they could raise their profits enormously, not by seriously attempting to increase yields but by expanding their holdings, often taking over the fields of nearby small landholders and land-reform beneficiaries.

With their ability both to lobby for higher prices and acquire more land, many large landowners scoffed at the idea of improved seeds for years after the much higher yield potential of the new seeds had been demonstrated. When they did begin to consider change, it was only when *all risk was removed* by a federal investment program that poured billions of pesos into irrigation works, roads, storage facilities, electricity, railroads, long-term agricultural credit, and ultimately, into a guaranteed price for wheat. Even so, it took the private wheat growers in Sonora fourteen years to reach the level of production already proven to be within their reach.[6] So much for the myth of the innovative, risk-taking big guy.

The Waste of Wealth

Continuing to pin hopes for genuine development on the contribution of the large landowners overlooks another critical question: What happens to the profit made by the large landowner? Is this profit as likely to be productively invested in agriculture as would the same profit spread among many smaller farmers or cooperatively controlled?

Concentrating the profits from agricultural modernization into a few hands has meant that much of what might have been returned to agricultural improvements goes instead for luxury items to satisfy the conspicuous consumption impulse of the rural *nouveaux riches*. Around the world the new agricultural entrepreneurs can be found "investing" surplus profits in tourist resorts, bars, taxi fleets, movie houses and travel agencies.

In studying Mexico we were astonished to find that the very landed elite, so pampered for 30 years by the Mexican government, was by the 1970s on the verge of bankruptcy. By 1971, reports Hewitt de Alcántara,

An estimated 80 percent of the large agricultural enterprises of the Hermosillo Coast [Mexico] were operating year after year in the red, and the situation was little better in the Yaqui Valley. One large farmer after another filed for bankruptcy.[7]

The financial collapse of the overextended commercial farmers was not a consequence solely of overinvestment in farm technology. On our research visits we found obviously frivolous expenditures by a few amid the equally obvious poverty of the majority: tasteless, sprawling ranch-style houses, swimming pools, multiple imported luxury automobiles, periodic shopping sprees across the border, Las Vegas junkets, private planes, and children in American boarding schools.

Large farmers are often the *least* reliable credit recipients. The World Bank reports that large farmers actually have *poorer* repayment records than small farmers in countries as diverse as Bangladesh, Colombia, Costa Rica, and Ethiopia.[8] Similarly, the U.S. Department of Agriculture tells us that rates of delinquency and foreclosure in the United States are greater on big loans for large-scale farm units than on smaller loans for family farms.[9]

A final factor to weigh is the literal waste of valuable land by large landholding interests. Plantations have always been noted for acquiring more land than they would ever use. But a recent study of land use in Central America tells us that the historic pattern holds true today: farmers who own up to 10 acres cultivate 72 percent of their land, but farmers with over 86 acres cultivate only 14 percent of their land. They use 49 percent for pasture, and leave 37 percent idle.[10] Similarly a 1968 study of Ecuador showed that farmers with less than 25 acres farmed about 80 percent of their land while the largest farmers with more than 2500 acres cultivated little more than a quarter of their land.[11] Since large landowners generally are the *most* wasteful of the land, what makes people now believe that they are the last best hope for agricultural development?

Inequality Thwarts Cooperation

The motivation of people to cooperate toward a common goal is ultimately what all development depends upon. But a social system that gives preferential access to land, agricultural inputs, and government programs to a few undercuts any possibility for cooperation and shared learning. It was thought, for example, that focusing the new seeds and other inputs on the large farmer would have such a powerful "demonstration effect" that all the smaller producers would seek to emulate the large landholder. But small farmers have more savvy than that. Rural development researcher Dr. Ingrid Palmer neatly sums up the perspective of the small farmer:

> It must be obvious to the small farmers that the successful farmers learned of the goodies first, were pals with the purveyors of same, and did all manner of string pulling for inputs. Since the whole deal is not open to public gaze, the small farmers see it as another example of the charmed circle excluding them, and if they are ever approached by technical authorities to do the same, they are damn sure it won't be on the same terms offered the large farmers.[12]

And such an intuition is ordinarily correct. The much-touted demonstration effect has thus been just the opposite of that intended. The simple fact that the large landowner is successful with the new approach is often enough to convince the smallholder that he himself could *not* be.

Finally, the suggestion that we simply cannot afford greater equality if we want to increase production ignores the most fundamental brake on production within a market system: the lack of buyers with the cash to pay for the increased production. One too often forgets that hunger alone is not enough to stimulate production in a market system. Only paying customers stimulate production and in most market economies today, their number is growing very slowly, if at all.

The question implies that "a little inequality is a good thing" or at least a necessary evil. In times of supposed scarcity it becomes even easier to accept the idea that we should turn to those who are "on top." The facts have, however, forced us to conclude that this is exactly the wrong approach. We have learned that the very power of the large landowners makes them less compelled to try to increase production, especially of locally needed food; that they divert resources out of agriculture into unnecessary consumption and unproductive investments; that they underutilize the land; and finally, that the constraints poverty places on motivation and consumption are the greatest blocks to increased production. Economic justice and economic progress are inseparable.

———————

Today, some sociologists view the large landowner with horror, arguing that the task of development should be to level incomes within particular countries, and this means concentrating on the small rather than the large landowner. This brings us once more to that question: Are we aiming at obtaining more food to feed a world with an exploding population? Or are we aiming at redistribution of incomes? I don't think we can do both.

Ray Vicker, *This Hungry World*

24. Is Small Always Beautiful?

Question: If small farmers have proven to be more productive, should not the primary concern of development be to channel more credit, equipment, seeds, fertilizers and irrigation to them?

Our Response: First of all, to focus on the small farmer is to miss entirely a large portion—in many countries 80 to 90 percent—of the rural labor force. A recent study from Cornell University concludes that the landless and near-landless constitute a majority of the rural labor force in Asia, approaching 90 percent in Java, Bangladesh, and Pakistan. In Latin America the landless and near-landless make up a majority in every country studied, exceeding 80 percent in Bolivia, El Salvador, Guatemala, and the Dominican Republic.[1]

Nor should one make the mistake of believing that the small farm is inherently more productive than the large. We have found that the size of the parcel of land matters less than the relationship of the people to it.

We have seen that small farms can be very productive—as in Japan—where the people working the land know that the productivity will benefit them. And we have seen exactly the opposite: small farms with low productivity when credit, debt, and tenancy arrangements deny those who work the fields the fruits of their labors.

Likewise with large farming units. They can be productive where those working the land know that their labor will benefit them. Thai Binh in North Vietnam is one example. Since 1965 a single cooperative involving 4000 people produces rice, small animals, such as ducks and geese, as well as fish in over 100 acres of village-controlled fish ponds. Harvesting two or even three rice crops annually, Thai Binh can produce almost 80 percent more than the annual production of the less-than-five-acre plot characteristic of India, for example.[2] But large units are not necessarily productive. We have just documented the inefficiencies of many privately owned, large landholder operations. Exchange these private landowners for antidemocratic bureaucrats and productivity will still remain low, as developments in Soviet agriculture have amply demonstrated.

25. But Hasn't Land Reform Sacrificed Production?

Question: Notwithstanding all that you have said about the low productivity of large landholders, hasn't land redistribution historically led to a fall-off in production? And in our own country, wouldn't land redistribution also mean higher food prices?

Our Response: The threat of lower production is certainly used to stave off land redistribution, but experience following genuine land reform proves just the contrary. Historically, genuine land reforms have led to greater production because they have redressed the "inefficiencies of inequality" that thwart production —those discussed in our last three responses. To illustrate the point concretely, we'll focus on the actual post-reform experiences in Vietnam, China, Cuba, and Portugal. Then our response will consider our own country: What would land reform mean here?

In 1945, over half of the farmland in Vietnam was held not by peasants but by large landlords and French colonists. The rents they extracted from the peasants amounted to as much as three-quarters of the harvest. After the defeat of the French in 1954, land reform in North Vietnam was immediately undertaken. By the end of 1957, about 45 percent of the North's arable land had been redistributed, with 77 percent of the rural households benefiting.[1]

Thoroughly redistributing control over resources helped to make possible production advances even during the height of the war against the United States. According to the FAO's Sixth Report on Land Reform, yields in North Vietnam were going up and irrigation was extended from 20 percent of the cultivated area in the mid-fifties to nearly 60 percent in the mid-sixties. Between 1960 and 1970, yields of rice went up 20 percent and other crops by 50 percent.[2]

China also demonstrates that national production advances follow once land reform has made control over the land more equal and democratic. After having progressed through four stages since the initiation of reforms in 1950, the ownership of land in China is vested in the production brigade, equal to one large village or several smaller ones. In practice, the production brigade turns over the land for cultivation to the village labor force, called the production team. Except where large tractors or combine harvesters are involved, the village production team is responsible for its own field management and accounting. Income is distributed according to a mutually agreed upon work-point system, and everyone is assured of the basic foodgrains and other essential items.

The share of production appropriated by the central government in taxes is small—only one to seven percent. These taxes are fixed rates based upon the income expected, considering the soil and climatic conditions of the commune. A commune with especially fertile land would have to allocate seven percent of its production to the central government, whereas a commune with poor natural resources like the famed

Tachai would have to contribute only one percent. This percentage does *not* rise even if the commune prospers beyond the expectations based on its natural endowment.[3] The greater the production, therefore, the greater the benefits to those who work the fields.

China's national production figures reflect these changes. By 1975 China was producing over 1700 pounds of grain per acre, 60 percent above corresponding per acre production in India[4] and almost double the yield per acre in China before the Revolution. According to Cornell's China watcher Dr. Benedict Stavis, compared to India, China feeds 50 percent more people 20 percent better with 30 percent less cultivated land (comparing per capita figures for grains and bean-type crops). Moreover, precisely because of China's far greater equality of access to productive resources, its per capita statistics much more accurately reflect the reality of food distribution.

The experience of land reform in Cuba is also instructive.[5] It demonstrates the real post-land reform problems that take time to overcome—the heritage of the old order—as well as the necessity for workers to participate in decision-making in order for production to rise.

Cuba's basic land reform was completed by 1963, having created over 100,000 additional independent landowners and having placed 60 percent of the country's agricultural land in public hands. Some economists studying Cuba have concluded that its agrarian reform "caused no major drop in production."[6] Others have pointed to the short-term production setbacks as the reorganization of agriculture was taking place.[7] In the years 1963 and 1964, the index of agricultural production dropped to 86 and 93 respectively, as compared to 100 in 1952–56. Although Cuba's overall agricultural progress during the 1960s was disappointing to Cuban planners, we should not lose sight of the fact that compared to levels before the beginning of the revolution, the production of important foods did rise: By 1971 rice had risen four times, fruit three and one-half times, egg production four and one-half times, and potatoes by 42 percent.[8]

Why did Cuba's agriculture progress more slowly than had been hoped during the 1960s?[9] Cubans attempted to rapidly diversify production away from sugar without the necessary skilled human resources, having inherited widespread illiteracy and a large labor force whose only skill was sugar harvesting. Thus investments in agriculture, such as more tractors, were largely wasted. In 1970 only one quarter of the tractor capacity was in use, due to lack of maintenance capability and administrative failures to get the tractors to where they were needed. The U.S.-imposed trade embargo also cut off the supply of needed spare parts. Moreover, Cuban agriculture experienced a labor shortage, especially in the grueling work of cane cutting, as other jobs opened up in the society. Perhaps more critically, during the 1960s decision-making appears to have been overcentralized; thus investments were not based enough on calculations made at a local level.

Cuba, during the 1960s, was attempting greater equality through agrarian reform and other means of controlling income differential. Greater equality is certainly one prerequisite for greater productivity, as we have already stated. But Cuba had not yet sufficiently followed through on the second prerequisite; namely, participation in policy decision-making by the Cuban people on a local level.

By the 1970s this had begun to change. Illiteracy had been almost wiped out through a national mobilization. Primary schools were graduating four times more students in 1970 than at the time of the revolution. This basic education was an essential ingredient of the more effective organization of work and decentralized participation that began to emerge in the 1970s. Mass organizations—labor unions, farmers' associations, and neighborhood clubs—widened their roles in the 1970s, not simply to carry out policy but to help formulate it. Although problems still remain in the agricultural sector, the increased participation in decision-making is being reflected in increased production. Between 1970 and 1974, non-sugarcane agricultural output grew at an annual rate of 8.4 percent, surpassing all previous years.

Portugal's recent agrarian reform points to still other key productive advances that can result from land redistribution.[10] Following the overthrow of fascism in Portgual in 1974, agricultural laborers seized almost 3 million acres of land held by huge estates in southern Alentejo. The expropriation of these big estates was then legalized by the new constitution. But, in 1977, in violation of the constitution, the Soares government passed a law dissolving the Units of Collective Production (UCPs) set up by the farm laborers and small farmers on the expropriated land and returning the land to its former owners. In the face of attack by specially trained police using electric nightsticks, water cannons, machine guns, and helicopters, the peasants refused to give up the land. As of mid-1978, the government has abandoned its efforts to disband the UCPs.

Members of the UCP's take their wages out of the sale of produce. Profits are then directed into social benefits such as shops, playgrounds, and daycare facilities by the General Assembly, which is made up of all members. Managers of the UCP's are elected.

What has been the impact of this spontaneous land redistribution? In two years, acreage actually under cultivation almost tripled in Alentejo. Even more significantly, many new jobs were created in an area previously plagued with chronic unemployment. The number of people fully employed in agriculture jumped fourfold after land reform. The new owners of the land supply 50 percent of all of Portugal's wheat and one-fifth to one-quarter of the meat for the domestic market.

Studying the actual experience of land reform in countries as different as Vietnam, China, Cuba, and Portugal, one consistent lesson emerges: rather than leading to a drop in production, genuine land reform can be a first step in long-term production advances.

Land Reform Misconceptions

Then why is it that so many believe the opposite—that land reform undercuts production?

First, deliberately half-hearted and ineffective land reform laws in countries like the Philippines, Pakistan, and India have obscured the potential productive returns from thoroughgoing land reform of the type carried out in three of the countries just discussed. On pages 313ff., we describe several features of these fake land reforms.

Second, most official measures of production commonly include only grain entering the national market. Yet, focusing solely on official production figures may seriously underestimate agricultural advances in societies undergoing genuine agrarian reform. When millions of formerly landless gain control over their own land, there is great likelihood—and FAO officials we queried concur—that a greater proportion of food production is consumed by the people who produce it. Thus it never enters into the national production figures used, for example, by the United Nations system.

A third factor causing an underestimation of post-reform gains is that progress is often measured in grain production *alone*. In countries undergoing basic restructuring of control, people realize that they need not live "by grain alone." Although the U.N. notes grain production per capita in China went up 19 percent between 1962 and 1975, this does not convey a complete picture of nutritional improvements according to a report from the Congressional Research Service of the Library of Congress.[11] People now eat more fruit, meat, and vegetables. "On the average, every Chinese eats half a kilo (just over a pound) of vegetables per day," the report notes. And the same can be said of Vietnam. Focusing on grain production ignores "a very important point in the strategy of food self-reliance of the Vietnamese," according to Vietnamese scholar Ngo Vinh Long. Under the French, rice alone occupied over 95 percent of the cultivated land, but by 1970 over 18 percent of the land was growing crops other than rice—corn, sweet potatoes, sesame seeds, and fruit.[12]

A fourth factor reinforcing the myth that land reform equals scarcity is simply our lack of familiarity with any system other than our own. Terms such as "rationing" are misunderstood. "Rationing" for most people implies scarcity. When outsiders learn of rationing in Cuba, they assume that there is less food available now—since they never heard of rationing before the revolution. Rationing, however, can best be understood in Cuba as a mechanism for insuring the minimal supply of basic food to all, as well as the means of channeling more food selectively to those with special needs—children, pregnant women, and the elderly. Ordinary Cubans we've spoken with feel that it works to their benefit more than would our rationing system: money.

On a research trip in northwest Mexico, we approached a community of landless laborers who had recently occupied and planted land that was legally theirs but for decades had been controlled by one of the area's largest landowners. As soon as they realized that we were North Americans, their first question was: "Don't you have land reform in the United States?"

We were a little taken back, as most North Americans would have been. Most of us have come to associate the need for land reform with the plight of underdeveloped countries. Yet the degree of concentration of land holdings in the United States is progressively reaching that of underdeveloped countries. Today 5.5 percent of all U.S. farms control over half of the farmland.[13] In some states, control is even tighter. In California, for example, only 45 corporations control over 30 percent of the prime cropland.[14] Indeed, in four states—California, Arizona, Florida, and Hawaii—the top ten percent of all farms account for over 90 percent of all farm sales. Landownership patterns are not the only measure of the concentration of effective control of production. In many food lines —poultry, fluid milk, vegetables for canning and freezing, and sugar beets for example—virtually all production is done under contract with a relative handful of large corporations.[15] Farmers thus are losing effective control over their production. (Part VIII details this problem with examples.)

Only in recent years has land reform even been

considered an issue in the United States. Only a handful of states have laws which in any way limit the unbridled movement of large, often non-farm corporations into farming. The state of Washington, for instance, passed a law in 1977 that would limit to 2000 acres the amount of land any owner could irrigate using the federally subsidized water system. The extensive citizens' campaign to pass the law was in part a response to efforts of the U and I Sugar Corporation to add an additional 117,000 irrigated acres to its 115,000-acre holding.[16] In 1975, national legislation was introduced by Senator James Abourezk and others that would prohibit any corporation with over $3 million in non-farm assets from operating farmland. The legislation has gotten nowhere. Indeed, there is not even a national inventory of our farmland that would reveal the true extent of concentration and control of farmland by non-farm interests. Why? Partly because Americans believe the many misconceptions about land reform we have just described. A good way to lay bare these misconceptions is to focus on one area of the country where much debate has been raging over the issue of land redistribution. Significant research has been done on the impact of possible redistribution.

In 1902, after a decade of agitation by western citizens, Congress passed the National Reclamation Act. It established a bureau to construct dams, reservoirs, and canals to irrigate the arid and semiarid land of the western states. As a condition for receiving water, provided by expenditures of the tax-paying public, the law stipulated that no owner had permanent right to more than 160 irrigated acres (320 for a couple). Although the congressional intent was clearly to favor family farms, actual policy throughout this century has been the opposite. Administrative and congressional negligence in enforcing the law and countervailing tax and agricultural subsidies have consistently favored the larger landholders. Thus, in the very areas entrusted to the family farm at the turn of the century, some of the world's largest agribusiness operations now control the land. Corporations like Southern Pacific (106,000 acres), J. G. Boswell, associated with the *Los Angeles Times* and Safeway (141,000 acres), and Standard Oil (10,000 acres) have reaped the largest share of the gain from the $9 billion investment of public funds irrigating the land.

Since the 1950's, a public interest group, National Land for People, has been fighting for enforcement of the Reclamation Act that would break up these large estates and give to small farmers the irrigation benefits that the law intended. In 1977, this group won several court and legislative battles that, while not yet achieving the enforcement of the law, did drive the issue into public view.

By 1978, big landholders were contributing $50,000 monthly to squash any enforcement initiative. Such interests would have us all be persuaded that redistribution of this land would be to our detriment. They would make consumers worry that prices would rise. Yet detailed studies such as one carried out at the University of California at Berkeley by agricultural economist Philip Leveen have indicated that enforcement of the law would not penalize the consumer with higher food prices.[17]

Defenders of large landholding interests have also tried to make the claim that a 320-acre farm is uneconomic. Yet because of the productivity of the irrigated soil, a 320-acre farm in this area could easily rank in the upper five percent of all farms in the nation—with total yearly sales in the neighborhood of $250,000.[18]

If the law were enforced, land redistribution in the federal irrigation districts would result in viable farms and would not raise our food prices. In addition, the communities in the irrigation districts would benefit by redistribution of the land. According to still other studies done by the University of California on the potential impact of land redistribution, communities in the area would benefit from more jobs, an increase in personal income, and greater business activity, as well as more community services.[19] In Part VII, pages 265–66, we discuss a classic comparison of two California towns that illustrate these many advantages of communities composed of small farms versus communities dominated by large farms.

Just as in underprivileged countries, those who control the food-producing resources in our country have much to gain by convincing all of us that reform would mean scarcity. We all must work to explode this myth, in regard to our own and other countries. In appendix A, we include the names and addresses of groups throughout the country now focusing on the need for land reform here.

Part VI

The Trade Trap

26. What About Their Natural Advantage?

Question: You have brought to light the food-producing potential of the underdeveloped countries. Yet there is another issue: Why is it necessary for these countries to grow their own food? Aren't certain regions better suited than others for growing particular crops? Underdeveloped countries cannot support themselves by exporting industrial goods. They just do not have the industry. It is only logical that these countries do what they can do best. If that turns out to be growing coffee, tea, or cocoa—why not let them exploit this natural advantage?

Our Response: The "natural advantage" argument does sound like common sense. But an apparently natural state of affairs may look that way simply because the economic forces molding our reality have been operating such a long time. Enjoying our morning cups of coffee or snacking on chocolate candy bars, we come to associate such pleasures with certain countries destined by nature to be able to grow only such crops as coffee and cocoa. We must begin, however, to erase the notion that there is anything "given" about the way the poor countries now use their land. Land use most often represents a choice by people, not by nature.

One of the most oppressive food myths is that underdeveloped countries can grow only "tropical crops." In reality they can grow an incredible diversity of crops—grains, high-protein legumes, vegetables, and fruits. The phrase "banana-republic" has made it easy to overlook that Latin America got along quite well without a single banana tree until the late 1830s. (The first banana did not arrive in the United States until 1866.) What United Brands, Standard Fruit (Dole), and Del Monte call "prime banana land" turns out to be first-class agricultural land—flat, deep soil, well-watered, suitable for a full range of food crops. In fact, when United Brands and Standard Fruit abandoned their larger banana plantations in Honduras' Rio Aguan valley (for "production consolidation reasons"), landless peasants settled in and grew corn, rice, and beans. When World War II restricted the coffee market, many coffee trees in Brazil were uprooted so that food crops could be planted on what was some of the country's best land.[1]

We repeat: There is nothing "natural" about the underdeveloped countries' concentration on a few, largely nonnutritious crops. And, as we shall see, there's no "advantage" either.

Most underdeveloped countries now depend for 50 to 90 percent of their export earnings on only one or two crops. Bananas in the period 1970–1972 accounted for 58 percent of the total export earnings of Panama, 48 percent of Honduras', and 31 percent of Somalia's.[2] Coffee has become crucially important for eleven countries that depend on it for 25 percent or more of their foreign earnings. In 1972, coffee brought in 53 percent of Colombia's foreign exchange; 78 percent of Burundi's; 50 percent of Rwanda's; 50 percent of Ethiopia's; and 61 percent of Uganda's.[3]

Concentration on a limited number of crops creates the vulnerability that characterizes underdeveloped countries. Vulnerability means an inability to control one's own destiny. Is there a more apt definition of underdevelopment itself?

In addition to the vulnerability to market changes inherent in being dependent on very few crops, there is the larger question of the overall decline in the value of the agricultural commodities most underdeveloped countries export. Bananas, the most important fresh fruit in international trade, serve as a good illustration of what this means. The price of bananas has fallen about 30 percent in the last twenty years while the price of manufactured goods has gone up. In 1960, three tons of bananas could buy a tractor. In 1970, that same tractor cost the equivalent of eleven tons of bananas.[4] (It is quite a treadmill if you have run almost four times as fast just to stay in the same place!)

A Roller Coaster Ride to Development?

But as much as the declining export income hurts the economies of underdeveloped countries, fluctuations in price are the real nemeses of economic planning. The high prices of one year can lure economic planners and farmers into continued reliance on a given crop, even to expand production. Wild price swings then wreak havoc with long-term development plans. Not only can prices fluctuate sharply from year to year but from week to week and even from day to day.

The colonizing powers chose those crops, you will recall from Part III, that did not require frequent planting. That was all well and good for the colonizer who wanted to minimize dependence on labor. But for those former colonies that now have their entire economies locked into coffee, palm oil, or bananas, the results can be disastrous. A coffee tree takes five years to mature; palm oil trees require three to four years. Likewise, you can't just go in and out of banana production in response to price changes, as an American farmer might with wheat and oats. A banana tree does not reach its full potential until two years after planting and even then the payoff, if any, comes over its next five to twenty years of yields. With cocoa trees you have to sit tight for a decade or more before your first harvest.

What happens then if you are encouraged by high current prices to rush into new coffee planting? By the time your first harvest of such crops is ready you might find the bottom has dropped out of the market. And it probably will have, since producers in your country and others will also have planted to meet the demand at the same time you did. The likely result is over-production once the new trees begin to bear more than the consumers are willing to buy even with a drop in price. (Remember a ten-cent drop in the retail price that General Foods charges you for Maxwell House is likely to represent a far greater price drop for the grower. And still, you probably won't drink more coffee.) There have been several coffee busts. In the Depression coffee prices fell by 80 percent. The Brazilian government tried unsuccessfully to bolster prices by burning 80 million bags (weighing 132 lbs. each!), or the equivalent of two years' total world consumption.[5]

Speculative activities are a major cause of extreme fluctuations in price. Take the case of cocoa. Most of the raw cocoa exported (about four-fifths of the total production is exported raw) is sold through dealers and specialized firms in New York, London, Paris, Amsterdam, and Hamburg on the basis of prices determined by bids and offers on the cocoa futures markets. What causes price swings on the cocoa futures market? Perhaps a meeting of cocoa producers has been called. That alone might be taken as bullish by the hard-core cocoa traders, thus inflating cocoa prices for a period as short as a day or as long as a month.[6] Rumors of a political change in the government of a major cocoa producer or a single report of some obscure cocoa pest can have the same instantaneous effect.

The point is that the range of price fluctuations due, say, to weather-caused variations in supply, are greatly magnified by a small number of people who usually have nothing to do with growing the crop. Their "business" is gambling. Their interest is in an actively fluctuating fast-changing market, since by playing it correctly one can make money whether prices go up or down. As an official of the Chicago Board of Trade told an agribusiness executives seminar in 1975, "Stability, gentlemen, is the only thing we can't deal with." Unlike fluctuations in stock market quotes that have no impact on the earnings of the corporations traded, speculation on the futures market directly hits the producers' earnings and the *predictability* of earnings.

Speculation also introduces an element of uncertainty that can discourage purchase of an underdeveloped country's product. Manufacturers of candy bars seek to reduce their profit risks by reducing the use of ingredients that fluctuate widely in price. A speculative commodity like cocoa is likely to be used less and less and to be eventually replaced by a more reliable synthetic substitute. If you flip through the advertisements of such publications as *Food Engineering* and *Food Technology,* you will discover that companies like Monsanto Chemical are already bragging to candy manufacturers that their chemical chocolate—Monodoad—is better than the real thing. Indeed the industrial countries spend at least $1 billion a year to develop substitutes for products from the underdeveloped countries. Natural rubber, jute, and hard fibers are the most vulnerable. Synthetic substitutes for coffee, tea, cocoa, and spices already exist. Can the artificial banana ("guaranteed not to rot") be far off?

"All Your Eggs in Two Baskets"

What can a national planner in Ghana do given that over half of his country's arable land is now planted with cocoa trees? In the late 1950s, when cocoa prices were high, Ghana decided to double its production. Development plans were drawn that counted on the increased foreign exchange earnings. But, as the prices that Ghana had to pay for its imports rose steadily, the price it could get for cocoa seesawed. Up to about $1000 per ton one year and down to less than $400 another; up to $1000 again and down to less than $600 later.[7] The overall decline from the mid-fifties peak has been estimated at 80 percent.[8] You can imagine what became of Ghana's development scheme. Income from sisal has been no more reliable. Tanzania's first five-year plan anticipated a minimum world sisal price of 90 pounds. Soon after, the price dropped to 60 pounds. In late 1976, Cuba announced that the sudden collapse of sugar prices (from 64 cents to 6 cents a pound in eighteen months) would make it necessary to revamp its five-year development plan.

Several years ago the government of Malaysia, in one of the most ambitious settlement schemes ever undertaken in Asia, transformed hundreds of thousands of acres of jungle into new settlements growing oil palm and rubber for export. It seemed to work. The settlers were able to improve their homes, buy some consumer items, and even save for their children's education. Then, in 1974, the entire picture changed. Recession in the industrial countries sent the price of rubber and palm oil plummeting. With no alternative crop to rely on, settlers' incomes also dropped sharply. Today none of the newly cleared land is being settled. A member of the Malaysian parliament observed that: "All our land-development eggs have been put in two baskets—rubber and palm oil. There is no diversification, we grow too little of our own food. Everything is for cash, and when the world prices that we do not control drop, it is our people who suffer."[9]

In addition to the vulnerability built into reliance on slow-maturing crops with highly unstable prices, the choice of crops handed down by the original colonizers contains another limitation. Many are commodities that appear to be reaching the saturation point among consumers. No matter how affluent the consumers or how low the prices drop, consumers seem to eat or drink only so much of products like cocoa, coffee, and bananas.

The "Rewards" of Export Agriculture

So what has export agriculture done for the underdeveloped countries?

Over half of the 40 countries on the United Nations list of those most seriously affected by the food crisis of the 1970s depend on agricultural exports for at least 80 percent of their export earnings.[10] That alone should tell us something.

The revenue from their agricultural exports has simply not kept pace with the cost of their mounting food imports from the industrial countries—in grain alone, up now to over 50 million tons a year. Ironically, the prices of the crops sold predominantly by the industrial countries, crops like grains and soybeans, have risen much faster than the prices of the commodities exported by the underdeveloped countries.

The reward for relying on agricultural trade as the main stimulus for growth has meant no growth. Almost half of the people in the Third World experienced no increase in per capita income in the last four years. Of course this average really means that a few have gained while the majority are worse off than they were four years ago.

Why shouldn't the underdeveloped countries exploit their "natural advantage" in producing a few tropical crops? We have had to conclude that there is nothing natural about it and there is no advantage in it. We have learned that economies dependent on narrow export agriculture are not natural, but the deliberate product of colonizing interests. And we have seen how the prices for colonial inheritance crops have declined, in some cases absolutely, and in every case relative to the industrial products they buy abroad; how price swings make development planning a nightmare; and how saturation of the consumer market in industrial countries makes the long and winding road a dead end.

What was originally designed as a system to transfer wealth *out* of subjugated countries is still promoted by many as the only road to development for those very same countries. Oddly enough, most observers do not see or do not wish to see a contradiction. To us, the contradiction is undeniable. Today export agriculture, dominating the economies of underdeveloped countries, serves foreign interests in the same way it has for hundreds of years. As such, how could it ever be thought of as the basis for self-determined development?

27. Don't They Have Cartels Now?

Question: Aren't some underdeveloped countries organizing producer associations, a polite term for cartels, to get a better price for their products? What is stopping the banana producers, the cocoa producers, and the tea producers from forming their own little "OPECs" (Organization of Petroleum Exporting Countries)?

Our Response: First of all, bananas are not oil. People in the industrial countries can get along much more easily without bananas, cocoa, and tea than they can without oil. Furthermore, most producing countries are pitted against each other for a share in stagnating markets dominated by a few buyers. Angola competes with Brazil for the coffee market. (This is a direct colonial inheritance. In the mid-twenties and again immediately after World War II, Britain, France, and Portugal encouraged the cultivation of coffee in their African colonies in a direct effort to break Brazil's dominance.) Ghana tries to stay on top of Cameroon in selling cocoa. Bangladesh desperately seeks an edge over India's jute. Jute from India and Bangladesh competes with kenaf from Thailand.

The industrial countries can also keep producing countries divided by punishing those who join producer associations. The United States inserted into its Trade Act of 1974 a clause denying trade preferences to any country that joined a producers' association for any commodity.

The Corporate Cartel

Most important, however, the governments of producing countries have been pre-empted: How can an underdeveloped country hope to organize an effective producers' cartel when the corporate cartels are already in charge? We hope that in our response to Question 26 we did not leave you with the impression that the price gyrations of agricultural commodities are just a matter of bad harvests, political unrest, and speculation. When a few corporations control the access to markets, there is very little to prevent them from manipulating the market to maximize profits, forcing prices down to buy up the commodity cheap from producers and then pushing them up so as to unload at a nice profit.

Cocoa serves as a good illustration of the contrast between the fortunes of the producing countries and those of the multinational corporate cartels that really control the production and marketing of most commodities. Cocoa processing, dominated by a small number of large firms in the industrial countries, remains one of the most profitable industries in the world. In 1967 the gross profit margin earned in chocolate production was 38 percent above the average margin for comparable food processing industries.[1] But how profitable is it for the producing countries?

According to a Ghanaian journal, in 1970–1971 Ghana lost $50 million because of manipulation of the cocoa market by the world's few large cocoa houses. One multinational corporation, Gill and Duffus, controls 40 percent of world cocoa trade. They manufacture chocolate, hedge and speculate in the cocoa futures market, and publish the *Cocoa Market News.* As the journal observes, "there are no checks and balances which can prevent Gill and Duffus from manipulating the market to maximize its profits."[2]

Palm oil is a similar story. We heard about a producers' entente for palm oil and looked into it to see how it might help underdeveloped countries that export palm oil. We discovered that the producers' entente was, in effect, none other than Unilever, one of the first corporations profiting on tropical agriculture. Unilever now controls 80 percent of the international oil seed market. The producers' entente has six members, but Zaire-Palm, an arm of Unilever in Zaire, exports over 80 percent of the group's total. We learned, too, that when the world market price for palm oil dips, the local government and the peasant producers suffer, not Unilever. The company simply "slows down their activities when the price goes down and appeals to the State for multiple [tax and other] exemptions."[3] Unilever thus buffers itself from the vagaries of the international palm oil market. A nice arrangement—for Unilever.

Coffee is not as tightly controlled as palm oil—yet. But Nestlé and General Foods already together control 30 to 40 percent of the world coffee trade.[4] Tight control over supplies gives corporations like General Foods, Nestlé, Coca-Cola, and Proctor and Gamble who process and market coffee a twofold method for increasing profits: lowering the return to the producers in the underdeveloped countries while increasing the price charged to consumers in the industrial countries. Take the price trends for Brazilian coffee in the 1960s. In 1968 American companies paid 30 percent less for Brazilian coffee than in 1964. But the coffee drinker in America paid more—13 percent more. The processors and distributors thus increased their cut by 43 percent! During this same period the return to the Brazilian producers was sliced in half.[5]

Bananas exemplify the same points. A United Nations investigative report on how the final retail banana dollar is divided up concluded that the producing countries get only an average of 11 cents out of every dollar we pay for bananas. Thus from the retail sale of a box of bananas in the United States at $5.93, the producers in Honduras would get a gross return of roughly 66 cents. The chain supermarkets, controlling 99.8 percent of retail banana sales in the United States, gross approximately $1.90 on the same box.[6] Workers on plantations in the Philippines receive only 1 to 2 percent of the retail price of a banana when it is sold in Japan.

Like the cocoa industry, the $2 billion plus banana industry is dominated by a few giant corporations—in this case really only three—United Brands (formerly United Fruit, with 35 percent of the world market), Castle and Cooke (Dole, with 25 percent), and Del Monte (a newcomer, with 10 percent).[7] We can appreciate the significance of this degree of corporate market power by looking at what happened when the banana-producing countries attempted to hold onto a larger share of the revenue earned from their products.

In 1974, the governments of five banana-producing countries organized for joint action and formed the Union of Banana Exporting Countries (UBEC). They decided on a uniform increase in export taxes on every box of bananas leaving their countries. But the corporations' market control made it easy for them to fight the tax. One corporation simply refused to export bananas, preferring to absorb the loss of 145,000 boxes of bananas. (Food-producing countries, unlike the OPEC countries, cannot opt to sit on their product for a while. Bananas have a lifespan of only twenty-one days from the time of cutting to the retail shelf.) After Hurricane Fifi in 1974, Castle and Cooke threatened not to replant their banana plantations if the export tax was not lowered. United Brands tried bribery. They admittedly paid Honduran officials $1.25 million to lower the tax. It worked. The bribe succeeded in getting the tax of 50 cents a box cut in half. Thus an outlay of $1.25 million saved United Brands $7.5 million in taxes. At this writing, only three of the five members of the banana producers' association have succeeded in levying any tax at all (ranging from 25 cents to 40 cents per box).[8]

The victors in the "banana war" were clearly not the five members of the banana producers' association but United Brands, Castle and Cooke, and Del Monte. In 1973, these corporations were making a profit of 20 cents on each box of bananas. But when the producers put on the tax and the corporations retaliated by cutting back purchases, the world price of bananas increased by 40 percent. The corporations were able to blame that "awful Third World cartel" for the price increase, while pocketing a profit of nearly 70 cents per box—more than three times their earlier profit. As *Newsweek* commented, "all of which goes to prove that sometimes organizing a cartel is just plain bananas!"[9]

Banana trees are like money trees. I wish we had more of them.

Alfred Eames, Jr., Chairman, Del Monte Corporation, *Forbes,* December 15, 1970

28. Doesn't Export Income Help the Hungry?

Question: Although the problems are indeed great, doesn't the income that underdeveloped countries receive from their agricultural exports ultimately help the hungry?

Our Response: On the contrary, some researchers have found that often when a country's earnings from export agriculture decrease, the well-being of the majority of the people in that country increases. Andre Gunder Frank, a well-known student of the process of underdevelopment in Latin America, writes:

When commercial agriculture's good times decline, as they did during the 1930s, this brings along a period of "good times" for subsistence agriculture. Thus, during that decade the trend toward land concentration was temporarily reversed as large owners sold off parts of their holdings to increase their liquid capital. In such circumstances, tenants are better able to enforce their demands for land and for permission to raise subsistence crops; and the "non-commercial" sector in general grows. But when the demand for one or more commercial crops expands, small owners begin to find themselves squeezed and bought out.[1]

A slight increase in income, if any, that peasant farmers in underdeveloped countries might acquire from a rising world price for their commodity has to be weighed against the increased threat of displacement by land-grabbing commercial farmers or corporations that see the higher prices as new grounds for profit.

The peasant producers or laborers have little to gain from increased export earnings of their country, partly because so little of the export price reaches them to begin with. Typically, in Guatemala, where 75 percent of all children under the age of five are underfed, migrant workers on the coffee plantations earn approximately $1 a day.[2] Like many other commodities, coffee boomed in 1973. Brazil's earnings shot up to $1,343,048,000. How much of that went to a worker on a typical coffee estate? About $58 a month. (Yet in "coffeeland" itself it takes $1.66 to buy a single pound of roasted coffee.) In 1975, Sri Lanka's tea exports amounted to $860 million and were produced by 650,000 workers on recently nationalized plantations. The maximum a male worker could earn was $14 a month; a woman, $11.40.[3]

In Mali, peasants are contracted to grow peanuts by a French multinational firm. They contribute the land and their labor and yet receive only the same amount per pound of peanuts as the profit per pound made by the corporation that merely sells the peanuts abroad.[4] The same pattern exists for peasants growing peanuts in Senegal. One Senegalese official reported that the net profit to the state exceeds the total amount the state cooperatives pay to the producers of peanuts.

Increases in the world price for a commodity may not translate into an increase in the price paid to peasant producers. A recent United Nations report on the "least developed countries" notes that while international coffee prices have advanced 58 percent from 1968 to 1973, producer prices in Rwanda have remained fixed.[5]

In fact, an increase in the world price for a commodity might actually mean less income for the plantation worker or the peasant producer. When the world price for peanuts went up in 1968–1969, the Senegalese government's price to farmers actually fell.[6] In the Ivory Coast the pattern is the same: between 1960 and 1971 the export price rose 11 percent while the price paid to producers dropped 6 percent.[7] When the price of sugar on the world market increased severalfold a few years ago, the real wage of a cane cutter in the Dominican Republic fell to less than it was 10 years earlier; even more significantly, it was not enough to buy an adequate amount of food.

Government policy makers everywhere push for greater production whenever the world price for an exported commodity goes up. What at first surprised us, however, is that some government marketing boards in Africa do so by paying peasant producers *less* for each unit produced. The reasoning is that the peasants will then have to produce even more just to maintain their incomes at the same level.

Moreover, in an economy dominated by the earnings of a single export commodity, a sudden international price boom for that commodity can trigger domestic inflation that will inevitably hurt the poor. During the 1977–78 period of unprecedented cocoa earnings in Ghana, for example, the price of a box of sugar shot up to $7.00 and a yam up to $4.00. Tomatoes, used in all traditional dishes for the last 500 years, were going for $1.00 each and were often unattainable.

Thus we have to erase from our minds the automatic connection between a poor country's rising export income and an improvement in the welfare of the majority of its people. We have found, moreover, that export crop production often directly undermines the local food supply. Not only does it monopolize the best land, but the demands of export crop production can interfere with the cultivation of food.

In Kenya, for instance, much effort was put into the production of a more productive variety of cotton. The seed strain finally developed was more productive but unfortunately less hardy. Food crops could no longer be planted in the same field with cotton, as was the tradition; the new cotton could not take the competition. So while cotton exports have gone up, we wonder what has been the impact on the diets of the people. In Upper Volta's drier regions the planting season is short. Where farmers are obliged by the government to grow a certain acreage of cotton, they have to find a crop that can be planted later but can still be squeezed into the planting season. Sorghum and millet, the traditional food crops, just cannot fit this schedule; but cassava, a much less nutritious food, will. Low-nutrition cassava is also taking the place of more nutritious food crops in Tanzania because of the need for labor in tobacco production during certain seasons; cassava requires less labor than other food crops.[8] Agricultural economist Ingrid Palmer has also noted an alarming increase in per capita cassava output in Latin America.[9]

World Bank rural economist Uma Lele writes of the substantial substitution of food crops with cash crops such as cotton, tea, and tobacco in Kenya and Tanzania. In one decade the acreage per family planted in tea increased more than two and a half times in Kenya. In Tanzania cotton acreage per family increased fivefold. Government resources allocated to developing agricultural extension techniques and incentive systems for cash crops have rarely been transferred to the production of traditional food crops. And the drop in food production in the cash-crop areas of these countries has not been matched by expansion elsewhere of food crops.[10]

In an effort to make Brazil a leading soybean exporter, soya production there has massively displaced the cultivation of black beans, the traditional staple of the people. By October 1976, stores serving Rio de Janeiro's poor simply ran out of black beans. In desperation the poor rioted, only to be suppressed by the police. Scarce black beans were available only on the black market. To buy one pound, however, would require a half day's labor at the minimum wage.[11] Doubly tragic is that now Brazil has begun to import black beans from Chile, where the government is also willing to sacrifice the nutritional well-being of the local people in order to earn foreign exchange.

As governments have put the pursuit of foreign exchange above the interest of the masses, more and more peasants have been forced into the position of having to sell cash crops, often highly nutritious, to obtain the money to buy empty calories just to keep their families alive. As one writer summed up the tragic reality of so many underdeveloped countries, "the small farmer sells the nitrogen, phosphorus, potassium and trace minerals from his soil in the form of tobacco or cotton and in return buys polished rice or noodles from the little . . . store down the road, thus selling the life-blood of his soil to buy starch and carbohydrates."[12]

Finally, giving priority to cash cropping means that a farming family's very survival through the year depends on the cash received only once or twice a year at harvest time. But such lump sum payments turn peasants into open targets for predatory merchants peddling gadgets and costly packaged foods. Diversified food cropping is the only guarantee of year-round food security for the rural family. In, for example, China it is said that when peasants step outside their front door they see from where their next meal is coming.

29. If It's So Bad, Why Does It Continue?

Question: You have documented the devastating impact on the Third World of a heavy dependence on export agriculture. But if it has been as bad as you say, the underdeveloped countries would certainly not have continued along this path. Why haven't they realized the trap they are in?

Our Response: The pervasive use of shorthand terms like "Third World," "poor world," "hungry world," makes us think of uniformly hungry masses in which all the people are equally affected by poverty and malnutrition—all with equal interest in eliminating hunger. It just is not so.

The fixation on export agriculture continues simply because, while harmful to most, it is highly advantageous to a few. The first beneficiaries are large producers and plantation owners.

The second group to benefit is the small class of better-off urban dwellers. Much of the foreign exchange earned ultimately gets spent on their food and consumer "needs." Zaire is a typical case. There, export agriculture has led to the decline of food production to such an extent that 30 percent of Zaire's foreign exchange now goes to buy imported foodstuffs. The staple foods of the people are in very short supply, but imported meat is still available for those who can pay. It comes from South Africa for the Zaire elite.[1] Another example is Ghana, heavily reliant on cocoa export earnings. When the world cocoa price shot up in 1977, one-quarter to one-fifth of the country's total foreign exchange earnings—once earmarked for capital development goods—actually went to import luxury consumer items for the urban classes.

Finally, export agriculture benefits those associated with the multinational corporations in their country and government officials who get paid for managing the export system.

By rewarding these elite groups, a small fraction of the entire population, export agriculture compounds the inequalities in wealth and well-being. A recent report from the United Nations confirms that

> Gains from foreign trade . . . and particularly from sharply increased export prices frequently tend to be concentrated among upper income groups to a much greater extent than is income from domestic production.[2]

Tending the Goose

If a government becomes convinced that export earnings are the *sine qua non* of development, export industries, whether domestic or foreign, appear as the salvation of the country. As political economist Cheryl Payer points out, the government will certainly refrain from "killing the goose that lays the golden eggs" and will tend the goose with a great deal of care.[3] But looking at their country with the interests of the goose in mind is hardly the same as keeping the interests of the people foremost; for what export agriculture most needs is cheap and docile labor and the control over large tracts of land with no requirement to invest in their conservation.

The myth that export agriculture is the path to development makes it possible for plantation owners, multinational corporations, and state marketing boards in underdeveloped countries to claim that they must keep wages of agricultural laborers low so that their products can compete in the international market. In 1973 the disclosure by British television of the appalling living conditions of Sri Lanka's tea estate workers met with protests from the government and the foreign estate owners (including Lipton's, the Unilever subsidiary, which markets over 50 percent of the tea sold in the United States). Improving the living conditions of the 650,000 workers—the majority of whom are women—and increasing their meager wages ranging from 36 to 48 cents a day would, they claimed, price Sri Lanka tea out of the market.[4]

Making similar excuses, governments have excluded large landowners from land-reform schemes. They argue that dividing up the large, cash-crop–producing estates would endanger the country's trade and monetary position. In the Philippines, for example, any land put to growing export crops, including over seven million acres with such crops as sugar and coconut, was exempted from land-reform legislation.[5] Government officials who make such decisions are themselves, of course, often large landowners.

Export Crops Expand

Given that multinational agribusiness and local elites benefit by the continuation of a focus on export agriculture and that export agriculture continues to be reinforced by international lending agencies, it is not surprising that export crop production is growing at a much faster rate than food crop production.

From the mid-fifties to the mid-sixties, the growth rate of export crops was 2.2 times faster than the total agricultural growth rate in the underdeveloped countries. In specific countries this trend was even more marked. Coffee production in Africa has increased more than fourfold in the last twenty years, tea production sixfold, sugar cane production has trebled, while cocoa and cotton production have doubled.[6] Between 1952 and 1967, the cotton acreage in Nicaragua increased fourfold while the area in basic grains was cut in half.[7]

Elite-controlled governments have encouraged this trend. In Colombia in 1965, 90 percent of all agricultural credit went to cash crops—coffee, cotton, and sugar.[8] As we found in the Sahel, many governments continue to use the techniques of past colonial regimes to enforce the production of cash crops. In East Java the government requires that as much as 30 percent of the land grow sugar cane.[9] Even in countries like Tanzania that have directed a large proportion of their resources to rural development and have talked of self-reliance, colonial laws have been reactivated specifying minimum acreages for export crops.[10] The rhetoric of many development planners about diversification of agriculture becomes in reality diversification among export crops.

"Hooked" on Exports

Once set out along the export agriculture path, it does indeed *appear* next to impossible to get off. In *Diet for a Small Planet,* I, Frances, likened the "export crop trap" to drug addiction. It seemed to me the only apt analogy. Once "hooked," it is terribly painful to get off. But at that time I did not understand the role that debt plays in maintaining this addiction, both for the individual farmer and for the nation.[11] Farmers growing export crops might want to compensate for sharply reduced income from falling crop prices by shifting to food crops for their families, but if they have gone into debt to obtain the inputs to grow export crops, they may no longer have that choice. They may be obliged to earn a cash income to repay their debts or face the possibility of losing their lands to a creditor.

Similarly, on a national level, when an underdeveloped country receives "aid" from abroad, even if the borrowed money does help to increase the country's production capacity, the debt cannot be paid back until the country has exported enough to earn the needed foreign exchange. Pesos and rupees do not help. Most so-called aid has to be repaid in the same currency in which it was given. The country is likely to be on a treadmill. If exports are not sufficient to acquire the needed foreign currency to pay back debts and to pay for necessary imports, the only immediate solution appears to be to seek yet another loan. This, of course, means only a greater push for export crops to pay back an even greater debt!

What we must remember is that this pattern continues not because the governments of the underdeveloped countries do not *understand* the nature of their trap. It continues because, as we have seen, export agriculture serves the interests of the elite landholding, government, and consumer groups in underdeveloped countries and the interests of multinational agribusiness and international lending agencies like the World Bank.

Thus, promoting trade justice must not lend credence to the idea that export agriculture can be the foundation for development. To do so would be to equate the country's balance of payments and its economic growth with the welfare of the people. Until fundamental restructuring occurs within the underdeveloped nations, higher prices and better export deals for their commodities are likely to work against the interests of the poor majority.

30. Is Export Agriculture the Enemy?

Question: You seem to be saying that agricultural exports cause hunger—that if a country did not export so much, the land now growing for foreign consumers could nourish local people. Is export agriculture, then, the enemy?

Our Response: Export agriculture is *not* the enemy. Agricultural exports from a country where many go hungry is largely a *reflection* of the problem, not the problem itself. Even if all agricultural exports stopped, there still would be hungry people—those who continue to be excluded from genuine control over their country's food-producing resources.

An export focus in countries where many go hungry reflects the impoverishment of much of the local population and the interests of the elite. An export focus is nonetheless an *active* force. Where productive assets are controlled by a few, export agriculture further exacerbates the deteriorating position of the majority. To sum up what we have said in the preceding pages, in such countries, export agriculture:

- makes it possible for the local elite to be unconcerned about the poverty at home that greatly limits the buying power of the local people. Export agriculture means the elite can profit anyway by finding buyers in the United States and other high-paying markets.
- provides the incentive to local and foreign elites to tighten their control over productive resources from which export profits are made and to resist firmly any attempts at redistribution of control over productive assets.
- necessitates miserable working conditions and wages. Underdeveloped countries can compete in export markets only by exploiting labor, especially women and children. Owners and export-oriented governments will stop at nothing to crush workers' efforts to organize themselves.
- throws the local population into competition with foreign consumers for the products of their own land, thus raising local prices and reducing the real income of the majority. (In Part VIII we discuss more fully this "Global Supermarket" phenomenon.)

A contrast between two countries in the Caribbean reveals why export agriculture itself is not the real enemy. In both Cuba and the Dominican Republic, a large portion of agricultural land produces sugar and other exports. Both countries rely on agricultural exports for foreign exchange and both import significant amounts of grain. Yet today in the Dominican Republic, at least 75 percent of the people are undernourished, while in Cuba there is virtually no malnutrition. What accounts for the difference?

First, the foreign exchange earned from sugar exports is controlled very differently in the two countries. In Cuba all the foreign exchange belongs to the public and is put to work implementing the country's development plans. Thus it is used to import productive goods that generate meaningful jobs such as building schools and homes and manufacturing basic home appliances and machinery. In the Dominican Republic a large part of the foreign exchange from sugar exports is treated as profit of private corporations such as Gulf and Western. Much of it is returned to the United States or wasted on projects such as G & W's tourist enclave. The few jobs created in such an enclave do not relate to the long-term development of the country but simply cater to the white man's colonial fantasies (chambermaids are dressed like Aunt Jemima). Such projects even represent an ongoing foreign exchange drain, for example, importing processed foods from home that tourists "need."

A second contrast can be drawn in terms of the employment impact of sugar. The Dominican Republic suffers from a 30 to 40 percent unemployment rate. Seventy-five percent of all who work in agriculture have less than 135 workdays a year.[1] In addition, Dominican workers' interests are further jeopardized by the sugar growers' importation of Haitian laborers, who now make up over half of the cane-cutting work force. The intensive seasonal labor demand of sugar cane (which spoils if not cut and milled within a short period of time) has created high population densities in cane monoculture areas and yet few year-round jobs.

With mechanization of cane harvesting, unemployment in the Dominican Republic deepens still further. Mechanization of the Cuban sugar harvest, expected to be completed by 1985, does not mean unemployment; instead farm mechanization in Cuba releases human labor from the backbreaking job of cane cutting for jobs in agriculture and other vital areas of the economy. The development of an economy oriented toward fulfilling basic social needs has meant that in Cuba there is no shortage of employment for the 180,000 cane cutters (nearly half the total) already freed from sugar production.[2]

These two countries illustrate that trade itself is not the enemy; the real question is "Trade in whose interest?" One crucial qualification, however. While we have concluded that trade itself is not the enemy, we have come to see clearly that *basic* food needs should be met locally. Basic food self-reliance—and by this we mean adequate local supplies to prevent famine if imports of food were abruptly cut off—is the *sine qua non* of a people's security. Moreover, no country can bargain successfully in international trade so long as it is desperate to sell its products in order to import food to stave off famine. Without basic food self-reliance, much-acclaimed "interdependence" becomes a smokescreen for food control of one country by another.

Cuba is an instructive case from which to learn about the tension between exports and such basic food self-reliance. Cuba is trying to expand sugar production while diversifying and expanding domestic food production. During the period 1971–1975 nonsugar agricultural production increased by 38 percent.[3] In the same period vegetable production for the local population more than doubled and fruit production increased by over 60 percent. Egg, poultry, and pork production have increased severalfold since the early sixties. There has been virtually no increase in food prices in the last ten years.[4]

At the same time Cuba is aiming for increased sugar exports, in part to import large quantities of grain. So far success with increasing sugar production has not been as great as with food. The reasons are complex and not entirely clear; almost certainly adverse weather for sugar growing has been one factor in recent years. Long-term sales contracts with the Soviet Union and other nations (like Canada and Japan) for much of its sugar have partially saved Cuba from the economic devastation caused by extreme international market price swings, experienced by most underdeveloped countries. This exceptional arrangement with buyers of its sugar makes Cuba a less useful model for other countries.

There are, then, tensions and unanswered questions. Will relying on exports to pay for a significant part of the national diet be judged feasible and consonant with the goal of political self-determination? Should the policy be to count on other socialist countries to meet food import needs? It will be important to watch what the Cuban people do over the next few years.

Certainly the concept of food self-reliance does not preclude exports. Most countries people now think of as having scarce resources, such as Bangladesh, could not only meet local food needs but also export considerable quantities of agricultural products, if that was judged desirable. Food self-reliance is not isolationist but recognizes that only *after* the redistribution of control over the resources used to produce exports would the income generated possibly serve the needs of all. In Part X, Question 46, we delve further into the implications of food self-reliance.

Part VII

The Myth of
Food Power

31. Don't They Need Our Food?

Question: The United States, with the best soils and the best climate in the world for growing grain, is one of the very few countries in the world with a surplus to export. Shouldn't we continue to export it to the world's hungry? Our unique endowment gives us a special obligation.

Our Response: America's primary role in world food trade is not to feed the hungry but to sell to the rich. The idea that the United States is the world's breadbasket is so deeply ingrained that we think of America solely as an exporter. The usual impression from the news media is that the United States exports large volumes of food under aid programs. But there are three gaping holes in this national self-image:

- First, what food we *do* export on an aid basis (that is, with long-term, low-interest financing) is only a tiny fraction of our commercial exports (6 percent in 1975).
- Second, less than 30 percent of our agricultural exports go to what the USDA terms the "less developed countries."
- Third, although it is true we are the world's leading food exporter, we are also one of the world's top food importers.

Keeping straight on these facts is not easy; everything one hears or reads seems to give exactly the opposite impression.

In the fiscal year 1975, the top four recipients of our agricultural exports were Japan, the Netherlands, West

237

Germany, and Canada. Contrast our exports to these countries with our exports to the underdeveloped countries listed by the United Nations as "most seriously affected" (MSA) by the food and oil price increases of the seventies.[1] The United States exported no agricultural products to nine of the forty MSA nations in either 1973 or 1974. Thirty-six of the forty MSA's export food and other agricultural products to us, including three that receive no agricultural exports from the United States.

To give you some idea of how little our trade has to do with feeding people in need, here is another example. In both 1973 and 1974, United States agricultural exports to Canada, itself a grain exporter, were greater in value than to all the MSA countries combined or to the entire continent of Africa. In fact, in 1973, such exports to Canada were almost twice as large as those to Africa. Our agricultural exports during the drought years 1973 and 1974 to four African Sahel nations—Mauritania, Mali, Niger, and Chad —were less than half (in terms of value) of those to *either* Sweden or Norway or Denmark.

When we consider the per capita quantities of our food going to poor countries versus those going to rich countries, the picture detracts even more from our "country bountiful" image of America. In 1974, the United States exported 114.5 pounds of wheat per person to Japan but only 7.5 pounds per person to India. Per person, Pakistan received only 18 percent as much wheat from us as did the Netherlands.[2]

We tend to pay much more attention to our food exports than to our imports. Contrary to popular notions, the industrial countries are the major food importers; not the underdeveloped countries. In 1974, the United States ranked third among the world's leading food importers, close behind Japan and West Germany. And over two-thirds of our imports come from underdeveloped countries.[3]

While we think of America as the world's beef capital, the United States is in reality the world's leading beef importer. The United States imports over 40 percent of all beef in world trade. In 1973 the

United States imported almost two billion pounds of meat. Often it is stressed that this is but a small amount since it represents only about 7 percent of our own production. The amount, however, is hardly small in relation to the needs of most other countries. It also means that a considerable portion of the food-producing resources in several countries with many hungry people go into producing beef for Americans. In international trade more meat flows from underdeveloped to industrial countries than the other way around.[4]

The United States is the world's principal importer of food from the sea. With only 6 percent of the world's population, the United States imported more than one quarter of the fish and one third of the shellfish in world trade.[5] In addition, the United States is a net importer of milk products.[6]

The next time you hear or read an article in which the author talks about how much the hungry "depend on" our exports and how we are the "breadbasket" of the world, recall some of these facts.

Who are the *real* food donors? They are many of the world's hungriest people.

32. Food Power to Save the Economy?

Question: You have said that the United States uses its food exports to make money and not to be charitable. That is certainly true. But isn't this absolutely necessary? Our oil import bill is so high because of the outrageous prices imposed upon us by OPEC that we must rely on food to balance our international payments. Since we have to export *something* in order to pay for the oil we need, isn't food our best bet?

Our Response: This question suggests that our ability to pay for oil imports depends on increasing our food exports. Indeed, we Americans are being made to believe that not only our monetary strength but also our diplomatic strength and even our moral persuasiveness hinge on our new-found Food Power.

We were told by an official of USDA that food exports are necessary to pay for "the imported petroleum and other goods we must import to maintain our standard of living."[1] We were told by President Ford that "our agricultural abundance helped open the door to 800 million people on the mainland of China. . . . It helped improve relations with the Soviets. It helped to build bridges to the developing world."[2]

We are told that our food will not only alleviate hunger but will even turn hungry people toward democracy. The past president of the Colorado Cattle Feeders Association hopes that by our improving diets abroad "nations will change their political feelings and move away from Communism to a more democratic form of government."[3] All in all, we are made to believe Food Power saves! The message is clear: For all these rewards we should be willing to tighten our belts.

The question expresses the feelings of many Americans who are willing to do just that: to make the best of an unavoidable situation. It disturbs us that the genuine good will of most Americans is being manipulated so that they do not see that the food export strategy of the seventies was not a necessary development but a promotion of certain interests at the expense of most of us.

Just what are the underlying reasons behind the American Food Power strategy in the seventies?

The Origins of Food Power: The Payments Crisis

By the late sixties, administration officials had decided that something had to be done about the nation's balance of payments deficits. To most Americans the balance of payments has no understandable link with their everyday well-being—certainly no connection with the price of food or the fate of the family farmer. The balance of payments is something bureaucrats have to worry about, not ordinary people.

But is this true? First we must understand what the balance of payments problem is and what caused it. How does it relate to the question about the need for food exports?

The meaning of a balance of payments deficit is no great mystery. Quite simply, a country has a deficit, an unfavorable balance, when more money goes out of the country than comes in. The balancing up takes into account government, corporate, and even individual transactions.

For years the United States government had been spending billions upon billions as the standing military force of the anti-socialist world. The Vietnam War alone cost the United States well over a half-trillion dollars.

In addition, United States-based corporations, beginning in the late fifties and throughout the sixties, made large capital investments in Western Europe and to a lesser extent in Latin America and Asia. Federal tax laws encouraged these corporations to keep their considerable earnings outside the United States since profits were not taxable until actually returned to the United States. Such corporations exacerbated the negative balance of trade by turning cheap-labor, low-tax countries like Mexico, Taiwan, and Singapore into "platforms" for exporting back to the United States consumer goods such as transistors, television sets, cameras, and textiles. Ironically, then, the United States was sending dollars abroad to import products made by U.S.-based corporations.

In the late 1960s, many European and Japanese firms also "went global" and began exporting to the United States, often from low-tax, low-wage plants side by side with competing subsidiaries of American multinational corporations. Before long, vast amounts of dollars were being drained out of the United States to pay for imported manufactured goods. A study in the early 1970s found that U.S.-based multinational corporations accounted for 42 percent of all imports, often "buying" from their own overseas subsidiaries.[4] (In the first five months of 1978 the United States imported an alarming $14 billion more in manufactured goods than it exported.[5] The cost of these imports was more than double the cost of imported oil during the same period.) United States corporations have also become increasingly dependent on foreign sources of critical raw materials. By 1970, the United States was importing 80 percent or more of eight basic raw materials. The trade deficit in raw materials had grown to $3.4 billion.[6]

In 1971, as a result of such capital drains, the United States experienced the first balance of payments deficit in the private sector (corporations and individuals) in a century. Thus, it was well *before* the price of imported oil increased that the balance of payments crisis developed.

The Myth of Oil Dependency

Most Americans nonetheless have been made to believe that oil imports are at the root of our international economic problems. Moreover, we have accepted the idea that we have become dependent on imported oil because the United States is running out of domestic sources; in fact, such an explanation does not fit the facts. In his *Poverty of Power,* Barry Commoner argues that after 1957, United States oil companies made less and less effort to look for domestic oil. Commoner notes that "exploratory expenditures per barrel of oil produced fell by some 25 percent in the next ten years."[7] According to a mammoth study by the American Association of Petroleum Geologists (with funds from the industry's National Petroleum Council), "none of the 11 regions [in the U.S.] has been adequately explored."[8] This study concludes that the United States has about 320 billion barrels yet to be discovered—*three* times more than has already been consumed.

It was not, therefore, that the United States started to run out of oil but that the oil companies had concentrated their efforts in countries where profits looked even better. Between 1956 and 1974, the profitability of foreign oil almost doubled while the profitability of domestic oil remained about the same.[9] Thus, while imported oil covered only 14 percent of domestic demand in 1954, by November of 1974 it had jumped to 40 percent.[10]

Commoner concludes that the United States has sufficient untapped oil reserves to get through a gradual transition period until we have developed renewable energy sources, such as solar radiation (No matter how big the reserves, fossil fuel is a *finite* resource.) The problem has been, not the lack of energy resources, but the lack of a national planning structure looking out for the interests of all Americans. Only such a structure could counter the narrowly profit-maximizing oil corporations that have made us increasingly dependent on foreign and finite oil. In this context, it is hard to accept the simplistic Food Power rationale that the lack of domestic energy resources is behind the need for an all-out push for agricultural exports.

The Birth of Food Power

By the late 1960s, the United States had approached the international equivalent of having its credit cards recalled. By then, other countries began to get uneasy about honoring dollars, as it was less certain whether they could always be converted. Foreign countries, furthermore, began to react to the takeover of their key industries by United States corporations using the power of good-as-gold dollars. Foreign treasuries, therefore, started demanding gold instead of paper in settling balance of payments deficits. By 1970, United States gold reserves had been reduced to less than one half of what they were in 1950.

For the Nixon administration, the question was: What exports from the United States could be stepped up in a really major way to compensate for the mounting import bill? In 1970, Nixon appointed a commission composed of corporation executives and their lawyers to come up with an answer. This Commission on International Trade and Investment Policy, known as the Williams Commission, concluded that there were only two trade categories that could earn the huge sums of foreign exchange needed to balance United States payments: high technology products and agricultural commodities.[11]

One type of high technology thought easy to push abroad was armaments. The Vietnam War had produced new "generations" of arms and every country just *had* to acquire the latest. American military attachés and corporate hustlers around the world doubled their efforts (and often their bribes) to compete with French and British armaments manufacturers. Vast credits were extended to underdeveloped countries. All went "well"; soon annual sales reached the multibillions. By 1975, armament sales amounted to $4.8 billion. Moreover, boosting arms sales had no awkward domestic repercussions for the administration.

But the second recommendation of the Williams Commission—boosting agricultural exports—was another matter. How could American farmers and consumers be made to go along with a plan to vastly increase agricultural exports? Just how do you get other countries to import enough American food to offset import expenditures that the United States was not willing to reduce? Equally crucial, how do you push up prices so that every bushel sold will do the most to help the United States balance of payments? And how do you increase exports to countries that want to protect the livelihood of their own farmers?

This was not easy. The Nixon administration, however, thought there might be one workable strategy. First, tempt potential buyers by making their initial purchases of grain cheap and by providing ample financing. Then persuade other countries to lower their protection against U.S. grain exports by offering, under the banner of free trade, to abolish domestic price supports for American farm products. And to ensure that prices go up, direct the Secretary of Agriculture to order cutbacks in United States crop acreage; then the final touch needed to raise grain prices would be bad weather in the major grain-producing countries.

Now let us look at the steps by which the Food Power strategy was actually implemented. Keep in mind that the first goal was to make exports as attractive as possible. Devaluing the dollar—first 11 percent in December 1971 and then a further 6 percent in early 1973—made the United States products less costly to foreign buyers. (Underdeveloped countries that had been encouraged to hold their reserves in dollars and to fix their currency to dollar values lost hundreds of millions overnight.)

A second way to make United States commodities more attractive would be simply to offer convenient financing. In July 1972, the United States announced a $750 million credit through the government's Commodity Credit Corporation to help the Soviets purchase our grain. Nixon had already courted the Soviets by rescinding the requirement that at least half of any grain sold to the Soviet Union or any Eastern European country be carried in American flag ships. And the Soviets were ready to buy. Although their grain production, somewhat exceeding that of the United States, was sufficient for direct consumption, many Soviet citizens clamored for more meat in their diets. Kremlin economic planners decided that 19 million tons of cheap United States grain for feed on such fine terms was the solution. Bad weather, which cut their harvest by a third, further convinced them.

The next step was to get prices to shoot up. The quickest way was simply to cut production back. Secretary of Agriculture Earl Butz ordered another five million acres of wheat lands taken out of production in September 1972. This put the total acreage kept out of production at 62 million, an amount equal in size to all the cultivated land in Great Britain. With the Soviets buying, the dollar devalued, and acute weather problems worldwide, this acreage cutback was enough to guarantee shortages, depleted reserves, and higher prices for any additional foreign sales.

Food Power and the "Free" Market

Still one question remained for the Nixon administration: How to make the strategy stick? The Williams Commission had concluded that the only way would be to negotiate a "free trade" policy that would open up protected European and Japanese markets to American farm products. The free trade doctrine thus became the strong arm of Food Power. You cannot, the commission said, have one without the other.

Only under free market conditions could the United States capitalize on its "comparative advantage" in grain and livestock feed. This meant the United States would have to prove its commitment to the "free market" by moving to scrap government-financed minimum price supports, acreage allotments, and other programs to regulate farm income and productive capacity.

The administration calculated it was a good moment to get hitherto reluctant farmers to support just such a move: The Soviet grain purchase had significantly reduced world grain reserves and weather conditions in many areas of the world were poor; it all added up to a very bullish market for U.S. farm products.

It was likewise easy to persuade Congress that the agricultural support programs were unnecessary. The 1973 farm bill virtually ended payments for land held out of production; established such low target prices (i.e. the market price below which the government would step in to help the farmer) as to be meaningless in protecting the small farmer; and, in effect, abolished government-held grain reserves. After the previous cutbacks designed to create scarcity prices, farmers were now being told that the United States government was releasing its agriculture—a significant part of the world food economy—to the speculative market where a small change in supply, indeed even a threat of such change, can set off huge price swings.

Drumming Up Customers

Between fiscal years 1970 and 1974, the quantity of American wheat exports increased about 90 percent while the *value* increased almost 400 percent![12] The pattern was almost as striking for feedgrains. But what would happen if widespread good harvests increased the worldwide availability of grain? To keep prices up, it was necessary to find some new customers.

In 1974, the Foreign Agricultural Service (FAS) spent over $10 million developing markets for American exports. In a recent issue of its periodical, *Foreign Agriculture,* FAS was conspicuously proud to explain how it is furthering an "aggressive foreign market development" to beat out the "stiff competition" in the race for increased agricultural exports.[13] An arm of the USDA, FAS is also the leading wedge for agribusiness penetration into the markets of other countries. FAS's "cooperation" with food export industries falls into three categories called "market intelligence," "trade servicing," and "product promotion."

If an American corporation wants to know whether it would be profitable to enter a certain market, it turns to its friend in FAS—one of the 96 U.S. agricultural attachés or officers in foreign countries—who jumps into action. First: Does the product meet the foreign government's import entry requirements? Second: Is it acceptable to local tastes? (Call in the "professional taste panel"!) If the company's product makes it past steps one and two, FAS helps sponsor a market test.

In addition, FAS sponsors exhibits around the world for the benefit of U.S. producers. One favorite exhibit is a lifelike reproduction of an American supermarket. Since the United States exports 44 percent of all the wheat in the world trade, FAS also helps sponsor schools to teach people how to cook with wheat in areas of the world where wheat is not a traditional food. In Japan, FAS has sponsored a beef campaign, noting that it is "aimed at better-class hotels and restaurants catering to the tourist trade."[14] Its efforts there have also helped to account for the success of fast-food outlets like McDonald's—90 percent of whose ingredients are imported. Although American-style fast-food outlets only began operating in Japan in 1970, FAS predicts that by 1979 these chains will have taken 70 percent of all such sales, displacing the traditional rice, fish, and noodle bars.[15]

Our Food Power strategy thus rests, not on shipping our food to a world of hungry people, but on molding the tastes and habits of a certain class of people to make them dependent on products and styles that they had never wanted before. American policy makers are encouraging other countries to become more and more food dependent on the United States and the United States itself is becoming more and more economically dependent on food exports. Reading the FAS material, one would think that the survival of our nation rested on its success in creating one more hamburger lover in the world.

Question 32 suggests that Food Power was born as the only possible response to the rising cost of oil imports. But the Food Power strategy predated the oil price increase response. Furthermore, Food Power was not the *only* possible response but the choice of policymakers who wanted to protect the economic status quo. Food Power, you will recall, was born out of the dollar drain caused by the Vietnam War, the overseas expansion of American corporations importing cheap-labor manufactured goods back into the United States, growing corporate dependence on foreign raw materials, and United States petroleum corporations' decision to import massive quantities of oil.

Today Food Power continues to be promoted as a way to buttress our balance of payments. Military expenditures are less of a foreign exchange drain now, in part because of increased arms sales abroad. But imports of consumer goods, largely by U.S. multinational corporations, continue as the single most important balance of payments drain after oil and industrial raw material imports. In 1976, the United States imported $15.9 billion in manufactured products from foreign plants owned by American corporations.[16] (This figure would be significantly higher, if we included other United States foreign investments with minority or licensing control.)

In addition, the United States now spends over $13 billion for agricultural imports.[17] Thus, while officials talk only of how our agricultural exports bring in almost $24 billion in foreign exchange, more than half of every dollar gained in agricultural exports is spent on agricultural *imports!* Ironically, about one-half of these agricultural imports are commodities that the United States can and does produce—meat, sugar, vegetable oil, vegetables, tobacco, wine and dairy products.

Because the largest U.S. corporations flock to wherever labor and other resources are cheapest, the United States thus winds up importing manufactured and agricultural goods that could be produced at home —at an import cost of more than one-half what the United States pays out for oil.* The place to start in confronting the oil import crisis is, therefore, not to launch a Food Power strategy but to seriously confront the forces that make us increasingly dependent. For we all pay a high price for Food Power, as we will see in the following pages.

---

* Half of agricultural imports plus manufactured products produced by foreign subsidiaries of U.S. corporations equal about $23 billion. Oil imports cost the United States about $44 billion.

33. At Least Food Power Works?

Question: But doesn't Food Power at least work in earning foreign exchange? Can't we expect high levels of agricultural exports to continue?

Our Response: In judging whether Food Power will work, even by the narrow measure of sustained high levels of export income, we must ask: Can the United States continue to underprice and outsell other countries that have cheaper land and labor costs, especially when U.S.-based corporations can profit by promoting exports from the very countries competing with U.S. domestic producers?

Take soybeans, the central pinion of the Food Power strategy. The business magazine *Forbes* called soybeans our "chief trump card." Dwayne Andreas, Chairman of Archer Daniels Midland, the largest soybean-processing firm, was even more unrestrained. "The soybean will be the savior of the dollar."[1] Soon, soybeans became America's second leading cash crop after wheat.

Such optimistic projections came in 1973 and 1974. By 1975, the picture looked a little different. It turns out that our climatic advantage for soybean production is not unique. The long summer days in southern Brazil are just what soybeans thrive on.

A few years ago Brazil's share of world soybean exports was only 1 percent. By 1975, Brazil had captured 30 percent of the world market, to become the world's third ranking soybean exporter. A coffee frost that killed many coffee trees only accelerated Brazil's movement into soybeans. The drought of 1978 is doubtlessly only a temporary set-back; huge investments in soy-processing mills have locked Brazil into a soybean push.

Ironically, among the greatest promoters of Brazil's soybean success are United States corporations. They are investing in Brazilian soybean production and processing for the very same customers to whom the United States has been selling. Anderson Clayton is doubling its current soybean processing capacity in Brazil. Cargill and Central Soya are also involved, and the agricultural loan office of the Chase Manhattan told us the bank couldn't invest enough.

And who would have thought that Paraguay would compete with U.S. soybean exports? It probably would not, without the help of United States corporations. The Florida Peach Corporation of America has put $12 million into a soya-processing plant there as only the first phase of a huge agribusiness complex. Gulf and Western has just purchased over 100 thousand acres of land in Paraguay to begin soy production.[2] In 1971, the Overseas Private Investment Corporation (OPIC), which is a quasi-official government agency, approached Cargill, the giant American grain corporation, to encourage it to take out a loan for a new soybean-crushing plant in Brazil. The next year they concluded a loan for $2.5 million.[3] Our balance of payments may be a problem for administration officials and for the citizens who will pay for both the cause and the "cure," but it is hardly a problem for United States–based multinational corporations. Profit seeking knows no national loyalties.

The market for soybean oil appears to be in even greater trouble than that for soybean meal. The trouble? Palm oil in countries like Malaysia, Indonesia and the Ivory Coast. An acre planted with palm oil trees can produce as much as seven to eight acres of soybeans. Now that's competition!

As a result of the competition from soy and palm oil producers, only a year after soybeans were called the American trump card to save the dollar, production in the United States dropped 19 percent. Thus in assessing the potential for Food Power on its own terms we would have to conclude that even in what the

United States thinks it does best—growing soybeans—it might still get crowded out of the market.

Finally, although Food Power may have "worked" in the sense of doubling the value of agricultural exports, it has not solved the U.S. balance of payments problem. In 1977, the U.S. trade deficit was over $31 billion, greater than before the era of Food Power. Agriculture should not be forced to try to pay the bill of $45 billion in oil imports. Solutions must be found elsewhere—first of all in an all-out drive to cut imports.

The Backlash

Some former high officials at USDA publicly question the Food Power strategy on other grounds. Two are Don Paarlberg, former chief economist for the Department of Agriculture, and his assistant, Patrick O'Brien. "Using food as a tool requires an extremely tight demand situation," says O'Brien. "If you happen to be sitting on a large supply in one short year, you're in good shape." But in the long run, he fears, high prices run the risks of creating a backlash as countries decide to grow their own. "You encourage every little producer to step up and do his duty." As examples, he cites Thailand's effort to increase its own production of corn and sorghum.[4]

What O'Brien implies to be the almost irrational response of "every little producer" is, of course, quite a realistic assessment by countries that do not want to make their survival dependent on a nation that has shown itself to be so ruthlessly willing to use food exports to serve its domestic interests and to grant political favors. Even European countries such as France are thinking twice now before becoming more dependent on American food imports.

Thus the Food Power strategy, aside from being unnecessary, is a risky operation; other countries, often with the help of U.S. corporations, can effectively compete with the United States, and more and more countries are perceiving that guaranteeing their own food supply is the basis for security. Still there is an even greater risk for the United States.

The Long-Run Cost of Food Power

The view that "well, at least Food Power works" is worse than shortsighted if it ignores the cost to America's agricultural resources. What do we mean? Simply that reports now coming in from this country's richest agricultural states show that the pressure for "fence-to-fence" planting has led to rapid soil deterioration that may be virtually irretrievable. The problem is manifold. The intense pressure to increase production brought more easily eroded soils into production, decreased or eliminated fallow periods that regenerate the soil, and led to the continuous planting of corn or other row crops that expose the soil to erosion, as opposed to crops such as hay that make the soil more erosion resistant.

According to a Soil Conservation Service official in Iowa, that state is now losing an average of ten tons of top soil per acre each year. Expressed another way, on much of the sloping land in Iowa, a farmer is losing two bushels of top soil for every one bushel of corn he produces! At this rate, all of the top soil in Iowa will be gone within less than a century.[5]

Moreover, once Food Power made agriculture the latest speculative industry, new irrigation technology started spreading to marginal soils. Former Nebraska pasturelands are being made into highly productive irrigated corn fields. But for how long and at what price? These are questions Nebraskans are asking about the rapid spread of center-pivot irrigation,[6] a method of tapping underground water, requiring a $60,000 investment but very little labor. Today there are 10,000 such units in Nebraska, over one-third owned by outside and even foreign investors. The farmers working the land often become mere sharecroppers, receiving only one fourth of their crop. In addition to the obvious shift in control of the land that accompanies such a capital-intensive investment as center-pivot irrigation, there is the question of the life of the soil itself. Center-pivot irrigation makes possible the cultivation of sandy, marginal soils not possible with other types of irrigation. But sandy soils are erosion-prone and leach soil nutrients into the ground, causing pollution of waterways. Moreover, center-pivot irrigation, a push-button sprinkler system of two rotating pipes, each one-quarter mile long, cannot accommodate trees. The trees must go. And indeed they do. Precious "shelterbelts," rows of trees planted by conservation-conscious farmers years ago, are now being pulled up to make way for the center pivots.

The center-pivot system, in widespread use only for the last ten years, has been associated with a ten-foot drop in the underground water table. The University of Nebraska has concluded that since water is being taken out of the ground faster than it is being naturally replenished, "groundwater mining is in progress." How long, then, will be the lifetime of center-pivot irrigation in Nebraska?

In 1973, state investigators in Montana reported another serious threat, exacerbated by the Food Power plant-it-all push. In Montana, North Dakota, South Dakota, and the Prairie provinces of Canada much land that has always served only as *grazing* land is now being planted every other year in grain. Even this moderate level of cultivation on these dry and vulnerable soils appears to have upset the soil's moisture balance. The result is that ground salts are being deposited on the soil surface, making it unusable for agriculture. Already by 1977, over 170,000 acres of land in Montana alone had been lost to saline seepage. And the investigators concluded that in the northern Great Plains 146 million acres may be threatened.[7]

So what will be left of family-farm agriculture and of the top soil itself once the Food Power push for production at all costs has run its course? To say "at least Food Power works" might turn out to be the equivalent of claiming that a sane way to build an addition to your house is with bricks from the foundation.

34. Who Gains and Who Loses?

Question: If the United States makes money selling food to countries that want it, and if American farmers are helped, isn't the end result of the Food Power strategy positive?

Our Response: If Food Power is so good, why did President Nixon and Secretary of Agriculture Butz try to keep the basic report on Food Power strategy out of the hands of Congress and, once it was leaked, why did they even try to disown the report? Perhaps their reason for being anxious to keep the Food Power strategy under wraps was that its "free-market-all-the-way" prescription amounted to an invigorating tonic for the larger farmers and big grain-exporting corporations—at the expense of a lot of belt-tightening by American consumers and foreclosure for thousands of family farms. Obviously the report did not spell things out in these words. But the implications for this country of so-called free market agriculture were clear enough.

The label "free trade" is insidiously misleading when applied to a system in which six giant grain-trading corporations control 85 percent of all U.S. grain trade. While the administration boosts an export-oriented agriculture in the name of family farmers, the exports are implemented not by farmers, not even by the national government, but by a handful of private corporations. Family farmers do not rendezvous with Kremlin bureaucrats and sign whopping sales contracts in Moscow, Tokyo, Bonn, and Cairo. Farmers sell to the likes of Cargill, Cook Industries, and Continental Grain. In 1974, Cargill alone controlled 29 percent of wheat exported from the United States, 16 percent of corn, 18 percent of soybeans, 22 percent of sorghum, 42 percent of barley, and 32 percent of oats. In the process, the balance of payments position of the United States Treasury is improved, but most of the profits end up with these few corporations and not on the family farm.

The farmer is the only one who has been put on the "free market." The farmer must rely on world production forecasts of the Department of Agriculture (USDA). But how reliable are they? In 1977 these forecasts shifted abruptly by 42 million metric tons! But the corporations have their own sources of information to judge government production estimates. They rely on insider information from their former executives now in government posts and on their own efforts to drum up foreign sales commitments. And they can even keep the government in the dark about what they learn. Moreover, their own intelligence networks constantly assess the agricultural prospects and likely food purchasing of other countries. According to *Business Week,* Continental Grain's worldwide intelligence network is so effective that agents of the CIA "often wine and dine the company's traders to pick their brains."[1]

The Soviet Grain Deal: A Case Study of an "Unfree" Market

Extreme cold, combined with inadequate snow cover during the Soviet winter of 1971–1972, killed 25 million acres of wheat—the equivalent of the entire United States wheat acreage. Despite many clear indications that the Soviets were in the market to buy in a big way and the indisputable evidence that bad weather nearly everywhere in the world meant there would be an exceptional demand for American grain, the USDA, contrary to law, did not inform the farmers. Instead, USDA warned farmers there would be a big surplus even after all foreseeable sales. Only a few

American government officials and grain company executives were in the know.

By early June 1972, Continental Grain, Cargill, and the other four members of the grain export club rushed out to the early-harvest Southwest to buy up wheat. The farmers knew that harvests were going to be big and since they did not know about the strong foreign market prospects, they were happy to unload their wheat. They got about $1.25 a bushel. A few weeks later the same wheat would have brought $2.25 to the farmer. (In early 1973, wheat would be hard to get at $5 a bushel.)

By July 5, Clarence Palmby, Continental Grain's vice-president, helped the firm to conclude the biggest grain sale in history—three days before the official announcement of the $750 million loan to the U.S.S.R. that made the deal possible and that had been negotiated by Palmby while he was an official of the USDA.* While still at USDA in May, Palmby had even attended meetings between Continental and the Russians and surely knew a big sale was in the offing. But Palmby and his bosses at USDA had still neglected to inform the farmers, despite their legal mandate to do so.

It was not until mid-July that the USDA informed the farmers. By then in the Southwest and the early-harvest areas of the Midwest, one quarter of all the wheat had already been sold.[3] In Oklahoma alone, the withholding of information by the Department of Agriculture cost wheat farmers about $47 million. Butz's rationalization? "Farmers didn't lose money because of early sales, they just didn't make the additional money they might have made."[4]

The Soviets kept buying and the grain companies kept selling. While huge commitments were being

---

* In early April 1972, Palmby headed an American trade delegation to the Soviet Union. Before his departure Continental Grain offered him a vice-presidency in their Manhattan headquarters. Although Palmby now says that he turned the offer down, the fact is that before leaving for Moscow he purchased a $100,000 Manhattan apartment, using the name of Continental's president as a reference.[2]

made, the August 1972 USDA newsletter *Wheat Situation* did inform farmers that the Soviets were buying but said that the likely total figure would be just half what Continental Grain alone had in fact *already* sold to the Soviets in early July. While the Soviets continued to buy wheat, Secretary Butz toured the country talking about *corn* sales.

In addition to extra profits made because uninformed farmers were willing to sell cheaply, the grain companies had yet another guarantee for unprecedented gain. In order to encourage exports the government at that time subsidized the exporting companies by making up the difference between the domestic price at which they bought the wheat and the lower price at which they sold it abroad. These subsidies went as high as 47 cents a bushel. (Clearly in the Soviet case there was no need for such an additional customer incentive.) As domestic prices finally began to rise, the companies claimed ever larger subsidies even though some of the wheat they were then selling in fact had been purchased earlier at lower prices.

A subsequent Senate investigation discovered that a grain export corporation sometimes collected the subsidy on sales to its wholly owned foreign subsidiary. The investigation documented sales by Cargill to its subsidiary in Panama. This subsidiary then sold to another Cargill subsidiary in Europe, which then sold the wheat at an unknown but doubtlessly higher price to a second party. In this way, headquarters collected a multimillion dollar subsidy not considered taxable income while the profits rung up by the foreign subsidiaries were sheltered from taxation as long as they stayed abroad (and that despite this country's drive to improve its balance of payments!). These transactions were in fact all on paper; the wheat never left the ship on which it was originally loaded.

Over a mere seven weeks taxpayers handed the six grain-exporting companies $300 million in subsidies. Food Power could indeed be profitable for some.

By contrast, the subsidies to farmers moved in the opposite direction. In 1972 subsidies were still paid to farmers to make up the difference between "parity," a price level considered fair in relation to the cost of machinery and supplies a farmer must purchase, and the average market price over a five-month period. The catch, in 1972, was that the government figured the period to begin in July, when most farmers in the Southwest and some in the Midwest had already sold out. As news of the big grain deal spread, wheat prices rose, narrowing the difference between average market prices and parity, thus cutting into the subsidies for the farmer. The farmers' lost subsidies have been estimated at $55 million.

Cook Industries, on the other hand, increased its annual profits fifteenfold between 1972 and 1974. Cook is the only firm with publicly held stock and therefore the only one required to disclose its earnings. Dan Morgan of the *Washington Post* reports, however, that privately held firms like Cargill and Bunge have doubled or tripled their net worth since 1972, according to reliable trade sources.[5] The General Accounting Office found the big traders had profits on those hundreds of millions of bushels ranging from 2 cents to 53 cents a bushel,[6] whereas normally a profit of 1.6 cents per bushel is considered good.[7]

So "free trade" and an all-out export drive worked well for the grain companies. Characteristically, Butz added insult to the farmers' injury by claiming that grain companies won and the farmers lost out in the 1972 grain sales simply because the farmers "weren't smart enough to take advantage of the situation." Some trading companies did make big money in the deal, he conceded, "but that's the name of the game."[8]

Butz is right. Big money is the name of the game. Under free trade export companies are able to extend their control and increase their profits. During the winter of 1972–1973, three of the large grain export corporations, Cargill, Continental, and Cook, were able to corner 90 percent of the soybean harvest for $4.00 a bushel, sending soybean prices up to $10.00 a bushel only a few months later.[9]

Free trade allows speculators to drive up prices out of all relation to actual supply. Speaking of food prices in 1973, Donald Paarlberg, then USDA's chief economist, said that his staff could account for only one-half to two-thirds of the sudden price rise. "The rest is psychological and speculative activity and these are not in our models," he explained.[10] But how real is any model of the free market that does not include speculation?

What free trade really does is free private multibillion dollar corporations to manipulate prices and supply to their advantage. When we say "private" we mean very private—with no room for public scrutiny. Five of the six largest grain conglomerates are closely held, private firms owned by a few individuals or families. None publish any detailed financial information. When Dan Morgan wondered why grain trade lobbyists are hard to find in Washington, one former grain trade lobbyist explained it to him this way: the grain companies "don't need to have powerful lobbyists—for they have no regulation."[11]

American consumers finally discovered that their wheat had been exported when they went to the grocery store that winter. Meat prices especially shot up because feedgrain prices rose so fast that many farmers cut back on their cattle- and hog-raising operations. The House Agriculture Committee concluded that higher food prices, directly attributable to the Soviet Union grain exports and the way they were handled, amounted to about $3 billion.

Hoping to avoid a repeat of the infamous "Russian grain deal," the USDA soon began requiring the reporting of large grain sales. Exempted from the reporting requirement are subsidiaries of U.S. grain trading corporations located in other countries. In order to capitalize on this loophole, the Soviets bought only through such subsidiaries when prices were most depressed in 1977. They made a killing before news of their buying pushed prices up. The USDA's crop estimators had sorely over-gauged the Russian crop. Again the primary losers were U.S. farmers who, assuming a low purchase by the USSR, had already sold their crop.[12]

Free Market and the Small Farmer

The USDA has invariably tried to sell us the idea of leaving American farmers to the workings of the free market as "getting the government off the farmer's back." What farmer could be against that? But, in fact, American farmers need some kind of controls to ensure against price declines caused by overproduction in relation to the ability of people to buy. As Jim Hightower, known for his in-depth investigations of the problems of American farmers, explained, without control of production, "American farmers regularly have the capacity to produce themselves out of business."[13]

The Department of Agriculture knew full well what would happen to rural America with free trade and no government protection. In 1975, the department initiated a study of what would happen to American farms under various trade and government support policies.[14] The study concluded that if the American farmer were left to the vagaries of the market with no income protection, America would lose over one and one-half million more farms by 1985! Of those farmers left, only nine percent would be full owners of their land, compared with the one-third who are full owners today. These projections of the inevitable results of a Food Power-free trade strategy were so embarrassing to the department that the office within USDA that carried out the study was summarily abolished.

The Department of Agriculture does admit that putting farmers on the free market means that they will experience "world-wide fluctuations" in demand and that their prices will "become more volatile."[15] But a family farmer cannot adjust to such fluctuation the way a corporation can. If market indicators look poor for General Motors, it simply lays off workers or even shuts down a plant. Given just the unpredictability of weather, a farmer's view of market prospects is hardly clear. But can the farmer simply lay himself off and not plant if prospects are poor?

Hightower recounts the not atypical story of how one department official, who never has to worry about his salary, which is paid by taxpayers, explained to some farmers the "new horizons" opened to them by United States Food Power:

> In one breath, an assistant secretary of agriculture told a farm group that in the new order of things each farmer must respond to signals of demand from world markets, that only their own forward-thinking management would protect them from the "ups and downs" of the market place. In the very next breath, this public servant told farmers that markets were changing on a daily basis, with doors opening and closing so fast that "what might happen next, no one can tell." Good luck, and good-bye.[16]

Often the case is made that family farmers should be forced to face the music. If they do not survive in the free market, it means they were not efficient enough to make it; therefore, it is all for the best for the country as a whole. Earl Butz described those farmers who have gone under in recent years as being either "unwilling to change or not wanting to compete."[17]

There is one big hitch, however. What makes it possible for the big producers to survive has nothing to do with their efficiency. Large amounts of capital and diversified investments allow big producers to survive an unstable market. In fact, an unstable market can work to the great advantage of the large producer, ready to buy out the small farmer who has nothing to fall back on during market busts. (This is the same shake-out process we have seen follow the introduction of modern commercial farming in underdeveloped countries.) In the eyes of one American farmer, government willingness to abandon farmers, as if they were all equal, to a boom and bust market is equivalent to an elephant in a chicken coop declaring, "O.K., fellows, everyone for himself."

Food Power's Victims

As part of its free market strategy, the administration encouraged farmers to plant "fence to fence," assuring them that the "hungry world" would take all the grain the U.S. could produce. With more acres in production than at any time in recent history, farmers did produce record harvests with record prices. Indeed Food Power looked good to many farmers in 1973 and 1974. The annual income per farm doubled between 1971 and 1973; even adjusting for inflation, income was up 60 percent.[18] But not every farm benefited equally. Gains in earnings accrued overwhelmingly to large farm operators. The nation's largest farms, representing only 4 percent of all farms, increased their average annual net farm income two and one-third times between 1971 and 1974, from $36,000 to over $84,000.[19] (This top 4 percent had gained control of 46 percent of all farm-produce sales even as early as 1973.[20]) But the majority of all farmers, those with sales of $20,000 or less, were able to increase their average net farm income only about 20 percent—from about $2000 in 1971 to less than $2500 in 1974.[21] Increases in the incomes of small-farm families have come only through off-farm jobs. This alone says a lot about the impact of the Food Power strategy.

In hopes of prospering on the new export markets —after a long period of stagnation—many farmers invested in more land and new machinery. To do this, most farmers had to take out big loans, especially since land and machinery costs were soaring. (A tractor equivalent to one costing $9,000 in 1966 cost $32,000 in the early 1970's.[22])

Then, once farmers had gone out on a limb on the promise of Food Power's ever increasing exports, markets became saturated. Farm prices started to plummet. Compared to 1973, net farm income dropped 65 percent by 1977.[23] Farmers were still increasing their borrowing, now not for expansion but just to keep afloat. Farm debt (sum of debts of all farmers) had doubled compared to 1971. By 1978 interest payments on an enormous $119 billion farm debt were eating up half of the farmers' shrunken income. "Such ratios of farm debt to farm income have no precedent in this century," observed a Federal Reserve economist.[24]

Food Power's production push and export strategy, moreover, set off a virtual land rush in the United States. In the four years following 1972, land values more than doubled. Just as we have seen in underdeveloped countries, those maneuvering to profit on the agricultural boom were not all farmers. Non-farm investors and even foreign investors began to perceive U.S. farmland investments as the best hedge against inflation. A Brussels investment consulting firm established that foreign investors bought up $800 million worth of U.S. farmland in 1977 alone. The Commerce Department notes that this figure, if correct, would amount to 30 percent of all direct foreign investment in the United States. A Commerce Department official told *Business Week:* "We simply cannot get a handle on farmland since ownership is disguised through the extensive use of trusts, partnerships, and corporations headquartered off shore." Foreign purchasers of U.S. farmland often buy through corporations headquartered in countries like the Dutch Antilles, for example, that levy little or no taxes.[25]

In part because of the pressure of non-farm and foreign investment, even when farm incomes began dropping in 1975, farmland prices kept on climbing steeply, slackening slightly only in 1977. Few Americans realize that 38 percent of all U.S. farmland is rented out.[26] The rising cost of land is particularly hard on farmers who rent their lands. As land prices rise, so do rents.

So, then, who has gained? In 1976 the U.S. farm population dropped at the fastest rate in 13 years. In Iowa that year 166 farms were going out of business each week.[27] Food Power strategies were thus accelerating the trend toward increasing concentration of control over the nation's farmland.

What Are We Losing?

The USDA obviously does not seek to prevent this increasing concentration of farm ownership. In the eyes of USDA, the decline of the small farmer is a fait accompli. Speculating on what American agriculture will look like in the future, USDA's Director of Agricultural Economics predicted a "highly coordinated industry of large farms very likely . . . operat[ing] in much the same fashion as nonfarm manufacturing industries."[28] Never mind that USDA has shown in its own studies that there are no economies of scale above the one- or two-operator farm[29] and that the greatest value per acre is produced on family-size farms.[30]

Often supporters of family farms are viewed as romantics who are yearning for the good old days that never really existed. Is it just nostalgia that makes many want to revitalize small-farm America? What is the difference between a rural America dominated by a few largeholders and corporations and a rural America dominated by family farmers and cooperatives?

In the 1940s a remarkable piece of sociological work was done in California. A researcher with the USDA selected two towns, Arvin and Dinuba, similar in the dollar value of production yet different in the average farm size—one with a few large farms and the other with many small farms. The differences between these two communities tell us a lot about the future of America if the present direction toward concentration of control is not reversed.

By every measure the quality of life in the small-farm community turned out to be significantly richer than in the large-farm community. The "quality of life," generally a vague term, was quantified by this study. For example, Dinuba, the small-farm community, supported:

- about 20 percent more people and at a higher level of income;
- a working population that was mostly self-employed in contrast to the large-farm community

where less than 20 percent were self-employed (and nearly two-thirds were agricultural wage laborers);
- many more democratic decision-making organizations and much broader representation in them;
- better schools, and more parks, newspapers, civic groups, churches, and public services;
- twice the number of small businesses and 61 percent more retail business.

Researcher Walter Goldschmidt had intended to continue the study by comparing other farm communities. He never got the chance. The implications of this study were so "hot" for the Department of Agriculture that Goldschmidt was ordered to stop his investigations. Then, in 1977, California officials visited Arvin and Dinuba to find that the contrasts in family income recorded by Goldschmidt in the 1940s had only continued to grow in the ensuing 30 years. In 1945 the median family income in the small-farm community Dinuba was 12 percent greater than in the big-farm town Arvin; by 1970 the difference had grown to 28 percent. In recent testimony before a Senate committee on land monopoly in California, Goldschmidt stated: "The vision of the future under increased corporate control of the land is the vision of Arvins rather than Dinubas—indeed of super-Arvins."[31]

Food Power, the Farmer and the American Consumer

By 1977, with the heaviest debt burden in this century and thousands of imminent foreclosures, farmers were desperate and angry. They were finding it increasingly difficult to make a living providing what any society needs above all else—food. This seemed neither logical nor just. In September a group of 2,000 farmers met in Pueblo, Colorado, to form the American Agriculture Movement (AAM). By December, with farm income compared to farm costs lower than even in the Depression years, AAM groups springing up around the country called for a nationwide strike by farmers. Refuse to plant, the AAM advised farmers, until the government guarantees parity. (Parity is the conventional measure of farm income in relation to the costs of production. 100 percent of parity implies a satisfactory return to farmers whereas in early 1978 farmers were getting only 65 percent of parity. The average during the Depression decade of the 30's was 78.)[32]

Although only a minority of farmers actually refused to plant, thousands participated in lobbying Congress and in demonstrations around the country. The sight of farmers parading their tractors in protest startled Americans. By March 30,000 determined farmers—plus their goats and donkeys and chickens—gathered on the steps of Congress to demand that the government step in to support their income. While not approaching the level of support demanded by the AAM, the Congress did then vote for higher price support loans and target prices* that would, when combined with acreage set-aside programs already underway, help to raise farm income.

Congress was thus reviving the old tools of limiting production and backstopping farmers' income. These are the very programs that have failed to prevent the historical trend toward ever greater concentration, as small farms have folded—on average 1400 each week between 1960 and 1976.[33]

The guiding principle of government farm support continues to be one of benefits accruing strictly according to the amount of land an individual farmer holds and his or her production. In other words, a farmer is compensated uniformly for each acre set-aside in a

---

* When market prices are low, price support loans allow farmers to put their crops in storage as security for a loan from the government. The farmer can pay off the loan and take the crop out of storage to sell it anytime the market price goes above the loan price. The "target price" system, on the other hand, triggers direct payment to farmers when the market price for their commodity falls below the government determined target price.

government program to control overproduction; and each bushel of grain receives the same compensatory payment when its market price falls below the government set target price. Thus the larger, higher-producing farmers always receive the bulk of the government benefits. Indeed, in 1976, the top 6 percent of all farmers received 37 percent of the government's direct payments. In 1977 the Congress increased the likelihood of uneven benefits by doubling the limitation on government payments to any one farmer from $22,000 to $55,000.[34]

The consumer, however, sees any government farm income support, especially acreage set-aside programs, as a threat. More government payments to farmers and fewer acres in production invariably read out to the consumer as higher prices. Americans are understandably troubled by rising food prices. The repeated assertion that they are fortunate because they pay only 16 percent of their income for food hides the fact that the bottom half of the population pays a significantly higher percentage. Those families with incomes in the middle (the mid-ten percent) spend at least 20 percent of their income on food. Those ten percent at the bottom spend 69 percent of their income to buy food.[35] So much for the simplistic view of America as a nation of people who do not properly appreciate their "cheap" food.

But the real fallacy is in assuming that farm income is the most important determinant of food prices. It is not.

Note first that the farmer's cut of each dollar we spend for food is only about 40¢.[36] Of course the bulk of that 40¢ goes not to the farmer's income but to buy the machinery, fertilizer, seeds, pesticides and all else needed to produce the food. With the Food Power push at its peak in the period 1972–1975 and farm income going up, it's true that food prices also were climbing. From January, 1972, just as Food Power got into full swing, to October, 1975, the Consumer Price Index for food rose 48 percent.[37] Between early 1972 and 1975 the increase in the nation's food bill averaged out to about $14 billion *each year*,[38] compared to $5 billion in the years 1970 and 1971. But who was getting those increases?

Between 1973 and 1975 the amount of money Americans were paying for their food that did *not* go to the farmer increased 26 percent. This sum—almost $104 billion by 1975—included the costs of non-farm labor, packaging, transportation, corporate profits, advertising and so on. The after-tax profits of food corporations, up 54 percent in these three years, rose faster than any other cost component of the food bill. The amount Americans were paying for their food that actually got to the farmer increased by only eight percent during these years—totalling about $55 billion.[39] In other words, the amount Americans paid for food that did *not* reach the farmer went up three times faster than what did.

What most reveals the fallacy of linking prices farmers get to the threat of rising retail food prices is that, even after farm income began to drop drastically in 1975, food prices still pushed upward. Whereas Americans were paying an average of $14 billion more each year for food in the early 1970's, this increment in the nation's food bill had jumped to $19 billion by 1976–1977.[40]

When farm prices are high, the giant processors and export companies are able to pass the costs right on to the consumer. When farm prices drop, consumer prices are miraculously insulated and the food companies' profits inflate. In a highly concentrated economy, a drop in food purchases, such as happened in 1973–1975, may not trigger a fall in food prices, as college economics classes led us to believe it would. In fact, a study of the Joint Economic Committee of Congress has found that when a few corporations control a whole sector, a drop in consumption can lead to an *increase* in prices by corporations seeking to make up for the drop in sales.[41]

It is not surprising, then, that in 1975, while farmers earned a 4.7 percent return on equity, food chains earned a 12.6 percent return and food processors a 24.6 percent return.[42] The Internal Revenue Service has found that grocery chains average 48 percent higher profits than all other retailers.[43]

Thus, identifying the connection between farm income and rising food prices as the crux of the food problem is to miss altogether the root problem: Neither the consumer nor the farmer controls our food system.

On the one hand, farmers are at the mercy of tightly controlled industries supplying all their machinery, fertilizers, and pesticides. In 1972, the Federal Trade Commission found that the lack of competition in the farm machinery industry had cost farmers an extra $251 million in overcharges.[44] On the other hand, farmers are dependent on a relative few buyers of their commodities. Farmers are in the unique position of having no bargaining position. A farmer comes to the market saying not, "This is what I will accept for my product," but rather "What will you give me for it?" In some food lines, canning vegetables and poultry broilers, for example, virtually all the producers are under contract with the major processors and distributors. They receive what the contract specifies— often very little. (See Part VIII, pages 304ff. for more detail.) Grain farmers have little choice but to sell to the major grain trading oligopoly we discussed earlier. Farmers are thus at the mercy of oligopolistic industry at both ends—both for buying what they need to produce our food and for selling their products.

Consumers are in no stronger position, they themselves victims of an increasingly concentrated food industry demanding more and more of their budget for less and less nutrition. The Select Committee on Nutrition and Human Needs of the United States Senate found that rising food costs produced "statistically significant declines" in per capita consumption of protein and many essential vitamins and minerals.[45] Nutritionists testified before the same committee that it is not possible to obtain a balanced diet on food stamps. Yet about 17 million Americans must depend on the food stamp program. And these millions represent at most one-half of those Americans whose poverty makes them eligible for food stamps.[46] This in a country with the greatest food bounty in history.

Food Power versus Food First

The most serious criticism of Food Power is that it moves the United States in the opposite direction from Food First. Just as in many underdeveloped countries where so many are hungry, agriculture is increasingly seen here as a prime arena for speculative investment and as a way to earn foreign exchange to ease an economic crisis whose roots are unrelated to agriculture. Food Power has not been a solution to a problem; it has been a way to avoid the solution. Relying on Food Power to earn foreign exchange has been a way out for a government unwilling to touch the power and profits of the large grain-trading and other corporations moving abroad in search of new markets and cheap land and labor. Indeed, a Food Power-free trade strategy reinforces the power of large corporations both directly and indirectly—by undercutting small farmers who cannot survive extreme market fluctuations and by increasing the price swings on which speculative companies thrive. Moreover, foreign exchange earned with agricultural exports is used to import agricultural and manufactured goods produced abroad often by American corporations—items that could have been produced at home. Finally, Food Power is a way to pay for a costly United States anti-people strategy that puts American military presence in every corner of the world to preserve "law and order."

By contrast a Food First agricultural economy in the United States would unite agricultural production with the development of viable rural communities and the long-term protection of the soil and water resources. It would look at food production, not as a source of speculative investment nor as merely a source of foreign exchange, but rather as a source of livelihood for millions of American farmers and the basic necessity of life for all Americans.

It would start with a national inventory of who controls our agricultural resources. Presently no comprehensive records exist. Pressing forward a Food First agricultural economy would then mean land reform legislation, excluding non-farm corporations from controlling farmland and stipulating a reasonable limit on the size of a farmholding, taking into account geographic factors influencing production. Putting food first would simply mean putting the family farmer and cooperative above the large corporate holding. Government income support programs, absolutely essential in the present if we are not to lose an ever increasing number of family farmers, would be designed to selectively support the smaller producer and cooperative.

A natural concomitant of land reform in America would be the development of local and regional food self-reliance. The United States, like underdeveloped countries today, must become more self-reliant in food both for the good of our own people and to make the nation less of a burden on the rest of the world. Pushing our food exports abroad, while it may be in the interests of foreign elites, ultimately undercuts production in other countries, the livelihood of their people, and their self-determination. In a world of extreme power differentials between countries there is no such thing as food interdependence. Interdependence, as we have said, becomes a smokescreen for the control of food by a few.

Greater regional and local food self-reliance here would make possible more direct marketing of products by the farmers themselves. The control of the giant food distributors would be undermined and a greater portion of the consumer's dollar would get to the farmer. Moreover, the vast sums spent in processing, packaging and transporting food over long distances could be reduced. Transporting our food alone cost $8.5 billion in 1975. Presently the U.S. food economy uses more energy in processing, packaging and transporting food than in growing it.

In place of mammoth transnational corporations controlling our food economy, a Food First agricultural economy would encourage worker-managed organizations producing and distributing our food. The

income generated would then go directly to those
growing and harvesting our crops, operating our can-
neries, and managing our retail stores.

What we have learned looking at countries where
so many go hungry is this: The increasing concentration of economic power, so vividly seen in our own
food economy, makes political democracy meaningless.
No matter how often we are allowed to go to the ballot
box, if fewer and fewer corporations have the power
to determine who gets to eat and at what cost—then
there can be no democracy.

The way to discredit a Food Power economy is to
show how it works against Americans and the majority
abroad. How can we make America safe for the
world? What would a food economy in America look
like in which all were eating well? These are the most
important questions.

We would be doing you a great disservice, however,
if we left you with the impression that this redirection
could be pursued by our present government. Indeed
this chapter demonstrates that our government is beholden to the very interests that *benefit* from the increasingly concentrated control of our food system.
The necessary restructuring of United States agriculture is, therefore, not something the government will
do for us. *We* must take the responsibility. Educating
ourselves and other Americans about the struggle for
control over farmland going on right now in America
is the first step toward the fundamental restructuring
that must take place.

We are at a national turning point. Will we allow
the basic necessity of human survival, food, to be controlled by a few and treated as any other commodity on which profit is enhanced by the creation of
"scarcity"?

Agriculture policy should be directed toward maintaining agriculture as a viable industry and not as
a way of life. The number of farms or farm popu-

lation size is irrelevant except as these influence performance of the agricultural industry.

U.S. Department of Agriculture,
"New Directions for U.S. Agricultural
Policy" (Report of the USDA's Young
Executive Committee, 1972), p. 11

Every new regulation that hampers agricultural production—every new bit of legislation that interferes with the individual farmer's management decisions, every new economic control that erodes his profit incentive—drives another nail into the collective coffin of mankind.

Earl Butz

Part VIII

World Hunger as Big Business

35. Don't They Need American Corporate Know-How?

Question: If underdeveloped countries are ever going to realize their food-growing potential, won't they need agricultural assistance from more advanced countries? Perhaps it is a mistake, however, to think that this assistance should come through government channels. There is too much politics, too many chances for bureaucratic red tape, too little business sense. Isn't what these countries need exactly what corporations have to offer: the know-how that comes out of the most successful agricultural system in the world?

Our Response: Agribusiness executives would certainly agree. If you ever weary of pessimistic assessments about world hunger, just listen to what corporate executives have to say. Hunger to them is clearly a "growth industry."

Charles Hall, a banker who chaired a 1974 conference entitled "Feeding the World's Hungry: The Challenge to Business," has proclaimed that the "diminishing self-sufficiency" of the underdeveloped countries can be reversed by applying a "systems approach" in which "multinational business concerns can play an essential role."[1] According to Hall, multinational corporations "either possess or have access to the organizational and management ability, the capital and the technology, to apply such systems right now." John H. Perkins, a bank president, described the challenge as one of bringing to the "hungry countries" the "technological revolution" that transformed "American ag-

277

riculture into the most amazingly productive system on earth."

Zeal, then, indeed missionary zeal, is not what agribusiness lacks. Even firms we would not normally think of as part of agribusiness have jumped aboard the agribusiness-has-the-solution bandwagon. At a 1974 United Nations-sponsored conference an executive from the St. Regis Paper Company expounded eloquently on how improved paper packaging could be the key to the solution to world hunger (what could he mean—that the trick is to devise a dry cereal container that will survive the Indian monsoon?).[2] Another would-be savior for the world's hungry is World Food Systems, Inc., an institutional catering service. Its president reported to the same conference that "large meal delivery system[s]" could deliver to the world's hungry millions "a satisfying eating experience" and at the same time carry out an "on-the-job consumer market analysis." Yes, why hadn't anyone thought of it before? All the hungry need is an efficient catering service and a taste preference survey!

A Global Farm for the Global Supermarket

The question contends that agribusiness firms possess a unique expertise to share with the poor in underdeveloped countries. But we ask, expertise for growing *what* kind of food and for *whom?*

In Part IV we discussed the mechanization and commercialization of agriculture in underdeveloped countries; in Part VI, the promotion of agriculture for export. Put the two together and we have the increasing worldwide penetration of agribusiness, the linking up of underdeveloped countries' farms with global food markets: a Global Farm supplying a Global Supermarket.

The world's hungry people are being thrown into even more direct competition with the well-fed and the over-fed. The fact that a food is grown in abundance right where they live, that their own country's natural and financial resources were consumed in producing it, or even that they themselves toiled to grow it will no longer mean that they will be likely to eat it. Rather, the food will go to an emerging Global Supermarket where everyone in the world, poor or rich, must reach for it on the same shelf. Every item has a price and that price, in large part, is determined by what the world's better-off customers are willing to pay. None without money will be able to move through the check-out line. Even Fido and Felix in the United States can outbid most of the world's hungry. This emerging Global Supermarket will be the culmination of food "interdependence" in a world of unequals.

As much as agribusiness firms talk of producing food in underdeveloped countries, they are not talking about the basic staples—beans, corn, rice, wheat, and millet—needed by the hungry. Instead they are referring to "luxury crops": asparagus, cucumbers, strawberries, tomatoes, pineapples, mangoes, beef, chicken, even flowers.

Furthermore, agribusiness "expertise" is not so much in producing as in marketing. They know who and where the world's affluent shoppers are—a small group in the underdeveloped world's urban centers such as Mexico City, Nairobi, Delhi, and Rio and a much larger group in New York, Tokyo, Zurich, and Stockholm. And agribusiness knows what they "demand."

Del Monte is but one example of agribusiness creating a Global Farm to service a Global Supermarket. Del Monte operates farms, fisheries, and processing plants in more than two dozen countries. Board Chairman Alfred Eames, Jr., wrote glowingly in a recent annual report: "Our business isn't just canning, it's feeding people." But which people? Del Monte is operating Philippine plantations to feed the banana-starved Japanese; contracting with Mexican growers to feed asparagus-cravers in France, Denmark, and Switzerland; and opening a new plantation in Kenya so that no Britisher need go without his or her ration of jet-fresh pineapple. Del Monte finds that a pineapple that would bring only 8 cents in the Philippines (still a significant portion of a worker's pay) can bring

$1.50 in Tokyo. No wonder that Del Monte exports 90 percent of its Philippine production. Yet the average Filipino has an even more inadequate calorie intake than the average Bangladeshi and serious protein-calorie undernutrition affects an estimated half of all Filipino children under four—one of the highest rates in the world.

There is nothing really new in food being grown for those who can afford to buy it. What is new is the agribusiness notion that *all* the world can be one Global Farm. Production of many low-nutrition crops that can fetch premium prices for the seller is being shifted out of the countries where most of the buyers live. These overseas production sites, in many countries with vast undernourished populations, are becoming mere extensions of the agricultural systems of countries such as the United States and Japan. In fact, the corporations themselves regularly refer to their farms and processing plants in underdeveloped countries as "offshore production units"—a revealing terminology.

This historic shift is occurring in our lifetime. Helping to create the agribusiness vision of One Global Farm has been the development of low-cost transportation technologies. One Bank of America executive noted the shift of agribusiness production out of the United States: "With the welcome mat out in many underdeveloped countries and with the lure of cheap land, cheap labor and ready international markets there has been a rush to get in on the ground floor." Moreover, tax concessions and tax havens beckon, and 360 days of sunshine can make farming easy.

The Mexican Connection

In Mexico the rush to link up with the Global Supermarket is far advanced. Traditionally, the American sunbelt and more northern greenhouses have supplied the United States with vegetables during the winter and early spring. But now agribusiness giants such as Del Monte, General Foods, and Campbell's, as well as numerous southwest-based "food brokers" and contracting supermarket chains such as Safeway and Grand Union, are changing all that.

Take the asparagus industry. Up until a few years ago you could bet the asparagus that you ate or that was exported from the United States to Europe was grown in central California. But now a significant part of production has been shifted to Irapuato, 150 miles northwest of Mexico City.[3] Since 1975, for instance, white asparagus is no longer grown in California. In Mexico, two firms control over 90 percent of asparagus production. One of them is Del Monte. In 1973, Del Monte paid American asparagus farmers 23 cents a pound for their crop; Mexican Del Monte contractors got 10 cents a pound.[4] The Mexican contractors pay the seasonal workers a mere 23 cents an hour.[5] Since labor costs account for up to 70 percent of the cost of growing vegetables, Del Monte translates cheap labor into bigger profit margins.[6]

Mexican soil and labor are already supplying one-half to two-thirds of the United States market for many winter and early spring vegetables.[7] The rate of increase has been phenomenal. One way of keeping tabs on it is the USDA's annual *U.S. Foreign Agricultural Trade Statistical Report*. (It is yours for the asking. The report is telephone-book size; but if you can get into it, your next trip to the supermarket will put you in touch with the Global Farm. Typical of United States government publications, however, it does not name the agribusiness firms that control the imported items.)

Here are a few examples of the shift in Mexico from cultivation for local consumption to production for the United States.[8] Most are operations contracted and financed by American firms. From 1960 to 1974, onion imports from Mexico to the United States increased over five times to 95 million pounds. From 1960 to 1976, cucumber imports soared from under 9 million to over 196 million pounds. From 1960 to 1972, eggplant imports multiplied ten times, and squash imports multiplied forty-three times. Frozen strawberries and cantaloupe from Mexico now supply a third of United States annual consumption. (The National Bank of Mexico notes that domestic strawberry consumption depends on "what's left over after exports.")[9] About half of all the tomatoes sold in the wintertime in the United States (about two-thirds of a billion pounds by 1976) come from Mexico, or, more precisely, from some 50 growers in the state of Sinaloa who in 1976 sold $100 million of tomatoes to the U.S. West and Midwest.

The shift is so far advanced that Ray Goldberg, of the Harvard Business School, in his 1974 study *Agribusiness Management for Developing Countries* notes, "If the recent rates of growth of imports from Mexico continue, in a relatively short time Mexico will account for almost the entire winter supply of most of these fruits and vegetables." The same study goes so far as to recommend that Mexico "seek further expansion" of vegetable exports.[10]

Multinational agribusiness is radically altering the availability of food for Mexico's poor, but in the wrong direction. Only a few years ago the national production of many fruits and vegetables was sufficient to keep prices low enough for lower-income families to eat some of these local products, at least occasionally. But now luxury crops grown for the Global Supermarket often crowd out more nutritious crops for local consumption,[11] taking over land that previously had grown up to twelve local food crops.[12] The land that is now contracted by Del Monte once grew corn, wheat, and sunflower seeds for local consumption. (Most significantly, crops for the Global Supermarket monopolize the funds and services of government agriculture programs.) As obvious as it may sound, we must remind ourselves that land growing crops for the Global Supermarket is land the local people cannot use to grow food crops for themselves. Higher prices of basic staples due to distortion of production priorities are making even beans a luxury Mexico's poor can no longer afford.

A Cucumber Republic?

In order to play off both U.S. and Mexican producers, agribusiness has started contracting with Central American businessmen-farmers for alternative sources for a wide variety of fresh fruits and vegetables. While banana exports barely increased, the volume of other fresh fruits and vegetables (such as cucumber, cantaloupe, honeydew, and okra) entering the United States from Central America rose thirteen-fold between 1964 and 1972. Focusing narrowly on gross production and revenue figures without asking who benefits and who loses, agricultural economists and international aid and lending agencies have applauded this diversification into "nontraditional" fruits and vegetables. ("Nontraditional" is in contrast to the great "tradition" of bananas, coffee, and cotton.)

Enthusiasts see this sharp increase as only the beginning for Central America. According to Goldberg, such nontraditional exports could jump from 18 million pounds in 1972 to over 100 million pounds per year by 1980. They could become a *new* tradition! Already by 1969 over 19 percent of the total crop area of Central America was planted with nontraditional fruits and vegetables.[13] If we combine this 19 percent with the 29 percent of the cropland devoted to coffee, cotton, and sugar exports[14]—not to mention untold acres for banana and cattle exports—we begin to understand why so many people in these countries are undernourished.

The utter inability of the Global Farm to meet the needs of the majority of the people—the absurdity of the whole scheme—came home to us in one fact, so calmly stated in the Harvard Business School study already mentioned: At least 65 percent of the fruits and vegetables produced in Central America for export is "literally dumped or, where feasible, used as animal feed"[15] because it either confronts an oversupplied market in the United States or does not meet the "beauty" standards of consumers here, while at home, where it is produced, people are too poor to buy it.

Strawberry Fields Forever?

In only fifteen years whole areas of Mexico have been turned into strawberry fiefdoms by U.S.-based suppliers to the Global Market: Pet Milk, Ocean Garden, Imperial Frozen Foods, Griffin and Brand, and Better Food Sales. Already by 1970 over 150 million pounds, three-quarters frozen, were being exported to the United States annually.

For two years Dr. Ernest Feder, formerly an FAO specialist on peasants in Latin America, painstakingly investigated the strawberry industry in Mexico. He was not particularly fascinated with strawberries—in fact, he is allergic to them—but he believed the industry would show how agribusiness affects rural people in an underdeveloped country.[16]

Dr. Feder's research makes clear that, first of all, we should not speak of the *Mexican* strawberry industry but of the U.S. strawberry industry located in Mexico. Officially, Mexican growers produce the berries and even own some of the processing facilities. The real control, however, remains with the American investors and food wholesalers. Using production contracts and credit facilities, these American firms make all the important decisions: the quantity, quality, types, and prices of inputs; how and when the crop will be cultivated; the marketing processes, including prices for the producers; the transportation and the distribution; and the returns on capital investments. U.S. marketing control is so powerful that, despite efforts by the Mexican government to develop markets in Europe, all Mexican strawberries pass through American exporters even when ultimately retailed in a third country such as Canada or France.

Even more revealing of this control, all strawberry plants come from nurseries in the United States. After fifteen years of commercial strawberry growing, Mexico does not yet have its own source of high-grade strawberry seedlings based on varieties best adapted to conditions in Mexico. Only two varieties are sold to Mexican producers; and they are not necessarily those best adapted to Mexico but the ones that meet the preferences of American consumers.

Although competition among strawberry producers might appear as a war between Mexican and Californian producers, in fact the rivalry is between two American groups, with different production sites. And the only way the Mexican production site can compete with the Californian one (where inputs and careful management give high yields per worker and per acre) is by keeping production costs extremely low. First, wages *must* be kept miserably low. Wages average only one seventh of those in California, even taking into account the higher cost of living in the United States. Feder is convinced that the very enforcement of Mexican minimum wage laws would "tend to drive the U.S. strawberry industry located in Mexico back to the U.S. or into some other Latin American country."

Second, the U.S. strawberry industry's interest in Mexico is strongly linked to cheap land and water. Water is "cheap" to the investors since its cost is largely paid for by federally funded irrigation schemes.

Third, the investors, Feder observes, bring in only enough technology to keep production going without raising costs. If they were to put in the type of money that would give yields comparable to those in California, they might as well stay in the United States.

Finally, the attraction of Mexico is that land obtained cheaply can be treated cheaply. Rather than requiring careful farming and applying inputs to increase yields, more land is simply plowed. The land, according to Feder, is "plundered"; bad plants, destructive use of irrigation, bad farming, and misuse of pesticides are in many places ruining the soils. But agribusiness knows that it can just move on to new land, eventually even into another country, where the whole process can be started again.

Because such an agricultural system is not oriented to the needs of the domestic population, it is, by that very fact, thrown into competition with production centers in other countries. To compete, commercial agriculture in Mexico must maintain underdevelopment (cheap wages and land) even at serious jeopardy to the longer term future. It is a vicious circle: this maintenance of underdevelopment ensures the continuing absence of a strong domestic market that alone could orient production toward local consumption.

The Desert May Bloom ... but for Whom?

It takes a lot of freight to fill a DC-10 jumbo jet. Yet three times a week from early December until May a chartered DC-10 cargo jet takes off from Senegal's dusty Dakar airport loaded with green beans, melons, tomatoes, eggplant, strawberries, and paprika. Ironically these food airlifts began just as the drought in Senegal was beginning and they dramatically increased even as it was getting worse.[17]

In the late 1960s, certain agribusiness firms circled Africa's semiarid regions on their world maps. Were they concerned about hunger there? No. What they saw in the Sahel was not hunger but low-cost production sites from which they might profit, given the European demand for fresh winter produce.

In 1971, Fritz Marschall, an executive of the European affiliate of the world-ranging, California-based Bud Antle Inc., visited Senegal. Bud Antle, one of the world's largest iceberg lettuce growers and now a subsidiary of Castle & Cooke ("Dole"), once filed a complaint, during a farmworkers organizing drive, that led to the jailing of Cesar Chavez for picketing. Marschall was struck by the similarity of the climate of Senegal to that of southern California, where only two generations ago United States government irrigation projects had made the desert bloom. Why couldn't Senegal, he mused, replace California as his company's source of vegetables for the high-priced European winter market? As a confidential World Bank report noted, "Senegal is the closest country to the European market where vegetables can be cultivated in the open, without glass or plastic protection during the winter."[18] By February of the following year, Marschall had set up Bud Senegal as an affiliate of Bud Antle's Brussels affiliate, the House of Bud.

Today, Bud Senegal operates giant garden plantations, using nothing but the latest technology. Israeli, Dutch, and American engineers have set up a drip irrigation system with miles of perforated plastic tubing. The water for this system comes over some distance from northern Senegal through pipelines installed at government expense. In order to make way for mechanized production, Bud uprooted scores of centuries-old baobob trees. To remove baobob, sometimes as much as twenty-five feet in diameter, required the power of two or even three Caterpillars. The local villagers explained to us the value of these unusual trees: Not only do they protect the soil, but they provide the local people with material for making everything from rope to houses.

Since the undertaking is billed as "development," Bud has had to come up with virtually none of its own capital. Major stockholders and soft-term creditors include the Senegalese government, the House of Bud, the World Bank, and the German Development Bank. The Senegalese government also helped by removing villagers from land that was to become Bud's plantations. Even four members of the Peace Corps helped develop the vegetable plantations for marketing through Bud.

Despite the rhetoric about development and the reality of widespread undernourishment in Senegal, all the production is geared to feeding consumers in the European Common Market. This, in spite of the fact that in 1974 alone European taxpayers spent $53 million to destroy ("withdraw from the market") European-produced vegetables in order to keep prices up. One year green bean prices in Europe went lower than the costs of picking, packing, and air freighting Bud's big crop in Senegal. Did that mean more food for hungry Senegalese? Hardly. As the director of Bud Holland, Paul van Pelt, admitted, "since the Senegalese are not familiar with green beans and don't eat them, we had to destroy them."

From May to December, European tariffs make it unprofitable to export any vegetables. Does Bud Senegal let its plantations lie fallow or allow the local people to grow food for themselves during those months? Again, no. Bud's better idea is to grow feed for livestock.

In July 1977, the Senegalese government fully nationalized Bud Senegal, reportedly because the government thought income was not being fully accounted for. The House of Bud, however, continues to handle the marketing of the plantation's vegetables in Europe —invariably the most profitable part of the operation. Visiting the Sahel in late 1977, we learned that Bud is breaking ground or planning to do so in nine other African countries.

American Foods Share Co., a multinational corporation owned by two Swedish shipping firms, also has its eyes on Africa. President Robert F. Zwarthuis states, "Anyone who says that 'we go to Ethiopia in order to help those poor things' is lying." The company is now "trying out" countries such as the Ivory Coast, Egypt, Kenya, and Ethiopia as production sites for supplying Europe. Investments in Africa, he estimates, can expect a yield on capital two to two-and-one-half times those in Sweden.[19]

Zwarthuis admits that the need for a "continuous supply" makes him favor countries like Ethiopia and Egypt "which do not have any local market for these products." He foresees that "Africa is going to become the world's biggest producer of vegetables, not only to Europe but also to America." Recent World Bank reports on Senegal and Mauritania also see the region's future in mango, eggplant, and avocado exports.

Why is Africa so attractive to agribusiness? Not only is it close to high-paying consumers in the Middle East and Western Europe but many African countries offer the prospect of unutilized land. Take Haile Selassie's Ethiopia, where, notwithstanding the recent severe famines, *most* of the arable land, held in large estates, was not utilized. The existence of large, uncultivated royal and church estates was an open invitation to agribusiness looking for cheap production sites. In the early 1970s, the Ethiopian government granted a concession to the Italian firm MAESCO to produce alfalfa to feed livestock in Japan. Ethiopia's climate makes possible several cuttings of alfalfa a year, compared to only two or three in the United States. MAESCO's plantation is in the area where thousands of people, evicted by such commercial plantations from their best grazing lands, starved to death in 1973 along with their herds of camels, sheep, cattle, and goats. That year MAESCO started to raise cattle and sheep for export.[20]

Exporting the Steak Religion

The question asserts that what the underdeveloped countries need is know-how. Certainly there is one activity in which a lot of American know-how is being applied abroad—cattle raising. United States firms have set out with missionary zeal to spread the American steak religion to the world. Yet, we ask, who benefits? Is the meat going to the hungry? Or does it merely mean low-cost imports for fast-food chains in the United States?

From one-third to one-half of total meat production in Central America and the Dominican Republic is exported—principally to the United States. Alan Berg, in his Brookings Institution study of world nutrition, notes that, despite dramatic gains in per capita meat production in Central America, the meat is "ending up not in Latin American stomachs but in franchised restaurant hamburgers in the United States."[21] Central America has become the chosen site for investment in meat export operations, first because it is so close to the United States and, second, because it is free from foot-and-mouth disease, not true of Argentina and Brazil whose fresh and chilled meat imports are not allowed into the United States. Should Central America consider itself fortunate?

In 1975, Costa Rica, with a population of 2 million, sent 60 million pounds of beef to the United States. Per capita beef consumption declined in Costa Rica from almost 49 pounds in 1950 to 33 pounds in 1971. If the 60 million pounds exported had stayed in Costa Rica, local meat consumption would have doubled.

Per capita consumption figures, however, are deceptive. Many Costa Ricans—those without land or jobs to earn money—can never afford meat no matter how much is available. One-half of the country's children do not get enough food tó eat, much less meat. True, however, to the Global Supermarket phenomenon, a few well-off Costa Ricans can afford to get some Costa Rican beef just like Americans—at one of the three McDonald's in San José. ("El Big Mac" is now in every Central American capital.)

The export market for beef has lured farmers, in countries like Costa Rica and Guatemala, away from raising dairy cows. The result has been sharp increases in the price of milk, putting it out of reach of most families.

We might think that, even though most of the meat gets exported because people are too poor to buy it, at least local folk are the ones who make money on these exports. But are we really talking about Central American small-time producers making good in the big-country market?

Not exactly. Those profiting in the meat export market are the traditional oligarchs as well as former United States diplomats (e.g., the ex-ambassadors to Nicaragua and British Honduras), a former Peace Corps director in Costa Rica, big western ranchers (including the lawyer for the country-sized King Ranch in Texas), and giant processors like United Brands' meat subsidiary John Morrell Co.[22] Even industrial multinational corporations like Volkswagen are getting into the beef business. As one Volkswagen executive pointed out, "You get a lot more for a pound of sirloin than a pound of beetle in Tokyo."

The World Bank, regional banks, and agribusiness corporations, working in projects costing several billion dollars, seem as committed as ever to increasing cattle production for export from Latin America and Africa. Several studies indicate it may be only the beginning.[23] The growth rate for world demand for beef has been higher than that for any other agricultural item.

Those who demand meat with every meal are capable of being coaxed on to a higher and higher price to get it. The American steak religion has already caught on in Japan and Western Europe and is becoming the "in" thing in Eastern Europe, the Soviet Union, and the oil-producing Middle East. In many Asian countries, a taste for grain-fed meat is being developed. But why is cattle production shifting to the underdeveloped countries? First, big U.S. ranchers have turned away from the higher land and labor costs of the United States. As one rancher put it: "Here's what it boils down to—$95 per cow per year in Montana, $25 in Costa Rica."[24]

Second, to avoid the rising costs of feedgrains, the beef industry is searching for areas where grazing is economical. Moreover, multinational conglomerates have recently taken over the major meat-processing firms. (Now Armour is really Greyhound, Wilson is L.T.V., Swift is Esmark, and Morrell is, as we just saw, another way of saying United Brands.) As meatcutters in the United States and Europe are just beginning to realize, these firms will now try to transfer labor-intensive meat preparation (boning, prepacking) right to the new production sites in cheap-labor countries. Finally, giant agribusiness firms do not want the bother of purchasing from several independent suppliers and competing among themselves for those supplies. Thus, United Brands is integrating backwards to ranching subsidiaries, especially attractive due to cheap labor, government incentives, and available development funds, in countries like Honduras. The Global Ranch is but a variant of the Global Farm.

Another impetus behind shifting the beef industry abroad is the U.S. government and corporate drive to build markets for American grain and soybean exports. Meat production may yet become the equivalent of the 1960s "screwdriver" industries for many Third World countries. Just as in the sixties underdeveloped countries began assembling consumer items that were machined in industrial countries for shipment *back* to industrial markets, cattle operations controlled by multinational corporations commonly import American grain to be fed to animals that then get shipped to the United States.

In their drive to increase exports to Western Europe, Japan, and the United States, many governments in underdeveloped countries have enacted a whole series of measures to *de*crease domestic beef consumption at home. Several Latin American countries, including even Argentina and Uruguay, have even decreed days and weeks of the year during which no beef can be sold. (The principal impact has been that the well-off suddenly decide it is time to buy a freezer!)

Africa has many of the same attractive features for livestock investors as Latin America. European corporations are reportedly considering numerous ranching projects in Kenya, the Sudan, and Ethiopia—some of the finest and cheapest grazing land near Europe. According to one FAO officer who is afraid to be quoted, the plan is to use Green Revolution inputs on fully mechanized farms to raise the feedgrains. This feed would fatten the animals brought in from ranches. The goal is export.

A Chicken in Every Pot?

Americans tend to think of chickens as a true "people's food" compared to meat. Promoting chicken in the underdeveloped countries might sound like a good idea: Isn't a low-cost source of protein just what they need?

But that is not how Ralston Purina sees it. Ralston Purina considered creating a poultry industry in Colombia, not so that the poor would have more chicken in their diet, but to create a need for its chief product, concentrated feeds. Experience had taught multinational feed companies like Purina that promoting poultry production was the fastest way to create customers for concentrated feed. The poultry business requires less initial capital and land than the cattle-feeding operations. Moreover, poultry feeds are among the most profitable for the feed companies.

First, Purina offered credit to commercial farmers to

buy baby chicks and feed. Soon there were more chicks than could be supplied by feedgrain. So the company offered credit to other commercial farmers to grow feed crops and encouraged the government and private creditors to do the same. Traditional food crops like corn gave way to sorghum for feed. A portion of the corn crop that had been for human consumption now brought a higher price as grist for Purina's mill. Beans, another staple of the poor, gave way to soybeans for feed. Between 1958 and 1968, the acreage planted with the traditional beans was halved while soybean plantings—all grown for animal feed—jumped sixfold.

The plight of the poor is compounded by the nature of the market. As livestock feed production takes up land that once grew beans and grain for human consumption, the prices of these staples go up.

Ralston Purina still likes to talk about how it was a prime mover in the production of new sources of protein: chicken and eggs. It is true that Colombia, an egg importer in 1957, was by 1961 no longer importing eggs. From 1966 to 1971, annual broiler production doubled from 11 million to 22 million. Yet, as the excellent Consumers' Union–sponsored study notes, "The displacement of cropland from pulses [beans] to feed crops did not simply replace a cheap source of protein with an expensive one. It also reduced the total availability of protein in the country, because animal sources of protein are less efficient to produce than are vegetable sources."[25]

A plot of land used to grow beans and corn can satisfy the protein requirements of significantly more people than when it is used for animal feed crops. Based on actual experience in the Valle region of Colombia, the Universidad del Valle arrived at the following estimates: One acre of land growing feed crops for chickens provides only one-third the amount of protein for people that the same land could provide if it grew corn or beans; if the acre grew soybeans for human consumption, it could provide sixteen times more protein than is produced by using that land to grow chicken feed.[26] Using the feed to produce eggs instead of chicken reduces these differences somewhat. But according to calculations based on Colombian government statistics for 1970, a dozen eggs would cost more than an entire week's earnings for over a quarter of the population.

Ralston Purina and the other feed companies in Colombia like to cite figures showing increases in per capita egg consumption. But, as usual, per capita figures are misleading. Higher averages merely reflect the increased consumption of eggs by the small middle- and upper-income groups, directly or in processed items such as snack foods and mayonnaise. For all the additional eggs Ralston Purina can count on a national basis, there is evidence that Colombia's protein gap is growing eight times faster than the population.[27]

Thus what looked like just the way to create a needed source of cheap protein for Colombians turns out to undermine the only accessible protein sources of the people. Ralston Purina helps teach us, as discussed earlier in Part IV, that "modern" techniques and production skills in themselves mean nothing. We must always ask: For what? For whom? At the cost of what alternatives? The answer to these questions will be determined by who is in charge of the production: the people themselves or multinational corporations.

Where Have All the Flowers Gone?

Another "know-how" that agribusiness is eager to bring to underdeveloped countries is the production of "ornamental crops"—the academic name for cut flowers and foliage.

If the local peasants cannot afford chicken or eggs, perhaps they can brighten their shacks with cut flowers. Since 1966 the value of cut flowers and foliage imported into the United States has increased over sixty times to over $20 million in 1975—over 90 percent coming from Latin America.[28] Some experts feel that by 1980 it will no longer be "feasible" to produce cut flowers in many current production areas in the United States.

The favored country so far is Colombia, where cut flowers are now a $17-million-a-year business. In 1973, a Colombian government economist estimated for us that one hectare planted with carnations brings in a million pesos a year; planted with wheat or corn, the same hectare would bring only 12,500.[29] Given that at least 70 percent of Colombia's agricultural land is controlled by a small group of wealthy farmers who need not think of land in terms of growing food to live by, it is not at all surprising that ornamental crops join feedgrain and cattle on their list of priority crops.

Ecuador and Guatemala, and to a lesser extent Mexico, are also being transformed into major flower production sites for the Global Supermarket. Already in 1972, Guatemala was supplying the United States with 159,278,421—the USDA counts them!—chrysanthemums, roses, pompoms, daisies, chamaedorea, and statice.

Agribusiness's shifting of flower production to underdeveloped countries to supply the Global Supermarket follows the twofold pattern we have seen with other crops.[30] First is the search for lower-cost production sites (land preparation costs for flower cultivation in Central America have been estimated to be less than 10 percent of comparable costs in Florida). Second is the corporate effort to integrate operations from the seed to the flower shop. The U.S. flower business has historically consisted of large numbers of independent enterprises: small growers, larger grower-shippers, and tens of thousands of retail shops. But certain agribusiness firms such as Sears, Green Giant, Pillsbury, and United Brands and the supermarket chains are beginning to eye the profits to be made by linking the retailing to low-cost foreign production sites[31]—an integration process that is a little out of the reach of your neighborhood florist. United Brands is known already to have production operations of several hundred acres in Central America and plans for major expansion. These corporations would seek to brand name flowers as United Brands did with Chiquita bananas in the 1960s. They will market the flowers through supermarket chains and franchised stores ("Flowers from Sears" and Backman's European Flower Markets, a subsidiary of Pillsbury). Neighborhood florist shops could well go the way of tens of thousands of other mom and pop stores—out of business.

So agribusiness firms are doing exactly what the question suggests: bringing their production know-how to the countries where many go without food. But what are they growing? Asparagus, cucumbers, strawberries, eggplant, beef, and flowers—"luxury crops." And for whom? For the well-fed to whom it is profitable to sell. More and more of the prime agricultural resources that the hungry people abroad need for their food get channeled into supplying Americans and other well-fed foreigners.

In answering this question we have not looked for the worst corporations. Those we use as illustrations are run by managers probably no better or more ill-intentioned than any others. But there is one fundamental obstacle: corporations must sell for a profit. You say that agribusiness firms cannot afford not to be successful. You are right. "The bottom line is what counts," James McKee, chief executive of CPC International, told us in an interview. "If we lose sight of that, no matter how much good we were doing, we wouldn't be around long." But that is exactly the reason they cannot help the hungry. No matter how many hungry people there are, as long as they are being impoverished, hungry people just do not add up to a market.

We find ourselves in the right business at the right time. Agriculture and the food industry will have top priority in a world of shortages. Rises in population and income will create unprecedented demand. Food will be the growth industry for at least the remainder of the century.

Heinz management, 1975

We must encourage the developing nations of the world to establish more sophisticated systems of food distribution, in order to eliminate the unnecessary waste and spoilage of vital foodstuffs between production sites and needy people. Our basic feed and food operations are aimed at these crucial objectives.

The Restaurant Group is composed of fast service Jack in the Box . . . and a network of specialty dinner house restaurants. . . . Both operations posted record sales. . . .

A new program of developing color-keyed interiors, custom designed for local areas, has been implemented. The Foodmaker Architectural and Graphics Departments have developed many new concepts for pleasing visual impact, both inside and outside the restaurants. Such furnishings as hanging flower baskets, stained glass partitions, semiconcealed trash containers and colorful and comfortable seating, are designed to increase customer satisfaction. New bright orange and yellow miracle fabric uniforms for restaurant employees, introduced during the second half of the fiscal year, are another step to improve visual impact!

> Ralston Purina Company, "Report to Shareholders," 1974, p. 12

I was sitting at a table beside the swimming pool of the Biltmore Hotel in Guatemala City writing up my log of the day's interviews, when I became aware that six men at the next table were discussing development plans for Guatemala.

When I went over later and introduced myself, I learned that the advisor of the group was the former executive director of a foundation whose effectiveness in providing overseas assistance had been endorsed by Presidents Kennedy, Johnson, and Nixon. Two of the men in the group were wealthy businessmen from upstate New York who had generously decided to contribute money and time to set up their own program to help feed the people of at least one hungry nation.

The sincerity of the men in the group and their basic Christian goodwill are also typical, and I urge that their conversation not be interpreted as a caricature of naivete. On the contrary, they were too highly motivated for that.

"What are the crops they raise here?"

"Don't know, but we can ask AID or the (U.S.) Department of Agriculture."

"World's going to starve to death in 1976, so we don't have much time."

"How much time do we have?"

"Two years."

"Let's work on that basis."

"That means we've got to have a crash program."

"How do they plant corn? Anyone here ever planted corn?" (Silence)

"Hell, the Dept. of Agriculture can tell us that. What we need to know is how to change the system here. It's bound to be lousy."

"You mean we don't have a contract to do this yet? How do we get one?"

"That's what we're talking about now. We've got to get a plan first."

"Right. That's what we need, a contract and a plan. The plan, I guess, comes first."

"These people (the Guatemalans) don't even know how to use a screwdriver. You can't imagine how easy it would be to double their food production once you get them to accept our ideas."

"What ideas do you mean?"

"You know, modern machinery. That's what they need."

"Right. Think what a tractor would do here!"

"How about strawberries? Hell, they use a lot of strawberries in the states."

"That's a great idea!"

"Strawberries grow ten months of the year, and all you do is plant them and cultivate. Wonder why they don't raise them here."

"Personally, I think this coconut idea is worth looking into. Of course, you can't use them all, but how about 15 or 20 million coconuts?"

"There ought to be a market for that many."

"Why not go into the cattle business or raise pigs. We could feed the coconuts to the pigs. We'll get the natives to harvest the coconuts to feed to the pigs."

W. Paddock and E. Paddock,
We Don't Know How, pp. 61–64

36. Still, Don't the People Benefit?

Question: But surely this is not the whole picture. Don't multinational agribusiness firms create thousands of rural jobs and bring greater income to small farmers whose produce the companies buy for export? So while agribusiness may look irrelevant to the development process, doesn't it in reality expand the local economy and further the development of the country?

Our Response: To answer this question, we must first understand how multinational corporations operate in underdeveloped countries. Traditionally foreign agricultural investment in an underdeveloped country meant owning and operating plantations. This is changing. Due to risk of "expropriation, revolution or insurrection" plantations are a "poor risk" says the Overseas Private Investment Corporation (OPIC),[1] the United States government agency insuring American firms against just such risks. Direct ownership of production, moreover, is not attractive to a corporation seeking to tie up as little capital as possible.

Contract Farming

It is not surprising, then, that by 1965 agribusiness investment in direct land ownership abroad was half the value of a decade earlier.[2] Nevertheless this decline has come at a time of a stepped-up interest in investment in Third World agriculture. Is this a contradiction? Not really: Many agribusiness firms are shifting from the plantation mode to that of "contract farming." Exceptions are found where military dictatorships make foreign corporations feel totally secure and when firms find that they must produce directly in order to control quality.

Instead of owning land and farming directly, contract farming means that the corporation gets local producers to sign a contract committing them to use certain inputs to produce a stipulated amount of specified products with the date of delivery to the corporation and the price fixed. The corporation obviously still maintains the control it requires, with little capital invested—and, best of all, there is nothing that can be nationalized.

United Brands (UB) pioneered the way to get out of direct ownership and still maintain control. It saw the light in 1960 when the Cuban government nationalized 271,000 acres.[3]

The company began to develop its "Associate Producer Program," which allowed it to sell much of its land. In Central America alone UB's direct ownership has fallen from close to two million acres in 1954 to a third of that by 1971. In Ecuador the company sold all its extensive holdings by the mid-sixties. But in every case UB maintained total control.

An associate producer is a local person who buys or leases land from the plantation company. Such an individual is hardly a struggling small farmer. In Guatemala Del Monte's one associate producer, formerly contracting with United Fruit, has over 3000 acres.[4] A United Nations study found that Del Monte's thirteen associate producers in Costa Rica own an average of 612 acres each.[5] The associate producers contract to buy their inputs and technical assistance from the company and to sell their entire production to it. If the company believes an associate is politically well placed, he or she might also receive a company loan to get started. The company splits the difference between the total cost of production and the purchase price *the company sets.* In addition, the company nets a further profit marketing the produce in what *Business Week* calls "the big, well-heeled market."[6] There are two additional bonuses to such contracting for the foreign companies: one economic and the other political. When the foreign market is booming, the companies rely on the associate producers to supplement their own direct plantation production. But when an oversupply might depress prices, the companies simply raise quality standards so as to reduce purchases from their associate producers. Politically, the system gives foreign companies an influential bloc of nationals who identify their welfare with that of the companies— the best insurance against nationalization of the remaining holdings or against national tax reforms, as the banana companies proved in 1974.

The corporation may not be called United Fruit anymore and soon there may be no more company plantations, yet little has changed for the ordinary people. The best lands still grow fruits like bananas and vegetables for the world's well-fed. Still the best that rural inhabitants can hope for are low-wage, seasonal jobs in an associate producer's field. Most of the value produced still goes to UB.

Former Secretary of Agriculture Orville Freeman, a leading agribusiness spokesperson, thinks this type of contract farming holds a bright future for Third World agriculture. He is now president of Business International and of a company called Multinational Agribusiness Systems, Inc. At a United Nations–organized conference on agribusiness and world hunger,[7] he shared his vision with other multinational executives of "a kind of contract farming" he prefers to call "satellite farming." He foresees "many agribusiness companies"—he named Del Monte, FMC, International Systems and Controls, the Hawaiian sugar companies, and Nestlé—with "the experience, technology and the management know-how" cultivating a "core-producing unit of optimum size, using the most modern technology," and providing "supervisory services" to "hundreds of adjacent small farmers" and contracting their production.

Such a vision is not new. Contract farming was not invented by agribusiness for underdeveloped countries. It is an already proven tool of agribusiness in gaining control over food production in the United States itself. To understand what contract farming now offers underdeveloped countries, we have to know what it has meant to American farmers.

The "New Slaves"

The food business in the United States is tightly controlled. Even though a food-industry lobbyist might argue that it is a highly competitive industry in that there are 28,656 food-manufacturing firms, just 50 brand-name giants own 60 percent of total food-manufacturing assets and take 90 percent of the industry's total profits.[8] Referring to them as giants, then, is hardly an exaggeration. But how does this affect life on the farm or the average consumer?

In this near-monopoly context the big processors like Del Monte, Campbell's Soup, General Foods, Heinz, and Coca-Cola aim at keeping the price they pay for farm goods at a minimum. Their principal tool is the contract. It is incredible to find that USDA does not categorize such processors as corporate farmers but as "subsistence" farmers—since they "consume" all of what they "produce." So much for statistics on corporate farming![9]

Del Monte directly owns fifty-five farms in the United States totaling 130,000 acres and, in addition, has hundreds of thousands of acres under production contracts with 10,000 farmers. Already over 22 percent of the total American food production is under direct corporate control, four-fifths of that by contract.[10] Of the vegetables processed in the United States, 78 percent are produced by farmers under contract and 10 percent by the processors themselves. This means that corporations control 88 percent of the American vegetable crop.[11] There is therefore no competitive market to which the individual farmer can turn. He has little choice but to sign up with a corporation. Almost all of such basic favorites as sweet corn, green beans, tomatoes, and even popcorn are grown under production contract.[12] The process resembles the oil companies' control of oil from the wellhead to the service station. As we have seen in Part VII, it is a disastrous arrangement for the family farmer, as well as for the consumer.

The American Agricultural Marketing Association enthusiastically estimates that 50 percent of the American food supply will be produced under corporate contract at the end of this decade and that by 1985 the agribusiness giants will have their grip on 75 percent of United States food production.[13] Is this something we should feel good about? Is this the "successful" model that agribusiness has to offer the underdeveloped countries?

We can only answer these questions by first finding out how a typical production contract in the United States works.

Before planting time a farmer signs up with a corporation to produce a specified amount of a certain product and to deliver it by a fixed date. Many of the contracts specify exactly what kind of inputs must be used and some offer credit.

"Farmers sign contracts because they are hard-pressed," states Gene Potter of the National Farmers Organization.[14] There are many sellers and few buyers. Already deeply mortgaged, the farmer is hardly in a position to negotiate. The preprinted contract prepared by a corporate lawyer is presented to him on a take-it-or-leave-it basis.

If farmers organize to pressure the corporation, in all likelihood the corporation only speeds up its shift of production to "offshore" sites. This is already happening in part. Asparagus growers in California, Oregon, and Washington produce most of their crop under contract to Del Monte. A few years ago the growers organized into a bargaining association and won a price boost from Del Monte. That is when Del Monte began moving some of its asparagus operations to Mexico.[15]

The processor's superior power does not end with getting farmers to sign up. The contracts they sign, after all, are written by the corporations for the corporations.

Jim Hightower reports the asparagus growers find that their contracts with Del Monte "allow the corporation to decide what part of the crop is 'acceptable.' " In 1972, 8 percent of the asparagus crop was rejected in this way. "With no open market to sell on," Hightower observes, "farmers literally had to eat that loss." He goes on to reveal how the farmers' loss is Del Monte's gain:

> In many cases, however, Del Monte will buy the rejected asparagus from the farmer—at cut-rate prices. In 1972, the price for "acceptable" canning asparagus was 23¢ a pound. The price for asparagus the corporation found unacceptable was .0005¢ a pound. Del Monte has sole power to decide whether a batch of asparagus is worth 23¢ or .0005¢, and the contract requires the farmer to offer any unacceptable asparagus to Del Monte. If the corporation does not want to buy it, then the farmer can take his rejects elsewhere. But there is nowhere else.
>
> Why would Del Monte want to write such a provision into its contract? Because there are windfall profits in those asparagus culls. The farmer may have to give the stuff away to Del Monte, but Del Monte certainly does not give it away to you. Del Monte packages and sells these rejects as asparagus soup, asparagus cuts and asparagus tips—all drawing a pretty penny at the supermarket.[16]

No examination of contract farming is complete without looking at the poultry industry: the first in the United States with contract operations on a large scale.

The production contract was the tool by which corporations like Ralston Purina, Cargill, Pillsbury, and Continental Grain took control of chicken production in the United States beginning in the late 1950s. Since at that time prices were only a few pennies a pound, an offer of credit from the corporation was one a hard-up independent farmer could hardly refuse. These same corporations controlled the feedgrain market and, sure enough, the contract required the farmer to use only his creditor's feed.

Within ten years the percentage of United States chicken production under contract went from 4 percent to 92 percent.[17] USDA nonetheless insists on calling these contracted farmers "family farmers." In reality they are little more than hired hands in a corporate factory. Only there is one big difference. It is they who must go into debt to build the "factory" and put in new equipment. As an official of the Mississippi Farm Bureau told USDA researchers, "Today a Mississippi farmer could not sell broilers in the market if he wanted to produce them. Farmers do not own the birds. They furnish only the labor and the houses. They do exactly what they are told."[18]

George Anthan, a first-rate investigative reporter for the *Des Moines Register,* described a recent visit to a poultry area in Northern Alabama after the "integrators" came in:

For farmers to get a contract, certain "improvements" specified by the corporation had to be made on their farms. These investments were financed by the farmers through local banks. Failure to meet the specifications would result in the contract being withdrawn, leaving the farmer virtually without a market. The integrators did not offer long-term contracts in exchange for the farmers making the changes the companies insisted upon.

The farmers I talked to said that every time it looked like they were going to get the loan paid off, the integrators would come up with a new "improvement" like gas heaters, insulated chicken houses, and automatic feeding equipment. Once in debt, the farmer had to stay in business, but to stay in business they had to get deeper in debt. One of the farmers described himself and other poultry farmers as the "new slaves."

Most of the farmers had to take jobs in town to supplement their incomes and usually had a wife or daughter working in the local poultry processing plant for minimum wages. Farmers were getting about 2¢ a pound for their chicken. I didn't find a

single farmer making more per pound than they
made five to ten years ago, but their costs had doubled.[19]

According to Harrison Wellford in the chapter
"Poultry Peonage" of his pioneering study *Sowing the
Wind,*[20] a USDA economist found Alabama chicken
growers making minus 36 cents an hour for their
service to the corporations. The same USDA study in
1967 concluded chicken farmers were pauperized because of their lack of bargaining strength in dealing
with the corporations. In 1962, some poultry growers
in Arkansas under contract to processing companies
tried to organize an association. The companies blacklisted the growers and ruined them by making certain
that they could never again receive a contract.[21]

Growers do not dare speak out against the unfair
trade practices for fear of being blacklisted. This fear
was dramatized in an interview with a contracting
chicken grower in Alabama on ABC-TV in 1973.[22]
The woman so feared reprisals that she would not allow her face to be shown or any mention of the corporation for which she raised chickens. At the end, the
interviewer asked, "Why do you stay in the business of
chicken raising?" The reply: "We have to! We'll lose
our house mortgaged to pay $29,600 for the chicken
houses. Our farm. Everything we've worked for."

In 1958, Earl Butz, just having left the post of
Assistant Secretary of Agriculture to become both Dean
of Agriculture at Purdue and a director of Ralston
Purina, wrote a widely disseminated article directed at
American farmers titled, "Don't Be Afraid of Integration" (certainly an eye-catching title in the South in
1958). Today agribusiness, the United States government, and the World Bank would have farmers in
underdeveloped countries trust the corporate hand, hoping they have not heard of the fate of small American
chicken farmers.

Tens of thousands of American farmers, hardly
naïve to the ways of the modern world and living in a
country with an array of antimonopoly and fair trade
laws as well as regulatory agencies, have not been able

to protect their interests against a few powerful poultry supply and marketing corporations. What then is the likelihood that farmers, even the better off, in countries like Pakistan, Mexico, Colombia, and Thailand will fare any better?

A retired official of the FAO invited us to consider two alternative visions of the world, both of which can already be foreseen in different countries. In the one, tens of thousands of entrepreneurial "farmers" receive corporate credit to raise chickens, using hired laborers and all the latest feedgrain and chemical techniques designed to bloat chicks in the shortest time (regardless of how tasteless and watery they become), for a few giant worldwide marketers like Ralston Purina and the Rockefeller-owned Arbor Acres. In the alternative vision, hundreds of millions of farmers have a few chickens each in their backyards eating insects and scraps, with some occasional input such as inexpensive chicken cholera vaccine. "In which world," asked our friend, "do you think more people are likely to eat chicken? Or are agricultural resources less likely to be used raising feed for animals instead of food for people? Or is less foreign exchange likely to be lost to the country on imported supplies and through repatriated profits and fees?" The FAO itself may already be committed to one vision; both Ralston Purina and Arbor Acres are key members of the FAO's Integrated Meat Development Working Group. Yet to us it was reassuring to realize there *is* an alternative and it is not starvation.

Popeye City

Agribusiness giants can turn whole towns, even regions, into company operations. The Agribusiness Accountability Project, an independent research group, did an in-depth study[23] of the "Spinach Capital of the World," Crystal City, county seat of Zavala County, Texas, where Del Monte owns 3600 acres of irrigated farmland producing an annual $14 million worth of spinach. Canning all the spinach grown in Crystal City,

Del Monte is by far Crystal City's biggest employer. There is no competition: Del Monte can buy the farmers' spinach without bidding against Green Giant, Bird's Eye, Libby—or anyone else. If farmers do not want to sell to Del Monte, they can, as Jim Hightower comments, "look forward to long days of eating lots of spinach."[24]

While billion-dollar-a-year Del Monte prospers, it refuses to contribute to Crystal City's welfare. Del Monte even built its plant outside the border of the town to avoid $11,987.61 in property taxes. The corporation argues that as the major employer it contributes sufficiently to community welfare. Del Monte has, it is only fair to note, donated to City Hall a statue of Popeye.

Even those who do find jobs with Del Monte can barely subsist. The 1970 census revealed half of the families in Zavala County had incomes below the official poverty level. Del Monte pays $2.12 to $3.09 an hour for processing spinach and $3.56 an hour in the can-manufacturing plant. If these wages were for *full-time* employment, yearly incomes would range from $4000 to $6800, somewhat below Del Monte's chief executive's $438,000. But most of Del Monte employees are not full-time but "seasonal" workers.

Del Monte has a long documented record of obstructing workers' legal rights not only to organize for decent wages and better working conditions but even to vote in municipal elections.

According to the study, Del Monte's plant is hellish in summer and bone-chilling in winter. It lacks adequate toilet and medical facilities. Conditions are no better in other Del Monte operations where the corporation houses its seasonal workers. George Ballis, a noted photographer, reported on workers' housing in Del Monte's "labor camp" in San Joaquin, California, the "Asparagus Capital of the World":

> The places—of cement blocks—don't look too bad ... except for the whole prison camp feel: high wire fence topped with barbed wire (a Del Monte trade-

mark), and huge "No Trespassing" signs at the gate.

The grounds are one big mudhole in the winter rains. There is no hot water in the units. No baths. No toilets. No heat.

When the workers complain, they are told the camp was made for summer use only, even though it has been used year round for 16 years.[25]

Is Crystal City or San Joaquin what Orville Freeman has in mind when he tells the world that Del Monte has "the experience, the technology and the management know-how to manage efficiently"? And what about Ray Vicker, of the *Wall Street Journal,* asserting in *This Hungry World* that Del Monte "has far more to gain through helping farmers in the developing countries to help themselves than through any exploitative method of operation"?[26]

Agribusiness Meets the Peasant

What is the real life condition of those who labor to supply the Global Supermarket? Has the coming of agribusiness meant decent jobs, income for adequate food and a secure foundation for development? Certainly not in the case of the thriving strawberry industry in Mexico studied in-depth by Ernest Feder in his book *Strawberry Imperialism: An Enquiry into the Mechanisms of Dependency in Mexican Agriculture* (see also Part VIII, Question 35).

As Feder relates, in the mid 1960s, before the strawberry boom hit the Zamora Valley, Zamora and the neighboring Jacona were small towns. Today Zamora has 100,000 inhabitants and Jacona 30,000. Thousands more come to the valley in search of work and return to their villages at night or sleep in the streets, since the cost of transportation for some represents 30 percent of their daily wage even if they find work. Over three quarters of the population lives in half-mile-wide carton-shack slums that ring the towns.

No sanitation, no running water, little electricity. All in all, a classic case of "overpopulation."

Yet in the Zamora valley you can also find the ranch-style houses of the new "strawberry millionaires." As employers, these few individuals and their American partners directly benefit from the desperate misery of the majority. Since the number seeking work far exceeds the number of jobs, the growers are able to hold down wages. Some growers, despite the large numbers of unemployed already in Zamora, send recruiter trucks to outlying villages because the peasants there are willing to work for still less.

In Zamora, during the four months of peak field work you can find over 5000 would-be workers gathering at 5:30 A.M. next to the railroad station. Guarded by the military armed with submachine guns, they wait for the growers or their agents to come in trucks. The largest growers come to pick up several hundred workers at a time. Still, many do not find a job. They must walk back to their villages only to return the next day hoping for better luck.

Those who do get hired get somewhat under the legal minimum wage of $3 per day. This is particularly true for women and children who, despite the law on equal wages for equal work, have to be content with two thirds of the wages paid to men. The employers say they prefer women and children "because they do not have to stoop so far," but fortunes have been made on such thoughtfulness. Like fieldhands in the fruit and vegetable industry in the United States (where the orange crate alone sells for more than the labor to fill it), a family must field every member, including young children, if it is to survive.

When the trucks do come, no workers dare to ask how much they would be paid, for, according to Feder, they would simply be told: "There is no work for you." The workers climb on board the truck without the slightest idea of where they will be taken, how much they will be paid, or whether they will have work the next day. As one worker put it, "In order not to starve, we don't ask any questions."

Employers are known to use a variety of tactics to

boost their profit on each worker such as shortening the lunch break and working the laborers overtime and seven days a week without extra pay. Everyday exposure to pesticides results in vomiting, fainting spells, severe headaches, and even death. Efforts to organize for better working conditions have always met with employer violence.

And what about the strawberry-processing and freezing factories? Do they through their famed "transfer of technology" develop new skills and provide decent employment?

The strawberry factories are geared to just one thing—strawberries. Since strawberries are harvested less than half the year, the factories lie idle six to seven months, employing no one. Despite this wasteful use of capital equipment, owning a factory can be quite lucrative. Feder reports that some companies have recovered their capital investment in a single year. During a few peak weeks the freezing factories in Zamora (most with United States capital) employ 10,000 to 12,000 women and girls, mostly between fourteen and twenty-five years of age. But the work for most is very short-term since the factories operate way below capacity during the beginning and end of the harvest.

Although child labor is illegal, Feder reports that in plants controlled by American capital he found up to sixty children working. The work is monotonous and the conditions are unconscionable. The workers must stand all day even though, during the peak season, that means standing up to eighteen hours a day, at 40 to 50 cents an hour. In some plants supervisors make extra money selling the obligatory white uniforms that cost four to five days' wages.

What about the small farmers in the region—can't they at least profit from growing strawberries? Only in theory. First of all, government permits, aimed at preventing massive overproduction, regulate who can plant how many acres. Since there is money to be made, those with political and economic influence make sure they get the permits.

In one *ejido* land-reform community, 19 out of 220 families received permits. Each recipient had a clear power connection. None actually worked on the land.

The processing factories, according to Feder's research, further narrow down the number of growers. Production contracts favor the larger suppliers, giving them priority and better terms in distribution of inputs and the purchase of their output.

Some larger growers use their influence literally to pocket the key to the watergates of the irrigation system. They can then use water in excess of the legal limit while the small producers are left to fight over the remaining water that trickles down to them. The district's small farmers growing food crops find they have less and less water. Mainly because of the flooding of the strawberry fields, the area irrigated by the Zamora system has actually shrunk. Strawberries use up 75 percent of the water on only 20 to 30 percent of the total area under cultivation.

In contrast to the agribusiness-controlled monoculture of today's Zamora, a peasant-controlled agriculture would naturally build on mixed cropping. Mixed cropping is not only environmentally sound (as discussed in the response to Question 17), but also means year-round food supply and work. Furthermore, when the rural population individually or collectively owns and controls the agricultural resources, it is likely to use its spare time to improve the agricultural resources—drainage, irrigation, terracing, tree planting, storage, and so on. By contrast, in Zamora today, most of the population can obtain at best only part-time seasonal work. The control of the valley's agricultural resources by an export-oriented industry with a pronounced seasonal peak and unstable export markets results in mostly part-time, insecure jobs and a plundering approach to the land.

In Zamora a single system produces millionaires and paupers. It adds up to a stunning waste of human life, as well as agricultural resources, and even the vast underutilization of investment capital. Hardly a foundation for development.

Counter Land Reform

Much of what we have learned points to one truth: People must control their agricultural resources if they are to free themselves from hunger. Yet supposed land redistribution programs in such places as Brazil, Colombia, Central America, Iran, and the Philippines have exempted agribusiness land, even though it is often the best land.

The Philippines, a country with an estimated 3,000,000 landless peasants, is a recent clear example. A "sweeping" land reform program—sometimes presented in the media as the justification for the martial law suspension of all human rights—exempted fully two-thirds of the country's agricultural land because it has been put into production for the global Supermarket.

In the Bukidnon region Del Monte is attempting to coerce self-provisioning smallholders to lease their land to the company. Armed company agents have fenced off and driven cattle onto the cultivated fields of those who refuse to lease.[27] An American priest, arrested for helping the peasants resist, described Del Monte's landgrabbing: "They bulldozed people right off the land. Now they're using aerial sprays, harming farm animals and giving people terrible rashes."[28]

Iran is also a prime example: a country where equating agricultural development with agribusiness investment has spelled the *reversal* of land reform. Consequences for the rural population have been disastrous.

In 1962 the Shah of Iran declared a substantial land reform that irrevocably broke the political power of the large landowners. "Land to the tiller," however, was taken literally. If a family was not well-off enough to own a plow and a draft animal—and many were not —they could not qualify for the broken-up estates.[29]

Throughout Iran, farmers who did receive land began to produce food. In the Khuzestan province, bordering on Iraq and the Persian Gulf, the farmers' productivity was extraordinary, especially considering the lack of technical assistance and irrigation and the 98 percent illiteracy. Traditional farming methods provided ample work for all.

Also during the 1960s, the government began to construct several large dams under the supervision of David Lilienthal, Franklin Roosevelt's designer of the Tennessee Valley Authority. The largest dam is on the Dez River in Khuzestan. It offered the prospect to the small farmers of over 200,000 acres of irrigated land. It sounded promising. Then, just when the dam was being completed, the shah and his elite advisors decided that what Khuzestan needed was foreign agribusiness corporations.

Today the farmers in Khuzestan no longer speak of land reform. Nor do they wait for the waters of the Dez to reach their parched lands. Irrigation channels, built for only *one-fifth* of the potential irrigated area, take water to the "farms" managed by such firms as Hawaiian Agronomics, the Diamond A. Cattle Co., Mitsui, Chase Manhattan, Transworld Agricultural Development Corp., Bank of America, Dow Chemical, John Deere & Co., Shell, Mitchell Cotts, and Hashem Naraghi (an Iranian émigré who became a major Californian grower).[30] For most of these firms, Khuzestan is but the latest venture out there on the Global Farm. Hawaiian Agronomics, for instance, is a subsidiary of C. Brewer—known in most western states by its C and H brand line—which in 1974 netted $3.8 million from agribusiness operations in Iran, Indonesia, Ecuador, and Guadalcanal.

Khuzestan today, instead of being an area of many small family farms utilizing the new irrigation, is a province dominated by large-scale (12,000 to 50,000 acres), highly mechanized, capital-intensive, cash crop units. Some 17,000 Iranians have been pushed off their lands.[31] Hawaiian Agronomics has boasted, "Land Barren for 23 Centuries Now Producing Food, Supporting Livestock."[32] The fact that peasants produced food there before the coming of agribusiness is ignored. Even more significantly, it was the massive irrigation system installed at public expense *before* agribusiness moved in that really made the parched lands productive. As one agribusiness executive remarked, "they develop the water first and we come in and farm it. It's an attractive arrangement."[33]

What might have looked to the shah like a way to achieve efficient, "sophisticated" agricultural production is not even working by the standards of the agribusiness firms themselves. So far only one firm is making a profit; already three firms have opted to sell out to the government. Productivity on these fully modernized tracts is lower than that of medium-sized Iranian farms in irrigated areas.[34] Two economists report that the firms "overestimated their ability." As one explained, "You just can't walk in, do a few soil samples and say these 10,000 acres should be artichokes." Another economist has pointed to the operating costs "due to the high salaries to technical experts and expatriate managers." Ironically, a 1975 study by an American consulting firm cites "management problems related to the large sizes of the production units."[35]

But do these problems discourage agribusiness? Some firms such as Chase Manhattan, John Deere, and Bank of America have kept on with their fumbling agricultural projects because of a series of government incentives, such as rebates from taxes on other income, and a desire to keep the shah happy. Mitsui is doing all right back home on selling as livestock feed the dehydrated alfalfa it exports out from the Khuzestan. The foreign corporations marketing inputs to cattle operations are doing all right, too. The shah wants cattle to such an extent that the government is paying World Airways to airlift 250,000 pregnant cows to Iran by 1979. One British firm, Fowler, Ltd., is importing cattle so ill-suited to the climate that the government must provide air-conditioned stables!

And how are the people of rural Khuzestan doing? Most are landless and jobless. Some see no alternative but to flee to the already overcrowded urban slums. Many of these refugees are in their teens and twenties. They would gladly farm if they had their own plots; their real skills are those of small rice farmers. The government has not even sought to train them for semiskilled jobs as construction workers, truck drivers, and machinists in Iran's supposedly boom economy. While urban unemployment soars, the government *imports* workers—80,000 South Koreans and innumerable Pakistanis for such jobs. Meanwhile the agribusiness refugees sit and wait around warehouses hoping for a few cents to lug a sack, sweep the floor, or shovel out the chicken droppings from the new British-owned ten-million-bird-a-year poultry factory in Teheran. Others who used to till fields have gone to the sparsely populated Arab states across the Gulf, proving to some that Iran is "overpopulated."

Those in Khuzestan forced to sell their land to agribusiness projects are winding up in one of the government's several "labor centers."[36] The purpose of these new labor centers is to provide the agribusiness projects with pools of labor—most of it on tap at $3 a day. As one foreign expert who out of fear wishes to remain anonymous wrote us, "You can see the government's theory that the agribusiness will require much more labor than they displace documented in government and even World Bank reports but not in the streets and houses where the idle gather." He has observed villagers, previously capable of self-initiated collective projects like building new villages, mosques, and schools, now demoralized, passive, and individualistic. He also reports that those families forced to work on agribusiness projects after they lost their plots eat even less well than before.

Reading such descriptions, all we could think of is that Khuzestan, Iran, might not be so far removed from Crystal City, Texas.

Sweet Corn

Of course not all contract agribusiness projects are export-oriented. At a symposium on world hunger in September 1975, CPC International presented the history of its investment in Pakistan to show what a positive contribution a foreign enterprise can make to a country's food supply. CPC International (known to you by its Thomas' English muffins, Skippy Peanut Butter, and Mazola Corn Oil) is no newcomer in underdeveloped countries. It has sizable operations in three dozen underdeveloped countries and therefore can be taken as a significant example of what agribusiness has to offer.

There are two ways of reading the CPC case study the company presented. The intended victory-over-hunger version is roughly as follows: In 1962, CPC International purchased control of Rafhan Maize Products, the largest corn grinding and processing company in Pakistan. By the late 1960s, Rafhan had expanded with loans from U.S. AID and the Pakistani government. But its mills just could not get hold of enough corn. So in January 1970 Rafhan "launched a corn development program." CPC decided it would use the agricultural expertise of its associated companies and brought in its subsidiary from the United States, the Funk Seed Company, to design a high-yielding hybrid. CPC has, the company notes, "people with know-how."

Rafhan worked out a contract system with the leading farmers whereby the company would supply on credit the right seed, pesticides, and fertilizers to be deducted at harvest from the contract price. "The contract farmers obtained average yields of more than twice the national average." Rafhan also built "modern facilities to shell, dry, and store the grain." So successful was Rafhan that it decided to expand yet further its processing plant.

Sounds good. But let's give it a second, more careful reading. Why was CPC not getting enough corn to its mills? According to the company:

Historically in Pakistan corn has been a food crop consumed by the underprivileged [*sic*] in the country and in the villages. It has been a popular food commodity because it was nearly always plentifully available during about six months of the year. . . . The price has been lower than the alternative food grains—wheat and rice. Corn has also been used for barter by farmers in the rural areas.[37]

In the 1960s, once CPC moved in, corn prices did increase and some better-off farms expanded total corn production. But still, according to the company, "the supply of corn available to the processors increased very little." The company sees three reasons for this: First, corn farmers "ate too much of their corn" or "bartered it for [other] food." Second, as the numbers of the poor grew rapidly they collectively "consumed increased quantities of corn as food." Third, the growing poultry industry was competing for the supply of corn.

In order to insure the corn supply it needed, Rafhan introduced a contract system that "completely changed the pattern of corn production." Corn farming is no longer the subsistence crop of the small farmer. CPC notes, "Corn had been cultivated on very small areas —not more than five acres for each farmer—now it was planted in larger fields."

As for storing the harvest, CPC states "there were two alternative methods." One was for the farmers to build narrow corn cribs where the air could circulate between the unshelled ears "preventing molding— *until the farmers wanted to sell*" [emphasis ours]. Rafhan, however, chose the other alternative: "Purchase the corn from farmers at the time of harvest, dry it in mechanical dryers and store it in [the company's] silos." Why? According to CPC, "the alternative of helping farmers obtain and own their corn cribs had two weaknesses." First, Rafhan "needs" corn, not cobs, and "the farmer-owned or community-owned shelling equipment is small, slow and inefficient." Second, when farmers store corn in their own cribs, there was always the chance that they might let family or friends consume the grain; or the farmers might sell or barter it to someone else!

Rafhan *will* have its corn. CPC indirectly notes an added advantage for the company, namely, that by buying up at harvest, rather than "when the farmers wanted to sell," the company is likely to get more and get it cheaper since the large supplies at harvest depress the price.

"Improved" corn farming has come to Pakistan.

Once a subsistence crop, corn is now grown by large farmers as just one link in a process controlled from seed to bin by CPC's Rafhan.

And what is it all for? To make "corn sweetener" as a sugar substitute in the fast-growing market for soft drinks and other snack foods among Pakistan's urban better-off classes.

Foreign corporations in an underdeveloped country's agriculture, then, are no help to the hungry, the landless or the small farmers. Natural resources like land and water, human resources and great sums of capital are spent on making profits for the corporations and their few local partners. The hungry do not benefit. It is not they who eat the food (if indeed it is food that is grown). It is not they who sell the products. Their wages must remain miserably low if production is to compete in the Global Supermarket. Their jobs, relatively few and seasonal compared to what could be the alternatives, are fundamentally insecure. Foods once relatively inexpensive become commercialized at prices affordable only by the world's well-fed. Agribusiness, furthermore, reverses and dooms agrarian reform.

Once a country's elite has opted to make agribusiness the engine of development, government must cater to agribusiness. The government is increasingly deprived of the capacity for independent economic and social planning. The interest of the state becomes indistinguishable from the interests of the multinational agribusiness firms within its territory. "Fiscal encouragements" lead to more "fiscal encouragements." There is the corporation's ever-present threat of pulling up stakes or turning to another country's supply.

Multinational agribusiness, often building on a colonial inheritance, is elite-controlled export agriculture under another name.

Among the most important reasons for the internationalization of the multinational corporation is to

increase its utility in the developing world of Latin
America, Asia and Africa. Its role in the development process becomes more urgently clear every
day, as we witness the limitations and handicaps of
local governments . . . even if local governments
were strong and assistance to them plentiful, the
fact is that the enormous complexities of the development process require abilities and attributes which are
as natural to the multinational corporation as they
are unnatural to government.

> Herbert C. Cornuelle, United Fruit Company
> Annual Report, 1968, Boston

The poor countries, on the other hand, have to try
to "denationalize" the subject of agribusiness investment and treat it for what it is: an amazingly
efficient way of institutionalizing the transfer of
technical knowledge in agriculture.

> Lester Brown, *Seeds of Change,* 1970

37. Better Than Beans and Rice?

Question: But aren't you overlooking something? Are
there not other types of agribusiness companies? What
about the food processors and distributors that have
perfected an efficient food delivery system in the
United States? Aren't these firms bringing to underdeveloped countries more nutritious and varied food
than their traditional, starchy diets?

Our Response: The beans and corn diet of Latin
America, the lentils and rice of India, and the soybean
and rice diet of China appear to most Americans as
starchy and nutrient poor. In fact, they are not. Such
diets evolved because they *work*. As basic dietetic

staples, these combinations are, in fact, quite ingenious. In each case the two items together give more biologically usable protein than if each were eaten separately.[1] Therefore, when we consider the problem of world hunger, we should always keep in mind that the traditional diet is adequate—*when* you can get enough of it. The problem is usually not quality. The problem is quantity.

What, then, do the food companies have in mind for "improving" the food of the poor?

Until several years ago the involvement of foreign firms in food processing in the underdeveloped countries was insignificant. With markets burgeoning at home and with so few urbanized consumer markets in the underdeveloped countries, there seemed little reason to bother. But suddenly multinational food processors have begun to take another look. The top 10 to 20 percent of the population in the underdeveloped countries constitute an emerging consumer class—but one lacking the servants who once made "convenience foods" unnecessary. At the same time the market in industrial countries for highly processed, more expensive, convenience items has become "saturated."

A 1973 *Business Week* article, "Starving for Profits," published a survey indicating that U.S. food processing companies had reported the lowest annual rate of domestic sales growth (5 percent) of any industry surveyed.[2] Each new dollar invested in advertising to get you to buy this or that exciting new convenience food was meeting with fewer and fewer market results. Population growth had plummeted. The middle classes in the industrial countries were unlikely to ever consume more than their 1700 to 2000 pounds a year of grain per person.

But perhaps the "worst" sign for American food processors, according to Joseph Winski of the *Wall Street Journal,* is that "After years of looking for the quick and easy way, Americans are returning to the basics in their food consumption." With more brown-bagging of lunches, more home gardening and canning, more homebaking and cooking "from scratch," convenience food sales have been plummeting. According to one estimate, unit sales of canned goods are down from 25 percent to 60 percent depending on the item. One large supermarket chain reported its frozen prepared food volume fell by 16 percent in one year alone. As its chairman Donald S. Perkins commented, "Today's consumers are willing to do it themselves." Even more disheartening to food-processing executives is that their own surveys show that the slump in the highly profitable convenience foods is not just a passing phase attributable to the recession. A *Better Homes and Gardens* survey revealed that 63 percent of the respondents agreed with the proposition that they were making "important and lasting changes" in the way they shop and the foods they eat regularly.[3]

The giant food companies have responded to the depressed home market in three ways. First, by diversifying into nonfood consumer products (such as toys —General Mills acquired Parker Brothers, Quaker Oats took over Fisher-Price and Marx). Second, by seeking to control cheaper sources of supply from foreign countries, as we have already seen. And third, by expanding into the new urban markets of Latin America, Asia, and Africa.

We have emphasized markets because that is what the food companies themselves emphasize. For the executive of a world-ranging food company, underdeveloped countries are not to be thought of in terms of the number of inhabitants, let alone the number of the malnourished. Countries *are* markets.

Peter Drucker, prolific corporate theologian, advises executives not to be put off by India's obvious poverty but to keep in mind that "within the vast mass of poverty that is India" there is "a sizeable modern economy, comprising 10 percent of the Indian population, or 50,000,000 who can consume on the level with most Americans and Western Europeans."[4] When we discussed the future of Nabisco in the underdeveloped world with Lee Bickmore, then chief executive of the corporation, he told us of his enthusiasm for the initial surveys indicating that Brazil could mean 20 million potential Ritz munchers, even though an estimated half of its 100 million people are so poor that they *never* handle money. In Mexico, considered one of the largest and most dynamic markets for food processing companies, less than one-third of the population has the means to buy some type of canned foods—as compared with 90 percent in the United States.[5]

André van Dam, who plans strategies for Hellmann's mayonnaise, Skippy's peanut butter, Knorr soup cubes, and other CPC products to "penetrate" Latin American markets, is quite aware what a large portion of the population is outside his industry's net. But he is not discouraged. With such large total populations van Dam is excited by the absolute numbers who could be made into customers. In a 1975 speech to top executives of food companies in Latin America he estimated the potential customers:

> Within ten years . . . Latin America will have 444 million inhabitants. . . . Of this number, a fifth will be able to buy, through their economic power, almost all the products which the gentlemen industrialists here presently manufacture, while a third will be able to buy some of these products only very infrequently. The rest of the population, about half of the total, are not customers except for the most simple and basic products and probably will continue on a subsistence basis. The potential market varies from country to country, from product to product, but those who have a continental vision realize that the potential market of 1985 in Latin America will double compared to today.[6]

No doubt Mr. van Dam would like to be concerned about the hungry. But with the "continental vision" of 89 million affluent Latin Americans ready to buy, he hardly need worry about those 208 million so miserably poor they could never buy a jar of Hellmann's mayonnaise or Skippy peanut butter.

At Home Away from Home

The question implies that food companies are bringing in new products and greater efficiency—that is, a better food system. But are multinational food processors really bringing something new and are they successful because they are more efficient?

Corporations, like people, behave much the same away from home as they do at home.[7] If anything, away from home there are fewer inhibitions. At home, firms have become giants not by offering a better product and greater efficiency but by a one-two punch of local takeovers and advertising expertise. And that is exactly how the multinational food companies are expanding throughout the underdeveloped world.

Rather than starting from scratch, the food companies gain an initial foothold by buying out a local firm that is already in at least one of the same product lines. Nabisco has taken over local biscuit and cracker companies in countries like Venezuela, Mexico, Iraq, Brazil, Nicaragua, and Puerto Rico. Pepsico, big in the United States snack market since its acquisition of Frito-Lay, has taken over an established Venezuelan bakery company. Borden bought out the largest maker of pastas in Brazil. In 1966, W. R. Grace, a conglomerate with an historical base in guano (fertilizer from bird droppings) and shipping in Latin America, bought Alimentos Korn in Guatemala. Grace developed it into a frozen-foods line. By 1969, Grace claimed to control 60 percent of the Central American market for packaged processed foods with sales increasing at the rate of 70 percent a year.[8]

General Foods is a star acquisition operator. Former president C. W. Cook reflected on the lessons of the company's experience. "With the rapid progress we made in England through acquiring Alfred Bird and Sons, we concluded that where possible we would find an ongoing business with a management that knew the country, the trade, the banking facilities, the governments and the people." He observed that "starting from scratch" in Germany had proven a "difficult experience." So the question was—where could profitable takeovers still be made? "When we looked around, Europe was pretty well combed over." Latin America, however, offered excellent prospects.[9]

In 1956, General Foods acquired La India, the largest chocolate processor and the best-known seafood processor in Venezuela. In 1960, it took over Kibon, the largest ice cream manufacturer in Brazil. Other acquisitions gave General Foods two-thirds of Brazil's chewing gum market. General Foods already had the gum market wrapped up in Europe through takeovers there (Hollywood and Maple Leaf). In Mexico, in the 1960s, General Foods acquired several coffee and soup manufacturers.

Expanding through acquisitions has advantages. Starting costs are minimized. In addition General Foods requires each new subsidiary to finance itself through retained earnings and local loans. With such a low-cost-to-headquarters strategy, a big food company can enter several country markets almost simultaneously. Politically there is an advantage, too. The new subsidiary can be "low-profile" American. Most Brazilians think that Kibon is as Brazilian as the Mardi Gras. Yet in terms of the benefits of support from the U.S. government, from government investment insurance—OPIC—or diplomatic or moral support, Kibon is as American as can be.

What Is Agribusiness Offering?

The food companies expanding overseas are not a cross section of the United States food industry, according to such major studies as *At Home Abroad,* but those whose American operations are concentrated in high-advertising products. "In investing abroad, these firms have sought out the faster growing, convenience foods where advertising, rather than price cutting, is the instrument of competition."[10]

The underdeveloped countries are thus getting our worst, not our best. They are getting those corporations *least* likely to fill real needs or to be useful models.

Underdeveloped countries are but the latest markets to conquer for those corporations that have made it big and are getting bigger because they have hit upon a formula for large profit margins, maximum processing, and advertising. Is this what either we or the underdeveloped countries need?

At least 92 percent of the "research and development" costs of these big food companies goes to develop quick preparation and consumer appeal or what the National Science Foundation calls "motivational research and product promotion."[11] "Quick preparation," "convenience" foods mean prewashed, prepeeled, precooked, premashed, premixed—almost preeaten foods! Take the common potato, a staple in human diets for centuries—and not just because it fills you up. It actually contains such a wide array of vitamins, minerals, and protein that you could practically live on the potato alone. This applies to the potato as it comes out of the ground: a cheap, nutritious food that you can eat for about 9 cents a pound. The more a potato gets processed, however, the more its price goes up and its nutritional value goes down (i.e., you get much more fat and chemicals per unit of real potato). Birds Eye (General Foods) frozen french fries are 66 cents a pound, Frenchs' instant mashed potatoes are $1.30 a pound, regular potato chips are $1.18 to $1.58 a pound, and Pringle's New Fangled Potato Chips (Proctor and Gamble) is the winner at $2.10 a pound.[12] Each processing step offers a new opportunity for profits.

Of course, the potato is just one example of a basic, inexpensive, low-profit staple turned into an expensive, high-profit "modern" food. Big profits are made the same way in the breakfast cereals industry, which the Federal Trade Commission has called a "shared monopoly," with the Big Four dividing up 91 percent of sales![13] In October 1975, General Mills was getting $75.04 per bushel for corn in the form of Cocoa Puffs. Farmers were getting $2.95 a bushel for corn. Quaker Oats was charging $69.44 a bushel for corn (Cap'n Crunch) and $110.04 per bushel for wheat that has been "puffed." Food industry investigator Jim Hightower did similar checking and found there is only 2 cents' worth of wheat in a regular-sized box of Wheaties (General Mills) selling for 53 cents. The box costs more than the wheat.[14] General Mills, in an effort not to lose the nutritionally conscious, also puts out Total. But, as Dr. Michael Jacobson of the Center for Science in the Public Interest points out, Total is merely Wheaties sprayed with vitamins. The additional cost to General Mills is half a cent; to you, 22 cents.[15] Not surprisingly, the breakfast food market has averaged almost twice the profit level of the food industry in general.

In highly processed foods, freshness, color, shape, and texture are frequently chemically induced. This makes it possible for big processors to get by with cheaper grades of farm products. In 1971 Alfred Eames, Jr., chairman of Del Monte, cited its pudding cup desserts as an example of a "continuing shift" to "higher-profit formulated or 'manufactured' products." "What do they have to offer?" he asked. "Among other things, above-average profit margins and little or no dependence on agricultural commodity prices."[16]

Ironically, according to a Federal Trade Commission study, most of the processing technologies were developed with public funds—many through Pentagon contracts—reminiscent of Napoleon's awarding of the first contract for canned food in 1810 for his far-traveling army. Your tax dollars bought the research for frozen concentrated juices, prepared mixes, low-calorie foods and drinks, baby foods, dried milk products, instant beverages, frozen poultry, and refrigerated biscuits.[17]

Advertising is the other part of the growth formula of the giants. In product lines dominated by only three or four corporations, advertising allows each company to increase its sales volume without lowering its price below a competitor's—an unsporting act that would narrow the comfortable profit margins of all "club" members.

The food processing industry puts a greater share of its budget into advertising ($13 a year for every man, woman, and child in America) and less into research than any other industry. The National Commission on Food Marketing reported that in 1966 the U.S. food industry spent, for basic food and nutrition research, only one tenth of 1 percent of what it spent on advertising. Already by 1962 the food industry's advertising accounted for more than a fifth of all advertising and was second in size only to cosmetics and toiletries. To be a big food processor a company has to advertise tremendously, but to afford to do this it has to be already well-established. Of the almost 30,000 food firms, the twenty biggest accounted for over 70 percent of all food advertising. The fifty largest food companies accounted for 63 percent of all advertising on television.

It is precisely these giant food companies, which have succeeded by maximum processing and all-out advertising, that have been expanding abroad—first into Canada, Latin America, Western Europe, and South Africa, then into the Far East, and now even into Africa.

Branded Consciousness

The immediate goal of a food company is brand consciousness: making consumers conscious of supposed differences between its product and Brand X. You can be sure you have brand consciousness if you reach for the brand-name product even though it seems identical (and probably is) with the one having the private label of the supermarket chain. It is the development of this brand loyalty, not feeding people, that is the goal of multinational companies in underdeveloped countries. The former chairman of Nabisco, Lee Bickmore, told us that his yardstick for measuring success of his company in Brazil would be whether people no longer ask for crackers but instead ask for Ritz. "That's what I call consumer demand," he said.

What a global food company, then, has to offer underdeveloped countries is not good food but good advertising. And as a multinational operator, it can repeat the same performance with each new audience

—recycling a successful advertising campaign based on research originally paid for by sales in the American market.

The costs of designing such a campaign could never be afforded by a local firm. As Robert Ledogar in his well-documented probe of American food and drug companies in Latin America observes, "Translating this success [of a U.S. advertising campaign] into another language is so much easier for a multinational firm than developing new products to meet specific local needs."[18]

General Foods brought in marketing and advertising experts when it acquired Kibon, its Brazilian ice cream subsidiary.[19] Why not, they reasoned, promote Kibon products in rural areas by offering toys made of popsicle sticks? But the real problem was how to get urban Brazilians to eat ice cream in the winter rainy season. One bright idea was "lucky visits": A Kibon representative might some evening call at your house and award you a gift certificate if you had a pint of Kibon's ice cream in the refrigerator. (The suspense was undercut for millions since they are too poor to have refrigerators.)

In Mexico, General Foods took over a dried-soup company to serve as its launching vehicle for Jell-O. It relied on a tried and true promotional gimmick: Put on the back of each three-pack carton a plastic Walt Disney figure (costing 6 cents each) and then saturate the media encouraging kids to aspire to be "the first to collect all 24." In one test market Jell-O sales jumped 1000 percent in one week. (Jell-O has virtually *no* nutritional value.)

Also in Mexico, General Foods masterminded a way to get Mexicans to pay more for one of their most traditional food items—chili powder. It added a few herbs like oregano and marjoram, figured out how small the packets had to be to get the cost within the reach of lower-income buyers (50 centavos each) and shaped the envelopes, called *triangulitos,* to imitate a locally popular stew flavoring. General Foods then topped it all off with a huge advertising campaign complete with a singing jingle, display signs in thousands of small shops throughout the countryside, and promotional gimmicks like a lottery and a TV contest.

Soft Drinks—Something for Everyone?

Although most multinational food processors aim their products at small upper-income groups, some are determined to market *something* to the poor—even to the very poor. But is it possible to find a product that the poor will want and that can be priced within the reach of millions while still producing a profit large enough to support the big advertising budget necessary to make the poor want it? Nothing fits this description better than soft drinks. The ingredients cost little— they're basically sugar and water. Yet the poor can be made to think of soft drinks as symbols of the good life.

The most extensive dietary impact of foreign corporations in the underdeveloped world is unquestionably coming from soft drinks. In many underdeveloped countries, as diverse culturally as Iran and Venezuela, the jump in sugar consumption is attributed largely to increased soft drink sales. Mexicans go through well over a staggering 14 billion bottles a year, or nearly five bottles per man, woman, and child *every week*.[20]

With such volume markets, even a small profit on each bottle translates into big advertising budgets and big profits. According to Albert Stridsberg, writing in *Advertising Age*, it is saturation advertising that makes the difference. He notes with satisfaction that "in the poorest regions of Mexico where soft drinks play a functional role in the diet [whatever that means!] it is the international brands—Coke and Pepsi—not local off-brands, which dominate." Coke, having taken over several local bottlers' brands, has "captured" 42 percent of the Mexican market. Stridsberg evidently thinks that Coca-Cola's advertisers should be commended that "a Palestinian refugee urchin, shining shoes in Beirut, saves his piastres for a real Coca-Cola, at twice the price of a local cola."[21]

To appreciate how deeply soft drinks can penetrate into the most remote regions of an underdeveloped country, we would like to quote from a letter written by a Mexican priest, Father Florencio, in June 1974:

It seems that soft drinks are a very important factor in the development of villages. I have heard some people say they can't live one day without drinking a soft drink. Other people, in order to display social status, must have soft drinks with every meal, especially if there are guests. . . .

Near the larger towns where daily salaries are a little higher, soft drinks are cheaper. But in the very remote villages where people earn much less, and where soft drinks have to be transported in by animals, soft drinks cost in many places up to twice as much. The typical family in Metlatonoc can't earn more than 1,200 to 2,000 pesos a year. But even the little they receive each year they spend drinking soft drinks. In the richest village in this area, Olinala, where the majority of people are artisans and earn from 25 to 70 pesos a day [$2.00 to $5.60], about 4,000 bottles of soft drinks are consumed each day. Olinala has 6,000 inhabitants.

The great majority of people are convinced that soft drinks must be consumed every day. This is mainly due to extensive advertising, especially on the radio which is so widespread in the mountains. . . . In the meantime, in these same villages, natural products such as fruit are consumed less—in some families just once a week. Other families sell their own natural products in order to buy soft drinks. . . .[22]

Robert Ledogar found Coca-Cola has also been busy in Brazil. Coca-Cola's competition came from a local popular soft drink with stimulant properties, made from the guaraná fruit, grown by small farmers in the Amazon basin. Unlike Coke, the caffeine in guaraná is a natural ingredient, extracted from the seeds of the guaraná tree. Because it is pasteurized it

avoids several controversial additives used by Coca-
Cola (and Pepsi Cola) products. In 1972, Coca-Cola
decided to undercut the popular local drink once and
for all. It began to produce Guaraná Fanta. It is entirely artificial, however, hardly the "real thing."

Fanta Orange is Coca-Cola's biggest seller in Brazil
after Coke itself. Despite its name Fanta Orange contains no orange juice. Yet Brazil is the world's largest
exporter of orange juice. Brazil sells almost all of its
orange crop to foreigners, mostly to the United States
where Coca-Cola is one of the prime buyers for its
Snow Crop and Minute Maid orange juice brands.
Brazilian consumption of oranges is very low and
many Brazilians suffer from a vitamin C deficiency.
A study in 1969–1970 of working-class families in
populous Sao Paulo found that poor working-class
families obtained only about half of the minimum daily
requirement of vitamin C.

Ledogar comments in his study that the companies
are "anxious to avoid adding costly nutritious [natural]
ingredients to their products" that might force them out
of an expanding "poor" market. Fanta-Uva ("Grape")
has not a drop of grape juice. Yet in southern Brazil
there is a chronic "surplus" of grapes—sometimes
over 200,000 tons—that necessitates government-sup-
port programs.

Another strategy is to reach a younger and younger
market of new consumers. Brazilian Robert Orsi who is
in charge of Pepsi's million-dollar advertising account
adapted Pepsi's American advertising campaign to the
"needs" of the Brazilian market. The "Pepsi Generation" became the "Pepsi Revolution." Orsi explains
the choice:

In this country the young don't have protest channels;
the present generation didn't receive any political
or social education. So we provide them with a
mechanism for protest. It is protest through consumption; the teenager changes from the old-fashioned Coca-Cola and adopts Pepsi, the Pepsi with
a young and new image, and he is happy, because
he is young and young people drink Pepsi.

The seduction of the youth market begins right at school. The cola companies provide or finance refrigerators and other appliances and provide free soft drinks at school events in exchange for permission to sell in the schools. Dr. Anne Dias of the Nutrition Institute in Rio de Janeiro surveyed six- to fourteen-year-old school children. She found high levels of consumption of Coke, Fanta, and Pepsi (one to two bottles per day) by all but the very poor with family incomes under $80 monthly. Dr. Dias also found vitamin deficiencies even in the diets of the rich children (who were the highest soft-drink consumers). Middle-class children showed symptoms of protein malnutrition as well as vitamin deficiency. The children of poor families, of course, suffered from both protein-calorie malnutrition and vitamin deficiencies. Virtually none of the children drank milk.

In Zambia babies have become malnourished because their mothers fed them Coke and Fanta, believing it is the best thing they can give their children. In the area of the country that produces much of the world's copper, Dr. Stevens, the only pediatrician, reports that 54 percent of the seriously malnourished children admitted to the Children's Hospital at Ndola have "Fanta Baby" written on the progress charts at the foot of their beds. The Zambian government now has reportedly banned Fanta advertisements "because of their influence on the poor."[23]

Canned Pineapple by the Slice

Besides soft drinks, some of the least nutritious foods the companies have been able to devise are now reaching the poor. While frozen foods and aerosol cans clearly can never be sold to the poor, there are other products that can reach them by being divided up into smaller units. A smaller salable unit means a smaller price—but, of course, higher cost per volume.

Just visit many of the shacklike stores in poor neighborhoods and rural areas throughout the Third World. You will see chewing gum sold by the stick and even the half stick; Ritz crackers counted out one by one; Kellogg's Frosted Flakes scooped out of regular boxes and sold by the cup; popsicles split; a roll of Charms divided up; cigarettes sold singly; a pack of two ITT's Hostess Twinkies cupcakes split open to sell separately. In pineapple-rich Mexico, you even find stores selling Del Monte's canned pineapple by the slice.

As we have seen, the strength of the multinational food company is not food, but advertising and marketing strategies. Advertising reaches into the most remote villages of the underdeveloped world. Mr. V. G. Rajadhyaksha, former chairman of Unilever (Lever Brothers, Good Humor Ice Cream, Lipton's in the United States) in India, is enthusiastic about the "new and exciting challenge" of "penetrating rural markets."[24] His goal is to sell Unilever's products in 565,000 Indian villages. Unilever has been persuading "dealers" in the larger towns to open branches, particularly in those villages where they have relatives. No promotional vehicle is beyond consideration, including cinema vans with advertising films, puppet shows, clowns, wall paintings, and sales personnel on stilts. Radio advertising is possible in the so-called well-to-do rural villages where 30 to 50 percent of the people have transistors. In any Third World country, go into the smallest shop in the most remote village and you will have a good chance of finding a placard for Nestlé or for Coca-Cola.

Lee Bickmore, the former Nabisco chairman quoted earlier, long ago saw the connection between media advertising and getting Ritz crackers into the smallest stores:

> Why, we plan someday to advertise all over the world. We might spend, say, $8 million for an advertisement on a communications satellite system. It might reach 359 million people. So what we are doing now is establishing the availability of our products in retail outlets all over the world.[25]

With this advertising effort, even those with very little money are reached. It persuades them that food in a package has special powers. Its subtle message is that their traditional diets of beans, corn, millet, and rice are worthless compared to what Americans eat.

Mexican nutritionist Joaquin Cravioto has studied the changing food habits in Mexican villages. He told us that the *compesinos* are switching from traditional corn tortillas to white breads like Pan Bimbo (ITT's name for Wonder Bread south of the border). ITT might argue that it has more vitamins ("enriched") but the reality is that a poor family's few pesos could buy much more nourishment if they were used to buy tortillas. As nutritionist Alan Berg notes, "Industrial processing inevitably elevates a product's cost beyond that of an equal quantity of the staple."[26] Berg, working for several years in India, found that "saturation food advertising convinced many low-income families they *must* buy certain high-priced nutritious products to keep their children well and alert." As a result, Berg found low-income families "seduced into spending a disproportionate amount of their income on canned baby foods and similar items *at the expense* of more needed staples."

If people in the United States insist on processed, branded food, they simply end up by spending more of the family income on food. Nobody starves, although nutrition suffers. But in underdeveloped countries where it is common for families to have to spend 80 percent of their income on food, the impact of shifting to more costly but less nutritious food is grave.

―――――――――――

How often we see in developing countries that the poorer the economic outlook, the more important the small luxury of a flavored soft drink or smoke . . . to the dismay of many would-be benefactors, the poorer the malnourished are, the more likely they are to spend a disproportionate amount of whatever they have on some luxury rather than on what they need. . . . Observe, study, learn [how to sell in rapidly changing rural societies]. We try to do it at

IFF. It seems to pay off for us. Perhaps it will for you too.

> H. Walter, Chairman of the Board, International
> Flavors and Fragrances, "Marketing in
> Developing Countries," *Columbia Journal
> of World Business,* Winter 1974

Lack of effective media in developing communities inhibits demand stimulation activities. Creative, adaptive applications of demand stimulating techniques are needed for the developing communities.

> Charles C. Slater, "Foreign Agribusiness
> Contribution to Marketing Agricultural
> Products," May 1972

What is it that GFC can contribute to a foreign subsidiary? Well, first we have more than 10 percent of all the food researchers in private industry in this country, and therefore we have a capability in food technology to contribute. Our Dream Whip and Gainsburger dog food products, for example, were technical achievements.

> President, General Foods

38. Do They Really Kill Babies?

Question: Some corporations have been criticized for marketing infant feeding formula in underdeveloped countries. And yet, isn't a high protein and vitamin-packed formula exactly what poor mothers need to get their babies started out on the right track?

Our Response: When the birth rate in industrial countries started to decline in the 1960s, articles in business magazines proclaimed the crisis: "The Baby Bust" and "The Bad News in Babyland."[1] One response of baby food corporations was to diversify into other products. Another was to market to the fast-growing population of infants in underdeveloped countries. Sales of infant formula in underdeveloped countries by Abbott Laboratories, American Home Products, and Bristol Myers (through its Mead Johnson Division) began to increase faster than sales at home. Nestlé, with 81 plants in 27 underdeveloped countries and 728 sales centers throughout the world, intensively promotes its Lactogen, Nan, and Cerelac. Borden and Carnation are also in on the growing business.

Most people would assume that sales of baby formula stand in dramatic contrast to the pushing of non-nutritious processed food. Why is it then that over five years ago international agencies such as the World Health Organization (WHO) began to look upon the increased sales of infant formula in underdeveloped countries as a serious health *problem?* Indeed, a public interest group in England, War on Want, in 1974 launched an international campaign claiming that the promotion of infant formula in underdeveloped countries was contributing to severe malnutrition and even to the death of infants.[2] When their pamphlet was translated into German as "Nestlé Kills Babies," Nestlé sought $5 million in damages in the Swiss courts. Nestlé charged that the accusations in the pamphlet—that its efforts were unethical and immoral, that its marketing techniques resulted in infant death, and that it disguised its representatives as medical personnel—were all defamatory. At the last minute Nestlé decided to drop these three claims of defamation. The only charge which Nestlé pressed was that the pamphlet's title "Nestlé Kills Babies" was defamatory. Although the judge ruled in favor of Nestlé on this count, he declared, "This verdict is no acquittal [of Nestlé]."

What did the judge mean? What is the evidence that links the marketing of bottled formula to increased infant death?

In underdeveloped countries the mortality rate for bottle-fed infants is about double that of breast-fed.

A recent Inter-American Investigation of Mortality in Childhood, checking on the causes of 35,000 infant deaths, has determined that "nutritional deficiency" as an underlying or associated cause of death was "less frequent in infants breast fed and never weaned than in infants who were never breast fed or only for limited periods."[3] In rural Punjab, India, according to a 1974 report in the medical journal, *The Lancet,* "in the study population virtually all infants died who did not receive breast milk in the first months of life."[4] Two decades ago when breast-feeding was widespread among the poor, severe malnutrition was usually held off beyond the absolutely crucial first year of a child's life. But now, according to World Bank nutritionist Alan Berg, the rapid decline in breast-feeding over the past two decades has caused the average age of the onset of malnutrition to drop from eighteen months to a more critical eight months in several countries studied.[5]

Baby formula displaces mother's milk. But because, as scientific research indicates, mother's milk has changed and evolved along with the human race, it, like nothing else, can sustain the newborn. It contains not the "highest amounts" but the *proper* amounts of proteins and fats for the human baby. Human milk contains only 1.3 percent protein; cow's milk, 3.5 percent.[6] The protein, mineral and fat levels in mother's milk, notes Dr. Hugh Jolly, a prominent London pediatrician writing in the London *Times,*[7] suits the capacity of a human baby's kidney perfectly. Calves need and can handle more protein because they grow much faster. A six-week calf is, after all, already a small cow. These are just some of the reasons why pediatrics professor Paul Gyorgy of the University of Pennsylvania likes to say, "Cow's milk is best for baby cows and human breast milk is best for human babies."[8]

If you still need to be convinced that nature knows what it is doing, please note that human milk comes complete with infection immunizers for humans, especially critical in unsanitary living conditions. Scientists hypothesize that the immunity probably results from the initial dose of antibodies in the colostrum (the yellowish fluid that comes from the mother's breast a few days after birth). Apparently colostrum protects the child against locally common infections, particularly those of the intestinal tract, and against food allergies. "This might explain why allergies are more common in artificially fed babies," comments Dr. Alan Berg. "Gastroenteritis is almost unknown in breast-fed babies, whereas it may be lethal in those fed on cow's milk, especially where sterilization of bottles may be impossible," notes Dr. Jolly.[9] Diarrhea, which can prevent the absorption of any nutrients at all, is rare among breast-fed babies.[10] A mother can adequately feed her infant for at least six months. Even mothers who are themselves malnourished can adequately breast-feed—although partially at the expense of their own tissues. Physiologists agree that the first months of life are crucial for normal brain development. The negative effects of later malnutrition, though highly undesirable, are far more remediable.

Actually a child can be well nourished on breast milk for two years or more if a few other foods are added—and they certainly need not be from a can. In some cultures children are breast fed much longer. As recently as forty years ago, Chinese and Japanese mothers nursed their children as long as five and six years; Caroline Islanders up to ten years; and Eskimoes up to fifteen years.

Several multinational companies, however, have not been satisfied with nature—or at least, not satisfied that nature seemed to leave no room for commercial exploitation. But to create a market where none seemed to exist, multinational corporations found they could play upon another aspect of human nature—the natural desire of parents to ensure a healthy baby. Exposed to countless billboards, newspaper advertisements, and color posters, parents in underdeveloped countries come to equate a happy, healthy baby with a bottle or can of Lactogen. They learn that educated and upper-class families use feeding bottles. They, too, want the best for their baby. The tragic irony, however, is that for most parents in underdeveloped countries, formula feeding actually endangers their baby's life.

First, most families simply cannot afford to buy the necessary amount. To feed one four-month-old infant in Guatemala would require almost 80 percent of the per capita income. To feed such a baby in Lima, Peru, adequately by bottle would take almost 50 percent.[11]

These cost estimates do not include bottles, artificial nipples, cooking utensils, refrigeration, fuel, and medical care (often ten times more needed for the formula-fed than for the breast-fed child). How can a family devote over half or more of its income to food for their youngest and totally unproductive member? The answer is that it cannot.

The seeming solution is to "stretch" the formula with water. Reports of dilution are commonplace. A 1969 survey in Barbados found that 82 percent of the families using formula as the sole food for two- or three-month-old babies were making a four-day can last five days to three weeks.[12] Dr. Adewale Omololu, a professor of nutrition in Nigeria, reported treating a severely malnourished baby whose mother had switched from breast-feeding to a bottle. For a month the child had nothing but water from the bottle because there was only enough money for the *bottle;* it took a month to save up to buy the can of formula!

On diluted formula, a baby loses weight and deteriorates progressively into the malnourished condition called marasmus. The child becomes increasingly susceptible to infection, a problem compounded by bottle-feeding, as we will see.

Second, formula-feeding requires clean water and conditions for sanitary preparation that often do not exist even for the middle classes in underdeveloped countries. "Wash your hands thoroughly with soap each time you have to prepare a meal for baby," reads the Nestlé's *Mother Book* distributed by the company in Malawi.[13] But 66 percent of the households even in the capital city have no washing facilities. "Place bottle and lid in a saucepan of water with sufficient water to cover them. Bring to the boil and allow to boil for 10 minutes," is the counsel of the Cow and Gate Company in its Babycare Booklet for West Africa. The text is accompanied by a photo of a gleaming aluminum saucepan on an electric stove. But you have to go far to find an electric stove in West Africa. Most West African mothers have to cope with a "three-stone" kitchen, that is, three stones supporting a pot above a wood fire. There is only one pot. One pot for sterilizing the baby's bottle and for cooking the family meal. To the mother's eye, putting the bottle in boiling water doesn't seem to do much, anyway; so sterilizing is probably forgotten.

The bottle, the nipple, and the formula are invariably found in the context of illiteracy, a contaminated water supply and the lack of washing, refrigeration or cooling facilities, and household hygiene. The combination, then, of malnutrition and exposure to bacteria sets up a vicious circle. The infant gets chronic diarrhea and therefore is unable to assimilate even the diluted formula. The infant's nutritional state worsens and it becomes even more vulnerable to respiratory infection and gastroenteritis. This is the state of millions of children who could have been adequately nourished by their mother's milk.

The companies like to argue that they are *fulfilling* and not creating a need. "Just think what the situation would be if we were to say, all right, we think these people [the critics] are right. What would the result be?" asks Ian Barter of Cow and Gate Company.[14] "It would be the death of thousands of children because there are tens of thousands of mothers in these countries who have got to have some substitute for their milk in order to feed their babies."

Let's look at the facts. Nutritionists recognize that there are some women who cannot feed for physiological reasons. But even the companies admit that at most such mothers are fewer than 5 percent.[15] Dr. David Morley surveyed a rural Nigerian village and found less than 1 percent of mothers had serious breast-feeding problems.[16]

Indeed, confidence—lack of anxiety—seems to be the key to breast-feeding without difficulties. Several doctors now believe that the typical company advertising does more than anything else to undermine the mother's confidence. By just mentioning "women who do not have milk" and "poor quality" milk, the companies place not so subtle doubts in a mother's mind about her ability to breast-feed.

The companies also stress that their products are needed by women who work. In fact, the percentage of Third World women who work away from their families is very low. (Countries where there is far greater employment for women, such as the Soviet Union and Cuba, provide extensive paid maternity leaves and day care centers at the workplace, which allow working mothers to breast-feed several times a day.)

But even if there is a need for artificial feeding, does it follow that a country needs a half dozen profit-oriented multinational firms? Is this the only alternative that you, say, as a minister of health, could think of for your country? Is the technology of making an equivalent baby food really so difficult? The United Nations Protein Advisory Group has recommended that underdeveloped countries come up with a product *better* than the expensive, easily contaminated products of the world's largest companies.[17] Various nutritionists have designed, for mothers who cannot breast-feed, nourishing artificial feeding regimes suitable to low-income homes with minimum hygiene, no refrigeration, and limited cooking facilities—and several would cost only a quarter of the current high-priced formulas.[18]

Finally, the companies try to defend themselves by claiming that they really aim their products only at the rich. According to Ross Laboratories' president David O. Cox, only "coincidentally" do his company's promotional activities reach the poor.[19]

This claim again does not fit the facts. The companies have actually devised sophisticated and often ingenious promotion strategies specifically for expanding sales down the income ladder. To begin with, colored wall posters of a healthy baby clutching a feeding bottle greet women, both rich and poor, who enter hospitals and clinics. The companies also employ milk nurses, women who commonly are fully trained nurses. In Nigeria 96 percent of mothers who used bottle-feeding thought they had been so advised by impartial medical personnel, mainly nurses. In fact, these nurses were company representatives. Nestlé employs 4000 to 5000 such "mothercraft advisors" in underdeveloped countries. Dressed in crisp white uniforms, they visit new mothers, no matter what their income level is. In many countries these nurses are allowed to enter maternity wards. Often they receive a commission in addition to salary. Moreover, higher pay offered by the companies diverts nurses trained at public expense from basic full-time health work.

In addition, the companies provide free samples, often through the hospitals. Surveys have shown that just as many illiterate mothers as literate ones receive samples, indicating there was no attempt to select mothers who were able to afford the product.[20] Companies often supply hospitals with free formula supplies, hoping that mothers will feel they must keep on using the products. Abbott Laboratories recently sold $300,000 worth of Similac to the New York City hospitals for only $100,000. A city spokesperson said, "For the company, it's an investment. They hope to get the future business."[21]

Another device clearly aimed at the poor are "milk banks,"[22] usually in hospitals and clinics. They sell the commercial formulas at discount prices to mothers who can prove they are really poor. In this way they can expand sales among the really poor without lowering the price in the normal commercial market. Milk banks in their hospitals just serve to convince women that they need something that they really don't. But even at discount prices (usually 30 to 40 percent), the formulas are too expensive for parents to buy enough. In Guatemala City, fifty mothers buying at a milk bank were questioned. Despite the discount, they could not afford enough so they "prepared the bottles with less milk and more water and in this way the milk lasted longer." Tea or chocolate drink is often substituted.

Radio is also an advertising vehicle to reach the poor. A typical day in Sierra Leone sees fifteen 30-second radio advertisements for Nestlé: "Now Lactogen a better food cos it don get more protein and iron, all

de important things dat go make pikin strong and
will. . . . Lactogen and Love." The use of the common
dialect of the poor makes it hard for Nestlé to convince us that they are directing their advertising at only
those who can afford it.[23]

Under the pressure of unfavorable publicity, the
companies say they have modified their advertisements.[24] Now the commercial product is pushed as
"the next best thing to mother's milk," for cases in
which "you find you need a substitute or a supplement
to breast milk." Nestlé now recommends "an occasional bottle-feed—if you cannot breast-feed Baby entirely
yourself."

The tactic is ingenious. As a Consumers' Union–
funded study comments, "By openly recommending
breast feeding, the companies can earn their public
relations credits. At the same time, the companies can
undermine breast feeding by implying repeatedly that
a mother may not have enough milk and may need
supplementary bottles of formula."[25] La Leche League
International, an organization devoted to helping
women breast-feed, comments, "This 'supplementary'
formula is one of the greatest deterrents to establishing
a good milk supply, and frequent nursing is one of
the greatest helps."[26]

Such ingenious modification of tactics serves to
emphasize how the solution to this grave situation is
not simply another "code of conduct" for the companies. One such code, already drawn up, would have
company milk nurses wear the company insignia on
their uniform. The companies must really think their
critics are simple-minded! All the codes condone the
use of medical facilities to market their products.[27]

Nestlé hoped to get some public relations mileage
out of its claim that it no longer would dress its salespeople in white uniforms. White uniforms obviously
gave the impression of medical authority. What Nestlé
neglected to say is that its salespeople now are wearing
blue and yellow uniforms. Now really. Doesn't a uniform, any uniform, still carry authority?

Not only is the decline in breast-feeding a personal

tragedy for babies who suffer malnutrition and disease, but it can be calculated as a loss to the natural resources of the country. In Kenya, notes Alan Berg, "The estimated $11.5 million annual loss in breast milk is equivalent to two-thirds of the national health budget, or one-fifth of the average annual economic aid."[28] In the Philippines $17 million was wasted on imported milk in 1958; by 1968, the number of mothers breast-feeding their babies dropped by 31 percent, and the national dollar loss had doubled. As breast-feeding declined sharply in the 1960s, Colombian milk imports soared; in 1968 they were seven times greater than the 1964–1967 average. Berg concludes that "losses to the developing countries more likely are in the billions."

An attack on the bottle-baby tragedy is now underway in some underdeveloped countries. Here are only a few examples. In Papua, New Guinea, the director of public health is enlisting the support of all health workers to persuade storekeepers not to display formula company advertisements.[29] Dar es Salaam University in Tanzania has put out a new guide on baby care for paramedical workers warning of the dangers of formula feeding. In Segbwena, Sierra Leone, a Nutrition Rehabilitation Unit is feeding malnourished children on locally available foods and showing mothers how to prepare well-balanced and inexpensive meals for their families.[30] The Nairobi City Council, Kenya, has banned milk nurses. Some African governments have even instructed rural health workers to destroy formula ads wherever they find them.

In contrast to the private multinational companies, a state-owned company in Zambia announces on its can of milk: "BREAST FEED YOUR CHILD." The label goes on to persuade the potential buyer not to buy the product unless the purchaser can afford to buy enough for many months.

Public action in the industrial countries to halt the ongoing tragedy did not stop with the Nestlé trial in the summer of 1976. Later that summer, groups from eight countries working on infant formula malnutrition met in Bern to plan and coordinate their efforts. That fall in New York the Sisters of the Precious Blood, working with the Interfaith Center for Corporate Responsibility (ICCR), brought suit against Bristol Myers. The Sisters charged Bristol Myers with committing fraud in its proxy statement to shareholders. In its statement Bristol Myers claimed to have been "totally responsive" to the concerns of the earlier stockholder resolution. Moreover, the company claimed that it does not promote its products to people who cannot afford to use them safely, that it does not sell directly to the consumer at all but only through professional medical personnel. The Sisters, working with ICCR, gathered over 1000 pages of testimony and other evidence from around the world that directly contradict these claims. This documentation demonstrated that Bristol Myers does use many techniques to reach the poor, including selling its products in poor people's stores, distributing free samples through health clinics, and using sales personnel dressed as nurses.

Even though the suit was not successful—the Sisters' appeal was dismissed by the U.S. District Court in 1977—the publicity of the suit, combined with the earlier Nestlé trial, launched the concern over infant formula malnutrition into an international campaign. The Infant Formula Action Coalition (INFACT, 1701 University Avenue, SE, Minneapolis, MN 55414) formed to coordinate the campaign. Its first move was to launch a boycott of Nestlé until the corporation agrees to stop all promotion of infant formula in the Third World. Many groups such as Clergy and Laity Concerned and Church Women United immediately backed INFACT and the Nestlé boycott. In addition, a Senate subcommittee held hearings on the problem in May of 1978. Thus news of the bottle baby tragedy is spreading rapidly. Church and community groups around the country are educating their constituencies using the film "Bottle Babies" (available from INFACT). The crisis of infant formula malnutrition is thus becoming for more and more people an example of how corporate economic motives not only can fail to serve the interests of people, but can directly contribute to their suffering.

We hope that by now we have given you an understanding of what the judge in the Swiss trial meant when, after ruling in favor of Nestlé, he added: "This verdict is no acquittal [of Nestlé]."

In an interview on West German radio in 1975 a pediatrician on the staff of Nairobi's Kenyatta National Hospital, Dr. Elizabeth Hillman, told this story:

> A short while ago . . . the Nestlé's representatives came to visit us at Nairobi's hospital to ask if we had any opinion about the publication "Nestlé Kills Babies." They really wanted us to say that Nestlé did not kill babies.
>
> We discussed this at length with them and were not able to say of course that Nestlé either does kill or does not kill, statistically speaking. But, to illustrate the point, I mentioned that there was a child over in our emergency ward . . . who was very near to death, because the mother was bottle-feeding with the Nestlé's product (Lactogen, a milk preparation), and out of interest I asked whether they would like to see the baby. I took the two representatives over into our emergency ward and as we walked in the door the baby collapsed and died. I had to leave these two non-medical gentlemen for a moment . . . and help with the resuscitation procedure. It was unsuccessful. And, after the baby was pronounced dead, we all watched the mother turn away from the dead baby and put the can of Nestlé's milk in her bag before she left the ward. . . . In a sense . . . it was a vivid demonstration of what bottle-feeding can do because this mother was perfectly capable of breast-feeding. The two gentlemen walked out of that room, very pale, shaken and quiet and there was no need to say anything more.[31]

Its broad geographical and product diversification,

its involvement with the population explosion in backward countries, where it makes cheap baby food, and finally, the fact that it keeps its cash in solid Swiss francs, make Nestlé *shares good insurance against depression, inflation, or revolution.*

Barrons, May 20, 1968

39. Agribusiness Abroad: A Boon for Americans?

Question: But if agribusiness shifts its production to underdeveloped countries, how does this hurt Americans? In fact don't we Americans at least get cheaper food?

Our Response: To understand what is the impact on Americans let us start with a look at the big plantation companies like Del Monte and Castle and Cooke (Dole).[1] They are spreading their production sites throughout the underdeveloped world. Most controversial is their shift of part of their pineapple production from Hawaii to the Philippines.

As recently as 1951 Hawaii produced three-fourths of the global supply. For years the big plantation companies imported thousands of low-wage workers from the Philippines and elsewhere. But, just as in an underdeveloped country, a dependence on tourism and importing goods rather than growing basic foods fueled inflation. In the 1960s plantation-worker unions struck several times for wages sufficient to cover the minimum cost of living. They eventually won the highest agricultural wages in the world: $2.85 an hour. These "high" wages combined with rising land values (due to competition from resort land speculators) have made Hawaii less attractive than other sites such as the Philippines, where wages can be as low as 15 cents an hour.

Over the past several years the Hawaiian state government has tried all the usual incentives offered by a typical underdeveloped country to keep Del Monte and Dole "home": defeat of a proposed minimum wage, weakened environmental protection standards, real property taxes permanently sliced in half, and tax-funded agricultural research.

While the plantation companies have snapped up these subsidies in the past, they now claim that they are not enough. Del Monte has already cut its Hawaiian production by 40 percent, expanded its production and canning in the Philippines, opened a new plantation in Kenya, and drawn up plans for pineapple production in Guatemala in 1977. The company now claims it will keep some operations open in Hawaii to supply the fresh pineapple market—in case the lid is blown off in the potentially politically explosive situation in the Philippines, Kenya, or Guatemala. Dole, with 100 percent of its operations in Hawaii as late as 1959, had only 25 percent there in 1975. Dole now operates 19,000 acres in the Philippines and in 1972 it expanded into Thailand.

What about the workers whose livelihoods have been made to depend on exporting pineapple from Hawaii? Their strike in 1974 in protest against the companies' shift of production was ineffectual, largely because of the difficulty of coordinating with pineapple workers in other countries.

The corporations talk about trying to get them jobs in hotels on the other islands. Responds Tony Hodges of the Life of the Land public interest lobby, "You don't take a 45-year-old guy (the average age of the pineapple workers) who's been picking pineapples all his life and, presto, put him in a suit and make him a night club entertainer."

Has the control of pineapple growing by a few giant corporations now shifting production abroad been in the interests of the people of Hawaii and of the United States as a whole? What if, alternatively, the United

States produced enough pineapples domestically, providing American workers—or even better, independent farmers—a decent income?

The shift by agribusiness of major segments of United States agriculture outside the United States, like the runaway manufacturing plants of the sixties and early seventies, will cost thousands of jobs. With Del Monte's shift of white asparagus production to Mexico that we already mentioned, over 6000 workers in California have lost their jobs. Moreover, as in manufacturing, the mere threat of such shifts acts as a check on the efforts of workers organizing for higher wages and better conditions here.

Displaced American agricultural workers and small farmers can no longer be conveniently thought of as being "absorbed" by a booming urban industrial economy. The unemployment and welfare rolls show that even now the economy is unable to absorb those *already* outside the rural sector. The defenders of agribusiness will assure us that new jobs in the United States will be created in machinery and other agricultural export factories selling to the modernized sectors in foreign countries. But how many? And how easily can someone be transformed from a truck farmer into a tractor factory worker? A middle-aged, unschooled tomato picker into an ammonia plant engineer?

The question suggests that the one thing we Americans could gain from the Global Supermarket is lower prices for food grown more cheaply abroad. But, while their foreign-produced products do, in fact, cost less to produce, we are very likely to pay the *same* price we did for the domestic product. The companies, not the consumer, pocket the savings.

Mushrooms are a good example. Only a few years ago several hundred competitive, family-owned companies canned mushrooms they bought from Pennsylvania farmers. Now many are being bought out or squeezed out by large corporations like Clorox (Mr. Mushroom), Green Giant (Dawn Fresh), and Castle and Cooke (Shady Oak West). These agribusiness giants are turning their backs on American growers and instead contracting in low-wage South Korea and

Taiwan.[2] As a result, mushroom imports have quadrupled. One out of three processed mushrooms is now an import. But does this loss of livelihood for American farmers and plant workers at least mean cheaper mushrooms for Americans? Not at all. Green Giant, which imports almost all of the mushrooms it sells in jars, admitted to the United States Tariff Commission that it could get plenty of high-quality mushrooms in this country but that the foreign imports mean greater profits for the Green Giant.[3] Now, as agribusiness watchdog Jim Hightower comments, "A few large food firms can fatten their profit margins on mushrooms, supposedly a low-calorie item."[4] Furthermore, the remaining American mushroom growers now give the excuse that they cannot pay decent wages to their workers because of competition from imports.

Similarly, in an investigation of pineapple profits, the federal Tariff Commission found that Del Monte and Dole "market the imported product at the same price that they ask for their domestically canned pineapple" despite the fact that wage costs at its foreign production sites are but a fraction of those in the United States. In fact, the small Maui Pineapple Co., which markets its entirely domestic-grown production through supermarket chain labels, sells for less than Del Monte and Dole foreign-grown imports.

The day might not be far off when multinational agribusiness firms will be able to manipulate prices as well as supply *on a global basis* through many of the "shared monopoly" practices corporations have already perfected in the United States. Once production has been shifted throughout the world, no national government would be able, even if it so desired, to know the truth about supply or costs.

United States Government Support of Agribusiness

Just because we ordinary Americans do not benefit from the expansion of U.S.-based agribusiness into underdeveloped countries does not mean that the

American government is not doing everything possible to encourage it. In addition to military, law and order, and financial support that helps keep governments in power that are favorable to American investment, the United States government provides a whole package of fiscal incentives and other inducements to corporate investment abroad.

Chief among the incentives are U.S. tax laws themselves. As stated earlier, a corporation can defer income earned by its subsidiary abroad as long as that income remains overseas. Even when earnings are brought back into the United States, taxes paid to foreign governments can be deducted from the total taxes owed. The upshot of these two rules is that a corporation has every incentive to open up overseas subsidiaries and to maximize—often through creative accounting—the portion of its total earnings that show up on its off-shore subsidiary's books. Corporations find they can also minimize taxes paid to foreign governments by simply setting up a one-room "subsidiary" in a tax-haven, such as Panama or the Bahamas. A corporation contracting for the production of vegetables in Mexico might technically sell the production to its Panama "subsidiary" only to sell it in turn to its headquarters in San Francisco. An additional encouragement for investment in Latin America was created by Congress in 1942 when it authorized U.S. corporations to conduct business there through what are called Western Hemisphere Trade Corporations that the government taxes at a reduced rate—34 percent instead of the usual 48 percent.[5]

Most significant, perhaps, is that the United States government puts itself, ultimately the American taxpayer, behind corporate investment abroad. The Overseas Private Investment Corporation (OPIC), a government initiated program backed by the United States Treasury, guarantees corporate investment abroad against losses incurred when a local currency cannot be converted into United States dollars, war damage, and expropriation. Through OPIC, the United States government has put a total of 3.2 billion tax dollars behind investment abroad by private companies. And it does so on easy terms: OPIC's rates average only 1.5 percent with terms as long as twenty years.

Nearly two-thirds of all U.S. private investment in underdeveloped countries, not including petroleum, is insured by OPIC.[6] Forty-one percent of OPIC insurance issued between 1974 and 1976 has gone to just eleven of the largest U.S. multinational corporations. OPIC has insured Del Monte's pineapple processing plant in Kenya and Ralston Purina's fast food chains in Brazil. In addition, OPIC provides loans to help corporations get started in underdeveloped countries. A recent loan went to establish an export-oriented vegetable processing plant in Costa Rica.

But OPIC is not a mere passive agent; it helps seek out investment opportunities. OPIC conducts investment-research trips to underdeveloped countries for corporate officers. It describes its own role as "brokerage": seeking out the most promising investments and making a "concerted effort to interest American companies in them." And in agriculture, the most promising investments involve large landholdings. As OPIC official Pat Counts explains, "our OPIC policy . . . limits our assistance to projects involving large land holdings."[7]

The most pernicious aspect of OPIC is, however, that it puts the United States government in opposition to any movement or government in an underdeveloped country that might even potentially expropriate American businesses, even if such movements are working in the best interests of the majority of local people. One of the motivations for United States covert support for anti-Allende forces in Chile in 1970–1973 was the belief that Allende's success would exhaust OPIC's reserves and be a drain on the United States Treasury, the final guarantor for OPIC-insured losses in cases of expropriation.

During 1977 the AFL-CIO led an attack against OPIC on the grounds that its promotion of U.S. agribusiness investment abroad robs Americans of jobs. Moreover, certain members of Congress were chagrined that OPIC was violating the human rights clauses of the 1975 Foreign Assistance Act. During the period 1974–1976 OPIC channelled more than 60 percent of its funds to only six countries, all of which have authoritarian regimes—Indonesia, the Philippines, South Korea, Brazil, Thailand and the Dominican Republic. Congress responded in 1978 by refusing to extend OPIC's authorization. Now OPIC is on the defensive. Through joint programs with the USDA, it is hoping to build support among farmers by convincing them that OPIC projects in cattle ranching and grain processing will expand markets for their grain.

Pitted Against the Hungry?

There is a more subtle but even graver problem for Americans. As multinational corporations expand into the underdeveloped world, American consumers are rapidly being made dependent on a whole range of imported agricultural products. Once this shift is made, there will no longer be hundreds of thousands of farms in the United States supplying the vegetables, fruits, meat, and even flowers Americans buy. *The food needs of American consumers will be made dependent on the active maintenance of a distorted land use system in underdeveloped countries.* We will be forced to translate our own legitimate food requirements into opposition to those of countries where hundreds of millions go hungry. Agribusiness, by putting American consumers at odds with the interests of the world's hungry, creates a type of interdependence no one needs.

The buying power of Americans—no longer able to find suppliers within the United States—will be a powerful suction force working against the land use changes that must be made now in underdeveloped countries if the hungry there are to eat. Already, of course, multinational agribusiness has made such changes more difficult, not only by giving the well-off a bigger stake in the *status quo,* but by encouraging governments' retreat on such basic issues as land reform, as we have seen in Mexico, the Philippines, and Iran to mention just a few countries.

This type of American food dependency fosters a certain foreign policy. American tax dollars are spent in both blatant and secret collaboration with regimes that repress efforts of the people to take control of the food resources they need to support themselves.

Once corporate interests put American farmers out of business, making America self-reliant in food will not be easy or accomplishable overnight. The implication, therefore, of an American food dependency created by corporate and government policies is that, when the oppressed in the underdeveloped countries do seize control and re-order their national priorities, we will be faced with shortages and higher prices— prices beyond the means of many of us.

The question therefore is: Will we continue to support policies of oppression to try to postpone that re-ordering or will we work now to put a halt to ever greater dependency both on monopolistic corporations and on the food resources that belong to other peoples?

In an earlier question (Question 35), it was suggested that agribusiness brought efficiency and production know-how to "backward" agricultural systems. In responding we have asked several key questions in an attempt to explain what agribusiness really offers:

- Which crops? They turned out to be luxury, non-essential items tying up valuable resources that could be producing staples.
- For whom? They turned out to be for the local and foreign elites.
- With what production model? It turned out to be contract farming—perhaps the very worst experience of American farmers with agribusiness.
- For whose benefit? Neither that of the majority in underdeveloped countries nor most Americans.

  The undernourished—usually a full 40 percent of the population in underdeveloped countries —are paying the cost of this kind of "modern agriculture." Not only do they not benefit, they find their lot deteriorating. The irony is that alternatives are not only possible; they are the very ones that are most accessible—as we will see in Part X.

Part IX

The Helping Handout: Aid for Whom?

40. Triage?

Question: Many people are talking about *triage*, the term coined on the battlefield to describe the sorting out of the wounded into three categories when it is clear that not everyone can be cared for. In order to save anyone at all, it is necessary to aid those with the greatest likelihood of survival. Those hopelessly wounded must be ignored for the sake of the survival of the others. Many experts are saying that we should apply the same principle in selecting countries that should receive our assistance. What is your opinion?

Our Response: In a very real sense our whole book is an answer to triage. The triage metaphor simply does not fit the reality of the world we have discovered through our research.

First, the triage concept is misleading because it implies that the United States has been giving aid according to some soft-hearted notion of need and that now we must be realistic, selecting recipients according to who is most likely to make it. But no one who has seriously looked at United States aid policies could accuse our country of being softhearted! As one member of the National Security Council put it, "To give food aid to countries just because people are starving is a pretty weak reason." No, as we will demonstrate in this Part, our aid is already highly selective, going to serve the narrow political and economic interests of certain groups in this country.

Second, triage assumes that the underdeveloped countries are on the receiving end only, when, in fact, many underdeveloped countries are net food exporters, particularly of high protein foods such as meat, seafood, and legumes. It reinforces the idea that these countries are the greatest burden because they have too many people. In fact, as we have shown in our response to Question 31, it is the industrial countries that are the major food importers. Between 1970 and 1974, four of the highest GNP countries—Japan, the United Kingdom, Italy, and West Germany—imported six times more grain than China and India, although these four countries have only one-fourth of the population of China and India.[1]

Third, triage is built on the scare notion that we are entering an era of absolute scarcity. According to the theory, food must be allocated judiciously to ensure the survival of—let's face it—ourselves.

Another analogy is suggested by biologist Garrett Hardin: that of the lifeboat. If we let everyone on board our lifeboat, we will all drown. But as we have seen throughout this book, the world has hardly reached this point. We have discussed what we call the "inefficiency of inequality"—that the main constraint on food production is the gross inequities in control over the earth's food-producing resources. The hungry have increasingly less control over the production process. The result? Tremendous waste: the underutilization of land, the expansion of nonfood and luxury crops to feed the already well-fed, and the feeding of over one-third of all the world's grain and at least one-quarter of the world's fish catch to livestock. As long as we have a system that is actively *creating* scarcity out of plenty, to say we are reaching natural limits is worse than merely misleading. The suggestion allows the present scarcity-generating system to go on unrecognized for what it is. Meanwhile people are manipulated with fear-evoking images of "shortages" and "overpopulation." Metaphors like triage thus work in the interests of those few who have seized power and wealth for themselves—forces that are steadily undermining the welfare of people both here and in underdeveloped countries.

41. Debt for Development?

Question: If agribusiness corporations cannot solve the problem of hunger, can the assistance given by the United States government do the job?

Our Response: One always hears about the United States "giving aid." In reality, however, more than half of American "aid" is not given at all but loaned with interest.[1] We all know a loan is not a gift even if the interest rates are low. Low interest rates have not prevented the debt obligation of the underdeveloped countries from becoming an increasingly unbearable burden. Between 1967 and 1976 the total debt burden of the non-oil producing underdeveloped countries, both public and private, increased over fourfold, from $43.7 billion to about $180 billion.[2]

Each year an ever greater portion of aid coming in must go out again just to repay loans received in previous years. By 1973, almost 40 percent of all loans and grants from foreign governments received by underdeveloped countries was spent on debt service payments on such past "aid."[3] But if debt service payments on loans from private lenders are also considered, by 1978 the sum paid out by non-oil exporting underdeveloped countries—over $13 billion—approached the *total* development assistance coming in from government sources in the industrial countries. In fact, according to AID official Abelardo L. Valdez, lenders in the industrial countries in some cases now receive more in loan repayments than they lend. In 1977, says

Valdez, the U.S. government received $150 million more in loan repayments from Latin American countries than it had provided in the form of AID and Export-Import Bank loans.[4]

Moreover, the debt service payments are growing faster than the rate of increases in aid. Between the mid-sixties and the end of the decade, the gross flows of external aid to Pakistan rose by 5 percent; but the debt service payments rose by 91 percent! (For many countries the level of aid is decreasing, not increasing.) Debt service payments are also going up twice as fast as the export earnings that bring in foreign exchange to repay the loan.[5] In some countries such as Bangladesh almost a quarter of export earnings must go out again just to pay off past debts. The percentage is growing rapidly. And a quarter is already far greater than what even bankers consider tolerable.[6]

It is an obviously no-win situation for the underdeveloped countries. Many Americans, nevertheless, are made to go on believing that all we can do to help is to increase aid. Not only will more aid of this type compound the debt burden, but it will also force a destructive all-out push for exports. The only way to get the foreign exchange to repay debts is to sell in the international marketplace. Internal development (building sanitation facilities, schools, and clinics, for example) based on local production and local currency does not count; it does not earn foreign exchange. Thus for most countries debt obligations lead right into the trade trap we discussed in Part VI.

In any discussion of development assistance these facts should never be forgotten: "Assistance" is largely loans and the debt they create can itself be the ultimate roadblock on the path to self-reliance. Debt takes an increasing bite out of development resources and ensures that a country's economic choices will be determined by foreign markets, foreign banks, and foreign development agencies often opposed to the internal needs of the country.

If development assistance were called "debt for development," the absurdity of thinking that this path could lead to self-reliant growth would be obvious.

42. Doesn't Our Food Aid Help?

Question: Throughout this book you seem to be talking about the potential of countries for food self-reliance. But what about the present? The United States has been the most generous country in the world trying to deal with present need through food aid. Since 1950 we have given over $25 billion in food aid. Doesn't food aid both help the hungry *now*— and even make it possible to build toward food self-reliance?

Our Response: The question suggests that U.S. food aid has been an expression of the concern of the American people. Undoubtedly the intentions of ordinary Americans supporting food aid have been genuine and praiseworthy. But the first thing we had to learn in trying to respond to this question is that the intentions of the American people may be very different from the actual design and impact of United States policy.

At different periods American food aid has served many purposes for diverse interest groups, but at no time has its primary aim been to feed the hungry. In fact, it was not until 1966 that humanitarian intent was even written into the food aid law. Food aid has been an extension of foreign policy, farm and business interests, which in most cases are mutually supportive.

To understand the origins of food aid you need look no further than an interview with the coordinator of United States food aid in the Ford administration, Robert R. Spitzer. After recounting how, in the early 1950s, farmers' organizations were calling for something to be done with the mounting surpluses threatening their incomes and how "humanitarians" hated to see food wasted, Spitzer continues:

There were other people who realized that there was a great potential for the products of the American agricultural community, and that perhaps by wisely placing some of these foods in certain countries, we would develop buyers for future commodities. Then we weren't thinking too much of oil, but I think some of our advanced thinkers were beginning to realize that we were not independent so far as many of the trace minerals are concerned. So someone had to do some thinking. Okay, what do we have to ship out? So the Public Law (P.L. 480) [food aid] was passed.[1]

Spitzer touched on virtually all the motives for food aid: the farmers' interest in unloading potentially price-depressing surpluses, the interest of agribusiness corporations in creating markets, and as a means to assure access to strategic materials. The only motive he neglected to mention was the use of food aid in support of United States military intervention, one of its principal functions since the mid-1960s.

Spitzer referred to the "advanced thinkers" who saw in food the leverage to obtain strategic raw materials. Therein, in fact, lay the rationale for the India Emergency Food Act of 1951, which is the direct predecessor of the current food aid authorization (P.L. 480) passed in 1954. In 1951, India made an emergency request to the United States for grain to stave off famine precipitated by monsoon failure. Since the end of World War II, India had embargoed exports of monazite sands that contain thorium, used in the production of atomic energy. Now the American government seized on the threatened famine as an opportunity to have the embargo lifted.

Congressman Charles J. Kersten, Republican of Wisconsin, put it bluntly, "In return for the wheat we are asked to give to India, the very least we should ask of India is that it permit the United States to buy some of these strategic materials."[2]

P.L. 480, later also named "Food for Peace," was born out of an even more immediate crisis. A greater problem than how to acquire needed materials was how to get rid of an unnecessary one. American farmers had too much food. During the 1940s, grain production in the United States had increased by about 50 percent, while domestic consumption lagged well behind, increasing only by about 30 percent. Productivity increases, based on more fertilizers and pesticides, plus better seeds, and price supports for farmers, created enormous surpluses that were costing taxpayers $1 million a day just for storage.

These surpluses represented a terrible dilemma. The farm lobby would not allow them to be put on the domestic market. And if dumped on the world market, grain prices would drop by a dollar a bushel. U.S. grain corporations were opposed to such a disruption of their international commercial market. In 1952, at their national convention, the American Farm Bureau, a group representing large- and medium-sized farmers, proposed a solution: Create a secondary foreign market by allowing food-deficit countries to pay for American food imports in their own currencies instead of in dollars. That is what P.L. 480 did. P.L. 480, then, was seen as a way to help low-income countries, which otherwise would not constitute a market at all, to buy surplus American food while keeping the commercial dollar price up for higher-income countries. P.L. 480 meant the United States would have its cake and eat it too.

Such are the mixed origins of food aid. But, despite all the varied and often questionable motives, has U.S. food aid gotten to the hungry?

Food to the Hungry

Over the last several years our Institute has received many letters and other reports from countries around the world revealing that food aid does anything but reach the hungry. Bangladesh, however, is a useful country on which to focus since it is a principal recipient of U.S. food aid and since most people think that food aid to such a needy country surely must be "humanitarian." Unfortunately, the story of food aid and the hungry in Bangladesh is by no means unique.

Today Bangladesh receives a full third of its food aid from the United States. Since 1974, 94 percent of U.S. food aid has been under Title I. Title I—dollar credits to buy food on a low-interest, long-term basis —gives the local government total control over what is done with the food.

The Bangladesh government sells most of the Title I food through a ration system that allows cardholders to buy a portion of their food at a 50 percent subsidy. Bangladesh researchers James Boyce and Betsy Hartmann point out that most of this food goes to those who could have afforded the market price: the urban middle class.[3] In 1976, 90 percent of the food aid was sold to this middle class.[4] Conservative World Bank figures are revealing: 27 percent of the food aid goes to the police, military and civil service; another 30 percent goes to the predominantly middle-class cardholders in the six major cities.[5] (In 1975 the government revoked all of the few ration cards held by the marginally employed living in Dacca's slums.[6]) Yet another 8 percent is supplied to mills for grinding flour for urban bakeries.[7]

While 85 to 90 percent of the people of Bangladesh live in rural areas and many of them are undernourished, a mere one-third of the ration cards are allotted to rural families. In theory, these cards allow for the purchase of half the amount of subsidized food allotted to an urban cardholder. In practice, rural cardholders can buy even less. First of all, fulfillment of their allotment depends on there being something left over after urban allotments are covered. Moreover, rural ration dealers sell a good part of the food on the black market, pocketing the cash. (Getting a dealership is a coveted political favor.)

The government's concentration of food aid on the urban middle class is deliberate. The ration system is designed, in the words of a 1976 U.S. Embassy cable, "to keep potentially active Dacca dwellers supplied with low-priced foodgrains."[8] "Active," of course, means politically active. (This use of food aid to keep middle class urban dwellers from wanting to revolt is a story often repeated around the world. In Upper Volta at least 75 percent of the relief aid during the drought—and during the political "unrest"—was distributed to the better-off dwellers in the capital city and the largest provincial towns, leaving very little for the hard-hit rural areas.[9] You will recall from Part I that at the same time moneylender-merchants exported to the Ivory Coast the grain they took from debt-burdened peasants.)

Food aid not only does not feed Bangladesh's hungry, but it also helps perpetuate hunger. Food aid is fundamental to the neglect of any serious efforts at increasing food production. The U.S. embassy in Dacca acknowledged in a 1976 cable to Washington that "The incentive for Bangladesh government leaders to devote attention, resources and talent to the problem of increasing domestic foodgrain production is reduced by the security provided by U.S. and other donors' food assistance."[10] This reduced incentive is welcomed, to say the least, by the government because in fact it is widely understood that meaningful production increases —and ensuring that everyone has access to the food produced—would require not so much the "attention, resources and talent" of government bureaucrats as a thorough restructuring of control over productive resources. And that this is the last thing the government wants is fully demonstrated by the brutal police and military repression it uses to crush popular movements by and for the poor.

Part of the ten percent of food aid to Bangladesh that winds up in the countryside is earmarked for a few rural works programs. Such seasonal "food-for-work" projects are certainly no long-term solution to the unemployment at the root of hunger. Moreover, in the opinion of some observers we spoke with, their main function is to take the edge off a potentially explosive rural situation by providing a few jobs during the slack agricultural season. A recent study by the F.A.O. stressed that food-for-work programs "lend themselves to misappropriation of grain, misuse of funds, false reporting of works, creation of a new class of profiteers, poor quality construction, etc."[11]

But most crucially such rural works almost exclusively benefit the already better-off part of the rural population, primarily the bigger landholders. According to an AID-sponsored study:

> Such projects (e.g., the building of a farm to market road) provide income to rural workers for a specified period, but do nothing generally to change the fundamental economic conditions that produce unemployment in the first place. At the same time, such projects tend to provide long-term benefits to landholders who, in this example, use the road to gain access to local markets.[12]

Our Institute has received in 1978 several communications, independent of each other, from American missionaries in rural Haiti who decry food-for-work programs using U.S. food aid. One wrote:

> In the village where we are living, for example, one family controls all the community and government offices including judge, mayor, community council president, etc. Besides owning vast tracts of land, "the family" speculates in coffee and controls all the illegal tree-cutting in the area. When CARE entered the village with a Food For Work soil conservation project, [using U.S. food aid] it came as no surprise that "the family" was the local administrator of the project and chose who would work on the project. "The family," through the auspices of the community council president, is also responsible for seeing to the actual food distribution. To the CARE people this project is a good grassroots effort, but in reality it is not helping those peasants in the area who really need it. CARE, for example, believes that the workers are mostly landless peasants. We have surveyed nearly all of the workers

on the project and have yet to find any landless peasants. The workers must work three days a week on the project, one day on the road for the community council and one day in the garden of one of the community leaders (i.e., "the family"). Thus, the projects take the farmers away from their own plots for five days of the week.

Market Development

In the first five years after it was passed, P.L. 480 succeeded in unloading abroad over $5 billion worth of American grain or 28 percent of total American agricultural exports. But even this was not enough to unload U.S. grain surpluses. By 1959 the United States held its highest stocks in history. Merely responding to food aid requests was not enough. Policy makers decided they had to take an active role in *creating* markets. The goal spelled out in the preamble to P.L. 480 included these words: "to develop and expand export markets for United States agricultural commodities." The goal was clear; the question was how to achieve it.

The answer was "development." P.L. 480, by allowing countries to import food *without* using dollars, made it more likely that poor governments would have dollars available to import American capital goods for light industrialization. Assistant Secretary of State W. L. Clayton testified that the World Bank financing for such capital goods "would certainly be a very good one for U.S. agricultural exports, because as you help develop them industrially, you will shift their economy to an industrial economy, so that I think in the end you would create more markets for your agricultural products."[13]

Congress in 1957 saw a way to reinforce this direction. Most of our food "aid" goes under Title I of P.L. 480. Title I, you will recall, provides for dollar credits (on a low-interest, long-term basis) to select governments to import food from the United States. The foreign government then sells the food. In 1957, the U.S. government agreed to accept the local currency generated by these food sales as repayment of the loans. (This lasted until 1972.)

This local currency modification of P.L. 480 was then turned into a direct aid to U.S. corporate investment. Up to 25 percent of the local currency accepted in exchange for food could be loaned at very low interest rates to U.S. corporations investing in those countries. Some companies, it was thought, could quite directly create demand for American agricultural exports. Eldrige Haynes, chairman of Business International, the service organization for multinational corporations, told the Congressional committee of the need for expanding the American food-processing industry into the underdeveloped world:

> We are not exporting bread, we are exporting wheat. Somebody has to convert it into bread. If they do not, if there are not more facilities to make bread, it will not be consumed.[14]

Haynes said the same is true of cotton and tobacco. He suggested, therefore, that American corporations get "Cooley loans" (named after a House Agricultural Committee chairman from North Carolina) in order to construct processing facilities for cloth and cigarettes.

Thus, U.S. agricultural surpluses were to be sold on credit to a foreign government that in turn sold the food for local currency. That local currency then in part financed American companies that would, it was hoped, generate the need to import yet more agricultural commodities. Under the Cooley loan provision, 419 subsidiaries of American firms in 31 countries established or expanded their operations at very low cost. In India, alone, Cooley loans have gone to Wyeth Labs, Union Carbide, Otis Elevator, Sylvania, Rockwell International, Goodyear, CPC International, Sunshine Farms, First National City Bank, the Bank of America, and American Express, among others.

In addition, the Department of Agriculture uses food loan repayments (in 1975 alone to the tune of $12 million) to support private trade associations such as the United States Feed Grains Council, whose members are the major grain-exporting companies. It uses the money to promote feedgrain, livestock, and poultry industries throughout the underdeveloped world.[15]

Building a Feedgrain Market: The Case of Cargill, Inc.

In 1968, Cargill, Inc.—the multi-billion dollar grain firm—decided to set up a complete poultry operation in South Korea breeding chicks, producing chicken feed, and retailing chickens. The American government—that is, the American taxpayers—provided 95 percent of the financing for what looked like a very profitable operation. Almost $500,000 came as a Cooley loan.

Cargill picked up an additional $1.9 million loan from the U.S. government under the Private Trade Entity provision of P.L. 480. (This provision allows the Commodity Credit Corporation, part of the USDA, to loan to a private corporation the money to purchase American agricultural commodities. The corporation then sells them in a foreign market, using the proceeds to establish its operations there. By 1976, over $120 million had gone to corporations under this P.L. 480 provision.)

All this help was not enough for Cargill. By 1972, the Cargill operation was in trouble. Cargill had used up all conceivable P.L. 480 credits for importing grain. Cargill approached its friends in the U.S. government to persuade South Korea to relax domestic price controls and import restrictions that interfered with its feedgrain import operations. The State Department instructed the embassy in South Korea to see that the "poultry and livestock industries" receive special consideration from the government. Finally, when all else failed, Cargill sought and received from the U.S. government a deferment of payment on its two P.L. 480 loans. P.L. 480 credits also enabled Ralston Purina and the Peavey Corporation to establish poultry operations in South Korea.

The net effect has been to make South Korea heavily dependent on imported feed. Whereas South Korea had earlier imported no feedgrain, by 1974 it imported about one million tons from the United States. Moreover, once having become dependent on American feedgrain, South Korea saw the United States raise the price three and a half times between 1970 and 1974.[16]

Building a Wheat Market

P.L. 480 has also succeeded in creating markets for wheat among the world's original rice lovers. P.L. 480 "was the best thing that ever happened to the wheat industry," observed one market development specialist, pointing to the tremendous increase in wheat consumption in such countries as Japan, Taiwan, and Korea. Wheat aid credits to the Taiwanese government allowed it to export the people's staple, rice, while it exhorted the population to embrace the new diet by such slogans as "eating wheat is patriotic."[17] South Korea now has 7000 bakeries, and Koreans eat Italian-style noodles made from wheat flour.[18] "We taught people to eat wheat who did not eat it before," bragged an official of USDA.[19]

P.L. 480 has perhaps proved that people like what they eat rather than eat what they like. At any rate American corporations have taught them to eat what they have to sell. This achievement was lauded, in 1974, in testimony before the Senate Foreign Relations Committee by former Secretary of Agriculture Orville Freeman, now president of Business International (the same organization whose chairman, Eldridge Haynes, you will recall, seventeen years earlier had urged the use of P.L. 480 to create markets for American agricultural exports). Freeman noted that, "In the last seven years, our agricultural exports to Taiwan have climbed by 531 percent and those to [South] Korea by

643 percent because we created a market." P.L. 480 "makes very good sense," he added.

Yet does it make good sense for South Korea?

Food Aid, Strings Attached

In a 1975 article entitled "P.L. 480—Humanitarian Effort Helps Develop Markets," USDA congratulates itself for helping to stimulate food sales abroad. "Many countries," it says, "have 'graduated' from P.L. 480 status."[20] Besides helping American corporations build import-demanding industries abroad, P.L. 480 created yet another method for helping countries "graduate" to commercial purchases. In order to receive food aid, the potential recipient had to accept one condition: agreement to purchase in the future on commercial terms American agricultural commodities. In 1973, our government made food credit to the Dominican Republic conditional upon much larger commercial purchases. In 1975, P.L. 480 loans to Egypt for wheat and to South Korea for rice were tied to additional commercial purchases of these commodities.

The United States applies this stipulation regularly for all commodities except wheat and reserves the right to apply it to wheat also. "The U.S. takes this seriously," emphasizes one American official. "If a country hasn't met its commercial requirements by the end of the year, the requirement is added on to the next year."[21] Apparently the compassion of the United States government is limited to future customers.

Food Aid and Local Production

South Korea has been the second largest recipient of American food aid and has purchased more U.S. agricultural goods than any other underdeveloped country. What has been the impact on South Korea's own agriculture? United States grain imported into Korea has allowed the government to maintain a "cheap food" policy, undercutting Korean farmers.

Prices that the government paid to rice producers barely approached the costs of production throughout the sixties. Pressure from farmers led to some increase in the government rice purchase price in the 1970s but, according to the Korean Catholic Farmer's Association, prices are still below farmers' costs.[22] Not surprisingly, then, the rural population fell from one-half to slightly more than one-third of the total population between 1963 and 1976 as farm people sought their livelihood in the cities, often with no success, as evidenced by the rising unemployment. Moreover, South Korea, 92 percent self-sufficient in grain in 1961, now must import one-third of its grain needs.[23]

The basic purpose of U.S. food aid, along with the more than $13 billion in direct economic and Security Supporting Assistance to Seoul since the Korean War, has been to maintain a low-paid disciplined labor force for use by export-oriented, multinational companies that dominate the Korean economy. Former Assistant Secretary of Agriculture Clayton Yeutter, however, claimed, "South Korea is the greatest success story worldwide of the Food for Peace [P.L. 480] program in terms of its contribution to the growth of the nation."[24]

Colombia is another dramatic case, showing the effects of P.L. 480 shipments. Between 1955 and 1971, Colombia imported over one million tons of wheat that could have been produced more cheaply at home.[25] The marketing agency of the Colombian government fixed the price of the imported grain so low that it undercut domestically produced wheat. This dumping resulted in 50 percent lower prices to Colombian farmers. From 1955, the first year of P.L. 480 shipments, to 1971, Colombia's wheat production dropped by 69 percent while its imports increased 800 percent to the point that imports came to account for 90 percent of domestic consumption.[26]

Moreover, two-thirds of the 407,550 acres that were pushed out of wheat production by subsidized wheat imports have not been compensated for by increases in other crops for local consumption. The fertile Sabana de Bogotá Valley, for example, which once grew wheat, is now used for cattle grazing—primarily for export.[27] Such poultry and cattle-feeding operations were abetted by P.L. 480 Cooley loans that went to subsidiaries of United States corporations such as Ralston Purina, Quaker Oats, Pfizer, and Abbott Laboratories to build plants for processing feed and producing drugs. Landlords, now making greater profits on beef, flowers, and vegetables for export, expand their operations, evict their tenants, and, in general, exclude more and more ordinary farmers from the land. Without land and without jobs, those needing food cannot buy the food "aid."

In this traditionally corn-eating country, the imported wheat goes to meet the "demand" of the "Americanized" minority who can afford processed, brand-name foods.

The impact of American food aid to Bolivia has been similar.[28] But an additional turn of the screw came when the United States stopped accepting payments in local currency and demanded dollars for food aid shipments, albeit on easy terms. Despite its rich agricultural potential and high rural underemployment, Bolivia had come to depend on United States imports, and local wheat production had stagnated. Millers had turned themselves primarily into flour-importing companies because importing was more profitable than milling. Thus, even after local currency was no longer accepted to repay P.L. 480 shipments (the final cutoff point being at the end of 1971), Bolivia had to continue to import flour. The big difference, however, was that Bolivia was forced to use up scarce foreign exchange to purchase the flour in dollars, foreign exchange that might have gone to purchase what it could *not* easily produce itself, such as productive industrial goods.

Even before we began our research for this book, we had long been familiar with the claim that United States food aid shipments depress the incentive of foreign farmers to grow their own food. We were tempted to reject this conclusion simply because it sounded like some "right-wing," unfounded critique of welfare ("If you feed 'em, they won't want to work").

We did not understand an important distinction. Many critics were saying that if you give people food they will not *want* to grow food for themselves; whereas the fact is that dumping large quantities of low-priced American grain on underdeveloped countries makes it economically *impossible* for the small domestic producers to compete—no matter how much they might want to. Unable to get a fair return for their grain, such producers are frequently forced to sell their land, becoming landless (and often jobless) laborers. A study published in an agricultural economics journal in 1969 concluded that for every pound of P.L. 480 cereals imported, there was a net decline in Indian domestic production over the following two years of almost one-half pound because of the reduced return to the farmer.[29]

Although this disincentive effect continues to be debated, a 1975 U.S. government (General Accounting Office) research survey concluded that: "Leading world authorities now indicate that such food assistance by the United States and other countries has hindered the developing countries in expanding their food production and thus has contributed to the critical world food situation."[30]

Food Aid Disaster

In visiting Guatemala, we learned that even in times of natural disasters, food aid can undermine the livelihood precisely of local poor farmers.

The rural people affected by the terrible 1976 earthquake were mostly smallholder farmers who, just before the earthquake, had brought in exceptional harvests. Following the earthquake, what they needed was cash to help rebuild their homes and farms. To get that cash, these farmers needed to dig out and sell part of their stored corn and other grain.

Immediately following the quake, however, food aid from the United States almost quadrupled. Distribution was largely through CARE and Catholic Relief Services (CRS). This increased distribution of free food from the United States was one factor helping to bring down the prices for locally grown grain *just when farmers selling grain most needed cash.* Thus food aid stood in the way of reconstruction, according to local witnesses.

Even when the Guatemalan government asked voluntary agencies to stop bringing grain into the country, the food aid kept on coming. CARE and CRS simply switched to grains pre-blended with other foods such as dry milk, since the ban specified "grain." One year after the quake, U.S. food aid was still 69 percent above pre-quake levels.

Ironically, two other voluntary organizations had to step in to counter the ill effects of the indiscriminate distribution of free food. First, Oxfam gave a special loan to a cooperative in the stricken Chimaltenango area that had been organized earlier with the help of World Neighbors. The loan was to be used to buy up crops from the farmers at a price above the depressed level and to establish a grainbank to help stabilize sinking grain prices. The scheme thus helped the farmers of the area get the cash they needed to rebuild their lives at a price that did not force them to take a severe loss.

Those on the scene at the time, such as William Rudell and Roland Bunch; both with long experience with rural cooperatives in Guatemala, told us that even where there was a need for food during the first days following the earthquake, before stored food could be recovered from the rubble, the food should have been bought from areas in Guatemala not affected by the earthquake. Such purchases could have been a boost to farmers in those villages. Moreover, supplies coming from within the country could be more easily curtailed once farmers in the recipient villages had dug out their stored harvests. As Bunch commented, "If the Guatemalans were sending wheat into the United States this year as their own version of a P.L. 480 donation and giving it out to American consumers, American farmers would be screaming bloody murder about it."[31]

Interestingly, it was the local people who most counseled against the distribution of free food and free materials. Instead they advised the outside agencies to provide building materials and to sell them at subsidized prices. Oxfam, World Neighbors and U.S. AID did just that—with extremely positive results.

Where disasters massively destroy food supplies, all the lessons inherent in the Guatemala food aid disaster might not apply. Still, the principle that emerges for us is that even for genuine short-term emergencies, the effort should be to purchase the relief food as locally as possible and from peasant producers whose families' livelihood depends on selling its grain.

Food as a Weapon

The political and military use of U.S. food aid is not a new story. In this century, immediately following World War I, future President Herbert Hoover put his support behind a food aid program for Germany to avert the danger of hungry Germans voting socialist (as well as to solve the American food surplus problem generated by the wartime agricultural effort).

In 1943, forty-three nations created what would become the United States–dominated United Nations Relief and Rehabilitation Administration (UNRRA) to give food aid to war victims. The aid was "not to be used as a political weapon and no discrimination was to be made in distribution for racial, religious or political reasons."[32] Despite this explicit provision, American food aid went to fascist forces in Greece and to Chiang Kai-shek in China.[33] India received no help following the great famine of 1943 in which 4 million Indians died, nor in the 1946–1947 famine. India, at that time, did not qualify as a priority anticommunist front zone, according to then Secretary of State Dean Acheson.

Following World War II, over one quarter of all United States funds spent on food aid was spent under the Marshall Plan. Enormous quantities of grain on credit flowed into Italy and France to help keep the impoverished working class from voting against capitalism. Marshall himself stated at the time: "Food is a vital factor in our foreign policy."

In 1959, Senator Humphrey criticized those who would have food aid serve only as a surplus disposal mechanism. He saw food as a potent political weapon:

> We have been told repeatedly that this is a world-wide struggle between the forces of evil and the forces of decency. . . . We all know we are engaged in the struggle of men's minds, for their loyalties. There is a struggle between ways of life, a system of values. Our values are different from those of the totalitarians. If it is a worldwide struggle, it would seem to me we would want to mobilize all the resources we possibly can in order to win it. And in a world of want and hunger what is more powerful than food and fibre?[34]

Since we have been told China, North Vietnam, and North Korea are "the forces of evil," naturally most of our food aid has gone to the bordering countries: India, South Vietnam, during the Vietnam War, Cambodia, South Korea, and Taiwan. By 1973, almost *half* of all U.S. food aid was going to South Vietnam and Cambodia. Between 1968 and 1973, South Vietnam alone received twenty times the value of food aid that the five African countries most seriously affected by drought received during that same period.[35]

The withdrawal of food aid can also be a powerful political weapon. Aid to Chile was abruptly discontinued when a government was elected that threatened American corporate interests, as we will discuss later. Because U.S. policymakers see food aid as a political tool, they do not like to contribute food to international agencies where its use might be less under their control. In October, 1974, the *Washington Post* reported on an unreleased government document, part of the preparation for the World Food Conference the following month. In it the United States opposed expansion of the World Food Program (WFP), a United Nations program to aid in famine areas. The document states that the United States has "not been able in recent years to influence appreciably the policies and procedures of the WFP or the distribution of aid to particular destinations. There would appear to be no advantage to the U.S. favoring a greater role and more resources for WFP."[36] The administration clearly wanted to have nothing to do with food aid projects it could not mold to its own purposes.

Food Aid as the Perfect Guise

By late 1973, with commercial sales booming, the amount of agricultural products shipped under P.L. 480 dropped to 3.3 million tons, one-fifth of the level of the mid-sixties. The Department of Agriculture no longer needed P.L. 480 to dispose of surpluses. But the National Security Council and the State Department under Kissinger were there to pick up the food aid baton.

Congress had begun to resist efforts by the administration to continue to prop up the regimes in South Vietnam and Cambodia as well as to aid the Chilean junta, which so flagrantly disregards human rights. P.L. 480 provided the administration with just the funding vehicle needed to skirt congressional controls.

First, the administration was confident that expanding food aid expenditures would be hard for Congress to oppose since so many well-meaning Americans think food aid is to feed hungry people.

Second, P.L. 480 country programs are not subject to annual congressional appropriations. The budget submitted is only an estimate that can change without congressional approval. For instance, in the fiscal year 1974, Cambodia was slated to receive $30 million in food aid but in fact received $194 million.[37] In addition, the Commodity Credit Corporation (CCC), established in 1957 to expand markets for American agricultural products, has its own capacity to extend credits for agricultural purchases to favored governments. Here, too, there is flexibility. During the course of the fiscal year 1976, the actual CCC credit sales were double the amount originally budgeted. All this gave the administration quite a bit of leeway.

Third, food aid can easily, yet discreetly, be turned into direct support for foreign military efforts. The food can be sold locally by foreign governments, thereby generating funds for that government's military budget. In the case of certain countries the administration does not require repayment of the food aid loan. It simply authorizes the recipient government to use the proceeds from the food resale as a grant for "common defense." In October 1973, an agreement signed with South Vietnam allowed all proceeds to the Saigon government from P.L. 480 sales to go to the military budget; in Cambodia the figure was 80 percent of food aid sales.

By 1975, $6 billion in local currencies generated by the sale of P.L. 480 food had been spent for military purposes; over one-third of this in South Korea and South Vietnam.[38] One study showed that in 1965 over 85 percent of South Korea's resale funds were used for military purposes.[39]

These three realities make food a handy tool indeed. In fiscal year 1974, for instance, Congress cut more than 20 percent out of the economic aid requested for Indochina by the administration. Undaunted, the White House more than doubled the P.L. 480 allocation to South Vietnam and Cambodia to $499 million, giving these two countries half of all food credits that year.[40] An American reporter in Cambodia documented a refugee camp where 70 percent of the small children went hungry while nearby the bags of food aid were being sold to pay the troops.[41] In contrast to Cambodia and South Vietnam, all of Africa received less than 15 percent of the food aid total that year.

In 1973, Congress, pressured by outraged citizens, tried to stop America's food for war program. It prohibited the use of any P.L. 480 resale funds for military purposes. The effect, however, was almost meaningless. Since the proceeds from the reselling of United States food often go into the general treasuries of the receiving countries, it is impossible to check how they get spent.

For fiscal year 1975, the administration was again budgeting half of all P.L. 480 credits for South Vietnam and Cambodia. In light of a growing image of America as indifferent to the plight of the hungry, Congress tried to balance the obvious military and political intent of U.S. food aid with some concern for the starving. It passed an amendment requiring that 70 percent of the food aid go to countries on the United Nations list of "most seriously affected" countries.

Here was a real challenge for the government: What steps should be taken? The first tack was to claim that the 70 percent rule applied only to food items—not to cotton and tobacco also shipped under P.L. 480. (The government was aware that these commodities could be turned into guns just as readily as food could.) Another strategy initiated by then Secretary of State Kissinger was simply to get Vietnam put on the United Nations list of "most seriously affected" countries; that one failed.

Finally, in order to get the amount of military support it wanted for Cambodia and Vietnam and to give its vote of confidence to other repressive regimes in Chile, South Korea, and the Middle East, the administration merely increased the total amount of food aid available. It could then support its client regimes and still stay within the new ruling requiring 70 percent of our food aid to go to the neediest countries, claiming to have generously acceded to the demands of the "humanitarians" by increasing food aid from $1 billion to $1.6 billion.

In 1975, in protest against the junta's repressive policies, Congress placed a $26 million limit on economic aid to Chile (still the second-highest amount granted by the United States to any country in Latin America) and cut off military aid altogether. All that meant little. By the end of the year, Chile's share of food aid was over $60 million. Other forms of "backdoor" aid to the junta include loans from the U.S. government's Export-Import Bank ($42 million in 1977) and from the USDA's Commodity Credit Corporation (a $38 million loan in April 1978).

With the defeat of the United States in Indochina, South Korea has taken on a new strategic significance in East Asia. The familiar pattern is being repeated: Congress tries to phase out military aid and the administration brings in food aid to fill the gap. South Korea's food aid credits for the fiscal year 1975–1976 were twice the level of the previous year.

The "New" Food Aid?

A new food aid provision (Title III) is supposed to help to insure that food aid benefits the poor. Under this provision, the United States forgives repayment of food aid loans *if* the foreign government uses the proceeds from its sale of food aid to undertake development programs in agriculture, nutrition, health services and population planning. At this writing (Fall 1978) agreements are being worked out with the governments of Bangladesh, Bolivia, and Haiti. Title III will undoubtedly succeed in reducing U.S. grain surpluses, but how is this program any more directed at the real poor than those already functioning by joint design of AID and the recipient government? Those projects we discuss in Question 44.

Congress has also tacked on yet two more "humanitarian" amendments to the food aid program. Both were supported by many citizens who would deeply like to see America's food bounty help the hungry.

The first decreed that 75 percent of P.L. 480 loans must go to the countries where the annual per capita gross national product is $550 or less.

First of all, this qualifier has very little significance. According to World Bank figures, such a cut-off line would exclude only 33 Third World countries.[42] The population of these ineligible countries is but a small fraction of that of the entire underdeveloped world and yet the amendment still allows the administration to allot 25 percent of U.S. food aid to those countries. So what's the practical application? And given all we have just learned about White House maneuvers, would a provision like this be enforced anyway?

More crucially, at least two fundamentally false assumptions would seem to be at work behind this amendment. First, that per capita GNP figures tell you anything about hunger. The per capita GNP of Brazil is $1030 and yet the majority of its 106 millions are undernourished. By contrast, the per capita GNP of China is $380; yet are there any in China who still go without at least the minimum they need? South Africa has a per capita GNP of $1270. But for the 71 percent of the population who are Black, the figure is $360; many of them are hungry. The second false assumption is that the GNP criterion tells you anything about which governments would use food aid to help the hungry. Bangladesh's per capita GNP is only $90 and we have seen that there food aid is more likely to hurt than help the hungry. By comparison, the only other country in the world with such a low per capita GNP is Laos. From what we have been told by American missionaries there the Laotian government might be one of the few that would use food aid to help those made hungry by the United States having brought its war into Laos. But as late as the spring of 1978 the Carter administration was resisting efforts of church groups and others to have at least some food sent to the Laotian people.

The second amendment states that food aid cannot be given to any government that "consistently violates recognized human rights." But there is a loophole. A government widely known to be violating human rights can still get food aid by simply agreeing to sign a special clause stating that the aid will directly (or indirectly through the sale of food) help the needy. This loophole would seem to be based on the naïve assumption that a government consistently violating the rights of its citizens would use food aid to benefit the needy. To stick with the case of Bangladesh: In late 1977 a special Carter administration committee determined that Bangladesh was indeed such a violator.[43] Has that meant a cut-off of food aid to Bangladesh? Not at all. After months of administration wrestling with the amendment and intense lobbying by the Bangladesh military government, a deal was made.

Bangladesh simply acquiesced to signing the special clause and promised that it would use food aid to help the hungry and got $56 million in food aid.

Finally, the case of Bangladesh illustrates that those who believe that "humanitarian" stipulations on food aid legislation will ensure that it gets to the hungry overlook one central fact: food aid helps to finance a narrowly based, unpopular, and therefore militarized government. Revenues from the sale of food aid through the ration system provide about 18 percent of the operating budget.[44] Fifty-four percent of the operating budget is financed by foreign aid.[45] Thirty percent of the operating budget—and the percentage is still growing—goes for "defense, justice, and peace."[46] Under that budget heading comes the operating of jails for what Amnesty International estimates are 10,000 to 15,000 political prisoners held under "inhuman conditions."[47] Since food aid revenue can be used for anything, some undoubtedly goes to the 12,500-man militarized police Special Task Force trained for "special drives and mopping-up operations" against civilian dissenters.[48] And to keep the revenue from food aid rolling in, government officials, by their own admission, underrepresent actual harvests.[49]

It is hard not to agree with the many who argue that the U.S. and other donors should terminate food aid to countries like Bangladesh. Even a 1976 U.S. Senate study mission concluded that food aid should be phased out over a five-year period. Without food aid, it is true that the well-off would have to buy their rice on the local market. This might mean higher prices for a while—if there is truly a fall in production —but only until greater production was triggered. And even in the case of interim higher prices it is not clear that more people would go hungry. For as researchers Hartmann and Boyce note, "Even when rice was plentiful and selling at a reasonable price in the local bazaar, the poor of our village went hungry."

We do not claim to have all the answers about food aid. A few points have, however, become clear to us.

First, hungry people should know that the United States can never be a source of food security. Indeed, food security is not something that can be given, even by a well-intentioned foreign government. Underdeveloped countries had better *assume* that the United States will use its food surpluses to help expand its commercial markets, to assist the penetration of agribusiness firms and to support the very regimes that work in direct opposition to the policies that would enable hungry people to free themselves from hunger. Let anything else be a pleasant surprise.

Second, food aid is useful and can prevent rather than cause tragedy *only* when it is in response to a short-term emergency—a severe drought or a flood, for example—that actually destroys food supplies. It should only be given after all means of garnering the food within the afflicted country have been pursued, including rationing and measures to prevent hoarding. A more appropriate form of "food aid" in many instances would be a donation of transportation to help a local government move the necessary supplies from an area within the country to the emergency site. What must be remembered is that even in famine-stricken countries seldom is there an absolute shortage of minimum supplies.

Third, concerned Americans should not think of food aid as *the* way to help the hungry. Dwelling on food aid—how much and what criteria should be used—diverts attention from the *process* of how hunger is created. It allows us to forget that the overriding impact of the United States on the ability of people to become food self-reliant is not through food aid but through the corporate, military, economic and covert involvement of the United States in their countries, as we will see in more detail in the following chapters. The proper agenda of Americans is to identify and help remove obstacles originating in our own country.

I have heard . . . that people may become dependent

on us for food. I know that was not supposed to be good news. To me, that was good news, because before people can do anything they have got to eat. And if you are looking for a way to get people to lean on you and to be dependent on you, in terms of their cooperation with you, it seems to me that food dependence would be terrific.

Senator Hubert H. Humphrey, 1957

During the last 10 years, the United States supplied 80 percent of the world's food aid. We did this, on the whole, without making the recipient nations deeply dependent upon our continued assistance—this danger has been, for the greater part, averted.

Don Paarlberg, USDA official

Food for Peace (P.L. 480) programs are designed to meet real food needs and AID's role is to assure that the programs also promote valid development objectives for the recipient.

AID 1979 Budgetary Proposal
to Congress

On only one occasion did we have the opportunity to see food aid reaching needy people. While visiting an adjacent area affected by floods, we saw a union council member handing out cornmeal biscuits from a tin dated 1963 and labelled, "Office of Civil Defense, U.S. Department of Defense." The biscuits had evidently been produced for American fallout shelters during the days of the bomb scares. After more than a decade, the U.S. government decided to dispose of them. They were reportedly on their way to Cambodia when Phnom Penh fell, at which point they were redirected to Bangladesh. Each villager received one rather stale biscuit. "The only reason these weren't sold on the black market is that no one would buy them," remarked a village elder.

Betsy Hartmann and James Boyce
reporting on nine months in a
Bangladesh village

43. What About the World Bank's "Assault on Poverty"?

Question: A few years ago the World Bank and other international lending agencies claimed to have learned from their past failures. "Trickle down" theory—the notion that overall economic growth eventually benefits the poor—is passé. Now they will directly help the poor meet their "basic needs." Shouldn't we lobby governments to increase their contributions to the World Bank?

Our Response: The World Bank cannot be taken lightly. It has rapidly emerged as the leading institution for development financing, with lending commitments for 1979 projected at $9.8 billion. President Carter asked American taxpayers to virtually double their contribution to the Bank. Our $2.2 billion in fiscal 1979, we were told, would help the Bank further its "assault on poverty."[1]

Putting on the Blinders

Important insights into the World Bank's battleplan can come from reading any of its confidential rural project planning documents ("gray covers").[2] Here the Bank staff seem to follow a ritual formula—one apparently unaffected by the Bank's "basic needs" rhetoric of the past five years.

Technical and statistical data are paraded forth. Poverty is quantified. Despite the stress on "participation" in publicly touted policy papers (for example,

388

"The rural poor must participate in designing and operating a program which involves so many of them"[3]), poor people, project documents imply, can be reached from the top down. The poor are not seen as the participants, much less the instigators, of their own development. In para-military language, the poor become the "target population."

Project proposals, nominally written by the local government, are in most cases ghost-written by Bank "missions" that fly in—at no small expense—from Washington for a few days.

The presumption throughout project design is that development can be achieved only by bringing in external resources. Foreign investment is thought of as essential. Everything should be done, therefore, to develop a favorable climate for foreign banks and corporations. That a project design includes ongoing reliance on imports is not seen as a problem.

The project implementation section of the "gray covers" amounts to a series of best-of-all-worlds projections. Statement of goals plus money equals success. Poverty is simply *there* with no hint that forces are at work creating and sustaining it. A project plan is an exercise in economics divorced from political, sociological and cultural factors. On the rare occasion that conflicts of interests are recognized, their implications for the implementation of a project are ignored. Government and other actors are all presumed to be working together to eliminate poverty.

Results of projects are measured only in statistics, not in the impact on the lives of real people.

"Going to the Big Boys"

With the Bank's project designs opting to ignore the social roots of poverty, is it surprising that they seem time after time to achieve the reverse of stated goals?

Take the Bank's credit to the government of Bangladesh to fund 3000 deep tubewells.[4] Each tubewell has the capacity to irrigate 60 acres, making possible an extra crop of rice during the dry winter season in northwestern Bangladesh. According to a Bank press release, each well would serve between 25 to 50 farmers joined together in a cooperative irrigation group. But independent researchers Betsy Hartmann and James Boyce who lived for nine months in one of the villages covered by the project found what was no secret to anyone in the village: the tubewell in reality has wound up as the property of one man, the richest landlord in the village. And the vaunted cooperative irrigation group amounted to a few signatures he had collected on a scrap of paper.

The World Bank (in reality the Bangladesh government) paid $12,000 for each well; and this landowner paid less than $300 for his, and that mostly in bribes to local officials. The landowner *will* allow smaller farmers tilling adjacent plots to use "his" water—but at his price, an hourly rate so high that few are interested.

Was the Hartmann and Boyce experience atypical? Apparently not at all. They expressed their shock to a foreign expert working on the Bank project. He told them,

I no longer ask who is getting the well. I know what the answer will be and I don't want to hear it. One hundred percent of these wells are going to the "big boys." First priority goes to those with the most power and influence: the judges, the magistrates, the members of Parliament, the union chairmen. If any tubewells are left over, the local authorities auction them off. The big landlords compete and whoever offers the biggest bribe gets the tubewell.[5]

But should the Bank have known this in advance? Are we just proving that hindsight is often clearer than foresight? Not at all. An evaluation carried out for the Swedish International Development Authority (SIDA) (that joined the Bank in financing the tubewell project) examined 270 tubewells and concluded:

It is not surprising that the tubewells have been situated on the land of the well-to-do farmers, or that it is the same well-to-do farmers who are the chairmen and managers of the irrigation groups. It [would have] been more surprising if the tubewells had *not* been located on their land, with the existing rural power structure, maintained largely because of the unequal distribution of the land.[6]

The Bank nonetheless will tell the world that the tubewell project is a success. The World Bank expert who told Hartmann and Boyce that the wells would only go to the "big boys" added:

> On paper it all sounds quite nice. Here are the peasants organizing to avail themselves of this wonderful resource. When the officials fly in from Washington for a three-day visit to Dacca, they look at these papers. They don't know what is happening out here in the field, and no one is going to tell them.[7]

And since the amount of land owned by the rich landowner is only half the area that the tubewell is minimally capable of irrigating, the tubewell will be greatly underutilized. (It is, in fact, this prevalent tubewell underutilization that most troubles World Bank technocrats.)

World Bank officials who find themselves forced to admit the failure of such a project invariably do not question its premises. "More managers," they say, are what is needed.

But what is the real tragedy here? That tens of millions of dollars (in reality loans that must be repaid by the work of the people of Bangladesh) have been wasted? That a resource has been grossly underutilized? That poor farmers have not been helped? Yes, all of these things, but much more.

The Bank's impact should not be understood as simply a failure to help the "target" group. By enriching their enemies, such a project actually *undercuts* those it is supposed to help. In the village studied, the

large landowner—like his counterparts in other villages
—is reported to "already have an eye on the plots
nearest his tubewell." Thanks to his new income from
the World Bank tubewell, he will be better positioned
to buy out the smaller farmers when hard times befall,
thus driving them into the growing ranks of the landless.

Not Neighbors, But Rivals

We ourselves investigated another Bank rural development program in Bangladesh, a major "pilot"
program called RD–1 (Rural Development Phase One).
The stated goal of the $16 million RD–1 is "to reduce
the domination of rural institutions by the more prosperous and politically influential farmers and to make
farm credits and agricultural inputs . . . available to
the small farmers through the cooperative system."[8]

Thus the Bank first of all presupposes that there
could be a cooperative system in which the well-off
participate but do not dominate. People in each village
we visited, however, told us that the so-called cooperatives were dominated by the well-off—generally
the top 10 percent owning six acres or more—who
controlled the records and determined who could join
and get credit. For the rest of the villagers, especially
the half owning one acre or less, not only are the repayment terms too stringent but even the membership
fees are too high. And without land, coming up with
collateral is virtually impossible. "Even if I did come
up with a scheme to pay back a loan," one landless
villager complained, "the cooperative would still not
give me credit."

For us, the SIDA evaluation of aid-funded village
cooperative programs rang true: "Democratically functioning cooperatives never can work, if land holdings
continue to be as unevenly distributed as they are today.
To try to keep the big landowners outside the cooperatives . . . is nothing but wishful thinking."[9]

Projects dreamed up in a social vacuum must nevertheless play themselves out in the real world of injustice

and conflict. As one FAO agronomist with 15 years experience in Bangladesh told us, "The thing to remember about the villages is that the people are not neighbors but rivals."[10] Similarly, an anthropologist[11] studying a disparate group of Bangladesh villages told us that the fundamental social reality is a struggle over land: the well-off do everything possible to get their smaller neighbors in debt to them in order to foreclose on their land; the poor farmers do everything possible to hold on to the little land they have, even hiring out wives and daughters for demeaning servant's work. Not only do the well-off landowners not want the small farmers or landless laborers to prosper, they want them to become *more* dependent, more indebted to them.

Thus the rural elite who usurp the tubewell—or the new machine or the extension worker's guidance or whatever the Bank projects supposedly earmark for the small farmer—will make sure the poor will not benefit. This is true even if it means vastly under-utilizing the new input. Ignoring this constant economic warfare, World Bank projects not only fail in narrow production terms (production in the RD–1 villages of Bangladesh, for example, is no higher than elsewhere) but also strengthen the oppressors of the already desperate small farmers and the landless.

Don't Rock the Boat

A 1975 Bank policy paper on rural development explains how projects should deal with "the existing social system." The paper states: "In many countries, avoiding opposition from powerful and influential sections of the rural community is essential if the Bank's program is not to be subverted from within."[12]

Bank President Robert McNamara tells us that the Bank's agricultural program "will put primary emphasis not on the redistribution of income and wealth—as necessary as they might be in many of our member countries—but rather on increasing the productivity of the poor, thereby providing for a more equitable sharing of the benefits of growth."[13]

But will increasing their output benefit the poor if merchants, moneylenders and other exploiters continue to siphon off the lion's share? Will not Bank programs to improve the productivity of the land (for example, by a dam-irrigation project) in a society structured against the poor only heighten the chances that smallholders will be bought out, tricked or otherwise forced off the land?

That the Bank is committed to "avoiding opposition from the powerful" is also clear when we discover that many of its rural programs do not even make the pretense of aiding poor smallholders. In *Assault on World Poverty* the Bank states that it is allocating almost half of its rural credit to small farmers.[14] Sounds good. But wait. This means then that more than half of the Bank's rural credit will still be going to medium and large farmers who at most constitute only 20 percent of all landholders in the underdeveloped countries.[15]

Moreover, closer examination of project appraisals has taught us you have to be on the alert about even the "almost half" supposedly going to "small farmers." For whether or not World Bank credit is getting to the rural poor depends, in part, on how the Bank defines "small." In Guatemala, for instance, a joint FAO/World Bank farm credit program would allocate one-half of the credit to the top three percent of the landholders, those owning 112 acres or more. The other half would go to what the Bank calls "small farmers," those owning less than 112 acres. To an American, 112 acres sounds small. But this cut-off point hardly separates out the rural poor in Guatemala where a full 97 percent of all farmers have less than 112 acres. With such a guideline, the Bank's project could bypass totally the real poor majority in Guatemala—farmers with less than even one acre and, of course, the many with no land at all. The size of the subloans provides another clue as to whom such projects are directed. In the "small farm" category the maximum would be $10,000. But what kind of collateral could the truly small farmers and the landless put up to qualify for loans on the scale suggested by such a figure?

Even where the stated purpose is to benefit truly smallholders, the Bank itself acknowledges that the credits go through national agricultural and development banks, primarily winding up in the hands of largeholders.[16] In the Philippines, for example, the World Bank made two loans to rural banks that were partially government-owned. Although the stated purpose was to help small farmers, smallholders with less than seven acres (who comprise 73 percent of all farmers in the area) actually received less than one percent of the credit extended.[17]

The Landless

And if the Bank is serious about attacking rural poverty what does it offer the millions of landless in countries where a few monopolize the land? Even in the Bank's own conservative estimate, the landless make up 40 to 60 percent of the population in many Third World countries. Here the Bank unabashedly revives the supposedly discredited "trickle down": we are told, for example, that millions of dollars for an irrigation dam will generate more farm employment— a boon to the landless. But, as Hartmann and Boyce ask, "Is giving aid to the rich so they can hire more poor at subsistence wages really the way to best help the poor?"[18]

As an utterly rare exception the Bank did design a program in Bangladesh to benefit landless villagers directly. Within the RD-1 project in Bangladesh, there is provision for a landless co-op in a single village. But even in that one village the program excludes two-thirds of the landless and does nothing to confront the structures that generate their poverty. The program has made available a meager $4000 loan and a pond for cultivating fish plus three acres of government land. (There is much more government land in the village but the well-off have usurped it.) Since the workers' income is still such that they must also work for the village landowners to survive, this pathetic program amounts to a wage subsidy for the rich landowners.

In visiting this single project for the landless, we could not avoid the feeling that it was consciously or not being used as a showcase. In signing the co-op's visitors book we noticed we had been preceded by visitors from several European countries and Canada. Were the poor people we met there being underpaid for their unwitting service to the Bank's image?

We suggest you contrast this landless "program" with one in another typical Bangladesh village where the landless were helped to organize to bring about change themselves (pp. 451–53).

The Bank goes out of its way not to rock the boat even in cases of outright corruption by elites. In Bangladesh the price tag on pumpsets for the Bank's deep tubewell project jumped from $9 to $12 million simply to meet the demand for super profits by the pumpset manufacturer, Bangladesh's richest citizen. According to the *Far Eastern Economic Review*, an effort by the resident Bank mission to cancel the contract was overruled by Bank headquarters in Washington:

> World Bank officials were apparently told that the highest Government authorities in Dacca were involved in placing the contract, and to cancel the whole scheme now would create embarrassing political problems in an area where the Bank hoped to have increasing influence in years to come.[19]

A Bank Is a Bank

While "feeding the hungry" might warm the heart of the Bank's president Robert McNamara, there is no column headed "full stomachs" on his ledger sheets. Hungry people who grow food so that they can eat better do not produce much money and foreign exchange. Only if they grow enough to sell, that is, a "marketable surplus," will loans get repaid with interest. And that is what the Bank is concerned about.

The World Bank, like any other bank, seeks to minimize its risk. The Bank itself notes, "Lending only to those with investment opportunities sufficient to produce a significant marketable surplus is perhaps the best way to reduce the level of default."[20] "Those with investment opportunities" is a euphemism for the larger farmer. It is rough to try to be a bank and a savior of the world at the same time!

Besides betting on the large farmer, the Bank also provides credit for non-food crops, thus ensuring a marketable surplus. Indeed, with crops like rubber and cotton, all of their production will go to market; it can't possibly be eaten by the producer. Furthermore, as the Bank notes, "Delinquencies [in loan repayments] have also been reduced when repayment has been coordinated with the marketing of crops that are centrally processed, for example, tobacco, cotton, cocoa, tea, and coffee."[21]

In 1978, in response to a newspaper article by our Institute, the World Bank denied it had provided any loans for nonfood export crops since 1973, the year the Bank marks as the beginning of its focus on the poor. You can imagine our disbelief! In 1978 alone the World Bank's annual report lists $258.5 million for loans for crops such as tea, tobacco, jute, and rubber. In addition, loans focused on food crops such as vegetables, sugar, and cashews—explicitly designated as going for export promotion—amounted to $221 million.[22]

Livestock is another "crop" that might be seen as a nutritious food. It is certainly one sector highly favored by Bank loans. Yet what Bank loans support is primarily commercial ranching, serving the local elite's and foreign consumers' growing taste for meat. The Bank claims to have de-emphasized livestock since 1975 when one-third of all agricultural lending was for livestock projects.[23] In 1978, however, the Bank's largest loan in agriculture and rural development went to livestock development in Mexico.

A large Bank-financed livestock project in Kenya currently allocates credits in the following manner: 54 percent for a few commercial ranchers; 33 percent for

a few company ranches; 9 percent for 42 individual
ranches; and 4 percent of the loans for 25 group
ranches supporting 1500 ranchers. Bank economist
Uma Lele notes that even the "employment potential
is low."[24] She gives a classic Bank rationalization for
so much money for the benefit of so few: "The tax revenues generated from these ranches are expected to
help the government provide rural services to other
needy areas." (Another example of how "trickle down"
theory is still believed in at the Bank.)

Cane sugar has become another Bank favorite. Visiting Indonesia, we learned that the Bank is bankrolling
(so far to the tune of $50 million) the rebuilding of
the sugar mills built by the Dutch colonizers. Unfortunately, local farmers do not want to raise sugar,
in part because they say they can make twice as much
cultivating rice. According to the *Wall Street Journal*,
sugar mill officials are "forcing the unhappy farmers
to grow cane at gunpoint."[25]

Similarly, the World Bank decided that what new
settlers in Way Abung, Sumatra (Indonesia), needed
was rubber trees.[26] But the farmers resisted. What are
their reasons?

"I'll make more money growing rice."

"I've never worked with rubber and I don't understand it."

"I want to plant food, not something I can't eat."

"The price of rubber fluctuates too much."

"There is no factory nearby so transportation costs
will be too high."

"If I spend time each day tapping rubber, I won't
have time for other crops."

As a crop in addition to rice, farmers and officials
much prefer coconut to rubber. Coconut oil is needed
for cooking; husks become fuel and leaves are used in
roofing and making walls. Coconut meat and milk are
food. If cash is needed, the market is local, not requiring costly transportation.

Rubber prevailed, however. One reason, we were
told, was simply that the World Bank expert on the
scene was a rubber not a coconut specialist. Farmers

now refuse to give up their land to the rubber scheme. At last count only 11 percent of the rubber area had been planted. As one confidential Bank review of the project noted, such problems result "when the development strategy overlooks the basic economy of the settlers themselves."[27]

Besides focusing on the large landholders and ranchers and on non-food crops, yet another way to insure that the marketable surplus does not get eaten is to send out "supervisors" to make sure it does not happen. Again we quote the Bank itself: "Supervision is designed to help the farmer but also to prevent loan funds from being misused for financing consumption and to ensure repayment . . . *But supervision can never completely eliminate increases in consumption* following the receipt of loans, even when credit is provided in kind" [emphasis added].[28] Even the World Bank can't always prevent people from eating what they grow!

We are not saying that agricultural exports are necessarily bad, as we have explained in Question 30, but that they tend to strengthen the mechanisms that cause hunger. To weigh the impact of export agriculture, one has to ask: Who is in control of the return from those export earnings? Does the decision to focus on exports represent a choice of the rural people themselves who have already achieved basic food security and who can deal with the uncertainties of the export market? And how does the conversion of small, self-provisioning farmers into commercial producers take into account the interests of the many more who have been deprived of land? Given the present powerlessness of the poor whom the World Bank says it is "targeting," is it realistic to think that they could genuinely participate in such choices? Not without prior mobilization and organization by the rural people —a development which World Bank-style projects stand directly against, as we have seen in the preceding examples.

Agriculture Only a Slice of the Pie

In all our discussion of agricultural development we fear that we may leave you with a false impression. Because World Bank speechmakers talk so much about helping the hungry, one might forget that more than 60 percent of its loans go not to agriculture or "rural development" but to transportation, telecommunications, industrial and power projects, tourism, and population control. These investments—most of which reinforce the economy's export orientation—are just what the local elites and foreign corporations need to make their own investments profitable. They are, of course, only too happy to have the World Bank foot the bill. Such Bank loans also aid corporations in industrial countries by financing their capital goods exports to the Third World. Moreover, "rural development" turns out to be a catch-all phrase encompassing loans for electrification, roads, motor vehicles, and so forth—projects that tend, as we have seen, to reinforce the position of those already in control of the productive assets.

All this is not to say that the Bank should loan more to agriculture but to point out yet another aspect of how the reality of the Bank's function contrasts with its "basic needs" rhetoric. What we have had to conclude is that since the Bank's strategy for development is counterproductive, encouraging the Bank to "live up to" its rhetoric is dangerous. Less, not more, of the World Bank is what is needed.

Pushing Money

We repeatedly hear in our investigations that the Bank is a "money pusher." What does that mean?

First of all, it has been explained to us that within the Bank, loan officers hold considerable power. They set target loan quotas for countries. They judge subordinates on how good they are at finding the project outlets to fill those quotas. Their complaint often is that there are not enough projects. Focusing on scaring up outlets for huge sums of money isn't exactly conducive to Bank officers reflecting on the social consequences of their projects. "Anyone who stops to raise questions," we were told by one Bank consultant who has worked with every department of the Bank, "is considered an obstructionist—not a good team man." (There are even repeated accounts of the Bank plunging ahead so fast that crucial technical and other implementation aspects are overlooked until it is too late.)

This "excess of funds syndrome," as those in the field speak of it, launches premature large-scale projects when smaller scale, slower-germinating projects would be at least less undesirable. Moreover, it lends itself to the perpetuation of extreme corruption in government. The *Wall Street Journal* reports that in Indonesia it is "authoritatively estimated" that 10 to 15 percent of the total cost of bank-financed projects (now running at over $500 million a year) is dissipated through "leakage."[29]

As the largest single lender in most countries, the Bank also can undermine the efforts of smaller official and voluntary agencies that try to circumvent corrupt and exploitative structures by placing tight conditions on aid. Why would a government bother with such agencies when the Bank is ready to lend large sums with no effective strings attached? In Bangladesh we learned of one aid agency laboring for four years to design a $4.5 million funding to the Agricultural Research Institute and then, at the last minute, the World Bank coming along and dumping in an additional $10 million to "beef up" the Institute. The aid agency officers were horrified; they feared that this sort of sudden money would be bad for the Institute. Indeed, they argued, had more money been in order, they themselves would have arranged it. The Bank, we have often been told, tends to be a "reckless donor."

In Tanzania, a major part of the funds in a World Bank urban garden project went to an outside contractor for building a storage unit. It cost four times as much per square foot, we were told by a community worker close to the project, as a comparable structure built by the participants themselves in a similar project nearby. The community worker also told us that the Bank this year has channeled into the project twice the amount of money needed. "The excess," she stressed, "leads to waste and inefficiency."

The Bank is pushing money, yes, but not giving it away. Loans must eventually be repaid—and with foreign exchange earned, as we have seen, largely by the labor of the rural population producing for export. At best the Bank, through its IDA operation, waives the interest charge, charges only .75 percent yearly service charge, and allows 40 to 50 years for repayment. Much of these loans, however, merely serve to create the cash flow that makes it possible to make payments on previous regular Bank loans.

Nor should we overlook that Bank projects invariably require the local government to put up "counterpart funds" amounting to 20 to 60 percent of the costs of the projects. Thus scarce financial resources—and human ones, too—are tied up by Bank projects.

Repaying mounting debts puts a country under ever greater pressure to orient every aspect of the economy toward exports. The "debt trap" (discussed on pages 361–62) pushes countries away from building a basis of self-reliance, the only foundation for a new international economic order.

Financing Exports

The World Bank was chartered at the close of World War II to stimulate and finance capital goods exports from countries like the United States. (In mid-1978 the State Department estimated that for every dollar the U.S. had paid into the Bank, $2 has been spent in the U.S. economy—which should lead some to ask who is aiding whom.)[30] "Development" then inevitably gets defined as things that cost large sums of money and must be imported—buildings, high-salary foreign technicians and the vehicles they need, dams, roads, laboratories, audio-visual equipment, and so forth. Thus it is not unusual that at least 50 percent of a Bank nutrition project in Indonesia goes to "bricks and mortar" and fancy equipment for fancy buildings, as one American technician working for the U.N. in Indonesia told us. Even under the heading of agriculture and rural development, World Bank loans go overwhelmingly to build infrastructures—from roads to dams—that enrich local and foreign contractors and consultants. Such projects leave intact or reinforce the economic stranglehold of the elites that prevents true agricultural progress and causes rural poverty.

Looking at some of the Bank's confidential planning documents, we found shockingly inflated prices for goods to be imported for projects. In a 1977 agricultural extension project in Thailand,[31] sophisticated audio-visual equipment and other electronic hardware, largely imported, make up over $1,000,000 out of the total budget. Sounds more like a Harvard graduate course in mass media than a rural development project in Asia!

Here are some of the Bank's "bargains" to be obtained for the project by "international competitive bidding": 420 hand calculators at $50 each; 30 desk calculators at $160 each; 30 16mm movie projectors at $1200 each; twelve 21 in. color television receivers at $1050 each; and on and on. (Business readers might wish to check into selling to the Bank.)

The World Bank and Agribusiness

Sometimes World Bank projects aid private corporations much more directly than just through creating a demand for their pesticides, fertilizers, tractors, roadgraders, desk calculators and so on. Part of the World Bank since 1964, the International Finance Corporation (IFC) was created to "act as a catalyst, to bring together private foreign and domestic capital and investment opportunities, and to facilitate investment with its own funds."[32] IFC provides loans for hotels and other profit-making ventures as well as for agri-business.

Recall the story of Bud Senegal's export vegetable operations from the African Sahel?* IFC helped Bud get started. In fact, IFC granted three loans to Bud Senegal. Other loans have gone to food processors and export crop estates, largely in Latin America and Africa.

In addition, the IDA, the soft-loan arm of the World Bank that is supposedly reserved for the "needy" governments, has apparently found some needy corporations. A 1978 loan, for instance, to rehabilitate commercial oil palm plantations in Zaire will, according to the Bank, "benefit three companies"—a subsidiary of the giant firm Unilever (known in the United States as Lever Bros.) and two Belgian firms.[33]

And benefit they will, in notable contrast to their Zairian employees. The plantation workers (3,500 jobs theoretically to be created by the project) will earn about $200 a year, which breaks down to $4.00 a week, low even for Third World plantation work. The net annual income of the participating companies, however, is expected to be $3 million at the time of the loan's maturity in 1987.[34]

In discussing its fears that the project's profitability might be reduced if unable to secure labor, the Bank's secret "gray cover" report on the project points out that better housing and social services for workers will be provided to "reduce the risk of labor shortage." Thus, while the World Bank talks publicly of its humanitarian motives, a reading of its private documents reveals that a better life for the poor is a goal when it serves the economic interests of the real beneficiaries, in this case multinational corporations.

Finally, it would seem at this point almost gratuitous to point out that the project completely overlooks the needs of Zaire's three to four million traditional small family farms. The rehabilitation of commercial oil palm plantations was selected instead because, the Bank says, it "offers the best prospects for future pro-

_____
* See page 286.

duction increases at the least cost."[35] Production maybe, development no.

More Than a Bank

The World Bank is not simply a provider of development loans. Over the past few years it has become a major force shaping the economic policies of various countries. In the Bank's own words:

> IDA's [part of the World Bank Group] borrowers, in particular, would be unlikely to obtain finance on terms as satisfactory as IDA's from any other source; they are therefore unlikely to disregard the kind of advice they may be given by Bank IDA missions whose periodic surveys of their economics include assessments of the soundness of their economic policies.[36]

The Bank has started establishing permanent missions in underdeveloped countries, often physically located right within national planning ministries and central banks. In an increasing number of countries the Bank puts together and chairs a consortium of the principal bilateral and multilateral lenders to coordinate donor contributions and policies. In many countries such as Bangladesh, the Bank is quietly placing and lending the funds for advisors in key ministries of the government. One trump card of the Bank is that it determines the government's international credit rating.

The Bank, in short, is increasingly spoken of as *the* power in many Third World countries we have visited.

A 1975 article in the British *Guardian* gives some notion of what that power is used for in a country like Bangladesh:

> . . . devaluation is only the most dramatic measure in the World Bank programme, which to be successful must be accompanied by fiscal and other changes which will restore monetary stability. An integral part of the programme is the creation of a "fa-

vourable investment climate" . . . In spite of the clinically neutral language . . . the stabilization programme is not simply a technical exercise in monetary management. It amounts to imposing lower real incomes mainly on the urban and other working classes . . .[87]

We should not be surprised then that loans go increasingly to the world's most repressive regimes, those willing to implement measures dictated by the Bank that penalize the working people with higher price and wage controls. Thus four countries that have undergone military takeovers or martial law since the early 1970's—Argentina, Chile, the Philippines and Uruguay—received a sevenfold increase in World Bank lending by 1979. Loans to all other borrowers increased only three times.[38]

The World Bank, the United States and the Human Rights Campaign

The U.S. government has been congratulated for trying to alter the trend of Bank loans going increasingly to the most repressive regimes. Since the Harkin "human rights" amendment to the International Financial Institutions Act of 1977, U.S. representatives in the international banks are required to oppose loans to governments that engage in "a consistent pattern of gross violations of internationally recognized human rights." Exempt from this law, however, are loans for projects that address "basic human needs."

Those who congratulate the United States for adhering to the Harkin amendment base their support on the fact that in the first year after enactment, U.S. representatives abstained on 17 votes and voted "no" only twice on World Bank loans to 12 countries officially recognized as "human rights violators" during that period. (In other international lending agencies, the U.S. representatives voted "no" 7 times and abstained 4 times.[39])

Most of these loans were approved anyway; "abstention" is not very effective opposition. But the uselessness of this record in proving that the administration is serious about forcing the Bank to stop supporting repressive regimes is revealed in one basic fact: During the first post-Harkin amendment year (FY 1978), a full quarter of all new World Bank (including IDA) loans went to just four countries, all well known for denying the economic and political rights of their people—Brazil, Indonesia, South Korea and the Philippines.[40]

How can this record of loans occur when the administration claims to adhere to the Harkin guidelines? First of all, the Harkin amendment loses much of its meaning when one realizes that the administration can decide which countries are "gross violators" and what are "internationally recognized" human rights, as well as which loans address "basic human needs" and are therefore exempt. Obviously there is great latitude for the administration to support loans to just about whichever government it wishes.[41]

Secondly, such "human rights" legislation unfortunately allows the criteria for judging who is and who is no longer a "human rights violator" to be narrowed down to the number of political prisoners being taken or released that week. Thus when martial law governments like those of the Philippines, Argentina, Chile and South Korea release some political prisoners, it is said that their human rights situation has improved. Pressure exerted by the United States through such stipulations as the Harkin human rights amendment is credited. But has the only true measure of human rights enforcement with lasting meaning been obscured? That is, whether or not a government's economic policies are denying the majority the "human right" to survive?

Finally, there are at least two false assumptions behind the efforts such as the Harkin amendment as ways to help the poor abroad. The amendment assumes World Bank projects claiming to serve "basic human needs" *can* actually further the interests of the poor majority instead of strengthening the mechanisms that make the poor poor. Throughout these chapters on aid we have questioned this assumption.

Efforts such as the Harkin amendment also assume that the U.S. government will and can be a global "social worker," pressuring "wayward governments" to "go straight." The reality, however, is that every administration—and the Carter administration is clearly no exception—will ignore even the most ruthless violations of elementary human rights whenever it is seeking to keep in power a government that is subservient to the needs and demands of U.S. corporate and military interests. It will go to great lengths to preserve an elite-controlled economy that does not present a threatening contrast to the concentration of economic power within the United States itself.

Mobutu's Zaire is just one case in point.[42] President Mobutu was installed in power with western connivance in 1965, following the Belgian-inspired murder of the popular Patrice Lumumba. He has kept Zaire (formerly the Congo) wide open for a multinational corporation mineral exploitation. A full 45 percent of the cobalt used in the U.S., for instance, is taken from Zaire.[43]

Despite Zaire's enormous mineral wealth, Mobutu's elitist, corrupt, and pro-foreign investment policies have generated even more widespread and wretched poverty for 20 million peasants and its inevitable partner— brutal repression. Hundreds of thousands of the rural poor have sought refuge in nearby countries. In January 1978, 700 to 1000 villagers—men, women and children—were massacred in the Bandundu province.[44] Yet only a couple of months later the White House proclaimed the Mobutu regime a "moderate government"[45] and President Carter rushed in U.S. military planes to transport Belgian and French troops to crush a revolt against Mobutu. At about the same time the World Bank, with U.S. support, approved yet another World Bank loan—this time for the palm oil plantation already discussed. World Bank and other international loans have come forth so readily to Mobutu that already by 1977 the servicing of those debts and tumbling copper prices combined to make the country to all intents bankrupt.[46]

Only when the brutal policies of a government cause the American government to fear that a revolutionary change will bring about a government no longer willing to serve U.S. corporate and military interests does it finally move to cut off aid. Such, for instance, is the case of the Carter administration's policy toward the Nicaraguan dictatorship of Anastasio Somoza, which we discuss in our next response.

No Accountability

The Bank is in no sense a democratic or even broadly representative institution. It is accountable to no one but itself. And it would be naive to expect that such a powerful institution can or will effectively monitor itself.

Bank documents are secret. The Bank is virtually unstudied even by social scientists; there are fewer than a dozen articles and books analyzing this powerful institution. No staff member will testify before any congressional or parliamentary hearings. Only recently has the Bank begun to go through the motions of evaluations (secret, of course) of all the projects it funds. Those who have seen some reports of the Bank's Operations Evaluations Department tell us that they were greatly "sanitized" when they were later summarized for public release.

Evaluations are sometimes commissioned of outside consultants; but how independent are they, given that their next contract might come from the Bank? One such major evaluation we heard of was critical. It has been suppressed and the author was ordered to do a "re-write." Public reports, we are told, must be upbeat in order to gain support in the congresses and parliaments of donor countries.

While in Bangladesh informed foreign sources told us that recently a mission had flown in from Washington and pronounced the RD-1 program we discussed earlier a success "because it is based on sound prin-

ciples" and that it should be expanded. Yet only the
day before a Bangladesh government official had shown
us an internal Bank memorandum indicting every aspect of the implementation of the project and conclud-
ing that the co-op system operates "excessively in
favor of the more wealthy farmers."

Moreover, many local government negotiators of
Bank loans often aspire to a position with the Bank in
Washington. Are they about to question a Bank project? As we were told in Sri Lanka—a country now
taking on massive Bank loans for a dam irrigation
project—government elites in the capital are already
expectant about "having a whiskey" with all the
foreign experts who come with such a project. In all,
a fairly closed circuit.

Accountable to no one, the Bank is free to make
whatever grandiose claims it wishes about the number
of people who benefit from its projects. Mr. McNamara, for instance, would have us believe the Bank's
agricultural and rural development program will
"reach" 60 million in the "poverty target group" by
lending during 1975-1979. The Bank, you see, likes
to count beneficiaries by totalling up the number of
people living in the area where a Bank project is to
take place. This is equivalent to arguing that a dam in
Paluba, California, benefits the population of California which is 20 million, and therefore the 4 million of
those who live below the poverty line. Soon the Bank's
calculations of the total number of poor beneficiaries
is likely to be more than the total number of poor people in the world.

Although the World Bank is blatantly unaccount-
able, this does not mean that responsibility cannot be
assigned. The U.S. government has the greatest voting
power—23 percent—of any member of the Bank.[47]
U.S. taxpayers have directly contributed 28 percent of
the funds to the "soft-loan" section of the Bank—the
International Development Association. Moreover, although the strictly commercial arm of the Bank does
not get its capital from government subscriptions but
from the public sale of bonds—many undoubtedly held
by universities, pension funds and churches—the fact

that governments back up these bonds is an important factor making them attractive to private investors.

The more we learn about the World Bank, the more astonished we are that the Bank has been so successful in convincing so many that it is promoting the interests of the poor and hungry. Since we as Americans are directly connected through the U.S. government to the World Bank, it is we who must take responsibility for revealing the true impact of World Bank programs and ending them. We must make it clear that the World Bank is still a bank; its concern is with the stability of current elite-controlled economies; its clientele will never be the world's hungry. Indeed, by strengthening the enemies of the hungry, World Bank programs are further undercutting the very poor they claim to be helping.

". . . perhaps more than any other institution in the world, [the World Bank] is helping large numbers of people move out of absolute poverty toward a more decent life."

> Robert S. McNamara
> President World Bank
> *The New York Times*, April 2, 1978

". . . filling (of the reservoir) began on schedule, and initially went according to plan, except that for a short period, the rise of the reservoir had to be slowed to allow some of the 80,000 people who had been slow to move out of the reservoir area, to get away from the rising waters."

> From World Bank Report on
> Tarbela Dam Project (Pakistan)
> July–August, 1975
> quoted in Susan George,
> *How the Other Half Dies*

"Rural Development is a new thing; it's only a few years old."

> Acting chief of World Bank mission,
> Bangladesh

"What isn't generally recognized and what I want to emphasize is that the salaries of the staff of the Bank are not paid for either in whole or in part by United States taxpayers but rather by the developing countries we serve."

Robert S. McNamara
The New York Times, April 2, 1978

44. And AID's New Directions?

Question: The United States Agency for International Development (AID) is not a bank and is not bound by the same constraints. In fact, now it has a clear mandate from Congress to gear its programs to the needs of the rural poor. Has AID taken "new directions"?

Our Response: Beginning in the mid-1970s, legislation empowering AID to carry out programs in our name reads as if it were written by the most enlightened development expert. Once again, the right phrases tumble forth—"participation of the poor," "labor-intensive production," "more equitable and more secure land tenure," and "intermediate technology." Moreover, Congress has legislated that no U.S. development assistance shall go to governments that use torture, prolonged detention without charges, or in other ways deny the right to "life, liberty and the security of person."[1]

All this might be enough to make you feel that AID is now finally on the right path. But our ongoing inquiry into the reality of AID leaves us with four major questions—ones not put to rest by fashionable phrases.

Our first question concerns whether AID has a model that could *ever* lead toward the ends reflected in its humanitarian rhetoric.

Second, can AID provide loans to powerful corporations, helping them to become partners with the elites in Third World countries, and yet serve the interests of the poor in the same countries?

Third, can AID cut off support where a government's economic programs are beginning to benefit the poor majority (such as was the dramatic case in Chile and Thailand) and provide massive support to governments undercutting the workers and peasants (such as in the Philippines and Nicaragua) and still claim to be on the side of the poor?

Fourth, direct economic assistance through AID is but a small fraction of the total impact of our government's policies in an underdeveloped country. Can not a narrow focus on AID ignore the overriding effect of U.S. military, intelligence, diplomatic, and economic operations—all helping maintain governments working to keep the majority of the people excluded from control over food-producing resources?

Now let us take each of these fundamental questions one by one. First, what is the model of development AID is offering?

What is AID's Model of Development?

Basic to AID's current model of development is a focus on the "small farmer." The unquestioned suggestion is that the "small farmer" represents the majority of the rural poor. While AID might find it easy to sell Congress and the American public on helping the world's small farmers, the facts abundantly show that "small farmers" are not the real poor.[2] A large proportion of the rural labor force are worse off than the small farmers. These are the landless and near-landless workers—day laborers, insecure tenants, sharecroppers, and squatters—who together make up 50 to 90 percent of the rural labor force. They are the majority of the hungry. What's more, as should be clear from

Part IV, their desperate plight is virtually everywhere deteriorating.

Neither will another favorite claim of AID's new directions—that its projects get more food grown— necessarily help the landless. For if they do not share in ownership of food-producing resources, or at least have an adequate income, they will not eat no matter how much food is grown.

Whenever we have questioned AID officials in Washington or in the field about what their programs will do for the landless, they seem at a loss. Sometimes they fall back on talking about welfare programs such as "food-for-work" that *at the very best* would mean perpetual funding to help but a handful of the poor. (And as we noted in Question 42, the longterm benefits accrue to the well-off landowners.)

AID simply has no strategy for the dispossessed. Worse still, we believe, the overriding impact of AID projects is to worsen their lot.

Does Commercialization Equal Development?

The new strategy of AID to help the rural poor thus turns out to be a focus on landholders who may be small by absolute or American standards but who in fact function as a middle level elite. To policymakers at AID, making these "small farmers" into commercial farmers seems to equal rural development. Those small farmers whom AID does succeed in making into rural entrepreneurs are likely to become part of the major rural power bloc. More numerous than large landlords, they are, in the words of an AID-commissioned 1978 Cornell study, "likely to be assertive profit-maximizers, politically active, determined in protecting their position and uninclined to recognize traditional obligations of patronage toward tenants and laborers."[3]

With our aid's focus on the profitability of the individual operation, farmers are, moreover, likely to mechanize and otherwise cut back on the use of labor, run tenants off the land, use the new profits to buy up more land, concentrate on one or two crops that bring the most money on local or foreign elite markets.

Thus in many countries a "small farmer" strategy threatens to be a replay of the "Modernizing of Hunger,"* but perhaps with a middle level elite. It is hard to imagine a more sure way to block efforts of the rural poor to organize themselves to demand a just re-distribution of control of productive assets.

Increased Risk

AID's goal is to create "successful commercial farmers." But for many small farmers near the bottom of an exploitative domestic economic structure and dependent on the vicissitudes of the world market, increasing the commercialization of their operations can bring increased vulnerability.

One example of a "small farmer" project about which the agency brags in its own magazine, *War on Hunger,* is a coffee project in Haiti. A $6 million loan plus a $700,000 grant will, we are told, increase the yields and therefore the income of one-third of Haiti's five million inhabitants.

Several reservations come readily to mind and several more have been raised for us by a thoughtful critique of the project done by the Washington consulting firm, Development Alternatives, Inc.[4]

The farmers who are the focus of the project are not, as AID would have us think, underproductive coffee growers. For they are not primarily coffee growers; they are self-provisioning farmers who happen to have a few coffee trees. Traditionally they spend most of their time producing yams, corn, and other food crops basic to their own needs. Whatever time and energy remains goes into coffee production and its cash return. AID would come in and reverse this food-cash relationship, making these peasant farmers primarily commercial coffee producers and buyers of the food they had been growing.

* See Part IV.

But where will this food come from? And, instead of digging up yams year around, will the coffee producer always have the cash to buy the food the family needs? With so many undernourished Haitians, is more coffee what the country needs?

Moreover, although coffee export prices might be up at the start of the project due to natural disasters that hit major coffee producers in other countries, what is to keep them high once recovery is underway? When production among the world's main producers is back to normal levels, the International Coffee Agreement will undoubtedly enforce quotas. Haiti in 1976 already greatly exceeded its "shadow" quota, the quota that would have been enforced under normal market conditions. Is AID setting Haiti up for a soon-to-be oversupplied market?

Such a market oversupply would be disastrous for small farmers who, if AID has its way, would for the first time be dependent on coffee sales for their food.

There are yet other ways in which, according to the Development Alternatives, Inc. report, AID's plan is "fraught with risks."

Part of AID's push to increase coffee yields requires reducing the shade coverage—a step extremely difficult to reverse. Shade coverage, while it might limit yields, does reduce the need for fertilizer. Once the coverage is removed, yields jump, but so does the need for fertilizer. A farmer who had been virtually self-reliant in his capacity to produce coffee will become "virtually dependent on an agricultural input, fertilizer, the source of which he does not control. If the supply of fertilizer dries up, so will his coffee trees," warns the Development Alternatives evaluation.

And even if the farmer can buy the fertilizer, how sure can he be that he will earn enough to justify the investment?

Finally, who will really benefit from the increased productivity if it is achieved in Haiti? The tax on coffee is the biggest source of revenue for the Baby Doc dictatorship. And it is the farmers, not the exporters or speculators, who carry that tax burden. Small, unorganized coffee producers get taxed heavily to pay for government services that, in an elite-dominated country like Haiti, benefit only the tiny upper strata.

And this is a "small farmer" project AID would brag about!

Can AID Reach the Poor?

Just as we learned in looking at the World Bank, it is not easy to selectively reach the poor no matter how the project is designed. But the first question is: does AID really try?

The U.S. Comptroller General in 1977 looked at a number of AID-financed agricultural schemes in Latin America and the Caribbean.[5] The eligibility criteria for loans is so broad, the report points out, as to include "many medium and large farmers." An AID loan in Panama to build cooperative credit groups defines a small farmer as one owning 50 acres or less and having assets of less than $15,000. But 50 percent of the landowners in that country work 12 acres or less!

In Bolivia AID acknowledged that its loan programs were going to the large landholders. AID did not apologize for contradicting its own rhetoric. Rather, it explained that "this target group could most effectively use production credit."

And even when AID sets the limit on its rural credit programs low enough to exclude the rural elite, a government that is allied with large landholders can simply ignore the guidelines. In Nicaragua, a loan limit was set at $120 according to AID's program guidelines. Yet, an AID-funded evaluation of the program showed that the government had pushed the limit up to $590, which is five times the annual income of 70 percent of the rural people in Nicaragua! Clearly, the majority would not qualify for such an AID-backed loan.

Well-intended credit schemes can even be much more grossly distorted in elite-controlled countries. An AID loan to Nicaragua was earmarked for building "community participation" through cooperatively controlled credit. But this involved local organizing which the Somoza dictatorship saw as a threat. So the money went instead for a computer that would make all credit decisions.[6] The computer bank with details of the local population has great potential for abuse. It could easily be a tool for the U.S.-trained National Guard who have killed many rural people, especially during the popular uprising against Somoza in 1979.

Electrify the Countryside

Furthermore, although AID talks of directing its projects selectively toward the needs of the poor, its biggest outlays build infrastructure—especially roads, dams, and electrification. Again: Who will benefit? Who will be harmed?

One good way to get a sense of AID's priorities is to pick a couple of countries and request through your Congressperson the AID Congressional Presentation and other project documents for those countries. We found, for instance, that AID's budgetary submission to Congress for Indonesia contains a "Preliminary Profile of Poverty," specifying the "Rural Target Group" as 33 million members of landless laborer families and 57 million members of smallholder families. The clear implication is that the multitude of proposed projects will help the poor, however vague the description. But many of the projects are massive electrification projects. A total of $125 million has been committed to "demonstrate that electrical power . . . provided to rural Indonesia . . . will contribute to productivity and improvement in the quality of life."[7] We asked the chief of the AID agricultural mission in Indonesia what he thought the impact would be. He predicted that the better-off farmers would use the electricity to mill rice mechanically. But what about the millions of landless laborers, especially women, who depend on this work for survival income? The project's net impact, he agreed, would be fewer jobs for the poor. And this in a country with already high unemployment!

In Bangladesh, AID is putting $50 million into

"rural electrification," its second largest program expenditure.[8] The main use of the electricity in the countryside will be to power irrigation pumps. But who has the pumps? A small group of farmers—all probably among Bangladesh's elite ten percent. AID's own evaluations of similar electrification schemes in Costa Rica and Colombia reveal a clear pattern: Benefits accrue to the better-off owners of the land, mills, dairy operations and to other members of the "non-target" population.

The AID rationale for such a large electrification expenditure in Bangladesh is that it will stimulate the development of rural industries. It is presumed that textile and food processing plants will spring up, providing jobs for the rural poor, 40 percent of whom are now jobless. But who will buy their products? Since most of the people in the countryside are too poor even to buy adequate food, how are they to constitute a profitable market for consumer goods?

Unless redistribution of control over agricultural resources is underway, in which the majority of people are gaining more equitable participation in the economy, rural industry cannot prosper. Only then would rural electrification serve to build rural-located industries integrated into the rhythms of agricultural work as well as the need for improved agricultural technology and consumer goods for the rural population.

Without such prior change, the only possibility is that electrification might allow the area to become an "export platform." There consumer items would be assembled for high income groups elsewhere—thus freezing an international division of labor and locking the rural poor into poorly paid factory jobs with as little security as they now have as day laborers.

In our experience, AID officials, when pushed, will concede the illogic of a focus on rural electrification. They then grasp for straws that might justify their huge commitment of funds. One AID official told us that rural electrification in Bangladesh would provide the amenities which will "induce government bureaucrats to get out into the countryside." Pamper the country's elite so they might be more willing to visit the country's poor? A mighty strange "basic needs" development strategy!

Appropriate Terminology

With the American public increasingly concerned about hunger, and some members of Congress questioning AID critically, the Agency has been working on its "appropriate terminology." Flipping through any AID presentation to Congress, you will find, for instance, a wide range of projects under the heading "Food and Nutrition."

- AID lists most electrification projects under the funding category "Food and Nutrition." One such project in Indonesia drawing on funds earmarked for Food and Nutrition is Rural Electrification I, a $36 million commitment by AID.[9] The Presentation states that of the two million villagers in the project area, about 500,000 will "benefit from street lighting and lighting in private and public buildings." Can anyone seriously believe that the majority of villagers—landless and underfed—participated in the decision that what they needed was street lighting? AID, à la World Bank, would have this project rack up another 2 million beneficiaries in the "rural target group": Congress is told that "all" of the two million people in the area will benefit from "increased economic activity." This despite the fact that everyone we interviewed in Indonesia, including the above mentioned AID official, predicted that the overall employment impact precisely on the poor would be negative. And without jobs, people go hungry—so much for electrification as "food and nutrition."

Looking closely at AID's Presentation on Indonesia, we often find the pious chant, "the beneficiaries ultimately will be the multitude of poor farmers." But the "direct beneficiaries," admits

AID, are Indonesian elites who will get degrees in the United States and work in local research institutes and U.S. universities. The enormous leap of faith here is that bureaucrats favored by AID will become more useful to the "multitude."

- Cameroon. "Satellite Application and Training" —$650,000 of "Food and Nutrition" funds.[10] One satellite specialist alone costs $90,000. In an elite-controlled society, who will benefit from a "more accurate knowledge of the natural resource base?" Similar satellite projects—all out of "Food and Nutrition"—are being promoted by AID around the world. In countries where the majority of the rural population is excluded from any form of ownership of agricultural resources, how can AID persist in claiming a remote sensing satellites project will mean better planning "which will ultimately further the economic development process"?

- A new $10.3 million project in the Philippines placed under the "Food and Nutrition" category is actually called a "Fund for Local Government."[11] Are we being asked to believe that in a country with notoriously corrupt martial law government, financing local government is a direct way to help the poor? This should cause as much incredulity as would a foreign donor claiming to help poor Blacks in Philadelphia by contributing to the Philadelphia City Council.

- Liberia. "Rural Roads Phase III"—$5,200,000 of "Food and Nutrition" funds.[12] According to Roy Prosterman and Charles Taylor of the University of Washington School of Law, it is a new interregional highway. "It may make it more convenient for Firestone (massive rubber operator plantation) vehicles to traverse the country, but its relationship to the small farmer's economic and social benefits, the avowed goal, is non-existent."[13]

- Pakistan. "Rural Roads Phase II"—$100 million in "Food and Nutrition" funds.[14] The project will build or rehabilitate 1600 miles of roads; that's $62,500 per mile—a sure signal that construction is low employment, capital-intensive. Each advisor will cost $7,500 per month. AID notes that it will assist in constructing or rehabilitating 120,000 miles of rural roads in Pakistan. That could mean that AID will be committing over $7 billion of "Food and Nutrition" funds to roads in Pakistan.

- Haiti. "Road Maintenance II"—$8.6 million in "Food and Nutrition" funds "to expand and strengthen the Government of Haiti's National Highway Maintenance Service."[15]

Better rural roads. Who could be against roads? Roads certainly sound neutral. Yet we have come to see that new roads in the context of sharp rural inequalities and repressive government can negatively affect the poor. Those who benefit from rural roads are the larger commercial growers able to get their crops to the cities and ports more efficiently. And the middleman who buys from the poor can also make his operation more lucrative with the help of better roads. (In most rural areas the middleman already profits more on each unit than the peasant who produces the crop.) Moreover, in countries such as Nicaragua or the Philippines where a dictatorship is trying to quell rural resistance, rural roads only make it easier to maintain control. Rural roads also open up the countryside to those pushing manufactured consumer items and processed foods. They can destroy the market for more nutritious local food and the livelihood of village craftspeople. (See our example of plastic shoes in Question 47.) Finally, roads allow for the exploitation of an area's natural resources, not for the benefit of the local inhabitants but for the local elite, or just as likely, for a foreign interest.

Some tell us that this perspective is paternalistic. Why should we deny people roads? But the real question is, when a society is structured against the poor, why should we make it even easier for those in power to reap further advantage?

The rural poor are often aware of the threat that a new road can represent. Last year a voluntary aid group in India presented a rural community with its plans for a road into its villages. To the dismay of the donors, the community resisted. They offered a counter-proposal: that in addition to the road, the donor provide loans to help a cooperative, to be formed by the community, purchase a bus and a truck to serve the area and also secure a license to operate quarries and cut wood in a nearby forest. At that point the donor agency lost interest in the whole project.[16]

AID and U.S. Corporations: Partners in Progress?

The second question we asked in the beginning of this chapter was: Can an agency that assists powerful corporations also help the poor majority in the under-developed countries? You will recall Part VIII in which we discussed the devastating impact of agribusiness on the lives and livelihood of the rural poor. Still, a recent administrator of AID openly promoted the expansion of agribusiness in order to bring the "unique reservoir" of talent in U.S. agribusiness corporations to underdeveloped countries. Moreover, the chief administrator of AID serves at the same time as the chairperson of OPIC, an insurance and lending agency that puts the U.S. government squarely behind investments by multinational corporations in underdeveloped countries. (See Question 39.)

AID directly aids some of the world's largest corporations. One case in point is the Latin American Agribusiness Development Corporation (LAAD), a holding company that numbers among its fifteen shareholders a Chase Manhattan agribusiness subsidiary, the Bank of America, Borden, Cargill, CPC International, John Deere, Gerber, Goodyear, Castle and Cooke, Ralston Purina, and ADELA (itself a multinational investment company whose 240 shareholders are large multinational corporations). By 1976, AID loans to LAAD totaled $17 million, at only a 3 to 4 percent rate of interest. (Let some small American business try to get loans on as favorable terms from the United States Government.)

By the end of 1977 LAAD had approved over $26 million in loans to 101 agribusiness projects in Latin America: processing and marketing beef, growing and exporting fresh and frozen vegetables, cut flowers, ferns, and tropical plants, wood products, seafood, and other specialty items.[17]

In 1975 alone, LAAD's net profit after interest payments was $519,757. Not bad, considering the total capital the corporate shareholders had invested was a mere $2 million. LAAD even used AID's low-interest loans to turn a cool profit: Latin American affiliates that borrow from LAAD pay back at rates up to 9 percent.

Shareholders' profits, which are hard to assess, of course, come from sales of their products by the 66 LAAD projects, and the business experience they gain. Although American taxpayers furnished two-thirds of LAAD's capital, the corporation pays no taxes to the United States: LAAD is incorporated in tax-haven Panama.

In 1974, AID hired an outside consulting firm to evaluate LAAD. Although not unsympathetic to LAAD's purposes, the firm commented that LAAD's presence has not produced additional food for those who need it. "The bulk of the product lines handled are either destined for upper middle, upper class consumption, or for export," according to the evaluation. Nor have small farmers and small businessmen been helped: "LAAD's efforts have not, for the most part, been diluted by social motives to 'reach the small man.'" Instead, according to the report, LAAD has been "supporting businessmen whose success is predictable."[18] In other words, one safe way not to fail in helping someone is to pick someone who would probably succeed anyway.

A principal country of LAAD's operations is Nicaragua. Besides interests in export-oriented cattle ranches, ice production, and American-style supermarkets, LAAD lent over $300,000, mostly from our AID tax money, to Industrias Amolonca. Industrias

Amolonca now ties up prime agricultural lands to produce black-eyed peas for stews and soups and freezing vegetables like okra for its major contractors, Safeway Stores and Southland (Seven-Eleven).

Amolonca employs a grand total of twenty-six people, ten of whom are salaried managers and administrators. The capital invested per employee is a phenomenal $47,817. All this in a country where even officially rural unemployment runs between 20 and 32 percent and over three-quarters of the rural people earn less than $120 a year. LAAD probably considers the Amolonca project not only profitable but a form of political insurance; the Nicaraguan partners are relatives of the dictator, Anastasio Somoza, a West Point graduate, whose father was described by FDR as a "son-of-a-bitch but he's our son-of-a-bitch."

LAAD's 1977 Annual Report boasts of ALCOSA, "a Guatemalan frozen food company" supplying the U.S. supermarkets with okra, broccoli, and cauliflower "grown by Indian communities."[19] A late 1977 investigation by Checchi and Co., however, found that everything is not as it sounds.[20] First of all, ALCOSA might sound Guatemalan but in fact it is an affiliate of the U.S. food multinational Hanover Brands. More importantly, the "Indian communities" turn out to be made up of not only Indian but also economically and socially better-off mestizos. And what has been the impact of ALCOSA coming in and contracting production? The Checchi investigation studied one village, Patzicia, and found that the already better-off small farmers, who had some capital to begin with, and who were "opportunistically entrepreneurial"—mostly mestizos—got the contracts. Their increased income has touched off a speculative land market in which the smallest landholders, mainly Indian, have lost their land and become seasonal laborers on farms growing cauliflower for ALCOSA. The net result, the evaluation concludes, is "an increase in economic inequality." The evaluation calls the harm done to the poor Indian families "ironic" since the ALCOSA field manager is considered "almost an Indianist." Once again we find that as long as a society's ground rules still allow for a few to get ahead at the real expense of the rest, agribusiness will harm the poor majority no matter how fine the intentions of persons with LAAD and AID.

At this writing LAAD is expanding its operations into the Caribbean with a fresh AID loan. One investment already made is a new affiliate of Hormel Meats in the Dominican Republic.[21] In the eyes of AID, LAAD has proved to be a success—a success that should be copied in other parts of the world. In 1977, AID (as well as the World Bank) contracted with LAAD for advisory services for agribusiness projects in Afghanistan, the Philippines, and the Sudan.[22]

Aid for Whom?

In selling its programs to Congress, AID explains why "we" have to help the underdeveloped countries. First of all, AID says, American corporations increasingly depend on underdeveloped countries for raw materials. Second, these corporations need the markets of the underdeveloped countries. And finally, according to AID, these countries provide "opportunities for productive and profitable investment of U.S. capital and technology."[23]

To fight back against attacks on foreign aid, AID regularly trumpets the value of aid to U.S. corporations and the economy. About three dollars out of four spent by AID purchase products and consultative services in the U.S.[24] Many American universities do particularly well by multi-million dollar AID contracts. A *typical* "Agricultural Development and Operations" project in Peru spent 54 percent of the funds at Iowa State for ten advisors and technicians at an average of over $40,000 each.[25] (You may wish to organize a group to investigate what your local university is up to with AID.)

It has become clear to us that exporting an American model of commercial agriculture or, as AID would say, "promoting profitable production," creates new customers for U.S. agribusiness corporations and in many cases helps tie the agricultural potential of underdeveloped countries into the Global Supermarket dominated by these companies.

On Whose Side?

The third question we asked in the beginning of this chapter was: Can AID still claim to be on the side of the poor when it cuts off aid to governments that are solidly behind basic reform and increases aid to governments blocking change that would benefit the poorer groups?

Take the case of the Popular Unity government in Chile, from 1970 to 1973. Only twenty months after President Allende's inauguration, the Popular Unity government had brought under its agrarian reform program more than 13 million acres of land benefiting 40,000 to 45,000 farm workers and small peasants. This was nearly twice the number that had benefited under the six years of land reform carried out by the previous administration.[26] The government encouraged development of participatory small farmer organizations. Their purpose was to allow the new landholders to pool their work and resources and, for the first time, to provide the rural poor with a strong voice in overall development policies.

In a short time, the Popular Unity government made great strides toward meeting basic human needs. Between 1970 and 1973, infant mortality fell from 79 to 65 per thousand; unemployment fell from 8 percent to 3.1 percent. The wage earners' share in the national income rose from 51 percent in 1970 to 76 percent by the end of 1972. Some expert observers claim that the poor had better food, shelter, medical attention and education than at any time in the history of Chile.[27]

What was the response of AID to a government doing exactly what the agency states to be its *own* primary goal—improving the lot of the poor? Within the first few months the United States drastically cut economic assistance, previously the highest amount to any Latin American country, to practically nothing.

The few programs left, we now know from Congressional investigations of the CIA, were in fact covers for subversive activity. In addition, the Nixon administration secretly organized a blockade of sales of parts for U.S.-made machines, including farm machinery. The United States wielded its virtual veto power in the World Bank and in the Inter-American Development Bank to block any loans to Chile, even for projects previously approved, and despite the fact that the Chilean government continued to meet the sizeable payments on loans taken out by previous administrations. The United States refused to send food aid to the Popular Unity government. It even refused to accept hard cash for food.[28]

After the Chilean military overthrew the constitutional government in September 1973, AID policies abruptly changed. Within hours of the bloody coup, ships loaded with American food set off from New Orleans for Chile. By 1975, Chile under the junta was receiving six times more food aid than the rest of Latin America put together. AID assistance and food aid together climbed twenty-fourfold, from $3.7 million in 1973 to $81.5 million in 1976.[29]

In the fall of 1976, the Chilean junta began to react to criticism from Americans questioning its human rights violations—not by changing its policies but by rejecting U.S. bilateral aid for 1978. But loans and guarantees from the U.S. Export-Import Bank continued as well as economic support from mutilateral sources dominated by the United States, such as the World Bank. Such indirect U.S. support, virtually cut off during the Allende period, was, in 1976, four times the level of 1972. Thus, the U.S. government allowed the junta's rejection of U.S. economic aid to be more apparent than real.[30]

In its 1976 fiscal year report to Congress, AID praised the economic measures of the junta—which have had a devastating impact on the poor majority and even on the middle class and small businesses. The military government not only halted but reversed land reform, driving small farmers and Indians off land which had, in some cases, been distributed to them even before the Popular Unity government came to power.

The junta's idea of development is modern commercialized farms exporting luxury fruits, vegetables, and even beans to the Global Supermarket. (Agricultural exports rank second, next to copper.) The lifting of tariffs has meant an influx of luxury goods affordable only by the rich. Investments in education and health have been drastically curtailed, with a corresponding rise in diseases like typhoid. The real wages of workers have plummeted.

The case of Chile reveals that AID is used by the administration to selectively support governments whose economic policies are not threatening to the status quo in our own country and favor the investment of U.S. business—regardless of the effect of these policies on the majority of the local population. Many have argued that what happened in Chile during the Nixon-Ford administration would not happen again and is certainly not happening now. But we have found AID's role as supporter of repressive regimes little different today from its backing of the brutal Chilean junta. We find AID enlarging its economic support even as it becomes clear that a recipient government is actively undermining the well-being of the majority and abolishing civil liberties in order to deal with those who protest.

A recent example is Thailand where during 1973–1976 AID sharply curtailed assistance and even prepared to eliminate it. During this period a civilian government was encouraging peasants who were organizing for reforms. Under the civilian government only AID's security assistance grew. Then, in 1976 a right-wing military coup brought severe repression to the student, labor, and peasant groups that had pressured for progressive reforms. AID's program in Thailand suddenly began expanding again and is now expected to increase severalfold over current levels.[31] Also significantly, in visiting Thailand in early 1978, we discovered AID's programs were concentrated in those provinces officially designated "sensitive" due to ongoing resistance.

Another example is found in the Philippines. Since the imposition of martial law in 1972, AID loans and grants have leapt fivefold.[32] But what kind of government is our AID money going to support in the Philippines?

Since 1972, the real income and nutrition of workers and peasants in the Philippines has declined steadily while the wealth and power of the ruling clique around President Ferdinand Marcos continues to grow. According to the Asian Development Bank the per capita calorie consumption in the Philippines has fallen to the *lowest in all Asia*.[33] The Food and Nutrition Research Institute in Manila reported that the percentage of people living in families with incomes too meager to purchase adequate diets increased from 56 percent in 1971 to 68 percent in 1975.[34] Thousands of Filipinos have been imprisoned and many tortured. Strikes are banned and organizing outlawed in key industries and in agriculture. The only newspapers left in Manila are those owned or controlled by the relatives of the President and by his key supporters. In the countryside, only those cooperatives organized by the government are recognized.

Land reform, proclaimed by Marcos as the cornerstone of his "new society," is a sham. After five years less than 1 percent of the country's tenants—and no landless laborers—have benefitted.[35] Land ownership in the Philippines appears to be growing more concentrated, not less.[36]

Looking at the AID Philippines program, we find that 42 percent of the proposed authorizations for fiscal 1978 are going to rural roads and agricultural research. But again, without *prior* restructuring of control over land and other productive resources, actively thwarted by the Marcos martial law regime, how can such improvements do anything but strengthen the hand of the current elites? AID even refers to its Philippine rural development program as a model of its "new directions" focus. But the fundamental question is: Because AID must work *through* channels of government in any host country, can it do anything other than reinforce the power that is clearly, in countries like the Philippines, a key obstacle to progress for the country's 8 million landless and 3 million tenants?

Aid and Human Rights

The human rights amendment to the aid legislation restricted U.S. economic aid from going to any country "which engages in a consistent pattern of gross violations of internationally recognized human rights . . . unless such assistance will directly benefit the needy people in such a country." Yet U.S. economic aid continues not only to Thailand and the Philippines but to more than a dozen other governments that have been either "officially" or "unofficially" denounced as violators of the human rights of their people.

Why is this happening? The truth is that, however abhorrent these regimes might appear to you and me, they have common interests with U.S. corporate executives and many of those in government who influence key decisions. Governments like the Marcos dictatorship provide an open door to U.S. corporate investments, exports, profit repatriation and provide a source of raw materials. The Marcos regime also allows the continued presence of U.S. military installations—the largest any nation has in a foreign country. Moreover, regimes such as Marcos' oppose efforts to redistribute control over their countries' productive resources.

Could the U.S. government do anything other than support such regimes? What if an arm of the U.S. government promoted economic democracy elsewhere —self-management by workers and peasants striving for national and regional self-reliance, with strict controls on foreign investment, and public planning selectively directing services toward previously disenfranchised groups? It is such alternatives—not regimes such as Marcos'—that many Americans are taught to see as threatening and tainted with totalitarianism. What if, through this government's genuine support of such alternatives elsewhere, Americans began to see them differently? What if they came to see that such alternatives might be fashioned to serve the interests of people like themselves? If this happened, would not those corporate and government officials who now make our foreign policy feel threatened?

Thus the U.S. government will cling to a regime favoring U.S. economic military and diplomatic interests—no matter how brutally it represses its own people—until, that is, the regime appears to be no longer viable. Only at this point is aid suspended in an effort to find a "moderate" solution that protects that structural status quo. One case in point is U.S. aid to Nicaragua.

Since the U.S. Marines helped to install the Somoza family in state power in 1933, the Nicaraguan government has been known as one of the world's worst human rights violators. In fiscal 1978 the Carter administration trebled what AID calls its "resource flow" to Somoza's Nicaragua. And even after popular uprisings began in early 1978, the administration fought to maintain funding at that level for fiscal 1979.[87] (Also add in funds going to Nicaragua through LAAD, discussed earlier.) Moreover, the administration sponsored a $32 million Inter-American Development Bank loan.

Only in early fall 1978 after prolonged general strikes of workers *and* business owners and a near-successful popular insurrection led by the National Liberation Front did the Carter administration change its policy toward Somoza. On September 23, the day after the U.S.-trained National Guard retook control of the liberated areas, the Carter administration announced a suspension of U.S. economic and military assistance.

Also revealing is the fact that the administration suspended rather than cut off aid. A suspension interrupts the planning of future projects but it allows all AID projects "in the pipeline" as well as the 11-member U.S. military advisory group to continue. (Contrast this to the actual cut-off of aid to Ethiopia following the overthrow of Haile Selassie and to Chile following the election of President Allende.) Clearly our government would like to maintain "somozismo" without Somoza. The human rights of the Nicaraguans have never been the determinant influence on U.S. policy.

Another way the administration deals with the growing outrage at U.S. aid supporting governments that are flagrant violators of political rights is by arguing that of course we do not want to support such governments, yet "we do not wish to deny our assistance to poor people who happen to live under repressive regimes." The State Department goes on to argue that in such countries we may properly have aid programs because they will directly benefit the poor.[38] Such a rationale sounds admirable. But the reality is that our government cannot promote economic rights where political rights are systematically denied. In Indonesia, for example, where AID has a massive program, even the *Wall Street Journal* (June 14, 1978) concludes that while the only hope for the hungry is "a realignment of power in the villages," it is unlikely to happen so long as "the government won't even allow the landless to organize pressure groups." Without political rights, the majority cannot achieve economic rights.

And we must never lose sight of the simple fact that a government that violates those rights is also the government that AID must work through if it wants to operate in that country. As an arm of the U.S. government, AID is constrained to work through the governing class that is the very obstacle to the necessary transformation. Thus, even if AID did have a theoretical model of development that worked, it could never confront the structures that generate and maintain poverty and hunger. As development authority Gunnar Myrdal notes, "It is with the people in this elite that all business has to be concluded. Even aid has to be negotiated through them." The effect, says Myrdal, is that "the power of the ruling elite . . . is then backed up." In part for this reason he concludes that aid from the industrial countries has "undoubtedly strengthened the inegalitarian economic and social power structure in underdeveloped countries that stands as the main impediment to institutional reforms."[39]

AID as a Political Tool

Thus AID is inevitably political. Moreover, its direct use as a tool in U.S. global military strategy becomes clear when we stand back and look at the big picture of where U.S. development aid flows.

Few Americans realize that development assistance linked to specific development projects and disaster relief is only about half of AID's spending overseas. The rest goes as "Security Supporting Assistance," which, according to aid legislation, "provides balance of payments, infrastructure and other capital and technical assistance to regions of the world in which the United States has special foreign policy and security interests." Since only two countries—Israel and Egypt —receive 83 percent of all Security Supporting Assistance, it turns out that Israel and Egypt receive almost as much from AID ($1.5 billion) as all other countries in the world receive ($1.7 billion), directly from AID or indirectly through AID contributions to international organizations.[40] Moreover, the Director of AID confessed that at least $300 million of this SSA money to Israel *goes totally unaccounted for*.[41]

Tip of the Iceberg

The fourth question we raised at the beginning of this response was this: Does not a focus on AID narrow our examination of how U.S. government policies relate to the problems of underdevelopment abroad?

Official development assistance, it turns out, represents the proverbial tip of the iceberg.

The role of AID is increasingly overshadowed by the much greater development impact of other channels through which funds flow with little if any congressional review and approval, channels such as the Export-Import Bank, OPIC, the World Bank, the regional development banks, and the International Monetary Fund. Over the last six years the share of the traditional aid outlets, those at least nominally reviewed and approved by Congress, has dropped from 46 percent to 31 percent of the total U.S. bilateral and U.S.-supported multilateral resource flows, according to James Morrell of the Center for International Policy.[42] In other words, *69 percent of such support goes without any congressional review*. Morrell documents these examples: In fiscal year 1976 only 22 percent of the credits, guarantees, and insurance going to the authoritarian regime in South Korea came through outlets that are subject to congressional control. In Chile in the same year the figure was 21 percent. The Philippines received $94 million, yet Congress specifically approved only 6 percent of that total. South Africa got $310 million from two United States programs and the International Monetary Fund in 1976 but Congress had not approved one cent.

Of the many financial institutions influencing the economies—and therefore the people—in underdeveloped countries, perhaps the most powerful while least in public view is the International Monetary Fund (IMF)—a fund from which 130 member nations can borrow foreign currency to help meet short-term balance of payments deficits. The United States holds the largest voting block. When Saudi Arabia joined the IMF in 1978, reducing the United States' voting power to less than 20 percent, the number of "yes" votes needed for action was also increased so that the United States would still hold veto power.

The leverage of the IMF over the economies of other countries is more than as a lender of its own funds. When an underdeveloped country faces a debt crisis and suffers a heavy trade deficit, it seeks loans to meet its international commitments. But first it must turn to the IMF. Before approving a loan, the IMF stipulates an economic "stabilization program" that must be carried out. Governments and private banks will hold off lending to the country in question until it has secured the IMF's stamp of approval.[43]

To get this approval, a country is usually obliged to:

- devalue its currency so as to boost exports and limit imports. If much food is being imported, the poor are the first to feel the squeeze.
- cut back government spending. The first to go are government health, housing and educational programs designed for the poor.
- introduce wage controls (hardly ever price controls), undercutting the already marginal income of the poor.
- raise interest rates, making it harder for farmers and small businesses to get credit. The result can be more unemployment and less food production.
- remove all barriers to foreign investment and free trade. Free trade means that luxury items are still allowed to enter even when scarce foreign exchange should be going for more needed basic items. An open door to foreign investment allows foreign corporations to get a foothold in the economy at bargain rates—just when land prices and wages are being held down by all of the above policies.

With some sense of the inevitable impact of these conditions on the poorest groups, it is not surprising that, for example, when Egypt was forced to end food subsidies and reduce fuel and clothing subsidies in 1977 to meet IMF stipulations, people rioted and seventy-eight were killed.[44]

Not only do IMF policies place the heaviest burden on the poorest groups but the IMF has also been attacked because its loan approvals reflect the ideological bias of its most powerful members. In 1977 Argentina, for example, was granted a $194 million loan without first having to bring under control one of the highest inflation rates in Latin America. Whereas, during the same period, Peru and Jamaica were forced to meet very rigid criteria.[45] In Jamaica, a country with a democratic government working toward land reform and more control by Jamaica over its natural resources, food prices shot up 40 percent in less than a year because of IMF-imposed policies.

Through such closed-to-public-view channels as the IMF, the U.S. administration can support the countries of its choice without relying on AID. Equally important, we must weigh the impact of development assistance against the powerful and overriding influence of our military assistance and sales programs and foreign covert operations (CIA) that go to maintain the status quo of hunger abroad.

In the face of explicit prohibition by our foreign assistance legislation against military assistance and sales to "gross violators of internationally recognized human rights," such assistance and arms sales continued in 1978 to at least eight regimes that have been widely denounced for their violation of human rights (Zaire, Paraguay, Nicaragua, Indonesia, the Philippines, Thailand, Bangladesh and South Korea). U.S. interference in each of these countries pits us against the movements for change we have come to learn are necessary. For thorough documentation on most of these countries we recommend to you the report, "Human Rights and the U.S. Foreign Assistance Program," prepared by the Center for International Policy, Washington, D.C.

In 1976 Congress tried to control our military's role in the Third World by limiting the number of military advisors that could be permanently stationed abroad. The effect has been negligible. By the time Congress passed the legislation, most U.S.-supported advice, training and technical assistance was being given by *roving* armed forces personnel (thus sidestepping the congressional limitations on permanent stationing) and by civilians—11,320 employees of the 50 U.S. arms manufacturers. In the era of highly sophisticated military hardware, technicians employed by Defense Department contractors are a major part of U.S. military presence in the Third World. United States military sales programs, including training, operate in 69 countries. But the heart of the new U.S. military presence abroad are Mobile Training Teams (MTTs) and Technical Assistance Field Teams (TAFTs). Team members, wearing civilian clothes despite their military status, can enter a country unobtrusively to do their jobs as advisors, trainers and maintenance specialists. Furthermore, U.S. military advisors are permanently stationed in seven countries that have had military aid sanctions placed on them by Congress for human rights violations: Argentina, Brazil, Chile, El Salvador, Nicaragua, Uruguay, and the Philippines.[46]

Finally, despite explicit prohibition by Congress, the U.S. government directly supports foreign police forces. The Philippines and Nicaragua are but two examples. The Philippines Constabulary (PC)—a military style police force recruited and trained through the armed forces—benefits directly from U.S. support to the Philippine armed forces. The PC and the armed forces rotate personnel and share facilities. The PC uses the regular army's logistics center supplied by the U.S. Military Assistance Program.[47] In Nicaragua, dictator Somoza has been kept in power by the brutal National Guard which operates as both an army and a policing force. The National Guard has had more U.S.-training than any other military or police force in the hemisphere on a per capita basis.[48]

The United States: a Model?

In AID's view of the world, all that needs to be done is to improve the existing situation. AID literature is full of words like "increase," "strengthen," "integrate," "localize"; no basic restructuring is necessary, just build on what is there. This is exactly the model of development most people accept for our own country. If we just keep going in the same direction, eventually everyone will have enough.

The new aid talks about alleviating hunger. Yet, after two hundred years of "development" in our own country, there are still over 20 million undernourished Americans. The new aid law talks about increasing the income of the poor abroad, yet the income of the poor in America is declining. According to the Department of Commerce, the number of poor Americans increased by 2.5 million in 1975 alone to total 26 million.[49]

The new aid talks about generating greater equity in income in underdeveloped countries. Yet, are we achieving greater equity here? A 1972 Labor Department study reveals "a slow but persistent trend toward inequality" in the United States for the period 1958–1970.[50] The poorest 20 percent of the country receives only 4 percent of all income whereas the wealthiest 20 percent receives almost 46 percent of all income.[51] In fact, the distribution of income in the United States today is about the same as that of India.[52]

The new aid talks about helping the small farmer. Yet in the United States over the last twenty years 1900 farms, most of them small, have gone out of business *each week*,[53] largely under the weight of ever more pervasive big business control of our food system. Landless agricultural laborers, including many children, are among the most underfed in America.

The new aid talks about land reform for the underdeveloped countries. Yet in the United States the largest 5.5 percent of all farms operate over half of all farmland while the bottom 40 percent of all farms operate only 4.5 percent.[54]

The new aid talks about the "participation of the poor." Yet the poor in our country are as marginal to economic and social decision making as in many underdeveloped countries.

So you can see why many might ask: What model does the United States have to offer the underdeveloped countries?

Lessons

The point of the preceding two chapters is not that our research has led us to be against roads, irrigation projects and rural electrification *per se*. Looking at such projects has clarified for us the real criterion: whose interests are served by these projects?

What we hope to have made clear is that for a

foreign government or international lending agency to direct aid to "the hungry" is extremely difficult, if not impossible. We could not phrase it better than an experienced rural development worker in Haiti who wrote to us:

> In Haiti, and I assume in most developing countries, there is a miniaturized, carbon-copy of the national distribution of wealth and power at the community level. Even conscientious aid organizations that can circumvent the corruption and pocketing of funds at the national level find their money or aid filling the coffers of the local elite.

He concludes that a project being "grassroots" doesn't help if that grassroots reality is structured against the poor.

AID officials must be aware that in such countries it is impossible for an outside government-to-government aid agency to assist only or even primarily the poor. Thus to persist in its programs, well-meaning AID policy-makers apparently cling to two beliefs: First, even though it is clearly impossible to design a project that does not benefit the rich, the same project can also help the poor. (Simply put, aiding the rich is inevitable if we want to "reach" the poor.) The second apparent belief is that even elite-dominated development is better than no development.

But what we have learned is that both of these beliefs are false. Aid cannot help both the rich and the poor simultaneously. Strengthening the elites (the overwhelming impact of even those projects supposedly designed specifically to exclude the rich) directly undercuts the poor. With outside assistance, the better-off are able to control more land, machines, and other inputs—reinforcing landlessness and joblessness. Moreover, the notion that such elite-dominated development is better than no development rests on an untenable definition of development. Yes, elite-dominated economic growth can occur, but the concept of development implies the betterment of the lives of minimally the majority—not rising affluence for a small minority and increasing misery for a swelling majority. As Brazil's President (General) Emilio Medici once commented on his country's "economic miracle," "Brazil is doing well but the people are not."

If we conclude that official assistance—as well as World Bank loans—can neither be by nor for the majority of people who lack economic power and, furthermore, can set back the possibility of their gaining that necessary control, then have we given up?

Far from it. A focus on official foreign assistance can cause us to overlook that in every country where people are hungry there are already those working in their own villages and cities to lay the groundwork for non-exploitative structures of self-government. A development worker with years of experience in rural Haiti wrote us that in that country such Haitian development workers cry in unison, "Keep out foreign aid!" And we have found the same among their counterparts in countries like the Philippines, Bangladesh, and Guatemala.

The first step of such local development workers is to help affirm with concrete information the intuitive understanding people have of how they are being impoverished. The next step is to actually build alternative structures of communication, defense and production to challenge the status quo.

The question then is, how can development agencies based in countries like our own help ally us with such indigenous forces for change? In the next chapter we suggest that a few small private organizations based in the industrial countries are successfully seeking out and supporting such groups genuinely challenging the status quo. Since such groups do challenge the status quo, the lives of their members are often endangered. They must work discreetly, often through officially sanctioned institutions such as churches. Giving support directly to such groups is therefore not easy. But it is not impossible.

In addition, the question "what can we do about world hunger?" often carries with it the notion that first we must *start* better foreign assistance programs.

But the real and long-term agenda is what we should *stop* our government from doing. The many groups here working to end military assistance and economic assistance to countries such as the Philippines, Iran and South Korea are helping to remove one significant prop to the forces now working against the hungry. Stopping present government economic and military assistance then should be seen as a positive, not a negative, step.

Finally, work in our own country is critical—work to make people aware that real alternatives exist by demonstrating through our own worker-managed organizations that self-government is possible. Only as we transform our own society through the democratization of control can we expect it to play a genuinely positive role in the world. There are, for example, governments that appear widely based and where the government appears to be working for the interests of the majority—countries such as Mozambique. And certainly there will be others. But, as long as we tolerate an anti-democratic economic system here, our government will be one that is threatened by their example. It will not assist such foreign governments but, indeed, will work to undermine them.

We thus discover that ending official government assistance to most countries does not close off opportunities to "do something" but rather opens up a long agenda, indeed. The final chapter of *Food First* also confronts the critical question of how we focus our outrage at needless hunger.

In one formal seminar we attended at the U.S. Embassy in Indonesia, AID officials listened to a report commissioned by AID. The authors concluded that aid programs have only worsened the plight of the poor, rural majority and that the only hope lies in the poor organizing themselves and gaining power. Following only a moment's pause, one AID officer asked, "But how could we see that such organizing wouldn't go too far?" "Yes," chimed in another, "how could we control such a process once it got started?"

Joseph Collins
David Kinley
February 1978

Not a nut or bolt will be allowed to reach Chile under Allende. Once Allende comes to power we shall do all within our power to condemn Chile and the Chileans to the utmost deprivation and poverty; a policy designed for a long time to come to accelerate the hard features of a communist society in Chile.

From a letter by U.S. Ambassador
Edward Korry to former Chilean President
Eduardo Frei, September 1970. Quoted in the
U.S. Senate Interim Report of the Select
Committee to Study Governmental Operations,
"Alleged Assassination Plots Involving
Foreign Leaders."

We should immediately pay greater attention to agribusiness aspects of our food and nutrition programs. . . . AID will place priority emphasis on this sector. . . . Agribusiness also seems to be the most promising area in which to begin a comprehensive across the board effort to involve the talents and resources of local and developed country private sectors in the development process.

Memorandum from Daniel Parker, Administrator,
AID, to Mission Directors, October 27, 1976

Democracy and communism are engaged in a struggle for objectives of worldwide significance. . . . The maintenance of military bases and the network of alliances that surround the communist world is not enough to stop revolutionary war, and, unfortunately, its field of battle is widening every day. Economic aid, another form of subtle penetration, is a particular phase of this struggle, in that the major powers try to obtain dominant influence over developing nations.

Lecture at the United States Army
School of the Americas

The refusal of *campesinos* [peasants] to pay rents, taxes or agricultural loans or any difficulty in collecting these will indicate the existence of an active insurrection that has succeeded in convincing the *campesinos* of the injustices of the present system, and is directing or instigating them to disobey its precepts.
Hostility on the part of the local population to the government forces, in contrast to their amiable or neutral attitude in the past. This can indicate a change of loyalty or of behavior inspired by fear, often manifested by children refusing to fraternize with members of the internal security forces.

Lecture at the United States Army
School of the Americas

45. Can Voluntary Aid Agencies Help?

Question: You have talked about aid as if it only comes through governments. That is just not true. Americans contribute as much money to overseas relief and development work through private, voluntary agencies as they do through official AID programs. Can't the many small, nongovernmental organizations be more effective exactly because they do not have all the conflicting interests you mention in regard to official aid?

Our Response: As we examined voluntary aid projects around the world, we felt ourselves in a quandary: Which organization or project should we recommend to our readers? Soon we realized that the most useful contribution we might make would not be to provide you with a catalog of critiques of all the voluntary aid organizations (an impossible task!) but to share with you the questions we found ourselves wanting to ask any development project.

Eight Questions to Ask a Development Project

1. Whose project *is* it? Is it the donor agency's?
   or
   Does it originate with the people involved?

2. Does the project define the problem to be tackled as a technical or physical deficiency (e.g. poor farming methods or depleted soils) that can be overcome with the right technique and skills?
   or
   Does it first address the underlying social, economic and political constraints that stand in the way of solving the physical or technical problem?

3. Does the project strengthen the economic and political position of a certain group, creating a more prosperous enclave which then becomes resistant to any change that might abolish its privileges?
   or
   Does it generate a shift in power to the powerless?

4. Does the project focus only on the needs of individuals?
   or
   Does it help individuals who are now powerless to see their common interest with others who are also exploited, thus leading to unified efforts through which cooperative strength is built?

5. Does the project merely help individuals adjust to their exploitation by such external forces as the national government or the international market?
   or

Does it encourage an understanding of that exploitation and a resistance to it?

6. Does the project, through the intervention of outside experts, take away local initiative?

or

Does it generate a process of democratic decision-making and a thrust toward self-reliance that can carry over to future projects?

7. Does the project reinforce dependence on outside sources of material and skills?

or

Does it call forth local ingenuity, local labor, and local materials, and can it be maintained with local skills?

8. Will success only be measured by the achievement of the pre-set plans of outsiders?

or

Is the project open-ended, with success measured by the local people as the project progresses?

It would be naive to assume that any organization could achieve "100 percent" in answer to these questions. The work of any development group undoubtedly will fall somewhere on a continuum. The first critical measure, however, is whether or not the outside development agency sees its role as going into another country to "set things right" or sees itself as a supporter of progressive indigenous forces already underway. In other words, does the outside group appreciate that in every country where people are hungry, something is *already* happening?

Our role, then, is not to start the train moving but to remove the obstacles in its way, especially those originating in our own countries that are outlined throughout this book. And to provide fuel for the train, *if needed*.

How the latter can be done will vary, depending in large part on the nature of the government in the country of our focus. In Third World countries allowing freedom of movement and speech, it is possible to work through legal organizations. (Tanzania is an example.) When the government is itself an active and central part of the redistribution of resources and power, it is possible to work directly with the government. (Guinea Bissau and Mozambique are examples.) In most countries, however, where the government is brutally repressing movements for change, it is necessary to work discreetly, supporting directly indigenous efforts that are building alternatives. (Bangladesh is an example.)

What U.S.-based groups do we know that take this approach and are struggling with the difficult questions we have just posed? Certainly we are not capable of endorsing all of the projects of any organization, but we can point to positive examples. It is up to all of us to learn more about such organizations and support what we find to be positive.

The Economic Development Bureau (EDB)* is one such organization. While working in Tanzania's Ministry of Planning, its founder, American economist Idrian Resnick, was struck by the Tanzanians' own capacity to do much of what they were asking foreigners to do. In 1975, he established a consulting service on development problems that would offer groups in the Third World an alternative to corporate, World Bank and AID "experts." The more than 200 consultants from over thirty-five countries now associated with the EDB have technical knowledge in varied areas but do not see the problem of development as merely a technical one. They understand that their knowledge can be a constructive one only after the local community has begun building a democratic and collective decision-making process.

The contrast between the EDB approach and that of a typical consulting agency is most revealing. In Tanzania, a country with one of the lowest nutritional levels in the world, 25 to 40 percent of the grain is lost each year due to mildew, vermin, and insect infestation. At the request of the Tanzanian government, the Swedish International Development Agency hired several consulting firms to examine the grain storage problem. In three years, the consultants produced four reports—

* See page 512 for address.

all recommending highly mechanized, extremely expensive silos and all requiring foreign technicians to run them. An additional three-quarters of a million dollars was recommended for further designs by consultants! Six years after the first report, no silos had been built.

Enter the EDB. Invited by the Community Development Trust Fund of Tanzania, the EDB decided to attack the problem at the village level and in such a way as to ensure the direct control by the villagers throughout the project. The EDB team, including a Tanzanian trained in the learning theories of exiled Brazilian Paulo Freire, and others with knowledge of village storage alternatives, entered the village. The villagers formed a storage committee. The team initiated a discussion in which the participants worked together to gain an understanding of the forces preventing them from adequately handling and storing their grains. The problem was not simply a matter of rats, mildew, and bugs, or of drying, spraying, and rebuilding. Uncovering and understanding the social and economic relations in the village were necessary before effective action was possible.

First, as one of the EDB consultants put it, "It was necessary to convince the villagers that we did not have a preconceived idea . . . 'up our sleeve' all the time just waiting for the little drama of village democracy to play itself out." The credibility of the EDB technicians was established only when, in response to serious criticism by the villagers, they dropped a design that they had put forward in discussion. Only then did the villagers believe that they had not come "with an answer."

The villagers soon came to realize that a great deal of effective technology already existed right there. But because the village is composed of many ethnic groups, neighbors were often unaware of each other's structures and methods. Through sharing experiences, the people became conscious of the richness of their varied knowledge and experience. Rather than introducing a foreign technology, the successful storage system that evolved turned out to be a recombination of the best elements in the traditional storage methods of the village. The people were part of a dynamic unfolding of events rather than on the receiving end of a technical exercise.

But the EDB was not totally satisfied with the results. The project did succeed in completing twenty rat-proof elevated sorghum storage structures in one harvest season but, without adequate follow-up, the process did not spread to other villages. Now the EDB is working in Guinea Bissau on similar grain storage problems, hoping to learn from past mistakes. First, in Guinea Bissau, women will be more fully involved. The dialogue leader in the initial project is, in fact, a woman. Also Guineans at the village level will be trained as discussion leaders during the first phase of dialogue and the identification of problems. Finally, as the project gets underway, the EDB will work with all relevant ministries of government to help develop a national program for village storage so that what is learned in the first project can be extended across the new nation. Such a possibility depends, as we have said, on the nature of the government in question. Unfortunately, few governments could be counted upon.

In most countries an outside development agency's role must be to support the indigenous forces resisting oppression and building alternatives. The Unitarian-Universalist Service Committee, for example, is supporting a newspaper in El Salvador called *Justice and Peace*. It is one of the few printed vehicles of dissent against the injustices and atrocities inflicted upon peasants struggling for survival. During 1975, for example, army units in El Salvador massacred unarmed peasants. In two cases the attacks were reported in the Salvadorian press as guerrilla attacks on army patrols. Only *Justice and Peace* published the peasants' side of the story.

Such resistance is going on not just in El Salvador but in virtually every country where people are hungry. Consider, for example, Bangladesh, where Americans have been made to see only passivity and hopelessness. Yet we have become aware of at least three organizations founded and directed by Bangladeshis that are

tackling problems such as landlessness, the oppression
of women, and the lack of credit and of health care
—the most difficult problems facing people in the
countryside. One organization, Gono Unnayan Pro-
chesta, is supported by the American Friends Service
Committee. Another is Gonoshasthaya Kendra, supported by a number of progressive foreign groups including Inter Pares (Canadian) and Terre des Hommes
(Holland and Switzerland).

Gonoshasthaya Kendra's work includes such village-
based programs as agricultural loans to sharecroppers
to help them become independent of their landlords
and local usurious creditors, a health insurance program
based on village paramedics, and the training of
women to fill the great need for carpenters, blacksmiths
and plumbers, jobs traditionally only performed by
men.[1]

Such groups have no illusions about the difficulty
of their work and the risks involved. In 1976 one of
the paramedics was killed by a local doctor who felt
his business threatened. The murderers, known by the
police, still roam free. But the obvious risk is paralleled
by the equally obvious bravery of the villagers. On the
anniversary of his death, all the paramedics organized
a five-mile walk to the site of the murder. One par-
ticipant wrote, "Along the way, about 300 villagers
spontaneously joined the procession; they had known
Nizam [the victim] well who had walked and cycled
the path to Simulia many times."

A third example in Bangladesh is the Bangladesh
Rural Advancement Committee (BRAC) supported
by Oxfam-America.[2] BRAC's projects focus on functional education for Bangladesh's poorest groups, meaning literacy achieved through discussion that focuses on
"real life problems." Literacy and therefore the chance
for a basic education are seen by BRAC as tools for
the poor villagers to grasp the forces limiting their
lives and as a first step for the poor in taking action
against those forces.

Functional education lays the basis, then, of BRAC's
action thrust. In forming cooperatives, such groups as
the landless, women, and exploited fisherpeople gain

strength through pulling together resources and working toward common goals. One example is BRAC's work with one landless group in the village of Atgaon.

Atgaon, a village of about 2000 in Northeast Bangladesh, is fairly typical: Two percent are rich landowners (with 40 to 50 acres) while 30 percent are very small farmers (with 2 to 7 acres). Fully 40 percent of the villagers are landless and very poor.

At stake in the village (particularly for the landless) was control of the "khas" land—mostly land confiscated from those who abandoned the country after the 1971 war of liberation from Pakistan. In theory, khas land—reportedly 10 percent of all cultivated land in the country—belongs to the government and any landless cultivator can apply for permanent rights. In fact, however, large landholders control much of the khas land, typically using it for grazing but sometimes for cultivation.

In 1974, 40 landless laborers applied individually for permission from the government to cultivate the khas land in Atgaon. The petitions were ignored.

Then in 1974, BRAC began its "functional education" classes in Atgaon. Those landless persons who participated became aware of their situation vis-à-vis the interests of others in the village. What emerged was the realization that to get the land from the government the landless would have to work together. Thus one night the landless of Atgaon, ranging in age from 25 to 70, came together and organized themselves into the Rajhasan Landless Cooperative Society. For the first time the landless were organized on the basis of common interest. Weekly cooperative meetings and village workshops, organized with the help of BRAC field workers, further heightened awareness of the social and economic realities of the village.

The cooperative then petitioned the government for the khas land. After persistent pressure by the cooperative, in 1976 the government finally granted the landless 60 acres, amounting to 1.5 acres for each family. The village's well-off farmers became alarmed, for many of them were illegally using the khas land. They might have put up more resistance at this point if many had not been convinced that the poor lacked the where-withal to cultivate the land profitably. The rich predicted that the land would eventually be mortgaged back to them anyway.

It's true that bringing the fallow land into cultivation requires a great deal of work and the purchase of seeds and good tools. But knowing its right to the land was secure, the cooperative was motivated to seek the credit it needed to get started. Lacking the proper collateral, it could not get credit from government agencies. But the cooperative was able to turn to BRAC, receiving a loan at 12 percent interest instead of the 50 to 200 percent interest demanded by the local moneylenders.

After much discussion, the cooperative decided to work the land as a collective farm, the first in the area. When the group had proved itself by actually leveling the land and planting the improved seed varieties, the large landlords started to worry. The success of the cooperative might instigate changes among other poor in the village. Moreover, if the cooperative succeeded there would be 40 fewer day laborers for the rich to hire. The well-to-do landlords therefore tried to thwart the cooperative by organizing other villagers to break the irrigation drainage canal on which the cooperative's land depended. They also tried to prevent the cooperative's use of river water for irrigation. But their efforts at sabotage failed. The rich landlords were divided. Those *not* occupying any of the khas land, and therefore not directly threatened by the cooperative's use of the land, were more sympathetic to the cooperative. They were mobilized against the efforts of the saboteur landlords.

Even though an early monsoon necessitated harvesting the crop before fully ready, the cooperative was able to pay back the entire BRAC loan plus interest. In 1977 the cooperative took out an even larger loan from BRAC and made arrangements with the government to purchase a power pump, normally possible only for the better-off farmers.

The members have also begun to work together in other economic activities—especially fishing during the rainy season. Furthermore, members of the co-operative participate in a health insurance program established by BRAC and are organizing for better childcare and health practices. In sharp contrast to pre-cooperative days, many of the landless families have decided to seek family planning assistance.

Over five years the changes in the lives of Atgaon's landless have followed this course: New literacy skills were gained in the process of achieving new awareness of the economic and social constraints on their lives. This process led to confidence that only through co-operative action could these limits be overcome. Cooperative action made possible the control of land which, for the first time, allowed some degree of self-determination and the ability to secure credit. This then opened doors to technical advances in production and the income necessary to participate in a health care system. The members of the cooperative are still poor. But real change has begun—and not only in their lives: The landless cooperative of Atgaon is now making contact with the landless in neighboring villages.

We in no way want to romanticize the work of any of the Third World groups mentioned here. Helping to liberate the will and the capacity of people for self-determination is arduous and often risk-laden. Neither do we want to suggest that our list of U.S.-based groups that are on the right track is exhaustive. In addition to the Economic Development Bureau, Oxfam, the Unitarian-Universalist Service Committee and the American Friends Service Committee that we have mentioned, others, such as the Mennonite Central Committee and World Neighbors, have been commended for supporting indigenous development efforts, often against great odds. Again, we are not giving our approval or disapproval but are pointing to some of the groups that seem to be confronting many of the difficult questions we posed early in the chapter. They are certainly worth examining.

Finally, we would ask you to compare the approach of the organizations we mention here—those trying not to go into another country with a pre-plan but to support local initiatives—with World Bank and AID projects described in earlier chapters. Mammoth official aid agencies can offer large sums of money but are structurally and ideologically incapable of helping the poor themselves to confront the powerful forces blocking their development. Small, non-governmental organizations do not require huge sums. The total annual budget of BRAC, covering work in literacy, health, and agricultural work in hundreds of villages, comes to about $300,000 compared, for example, to AID's $50 million electrification project in Bangladesh.

Highly selective voluntary aid, not official U.S. foreign aid, appears to be the channel through which Americans' direct support of efforts of the poor in the Third World countries has a chance of helping, rather than hurting. Such aid should go to indigenous groups already based in village realities—using local field workers, starting with the most immediate problems at hand. It is a most difficult path but the only one through which an outsider can help along the process of greater self-determination for those who now appear powerless to change their lives.

Part X

Food Self-Reliance

46. What Is Food Self-Reliance?

Question: Throughout this book you have mentioned food self-reliance. What does food self-reliance mean and how can it be achieved?

Our Response: Food self-reliance is not a new concept; it is as old as humanity itself. Throughout history, people have assumed that producing their food was the basis of their survival.[1] Food self-reliance is the foundation of genuine food security for all.

Not Necessarily Self-Sufficiency

Food self-reliance does not necessarily mean producing everything the nation eats but producing enough of its basic foods to be independent of outside forces. Food self-reliance calls for the maximum utilization of local resources—physical and human—before seeking out foreign resources. While food self-reliance is not necessarily food self-sufficiency, it does imply the ability to become, in short order, self-sufficient enough to survive a sudden cut-off of imports. No people should allow themselves to be vulnerable to the disruption of their food supply due to natural disasters or wars elsewhere, or to the political manipulation of food exports by foreign governments.

It is crucial not to confuse food self-reliance with simply a sufficient per capita production of basic food. Today both India and the Philippines, countries where many suffer chronic malnutrition, claim self-sufficiency in basic grain. In fact, the Philippines became a rice exporter in 1977. And India now has bufferstocks of at least 22 million tons of grain stored on old World War II airstrips. Soldiers parade around it with orders to shoot anybody who comes to steal the grain—even as it rots for the lack of adequate tarpaulin cover.

Thus food self-reliance is measured not in terms of production totals. The real criterion of self-reliance must rather always be: Do all the people have access to an adequate amount of food?

Fundamentals of Food Self-Reliance

Keeping this meaning of food self-reliance in mind, we have learned that re-achieving food self-reliance involves at least eight fundamentals. These fundamentals are not speculative points. They have proven to be crucial in countries that have achieved or are well on the way toward achieving food self-reliance —countries, we should not forget, that contain over 40 percent of all people living in the underdeveloped world.

1. *Food self-reliance requires the allocation of control over agricultural resources to local, democratically organized units.*

Since food self-reliance involves not only adequate production but adequate consumption realized by everyone, a society will never achieve food self-reliance unless the control of agricultural resources is shared democratically. A re-allocation of control over productive assets is crucial for the redistribution of purchasing power; this alone will insure that agricultural (and industrial) production benefits the local population instead of just local and foreign elites. For only by sharing the control over productive assets will the local majority make up the priority market toward which production is oriented.

Land Reform

Part of the re-allocation of control is land reform. But many so-called land reforms in the last thirty years have actually tended to "consolidate the prevailing social order," notes economist J. B. W. Kuitenbrouwer.[2] Loopholes have been commonplace. In several states in India, for example, reform legislation did not apply to fruit cultivation. A landowner with several hundred acres of rice cultivation could plant six mango trees in his rice field and—bingo—his land was exempt.[3] Reforms have often affected only a small fraction of the land. Over five years after the land reform decree in the Philippines, less than one percent of the cropped land has been "redistributed"—and then only to tenants who must meet the payments of a 15-year mortgage.[4] The plight of the landless has been ignored by land reform laws in countries like the Philippines, Pakistan, India, and Egypt.

Many land reform laws have aimed explicitly at promoting tenant security by granting permanent lease rights to tenants who cultivate a given piece of land over a certain period of years. But they have often had just the opposite impact. Afraid of eventually losing their land to their tenants under such laws, landlords change tenants every year or switch to day laborers.

Even when some of their land is taken away, the large landowners can still be the real beneficiaries of the "reforms." A 1959 land reform in Pakistan compensated landlords handsomely for poor, unirrigated land that had previously brought them little or no income.[5]

Such fake reforms obscure an appreciation of what the effects of real distribution could be. Production advances have not been sacrificed in countries that have authentically redistributed the land and other food-producing resources, countries as different as Japan, Cuba, Taiwan, China, and North Vietnam.* Indeed,

---

* To be sure, there are telling differences in the land reforms carried out in these countries, differences that will determine their long-term effectiveness.

to the contrary, people who own the land they work, either individually or as a group, naturally invest more time, labor, and money in it than do non-owners. In Japan in 1940, only about 31 percent of the landholdings were worked by people who owned the land. By 1960, over 75 percent of the holdings were operated by owner farmers.[6] This shift goes a long way toward explaining why recent yields per acre of foodgrains in Japan were as much as 60 percent greater than in the United States.[7]

But land redistribution in itself will not prevent a regression to old inequalities, leading some to logically ask: How could land redistribution fail to redistribute power if considerable power rests in land ownership itself? Part of the answer is that power also rests in control of all the resources, from water to fertilizer to credit, that make the land produce, as well as in access to markets that make that production profitable. The South Korean reform ended tenancy, at least in theory, by giving small amounts of land to former tenants. But rich peasants illegally retained large holdings. Moreover, credit systems, marketing, and irrigation were not reorganized cooperatively to meet the needs of the new small landholders. There existed no built-in mechanism for the poorer peasants to overcome the privileges clung to by the rural elites. Twenty years later the results are predictable: by 1970, 54 percent of those farmers who had received land under the land reform had become tenants again.[8]

Moreover, landowners who are compensated for their land through land reform programs can invest that gain in urban consumer and export industries. Money that might have gone into rural development instead goes into other sectors, further exacerbating the pre-existing urban export bias. Such "reform" in no way mitigates the concentration of wealth.

Fake and partial land reform cannot therefore lead to food self-reliance. But two fears seem to haunt many Americans in any discussion of a thorough-going land redistribution—the "wholesale slaughter" of the land-owning elite and "forced collectivization." Neither generalization captures the lessons to be gained from the many land reforms carried out in this century.

During land reforms, retribution against individual landlords by outraged peasants has occurred, especially when those landlords fought to hold onto their privileges. Some landlords, in Cuba for example, have been brought to trial for particular crimes such as the murder of tenants. When not convicted of heinous crimes against those previously under their control, however, former landlords have often been integrated into the new social order. Many have received regular compensatory payments from the state. (In countries where the land is tightly held, the number of individuals who actually must give up land because of redistribution is relatively small. Moreover, many landlords, precisely because of their economic resources, are able to flee into exile.) Seldom, if ever, have land redistributions triggered the wholesale liquidation of a landlord class.

Forced collectivization, moreover, has nowhere worked successfully. Where attempted, it has often later been reversed.[9] By the early 1950s, Yugoslavia and Poland abandoned a top-down approach to creating agricultural cooperatives. For one thing, the agricultural machinery—which could have increased production and lightened work on the larger cooperative units and thus compensated the peasant farmers for the feeling of loss of the ownership of their land—was simply not in adequate supply. Farming in both countries is now mainly by small holdings served by extensive networks of cooperatives for sharing machinery and for marketing. Both countries have protected these small holdings by setting a ceiling on farm size—a maximum of 37 acres and 248 acres (less on good soils) in Yugoslavia and Poland respectively.

Where a forced or top-down approach to collectivization has continued, development has suffered. Production stagnation on the state farms in the Soviet Union, as compared to the obvious productivity of private garden plots, can be seen as peasant resistance to a system in which they are mere employees of the state—and underpaid at that.

By contrast, successful collective agricultural development has been the result of a transition through progressive stages in which people can come to appreciate the advantages to themselves of cooperative work.

In China, the first stage was the "mutual aid team" in which families shared tools and labor—a traditional practice in much of the world. The organization of rural life has now moved in China to the three-tiered commune in which effective control of the land resides in the production team comprised of 20 to 30 families. An FAO report referred to the production team as "an extended family farm."[10] Everyone is expected to contribute and the rewards are determined by the entire "family," based on work done—with a guarantee of the basic food requirements to all.

Likewise, in Vietnam (formerly North Vietnam) cooperative control of the land was not brought about in one fell swoop but step by step. The 1953 reform act distributed land primarily to the landless and small peasant households; by the end of 1957, 77 percent of the rural households had benefited from the distribution of 2 million acres. The movement toward collective work was built on the tradition of individuals joining together to construct and maintain dykes.

Collective modes of work were reinforced by the war. By 1956, half of the peasants belonged to labor-pooling groups and mutual aid groups. The movement toward collective control passed through four stages of organization. It was not until the mid-sixties that most cooperatives actually pooled land and determined the individual's income by his or her work. By 1967, 90 percent of the cropland was worked cooperatively.[11]

The advantage of cooperative development of the land in contrast to individually worked plots depends also on the size of the plots in question. And this factor varies greatly. Many who have studied Asian agriculture have concluded that in countries such as Bangladesh, where the typical holding is less than two acres, cooperative agriculture is the only hope of lightening labor and increasing production. Even small-scale power tillers and tubewells are beyond the capacity of many individual small farmers. Pre-existing cultural patterns of cooperative work, particularly in Asia, play a part too, as we see in China and Vietnam.

Participation

A final point remains. Rural people must not only control the land they work but effectively participate in wielding national political and economic power. They must exercise a strong voice through their co-operatives and political organizations in the control of credit and marketing institutions. As part of this taking charge, they will need to acquire the knowledge and skills to manage their own affairs. Thus literacy and basic education for *all* men and women must be a high priority to help make and keep their organizations democratic. While including bookkeeping and administrative skills, this basic education should not be seen merely as a means of increasing people's productivity. Education is the process by which the rural majority can develop cooperative values and discover their own range of capacities.

Effective *campesino* (peasant) organization was becoming a reality in Chile during the Popular Unity government before its overthrow by the military in September 1973. The government promoted democratically elected *campesino* councils for each country and province as well as for the nation as a whole. Jointly with the state, these councils were beginning to plan and carry out agrarian programs such as credit and marketing. Pressured by many *campesinos,* the government also actively encouraged campesino-controlled unions and cooperatives.

Only the redistribution of control of the land and the participation by farmers in national political and economic power can create new kinds of farmers, able to cooperate as equals and to face difficult challenges, no longer afraid of bosses, moneylenders and landlords.

2. *Food self-reliance depends on the initiative of the people, not on government directives.*

Only when the transformation of the agrarian structure takes place under the overwhelming pressure of organized peasants will the changes favor them. Mass initiative is the opposite of government-managed "development." If food self-reliance is managed from above, people feel they are working "for the government," not for themselves. People become "clients," not the motive force.

A government policy of simply parceling out land to the peasants is not, for example, self-reliant development. Land reform must not only redistribute land but must be the first step in the creation of real democracy.

"Bureaucratic devices may be able to crush the landlord power, but they will not be able to help the peasants establish their own power," observes China scholar Yu-Hsi Chen.[12] During Taiwan's land redistribution (1949–53), the peasants remained passive recipients while the government acted as the insulating agent between the landlords and the peasants. The land reform did not give birth to independent peasant organizations able to look out for their own interests. The post-reform era, therefore, left Taiwanese peasants at the mercy of their new exploiter—the state. Twelve years after the reform, the land tax more than tripled while the price of rice increased less than 20 percent.[13]

Similarly in Bolivia, the 1952–53 land reform did succeed in a fairly just redistribution of land. But the newly created owners of small plots who had been dependent on exploitative landlords prior to the reform became, in the years following, dependent on a new class of exploiters—the middlemen who purchased their crops cheaply and sold them in the cities at a handsome profit.

Since the development of any society is based entirely on the development of the individuals within it, the program of redistribution must break the pattern of dependency. It must initiate a process of people themselves taking more and more control over their own lives. Only when the people are in control is there hope of preventing a fall back into exploitative patterns.

Even progressive Tanzania has, in part, fallen into the trap of trying to "manage" self-reliance. Political economist P. L. Raikes, in his detailed study of *ujamaa* villages in Tanzania,[14] finds that bureaucratic,

external interventions have thwarted release of the enthusiasm and productive energy of the peasants. Under
urban- and foreign-oriented administrators, the peasants
treat the communal lands as if they were government
farms. The use of coercion leads to passive resistance.
Raikes notes, for example, that all too often administrators present villagers with a plan that is primarily
a set of production targets. The allocation of needed
farming inputs and social services is made to depend
upon acceptance of this plan. The villagers know that
to question its merits will probably displease the bureau-
crat, thus reducing the likelihood of their getting any
assistance.

The *process* of land reform is therefore as important
as the reform itself. The people must together deliberate and decide how they want to distribute the land
and resolve any conflicting claims that arise. The experience of land reform will then be one of a valuable
social education, training the people for the new task
of cooperative administration. Such is the conclusion
of a group of Asian rural economists reflecting upon
what the Chinese experience has to teach. Their report
observes: "Land reform through mass . . . action also
gives an opportunity for other dominance-dependence
relations to be shaken up: Women and youth, the low
castes, even the children, will be in the thick of this
experience which will shock them emotionally and help
remove deep-seated inhibitions in their minds as well."[15]

3. *Food self-reliance based on popular initiative
presupposes group solidarity and therefore equality.*

Popular initiative is not simply the sum total of
individual self-seeking. It rests in awakening the confidence of the people that their natural self-interest and
the goals of cooperative struggle are not in conflict but,
indeed, share common ground.

Current dependency relationships that tie the poor
to the rich—as tenant, laborer, debtor—engender dis-
unity among the poor. Competition for survival means
that the poor often see each other, rather than the elite
classes, as the threats. The struggle for self-reliant
development must therefore begin with cooperative

activities that reduce the dependency of the poor on the rich and allow the oppressed to grasp how solidarity can benefit them.

People have proved themselves willing to sacrifice and work hard for future reward when they can see that all are sacrificing equally. Thus, equality is a necessary prerequisite for popular initiative. (In countries with great inequalities in wealth and income, appeals for national sacrifice are correctly perceived by the poor majority as a way for the controlling elite to extract yet more wealth through the extra exertion of the people.)

What does equality mean? How is it achieved? And, once advancements toward equality are achieved, how are they maintained? We do not claim to have the answers. But we do believe that now, perhaps more than at any time in human history, people are struggling with these questions. One reason to try to learn as much as possible about China is that the Chinese, perhaps more seriously than any other people, are tackling such questions. Within 5 or 6 years after the 1949 land redistribution in China, the old rural inequalities were reappearing. In direct response came the initiative for cooperative control of both the land and needed farm inputs. Cooperative control was thus an attempt to prevent the re-emergence of an elite-controlled economy. But what about the inequalities among geographic regions, as well as differences in human resources? Given these differences, why would not one cooperative organization tend to move ahead of another? Attempts to enlarge the size of the accounting unit so as to even out these differences as much as possible were tried—and resisted by those who felt it unjust that they should have to share their hard-earned success with the less well-endowed—and were tried again as the wealth base has increased.[16]

Even by the early mid-sixties, the gap between the richest 20 percent and the poorest 20 percent was one-third what it was before the revolution began. Today in China you find spirited debate over such issues as the size of the accounting unit and the use of material incentives. Although not all Chinese agree as to the role of material incentives, there is a widespread agreement that the reduction of inequality has been essential to their society's achievements.

4. *With food self-reliance, trade becomes an organic outgrowth of development, not the fragile hinge on which survival hangs.*

To our surprise one of the most controversial propositions in our writing has been that trade is not universally positive. Trade *can* play a positive role, but dependency on imports for basic survival puts whole populations at risk of famine and makes national self-determination an illusion.

Perhaps most of us are unaware of how totally we accept the notion that "free trade" is by definition "progressive" and that anti-trade sentiment could only throw us "back to the stone age." With only partial tongue in cheek, economist Samir Amin claims that if one were to follow prevailing attitudes of the world powers, "one would have to add to the Charter of the United Nations a new crime of aggression against civilization: The refusal to trade."[17]

We are not against trade; we only question whether trade can be accepted as a universal good. Agricultural exports should come only after the agricultural resources are in the hands of people first meeting their own food needs. No country can hope to "win" in the game of international trade, as we say in Part VI, as long as its very survival depends on selling its one or two products every year. A country simply cannot hold out for just prices for its exports if it is desperate for foreign exchange with which to import food. When the basic needs are met, however, trade can become a healthy extension of *domestic need* instead of being determined strictly by *foreign demand*.

Such trade—trade that would supplement domestic production with items needed by the majority for their own development—is a far cry from the trade-oriented economies of most Third World countries today. In elite-dominated economies, a fixation on trade as the road to development represents an option against the creation of a domestic market—for that would require the elimination of mass poverty. Theories of "comparative trade advantage" (exporting cocoa, for example, theoretically to import basic foods) end up being an advantage to the domestic elite and a disadvantage to the majority of the people.

A people working for basic self-reliance is thus the only context in which trade can play a positive role. Only then will trade help to broaden people's choices rather than, as is so often the case now, help to concentrate economic power in the hands of the few.

Moreover, only when all avenues for local production have been tried should imports be sought. This principle will lead to diversity, giving rise to unique models for unique localities. As development economist Johan Galtung notes, any loss in efficiency that might result from reinventing something already invented somewhere else "is more than offset by the gain in self-confidence in accepting the challenge of being the innovator."[18]

5. *Food self-reliance means reuniting agriculture and nutrition.*

If colonialism's plantations first converted food into a mere commodity, production contracted by multinational agribusiness for the Global Supermarket completes the divorce of agriculture and nutrition. Self-reliance would make the central question not "What crop might have a few cents' edge on the world market months or even years hence?" but "How can the people best feed themselves with this piece of land?"

As obvious as it may seem, the policy basing land use on nutritional output is practiced in only a few countries today. For these countries food is no longer just a commodity. As a necessity of life, it is considered as precious as life itself.

With Food First self-reliance, industrial crops (like cotton and rubber), livestock feed crops, and luxury fruits and vegetables are planted *after* meeting the basic needs of all the people.

6. *Food self-reliance makes agriculture an end, not a means.*

In countries where so much of the population today is hungry, agriculture has been seen, since the onslaught of colonialism, as the sector from which to extract wealth to serve urban, industrial, and foreign interests. Theoretically things have changed. But have they really?

In most underdeveloped countries the government keeps the prices of the main farm products low—either directly or through food imports—while the prices of industrial goods inflate. An elite-controlled government is pleased if low food prices mean that industrial wages can also be kept low, but the result for farmers is declining real income and mounting debt.

Although agriculture in underdeveloped countries ordinarily generates most of the national product and foreign exchange, a recent survey found that, on the average, agriculture receives only 11 percent of all investment. On the other hand, mining and manufacture receive over one-quarter of all investment.[19] A United Nations study of Africa notes that although agriculture contributes 20 to 50 percent of the GNP, it receives only 10 to 30 percent of the public investment.[20]

The Chinese people have chosen a different path. They have decided quite deliberately to reject the Soviet approach of squeezing peasant producers through low prices for their products and high prices for consumer goods and farm inputs. They have chosen a policy of relatively high and slowly increasing prices for agricultural commodities along with low prices for farm supplies. Between 1950 and 1970, the exchange power of a given amount of agricultural goods increased 68 percent.[21] In addition, the farm taxation rate has been effectively cut in half.[22] Rather than extracting a surplus from agriculture, the rest of the society contributes 23 percent in excess of what it receives from agriculture.[23]

With food self-reliant policies, the goal of agricultural progress is first and foremost rural development, not the draining of surplus to subsidize the industrial sector.

7. *With food self-reliant policies, industry will serve agriculture; town and country will meet.*

If the majority of people are in command—and their income is growing—invention and production will be based on their *needs*. A rural, dispersed, small-scale industrial network will grow to fill the need for fertilizer, farming equipment, and other simple manufactures. We are not talking about plopping factories producing for urban markets in the middle of a rice field just for the sake of "decentralization," but of developing industry as an organic outgrowth of the needs of labor-intensive agriculture and those of the local population.

In India decentralization of industry became official policy but with no understanding of the process. Clock and radio factories were established in rural areas. But since both the production materials and the market for the finished product were in the cities, a lot of money was spent shipping springs to the country and clocks to the city. The problem was that a clock factory did nothing to stimulate the growth of agriculture and that agricultural growth did not give impetus to the clock factory.

Moreover, Food First self-reliance will halt, even reverse, the flow of landless refugees who daily migrate to cities in hope of work. The wide gap in income between rural and urban workers will begin to close. Rural life will no longer be looked upon as backward. The Cuban people, for example, understood the need to bring to rural areas the health, educational, and cultural facilities—dance, film, library, theater—invariably associated, especially by the young, with city life. Over the past several years more than 500 boarding high schools have been constructed in the countryside for students from both rural and urban areas. These schools are among the country's finest and offer not only a regular high school education but also daily work in food production. Through such schools in the countryside tens of thousands of young people come to appreciate the difficulties and rewards of rural work and to realize that they too can contribute to their country's development.

Not only can urban dwellers go to the countryside but the countryside can come to the city. In Cuba a substantial area around each large city is reserved for agricultural and livestock production. Root crops, vegetables and coffee are cultivated by volunteer workers and school children from nearby cities. Surrounding pastures graze cows that provide milk for the cities.

Sending students to the countryside, as is the policy in countries like Cuba, Somalia, and China, has often appeared to Western observers as a form of anti-intellectualism. Rather it is the recognition that the entire population, and especially the young, must appreciate the importance of agriculture. If not, rural development will likely be sacrificed by urbanized, white-collar bureaucrats who go on believing that agriculture should be the handmaiden to other sectors and to the needs of an elite (including themselves).

8. *Food self-reliance requires coordinated social planning.*

Social planning need not mean authoritarian rule from the top. In fact, effective social planning can only result from the decentralization of authority that allows each region to work out appropriate solutions. As Johan Galtung suggests, self-reliance does not exclude planning but uses it in a way that "sets into motion a process of diagnosis . . . by local people formulating practical proposals for action."[24]

Planning is not a mere technical activity. Effective planning is not simply establishing quotas, targets and tasks; it is the organization of a sensitive and flexible structure of communication between government bodies and communities. This structure of communication serves optimum feedback and agreement on joint action —which then provides the basis for planning as a technical activity.[25]

The Chinese call this "from the people/to the people" social planning. Food self-reliance starts with the nutritional needs of all the people and translates them into a national agricultural plan. A Canadian report on agriculture and nutrition in Cuba describes how local farmers participate in this translation: "Meetings take place with all the farm workers and small farmers at the local level to discuss the plan and the production quotas allocated to their area. Suggestions for revisions or changes are made. This feedback process is very important because it is the local farmers and workers who know best what crops will grow in their area."[26]

Such planning presupposes common goals among the communities and the government. It substitutes conscious intervention and cooperation for the free market. This does not mean that social planning precludes the market altogether. The difference is that in a society whose conscious goal is to meet the needs of the people, social planning can "utilize the market instead of being governed by it," observes U.N. development analyst J. B. W. Kuitenbrouwer.[27] With social planning, prices of necessary items might be fixed to guarantee their availability to all; and the production of key industrial and consumer goods might be subsidized out of the profits from other lines of production, all with an eye to maximally stimulating both economic and social progress.

Planning for self-reliance, however, may well require both a short-term as well as a long-term strategy. The fundamental principles of self-reliance we have so far outlined represent the long-term thrust that appears to be necessary for self-determination and food security. Real life, however, does not often leave every policy option open. Countries now working genuinely toward food self-reliance often find they face immediate crises presented both by the inheritance of the old colonial order (see Question 13) and the collapse of its structures.

Vietnam and Mozambique are good examples. The Vietnam war forced the abandonment of about 2.5 million acres of cultivated land—or between 20 and 25 percent of all arable land throughout Vietnam. Reclaiming agricultural land, the Vietnamese faced the threat of unexploded mines and bombs still in the fields. At the end of the war several million tons of American explosives still lay unexploded. The task of agricultural reconstruction could not happen overnight. Thus in the immediate aftermath of the war, Vietnam urgently requested food aid (which the United States refused to contribute), not, as in so many countries, to avoid agricultural restructuring but in order to sustain people while they worked at carrying out their development plans.

Mozambique, having won its independence from Portugal in 1975, also faced staggering agricultural problems. Portuguese settlers had been the main suppliers of food to the capital city. After independence most of these Portuguese fled the country, but not without first sabotaging farm machines and irrigation and transportation equipment. Thus, although the stated policies of the new Mozambique government stressed the development of cooperative villages, the immediate policy was to focus first on state farms as the only quick way to bring into production the abandoned land that had been feeding the cities. Moreover, the new government imported wheat and beef primarily so that the food habits of the city dwellers would not be overly altered. It was feared that those who lived in the city, because they had not, for the most part, experienced the liberation struggle directly, would be less willing to accept any sacrifices. Moreover, there continued to be many in the cities whose support for the new government was only marginal but whose skills Mozambique felt it could not afford to lose, at least in the early years. (The colonial system had so blocked the education of Mozambicans that the flight of Portuguese left the new country bereft of many essential technical skills.) Thus the focus on feeding the cities was a carefully weighed political choice. Only in 1978 was the government in a position to turn its attention to the working out of a national structure to promote the development of cooperative villages. (It should be noted that from the beginning, a national literacy and health campaign reached deep into the countryside, helping to establish the prerequisites for building productive and self-reliant villages.)

For such countries, struggling first for their survival, the challenge is to be able to make short-term compromises demanded by the exigencies of immediate crises without losing sight of the long-term strategy for democratic, equitable, and self-reliant development.

The Food Self-Reliance Bandwagon

As forced food dependency continues to translate into food shortages and rising prices for people throughout the world, national politicians will increasingly call for food self-reliance. They will claim that their new agricultural policies will make their countries independent. But the food self-reliant policies we have described simply cannot be implemented by the present governments of most underdeveloped countries. Why not? Simply because these policies directly counter the self-interest of the propertied elite now in power. Food First, then, is not a simple call to put food into hungry mouths. It is the recognition that, if enabling people to feed themselves is to be the priority, then all social relationships must be reconstructed.

If present governments will not implement Food First policies, what, then, is the value of this prescription for food self-reliance? Its value, we think, lies in showing what is possible—in giving evidence to groups struggling for self-determination that food self-reliance is a *viable* alternative. A prescription for food self-reliance and a continuing effort to garner the proof of experience that it is possible will serve to discredit all governments that now rationalize continuing dependency as necessary for survival. Indeed the strongest weapon of oppression is the belief, by oppressor and oppressed alike, that while dependency may not be desirable, it is better than starvation. Food self-reliance is the cornerstone of genuine self-determination and it is possible for every country in the world.

Food Self-Reliance and the Industrial Countries

How would food self-reliance in the underdeveloped countries affect those of us in the industrial countries? Many might assume that the citizens of the industrial countries benefit by the continued dependency of the underdeveloped countries.

The answer, we have seen, is an emphatic no. Self-reliance for the now dependent countries would strike at the heart of the Global Supermarket phenomenon, that is, the collaboration of elites in both industrial and underdeveloped countries to profit from the land and people of underdeveloped countries by supplying those locally and abroad who can afford to pay the most. Although citizens of the industrial countries might be told by the apologists of agribusiness that the Global Supermarket exists to serve them, it does not. We have already seen, in Part VIII, that it serves only its creators.

But would Food First self-reliance in the underdeveloped countries close important markets for the agricultural exports of countries such as the United States and Canada? Obviously it would. Does that mean, then, that every means must be used to keep other countries food-dependent, or otherwise American family farmers will be unable to make a decent and secure living? We think not. In Part VII we began to sketch the rebalancing of the structures in the American agriculture and food industry. (Not the least significant thing we pointed to is that the United States is importing enormous quantities of agricultural products that could easily and profitably be grown by American farmers without boosting prices to consumers.) Furthermore, the proper goal of the family farmer is not maximum volume but earning a satisfactory and steady income. It is urgent to work now to understand and implement those policies that would make farming a good, reliable livelihood without having to push our "abundance" onto others who could and would provide for themselves.

The prescription for food self-reliance presented here is not simply what "those poor, hungry countries" should do. Redistribution of control over food-producing resources is the only path toward true self-reliance for the industrial countries as well. By understanding the parallels, the majority in the industrial countries will come to see that the hungry masses they are often made to fear are, in reality, their natural allies. We are all in a common struggle for control over the most basic human need—food.

47. But Where Would Funds for Development Come from?

Question: But with self-reliant policies, where do you think underdeveloped countries would get the development funds they need? Where would underdeveloped countries get foreign exchange to buy building materials, fertilizers, farm machinery, fuel, and so on? Not only do they need foreign exchange, but they need the wealth of their upper classes to invest in growth. If underdeveloped countries attempt self-reliance or redistribute their wealth, I'm afraid they will be resigning themselves to a state of miserable stagnation.

Our Response: The question implies that the Food First alternative we have just outlined would make accumulating development funds more difficult than it is today. But shouldn't we evaluate any proposal for change first by comparing it to what exists? We think if you truly examine the "what is" now in underdeveloped countries, you will soon realize that no one could devise a system with *less* chance for accumulating wealth.

Wealth is not simply money in the bank. Most workers in every underdeveloped country, no matter how poor and undernourished the majority of its population, produce more than they consume. This surplus generated by their work is the root of wealth. The real question is who will control the accumulated goods and the means to produce more.

In most underdeveloped countries the surplus is not available to the majority of the people who produce it, for it is drained off by landlords, moneylenders, merchants, industrialists, state bureaucrats, and foreign corporations. Traditionally it is argued that unequal control over the surplus is "good" for a society because only the rich will save the surplus and invest in a society's future. Recently, however, respected economists studying underdeveloped countries have independently concluded that in reality such a rationalization of unequal control simply does not hold up.[1] They find that in the countryside, the landlords, moneylenders, and merchants who appropriate so much of the surplus generally do *not* reinvest it; rather, they tend to spend it on imported luxury goods and expensive consumer items manufactured in foreign-style factories that use up large amounts of capital and provide little employment. Even when they do invest, as we noted in Part V, it is invariably abroad or nonproductively, for instance, in hotels, bars, restaurants, rental property, taxis and the like.

One of us lived for several months in a village in the remote southern Yucatan jungle of Mexico. The Indians were poor farmers—former chicle gatherers for Wrigley's chewing gum until Wrigley came up with a synthetic gum—who were gravely exploited by the village's general storeowner and moneylender. We will call him Don Eziquiel. One day Don Eziquiel used his accumulated profits to import what had been his heart's desire since the day he saw an ad in a newspaper—a Ford Galaxie—and there wasn't even a single paved road in the jungle!

What About Foreign Investment Capital?

Foreign corporations like to claim that underdeveloped countries need them because they need investment funds. But numerous studies[2] now have demonstrated that a multinational corporation usually brings in precious little initial investment funds to those countries. Why should a corporation bother when it finds it can tap the local savings since everyone wants to lend to, say, General Foods. Often a large part of the equity contribution by a foreign corporation to a joint venture with a local partner or the state consists not of money, but of technical and marketing "know-how." In addition, all or part of the profit is frequently not reinvested but is "repatriated," that is, returned to the home country.

We have seen that agribusiness corporations, whether operating plantations or through contracts, appropriate the lion's share of the value of produce through their monopoly hold on foreign marketing. All types of foreign corporations regularly siphon off foreign exchange (in addition to declared profits) through untaxed royalties, debt payments, and inflated charges by headquarters for management advice, research, and the like. All the devices open to them rely on the marvels of modern corporate accounting (recently defined by one accountant as a subdivision of creative writing).

It is doubtful if even a country like the United States has enough skilled civil servants to monitor the accounting alchemies of the multinational corporations operating across its borders. Certainly no underdeveloped country can even come close to doing so. The chief accounting alchemies are overpricing imports from headquarters (including depreciated machinery) and underpricing exports to another subsidiary of the same company. These devices enable the local subsidiary to claim it is losing money. It can then threaten to pull up stakes if it does not receive even more subsidies, "tax holidays," no-strike guarantees, free roads, water, and so on.

Some governments are finally realizing therefore that

a foreign "investor" is often a net drain on funds. Ironically, one such government is that of Brazil. We say "ironically" because the military government of Brazil since 1964 has sought above all to provide the proper "climate" for foreign investment. An official study late in 1975 showed that the eleven most important foreign firms have remitted more capital out of Brazil than they have brought in. Since 1965, the giant agribusiness firm, Anderson Clayton, for example, has brought $1.6 million in foreign exchange into Brazil. By 1975, it had generated a surplus 32 times greater, $16.8 million of which was sent abroad in the form of profits and dividends.[8]

Plastic Shoes for Development?

Nonagribusiness firms also can appropriate the surplus that the peasants produce and perpetuate a distortion of the country's potential food resources. A good example of this was sent to us by a missionary in the Cameroon. The Bata Shoe Company, a ubiquitous Canadian-based multinational corporation, a few years ago started manufacturing plastic shoes in the coastal town of Douala. The shoes are heavily advertised throughout the predominantly rural country and they have become one of those symbols of status that poor people buy. Tourists in Douala seek out traditional handcrafted shoes while the peasants save up money from the export of their cocoa, peanuts, and cotton to buy plastic shoes. With such "incentives" the peasants expand their production of export crops (thereby often lowering market prices) on land well suited for food crops, despite serious rural undernutrition. The Bata Shoe Company (and similar multinationals) therefore are in fact recouping part of the foreign exchange paid to the Cameroon for its agricultural exports—foreign exchange that theoretically goes for development needs. At the same time several thousand village shoemakers, perfectly capable of meeting the country's needs, are being put out of work and will likely go hungry. The plastic shoe factory itself, the missionary noted, employs all of thirty workers.

Over the past few years European textile firms, like their New England counterparts years ago, are moving south, but, in their case, to central Africa to avoid labor unions and higher labor costs. The first impact, already dramatic in countries like Mali and. Chad, is an increased push for cotton production at the expense of food staples. In addition, through the firms' repatriations and remittances for machinery, loans and service fees, much of the foreign exchange earned by the export of agricultural products and textiles leaves the country. In other words, foreign exchange is not being spent on the type of development that decreases poverty, unemployment, inequality, and hunger. Tens of thousands of local craftspeople, formerly tailors, makers of cotton and wool thread and cloth, are being put out of work. Such companies perpetuate underdevelopment by sopping up, displacing, and mischanneling the country's actual and potential wealth.

Wealth Begins with Land and People

In a Food First economy people would mobilize the potential wealth of their labor power and of underutilized land. Vast tracts of underused land exist on large estates, monocultural plantations, and mechanized farms that employ capital to displace people.

Moreover, the redistribution of income that is the product of the Food First economy we described in our response to Question 46 can mean greater savings for investment, not less. We have seen, in Part VI, that even under present conditions poor farmers, especially if they have some land, often turn out to be better savers than the rich. And if poor peasants are given reason to believe that their savings will benefit them, they can save at impressive rates. After the Chinese revolution the net savings ratio in China rose from 1 to 2 percent in 1949 to 20 percent in 1953.[4]

The Chinese people have learned through their own struggle to overcome hunger that neither money nor the natural geographic endowment of an area are the determining factors. In the 1950s, Tachai and Wu Chai-Ping were two neighboring villages with very disparate natural qualities. Wu Chai-Ping wanted to separate itself from Tachai because it felt that the potential of its superior natural endowment would be held back by its neighbor, the resource-poor Tachai. They did split up. But Tachai, through intensive collective work, has more than made up for its inferior natural resources. Tachai now produces better harvests and enjoys a considerably higher income than the other village. The people of Tachai overcame an extremely hostile environment *without outside material support.*[5]

The point is that where people are organized, share in the decision-making, and know that their work will benefit them, resources will be available which before were siphoned off. Kathleen Gough, author of *Ten Times More Beautiful* and an anthropologist with 30 years' experience in the field, compared in some detail two geographically comparable rice growing regions of Asia—one in southeast India, Thanjavur, and one in the Red River region of Vietnam, Thai Binh.[6]

In Thanjavur, land ownership is tightly concentrated, and in some areas as much as three-quarters of the land is controlled by absentee owners. Gough estimates that under these conditions one-half to three-fourths of the value of agricultural production is drained off by landowners and merchants for personal consumption and investment outside of agriculture.

In a typical village in Thai Binh, however, where the agricultural land is cooperatively worked, 45 percent of the harvests and a good portion of the livestock products and crafts goods are bought by the national distribution system. The money received, plus the remaining 55 percent of the production, is divided up among the villagers. Seventy percent goes for wages and running expenses such as hand tools; 20 percent is spent on engineering projects and machinery and fertilizer, and 10 percent on social welfare, including housing and medical care. Thus *all* of what is produced goes to the development of the village.

Where people are working cooperatively toward

mutually agreed-upon goals, the resources that do exist are put to much greater use than where most resources are controlled by a few. In Vu Thang, a Vietnamese village in the Thai Binh area visited by Gough, 12 irrigation pumpsets irrigated 300 acres whereas a typical Indian village in Thanjavur needed 18 pumpsets to cover only 175 acres of rice land—that is 50 percent more pumpsets to irrigate 42 percent less land.

Vu Thang's pumps were more efficiently used in part because their location was determined by the cooperative, based on maximum irrigation potential. By contrast, the privately owned pumps in Thanjavur were located to benefit only the owners, who often diverted water from others into their own fields. Moreover, irrigation is a delicate and sophisticated operation, needing continual maintenance. But in Thanjavur, Indian agricultural officials find it difficult, according to Gough, "to move an embankment or channel even one foot in order to improve irrigation because they cannot obtain permission from the numerous village owners." Just as it became clear in Part V, "The Inefficiency of Inequality," the cooperation essential to development is not possible where a few control the resources, forcing the majority into competition and dependency.

But the question asks, What about resources that don't now exist in the villages or even in the underdeveloped countries? Don't development needs such as fertilizer have to be imported? In answering this question, we learned that local resources, there all the time but unused and even unrecognized, can be mobilized for development—if a cooperative organization of the people turns that development into a priority.

Take fertilizer. First of all we must keep in mind that shifting from monoculture to a variety of crops and instituting crop rotation will, as first steps, reduce the need for fertilizer. More important, however, the local potential for producing fertilizer from indigenous waste material is estimated to represent six to eight times the amount of nutrients in costly, largely imported, chemical fertilizers actually used by the underdeveloped countries.[7] This energy and fertilizer potential can be tapped right at the village level, using materials that are often wasted.

Biogasification, mentioned in Question 20, is a simple method of fermenting organic raw material such as crop residues and manure to produce methane (for fuel) and a nutrient-rich effluent (for fertilizer). The fertilizer produced through the biogas technique is many times richer in nutrients than the waste products that went into it. By fermenting the village wastes of 500 human beings and 250 cattle, a biogas "plant" can supply the average cropped land of a typical Asian village with two and one half times the present nitrogen applied in the form of chemical fertilizers. Moreover, it can supply almost double the present daily energy needs of the village for cooking, water pumping, electricity, and industries.[8]

Again, a comparison of villages in Vietnam and India is useful. In the Vietnamese village studied by Gough, every scrap of human and animal excrement is collected for fertilizer. Moreover, 46 hectares of bomb craters are used not only for fish breeding but for growing algae for fertilizer. Trees are planted around the cooperatives to provide fuel and as shelter for crops and green manure. In Thanjavur, India, however, excrement is not a fertilizer resource. Dropped haphazardly, it is instead a health hazard. Cow dung is burned as fuel instead of being fermented to produce much more potential fertilizer and fuel in the form of methane gas.*

Both villages studied by Gough would be considered by many to be without adequate resources—both in need of outside sources of funds for development. Yet in both, wealth currently exists, not to mention the much greater potential. The questions are: How is that potential to be mobilized? And how is the wealth to be used? The answers to both depend entirely on the economic system. Is the economic system used to drain off the wealth produced by the villagers? Or is it used to channel that wealth to the villagers themselves (thus

* See p. 178 for a comparison of the impact of biogas in India and China.

promoting their well-being and their willingness to cooperate and to work) as well as to the development
needs (irrigation, schools, clinics) of the community
as a whole?

But an economic system based on cooperative control over resources and on cooperative work may seem
unreal in a culture such as ours—or in most underdeveloped countries today for that matter. What could
make people work to mobilize the potential resources
at hand, many would find themselves wondering. And
how could people ever be made to work cooperatively?

Such reservations in part reflect our experience of
seeing people's reaction when they are called upon to
"sacrifice for the sake of their country."

People sense intuitively and correctly that in highly
inequitable societies, such calls are usually a convenient way for the rich to blind the nonrich to the
fact that only *they* are being made to give up something. In the Vietnamese village of Vu Thang we have
been discussing, the income gap between the lowest
and the highest paid peasant is only about 20 percent.
Contrast this with the 1000- to 8000-fold difference
between the income of the rich landowner in Thanjavur, India, and that of a landless laborer there. Thus
in the first village, appeals to eschew selfishness for
cooperative work make sense because all gain relatively equally. But in Thanjavur, peasants know that the
wealth they produce will principally benefit others.

The next time you hear or read a discussion on the
lack of aid, poor terms of trade or the poor natural
endowment of the underdeveloped countries, don't
conclude that such are the causes of underdevelopment.
Lack of development funds is really not the problem.
The fundamental problem is the unjust social structures that block the development of the great potential
wealth that does exist—structures of control described
throughout this book that prevent the poor majority
from mobilizing that potential for their own benefit.

48. Aren't Poor Peasants Too Oppressed Ever to Change?

Question: But aren't peasants in the underdeveloped countries so underfed, so ignorant of the real forces oppressing them, and conditioned into a state of passivity that they are not able to mobilize? Even if you are right that any real change must involve the mobilization of the peasantry, isn't this just plain unrealistic?

Our Response: Bombarded with pictures showing the poor as weak and hungry, we should not lose sight of the obvious fact that they often must exert themselves tremendously just to stay alive—traveling long distances and working 10 to 14 hours a day. In that sense, the poor are hardly passive. They represent great potential energy that, once released, can be applied to their own development.

Moreover, those living and working with the poor in underdeveloped countries have found that they comprehend quite well the forces oppressing them. In a report for the U.N. Asian Development Institute, the four Asian authors with much experience in organizing with the rural poor concluded that the poor "have an understanding of the working of the economic system and can describe in detail the processes (wage exploitation, money lending, bribery, and price discrimination) through which exploitation takes place."[1]

Those with direct experience working with poor peasants also counter the notion that it is mainly superstitious religious beliefs that keep the poor down. Lasse and Lisa Berg, writing of their experiences in India, in their book *Face to Face* observe that, while reasoning based in religious beliefs might characterize India's middle class, the poor almost never cite religion to explain their daily actions. "If asked why they do not revolt," note the Bergs, "they do not answer that they want to be reborn to a better position; they answer that they are afraid of the landowner or the government or the police."[2]

But stressing both the powerful structure of control over the lives of the poor and their understandable fear can cause us to ignore the fact that in every country in the world where people are hungry there is a struggle going on right now over who controls food-producing resources—in Mexico, the Philippines, South Africa, Brazil, Chad, the United States, El Salvador, Bangladesh, Thailand, and we could go on and on. Those standing up to resist are the very people who have been perceived by so many as "too oppressed ever to change."

Moreover, so many who would question what peasants can do seem unaware that since only the early 1950s over 40 percent of the population of the underdeveloped world have freed themselves from famine through their own efforts. The Chinese alone, of course, account for the major portion of those who have achieved this remarkable success. In addition, there are countries—such as Vietnam, Mozambique, Guinea Bissau, and Angola—where after decades of intense struggle, mainly by peasant-based organizations, independence has recently been won. Now these people are able to turn their energies into building the basis of food self-reliance.

Because of the selective way news is transmitted to us, we in countries like the United States are often unaware of the courageous struggles of millions of people everywhere to gain control over food-producing resources rightfully theirs. Events often come to us filtered through a lens that causes us to identify not with people like us, but with the governing elites in underdeveloped countries. We once read, for example, a news account of the depressed economy of Senegal, ruined by a fall-off in the production of the main export crop, peanuts. Simply presented this way, our natural response was to ask: What can be done to spur the lagging production of this crop? How can we get the economy rolling again? We thus were made to identify with the export economy of Senegal, not with the *people*.

The real story was that many Senegalese peasants had purposefully spurned cash-cropping in order to grow food for themselves, particularly millet and sorghum. This shift was interpreted by some as the reaction of tradition-bound peasants. On the contrary, this example of peasant resistance can be seen as a positive break away from tradition, if being traditional means doing what the political and social hierarchy has always demanded. These lessons are seldom, if ever, drawn for us; such is the power of selective news that reinforces the notion of the passivity of the world's disenfranchised.

To counter the myth of the passive poor we must find ongoing sources of news that go behind the selective, filtered information offered us by most of the media. At the end of this book we therefore include a list of some of the publications and organizations that provide news and analysis of the struggles of ordinary people in countries around the world for their food rights. We find these sources invaluable in uprooting the myth of the passive poor and the companion myth, that of our own powerlessness.

49. Food Versus Freedom?

Question: Societies that have eliminated hunger have done so only by denying people's rights. Is there not an inevitable trade-off between freedom and ending hunger?

Our Response: This question, perhaps more than any other, paralyzes well-meaning people. It raises critical issues that must be grappled with. But a clear formulation of these issues is clouded by the multiple distortions contained in the "food versus freedom" formulation.

First, it implies that societies that are not making structural changes to end hunger at least have more freedom, Even in terms of *theoretical* freedom, this is often false. People in countries with widespread hunger and other forms of poverty, such as the Philippines, Chile, or Nicaragua, do not have even the theoretical freedom of free assembly or the right to vote.

Moreover, learning more about countries where many, often the majority, face hunger, has forced us to confront the difference between theoretical freedoms and effective freedoms. In countries such as India or Mexico, more and more people are losing control of their land. Still more find it hard to get any kind of job, even at slow starvation "wages." In such countries people have the theoretical freedom to organize and to vote. But do they effectively have the freedom? Given the violent reaction of the elite threatened by any mobilization of the poor, we doubt it. And while perhaps the most basic freedom is the freedom to achieve security for one's self and one's loved ones, in such countries—now the majority of the world's countries—life is increasingly insecure.

In other words, with absolutely no share in control over their country's productive assets, how much *effective* freedom do people have? This contradiction between theoretical freedom and effective freedom applies here in the United States as well.

Second, the myth seems to suggest that in eliminating hunger, countries have moved from a state of "more freedom" to less freedom. But when we study societies in which the majority are achieving greater food, job, and old-age security—as in China or Cuba, for example—we find, of course, that most people have not moved from a state of freedom to a state of repression in the process of achieving that security. No, the political and economic structures that preceded the present ones were among the most repressive in the world.

Studying these societies today, we find many problems, including the incredible difficulties resulting from hundreds of years of internal and external exploitation. Their problems are not only physical but human—how people can transform their consciousness of themselves in order to make true self-government possible. We also find the drive for greater self-government accompanied by some restrictions on people's individual choices.

In societies attempting to create structures to meet the needs of all, the legal definition of what is socially harmful might have to be enlarged. In our system we allow speculation in land and food that insures that some persons go hungry while others become profiteers and many overconsume. In a system attempting deliberately to plan for the needs of all, hoarding and speculation are not accepted. (Most important, of course, the majority of people seem not so motivated to hoard and speculate when their basic needs for a job and for food are assured.) Moreover, individual choices may sometimes have to be adjusted in order to fulfill the community's needs. At least during the primary period of overcoming underdevelopment, some may not be able to choose whatever job or area of residence they prefer. (We must keep in mind, of course, that few even in supposedly free-market societies have such absolute freedom.) Clearly, every society places limits upon the individual's choices. The real issues, then, are these: How can those restrictions be made fairly? Are these restrictions imposed by an elite for their own benefit or by the community for the good of all? Is the goal to achieve a society in which the individual's legitimate self-interest and the community's needs are more and more complementary?

Freedom for critical expression is also of pivotal concern. In countries that choose to break with private control over productive assets, this issue is made considerably more problematic by the denunciation, aggressive posturing, and even subversive intervention of foreign powers like the United States. Such external hostility creates the worst possible environment for the fostering of internal critical expression (and individual variety). Americans should know this all too well from the years following Pearl Harbor. Any individual or grouping of individuals differing with the commonly held view runs the risk of being labeled a collaborator of the foreign enemy. The challenge for a society in the difficult period of restructuring is both to recognize the vulnerability caused by a lack of unity, and yet to develop effective means for constructive critical thinking. Critical thinking must be encouraged, thinking that can speak out and be heard, *even* when, at first, few acknowledge the very existence of an issue, as with nuclear power or sexism.

Thus, instead of the simplistic notion that "freedom" must be sacrificed to eliminate hunger, we find tremendous complexity. But we also find grounds for hope. While no people on earth have achieved a model society that ideally melds individual and community needs, we do have much to learn from people engaged in the *process* of attempting that goal. Some of the most critical lessons we have discussed are in Chapter 46.

We wish to underline that these lessons represent a *process* and not simply goals to be achieved once and for all. And within this process are profound tensions—the tension between the individual's wishes and the community needs; the tension between democratic, participatory decision-making and the need for leadership based on specialized skills, knowledge, and experience; the tension between a focus on agriculture and the need to build up industry in order to increase agricultural productivity.

These are just a few of what we have come to believe are *necessary* tensions in creating a social, economic, and political system designed to maximize both individual fulfillment and community progress. The trouble with a "freedom versus food trade-off" is that by over-simplifying and distorting, it frightens people, preventing them from being able to learn from the concrete experiences of their counterparts in other countries.

50. What Can We Do?

Question: If you say that it is up to the underdeveloped countries themselves, then what role is left for us?

Diet for a Small Planet implies that social change starts with the individual. Do you still feel that way? Aren't individual acts no more than symbolic gestures against the enormity of the economic and political reality of hunger?

Our Response: Saying that self-reliance means "let them take care of themselves" could be the most convenient way of escaping our responsibilities. Or, the concept of self-reliance could free us for the first time to perceive clearly the paths of effective action.

When *Diet for a Small Planet* was first published there were few group initiatives for change grounded in the issues of food and hunger. At that time it seemed necessary to focus on what the individual could do. But today it is no longer necessary to speak only of the individual. We are in touch with hundreds of groups all over the country who have emerged spontaneously in the last few years. On college campuses, in religious organizations, among certain state and national legislators, in co-op movements, and among ecology and natural food groups there is a feeling that food is the right place to start to focus attention and energy for change. It is not a movement only of young people. It includes farmers: groups that have been fighting for decades many of the battles others have just discovered. Now they have new allies.

Wherever you are, it is possible to make your impact felt. But what should the impact be? What are the most important issues to focus on? What are the pitfalls? These questions we ask ourselves continually. We hope some of our answers will be helpful to you.

Grasp the Root Causes—Don't Assume We Already Know Enough

It is important to keep in mind where most Americans are starting—how deeply imbedded the myths are in all our psyches. Do not assume there is a common understanding even among "food activists." There is a wide divergence of views, many of them rooted in the old myths we have tried to dispel in this book.

Most of what you read elsewhere will not reflect the reality that we have tried to convey here. Questions will still be framed in the old way. You will go on hearing that the United States is the world's "breadbasket," that the problem is simply "population pressure," "droughts," "backwardness," "lack of incentives for foreign investment," or "not enough foreign aid."

One of the most important lessons learned in writing this book has been that acting out of ignorance can strengthen the very forces we must counter. Focusing on the small farmer sounds good until we realize that in many countries up to 60 percent of the people in the countryside have no land. Focusing on increasing production sounds good until we ask how the hungry will ever partake of it if they are excluded from participation in or control over the productive assets. Introducing mechanization sounds like progress until we ask whose jobs are being eliminated. Sending food abroad sounds good until we look at the impact on local producers and ask what is being done with the money local governments raise by selling the food we send as aid. Our government as helper of the poor abroad sounds noble until we remind ourselves of the overriding impact of U.S. economic and counter-insurgency activities that sustain the very forces most oppressing the hungry. Agribusiness banter about feeding the hungry sounds admirable until we recall that corporations can make a profit only by allying themselves with the forces that keep the hungry marginal and by diverting resources to market to the already well-fed.

Redefining "Help"

The question suggests that there may be a contradiction between self-reliance as the first goal of the hungry and our ability to help. But there is no contradiction if we keep in mind that *people will feed themselves*. If they are not doing so, you can be sure that mighty obstacles are in the way. These obstacles are not, as we have seen, the "hunger myths"—overpopulation, poor climate, inappropriate technology, discriminatory trade practices, or insufficient capital. The real obstacle in the way of people liberating themselves from hunger is that the majority of citizens are increasingly cut out from control over productive resources. Thus the broad agenda for us is three-fold.

First: We cannot solve the problem of world hunger *for* other people. We can, however, work to remove the obstacles that make it increasingly difficult for people everywhere to take control of food production in order to feed themselves. We should concentrate on those obstacles that are being reinforced by forces originating in our country, often in our name and with our tax dollars.

Second: We should support people everywhere already resisting forced food dependency and those now building new self-reliant societies in which people democratically control the food-producing processes. Direct financial assistance, without strings, is important. At the same time we must communicate the very existence of such groups to Americans still believing that "people are too oppressed ever to change."

Third: No matter how well we learn to support indigenous groups in the Third World that are struggling for self-determination, our greatest impact on them still will come through U.S. government and corporate policies using our tax and consumer dollars. Working to construct a democratically controlled, self-reliant economy at home is not merely the only way to end hunger and deprivation in America. It is the only way to make America "safe for the world."

The forms that our energies will take acting in these areas will of course be the outgrowth of our labors together in the coming years. They will differ depending on where you are, who you are, and whom you are trying to reach. Let us welcome a multiplicity of approaches at this stage. Here are some possibilities:

Hunger Re-education

Some would claim that education is merely passive while what we need is action. For us, however, there is no division between the two. Education is not something that is completed as the first step toward action, but is a process that never ends; it is an ongoing source of our energy and direction.

True education is not passive because it does not leave us the same as we were. Education is that which changes us. But most of us were brought up to fear change, to think that the good life had to do with getting oneself so situated that change could be avoided. In learning about the roots of the tremendous suffering we see around us, we have come to exactly the opposite conclusion. We have come to see that the world must change profoundly to end the suffering that is so evident; and how can we believe that the world can change if we don't experience ourselves changing?

Trying the untried, and the continuous self-evaluation that formerly appeared to threaten our stability, and therefore our happiness, are now perceived as sources of vitality and strength. Once willing to take risks, we stop seeing ourselves as responders; new self-respect grows as we experience ourselves as doers.

Learning, defined this way, is not confined to study, although the many reading suggestions that follow reveal that ongoing study—as individuals and in groups —is invaluable. Education means exposing ourselves to learning situations. We can, for example, learn and perhaps even work alongside people most abused by our own country's food and agricultural systems— farmworkers, cannery workers, poor farmers, and others. We can travel, trying always to learn about the forces affecting people's lives in other countries.

The first step, of course, in doing anything is finding out what we need to know to do it well. Our educational system mimics our economic system; it makes us passive consumers of information. By contrast, we all can begin to take charge of our own learning. Assuming that mass media largely reflect the economic status quo, we should seek out alternative sources of information that tell us of the efforts of our counterparts here and in other countries working for their own economic self-determination. For recommendations of some such publications, see Appendices A and B at the end of the book.

Our own re-education work will continue in the form of in-the-field research, the writing of articles and pamphlets and the development of audio-visual materials. To be put on our mailing list, please write:

Institute for Food and Development Policy
2588 Mission Street
San Francisco, CA 94110

With your own re-education under way, you may choose to:

- Find out how "hunger" is taught in your school or in the school in your community. Are your peers or your children being taught to fear scarcity and hungry people? Examine textbooks and classroom materials. Then join with others to develop alternative curricula and special events that present another view—a positive view that the problem is firmly in *our* hands.
- Form a counter-media group to provide an ongoing answer to your local media's interpretation of hunger here and abroad—through letters to the editor, a regular column, or radio shows sponsored by your group. In the future we ourselves will be developing slide shows and study guides.
- Instead of trying to tackle "world hunger" you or your organization might choose to become thoroughly familiar with the forces causing hunger in *one* country. Get hold of all U.S. AID and World Bank documents on their programs in that country. What military and international financial supports go to the country? Find out what U.S. corporations operate there. What is their impact? What indigenous groups are working for change? How can they be supported? Get in touch with people who have been there. Read first-hand accounts. Focusing on one country in depth may be the most useful way to understand and act on everything we discuss in *Food First*.

Work for Self-Reliance Here

- Work now to open a national debate on the issue of democratic, national planning in food production and processing to ensure that America's abundance is available to all its people.
- Opt out of the "food only for profit" system that creates scarcity. Organize a worker-managed co-operative. Grow some of your own food, and get

behind a network to directly link farmers to consumers in your area. It is a sure way to learn
about farmers' problems. Worker-managed food
systems are evolving in cities large and small
around the country. In Minnesota almost 10 percent of all food purchases are now through cooperatives.

- Work for regional food self-reliance policies within the United States that will carry with them a
message for all Americans. We do not have to
import food from countries where many go hungry or waste our fossil fuel transporting food
thousands of miles. (Energy use for food transportation has *tripled* in the last thirty years.)
Four states that have begun at least to move toward greater self-reliance are Massachusetts, Vermont, Pennsylvania, and West Virginia. (A special
Massachusetts commission on food policy recently
found that the state imports 84 percent of its
food.)

Democratize the U.S. Food Economy

- Work for land reform in the United States, including a ceiling on the amount of land one person
or one family can hold. In 1969, the largest 5.5
percent of all farms operated 54 percent of all
farmland, while the bottom 40 percent operated
only 4.5 percent.[1] The proportion of farmland
rented was 38 percent, mostly from nonfarm landlords. An appropriate beginning is the breaking
up of large holdings and the banning of absentee
ownership in federally subsidized irrigation districts.
- Work for a national agricultural policy that would
support family farms and cooperatives—through
price supports, when necessary, government research priorities, and credit programs.
- Prohibit corporations with significant nonfarm
investment from entering agriculture. Today at
least 22 percent of all farm production is con-

trolled directly or through contracts by large corporations. Minnesota and North Dakota are two states with significant laws to keep corporations out of farming. National anti-corporate farming legislation was first introduced in Congress in 1973.

- Remove tax laws that encourage farm investment by non-farmers seeking to offset their taxable income.
- Alter inheritance tax laws that force surviving farm families to sell their farms to pay an inheritance tax on highly inflated farmland. (The average farm today is valued at $170,000; farmland is assessed at its real estate value, as if subdivision is intended, rather than at its value as food-producing land.)
- Work for anti-trust enforcement in the food processing sector.
- Require all food products to carry the name of the parent company. This would help to dispel the myth of a competitive food industry, a myth perpetuated by a handful of corporations selling under hundreds of different names.
- Work to limit the influence of media advertising by a handful of food corporations, starting with the prohibition of commercials for low-nutrition foods during children's television programming.

Make America "Safe for the World"

- Outlaw government assistance through AID and OPIC and indirectly through the World Bank to U.S. private corporations investing in underdeveloped countries. Minimally such corporations should be self-reliant.
- Abolish all tax laws that encourage American corporations to locate abroad in order to escape environmental, wage, and tax laws here.
- Stop all military aid to regimes blocking their people's efforts to redistribute economic control and achieve food self-reliance—countries such as

the Philippines, Indonesia, Bangladesh, and Nicaragua.

- End economic assistance to any country not actively democratizing control over food-producing resources (including countries like the Philippines and Pakistan) where land reform is in rhetoric only.
- Promote economic assistance, not as loans but as grants untied to purchases in the United States, to countries where steps are being taken to democratize control over agricultural resources, such as Vietnam and Mozambique.
- Supply food aid only to meet emergencies and where it directly contributes to creating the preconditions for food self-reliance.

We do not hold out the naive promise that groups working independently on each of these initiatives across the country will bring into being a new economic structure, one in which average citizens are in active control of economic and social planning. To accomplish such a thorough reconstruction will require the evolution of a broad-based political organization, able to confront the power of the elite who benefit from the system as it now operates.

We do believe, however, that working on these many initiatives today can awaken a wide number of Americans to the built-in failure of our present system to meet human needs, and can transform more and more of us from passive responders into active agents, as well as teach each of us the process of effective organizing. We then are laying the necessary groundwork for structural change.

A key to building toward structural change is to communicate in all of our educational and organizing work that the many separate crises we are tackling (the world food crisis, the energy crisis, the nuclear reactor crisis, the armaments crisis, etc.) have a common root. Working on a food and agriculture-related problem is not the *only* way to fight hunger. If the root of the problems is common—the highly inequitable structure of economic control that excludes the majority of Americans from exercising power over decisions most affecting them—any number of critical issues can point to this root. You must decide in which issue and through which channels you can best take greater responsibility for change.

Remember also that we are not alone—within virtually every Third World country there are individuals and groups working to establish Food First policies. Anything that we can do to reveal how corporations and government policies are interfering with their efforts will give strength and credibility to these helpful forces.

Finally, don't be afraid to be controversial. It is in controversy that people begin to learn that something new is being said.

The Significance of Individual Life Choices

How important are individual life choices—what we eat, where we shop, etc.—if the analysis in this book is that the problems are rooted in economic and political systems much larger than the individual?

Making a conscious choice to consume in a manner more consistent with our understanding of systemic problems need not be to diminish guilt but rather to diminish our sense of powerlessness. To realize that we can make some real choices is a first step in regaining a sense of personal power in face of a system that denies individual responsibility for our choices. It is in this spirit that the message of *Diet for a Small Planet* has great significance for us.

The American meat-fixated diet came to represent to us an extreme example of how resource use based solely on profit considerations places a burden on our food production resources and reduces the potential food supply. Over half of U.S. harvested acreage goes to feed livestock who return only a small fraction of the potential nutrients to us. Converting livestock from their historical role as protein factories into protein disposals has been the preferred way to get rid of grain in a domestic and world market where those who need

the grain itself are too poor to buy it. And in the
process Americans have been hooked on a meat-
centered diet—now consuming on average at least
twice the protein their bodies need. Eating less meat
and less processed food—eating in a way that reflects
our bodies' real needs—is thus one way of saying "no"
to a system that looks at food like any other profitable
commodity—totally divorcing it from human need.

What Motivates Us?

After a talk we gave while writing this book, students
asked: But what makes you think people can change
—that anything can change? You say that your position
counters the fatalistic overpopulation and weather
theories of hunger; that it puts control of our fate back
into the hands of the people. But aren't the forces of
concentrated wealth and power just as hard to confront, or more so?

First, the very phrasing of the students' questions
reflects their sense that the elites dominating the food
economy both here and in the underdeveloped countries have completely taken charge. Yet we have seen
over and over again that the dominant groups are
constantly on the defensive, trying to protect their
power as more and more of us become aware of our
worsening position. The mechanization of agriculture
can be seen, in part, as a defensive move. Large landowners, for instance, mechanize in order to no longer
have to deal with the legitimate, militant demands of
laborers and tenants.

The phenomenon of the Global Supermarket—U.S.
firms moving abroad in search of cheap land and labor
—can also be seen in part as a reflection of the effort
of multinational firms to deal with the strength of farm
labor movements in the industrial countries demanding
decent wages for their work. Even the considerable
expenditures by corporations on advertisements por-
traying themselves as helping to solve world hunger
mean that they themselves are worried. They recognize
that Americans are beginning to question the power of

corporations. Perhaps those who control the food economy appreciate the power of the awakening people more than we ourselves do.

Second, we believe that anyone who is privileged enough to become aware must make a choice. We either choose to be observers of history, thereby lending our weight to the forces now in control, or we choose to be participants, actively building a new culture based on human values. Seen this way, do we really have a choice?

Human society is, after all, only a product of the collective struggle of all people. If we say that *we* have no power to change things, who does?

If we answer that the power is in the hands of an elite who alone are making the decisions, we will be doing exactly what the established forces of power want of us. We will have folded our arms in defeat, saying that we prefer to build shells to protect ourselves from reality, to keep out the bad news.

Based on our own experience we have come to believe that people prefer a protective shell only because they are overwhelmed with negative information that they cannot integrate. They cannot integrate facts into useful action because they are made to feel guilty about and fearful of the hungry. Too often, the problem of hunger gets turned into a contest between them and us —all of us in the rich world versus all of them in the poor. In fact, the majority of the American people are *not* pitted against the hungry people; these are not the battle lines of the hunger struggle. The struggle is against a system that increasingly concentrates wealth and power. The struggle is against a system profiting on hunger in the Philippines or Brazil just as it is in the United States. The real forces creating hunger span almost all nations in the world. Once the lines of struggle are clear we can no longer be manipulated by profferers of guilt and fear.

But some would say that our choices, if we do indeed have them, are limited—that since human nature is basically self-centered, all we can do is build on that trait. But in our experience, debates on "human nature" have been unproductive—for who can *prove* anything?

There is no need to prove that human beings are basically good. Rather, history has shown human potential for cooperation *as well as* our potential for cruelty and cut-throat competitiveness. With this view, the most pressing question becomes: What kind of structures of human organization can we help create that will elicit our best, not our worst qualities?

Nor do we say that people must extinguish their self-interest for the sake of the larger community. Rather, we are learning that there need not be the often-assumed contradiction between self-interest and community interest. We then ask: What kind of structures allow an individual's natural self-interest to contribute to the community's progress?

Many people here and in other countries are asking these questions, and, moreover, are actively working to build such social structures. There is no more important work today than explaining this to people in countries like our own. Before they would work for change they have to believe that change is possible, that a culture fixated on individual profit-seeking alone is not "natural." The tragedy is that we have had to reach the point where so many people are hungry and malnourished, including millions here at home, before we could begin to see that our system—a system built on the vulnerabilities of the human personality instead of its strengths—can never create a humane society.

Finally, we must not allow our appropriate sense of urgency to lead to frustration and despair. It took centuries to create the structures that cause the worldwide deprivation we now witness. It will take time to construct a human world. That does not belittle our task; that makes it all the more important. Our personal time frames have changed. We must come to understand today's struggle in light of the entire scope of human history. We must not limit our vision by what we see around us today. What we see today may tell us little about what our children and their children are capable of creating.

When we say that we are learning, through studying hunger, where our own self-interest really lies, we are not saying simply that we are learning how our lives are limited by the same forces exploiting the hungry peasant in Africa or India. We are also saying that understanding the forces that generate hunger is in our own self-interest because through this understanding we are made freer. The more we grasp the system we are part of, the more able we are to make conscious choices to alter it.

We want you to join us, not simply because of the urgent struggle to construct a just and life-giving society, but because through our own experience we have become certain that none of us can live fully today as long as we are overwhelmed by a false view of the world and a false view of human nature to buttress it. Learning how a system can cause hunger then becomes not a lesson in misery and deprivation, but a vehicle for a great awakening in our own lives.

Appendix A

Organizing for Change

We must do more than critique, as this book has done, the forces generating hunger today. Positive change depends on developing the collective self-confidence in our capacity to overcome the messages that would have us believe we are powerless. Any society develops only to the degree that enough individuals within it realize their capacity to mold new and more satisfying forms of social organization. In our work for change we must become living proof of the human potential our current system would deny and negate.

How can we become increasingly self-determining? How can we become that which we have been taught to believe is not possible? In our own work, we have found the answer lies—above all else—in learning to work together toward common goals.

No one changes alone. Change comes as a result of contact with others. Not only do we need others for the ongoing challenge that they represent, but for their help in our self-questioning in order to sharpen our unique contributions. We also must have the support of others when our risk-taking results in disappointments, as it inevitably will at times.

Thus, wherever we are, whoever we are, we must not be resigned to working alone. Perhaps the first step in our self-education for social change is to take the initiative to reach out to others with whom we can work. When we are working with others, we can experience daily the lessons of cooperative organization that reflect the transformation needed in the economic sphere.

What follows is a selected listing of organizations, grouped according to issues, that are working on many of the problems we have written about. Get in touch. Explore their programs. Find out how to participate. Or initiate your own organization.

Action Groups and Their Publications by Issue

U.S. Agricultural Policies

1. Agribusiness Accountability Project, P.O. Box 5646, San Francisco, Calif. 94101 (415) 626–1650. Publications: *AgBiz Tiller* (periodical), *Major U.S. Corporations Involved in Agribusiness*, 1978 Edition; *The Agribusiness Accountability Project Reader; The Fields Have Turned Brown* (Susan DeMarco and Susan Sechler 1975).

2. Agricultural Resources Center, P.O. Box 646, Chapel Hill, N. C. 27514. Education on the causes of hunger with special focus on the American South.

3. American Agriculture Movement. Publication: *American Agriculture News,* P.O. Box 100A, Iredell, Tex. 76649.

4. Center for Rural Affairs, P.O. Box 405, Walthill, Neb. 68087. Publications: Newsletter, *New Land Review* and research studies.

5. Community Land Trust Center, c/o CCED, 639 Massachusetts Ave., Cambridge, Mass. 02139. Publication: *Community Land Trusts.*

6. Exploratory Project for Economic Alternatives, 2000 P St. NW, Suite 515, Washington, D.C. 20036 (202) 833–3208.

7. National Catholic Rural Life Conference, 3801 Grand Ave., Des Moines, Iowa 50312. Publication: *Catholic Rural Life.*

8. National Farmers Union, 1012 14th St., NW, Washington, D.C. 20005. Publication: *Washington Newsletter.*

9. National Land for People, 2348 North Cornelia, Fresno, Calif. 93711 (209) 237–6516. Publications: *People, Land, Food* (monthly), *Who Owns the Land* (monograph). Slide show available.

Direct Farmer-Consumer Marketing

10. Agricultural Marketing Project, Center for Health Services, Station 17, Vanderbilt Medical Center, Nashville, Tenn. 37232.
11. Earthwork—Center for Rural Studies, 3410 19th St., San Francisco, Calif. 94110. Publication: A complete directory of books and films on food and land.

Alternative Food Systems

12. Arizona/New Mexico Federation of Co-ops, Albuquerque Outpost, 106 Girard SE, Albuquerque, N.M. 87106 (505) 265–7416.
13. CC Grains Collective Warehouse, 4501 Shilshole Ave. NW, Seattle, Wash. 98107.
14. Co-op Federation of Greater New York, Richard Parsekian, 378 Pacific, Brooklyn, N.Y. 11217.
15. Chicago Loop College, Food Co-op Project, 64 East Lake St., Chicago, Ill. 60601.
16. DANCE, 1401 South 5th St., Minneapolis, Minn. 55454 (612) 338–5232.
17. Earthwork (see no. 11).
18. Federation of Ohio River Co-ops, 80 East Swan, Columbus, Ohio 43215 (614) 228–3672. (Also: World Food Group, c/o FORC)
19. Leon County Food Co-op Warehouse, 649 West Gaines St., Tallahasee, Fla. 32304 (904) 222–9916.
20. NEFCO, 8 Ashford, Allston, Mass. 02134 (617) A–Living (617) 254–8464.

Sources of Literature on Cooperatives

21. Community Services Administration, 1200 19th St. NW, Room 318 B, Washington, D.C. 20506 (202) 254–5770. Publications: *How to Organize a Co-op—Moving Ahead Together,* and others.
22. *Food Co-ops for Small Groups,* Tony Velella, Workman Publishing Company, 231 East 51st St., New York, N.Y. 10022.
23. *Food Co-op Handbook,* NEFCO Collective, Houghton Mifflin Company, 2 Park St., Boston, Mass. 02101.
24. *Non-Profit Food Stores* and *D.C. Food Buying Club Handbook.* Strongforce, 2121 Decatur Pl. NW, Washington, D.C. 20008 (202) 234–6883.

Building Alliances—Farmer, Food Worker, Consumer

25. Consumers Federation, 5516 South Cornell, Chicago, Ill. 60637. Contact: Dan McCurry.
26. Earthwork (see no. 11).

Local Self-Reliance

27. Coalition for Alternative Agriculture and Self-Sufficiency, c/o SCER, Campus Center, P.O. Box 18, University of Massachusetts, Amherst, Mass. 01003 (415) 545–2892.
28. Institute for Local-Self Reliance, 1717 18th St. NW, Washington, D.C. 20009. Publication: *Self-Reliance.*

Problems of Farmworkers and Food Workers

29. California Agrarian Action Project, P.O. Box 464, Davis, Calif. 95616 (916) 756–8518. Farmworker job loss caused by mechanization. Publications:

Newsletter, Pamphlet "No Hands Touch the Land."
Slide Show: "No Hands Touch the Land."
30. United Farm Workers (AFL/CIO), P.O. Box 62, Keene, Calif. 93531 (805) 822–5571.

Agricultural Research

31. The Action Center, 1028 Connecticut Ave. NW, Room 302, Washington, D.C. 20036. Responsible Agriculture Project looks at research in land grant colleges.
32. California Agrarian Action Project (see no. 29).

Research on Agricultural Alternatives

33. Center for the Biology of Natural Systems, P.O. Box 1126, Washington University, St. Louis, Mo. 63130.
34. Institute for Local Self-Reliance (see no. 28).

Nutritional Decline, Government Food Programs, and Corporate Penetration of Institutional Food Systems

35. The Action Center (see no. 31).
36. Center for Science in the Public Interest, 1757 S Street NW, Washington, D.C. 20009 (202) 332–9110. Publication: *Nutrition Action*.
37. Children's Foundation, 1082 Connecticut Ave. NW, No. 1112, Washington, D.C. 20036 (202) 296–4451.
38. Community Nutrition Institute, 1910 K St. NW, Washington, D.C. 20006 (202) 833–1730.
39. Food Research and Action Center (FRAC), 2011 I St. NW, Washington, D.C. 20006 (202) 452–8250.

Other Resources

40. Katz, Deborah, and Goodwin, Mary. *Food: Where Nutrition, Politics and Culture Meet* (An Activities

Guide for Teachers) from Center for Science in the Public Interest (see no. 36) 1977.

41. Kinsella, Susan, and The Action Center. *Food on Campus: A Recipe for Action*. Rodale Press, Emmaus, Pa. 18049, 1977.

The Media and Food/Hunger

42. Action for Children's Television, 46 Austin St., Newtonville, Mass. 02160 (617) 527–7870.
43. Food Media Center, c/o Earthwork (see no. 11).
44. World Hunger Year (WHY), P.O. Box 1975, Garden City, Long Island, N.Y. 11530 (516) 742–3700. Organizes educational "radiothons" on hunger issues. Publication: *Food Monitor*. See also: WHY of New Jersey, 27-06 High St., Fairlawn, N.J. 07410 (201) 791–3828. Publication: *A Guide for Action on Food and Hunger in the School and Community*.

Development, Trade, and Government Aid

45. Boston Industrial Mission, 56 Boylston St., Cambridge, Mass. 02138 (617) 491–6350. Publications: *Vectors; Women and Hunger*.
46. Bread for the World, 207 East 16th St., New York, N. Y. 10003 (212) 260–7000. Publication: Newsletter. Christian citizens' lobby on hunger issues.
47. Center of Concern, 3700 13th St. NE, Washington, D.C. 20017 (202) 635–2757. Publication: *Center Focus*.
48. Center for Community Change, 1000 Wisconsin Ave. NW, Washington, D.C. 20007.
49. Center for Development Policy, 401 C St. NE, Washington, D.C. 20002 (202) 547–1656.
50. Center for International Policy, 120 Maryland Ave. NE, Washington, D.C. 20002 (202) 544–4666.
51. Development Groups for Alternative Policies, 2200 19th St. NW, no. 206, Washington, D.C. 20009 (202) 332–1600.

52. Food Policy Center, 538 7th St. SE, Washington, D.C. 20003 (202) 547–7070.
53. Institute for Food and Development Policy, 2588 Mission St., No. 201, San Francisco, Calif. 94110 (415) 648–6090. Publications: *see coupon at back of book.*
54. Institute for Policy Studies, Transnational Institute, 1901 Q St. NW, Washington, D.C. 20008 (202) 234–9382. Publication: *The Elements.*
55. Interreligious Taskforce on U.S. Food Policy, 110 Maryland Ave. NE, Washington, D.C. 20002 (800) 424–7292. Publication: *Impact.*
56. Network, 1029 Vermont Ave. NW, Suite 650, Washington, D.C. 20005 (202) 347–6200. Publication: Newsletter.

U.S. Corporate Penetration in the Third World

57. Corporate Data Exchange, 198 Broadway, Room 707, New York, N. Y. 10038. Study of ownership of agribusiness corporations.
58. INFACT, The Newman Center, 1701 University Ave. SE, Minneapolis, Minn. 55414.
59. Interfaith Center for Corporate Responsibility, 475 Riverside Dr., Room 566, New York, N. Y. 10027. Film: *Bottle Babies* (see Question 38).
60. North American Congress on Latin America (NACLA), P.O. Box 57, Cathedral Station, New York, N. Y. 10025. Publication: NACLA's *Report.*
61. Northern California Interfaith Committee on Corporate Responsibility (NC–ICCR), 3410 19th St., San Francisco, Calif. 94110 (415) 863–8060.

Ending U.S. Government Economic and Military Support to Anti-Democratic Regimes

62. Anti-Martial Law Coalition (Philippines), 41–32 56th St., Woodside, N. Y. 11377.

63. Clergy & Laity Concerned, 198 Broadway, New York, N. Y. 10038 (212) 964–6730.
64. Coalition for a New Foreign & Military Policy, 120 Maryland Ave. NE, Washington, D.C. 20002 (202) 546–8400. Publications: *Legislative Update and Key Votes; Action Alerts.*

Direct Assistance to Self-Help Efforts Abroad

65. American Friends Service Committee: *National Office,* 1501 Cherry St., Philadelphia, Pa. 19102 (215) 241–7000. In *New York:* 15 Rutherford Pl., New York, N. Y. 10003 (212) 777–4600. Publication: *World Hunger Action Letter.* In *San Francisco:* 2160 Lake St., San Francisco, Calif. 94121 (415) 752–7766. Slide Show: "Hamburger, U.S.A." (Agribusiness in control of food system).
66. Economic Development Bureau, 234 Colony Rd., New Haven, Conn. 06511. An alternative to corporate consulting services, the EDB puts people with technical skills in touch with progressive Third World groups.
67. Oxfam-America, P.O. Box 288, Boston, Mass. 02116 (617) 247–3304. Sponsors self-help projects domestically and in the Third World.
68. Unitarian Universalist Service Committee, Inc., 78 Beacon St., Boston, Mass. 02108 (617) 742–2120. Publication: A hunger action study kit.

Acquiring Organizing Skills

69. The Action Center (see no. 31).
70. Mid-West Academy, 600 West Fullerton, Chicago, Ill. 60606.
71. Movement for a New Society, 4722 Baltimore Ave., Philadelphia, Pa. 19143 (215) 724–1464. Publication: *Dandelion.*
72. The New School for Democratic Management, 256 Sutter St., San Francisco, Calif. 94108.

Other Organizations

73. Public Interest Research Group (PIRG), U.S. (regional network): National Clearinghouse, 1329 E St. NW, Washington, D.C. 20004 (202) 347–3811. Publication: Newsletter. Multi-issue clearinghouse for student funded research.

Canadian Organizations

Canadian Council for International Cooperation (National), 75 Sparks St., Ottawa, Ontario KIP 5A5.

Development Education Center, 121 Avenue Rd., Toronto, Ontario.

DEVERIC, 1539 Birmingham St., Halifax, Nova Scotia.

GATT-fly (National), 11 Madison Ave., Toronto, Ontario M52 252.

IDEA Center, P.O. Box 32, Station C, Winnipeg, Manitoba.

IDERA, 2524 Cypress Ave., Vancouver, British Columbia.

National Farmers Union (National), 250-C Second Ave., Saskatoon, Saskatchewan, S7K 2M1.

One Sky Center, 134 Avenue F South, Saskatoon, Saskatchewan.

Ontario Public Interest Research Group (OPIRG), Room 226–Physics Bldg., University of Waterloo, Waterloo, Ontario.

People's Food Commission, 4th floor, 75 Sparks St., Ottawa, Ontario. Publication: Newsletter. A cross Canada inquiry into the food system in communities.

Appendix B

Recommended Books, Periodicals, and Films

FOOD FIRST RESOURCE GUIDE: Documentation on the Roots of World Hunger and Rural Poverty. Prepared by the staff of the Institute for Food and Development Policy, 2588 Mission St., San Francisco, Calif. 94110, 1979.

Part I   The Scarcity Scare

Arens, Jenneke, and van Beurden, Jos. *Jhagrapur: Poor peasants and women in a village in Bangladesh.* Amsterdam, The Netherlands: Arens & Van Beurden, 1977.

Bryan, Helen. *Fertilizer: Part of the Solution, or Part of the Problem?* War on Want, 467 Caledonian Rd., London N7 9BE, 1976.

Farvar, M. Taghi, and Milton, John P., eds. *Careless Technology.* Garden City, N. J.: The Natural History Press, 1972.

Food and Agriculture Organization. *Progress in Land Reform—Sixth Report,* 1975.

Hartmann, Betsy, and Boyce, James. *Needless Hunger: Voices from a Bangladesh Village.* Institute for Food and Development Policy, 2588 Mission St., San Francisco, Calif. 94110, 1979.

Kocher, James. "Rural Development, Income Distribution, and Fertility Decline." An occasional paper of the Population Council, New York, 1973.

Mamdani, Mahmood. *The Myth of Population Control —Family, Class, and Caste in an Indian Village.* New York and London: Monthly Review, 1972.

Orleans, Leo A. "China's Experience in Population Control: The Elusive Model," 1974, and "The Role of Science and Technology in China's Population/Food Balance," Library of Congress, Washington, D.C., 1977.

Pimentel, David. "Realities of a Pesticide Ban," *Environment* 15 (March 1973): 18–31.

Shea, Kevin P. "Nerve Damage," *Environment* 16, 9 (November 1974).

Swedish International Development Authority and Food and Agriculture Organization. *Organic Materials as Fertilizers.* Soils Bulletin 27, 1975.

Turner, James S. *A Chemical Feast: Report on the Food and Drug Administration,* (Ralph Nader Study Group Reports). New York: Grossman, 1970.

United Nations Research Institute for Social Development (UNRISD). *Famine Risk and Famine Prevention in the Modern World,* 1976.

van den Bosch, Robert. *The Pesticide Conspiracy.* New York: Doubleday, 1978.

Ware, Helen. "The Sahelian Drought: Some Thoughts on the Future," Research Fellow, Department of Demography, Australian National University, March 26, 1975.

Part II Blaming Nature

Frankie, Richard, and Chasin, Barbara. *The Political Economy of Ecological Destruction: Drought, Famine and Development in the West African Sahel.* Montclair, N.J.: Allanheld, Osmun and Co., 1979.

Part III Colonial Inheritance

Beckford, George L. *Persistent Poverty—Underdevelopment in Plantation Economies of the Third World.* New York: Oxford University Press, 1972.

Feldman, David, and Lawrence, Peter. *Africa Report,* Global II Project on the Social and Economic Implications of Large-Scale Introduction of New Varieties of Foodgrains, UNDP/UNRISD, Geneva, 1975.

Rodney, Walter. *How Europe Underdeveloped Africa.* Bogle—L'Ouverture Publications, 141 Coldershaw Rd., London W. 13, 1972.

Williams, Eric. *Capitalism and Slavery.* New York: Putnam, 1966.

Part IV   Modernizing Hunger

Center for International Studies. *Landlessness and Nearlandlessness in Developing Countries.* Ithaca, N. Y.: Cornell University, 1978.

Dahlberg, Kenneth A. *Beyond the Green Revolution: The Politics of Global Agricultural Development.* New York: Plenum Press, 1979.

George, Susan. *How the Other Half Dies.* Montclair, N.J.: Allanheld, Osmun & Co., 1977.

Griffin, Keith. *Land Concentration and Rural Poverty.* New York: Macmillan, 1976.

———. *The Political Economy of Agrarian Change.* Cambridge, Mass.: Harvard University Press, 1974.

Griffin, Keith, and Khan, Azizur Rahman, eds. *Poverty and Landlessness in Rural Asia.* A Study by the World Employment Programme, International Labor Office, Geneva, 1977.

Hewitt de Alcántara, Cynthia. Global II Project on the Social and Economic Implications of the Introduction of New Varieties of Foodgrains, *Country Report—Mexico,* Geneva: UNDP/UNRISD, 1974.

———. "The Green Revolution as History," *Development and Change* 5, 2 (1973–1974).

International Labor Office. *Mechanization and Employment in Agriculture,* 1974.

Owens, Edgar, and Shaw, Robert. *Development Reconsidered: Bridging the Gap Between Government and People.* Lexington, Mass.: Heath, 1972.

Palmer, Ingrid. *Science and Agricultural Production,* UNRISD, 1972.

Pearse, Andrew. Global II Project on the Social and Economic Implications of the Introduction of New

Varieties of Foodgrains, Parts I–IV, Geneva: UNDP/UNRISD, April–July, 1975.

Perelman, Michael. *Farming for Profit in a Hungry World: Capital and the Crises in Agriculture.* Montclair, N. J.: Allanheld, Osmun & Co., 1977.

Swedish International Development Authority and Food and Agriculture Organization. *Organic Materials as Fertilizers.* Soils Bulletin 27, 1975.

Part V   The Inefficiency of Inequality

Bergmann, Theodore. *Farm Policies in Socialist Countries.* Lexington, Mass.: Heath, 1975.

Fellmeth, Robert C. *Politics of Land.* New York: Grossman, 1973.

Griffin, Keith. *Land Concentration and Rural Poverty.* New York: Macmillan, 1976.

International Labor Office. *Poverty and Landlessness in Rural Asia.* A Study by the World Employment Programme, Keith Griffin and Azizur Rahman Khan, eds. Geneva: 1977.

Jacoby, Erich, and Jacoby, Charlotte. *Man and Land.* New York: Knopf, 1971.

Orleans, Leo A. "China's Experience in Population Control: The Elusive Model," Washington, D.C.: Library of Congress, 1974.

Owens, Edgar, and Shaw, Robert. *Development Reconsidered: Bridging the Gap Between Government and People.* Lexington, Mass.: Heath, 1972.

Perelman, Michael. *Farming for Profit in a Hungry World.* Montclair, N.J.: Allanheld, Osmun & Co., 1977.

Part VI   The Trade Trap

Galeano, Eduardo. *Open Veins in Latin America: Five Centuries of the Pillage of a Continent.* New York: Monthly Review, 1973.

Gallis, Marion. *Trade for Justice: Myth or Mandate?* Geneva: World Council of Churches, 1972.

Jonas, Susanne, and Tobis, David, eds. *Guatemala.* New York and Berkeley: North American Congress on Latin America (NACLA), 1974.

Palmer, Ingrid. *Food and the New Agricultural Technology,* UNRISD, 1972.

Payer, Cheryl, ed. *Commodity Trade in the Third World.* New York: Wiley, 1975.

Part VII   The Myth of Food Power

Barnes, Peter, ed. *The Peoples' Land.* A reader on land reform in the United States. Emmaus, Pa.: Rodale Press, 1975.

Belden, Joe, with Forte, Gregg. *Toward a National Food Policy.* Exploratory Project for Economic Alternatives, 1519 Connecticut Ave. NW, Washington, D.C. 20036, 1976.

Burbach, Roger, and Flynn, Patricia. Forthcoming book on agribusiness to be published by the North American Congress on Latin America, 464 19th St., Oakland, Calif. 94612.

Commoner, Barry. *The Poverty of Power.* New York: Knopf, 1976.

DeMarco, Susan, and Sechler, Susan. *The Fields Have Turned Brown—Four Essays on World Hunger.* Washington, D.C.: Agribusiness Accountability Project, 1975.

Goldschmidt, Walter. *As You Sow: Three Studies in the Social Consequences of Agribusiness.* Montclair, N.J.: Allanheld, Osmun & Co., 1978.

Hamilton, Martha. *The Great Grain Robbery and Other Stories.* Washington, D.C.: Agribusiness Accountability Project, 1972.

Hightower, Jim. *Eat Your Heart Out: How Food Profiteers Victimize the Consumer.* New York: Crown, 1975.

North American Congress on Latin America (NACLA), "U.S. Grain Arsenal," *Latin America and Empire Report* 9, 7 (October 1975).

Part VIII World Hunger as Big Business

Berg, Alan. *The Nutrition Factor*. Washington, D.C.: The Brookings Institution, 1973.

Cullen, Vincent C. "Sour Pineapples," *America* (November 6, 1976).

DeMarco, Susan, and Sechler, Susan. *The Fields Have Turned Brown—Four Essays on World Hunger*. Washington, D.C.: The Agribusiness Accountability Project, 1975.

Feder, Ernest. *Strawberry Imperialism*. Distributed by *America Latina,* 71 Fleet St., London, England, 1978.

The Food Action Campaign Papers. "Crystal City, Texas—A Del Monte Company Town." Washington, D.C.: Agribusiness Accountability Project, 1973.

Hightower, Jim. *Eat Your Heart Out: How Food Profiteers Victimize the Consumer*. New York: Crown, 1975.

Interfaith Center on Corporate Responsibility. *The Agribusiness Manual,* 475 Riverside Drive, New York 10027.

Jonas, Susanne, and Tobis, David, eds. *Guatemala*. New York and Berkeley: North American Congress on Latin America (NACLA), 1974.

Latham, Michael C. "Introduction," *The Promotion of Bottle Feeding by Multinational Corporations: How Advertising and the Health Professions Have Contributed,* Ted Greiner, ed. Ithaca, N.Y.: Cornell University Monograph Series, no. 2, 1975.

Ledogar, Robert J. *Hungry for Profits: U.S. Food and Drug Multinationals in Latin America*. New York: IDOC, 1976.

Muller, Mike. *The Baby Killer*. London: War on Want, 1975; 467 Caledonian Rd.

North American Congress on Latin America (NACLA), "Bitter Fruits," *Latin America and Empire Report*. Berkeley, Calif.: September 1976.

Wellford, Harrison. *Sowing the Wind*. New York: Grossman, 1972.

Part IX   The Helping Handout: Aid for Whom?

Center for International Policy. *Human Rights and the U.S. Foreign Assistance Program,* 2 parts, Washington, D.C., 1978.

Center for International Policy. "Foreign Aid: Evading the Control of Congress," *International Policy Report,* Washington, D.C.

Chonchol, Jacques, et al. *World Hunger: Causes and Remedies.* Washington, D.C.: Transnational Institute Report, Institute for Policy Studies, 1974.

Feder, Ernest. "Capitalism's Last-Ditch Effort to Save Underdeveloped Agricultures," *Journal of Contemporary Asia* 7, 1, 1977.

Hartman, Betsy, and Boyce, James. *Aid to the Needy?* International Policy Report Center for International Policy, Washington, D.C., June 1977.

Hayter, Theresa. *Aid as Imperialism.* Harmondsworth, Middlesex, England: Penguin Books, 1971.

North American Congress on Latin America (NACLA), "U.S. Grain Arsenal," *Latin America and Empire Report,* 9, 7 (October 1975).

National Action/Research on the Military-Industrial Complex (NARMIC). *Food as a Weapon—The Food for Peace Program.* 112 South 16th St., Philadelphia, Pa., 1975.

Payer, Cheryl. *The Debt Trap: The IMF and the Third World.* London: Penguin, 1974.

Weissman, Steve. *The Trojan Horse: A Radical Look at Foreign Aid.* San Francisco: Ramparts, 1974.

Yost, Israel. "The Food for Peace Arsenal," *NACLA Newsletter* 5, 3 (May-June 1971): 1–13.

Part X   Food Self-Reliance

Ahmad, Zubeda. "The Chinese Approach to Rural Development," *International Development Review* 15, 4, 1973.

Bergmann, Theodore. *Farm Policies in Socialist Coun-*

tries. Lexington, Mass.: Lexington Books, Heath, 1975.

Food and Agriculture Organization. *Progress in Land Reform—Sixth Report,* 1975.

Food and Agriculture Organization. *Report on China's Agriculture,* prepared by H. V. Henle, 1974.

Galtung, Johan. "Self-Reliance: Concepts, Practice, and Rationale," Ecumenical Institute, Château de Bossey, CH-1298, Celigny, Switzerland, April 1976.

Gough, Kathleen. *Ten Times More Beautiful: Rebuilding the Republic of Vietnam.* New York: Monthly Review, 1978.

International Labor Office. *Land Reform in Asia,* edited by Zubeda Ahmad. World Employment Programme Research, Working Papers, 1976.

MacEwan, Arthur. *Agriculture and Development in Cuba,* prepared for the International Labor Office, Geneva, 1978.

U.N. Asian Development Institute. "Towards a Theory of Rural Development," prepared by Wahidul Haque, December 1975.

General Reading

Berg, Lasse, and Berg, Lisa. *Face to Face: Fascism and Revolution in India.* Berkeley, Calif.: Ramparts, 1971.

George, Susan. *How the Other Half Dies: The Real Reasons for World Hunger.* Montclair, N.J.: Allanheld, Osmun & Co., 1977.

Gussow, Joan Dye. *The Feeding Web: The Issues in Nutritional Ecology.* Palo Alto, Calif.: Bull Publishing Co., 1978.

Other Resources

Study Action Guides:
Moyer, William, and Thorne, Erika. Food/Hunger Macro-Analysis Seminar: A *Do It Yourself Manual* for college courses and action groups. Details or-

ganizing technique and curriculum for a participatory seminar examining the structural roots of hunger. $2.50 each or $2.00 for orders of 10 or more. Transnational Academic Program, Institute for World Order, 1140 Avenue of the Americas, New York, N. Y. 10036.

Other Important Publications

Ag World, 1186 West Summer St., St. Paul, Minn. 55113.

Asian Action, Newsletter of the Asian Cultural Forum on Development, Room 201, 399/1 Soi Siri, off Silom Rd., Bangkok-5, Thailand.

Ceres, FAO Review on Development, UNIPUB, 650 First Ave., P.O. Box 433, Murray Hill Station, New York, N. Y. 10016.

Ideas and Action, Action for Development, FAO, 00100 Rome, Italy.

International Bulletin, P.O. Box 4400, Berkeley, Calif. 94704.

Latin America and *Latin America Economic Report,* Latin American Newsletters Ltd., 90–93 Cowcross St., London EC1M 6BL.

New Internationalist, published in England but subscribe through the New World Coalition, Room 209, 409 Boylston St., Boston, Mass. 02116.

Strongforce Publications, 2121 Decatur Pl. NW, Washington, D.C. 20008. Publications: *Democracy in the Workplace, NonProfit Food Stores, Women & Self-Management,* and others.

Films

Earthwork/Newsreel Food Media Center distributes films and program suggestions on land and food issues. For their bibliography, "Films on Food and Land", including ideas and suggestions for film programs, write Earthwork/Newsreel Food Media Center, 1499 Potrero, San Francisco, Calif. 94110.

To book films or slide shows, call or write Earth-work/Newsreel Food Media Center, 630 Natoma, San Francisco, Calif. 94103 (415) 621-6196.

"The Land" is an NBC documentary examination of the history of land use in the United States from colonial times to the present (color, 60 min.); film and study guide available from Office for Film and Broadcasting, USCC, 1011 First Ave., Suite 1300, New York, N. Y. 10022 ($35 plus $5 for postage and insurance).

Notes

PART I. THE SCARCITY SCARE

1. Too Many People?

1. Calculated from Food and Agriculture Organization, *Trade Yearbook*, vol. 28; *Production Yearbook*, vol. 28-1; and *Yearbook of International Trade Statistics*, 1974.

2. *Ceres* (July-August 1978): 13-16.

3. Nelson A. Rockefeller, *Vital Resources: Critical Choices for Americans, Reports on Energy, Food & Raw Materials, Volume I* (Lexington, Mass.: Heath, 1977), p. 101.

4. World Bank, *Assault on World Poverty*, 1975, p. 244.

5. Keith Griffin, *Land Concentration and Rural Poverty* (New York: Macmillan, 1976), p. 135.

6. Calculations based on Food and Agriculture Organization, *Production Yearbooks*.

7. Comparisons regarding MSA countries are calculated from U.S. Department of Agriculture, *Foreign Agriculture Trade Statistical Report*, Calendar Year 1974, May 1975.

8. Calculations based on Food and Agriculture Organization, *Production Yearbooks*, 1965-1972.

9. Alan Riding, "Malnutrition Taking Bigger Toll Among Mexican Children," *The New York Times*, March 6, 1978, p. 2

10. *Foreign Agriculture*, February 20, 1978, pp. 8ff.

11. *Bangkok Post*, January 26, 1978.

2. But What About the Real "Basketcases"?

1. Calculated from Food and Agricultural Organization, *Production Yearbook*, vol. 28-1, 1974.

2. Ibid., *Production Yearbook*, 1975.

3. Samir Amin, "L'Afrique sous-peuplée," *Développement et Civilisation*, nos. 47-48 (March-June 1972): 60-61.

4. Food and Agriculture Organization, *The State of Food and Agriculture—1974*, p. 145.

5. Calculated from FAO *Production Yearbook*, 1974.

6. Ibid.

7. Institute of Nutrition and Food Science, *Nutrition Survey of Rural Bangladesh*, University of Dacca, Bangladesh, 1977.

8. Steve Raymer, "The Nightmare of Famine," *National Geographic*, July 1975.

9. *World Hunger, Health, and Refugee Problems*, Summary of a Special Study Mission to Asia and the Middle East (Washington, D.C.: U.S. Government Printing Office, 1976), p. 99.

10. F. T. Jannuzi and J. T. Peach, "Report on the Hierarchy of Interests in Land in Bangladesh," AID, September 1977.

11. Ibid.

12. Food and Agriculture Organization, *Bangladesh: Country Development Brief*, 1973, pp. 7, 31-32.

13. United Nations Report (confidential), "Some Notes on Agriculture in Bangladesh," Dacca, November 18, 1974, p. 4.

14. Food and Agriculture Organization, *Progress in Land Reform*, Rome, 1975, pp. iii-82, emphasis added.

3. Are People a Liability or a Resource?

1. Robert d'A. Shaw, *Jobs and Agricultural Development* (Washington, D.C.: Overseas Development Council, 1970), Table 2, p. 10.

2. World Bank, *The Assault on World Poverty* (Baltimore: Johns Hopkins University Press, 1975), pp. 242-243.

3. Wolfgang Hein, "Over-unemployment or Marginality," a review of *Urban Unemployment in Developing Countries, The Nature of the Problem and Proposals for Its Solution* by Paul Bairoch (Geneva: ILO, 1973), in *Ceres* (May-June 1976): 61.

4. Edgar Owens and Robert Shaw, *Development Reconsidered* (Lexington, Mass.: Heath, 1972), p. 54.

5. Richard Barnet and Ronald Mueller, *Global Reach* (New York: Simon & Schuster, 1974), p. 169.

6. Colin Tudge, *The Famine Business* (New York: St. Martin's Press, 1977), Chapter 1.

7. Robert Maurer, "Work: Cuba," in *Cuba: People—Questions,* W. L. Kaiser, ed. (New York: Friendship Press/IDOC/North America, 1975), p. 22.

8. *New York Times,* November 1, 1970.

9. International Labor Organization, "Agricultural Mechanisation and Employment in Latin America," prepared by K. C. Abercrombie, in *Mechanisation and Employment in Agriculture,* 1974, pp. 61-63.

10. Steve Hellinger and Doug Hellinger, Overseas Development Council, unpublished manuscript, 1975, Part II-D, p. 46.

11. Gordon Gemmill and Carl K. Eicher, "A Framework for Research on the Economics of Farm Mechanization in Developing Countries," African Rural Employment Research Network, paper no. 6, p. 2, 1973, Department of Agricultural Economics, Michigan State University, East Lansing, Mich.

4. Does Ignorance Breed Babies?

1. Helen Ware, "The Sahelian Drought: Some Thoughts on the Future," Special Sahelian Office, Food and Agriculture Organization, March 1975, p. 13. See also Ben White, "Children: The Benefit to the Poor and the Cost to the Rich," *New Internationalist,* no. 52 (June 1977): 16-17.

2. Mahmood Mamdani, *The Myth of Population Control: Family, Class and Caste in an Indian Village* (New York and London: Monthly Review, 1972), pp. 78, 113.

3. Ware, "The Sahelian Drought," p. 13.

4. Mamdani, *The Myth of Population Control,* p. 111.

5. David Heer and David May, "Son Survivorship Motivation and Family Size in India: A Computer Simulation," *Population Studies* 22 (1968): 206, cited by William Rich, *Smaller Families Through Social and Economic Progress* (Washington, D.C.: Overseas Development Council, 1973).

6. Perdita Huston, "Power and Pregnancy," *New Internationalist,* no. 52 (June 1977): 10-12.

7. Betsy Hartmann and Jim Boyce, "The View from the Village," *New Internationalist* (March 1977): 15.

5. Sophisticated Fatalism?

1. Roger Revelle, Center for Population Studies, Harvard University, Letters, *Science* 187 (March 21, 1975).

2. Dr. Parker Maudlin of the Population Council, Washington, D.C., presentation to the symposium entitled "Fertility Decline in Less Developed Countries: The Emerging Patterns," Annual Meeting of the American Association for the Advancement of Science, February 12-17, 1978.

3. Ibid., Nick Eberstadt, "Background on Population Conference."

4. William Rich, *Smaller Families Through Social and Economic Progress* (Washington, D.C.: Overseas Development Council, 1973), Chapter 1.

5. Alan Berg, "The Trouble with Triage," *New York Times Magazine* (June 15, 1975): 22ff.

6. Leo Orleans, "China's Experience in Population Control: The Elusive Model," *World Development* 3 (July-August 1975): 507.

7. Lester Brown, "World Population Trends," Appendix B. Our estimate is also based on discussions with Leo Orleans, China scholar at the Library of Congress.

6. Controlling Births or Controlling the Population?

1. Leo A. Orleans, "China's Experience in Population Control: The Elusive Model," prepared for the Committee on Foreign Affairs, U.S. House of Representatives, by the Congressional Research Service, Library of Congress, September 1974, GAO, Washington, D.C.

2. Barry Commoner, *The Closing Circle* (New York: Knopf, 1971), p. 249.

7. Population Pressure on the Environment?

1. Lester Brown with Erik Eckholm, *By Bread Alone* (New York: Praeger, 1974), p. 87.

2. Howard E. Daugherty, *Man-Induced Ecologic Change in El Salvador* (Ph.D. dissertation, University of California, Los Angeles, 1969).

3. *El Salvador Zonificacion Agricola* (Fase I), Organization of American States, Washington, D.C., 1974, cited

by Erik Eckholm, *Losing Ground* (New York: Norton, for Worldwatch Institute, 1976), p. 167.

4. Georg Borgstrom, "Ecological Aspects of Protein Feeding—the Case of Peru," in M. Taghi Farvar and John P. Milton, eds., *The Careless Technology: Ecology and International Development* (Garden City, N.J.: Natural History Press, 1972), p. 901.

5. Food and Agriculture Organization, *Production Yearbook*, vol. 28-1, 1974.

6. Erik Eckholm, *Losing Ground* (New York: Norton, for Worldwatch Institute, 1976).

7. *The Economic Development of Colombia* (Baltimore: Johns Hopkins University Press, 1950), pp. 63, 360, cited by Michael Hudson, *Super Imperialism* (New York: Holt, Rinehart and Winston, 1972), pp. 103-104.

8. Ibid.

9. René Dumont, *False Start in Africa* (New York: Praeger, 1966), p. 69; originally, *L'Afrique est mal partie* (Paris: Seuil, 1962).

10. Jeremy Swift, "Disaster and a Sahelian Nomad Economy," in *Drought in Africa*, David Dalby and R. J. Harrison, eds. (London: Centre for African Studies, 1973), pp. 71-79; Douglas L. Johnson, "The Response of Pastoral Nomads to Drought in the Absence of Outside Intervention," paper commissioned by the United Nations Special Sahelian Office, December 19, 1973; F. Fraser Darling and M. T. Farvar, "Ecological Consequences of Sedentarization of Nomads," in *The Careless Technology;* D. J. Stenning, *Savannah Nomads* (London: Oxford University Press, 1959).

11. Ibid., especially Stenning.

12. Helen Ware, "The Sahelian Drought: Some Thoughts on the Future," Special Sahelian Office, Food and Agriculture Organization, March 26, 1975, especially 3ff.

13. Claire Sterling, "The Making of the Sub-Saharan Wasteland," *Atlantic Monthly* (May 1974): 98-105.

14. Ibid.

15. Eduardo Cruz de Carvalho, " 'Traditional' and 'Modern' Patterns of Cattle Raising: A Critical Evaluation of Change from Pastoralism to Ranching," *The Journal of Developing Areas* 8 (January 1974).

16. Frank L. Lambrecht, "The Tsetse Fly: A Blessing or a Curse?" in *The Careless Technology*, 72ff., 775ff.

17. Frances M. Foland, "A Profile of Amazonia," *Journal of Inter-American Studies and World Affairs* (January 1971): 72ff.

18. Cited by Vic Cox, "Brazil: The Amazon Gamble," *The Nation* (October 11, 1975): 328.

19. Dr. Nelson Chaves, Head of the Nutrition Institute at the University of Pernambuco.

20. *World Environment Report,* Center for Environmental Information, New York, vol. 1, no. 8 (May 12, 1975).

21. José S. Da Veiga, "Quand les multinationales font du ranching," *Le Monde Diplomatique* (September 1975): 12.

22. Ibid., p. 13.

23. See Erik P. Eckholm, *Losing Ground,* pp. 136-141.

8. The Price Scare?

1. U.S. Department of Agriculture, *Agricultural Statistics—1972* (Washington, D.C.: Government Printing Office, 1972), Tables 650, 755, and 759.

2. Lester Brown with Erik Eckholm, *By Bread Alone* (New York: Praeger, 1974), p. 60.

3. *Wall Street Journal,* September 2, 1975.

4. Helen Bryant, *Fertilizer: Part of the Solution, or Part of the Problem?* (War on Want, 467 Caledonian Rd., London N7 9BE, 1975), quoting Edwin Wheeler, president of the Fertilizer Institute, at its annual meeting, February 3, 1975.

5. Joe Belden with Gregg Forte, *Toward a National Food Policy* (Exploratory Project for Economic Alternatives, 1519 Connecticut Ave. NW, Washington, D.C. 20036), p. 132, citing USDA *Agricultural Statistics,* 1974, p. 210.

6. U.S. Department of Agriculture, *Foreign Agricultural Trade of the U.S.* (FATUS) (Washington, D.C.: Government Printing Office, April 1975), p. 30.

9. The Food vs. Poison Trade-off?

1. David Pimentel, et al., "Pesticides, Insects in Foods, and Cosmetic Standards," *BioScience* 27 (March 1977): 3, 180.

2. Ibid.

3. David Pimentel, "Extent of Pesticide Use, Food Supply and Pollution," *Journal of the New York Entomological Society* 81 (1973): 3-33.

4. Ibid.

5. Pimentel, "Pesticides," p. 182.

6. David Pimentel, "Realities of a Pesticide Ban," *Environment* (March, 1973).

7. J. P. Hrabovszky, Senior Policy and Planning Coordinator, Agriculture Department, FAO, Rome, letter dated March 18, 1976, quoting Dr. W. R. Furtick, Chief, Plant Protection Service.

8. Teodoro Boza Barducci, "Ecological Consequences of Pesticides Used for the Control of Cotton Insects in Cañete Valley, Peru," in *Careless Technology, Ecology and International Development,* M. Taghi Farvar and John P. Milton, eds. (Garden City, N.J.: Natural History Press, 1972), pp. 423ff.

9. M. Taghi Farvar, "Relationship Between Ecological and Social Systems," speech delivered to EARTHCARE conference, New York, June 6, 1975, p. 4.

10. M. Taghi Farvar, "Ecological Implications of Insect Control," Center for the Study of Biological Systems, Research Report, February 6, 1970, pp. 6-8.

11. Ibid., p. 11.

12. Robert F. Luck, et al. "Chemical Insect Control, A Troubled Pest Management Strategy," *BioScience,* September 1977.

13. Farvar, "Ecological Implications of Insect Control," p. 15.

14. Erik Eckholm and S. Jacob Scherr, "Double Standards and the Pesticide Trade," *New Scientist,* February 16, 1978, pp. 440 ff.

15. *New York Times,* December 5, 1976, p. 39 and Eckholm, "Double Standards and the Pesticide Trade," p. 443.

16. Eckholm, "Double Standards and the Pesticide Trade," p. 443.

17. Farvar, "Relationship Between Ecological and Social Systems," p. 4.

18. Farvar, "Ecological Implications of Insect Control," p. 10.

19. *Environment* 17 (April-May 1975): 22.

20. *New York Times,* February 6, 1976, p. 12.

21. Richard Franke, "The Green Revolution in a Javanese Village" (Ph.D. dissertation, Department of Anthropology, Harvard University, 1972), pp. 39ff.

22. See James S. Turner, *A Chemical Feast: Report on the Food and Drug Administration* (Ralph Nader Study Group Reports) (New York: Grossman, 1970), for a study of the influence in government of the chemical and drug companies; David Pimentel, "Realities of a Pesticide Ban," *Environment* 15 (March 1973), gives extensive reference notes.

23. Fred Willman, "Biodegradable Pesticides," *R. F. Illustrated* (Rockefeller Foundation) 2, 1 (March 1975): 5.

24. Environmental Protection Agency, "Strategy of the Environmental Protection Agency for Controlling the Adverse Effects of Pesticides," EPA Office of Pesticide Programs, Office of Water and Hazardous Materials, Washington, D.C. 36 pp., p. 3.

25. Ibid.

26. David Burnham, "Pesticide Work Suggested for Those Seeking Sterility," *New York Times,* September 27, 1977.

27. *New York Times,* February 14, 1975, citing Dr. G. M. Woodwell, Marine Biology Laboratory, Woods Hole, Mass.

28. "Man's Impact on the Global Environment," report of the Study of Critical Environment Problems (Cambridge, Mass.: Massachusetts Institute of Technology, 1970), cited by Erik Eckholm, *Losing Ground* (New York: Norton, 1976), p. 162.

29. Harold M. Schmeck, Jr., "Pesticides: Control of Insects is Found to Decline Sharply," *New York Times,* February 6, 1976, p. 1.

30. Martin Brown, "An Orange Is an Orange," *Environment* 17 (July-August 1975): 6ff.

31. Van den Bosch, et al., "Investigation of the Effects of Food Standards on Pesticide Use," draft report, Environmental Protection Agency, Washington, D.C., cited by Pimentel, 1977, p. 180.

32. Pimentel, "Pesticides," pp. 178ff.

33. Michael Jacobson, "Agriculture's New Hero: IPM," *Nutrition Action,* January 1978, p. 4.

34. *New York Times,* February 6, 1976, p. 12.

35. Ibid., citing National Academy of Sciences study, 1976.

36. Smith and Reynolds, "Effects of Manipulation of Cotton AgroSystems on Insect Pest Populations," *Careless Technology,* p. 389.

37. A. Ayanaba and B. N. Okigbo, "Mulching for Improved Soil Fertility and Crop Production," *Organic Materials as Fertilizers,* Soils Bulletin 27, Swedish International Development Authority and FAO, Rome, 1975, p. 101.

38. *Pesticides* (The Journal of the Indian Pesticides Industry), February 1968, entire issue.

39. Personal communication of L. More and T. F. Watson with Dr. Robert van den Bosch, Division of Biological Control, University of California, Berkeley, cited by Dr. van den Bosch in "The Politics of Pesticides," speech, 1973.

40. Richard Norgaard, "Evaluation of Pest Management Programs for Cotton in California and Arizona," Appendix C in *Evaluation of Pest Management Programs for Cotton, Peanuts and Tobacco,* Rosemarie von Rumker, consultant, RVR Project 66, Contract #EQ4Ac036, Environmental Protection Agency and the Council on Environmental Quality, October 1975. See also D. C. Hall, R. B. Norgaard, and P. K. True, "The Performance of Independent Pest Management Consultants in San Joaquin Cotton and Citrus," in *California Agriculture,* Division of Agricultural Sciences, University of California, 29 (October 1975).

41. John S. Steinhart and Carol E. Steinhart, "Energy Use in the U.S. Food System," *Science* (April 1974): 3-4.

42. Jacobson, "Agriculture's New Hero," p. 4.

43. Erich H. Jacoby, *The Green Revolution in China* (Geneva: UNRISD, December 18, 1973), pp. 11-12.

44. Robert F. Luck, et. al., "Chemical Insect Control, A Troubled Pest Management Strategy," *BioScience* 27, no. 9 (September 1977): 606-611.

45. Peter Feldman and David Lawrence, "Social and Economic Implications of the Large-Scale Introduction of New Varieties of Foodgrains," Africa Report, preliminary draft (Geneva: UNRISD, 1975), pp. 198ff.

PART II. BLAMING NATURE

10. Haven't There Always Been Famines?

1. M. Ganzin, "Pour entrer dans une ère de justice alimentaire," UNESCO *Courrier,* May 1975, cited by Susan George, *How the Other Half Dies* (London: Penguin, 1976), p. 139.

2. "Famine-Risk and Famine Prevention in the Modern World: Studies of food systems under conditions of recurrent scarcity" (Geneva: UNRISD, June 1976), p. 36.

3. Royal Famine Commission, *Report on Bengal* (Delhi: Government of India Publication, 1945), p. 28.

4. Ibid. pp. 106, 198.

5. George Blyn, *Agricultural Trends in India, 1891-1947* (Philadelphia: University of Pennsylvania Press, 1966), p. 102, cited by Gail Omvedt in "The Political Economy of Starvation," unpublished manuscript, 1974.

6. ———. *The Agricultural Crops of India, 1893-94 to 1945-46* (Philadelphia: University of Pennsylvania Press, 1951).

7. Lester Brown and Gail Finsterbusch, *Man and His Environment: Food* (New York: Harper and Row, 1972), p. 7, cited by Omvedt, "Political Economy of Starvation."

8. Special Publication of the American Geographical Society, no. 6, p. 1.

9. *The Report of the American Red Cross Commission to China,* ARC 270, October 1929.

10. Joseph Needham, "The Nature of Chinese Society: A Technical Interpretation," a public lecture published in University of Hong Kong *Gazette,* May 15, 1974, cited by Harry Magdoff, "China: Contrasts with the U.S.S.R.," in "China's Economic Strategy," *Monthly Review* 27 (July-August 1975): 15-16.

11. *China Reconstructs* 23, no. 2, pp. 2ff.

12. Richard Greenhill, "Coping," *New Internationalist* (June 1973): 14-15.

13. *China Reconstructs* 23, no. 2, pp. 2ff.

14. Personal communication with A. de Vajda, Senior Advisor, FAO, Rome.

15. Greenhill, "Coping."

16. Ibid.

11. Can We Hold Back the Desert?

1. U.S. Agency for International Development, Office of Science and Technology, *Desert Encroachment on Arable Lands: Significance, Causes and Control* (TA/OST 72-10) (Washington, D.C.: Government Printing Office, August 1972).

2. Helen Ware, "The Sahelian Drought: Some Thoughts on the Future," paper commissioned by the United Nations Special Sahelian Office, March 26, 1975, especially pp. 2-5.

3. Douglas L. Johnson, "The Response of Pastoral Nomads to Drought in the Absence of Outside Intervention," paper commissioned by the United Nations Special Sahelian Office, December 19, 1973, p. 3.

4. Ware, "The Sahelian Drought," pp. 2ff.

5. A. T. Grove, "Desertification in the African Environment," in David Dalby and R. J. Harrison, *Drought in Africa* (London: Centre for African Studies, 1973), pp. 33-45.

6. *Christian Science Monitor,* quoted in *Environment* 1 (December 1974).

7. "Deserts," *China Reconstructs* 23 (October 1974): 46ff.

8. D. Stamp, "Some Conclusions," in *A History of Land Use in Arid Regions* (Paris: UNESCO, 1961).

9. Thurston Clarke, *The Last Caravan* (New York: Putnam, 1978), pp. 7, 84-90.

10. "Les ravages de la culture du coton," *Le Monde Diplomatique* (May 1976): 11.

11. Claude Raynaut, "Le Cas de la region de Maradi (Niger)," in *Sécheresses et Famines du Sahel* (Paris: François Maspero, 1975), especially pp. 8-18.

12. Ware, "The Sahelian Drought," p. 21, citing a personal communication from S. Lallemand, "A Yatenga Village in the Course of the 1973 Drought." See also René Dumont, *False Start in Africa* (New York: Praeger, 1966).

13. Gert Spittler, "Migrations rurales et développement economique: Example du Canton de Tibiri," an unpublished paper discussed in "Social Institutions," a study commissioned by the United Nations Special Sahelian Office, March 28, 1974, p. 93.

14. Calculations based on Food and Agriculture Organization, *Yearbook of International Trade Statistics,* 1974.

15. Food and Agriculture Organization, *Production Year-book* vol. 28-1, 1974, pp. 117ff.

16. Food and Agriculture Organization, *Trade Year-book,* 1975.

17. Ibid., and *Production Yearbook,* 1975.

18. Personal communication from Dr. Thierry Brun, Institut National de la Santé, Paris, Hôpital Bichat, November 17, 1975.

19. Lofchie, "Political and Economic Origins of African Hunger," pp. 554, 561ff.

20. "Social Institutions," a study commissioned by the Special Sahelian Office, March 28, 1974, pp. 79ff.

21. International Bank for Reconstruction and Development, *Senegal: Tradition, Diversification, and Economic Development,* 1974, pp. 66ff.

22. *Trade Yearbook,* 1975.

23. "Social Institutions," p. 80.

24. Calculations based on the Food and Agriculture Organization, *Yearbook of International Trade Statistics,* 1974.

25. Interview with Dr. Marcel Ganzin, Director, Food Policy and Nutrition Division, FAO, April 20, 1976.

26. Letter from Dr. Marcel Ganzin, Director, Food Policy and Nutrition Division, FAO, dated December 18, 1975, emphasis added.

27. Food and Agriculture Organization, *Progress in Land Reform—Sixth Report,* 1976, especially p. 24. See also Grigori Lazarev, "Rural Development in the African Countries of the Sudano-Sahelian Africa," paper commissioned by the United Nations Special Sahelian Office, July 23, 1974, p. 5.

28. Claude Meillassoux, "Development or Exploitation: Is the Sahel Famine Good Business?" *The Review of African Political Economy* 1 (August-November 1974): 27-34.

PART III. COLONIAL INHERITANCE

12. Why Can't People Feed Themselves?

1. Radha Sinha, *Food and Poverty* (New York: Holmes and Meier, 1976), p. 26.

2. John Stuart Mill, *Political Economy,* Book 3, Chapter 25, emphasis added.

3. Peter Feldman and David Lawrence, "Social and Economic Implications of the Large-Scale Introduction of New Varieties of Foodgrains," Africa Report, preliminary draft (Geneva: UNRISD, 1975), pp. 107-108.

4. Edgar Owens, *The Right Side of History,* unpublished manuscript, 1976.

5. Walter Rodney, *How Europe Underdeveloped Africa* (London: Bogle-L'Ouverture Publications, 1972), pp. 171-172.

6. Ferdinand Ossendowski, *Slaves of the Sun* (New York: Dutton, 1928), p. 276.

7. Rodney, *How Europe Underdeveloped Africa,* pp. 171-172.

8. Ibid., p. 181.

9. Clifford Geertz, *Agricultural Involution* (Berkeley and Los Angeles: University of California Press, 1963), pp. 52-53.

10. Rodney, *How Europe Underdeveloped Africa,* p. 185.

11. Ibid., p. 184.

12. Ibid., p. 186.

13. George L. Beckford, *Persistent Poverty: Underdevelopment in Plantation Economies of the Third World* (New York: Oxford University Press, 1972), p. 99.

14. Ibid., p. 99, quoting from Erich Jacoby, *Agrarian Unrest in Southeast Asia* (New York: Asia Publishing House, 1961), p. 66.

15. Roger Burbach and Pat Flynn, "Del Monte: Bitter Fruits," *North American Congress on Latin America (NACLA) Report,* X, 7, September 1976, p. 26.

16. Feldman and Lawrence, "Social and Economic Implications," p. 103.

17. Special Sahelian Office Report, Food and Agriculture Organization, March 28, 1974, pp. 88-89.

18. Alan Adamson, *Sugar Without Slaves: The Political Economy of British Guiana, 1838-1904* (New Haven and London: Yale University Press, 1972).

19. Ibid., p. 41.

20. Eric Williams, *Capitalism and Slavery* (New York: Putnam, 1966), p. 110.

21. Ibid., p. 121.

22. Gunnar Myrdal, *Asian Drama,* vol. 1 (New York: Pantheon, 1966), pp. 448-449.

23. Feldman and Lawrence, "Social and Economic Implications," p. 189.

13. Isn't Colonialism Dead?

1. Eduardo Galeano, *Open Veins in Latin America: Five Centuries of the Pillage of a Continent* (New York: Monthly Review, 1973), p. 282.

2. Walter Rodney, *How Europe Underdeveloped Africa* (London: Bogle-L'Ouverture Publications, 1972), p. 240.

3. Peter Feldman and David Lawrence, "Social and Economic Implications of the Large-Scale Introduction of New Varieties of Foodgrains," Africa Report, preliminary draft (Geneva: UNRISD, 1975), p. 107.

4. Rodney, *How Europe Underdeveloped Africa*, p. 106.

5. George Beckford, *Persistent Poverty: Underdevelopment in Plantation Economies of the Third World* (New York: Oxford University Press, 1972), p. 82.

6. Robert E. Gamer, *The Developing Nations, A Comparative Perspective* (Boston: Allyn and Bacon, 1976), Chapter 2.

7. Edgar Owens and Robert Shaw, *Development Reconsidered* (Lexington, Mass.: Heath, 1972), p. 150; see also Gunnar Myrdal, *Asian Drama*, vol. 1 (New York: Pantheon, 1966), Part III, Chapter 10.

8. Francine R. Frankel, "The Politics of the Green Revolution: Shifting Patterns of Peasant Participation in India and Pakistan," in *Food, Population and Employment*, Thomas T. Poleman and Donald K. Freebairn, eds. (New York: Praeger, 1973), p. 124.

9. Thomas P. Melady and R. B. Suhartono, *Development: Lessons for the Future* (Maryknoll, New York: Orbis, 1973), p. 209.

PART IV. Modernizing Hunger

14. Shouldn't Production Be the Priority?

1. Radha Sinha, *Food and Poverty* (New York: Holmes and Meier, 1976), p. 7.

2. Cynthia Hewitt de Alcántara, "A Commentary on the Satisfaction of Basic Needs in Mexico, 1917-1975," prepared by the Dag Hammarskjöld Foundation, May 7, 1975, pp. 1, 9.

3. Cynthia Hewitt de Alcántara, "The Green Revolution as History," *Development and Change,* 5, 2 (1973-1974): 25-26.

4. Hewitt de Alcántara, "Commentary on the Satisfaction of Basic Needs," p. 10.

5. Hewitt de Alcántara, "The Social and Economic Implications of the Large-Scale Introduction of New Varieties of Foodgrains," *Country Report—Mexico* (Geneva: UNDP/UNRISD, 1974), p. 30.

6. Ibid., p. 19.

7. Ibid., p. 129.

8. Ibid., p. 156.

9. "Mexico: Roosting Chickens," *Latin America* (Nov. 28, 1975): 375.

10. Andrew Pearse, "Social and Economic Implications of the Large-Scale Introduction of New Varieties of Foodgrains," Part 4 (Geneva: UNDP/UNRISD, 1975), pp. XI-19, XI-20.

11. Cited by Keith Griffin, *The Political Economy of Agrarian Change* (Cambridge, Mass.: Harvard University Press, 1974), p. 55.

15. But Isn't Nature Neutral?

1. Ingrid Palmer, *Science and Agricultural Production* (Geneva: UNRISD, 1972), pp. 6-7.

2. World Bank, *The Assault on World Poverty—Problems of Rural Development, Education, and Health* (Baltimore: Johns Hopkins University Press, 1975), pp. 132-133.

3. Andrew Pearse, "Social and Economic Implications of the Large-Scale Introduction of New Varieties of Foodgrains," Part 2 (Geneva: UNDP/UNRISD, 1975), p. II-7.

4. S. Ahmed and S. Abu Khalid, "Why did Mexican Dwarf Wheat Decline in Pakistan?" *World Crops* 23: 211-215.

5. Charles Elliott, *Patterns of Poverty in the Third World —A Study of Social and Economic Stratification* (New York: Praeger, 1975), pp. 47-48.

6. Cynthia Hewitt de Alcántara, "The Social and Economic Implications of the Large-Scale Introduction of the New Varieties of Foodgrains," *Country Report—Mexico* (Geneva: UNDP/UNRISD, 1974), p. 181.

7. North London Haslemere, *The Death of the Green*

Revolution (London: Haslemere Declaration Group; Oxford: Third World First), p. 4.

8. Victor McElheny, "Nations Demand Agricultural Aid," *New York Times,* August 3, 1975, p. 20.

9. Keith Griffin, *The Political Economy of Agrarian Change* (Cambridge, Mass.: Harvard University Press, 1974), p. 205.

10. Pearse, "Social and Economic Implications," Part 1, pp. 111-118.

11. Nicholas Wade, "Green Revolution I: A Just Technology Often Unjust in Use," *Science* (December 1974): 1093-1096.

12. Hewitt de Alcántara, *Country Report—Mexico,* p. 87.

13. Pearse, "Social and Economic Implications," Part 4, pp. XI-52, XI-53.

14. Pearse, "Social and Economic Implications," Part 3, pp. IX-23, IX-24.

15. Palmer, *Science and Agricultural Production,* p. 47.

16. Erich M. Jacoby, *The "Green Revolution" in China* (Geneva: UNRISD, 1974), p. 6.

17. Food and Agricultural Organization, *Report on China's Agriculture,* prepared by H. V. Henle, 1974, pp. 144-145.

16. Hasn't the Green Revolution "Bought Us Time"?

1. Erna Bennett, Department of Plant Genetics, FAO, Rome, personal communication, April 1976.

2. Francine R. Frankel, "The Politics of the Green Revolution: Shifting Patterns of Peasant Participation in India and Pakistan," in *Food, Population, and Employment— The Impact of the Green Revolution,* Thomas T. Poleman and Donald K. Freebairn, eds. (New York: Praeger, 1973), p. 133.

3. Joan Mencher, "Conflicts and Contradictions in the 'Green Revolution': The Case of Tamil Nadu," *Economic and Political Weekly* 9, nos. 6, 7, 8 (February 1974): especially 315.

4. Andrew Pearse, "Social and Economic Implications of the Large-Scale Introduction of New Varieties of Foodgrains," Part 2 (Geneva: UNDP/UNRISD, 1975), pp. VI-14, VI-15.

5. "Tamil Nadu—Starvation Deaths in a Surplus State," *Economic and Political Weekly* 10 (February 22, 1975): 348.

6. H. P. Singh, "Plight of Agricultural Labourers. II, A Review," *Economic Affairs* 16 (June 1971): 283.

7. Wolf Ladejinsky, "Ironies of India's Green Revolution," *Foreign Affairs* (July 1970): 762.

8. Robert d'A. Shaw, "The Employment Implications of the Green Revolution" (Washington, D.C.: Overseas Development Council, 1970), pp. 3-20.

9. A. Eugene Havens and William Flinn, *Green Revolution Technology—Structural Aspects of its Adoption and Consequences* (Geneva: UNRISD, 1975), p. 25.

10. Ibid., p. 35.

11. Keith Griffin, *Land Concentration and Rural Poverty* (New York: Macmillan, 1976), p. 74.

12. A. Rudra, A. Majid, and B. D. Talib, "Big Farmers of the Punjab: Some Preliminary Findings of a Sample Survey," *Economic and Political Weekly,* Review of Agriculture, 4 (September 27, 1969).

13. A. R. Khan, "Poverty and Inequality in Bangladesh," in *Poverty and Landlessness in Rural Asia,* Keith Griffin and Azizur Rahman Khan, eds., A Study by the World Employment Programme, manuscript (Geneva: ILO, 1976), pp. 7-41.

14. Cynthia Hewitt de Alcántara, "Social and Economic Implications of the Large-Scale Introduction of New Varieties of Foodgrains," *Country Report—Mexico* (Geneva: UNDP/UNRISD, 1974), p. 148.

15. Gordon Gemmill and Carl K. Eicher, "A Framework for Research on the Economics of Farm Mechanization in Developing Countries," African Rural Employment Paper no. 6, African Rural Employment Research Network, Department of Agricultural Economics, Michigan State University, East Lansing, Mich., 1973, pp. 32-33.

16. Susan George, *How the Other Half Dies* (London: Penguin, 1976).

17. Edgar Owens and Robert Shaw, *Development Reconsidered: Bridging the Gap Between Government and People* (Lexington, Mass.: Heath, 1972), p. 74.

18. Hewitt de Alcántara, *Country Report—Mexico,* p. 215.

19. Food and Agriculture Organization, *Agricultural Development and Employment Performance and Planning:*

A Comparative Analysis (Agricultural Planning Studies, no. 18, 1974), pp. 100, 102.

20. A. R. Khan, "Poverty and Inequality in Bangladesh," pp. 7-36.

21. Pearse, "Social and Economic Implications," Part 3, p. IX-25.

22. Ingrid Palmer, *Food and the New Agricultural Technology* (Geneva: UNRISD, 1972), pp. 64-65.

23. T. J. Byres, "The Dialectic of India's Green Revolution," *South Asian Review* 5 (January 1972): 109.

24. Donald K. Freebairn, "Income Disparities in the Agricultural Sector: Regional and Institutional Stresses," in *Food, Population, and Employment—The Impact of the Green Revolution,* Thomas Poleman and Donald Freebairn, eds. (New York: Praeger, 1973), p. 108.

25. Rodger D. Hansen, *The Politics of Mexican Development* (Baltimore: Johns Hopkins University Press, 1971), p. 81.

26. Hewitt de Alcántara, *Country Report—Mexico,* p. 267.

27. Douglas Zoloth Foster, "Weeding Workers: How the University of California is Underwriting the Loss of 170,000 Jobs," *In These Times* May 10-16, 1978, p. 12.

28. Michael Perlman, *Farming for Profit in a Hungry World* (Montclair, N. J.: Allanheld, Osmun & Co., 1977), p. 88.

29. For further discussion of women's issues, see Mary Roodkowsky and Lisa Leghorn, *Who Really Starves? Women and World Hunger* (New York: Friendship Press, 1977).

30. A. R. Khan, "Growth and Inequality in the Rural Philippines," in *Poverty and Landlessness in Rural Asia,* pp. 11-13, 11-24.

31. ———. "Poverty and Inequality in Bangladesh," in *Poverty and Landlessness in Rural Asia,* pp. 7-21, 7-22.

32. E. Lee, "Rural Poverty in West Malaysia," in *Poverty and Landlessness,* p. 5.

33. ———. "Rural Poverty in Sri Lanka, 1963-1973," in *Poverty and Landlessness in Rural Asia,* pp. 8-13.

34. *New York Times,* March 3, 1976, p. 2.

17. Wasn't the Green Revolution a Vital Scientific Breakthrough?

1. Andrew Pearse, "Social and Economic Implications of the Large-Scale Introduction of New Varieties of Foodgrains," Part 1 (Geneva: UNDP/UNRISD, 1975), pp. III-9, III-10.

2. Ibid., Part 1, pp. III-12.

3. Edgar Owens, U.S. AID, personal communication, June 1976.

4. Pearse, "Social and Economic Implications," Part 1, pp. III-6, III-7.

5. Ingrid Palmer, *Food and the New Agricultural Technology* (Geneva: UNRISD, 1972), p. 43.

6. Roger Blobaum, "Why China Doesn't Starve," *Ramparts* (July 1975): 42.

7. Pearse, "Social and Economic Implications," Part 1, p. III-17.

8. *New York Times*, August 22, 1975, p. 4.

9. Ingrid Palmer, *Science and Agricultural Production* (Geneva: UNRISD, 1972), pp. 37-38.

10. Cynthia Hewitt de Alcántara, "Social and Economic Implications of the Large-Scale Introduction of New Varieties of Foodgrains," *Country Report—Mexico* (Geneva: UNDP/UNRISD, 1974), pp. 115-116.

11. Pearse, "Social and Economic Implications," Part 1, p. III-14.

12. Palmer, *Food and the New Agricultural Technology*, pp. 59-62.

18. Hasn't the Green Revolution Strengthened Food Security?

1. Jon Tinker, "How the Boran Wereng Did a Red Khmer on the Green Revolution," *New Scientist* (August 7, 1975): 316.

2. Nicholas Wade, "Green Revolution (II): Problems of Adapting a Western Technology," *Science* 186 (December 27, 1974): 1186-1187.

3. John Prester, "The Green Revolution Turns Sour," *Reports* (December 7, 1974).

4. Andrew Pearse, "Social and Economic Implications of the Large-Scale Introduction of the New Varieties of

Foodgrains," Part 1 (Geneva: UNDP/UNRISD, 1975), pp. II-8, II-9.

5. *Des Moines Register,* April 17, 1974.

6. Ibid.

7. D. H. Timothy and M. M. Goodman, "Plant Germ Plasm Resources—Future Feast or Famine?" paper (Journal Series of the North Carolina State University Agricultural Experiment Station), cited by P. C. Mangelsdorf, *Proceedings of the National Academy of Science* (1966): 56, 370; and H. Garrison Wilkes, "Too Little Gene Exchange," letter to the editor of *Science* 171 (March 12, 1971): 955.

8. H. Garrison Wilkes and Susan Wilkes, "The Green Revolution," *Environment* 14 (October 1972): 33.

9. Robert A. Ginskey, "Sowing the Seeds of Disaster?" *The Plain Truth* 61 (June 1976): 35, quoting Wilkes.

10. Ibid.

11. Wade, "Green Revolution," p. 1191.

12. Bettina Conner, "Seed Monopoly," *Elements* (Washington, D.C.: Transnational Institute for Policy Studies, February 1975).

13. Ibid.

14. Frank B. Viets, Jr., and Samuel R. Aldrich, "The Sources of Nitrogen for Food and Meat Production," in *Sources of Nitrogenous Compounds and Methods of Control,* Environmental Protection Agency Monograph, pp. 67, 73ff.

15. William Brune, State Conservationist, Soil Conservation Service, 823 Federal Building, Des Moines, Iowa 50309, testimony before the Senate Committee on Agriculture and Forestry, July 1976.

16. Ramon Garcia, "Some Aspects on World Fertilizer Production, Consumption and Usage," paper, University of Iowa, 1975.

17. Swedish International Development Agency and Food and Agriculture Organization, "Organic Materials as Fertilizers," Soils Bulletin 27, 1975.

19. Where Has All the Production Gone?

1. Robert J. Ledogar, *Hungry for Profits: U.S. Food and Drug Multinationals in Latin America* (New York: IDOC/North America Inc., 1975), p. 96.

2. *Ceres* (May-June 1976): 8.

3. Ray Goldberg, *Agribusiness Management for the Developing Countries—Latin America* (Cambridge, Mass.: Ballinger, 1974), p. 87.

20. Don't They Need Our Machines?

1. Robert d'A. Shaw, *Jobs and Agricultural Development* (Washington, D.C.: Overseas Development Council, monograph no. 3, 1970), pp. 34-35.

2. Andrew Pearse, "Social and Economic Implications of the Large-Scale Introduction of New Varieties of Food-grains," Part 3 (Geneva: UNDP/UNRISD, 1975), pp. IX-12.

3. Jennifer E. Miller, "Automatic Harvesters Mechanize North Carolina's Tobacco Industry: The Effect on the Tobacco Farmer," University of North Carolina, February 25, 1975, p. 11.

4. USDA study, quoted in *CNI Weekly Report* (Community Nutrition Institute, February 21, 1974), p. 4.

5. International Labor Office, *Mechanization and Employment in Agriculture* (Geneva, 1974), p. 8.

6. S. R. Bose and E. H. Clark, "Some Basic Considerations on Agricultural Mechanization in West Pakistan," *Pakistan Development Review* 9, 3 (Autumn 1969), cited by Owens and Shaw, *Development Reconsidered: Bridging the Gap Between Government and People* (Lexington, Mass.: Heath, 1972), p. 62.

7. Randolph Barker, et al., "Employment and Technological Change in Philippine Agriculture," *International Labour Review* 106, 2-3 (August-September 1972): 130.

8. Frank C. Child and Hiromitsu Kaneda, "Links to the Green Revolution: A Study of Small-Scale, Agriculturally-Related Industry in the Punjab," *Economic Development and Cultural Change* 23 (1974): 5.

9. Roger Blobaum, "Why China Doesn't Starve," *Ramparts* (July 1975): 41.

10. Amir U. Khan and Bart Duff, "Development of Agricultural Mechanization Technologies at the IRRI (Manila)," paper no. 72-02, mimeographed (International Rice Research Institute), cited in *Mechanization and Employment in Agriculture,* 1974, p. 11.

11. Lester Brown, *Seeds of Change* (New York: Praeger, 1970), p. 59.

12. "Companies—Massey-Ferguson's Success Story," *Business Week,* February 2, 1976, p. 44.

13. *Mechanization and Employment in Agriculture,* p. 11.

14. Keith Griffin, *The Political Economy of Agrarian Change* (Cambridge, Mass.: Harvard University Press, 1974), p. 54.

15. Francine .R. Frankel, "The Politics of the Green Revolution: Shifting Patterns of Peasant Participation in India and Pakistan," in *Food, Population, and Employment—The Impact of the Green Revolution,* Thomas T. Poleman and Donald K. Freebairn, eds. (New York: Praeger, 1973), pp. 132-133.

16. M. Taghi Farvar, "The Relationship Between Ecological and Social Systems," Speech delivered to EARTH-CARE conference, New York, June 6, 1975, p. 9.

17. Ma Chu, "Something on the Side," *Far Eastern-Economic Review,* April 14, 1978, p. 30.

18. Joseph Hanlon, "India Back to the Village: Does AT Walk on Plastic Sandals?" *New Scientist,* May 26, 1977, pp. 467ff.

19. *Christian Science Monitor,* August 3, 1977.

20. Hanlon, "India Back to the Village," p. 469.

PART V. THE INEFFICIENCY OF INEQUALITY

21. Isn't the Backwardness of Small Farmers to Blame?

1. Edgar Owens and Robert Shaw, *Development Reconsidered: Bridging the Gap Between Government and People* (Lexington, Mass.: D. C. Heath, 1972), p. 60. .

2. World Bank, *The Assault on World Poverty—Problems of Rural Development, Education, and Health* (Baltimore: Johns Hopkins University Press, 1975), p. 215.

3. Owens and Shaw, *Development Reconsidered,* p. 60.

4. World Bank, *Assault on World Poverty,* pp. 215-216.

5. Food and Agriculture Organization, *Report on the 1960 World Census of Agriculture,* Rome, 1971, cited in *The Assault on World Poverty* (Baltimore: World Bank, Johns Hopkins University Press, 1975), p. 244.

6. U.S. Department of Agriculture, "The One-Man Farm," prepared by Warren Bailey, USDA/ERS-519

(Washington, D.C.: Government Printing Office, August 1973). See also Angus McDonald, "The Family Farm is the Most Efficient Unit of Production," in Peter Barnes, ed., *The People's Land* (Rodale Press, Emmaus, Pa., 1975).

7. Calculated from U.S. Department of Agriculture, *Statistical Bulletin,* no. 547, *Farm Income Statistics,* Table 3D, USDA/ERS (Washington, D.C.: Government Printing Office, July 1975), p. 60; and "The Balance Sheet of the Farming Sector, by Value of Sales Class, 1960-1973," supplement no. 1, *Agricultural Information Bulletin,* no. 376, Table 2, USDA/ERS (Washington, D.C.: Government Printing Office, April 1975), p. 30.

22. Why Don't Small Farmers Produce More?

1. *New York Times,* November 5, 1974, p. 14.

2. Keith Griffin, *The Political Economy of Agrarian Change* (Cambridge, Mass.: Harvard University Press, 1974), p. 27.

3. World Bank, *Assault on World Poverty,* 1975, p. 105.

4. Sudhir Sen, *Reaping the Green Revolution* (Maryknoll, New York: Orbis, 1975), p. 11.

5. Andrew Pearse, "Social and Economic Implications of the Large-Scale Introduction of the New Varieties of Foodgrains," Part 2 (Geneva: UNDP/UNRISD, 1975), pp. 8-9.

6. Griffin, *Political Economy,* p. 28.

7. Keith Griffin, *Land Concentration and Rural Poverty* (New York: Macmillan, 1976), p. 122.

8. International Labor Office, *Poverty and Landlessness in Rural Asia,* A Study by the World Employment Programme, Keith Griffin and Azizur Rahman Khan, eds., 1976, pp. I-31.

9. Erich Jacoby and Charlotte Jacoby, *Man and Land* (New York: Knopf, 1971), p. 79.

10. Hugh Brammer, FAO, Bangladesh, interviewed by Joseph Collins, January 1978.

23. Isn't Bigger Better?

1. Erich Jacoby and Charlotte Jacoby, *Man and Land* (New York: Knopf, 1971), p. 79.

2. C. H. Gotsch, "Technological Change and The Dis-

tribution of Income in Rural Areas," *American Journal of Agricultural Economics* 54 (May 2, 1972): 326-341.

3. Cynthia Hewitt de Alcántara, "Social and Economic Implications of the Large-Scale Introduction of New Varieties of Foodgrains," *Country Report—Mexico,* (Geneva: UNDP/UNRISD, 1974), p. 146.

4. Ibid., p. 90.

5. Ibid., p. 146.

6. Ibid., p. 260.

7. Ibid., p. 160.

8. World Bank, *Assault on World Poverty,* 1975, p. 142.

9. Don Paarlberg of USDA, speech before the 55th Annual Convention of Milk Producers, November 30, 1971.

10. Food and Agriculture Organization, *Agricultural Development and Employment Performance: A Comparative Analysis* (Agricultural Planning Studies no. 18, 1974), p. 124.

11. Keith Griffin, *Land Concentration and Rural Poverty* (New York: Macmillan, 1976), p. 190.

12. Ingrid Palmer, personal communication, May 1976.

24. Is Small Always Beautiful?

1. Milton J. Esman, *Landlessness and Nearlandlessness in Developing Countries,* Center for International Studies (Ithaca, N.Y.: Cornell University, February 15, 1978), 664 pp.

2. Kathleen Gough, "The 'Green Revolution' in South India and North Vietnam," *Social Scientist,* Kerala, India, August 1977, no. 61. See also Gough, *Ten Times More Beautiful* (New York: Monthly Review Press, 1978).

25. But Hasn't Land Reform Sacrificed Production?

1. Theodore Bergmann, *Farm Policies in Socialist Countries* (Lexington, Mass.: Heath, 1975), pp. 203-204, 206.

2. Food and Agriculture Organization, *Progress in Land Reform—Sixth Report,* Rural Institutions Division, Rome, 1975, pp. III-8; and *Agricultural Problems: Agronomical Data,* Vietnamese Studies, Hanoi, pp. 19-20.

3. Food and Agriculture Organization, op. cit.

4. Food and Agriculture Organization, *Production Yearbook,* 1975.

5. Arthur MacEwan, *Agriculture and Development in Cuba,* a manuscript prepared for the International Labor Office, 1978.

6. Bergmann, *Farm Policies in Socialist Countries,* p. 225.

7. MacEwan, *Agriculture and Development in Cuba,* especially Chapter 16.

8. Bergmann, *Farm Policies,* p. 219, and MacEwan, *Agriculture and Development,* pp. 16-3.

9. MacEwan, *Agriculture and Development,* Parts VI and VII.

10. Wilfred Burchett, "Portuguese Defend Land Reform," *Guardian,* April 26, 1978, p. 24.

11. Leo Orleans, "The Role of Science and Technology in China's Population-Food Balance," prepared for the Subcommittee on Domestic and International Scientific Planning, Analysis and Cooperation of the Committee on Science and Technology of the U.S. House of Representatives, September 1977, p. 55.

12. *Agricultural Problems,* pp. 19ff.

13. U.S. Department of Agriculture, *Our Land and Water Resources* (USDA/ERS, Miscellaneous Publication, no. 1290, 1974), p. 32.

14. Robert C. Fellmeth, *Politics of Land* (New York: Grossman, 1973), p. 12.

15. Michael Perelman, *Farming for Profit in a Hungry World* (Montclair, N. J.: Allanheld, Osmun & Co., 1977), p. 90.

16. Steve Bossi, *New Land Review,* Winter 1978, p. 10.

17. Bruce F. Hall and E. Phillip Leveen, "Farm-Size and Economic Efficiency: The Case of California," Working Paper No. 53, Division of Agricultural Sciences, University of California, Berkeley, February, 1978, pp. 27ff.

18. Ibid., pp. 26ff.

19. "Communities of the San Joaquin Valley: The Relation Between Scale of Farming Water Use and the Quality of Life," University of California, Davis, 1977.

PART VI. THE TRADE TRAP

26. What About Their Natural Advantage?

1. Cheryl Payer, "Coffee," in Cheryl Payer, ed., *Commodity Trade in the Third World* (New York: Wiley, 1975), p. 159.

2. Frederick Clairmonte, "Bananas," in Payer, *Commodity Trade*, p. 131.

3. Payer, "Coffee," in *Commodity Trade*, 156ff.

4. UNDP, "Changing Factors in World Development," prepared by Don Casey, (Development Issue Paper 5, Global I), UNDP, August 1975, p. 2.

5. Payer, "Coffee," in *Commodity Trade*, p. 158.

6. UNCTAD, "Marketing and Distribution System for Cocoa," (Report by the Secretariat), January 1975, p. 9.

7. Ibid., p. 6.

8. Payer, *Commodity Trade*, p. 185.

9. David Andelman, "Malaysian Land Plan Thriving, but Snags Arise," *New York Times*, September 4, 1976.

10. Susan DeMarco and Susan Sechler, *The Fields Have Turned Brown—Four Essays on World Hunger* (Agribusiness Accountability Project, 1000 Wisconsin Ave. NW, Washington, D.C.), 1975, p. 8.

27. Don't They Have Cartels Now?

1. UNCTAD, "Marketing and Distribution System for Cocoa" (Report by the Secretariat, January 1975), p. 89.

2. John Freivalds, "Future Market—A New Way to Price Stability," *African Development* 9 (September 1975): 27.

3. Carl Widstrand, ed., *Multinational Firms in Africa* (African Institute for Economic Development and Planning, Dakar; and Scandinavian Institute of African Studies, Uppsala, 1975), p. 308.

4. Keith Griffin, *Land Concentration and Rural Poverty* (New York: Macmillan, 1976), p. 153.

5. Eduardo Galeano, *Open Veins in Latin America: Five Centuries of the Pillage of a Continent* (New York: Monthly Review, 1973), pp. 113-114.

6. Frederick Clairmonte, "Bananas," in Cheryl Payer,

ed. *Commodity Trade in the Third World* (New York: Wiley, 1975), pp. 138-139.

7. Ibid., p. 136.

8. UNDP, "Changing Factors in World Development," prepared by Don Casev (Development Issue Paper 5, Global I), August 1975, p. 5.

9. *Newsweek,* "Cartels: Just Bananas," August 26, 1974, p. 38. See also "Multinationals: A Banana Brouhaha over Higher Prices," *Business Week,* July 6, 1974, p. 42.

28. Doesn't Export Income Help the Hungry?

1. Andre Gunder Frank, *Capitalism and Underdevelopment in Latin America* (New York: Monthly Review, 1969; London: Penguin, 1971), pp. 286-287.

2. Susanne Jonas and David Tobis, eds., *Guatemala* (New York and Berkeley: North American Congress on Latin America, 1974), pp. 9, 16.

3. Gamini Navaratne, "Tea," *New Internationalist* (April 1976): 11.

4. Thierry Brun, "Démystifier la famine," *Cahiers de Nutrition et de Dietique* 9 (2): 115, no date.

5. UNCTAD, "Report of Intergovernmental Group on Least Developed Countries," Geneva, 1975, p. 43.

6. Donal B. Cruise O'Brien, "Cooperators and Bureaucrats: Class Formation in a Senegalese Society," *Africa* (Journal of the International African Institute) 61 (October 1972): 273.

7. UNCTAD, "Marketing and Distribution System for Cocoa," (Report of the Secretariat, January 1975), p. 34.

8. Derek Byerlee and Carl K. Eicher, "Rural Employment, Migration and Economic Development: Theoretical Issues and Empirical Evidence from Africa," African Rural Employment Study, paper no. 1, Department of Agricultural Economics, State University, East Lansing, Mich., September 1972, pp. 13-14.

9. Ingrid Palmer, *Food and the New Agricultural Technology* (Geneva: UNRISD, 1972), p. 53.

10. Uma Lele, "A Conceptual Framework for Rural Development," paper presented to the Development from Below Workshop, the Association for the Advancement of Agricultural Sciences in Africa (AAASA), October 1973, pp. 8-9.

11. *Latin America* 10 (October 22, 1976): 326.

12. Roger Wertling, Jr., *Organic Gardening and Farming* (Emmaus, Pa., September 1972), p. 76.

29. If It's So Bad, Why Does It Continue?

1. Walter Hink, "Mobutu on Tightrope as Crisis Hits Zaire," *African Development* (September 1975): 48.

2. United Nations Economic and Social Council, Preparatory Committee for the Special Session of the General Assembly Devoted to Development and International Cooperation, Second Session, June 16-27, 1975 (E/AC. 621/8) May 5, 1975, p. 7.

3. Cheryl Payer, ed., *Commodity Trade in the Third World* (New York: Wiley, 1975), pp. 180, 184.

4. Gamini Navaratne, "Tea," *New Internationalist* (April 1976): 11.

5. Robert Shaplen, Letter from Manila, *The New Yorker,* May 3, 1976, p. 92.

6. David Feldman and Peter Lawrence, "Global II Project on the Economic and Social Implications of Large-Scale Introduction of New Varieties of Foodgrains," Africa Report (Geneva: UNDP/UNRISD, 1975), p. 52.

7. Peter Dorner, "Export Agriculture and Economic Development," Land Tenure Center, University of Wisconsin, Madison, statement before the Interfaith Center on Corporate Responsibility, New York, September 14, 1976, p. 6.

8. Keith Griffin, *Land Concentration and Rural Poverty* (New York: Macmillan, 1976), p. 162.

9. Keith Griffin, *The Political Economy of Agrarian Change* (Cambridge, Mass.: Harvard University Press, 1974), p. 105.

10. R. L. Raikes, "Ujamaa and Rural Socialism," *Review of African Political Economy* (May-October 1974): 36.

11. Cheryl Payer, *The Debt Trap—The IMF and the Third World* (London: Penguin, 1974).

30. Is Export Agriculture the Enemy?

1. Interview conducted by Joseph Collins with U.S. AID Mission, Santo Domingo, Dominican Republic, November 26, 1976.

2. Arthur MacEwan, *Agriculture and Development in*

Cuba, manuscript prepared for the International Labor Organization, 1978, Chapter 27, p. 2.

3. Pedro Alvarez Tabio, ed., *The Overall Situation of the Cuban Economy* (Havana: Instituto Cubano de Deportes, September 1975), 39ff.

4. Ibid., 2ff.

PART VII. THE MYTH OF FOOD POWER

31. Don't They Need Our Food?

1. The following comparisons regarding MSA countries are calculated from U.S. Department of Agriculture, *Foreign Agricultural Trade Statistical Report*, Calendar Year 1974, May 1975.

2. Calculated from Food and Agriculture Organization, *Production Yearbook*, 1974, and *Yearbook of International Trade Statistics*, 1974.

3. Calculated from U.S. Department of Agriculture, *Foreign Agricultural Trade Statistical Report*, Calendar Year 1974.

4. Calculated from *Yearbook of International Trade Statistics*, 1974.

5. Food and Agricultural Organization, *The State of Food and Agriculture*, 1972, pp. 182-186.

6. "Commodities," *Ceres* 7 (January-February 1974): 21.

32. Food Power to Save the Economy?

1. Richard Bell, Assistant Secretary for International Affairs and Commodity Programs, USDA, cited by Norman Faramelli, "A Primer for Church Groups on Agribusiness and the World Food Crisis," Boston Industrial Mission, Boston, Mass., 1975.

2. *New York Times*, August 19, 1975, p. 16.

3. *Feedstuffs* 47 (September 8, 1975): 4.

4. Richard Barnet and Ronald Mueller, *Global Reach: The Power of the Multinational Corporations* (New York: Simon and Schuster, 1973), p. 266.

5. United States Commerce Department, Guide to

Foreign Trade Statistics (Washington, D.C.: Government Printing Office, June, 1978).

6. North American Congress on Latin America (NACLA), "U.S. Grain Arsenal," *NACLA Report* 9, 7 (October, 1975), p. 4.

7. Barry Commoner, *The Poverty of Power* (New York: Knopf, 1976), p. 54.

8. *Future Petroleum Provinces of the United States—Their Geology and Potential,* 2 vols. (Washington, D.C.: National Petroleum Council, July 1970), cited by Commoner, pp. 53-54.

9. Barry Commoner, "Reporter at Large (Energy-1)," *The New Yorker,* February 2, 1976, p. 56.

10. Commoner, "Reporter at Large," p. 52.

11. *United States International Economic Policy in an Interdependent World,* Report to the President submitted by the Commission on International Trade and Investment Policy (Washington, D.C., July, 1971).

12. U.S. Department of Agriculture, *Foreign Agricultural Trade Statistical Report,* Fiscal Year 1971 and Fiscal Year 1974, Table 10.

13. Jimmy Minyard, "Market Development Looks Ahead to New Markets and Programs." See also Darwin Stolte, "Team Effort Boosts U.S. Farm Exports," *Foreign Agriculture* 13 (May 26, 1975): 6, 9.

14. C. W. McMillan, "Meat Export Federation to be Newest Cooperator," *Foreign Agriculture* 13 (May 26, 1975): 14.

15. Philip B. Dwoskin and Nick Havas, "Fast Foods in Japan—A Billion-Dollar Industry?" *Foreign Agriculture* 13 (May 26, 1975): 33.

16. William K. Chung, "Sales by Majority-Owned Foreign Affiliates of U.S. Companies, 1976," *Survey of Current Business,* March 1978, vol. 58 no. 3, U.S. Dept. of Commerce, p. 32.

17. U.S. Department of Agriculture, *Foreign Agricultural Trade Statistical Report,* Calendar Year 1976, June 1977, p. 192.

33. At Least Food Power Works?

1. "Can Agriculture Save the Dollar?" *Forbes,* March 15, 1973, pp. 38-39.

2. *Latin America Economic Report* 4 (January 23, 1976): 16.

3. Dan Morgan, *Washington Post,* January 2-3, 1976.

4. "U.S. Food Power: Ultimate Power in World Politics?" *Business Week,* December 15, 1975, p. 58.

5. William Brune, State Conservationist, Soil Conservation Service, Des Moines, Iowa, testimony before Senate Committee on Agriculture and Forestry, July 6, 1976. See also Seth King, "Iowa Rain and Wind Deplete Farmlands," *New York Times,* December 5, 1976, p. 61.

6. "Wheels of Fortune: A Report on the Impact of Center Pivot Irrigation on the Ownership of Land in Nebraska," Center for Rural Affairs, P.O. Box 405, Walthill, Neb. 68067. See also "No One Knows the Value of Water Until the Well Runs Dry," *New Land Review* (Spring 1976): 3 (also published by the Center for Rural Affairs).

7. Report to the 1977 state legislature on the State Saline Seep Control Program funded by the 1974 and 1975 state legislatures, available from Department of State Lands, State of Montana, Helena, Mont. 59601.

34. Who Gains and Who Loses?

1. "The Incredible Empire of Michael Fribourg," *Business Week,* March 11, 1972, p. 84.

2. James Trager, *The Great Grain Robbery* (New York: Ballantine Books, 1975), p. 27.

3. William Robbins, *The American Food Scandal— Why You Can't Eat Well on What You Earn* (New York: Morrow, 1974), p. 185. See also A. V. Krebs, "Of the Grain Trade, by the Grain Trade, and for the Grain Trade," in *The Great American Grain Robbery and Other Stories,* Martha Hamilton, ed. (Washington, D.C.: Agribusiness Accountability Project, 1972), p. 289.

4. Jim Hightower, *Eat Your Heart Out: How Food Profiteers Victimize the Consumer* (New York: Crown, 1975), p. 194.

5. Dan Morgan, *Washington Post,* January 2, 3, 1976, p. A5.

6. U.S. General Accounting Office, *Exporters' Profits on Sales of U.S. Wheat to Russia* (B-176943, February 12, 1974), pp. 15ff.

7. Hightower, *Eat Your Heart Out,* p. 194.

8. Steven Bennett, "U.S. Food Policy for Whom?" *Center Survey* 4(1): 6, Center of Concern, Washington, D.C.

9. Cliff Connor, "U.S. Agribusiness and World Famine," *International Socialist Review* (September 1974), quoting James McHale, Secretary of Agriculture for the State of Pennsylvania.

10. Lawrence A. Mayer, "We Can't Take Food for Granted Anymore," *Fortune,* February 1974, p. 86.

11. Morgan, *Washington Post,* January 2, 1976.

12. *The NFO Reporter,* Corning, Iowa, January 1978, p. 9.

13. Hightower, *Eat Your Heart Out,* p. 197.

14. U.S. Department of Agriculture, *Alternative Futures for U.S. Agriculture—Part I* (USDA, Office for Planning and Evaluation for the Committee on Agriculture and Forestry, United States Senate, September 25, 1975).

15. Don Paarlberg, Director of Agricultural Economics, USDA, "Agricultural Trade and Domestic Adjustments in Agriculture," speech, March 21, 1974, p. 4.

16. Hightower, *Eat Your Heart Out,* pp. 198-199.

17. Earl Butz, "A Policy of Plenty," *Skeptic,* no. 10 (November-December 1975): 57.

18. James Flanigan, "Question for Congress," *Forbes,* May 1, 1978, p. 36.

19. Calculated from U.S. Department of Agriculture, *Farm Income Statistics,* Annual Statistical Bulletin 557, Table 3D (July 1976), p. 60.

20. Ibid., Table 4D, p. 61.

21. Ibid., Tables ID-4D.

22. *Time,* October 24, 1977, p. 28.

23. Ibid.

24. *Forbes,* pp. 35, 40.

25. *Business Week,* March 27, 1978, p. 79.

26. U.S. Department of Agriculture, *Farmland Tenure Patterns in the United States,* (USDA/ERS, February 1974), p. 3.

27. *Ag World,* 4, 3 (March 1978): 13.

28. Don Paarlberg quoted in *Feedstuffs,* August 16, 1976, p. 10.

29. U.S. Department of Agriculture, *The One-Man Farm,* prepared by Warren Bailey (USDA/ERS-519, August 1973).

30. Calculated from *Farm Income Statistics,* Statistical Bulletin, no. 547, Table 3D (USDA/ERS, July 1975), p. 60; and "The Balance Sheet of the Farming Sector, by Value of Sales Class, 1960-1973," supplement no. 1, *Agricultural Information Bulletin,* no. 376, Table 2, USDA/ERS (Washington, D.C.: Government Printing Office, April 1975), p. 3.

31. Walter Goldschmidt, "A Tale of Two Towns," in *The People's Land,* Peter Barnes, ed. (Emmaus, Pa.: Rodale Press, 1975), pp. 171ff.

32. Parity figures from Jim Thorp, USDA/ERS, telephone conversation, December 9, 1976.

33. U.S. Department of Agriculture, *Handbook of Agricultural Charts,* Agricultural Handbook, no. 504, 1976, p. 25.

34. "A Primer on Farm Policy," *New Land Review,* Winter 1978, p. 5.

35. U.S. Department of Labor, *Bureau of Labor Statistical Report 448-2* (Consumer Expenditure Survey Series: Diary Survey, 1973).

36. 1976 *Handbook of Agricultural Charts,* p. 32.

37. U.S. Department of Agriculture, *1975 Handbook of Agricultural Charts,* Handbook, no. 491, (Washington, D.C.: Government Printing Office, 1975), p. 65.

38. 1976 *Handbook,* p. 30.

39. 1976 *Handbook,* pp. 30, 33.

40. U.S. Department of Agriculture, *National Food Review,* 1978.

41. "Achieving the Goals of the Employment Act of 1946—Thirtieth Anniversary Review," vol. 3, Inflation and Market Structure, paper no. 1, "The Inflationary Impact of Unemployment: Price Markups During Postwar Recessions, 1947-70," Joint Economic Committee, Congress of the U.S. (Washington, D.C.: Government Printing Office, November 3, 1976), pp. 2ff.

42. National Farmers Union, *Washington Newsletter,* November 29, 1976.

43. U.S. Internal Revenue Service, *Source Book, Statistics of Income, Corporate Income Tax Returns,* quoted in Economic Report on Food Chain Profits, Staff Report to the Federal Trade Commission, 1975, p. 16, cited by Joe Belden, "New Directions For United States Agricultural Policy," Exploratory Project for Economic Alternatives (1519 Conn. Ave. NW, Washington, D.C. 20036), Chap-

ters 2, 4. (Supermarkets often claim low profits—only
1% profit on sales. What is neglected here is that the
supermarket makes that 1% each time it turns over its
stock which may be 12 or more times a year. Thus a 1%
profit on sales may become an actual profit of 12% annually, or what economists call "return on investment.")

44. Hightower, *Eat Your Heart Out,* p. 172.

45. U.S. Congress, Senate Select Committee on Nutrition and Human Needs, *Food Price Changes, 1973-1974
and Nutritional Status,* Part 1, 93rd Congress, 2nd Session (Washington, D.C.: Government Printing Office,
1974) pp. 12, 14.

46. Kathy Bishop, Food and Nutrition Service, U.S.
Department of Agriculture, personal communication, May,
1978.

PART VIII. WORLD HUNGER AS BIG BUSINESS

35. Don't They Need American Corporate Know-How?

1. "Feeding the World's Hungry: The Challenge to
Business," transcript of the Proceedings of an International
Conference sponsored by the Continental Bank, Chicago,
May 20, 1974.

2. Consultation with agroindustrial leaders in preparation for U.N. World Food Conference, Toronto, Canada,
September 10-11, 1974.

3. George L. Baker, "Good Climate for Agribusiness,"
The Nation, November 5, 1973, p. 460; NACLA, *Bitter
Fruits,* September 1976, *Latin America and Empire Re-
port,* pp. 12ff.

4. Baker, "Good Climate for Agribusiness," p. 460.

5. "Poverty in American Democracy: A Study of Social
Power," U.S. Catholic Conference, November 1974, cited
in *CNI Weekly Report,* Community Nutrition Institute,
Washington, D.C., September 2, 1976, p. 8.

6. Baker, "Good Climate for Agribusiness," p. 460.

7. Ernest Feder, "The Penetration of the Agricultures of
the Underdeveloped Countries by the Industrial Nations
and Their Multinational Corporations," Institute of Social
Studies, The Hague, 1975, p. 8.

8. For commodity breakdowns see Ray Goldberg, *Agribusiness Management for Developing Countries—Latin America* (Cambridge, Mass.: Ballinger, 1974), 69ff. Calculations based on Goldberg, *Agribusiness Management*, Chapter 2; and U.S. Department of Agriculture, *Foreign Agricultural Trade Statistical Report Fiscal Year 1975* and *1976* (Washington, D.C.: Government Printing Office, 1975, 1976).

9. Cited by Goldberg, *Agribusiness Management*, p. 70.

10. Ibid., p. 70.

11. Ibid., pp. 150ff. gives some figures. See also Food and Agricultural Organization, *Production Yearbooks*.

12. Ernest Feder, *Strawberry Imperialism: An Enquiry into the Mechanisms of Dependency in Mexican Agriculture* (The Hague: Institute of Social Studies, 1978).

13. Goldberg, *Agribusiness Management*, p. 147.

14. Ibid., p. 150.

15. Ibid., p. 87.

16. Ernest Feder, *Strawberry Imperialism;* unless otherwise noted, the facts on the strawberry industry in Mexico are drawn from Dr. Feder's comprehensive documentation.

17. Unless otherwise noted, the sources for the analysis of Bud Senegal are: Kees Pels, "Stijgende invoer van Afrikaanse groenten," 1975; Jan Bunnik, "Bud maakt Senegal groen," *Vakblad voor groothandel in aardappelen, groeten en fruit,* February 6 and 13, 1975, pp. 11-15 and pp. 13-16; transcript of KRO (Netherlands) televised documentary March 3, 1975; "Une remarquable reussite," *Senegal 1960-1973: 14 ans de développement;* "De situatie in Senegal," *Landbouw Wereldnieuws,* October 15, 1974; "Liefermoeglichkeiten Senegals," *Mitteilungen der Bundesstelle fuer Aussenhandelsinformation,* July 1974, 1ff.; and personal communication from Maureen M. Mackintosh, The Institute of Development Studies, completing a study of Bud Senegal, dated October 5, 1976.

18. International Finance Corporation, IFC T162, Appraisal Report for Bud Senegal, February 24, 1976.

19. Lars Bondestam, "Notes on Foreign Investments in Ethiopia," in *Multinational Firms in Africa,* Carl Widstrand and Samir Amin, eds. (Uppsala: Scandinavian Institute for African Studies, 1975), 139ff. The interview referred to is in *SIDA-rapport,* no. 8, Stockholm, 1972.

20. Bondestam, "Notes on Foreign Investments."

21. Alan Berg, *The Nutrition Factor: Its Role in Nation-*

al Development (Washington, D.C.: The Brookings Institution, 1973), p. 65.

22. *Wall Street Journal,* July 27, 1972 and January 7, 1970.

23. José da Veiga, "Quand les multinationales font du Ranching," *Le Monde Diplomatique,* September 1975, p. 13.

24. *New York Times,* July 4, 1972.

25. We are greatly indebted to the excellent study of Ralston Purina in Colombia researched by Rick Edwards and largely forming Chapter 6 in Robert J. Ledogar, *Hungry for Profits: U.S. Food and Drug Multinationals in Latin America* (New York: IDOC, 1976). Unless otherwise noted, data on Ralston Purina in Colombia comes from this study.

26. Giovanni Acciarri, et al., "Produccion Agropecuaria y Desnutricion en Colombia," (Cali: Universidad del Valle, Division de Ingenieria, 1973).

27. Ibid.

28. Calculations are based on figures in the U.S. Department of Agriculture, *Foreign Agricultural Trade Statistical Report, Fiscal Year, 1975.*

29. Interview with Gabriel Misas, D.A.N.E. (National Department of Statistics) Bogotá, Colombia, April 30, 1973, confirmed as "more or less correct" by the Embassy of Colombia in Washington, D.C., January 14, 1974.

30. A helpful source of data, largely compiled from U.S. government statistics, can be found in Appendix J in Ray A. Goldberg, *Agribusiness Management,* pp. 359-374.

31. Ibid.

36. Still, Don't the People Benefit?

1. Overseas Private Investment Corporation, Annual Report, 1973.

2. Calculation taken from Henry Frundt, *American Agribusiness and U.S. Foreign Agricultural Policy* (Ph.D. dissertation, Rutgers University, May 1975).

3. Unless otherwise noted, the data in this section is from Susanne Jonas and David Tobis, *Guatemala* (NACLA, P.O. Box 226, Berkeley, Calif. 94701), pp. 127-131.

4. "Bitter Fruits," *Latin America and Empire Report,* NACLA, 10 (September 1976): 30.

5. UNCTAD, *The Marketing and Distribution System for Bananas,* December 24, 1974, p. 24.

6. *Business Week,* January 18, 1969, p. 54.

7. Consultation with agroindustrial leaders in preparation for the U.N. World Food Conference, September 10-11, 1974, Toronto, Canada.

8. Dr. Russell C. Parker, testimony before U.S. Congress, Senate, Consumer Economics Subcommittee of the Joint Economic Committee, May 21, 1974, p. 4. For an estimate of 90 percent, see also Russell C. Parker and John M. Connor, "Estimates of Consumer Loss Due to Monopoly in the U.S. Food Manufacturing Industries," Food Systems Research Group of North Central Research Project NC-117, University of Wisconsin, Madison, Wisconsin, 1978.

9. Jim Hightower, *Eat Your Heart Out: How Food Profiteers Victimize the Consumer* (New York: Crown, 1975), p. 163.

10. U.S. Department of Agriculture, prepared by Ronald L. Mighell and William S. Hoofnagle, *Contract Production and Vertical Integration in Farming, 1960 and 1970* (Economic Research Service), p. 4.

11. U.S. Department of Agriculture, *Interrelationships in Our Food System,* prepared by William T. Manley and Donn. A. Reimund (Economic Research Service) February 21, 1973, p. 6.

12. U.S. Congress, Senate, House Antitrust Subcommittee Hearings, "Family Farm Act," testimony of Undersecretary J. Phil Campbell, March 22, 1972, 28ff.

13. *Feedstuffs,* December 12, 1970, p. 4, cited by Jim Hightower, *Eat Your Heart Out,* p. 165.

14. Cited by Hightower, *Eat Your Heart Out,* p. 164.

15. Ibid., 149ff.

16. Ibid., p. 170.

17. Ibid., p. 165.

18. U.S. Department of Agriculture, *Packers and Stockyards Administration,* prepared by Marvin L. McLain, May 14, 1974, p. 28.

19. Cited by Susan DeMarco and Susan Sechler, *The Fields Have Turned Brown—Four Essays on World Hunger* (Washington, D.C.: The Agribusiness Accountability Project, 1975), pp. 73ff.

20. Harrison Wellford, *Sowing the Wind* (New York: Grossman, 1972), pp. 101ff.

21. Hightower, *Eat Your Heart Out,* p. 168. See also U.S. Department of Agriculture, "The Broiler Industry," *Packers and Stockyards Administration* (August 1967).

22. ABC-Television News, "Food: Green Grow the Profits," documentary, December 21, 1973, transcript, pp. 46ff.

23. The Food Action Campaign Papers, "Crystal City, Tex.—A Del Monte Company Town" (Agribusiness Accountability Project, 1000 Wisconsin Ave. NW, Washington, D.C. 20007; $1). Unless otherwise noted, data on Crystal City are from this valuable study.

24. Hightower, *Eat Your Heart Out,* p. 149.

25. San Francisco, *Consumer Action News,* October, 1975.

26. Ray Vicker, *This Hungry World* (New York: Scribner's, 1975), p. 224.

27. Vincent G. Cullen, "Sour Pineapples," *America* (November 6, 1976): 300ff.

28. Liberation News Service, June 22, 1974.

29. Ismail A. Jami, "Land Reform and Modernization of Farming Structure in Iran," *Institute of Agricultural Economy* (no. 2, December 1973): 118-121. See also Julian Bharier, *Economic Development of Iran, 1900-1970* (London: Oxford University Press, 1971), especially p. 138.

30. *Agriculture and Agribusiness in Iran: Investment Opportunities* (New York: Paul R. Walter & Associates, Inc., March 1975), p. 39. Also, much information was obtained through correspondence with two Iranian economists who, for reasons of their personal safety, have asked to remain anonymous. Also helpful was an interview with John Tobey, a senior investment officer of the Chase Manhattan Bank, July 16, 1975.

31. Frances FitzGerald, "Giving the Shah Everything He Wants," *Harper's,* November 1974, p. 55.

32. *International Agribusiness,* published by Hawaiian Agronomics (a subsidiary of C. Brewer and Company), Winter 1975, p. 3.

33. "How Iran Spends Its New Found Riches," *Business Week,* June 22, 1974.

34. FitzGerald, "Giving the Shah Everything He Wants."

35. *Agriculture and Agribusiness in Iran: Investment Opportunities,* p. 4.

36. While our information was gathered from correspondence, these "labor centers" are discussed at some length in FitzGerald, "Giving the Shah Everything He Wants," pp. 74ff.

37. Presentation by CPC International at the World Food System Symposium, University of California, Berkeley, September 17-19, 1975. All quotes in this section are from this case presentation by CPC International.

37. Better Than Beans and Rice?

1. See Frances Moore Lappé, *Diet for a Small Planet* (New York: Ballantine Books, revised edition, 1975).

2. *Business Week,* December 1, 1973, p. 89.

3. Joseph M. Winski, "Back-to-Basics Trend," *Wall Street Journal,* May 29, 1975, pp. 1, 25. See also Peter T. Kilborn, "Food Industry Finds Shoppers' Tastes Are Changing," *New York Times,* April 28, 1975, pp. 45, 49.

4. Peter Drucker, *The Age of Discontinuity* (New York: Harper and Row, 1969), p. 107.

5. *Food Processing and Packing Machinery and Equipment: Mexico,* Office of International Trade Promotion, April 1971.

6. Andre van Dam, "El Futuro de la Industria Alimenticia en America Latina," speech delivered in Porto Alegre, May 14, 1975.

7. Thomas Horst, *At Home Abroad* (Cambridge, Mass.: Ballinger, 1974).

8. W. R. Grace and Co., *Annual Report,* 1969.

9. Quotations are from David F. Hawkins and Derek A. Newton, *Case Study on General Foods Corporation* (Harvard Business School course materials), 1964.

10. Horst, *At Home Abroad,* p. 127.

11. Federal Trade Commission, "Structure of Food Manufacturing," Technical Study, no. 8 (Washington, D.C.: Government Printing Office, June 1966), p. 80.

12. Research carried out in October 1976, New York State, suburban supermarket.

13. Federal Trade Commission, "Structure of Food Manufacturing," June 1966.

14. Jim Hightower, *Eat Your Heart Out: How Food Profiteers Victimize the Consumer* (New York: Crown, 1975), p. 52.

15. Michael F. Jacobson, *Nutrition Scoreboard* (Wash-

ington, D.C.: Center for Science in the Public Interest, July 1973), p. 88.

16. Cited by Hightower, *Eat Your Heart Out*, p. 52.

17. Federal Trade Commission, "Structure of Food Manufacturing," p. 81, n. 33.

18. Robert J. Ledogar, *Hungry for Profits: U.S. Food and Drug Multinationals in Latin America* (New York: IDOC, 1976), pp. 111ff.

19. We gratefully acknowledge the research on General Foods as coming from Henry Frundt, *American Agribusiness and U.S. Foreign Policy* (Ph.D. dissertation, Rutgers University, 1975), especially pp. 194-198.

20. We gratefully acknowledge much of the research for this section as that of Bernardo Kucinski, carried out for Robert Ledogar, *Hungry for Profits,* pp. 111-127. While the analysis may differ, the facts, unless otherwise noted, are from this source.

21. Cited by Richard Barnet and Ronald Mueller, *Global Reach* (New York: Simon and Schuster, 1974), pp. 183ff.

22. Letter to Robert Ledogar from Rev. Crisoforo Florencio, parish priest of Olinala, Guerrero, Mexico, June 1974, cited by Robert Ledogar, *Hungry for Profits,* p. 113.

23. *New Internationalist,* no. 7, September 1973, p. 2.

24. Ibid.

25. Quoted in *Forbes,* November 15, 1968.

26. Alan Berg, "Industry's Struggle with World Malnutrition," *Harvard Business Review* 50 (January-February 1972): 135.

38. Do They Really Kill Babies?

1. Roy J. Harris, Jr., "The Baby Bust," *Wall Street Journal,* January 4, 1972; "The Bad News in Babyland," *Dun's Review* 100 (December 1972): 104.

2. Mike Muller, *The Baby Killer,* pamphlet (London: War on Want, 1975; 467 Caledonian Rd.). Contains extensive references and bibliography.

3. Ruth Rice Puffer and Carlos V. Serrano, *Patterns of Mortality in Childhood,* Scientific Publication, no. 262 (Washington, D.C.: Pan American Health Organization, 1973), p. 161.

4. William A. M. Cutting, *The Lancet* 7870 (June 29,

1974): 1340, citing J. B. Wyon and J. E. Gordon, *The Khanna Study* (Cambridge, Mass.: Harvard University Press, 1971), p. 187.

5. Alan Berg, *The Nutrition Factor* (Washington, D.C.: The Brookings Institution, 1973), p. 95, citing D. S. McLaren, in *The Lancet* 7461 (August 27, 1966): 485.

6. Derrick B. Jelliffe and E. F. Patrice Jelliffe, "An Overview," in *The Uniqueness of Human Milk,* symposium reprinted from *The American Journal of Clinical Nutrition* 24 (August 1971).

7. London *Times,* June 29, 1974.

8. Paul Gyorgy, "Biochemical Aspects of Human Milk," *The American Journal of Clinical Nutrition* 24 (August 1971): 970.

9. Hugh Jolly, "Why Breast Feeding Is Food for Mother and Baby," London *Times,* March 26, 1975.

10. Michael C. Latham, "Introduction," in *The Promotion of Bottle Feeding by Multinational Corporations: How Advertising and the Health Professions Have Contributed,* Ted Greiner, ed. (Ithaca, N.Y.: Cornell University Monograph Series, no. 2, 1975), pp. iiff.

11. Data from affidavit submitted for *Sisters of the Precious Blood, Inc.* vs. *Bristol Myers Co.,* U.S. District Court, Southern District of New York, 1976. See also V. G. James, "Household Expenditure on Food and Drink by Income Groups," paper delivered at Seminar on National Food and Nutrition Policy of Jamaica, Kingston, May 27-31, 1974 and Latham, "Introduction," p. ii.

12. The National Food and Nutrition Survey of Barbados, Scientific Publication, no. 237 (Washington, D.C.: Pan American Health Organization, 1972), cited by Robert J. Ledogar, *Hungry for Profits: U.S. Food and Drug Multinationals in Latin America* (New York: IDOC, 1976), 130ff.

13. This and the next example are from Muller, *The Baby Killer,* p. 7.

14. Ibid., p. 6.

15. Ibid.

16. Ibid.

17. *Report of an Ad-Hoc Committee on Young Child Feeding* (New York: United Nations Protein Advisory Group, 1971).

18. Ledogar, *Hungry for Profits,* p. 132, cites M. D. Samsudin, et al., "Rational Use of Skim Milk in a Com-

plete Infant Formula," *The American Journal of Clinical Nutrition* 20 (1967): 1304; and John McKigney, "Economic Aspects," in *The Uniqueness of Human Milk*, p. 1009.

19. David O. Cox, "Economics of Feeding Infants and Young Children in Developing Countries," paper presented at the U.N. Protein Advisory Group Ad-Hoc Working Group meeting, Geneva, December 11-13, 1972.

20. Muller, *The Baby Killer*, pp. 11ff.

21. *New York Times*, September 14, 1975.

22. This and more extensive information on milk banks can be found in Ledogar, *Hungry for Profits*, pp. 138ff.

23. *New Internationalist*, March 1975, p. 2.

24. From various company promotion, all books cited and noted in Ledogar, *Hungry for Profits*, pp. 133ff.

25. Ibid., p. 135.

26. *The Womanly Art of Breast Feeding* (Franklin Park, Illinois: La Leche League International, 1963), p. 54.

27. Information obtained from Leah Margulies, Interfaith Center on Corporate Responsibility, New York.

28. Alan Berg, "The Economics of Breast-Feeding," *The Saturday Review of the Sciences* 1 (May 1973): 30.

29. *New Internationalist*, March 1975.

30. Ibid.

31. *Development Forum*, July-August 1976, Geneva: United Nations, Council for Economic and Social Information.

39. Agribusiness Abroad: A Boon for Americans?

1. The information and data for this section are derived from Mary Alice Kellogg, "Hawaii Without the Pineapple," *The Nation*, March 16, 1974; "Hawaii: Pineapples or Parking Lots?" *Newsweek*, February 25, 1974; "Plantation Decline in Hawaii Spurs Exodus," *New York Times*, November 11, 1975; "Bitter Fruits," *Latin America and Empire Report*, NACLA, 10 (September 1976): 21ff.

2. Jim Hightower, *Eat Your Heart Out: How Food Profiteers Victimize the Consumer* (New York: Crown, 1975), pp. 151ff.

3. Mushroom Processors Association, "Memorandum to Trade Staff Committee of the U.S. Tariff Commission,"

June 26, 1973, Investigation 332-72, p. 15, cited by Hightower, *Eat Your Heart Out*, p. 152.

4. Hightower, *Eat Your Heart Out*, p. 152.

5. Robert J. Ledogar, *Hungry for Profits: U.S. Food and Drug Multinationals in Latin America* (New York: IDOC, 1976), pp. 150ff.

6. OPIC, Country List, brochure of OPIC, 1975.

7. OPIC, *Topics* (June 1975): 4a.

PART IX. THE HELPING HANDOUT: AID FOR WHOM?

40. Triage?

1. Radha Sinha, *Food and Poverty* (New York: Holmes and Meier, 1976), p. 8.

41. Debt for Development?

1. Food Policy Notes, Interreligious Taskforce on U.S. Food Policy (110 Maryland Ave. NE, Washington, D.C. 20002), October 1976, p. 4.

2. Howard M. Wachtel, *The New Gnomes: Multinational Banks in the Third World* (Washington, D.C.: Transnational Institute, 1977), p. 11.

3. UNCTAD, *Money and Finance and Transfer of Real Resources for Development*, International Financial Cooperation for Development (Report by the UNCTAD Secretariat, TD/188/Supplement), February 1976, p. 32.

4. "What one hand giveth . . . ," *International Bulletin*, May 22, 1978, p. 7

5. UNCTAD, *Debt Problems in the Context of Development* (Report by the Secretariat) 1974, pp. 1, 16.

6. Marcel Barang, "Latest Theories Tested Here," *Far Eastern Economic Review* (May 19, 1978): 30

42. Doesn't Our Food Aid Help?

1. John McClung, "Dr. Spitzer Views Food Resources as Tool in Defending Nation's System," *Feedstuffs* (December 8, 1975): 7.

2. James Reibel, "Food Aid to India" (Mt. Airy Rd., Croton-on-Hudson, N.Y. 10520), 1975, p. 1.

3. Betsy Hartmann and James Boyce, *Bangladesh: Aid to the Needy?* (Washington, D.C.: Center for International Policy, June 1978).

4. Donald F. McHenry and Kai Bird, "Food Bungle in Bangladesh," *Foreign Policy,* Summer 1977, p. 74.

5. *Bangladesh: Food Policy Review,* World Bank (December 12, 1977), p. 39.

6. McHenry and Bird, "Food Bungle in Bangladesh."

7. *Bangladesh: Food Policy Review,* op. cit.

8. Cited by McHenry and Bird, "Food Bungle in Bangladesh," p. 75.

9. Communication on file, Dec. 1977.

10. Cited by McHenry and Bird, "Food Bungle in Bangladesh," p. 78.

11. Cited in *Far Eastern Economic Review,* May 19, 1978, p. 35.

12. F. Thomasson Jannuzi and James T. Peach, *Report on the Hierarchy of Interests in Land in Bangladesh* (USAID, September 1977), p. 88.

13. W. L. Clayton, Assistant Secretary of State, U.S. Congress, House of Representatives, *Hearings on H.R. 2211, Bretton Woods Agreement Act,* Committee on Banking and Currency, 79th Congress, 1st Session (March 9, 1945), pp. 275, 282, cited by Michael Hudson in *Super-Imperialism—The Economic Strategy of American Empire* (New York: Holt, Rinehart and Winston, 1972), pp. 92-93.

14. Eldridge Haynes, ed. and pub., *Business International* and testimony before the Senate Committee on Agriculture and Forestry, *Policies and Operations under P.L. 480* (Washington, D.C.: Government Printing Office, 1957), p. 395.

15. "U.S. Grain Arsenal," Latin America and Empire Report, North American Congress on Latin America (NACLA) 9, 7 (October 1975), p. 9.

16. Ibid.

17. Dan Morgan, "Opening Markets: Program Pushes U.S. Food," *Washington Post,* March 10, 1975.

18. Dan Morgan, "Impact of U.S. Food Heavy on South Korea," *Washington Post,* March 12, 1975.

19. North American Congress on Latin America (NACLA), interview with George Shanklin, Assistant Administrator, Commercial Export Programs, "U.S. Grain Arsenal," *NACLA Reports,* October, 1975, p. 23.

20. Arthur Mead, "P.L. 480—Humanitarian Effort Helps Develop Markets," *Foreign Agriculture* (USDA) 13 (May 26, 1975): 29.

21. Dan Morgan, "Self-Interest, Markets Bedevil World Food Aid," *Washington Post*, July 5, 1975.

22. Kim Chang Soo, "Korean Farmers Betrayed," *New Asia News*, Nov. 25, 1977 [Tokyo].

23. Loren Fessler, "Population and Food Production in South Korea," *Fieldstaff Reports* XXII, 2, East Asia Series, American University Fieldstaff Inc., New York, 1975.

24. Morgan, "Impact of U.S. Food Heavy on South Korea."

25. Leonard Dudley and Roger Sandilands, "The Side Effects of Foreign Aid: The Case of P.L. 480 Wheat in Colombia," *Economic Development and Cultural Change* (January 1975): 321.

26. Ibid., pp. 331, 332.

27. Ibid.

28. Melvin Burke, "Does 'Food for Peace' Assistance Damage the Bolivian Economy?" *Inter-American Economic Affairs* 25 (1971): 9, 17.

29. J. S. Mann, "The Impact of Public Law 480 on Prices and Domestic Supply of Cereals in India," *Journal of Farm Economics* 49 (February 1969): 143.

30. U.S. General Accounting Office, *Disincentives to Agricultural Production in Developing Countries*, report to the Congress (November 26, 1975), p. 25.

31. We are grateful to William Ruddell and Roland Bunch for interviews, August 1977, Antigua, Guatemala.

32. Pierre Spitz, "L'Arme de l'Aide Alimentaire: Les Années d'Apprentissage 1917-1947," *Critiques de l'Economie Politique* (January-March 1974).

33. Pierre Spitz, "Les aides alimentaire, technique et culturelle dans la politique agricole des Etats-unis en Inde depuis la défaite du Kuomintang," *Monde et Developpement*, No. 4. Paris, 1973.

34. Hubert Humphrey, testimony before the Senate Committee on Foreign Relations, 1959.

35. U.S. AID, *U.S. Overseas Loans and Grants and Obligations from International Organizations: Obligations and Loan Authorizations, July 1, 1945-June 30, 1973*, Office of Financial Management.

36. *Washington Post*, October 26, 1974, p. 7.

37. North American Congress on Latin America, p. 13.

38. Ibid., p. 14.

39. Morgan, "Impact of U.S. Food Heavy on South Korea."

40. North American Congress on Latin America, p. 14.

41. Editorial, *The New Republic,* December 7, 1974.

42. Per capita GNP figures are taken from *World Bank Atlas,* 1977, and *World Economic and Social Indicators,* World Bank, April 1978.

43. Seth S. King, "Link to Food-Aid Program Helping Carter's Human Rights Campaign," *New York Times,* December 18, 1977.

44. McHenry and Bird, "Food Bungle in Bangladesh," p. 78.

45. *Bangladesh: Current Economic Situation and Development Policy Issues,* May 19, 1977. World Bank.

46. Ibid.

47. Amnesty International, *Report of an Amnesty International Mission to Bangladesh* (41-12 April 1977), February 1978.

48. Michael Chinoy, "Dacca's Strongman Consolidates," *Far Eastern Economic Review,* January 16, 1976, cited by Hartmann and Boyce, op. cit.

49. McHenry and Bird, "Food Bungle in Bangladesh," pp. 78ff.

43. What About the World Bank's "Assault on Poverty"?

1. Communication from Allison B. Herrick, State Department, Office of Planning and Budget, dated February 24, 1978.

2. We are greatly appreciative of the paper "Development vs. the World System: A Model Policy Planning Country Study of Peru," prepared by development consultant Guy Gran (Washington: AID, March 1978). It catalyzed for us the discussion here of World Bank appraisal reports.

3. World Bank, *Rural Development: Sector Policy Paper* (Washington, D.C., February 1975), p. 18.

4. Betsy Hartmann and James Boyce, *Bangladesh: Aid to the Needy?* (Washington, D.C.: Center for International Policy, June 1978).

5. Hartmann and Boyce, ibid., p. 7.

6. Per-Arne Stroberg, "Water and Development: Orga-

nizational Aspects of a Tubewell Irrigation Project in Bangladesh," Dacca, March 1977, pp. 80-81.

7. Hartmann and Boyce, *Aid to the Needy?* p. 7.

8. IDA News Release, no. 76/22, May 24, 1976.

9. Stroberg, "Water and Development," p. 82.

10. Interview with Hugh Brammer, FAO, Dacca, January 25, 1978, conducted by Joseph Collins.

11. Interview with Errik Jansen, Dacca, January 26, 1978, conducted by Joseph Collins.

12. World Bank, *Rural Development: Sector Policy Paper*, p. 40.

13. Speech by President Robert McNamara to the World Bank Board of Governors, Nairobi, 1973.

14. World Bank, *Assault on World Poverty* (Baltimore: Johns Hopkins University Press, 1975), pp. 106, 118.

15. Ibid., p. 194.

16. Ibid., pp. 154-155.

17. Ibid., pp. 159-160.

18. Hartmann and Boyce, *Aid to the Needy?*, p. 15.

19. "Letter from London," *Far Eastern Economic Review*, February 7, 1975.

20. World Bank, *Assault on World Poverty*, p. 143.

21. Ibid., p. 143.

22. World Bank Annual Report, 1978, pp. 72-79.

23. World Bank, *Assault on World Poverty*, p. 125.

24. Ume Lele, *The Design of Rural Development*, A World Bank Research Publication (Baltimore: Johns Hopkins University Press), pp. 204ff.

25. Barry Newman, "In Indonesia, Attempts by World Bank to Aid Poor Often Go Astray," *Wall Street Journal*, November 19, 1977, p. 1.

26. We have received various communications (some anonymous) from Indonesia on the peasants' resistance to the imposition of this World Bank project. One is an internal World Bank document (C18700/J23823/D2168 Annex 1).

27. World Bank internal document C18700/J23823/D2168, especially pp. 51ff.

28. World Bank, *Assault on World Poverty*, pp. 139-140.

29. Newman, "In Indonesia."

30. Cyrus Vance, "Foreign Assistance and U.S. Foreign Policy," U.S. Department of State, Office of Public Information, May 1, 1978, p. 2.

31. World Bank, *Thailand: Appraisal of the National Agricultural Extension Project*, report no. 1256a-TH., March 10, 1977.

32. World Bank, *Policy and Operations: The World Bank Group*, September 1974, pp. 12f.

33. World Bank, *Zaire—Appraisal of the Oil Palm Project.* Report no. 1592-ZR, March 29, 1978, unpublished.

34. Ibid.

35. Ibid.

36. World Bank, document cited by Susan George, *How the Other Half Dies* (Montclair, N.J.: Allanheld, Osmun & Co., 1977), p. 260.

37. Paul Boucher, in the *Guardian*, June 12, 1975, cited in Susan George, op. cit.

38. "World Bank Sets $2.9 Billion in Loans to Human Rights Violators for Fiscal Year 1979," a research study published by Center for International Policy, Washington, D.C., p. 2.

39. Hon. Tom Harkin, "Human Rights and International Financial Institutions," *Congressional Record*, September 7, 1978, p. E4847.

40. World Bank Annual Report, 1978, pp. 26ff.

41. Hon. Tom Harkin, "Human Rights and International Financial Institutions," p. E4848.

42. Geoffrey Barraclough, "The Struggle for the Third World," *New York Review of Books*, November 9, 1978, pp. 47-49.

43. Howard M. Wachtel, *The New Gnomes: Multinational Banks in the Third World* (Washington, D.C.: Transnational Institute, 1977), p. 39.

44. *Manchester Guardian Weekly*, June 11, 1978.

45. *The Washington Post*, May 19, 1978.

46. Guy Gran, "Zaire 1978," a paper presented at 21st Annual Meeting, African Studies Association, November 4, 1978, unpublished.

47. World Bank Annual Report, 1978, Appendix F, p. 147.

44. And AID's New Directions?

1. H.R. 9005 passed by the Senate, November 1975, p. 35.

2. The most recent survey of studies that comes to this conclusion is *Landlessness and Nearlandlessness in Developing Countries,* Center for International Studies (Ithaca, N.Y.: Cornell University, February 15, 1978), 664 pp.

3. Ibid.

4. Evaluation of Haiti Small Farmer Project, Development Alternatives, Inc., Washington, D.C., June 30, 1977.

5. Credit Programs for Small Farmers in Latin America Can Be Improved, Report to the Congress by the Comptroller General of the United States, December 9, 1977.

6. "The Nicaraguan AID Program: Rural Development Loan—INVIERNO," Washington Office on Latin America, Washington D.C., May 1977, citing "An Evaluation of AID Loan 524-T-031, INVIERNO," ATAK, October, 1976 and "INVIERNO, A Case Study," INCAE (Harvard affiliated Business School), Managua, Nicaragua, 1977 and interviews with Nicaraguan government officials.

7. Agency for International Development, Congressional Presentation Fiscal Year 1979, Annex A, p. 481.

8. Ibid., p. 452.

9. Ibid., p. 481.

10. Ibid., p. 251.

11. Ibid., p. 529.

12. Ibid., p. 330.

13. R. L. Prosterman and C. A. Taylor, "Grading Bureaucratic Compliance: A Briefing Paper on AID's Fiscal Year 1977 Presentation to Congress," unpublished manuscript, March 11, 1976, pp. 12ff.

14. Agency for International Development, op. cit., p. 508.

15. Ibid., p. 733.

16. Baljit Malik, "More Than Just Survival," *Development Forum,* March, 1978, pp. 1-2.

17. LAAD, *Annual Report,* 1974.

18. Jack C. Corbett and Ronald J. Ivey, *Evaluation of the Latin-American Agribusiness Development Corporation,* Checchi and Co., Washington, D.C., July 31, 1974.

19. LAAD, *Annual Report,* 1977.

20. "Evaluation of LAAD De Centroamerica," Checchi and Co., Washington, D.C., November 23, 1977.

21. LAAD, *Annual Report,* 1977, and interview with LAAD Operations Manager Mark Horsky, Santo Domingo, November 27, 1976.

22. LAAD *Annual Report,* 1977.

23. *AID in an Interdependent World,* A Summary of the Presentation to Congress, Agency for International Development, Fiscal Year 1976.

24. AID's Challenge in an Interdependent World, Office of Public Affairs, Agency for International Development, Washington, D.C., 1977.

25. See the appraisal of AID in Peru by Guy Gran, "Development vs. the World System: A Model Policy Planning Country Study of Peru," Agency for International Development, Washington, D.C., March 1978.

26. COFFLA, Special Correspondent's Report from Santiago, November 24, 1972.

27. Patricia Weiss Fagen, "The Links Between Human Rights and Basic Needs," *Background,* Center for International Policy, Washington, D.C., Spring 1978.

28. Joseph D. Collins, "Tightening the Financial Knot," in *Chile: The Allende Years* (New York: IDOC, 1973), 70ff.

29. Center for International Policy, *Human Rights and the U.S. Foreign Assistance Program: Fiscal Year 1978* (Part I—Latin America), Center for International Policy, Washington, D.C., 1978.

30. Ibid.

31. Interviews with U.S. AID officials in Bangkok, Mission of AID, February 1978.

32. Center for International Policy, *Human Rights and the U.S. Foreign Assistance Program: Fiscal Year 1978* (Part II—East Asia), Center for International Policy, Washington, D.C., 1978.

33. Keith Dalton, "The Undernourished Philippines," *Far Eastern Economic Review,* September 1, 1978, p. 35, citing the Asian Development Bank.

34. Ibid., citing the Food and Nutrition Research Institute, Manila.

35. Interview with Joel Rocamora, Philippine scholar, at the Southeast Asia Resource Center, Berkeley, Calif., March 19, 1978.

36. David Wurfel, "Philippine Agrarian Policy Today: Implementation and Political Impact," Institute of Southeast Asian Studies, Singapore, Occasional Paper No. 46, May, 1977.

37. Agency for International Development, Congressional Presentation Fiscal Year 1979, p. 774.

38. See Secretary of State Cyrus Vance, "Foreign Assistance for U.S. Foreign Policy," May 1, 1978, p. 5, and "U.S. Foreign Assistance Programs for Fiscal Year 1979," March 2, 1978, p. 3.

39. Gunnar Myrdal, "Need for Reforms in Underdeveloped Countries," Institute for International Economic Studies, S-106 91, Stockholm, Sweden, 1978, p. 35.

40. Agency for International Development, Congressional Presentation, Fiscal Year 1979, Main Volume, p. 22, 103, 139ff.

41. Testimony of John J. Gilligan, Foreign Assistance and Related Agencies Appropriations for 1979: Hearings before a Subcommittee of the Committee on Appropriations, House of Representatives, p. 707.

42. James Morrell, "Foreign Aid: End Run Around Congress," Center for International Policy, Washington, D.C., 1977.

43. "Human Needs and the International Monetary Fund," Food Policy Notes, Note 78-25, Interreligious Taskforce on U.S. Food Policy, August, 1978; for a general discussion of the role of the IMF, see Cheryl Payer, *The Debt Trap: The IMF and the Third World*, London: Penguin, 1974.

44. Patricia Weiss Fagen, "The Links Between Human Rights and Basic Needs," *Background*, Center for International Policy, 1978, p. 7ff.

45. Jim Morrell, "Behind the Scenes at the IFM," *The Nation*, September 16, 1978.

46. John Markoff and Christopher Pain, "Advice Without Consent: The U.S. Military Abroad," *Pacific Research*, Pacific Studies Center, Mountain View, Calif., January-February, 1978, based on data from "Table B—Human Rights Related Legislative Sanctions on Specific Countries (1976-1977)," Congressional Record, Senate, December 7, 1977, p. S19421; Nancy Stein, Response to FOIA on Special Forces Mobile Training Teams: Department of the Army, September 26, 1975; Harry O. Amos, "The MAAGS Live On," *National Defense*, November-December, 1977, p. 233.

47. Center for International Policy, *Human Rights and the U.S. Foreign Assistance Program: Fiscal Year 1978* (Part II—East Asia), p. 35.

48. Coalition for a New Foreign and Military Policy, "International Human Rights and the Administration's

Security Assistance Program for Fiscal Year 1979," Washington, D.C., March 1978, Nicaragua, p. 2.

49. U.S. Department of Commerce, *Money Income and Poverty Status of Families and Persons in the United States: 1975 and 1974 Revisions* (Advance Report) (Series P-60, no. 103), September 1976.

50. Peter Henle, "Explaining the Distribution of Earned Income," *Monthly Labor Review,* U.S. Department of Labor, December 1972.

51. World Bank, *Size Distribution of Income: A Compilation of Data,* prepared by Shail Jain, 1975, pp. 51, 116.

52. Ibid.

53. U.S. Department of Agriculture, *Farm Income Statistics,* Statistical Bulletin no. 547, July 1975; and U.S. Department of Agriculture, *Agricultural Statistics 1972.*

54. U.S. Department of Agriculture, *Our Land and Water Resources* (USDA/ERS Miscellaneous Publication, no. 1290, May 1974), pp. 23, 32.

45. Can Voluntary Aid Agencies Help?

1. Manzoor Ahmed, *The Savar Project: Meeting the Rural Health Crises in Bangladesh,* International Council for Educational Development, P.O. Box 217, Essex, Connecticut 06426 USA

2. Manzoor Ahmed, *BRAC: Building Human Infrastructures To Serve the Rural Poor,* International Council for Educational Development.

46. What Is Food Self-Reliance?

1. "The Struggle for Self-Reliance in Asia Today," Pan Asian Assembly, May 1976, published by the World Student Christian Federation and the International Movement of Catholic Students Asia Region, P.O. Box 11-1473, Bangkok, Thailand, p. 8.

2. Joseph B. W. Kuitenbrouwer, "Self-Reliance Without Poverty (An Analysis of Pakistan's Fifth Five-Year Plan, 1976-1981)," U.N. Economic and Social Commission for Asia and for the Pacific, Bangkok, Thailand, 1976, p. 94.

3. Lasse Berg and Lisa Berg, *Face to Face* (Berkeley: Ramparts, 1971), p. 174.

4. Joel Rocamora and David O'Conner, "The U.S. Land Reform and Rural Development in the Philippines," in *Logistics of Repression,* Walden Bello and Severina Rivera, eds. Southeast Asia Resource Center, P.O. Box 4000D, Berkeley, Calif., 94704.

5. International Labor Office, *Land Reform in Asia,* Zubeda Ahmad, ed., World Employment Programme Research, Working Papers, 1976.

6. Takedazu Ogura, ed., *Agricultural Development in Modern Japan* (Tokyo: Japan FAO Association, 1976), p. 25.

7. Edgar Owens and Robert Shaw, *Development Reconsidered* (Lexington, Mass.: Heath, 1972), p. 73.

8. *Captives on the Land,* Report of a Consultation on Land, Colombo, Sri Lanka, February, 1976, Christian Conference on Asia—Urban Rural Mission Office, 2-3-18 Nishi-Waseda, Shinjuku-ku Tokyo 160, Japan, p. 11.

9. Theodor Bergmann, *Farm Policies in Socialist Countries* (Lexington, Mass.: Heath, 1975), pp. 129ff.

10. Food and Agriculture Organization, Mission to China, confidential report, 1977.

11. Bergmann, *Farm Policies,* pp. 197ff.

12. Yu-Hsi Chen, "Rural Transformation in Mainland China and Taiwan: A Comparative Study," May, 1976, manuscript, p. 7.

13. Ibid., p. 17.

14. P. L. Raikes, "Ujamaa and Rural Socialism," *Review of African Political Economy,* no. 3, May-June 1975.

15. U.N. Asian Development Institute, "Toward a Theory of Rural Development," prepared by Wahidul Haque, et al., December 1975, 66ff.

16. Azizur Rahman Khan, "China: The Great Exception," in *Poverty and Landlessness in Rural Asia,* a study by the World Employment Programme, International Labor Office, 1977.

17. Roy Preiswerk, "Sources of Resistance to Self-Reliance," manuscript, Institut d'etudes du Developpement, Institut Universitaire de Hautes Etudes Internationales, Geneva, quoting an interview with Samir Amin in *Politique Hebdo,* no. 225, June 3, 1976.

18. Johan Galtung, "Self-Reliance: Concepts, Practice, and Rationale," Ecumenical Institute, Château de Bossey, CH-1298, Celigny, Switzerland, April 1976.

19. Dudley Jackson, "Third World Food Crisis," *New Society* (May 16, 1974): 380.

20. David Feldman and Peter Lawrence, "The Social and Economic Implications of the Large Scale Introduction of New Varieties of Foodgrains," *Africa Report* (Geneva: UNRISD, 1975), p. 215.

21. Chen, "Rural Transformation," p. 21.

22. Sartaj Aziz, "The Chinese Approach to Rural Development," *International Development Review* 15 (1973): 4.

23. Food and Agriculture Organization, "First FAO Professional Study Mission to China: Some Preliminary Observations," October 1975, p. 7.

24. Preiswerk, "Sources of Resistance," p. 10.

25. Kuitenbrouwer, "Self-Reliance Without Poverty," p. 93.

26. Latin America Working Group Letter, vol. 2, no. 7 (February-March 1975): 18-19.

27. Kuitenbrouwer, "Self-Reliance Without Poverty," p. 45.

47. But Where Would Funds for Development Come from?

1. See Dudley Seers, "The Meaning of Development," in *The Political Economy of Development*, Norman T. Uphoff and Warren Ilchman, eds. (Berkeley: University of California Press, 1972).

2. Richard J. Barnet and Ronald Mueller, *Global Reach: The Power of the Multinational Corporations* (New York: Simon and Schuster, 1974).

3. Banco Central, cited in *Latin America Economic Report*, January 9, 1976, vol. 4, no. 2, p. 6.

4. J. Gurley, "Rural Development in China," in *Employment in Developing Nations*, E. D. Edwards, ed. (New York: Columbia University Press, 1974), p. 385.

5. Food and Agriculture Organization, *Progress in Land Reform—Sixth Report*, Rural Institutions Division, Rome, April 1975, pp. III-69, III-70.

6. Kathleen Gough, "The 'Green Revolution' in South India and North Vietnam," *Social Scientist*, Kerala, India, August 1977, no. 61; and the *Bulletin of Concerned Asian Scholars* (forthcoming). See also Gough, *Ten Times More Beautiful* (New York: Monthly Review, 1978).

7. Swedish International Development Authority and Food and Agriculture Organization, "Use of Organic Materials and Green Manures as Fertilizers in Developing Countries" prepared by Ambika Singh, in *Organic Materials as Fertilizers,* Rome, 1975, p. 29.

8. Amulya Kumar and N. Reddy, "The Trojan Horse," *Ceres* (March-April 1976): 43; for greater detail see Arjun Makhijani with Alan Poole, *Energy and Agriculture in the Third World* (Cambridge, Mass.: Ballinger, 1976), Chapter 4.

48. Aren't Poor Peasants Too Oppressed Ever to Change?

1. Wahidul Haque, et al., "An Approach to Micro-Level Development: Designing and Evaluation of Rural Development Projects," United Nations Asian Development Institute, February 1977, p. 15.

2. Lasse Berg and Lisa Berg, *Face to Face* (Berkeley, Calif.: Ramparts, 1970), p. 154.

50. What Can We Do?

1. U.S. Department of Agriculture, *Our Land and Water Resources* (USDA/ERS, Miscellaneous Publication, no. 1290, 1974), pp. 23, 32.

Index

A

Abbott Laboratories, 337, 343, 375
Abourezk, Senator James, 203
Accountability, lack of
  grain corporations, 260
  World Bank, 435
  P.L. 480, 380-81
Adamson, Alan, 108
ADELA, 423
Advertising
  in food industry, 324, 327-29, 333, 334-35
  of infant formula, 342-48
Africa (see also individual countries; Colonialism;

Sahel; Cash Crops)
  agribusiness in, 286-89, 404
  commercial agriculture vs. subsistence, 102-103, 110
  contribution of agriculture to GNP, 469
  game animals in, 47
  pastoral nomadism, 44-47, 86
  people-to-cultivated acre ratio, 18-19
  protein-calorie malnutri-dividual corporations, tion, 18-19
  slave trade, 86, 113-14
Afghanistan, 426
Agribusiness (see also in-

food processing, Cartels, export agriculture)

Advertising in underdeveloped countries, 321, 324, 326, 328

in Africa, 286-88

in Bangladesh, 280

in Central America, 283, 300

commodities trade, 216-24

contract farming, 280-86, 299-302, 303-304, 318

corporate farms, 302-303

and employment, 299-319

flowers, 155, 294-95, 296

Global Farm/Supermarket, 278-81, 350, 404

in Hawaii, 348-50

impact of, 348 ff., 478-80

in Iran, 313-16

land reform, 312-16, 318-19

livestock, 289-92

Mexico, 126-27, 155-56, 280-82, 284-86, 350, 352

monopoly of farm inputs, 270

myth of productivity, 277-78

in Philippines (see Del Monte), 279-80, 348-49

poultry industry, 293-94, 304-306, 371

U.S. consumers, 354-55

and U.S. foreign policy, 355, 386

U.S. government support for, 74, 175, 247, 258-59, 352-54, 498-99

Agribusiness Accountability Project, 307-308

Agricultural Adjustment Act, 54-55

Agricultural Minimum Wages Act (Kerala, India), 174

Agriculture
and employment, 24-27
and industry, 25-27, 168, 252, 270, 419, 469-71

Aid, foreign (see U.S. AID, World Bank)
and debt, 361-62
and export cropping, 90-91, 396-400
redefining, 493-94

Aid, voluntary (see Voluntary Agencies)

de Alcántara, Cynthia H., 190, 191

Algeria, 85

Amazon River basin, 48-52

American Agriculture Movement, 266-67

American Foods Share Co., 288

American Friends Service Committee, 450, 453

American Home Products, 337

Americans, responsibilities of, 6-7, 8-9, 491-93, 503-504
democratize U.S. food economy, 497-99
grass root causes, 492-93
hunger re-education, 494-97
life choices, 500-504
make U.S. "safe for the world," 498 ff.
redefining "help," 493-94
work for self-reliance, 496-97

Amin, Samir, 467

Amnesty International, 385

Anderson, Clayton, 50, 251, 479

Angola, 110, 486

Andreas, Dwayne, 250

Anthan, George, 305-306

Appropriate technology, 171-74, 178-79
biogas, 178-79, 483

Arbor Acres, 307

Argentina, 56
and the IMF, 436
and World Bank, 406

Arizona, 72

Arvin and Dinuba (California) study, 265-66

Asian Development Bank, 430

At Home Abroad, 325

B

Bahamas, 352

Balance of payments, 240 ff.

Ballis, George, 308-309

Bananas (see also Castle & Cooke, United Brands, Del Monte)
in Central America, 209 ff.
corporate control, 218-19
cost breakdown, 218
mechanization of industry, 28
in Philippines, 218-19, 279

Bangladesh, 19-24
Bangladesh Rural Advancement Committee, 450-54
birth rates, 32
cooperative agriculture, 462
debt, 362
fish resources, 22-23
Gonoshasthaya Kendra, 450
Green Revolution in, 131-32, 138, 139
irrigation, 21, 22
landless laborers, 20, 141
landownership, concentration, 139, 391
population control, 37
rice after 1974 floods, 20
rice varieties, 160
sharecroppers, 21, 393

speculation of food, 20
Voluntary Agency &
   Programs, 449-54
underutilized resources,
   20
U.S. AID, 418-19, 437
U.S. food aid, 366-68,
   384, 384-85
World Bank programs,
   389-93, 401, 405-406,
   409-10
Bank of America, 280, 314,
   370, 423
Barbados, 42
Barrons, 348
Bartol, Ian, 341
Basic needs (see also World
   Bank)
   and human rights, 406-
   409
   met in Cuba, 231-32
   as strategy of World
   Bank, 388 ff., 398
"Basketcase" countries
   (see Bangladesh,
   MSA's, Sahel)
Bata Shoe Co., 479
Beef (see also Livestock)
   consumer demand for,
   45, 50, 165-66, 290-
   91
   as export commodity, 47,
   50, 94, 168, 289-92,
   424
   U.S. importer of, 238-39
Bengal famine, 80, 81
Berg, Alan, 289, 335,
   338 ff., 345
Berg, Lasse & Lisa, 485-86

Better Homes and Gardens,
   survey, 322
Bibliography (see Appen-
   dix B)
Biogasification, 179, 483
Birth control, 36-39
Birth rates, 33-39
   decline in, 34 ff.
   and infant formula,
   336 ff.
Blobaum, Roger, 174
Bolivia, 19, 375, 383, 417,
   464
Borden, 50, 74, 337, 423
Borlaug, Norman, 134-35,
   185
"Bottle Babies," 346-47
Boyce, James, 366, 385,
   387, 390
Brady, Nyle C., 131
Brazil, 440
   Amazon River basin, 48-
   53
   coffee, 218
   commercial agriculture
   vs. subsistence, 223-24
   grain for beef, 16
   industrial development,
   479
   infant mortality, 49
   land ownership, 49
   land reform, 313 ff.
   livestock, 16, 50
   locally improved varieties
   (wheat), 149
   market for processed
   foods, 322-23
   multinationals, 49-50
   OPIC, 353, 354

people-to-cultivated land ratio, 48
soft drinks, 331-33
soybean exports, 223-24, 250-51
World Bank Loans, 407, 437, 441
C. Brewer and Company, Ltd. (Hawaiian Agronomics), 314
Bristol Myers, 337, 346
Brown, Lester R., 5, 81, 95, 168, 175, 320
Bruyznell, 50
Bud Antle, Inc. (Bud Senegal), 286 ff., 404
Bunch, Roland, 377
Burundi, 210
Business International, 370
Business Week, 57, 256, 264, 321
Butz, Earl, 50, 245, 255, 257, 274
By Bread Alone, 40

C

Cadbury, 104-105
California
competition from Mexico, 350
land concentration, 202
large farm vs. small farm community, 265-66
mechanization, 143
pesticides in, 69, 73, 76

Cambodia, 379, 380, 381, 382
Camacho, Avila, 125 ff.
Cameroon, 421, 479
Canada
Food First policies, 475
grain production, 254
Mexican strawberries, 284
resource groups in, 513
Cárdenas, Lázaro, 123-26
CARE, 368-69, 376-77
Cargill, Inc., 251, 257, 258, 259, 371, 423
Caribbean (see also individual countries)
environmental destruction, 41-42
land use, 41-42
Carnation Co., 337
Cartels, 216-20
Carter, James, 408, 409
Cash crops (see also colonialism, export crops, agribusiness, monoculture)
commercial agriculture vs. subsistence, 220-21, 228-29, 279-80, 396-99, 486-87
dependence on single crop, 209 ff., 213-14, 222-24
and environmental destruction, 43, 52
food production decline, 225, 227-29
and land use, 209 ff.
"rewards" of, 214 ff.

World Bank policy on, 397

Cassava, 16-17, 144, 223

Castle and Cooke (Dole and Standard Fruit), 219, 220, 286, 348, 350, 424

Caterpillar Tractor, 48, 176

Catholic Relief Services, 376

Cattle Production (see beef, livestock, overgrazing)

Center for International Policy, 435, 437

Center-pivot irrigation (see irrigation)

Central America (see individual countries)
  export agriculture, 167-68, 283, 289-90
  land reform, 313 ff.
  land use, 192

Central Soya, 251

Chad, 90-91, 480

Chase Manhattan Bank, 251, 314

Chavez, Cesar, 286

Checchi & Co., 425

Chemical corporations (see individual companies, fertilizers, pesticides, ecological destruction)
  pesticide corporations, 74-75
  Pesticide Working Group (FAO), 74-75

Children, economic value of, 30-31, 34-35, 37
  labor of, 30-31, 310
  target of advertising, 329

Chile,
  agrarian reform in, 427-29, 463
  human rights in, 406, 428, 429, 438
  mechanization, 28
  OPIC, 353
  U.S. AID, 379, 382, 413, 435, 443
  and World Bank, 406

China,
  agricultural planning process, 173-74, 469, 472
  biogas, 178-79
  communes, 197-98, 462-63
  comparison with India, 198
  desert reclamation, 85
  end of hunger, 18
  famine in, 81 ff.
  fertilizer, 163
  greater production from greater equality, 201
  industry and agriculture, 469-70
  labor force, 26, 172
  labor productivity, 25
  land reform, 197-98, 462, 465, 466-67
  mechanization, 176-77
  new seed varieties, 133-34, 149, 150
  people-to-cultivated acre ratio, 18
  pest control, 73
  pig raising, 58
  price stability, 469

rural industry, 170, 173-74
Tachai, 198, 481
taxation, 469
water control, 81-83
China, Land of Famine, 81
Chinese Academy of Science, 150
Church Women United, 346
Clarke, Thurston, 87
Citrus fruits, 69 ff.
Clergy and Laity Concerned, 346
Closing Circle, The, 38
Coca-Cola Company, 302, 330, 331, 332, 333, 334
Cocoa, 105, 209, 212-13, 216-17, 225-26
Coffee,
   competition among producers, 216
   expansion in Africa, 227
   and foreign exchange, 210
   in Haiti, 416
   high-yield varieties, 138, 139
   land devoted to, 41, 42, 139, 210
   mechanization of, 28
   price fluctuations, 211-12, 221
   U.S. corporations' control over, 218
Collier, Peter, 7
Colombia, 113
   flowers, 294-95

government credit for cash crops, 227-28
Green Revolution, 138, 141, 166-67
land ownership, 42-43
land reform, 313 ff.
landless laborers, 141
mechanization, 28
milk imports vs. breast-feeding, 345
poultry-feed industry, 292-94
wheat production and U.S. food aid, 374-75
and U.S. AID, 374, 419
Colonialism, 99-117 (see also individual countries, regions, underdeveloped countries)
   in British Guyana, 108-109
   cash crops, 41, 103-104, 108-109, 211
   dualism, 116-17
   ecosystem, destruction of, 5, 40-41
   elite, creation of, 114
   forced migration, 107-108
   imported foodstuff dependency, 109-10
   in India, 79-81, 114-15
   in Indonesia, 104, 106, 110, 115
   marketing boards, 104-105, 222
   mentality, 101-102
   moneylenders, 114-15
   monoculture, 108-10

plantations, 103, 105-107, 404

precolonial social structures, 100

slavery, 86, 113

suppression of peasant competition, 106-107, 110

taxation, 45, 87, 107, 114-15

traditional society disruption, 86, 103-109, 111-12, 114

trade, 109

in Vietnam, 103, 114

in West Indies, 109-10

Colorado Cattle Feeders Association, 240

Commercial agriculture vs. subsistence, 107-21, 144, 220-21, 228-29, 279-80, 289-96, 335, 396-99, 487

Commodities (see individual commodities; cash crops, trade)

producers associations, 216, 219

United States imports, 249

Commodity Credit Corporation (see U.S. Dept. of Agriculture)

Commodity prices (see also trade)

instability of, 56-58, 213-14

market control, 216-20

Commoner, Barry, 38, 242

Competition, 22, 31, 216, 226

Consumers Union, 344

Continental Grain, 256-60

Contract Farming (see also Agribusiness), 281-86, 299-302, 304, 317-18

convenience foods, 321-26

Cook Industries, 255, 259

Cooperation (see also China, Vietnam), 15, 22, 23, 93, 193-94, 451, 453

Cooperative farms, 452, 461, 481-84

Corn, 152, 153, 157, 159-60, 161, 166 ff., 317-19

Cornuelle, Herbert C., 320

Costa Rica, 71, 289-91, 300, 353, 419

Cotton, 16, 41, 87, 89-90, 91, 171, 223

and insecticides, 60, 61-62, 71

in Nicaragua, 62, 227

Cox, David O., 342

CPC International, 166 ff.

advertising, 323

and AID, 423

Cooley loans, 370

corn, in Pakistan, 316-19

Credit (see also U.S. AID, World Bank, landlords)

access to, 15, 185, 186, 188 ff., 394, 436

debt bondage, 143-44, 187

export production, 227, 397

and World Bank, 290, 391-95, 397, 403-404, 406-408

Crop rotation, 71, 151, 188

Cuba

agrarian reform, 198-99, 461

decision-making, 199, 472

employment, 28

export agriculture (compared to Dominican Republic), 230-31

mechanization, 177, 199

national diversification of agriculture, 232-33

people-to-land ratio, 19

rationing, 202

rural development, 470

schools in the countryside, 199, 470

sugar, 199, 230-33

tractors, 177

Cucumbers, 283

Cow and Gate Co., 340-41

Cravioto, Joaquin, 335

Crystal City, Texas, 307-309

D

Dahomey, 103

Dasmann, Raymond F., 47

David, Raymond, 65

DBCP, 67 (see Pesticides)

DDT (see Pesticides)

Debt, 228 (see also Underdeveloped countries; Credit)

Debt-service payments, 228-29, 361, 435

Deep water wells, 46

Deere and Company, 175, 176, 314-15, 424

DeKalb Ag Research, 160

Del Monte, 210, 219, 279-80, 334

in California, 308

in Costa Rica, 300

in Crystal City, Texas, 307-308

employment, 308-309

in Guatemala, 107, 300

in Hawaii, 348-49, 351

in Kenya, 353

in Mexico, 280-82, 303, 334

in Philippines, 65-66, 279-80, 313

in U.S., 302-303, 327

de Pury, Pascal, 173

Democracy, 23, 240, 273 (see also Food Producing Resources, Control of)

Desert, 84-96 (see Sahel)

and overgrazing, 44-48

Devaluation of currency, 245, 436

Development Alternatives Inc., 415

Development capital, 476-84

Development models, 215, 229, 402-403, 408, 410

Dias, Anne, 333

Diet for a Small Planet, 7, 99, 152-53, 228, 491-92, 500

Direct marketing (food), 272-73

Dollar devaluation, 245-46

Dominican Republic, 19
 contrasted with Cuba, 230 ff.
 food exports, 289
 food aid, 373
 sugar exports and well-being of people, 222

Drought, 79-96
 in China, 81-82
 in Sahel, 56, 84-85, 89
 worldwide (1972-73), 56

Drucker, Peter, 322

Dumont, Rene, 127

duPont, 66

Dwarf seed varieties (see Seeds)

E

Eames, Alfred J., 279

Eckholm, Erik, 42

Ecological destruction, 40-52, 67-68 (see also Fertilizers; Pesticides)
 in Africa, 42, 87-88
 in Brazil, 50-52
 center-pivot irrigation, 253-54
 colonialism, 40-41
 destruction of shade cover, 416
 destruction in Caribbean, 41 ff.
 in El Salvador, 41
 and increased roads, 421-22
 genetic loss, 132, 157-60
 overgrazing, 44-48
 preventive measures in China, 82-83
 saline seepage, 254
 soil depletion, 16-17, 40-43, 51-52, 161-62, 253-54, 285
 in South America, 42-43, 50
 tropical forests, 48-53

Economic Development Bureau (EDB), 447, 448, 449, 453

Economic value of children, 30-33

Ecuador, 184, 192, 295

Education and literacy, 450 ff., 463, 470

Economist, 94

Eggs, in Colombia, 292-94

Egypt, 62, 65
 AID program, 434
 food aid to, 373
 and the IMF, 436
 land reform, 459
 locally improved seeds, 149-50

El Salvador, 41, 438, 449

Employment (see also Mechanization; Industrialization)
agricultural workers, 25
in Cuba, 28, 232
industrial, 25-27
monoculture and, 27-28
multinational corporations, 26
unemployment, 171, 231-32
U.S. AID, 224-25, 419

England, 27

Environment (see Ecological Destruction)

Ethiopia, 210, 288-89, 432-33

European Common Market, 58-59, 287

Export Agriculture, 15-17 (see also Colonialism; Cash crops; Luxury Crops, Trade; Agribusiness)
benefit to elites, 91-92, 225, 227-30, 400
Central America, 16, 283, 289, 290
the enemy?, 229-33, 399
expansion of, 45-46, 80-81, 167-68
flowers, 155, 294-95
forced cultivation, 87, 227-28
foreign exchange earnings, 220-24
grapes, 155
growth rates of, 227-28
Mexico, 280-86, 309-12, 350
Philippines, 279-80, 348-49
plantations, 105-106
Sahel, 89, 93 ff., 286, 288
U.S. support of, 351-54
World Bank support of, 396-99, 403-405

Export Platform, 241, 419

Extension services, access to, 15

Exxon (Standard Oil), 124, 204

F

Face to Face, 485-86

Family farms (see Small farms)

Family planning, 30-39 (see also Population)

Famine (see also Sahel, Bangladesh)
in Bengal, 80-81
history of, 79-83
in Jamaica, 109-10

Far Eastern Economic Review, 396

Farm debt, 20, 114-15, 187, 263-64

Farm efficiency and size, 183-96 (see also Small farms; Mechanizaton)

Farm labor (see also Landless laborers; unemployment)

child labor, 311
low cost of in Mexico,
281-85
migrant workers, 231
on plantations, 103, 106-
108, 404
slavery, 86, 113
Farvar, M. Taghi, 64, 66
Feder, Ernest, 284-85, 309-
10
Fertilizers (see also Soil
Depletion; Green Rev-
olution)
dependence on, 88, 157,
161-62, 172, 416
nitrogen-fixing crops,
150-51
organic sources, 178
rising prices, 57, 88, 162
use in India, 483
use in U.S., 161-62
use in Vietnam, 483
Firestone Tire and Rubber
Co., 103, 179, 421
Fishery resources
in Bangladesh, 22-23
effects of pesticides on,
66
Florida Peach Corporation
of America, 251
Flowers, as export crop,
155, 294-95
FMC, 176, 180
Food
energy consumption, 272
global supply, 13, 121-
22, 154-55
high cost of, 335, 340,
342

incentives to produce,
14-15, 22-23, 123-24,
164, 187, 451-52
instability of, 54-55, 56-
57, 93, 164-65, 211 ff.,
215, 246-47, 259-60,
268, 416, 436-37
more food, more hunger,
145-47, 165-68, 457-
58
overproduction and sur-
plus, 54, 57-58, 165-
68, 256 ff., 261, 267-
68, 283, 365 ff., 457-
58
prices compared to U.S.
costs, 268-69
prices and instability, 57-
58, 93, 164-65, 416,
436-37
Food Aid (see also U.S.
AID; World Bank)
as aid to corporate in-
vestment (Cooley
Loans), 370, 372-75
as production disincen-
tive, 373 ff.
in Bangladesh, 384-85,
387
in Bolivia, 375
building markets, 371
in Cambodia, 380, 381
in Colombia, 374 ff.
after Chile coup, 379,
380
as extension of foreign
policy, 373, 378 ff.
Food for Peace, 363-83
Food for work, 367-69

in Guatemala, 377
guise for military support, 374, 380-82
market development, 369-72, 386
"new directions," 383-86
relief aid, 367, 376-78, 386
in South Korea, 373, 379
in South Vietnam, 380-82
stabilizing governments, 366-69, 385, 386-87
surplus disposal, 365 ff., 379
triage, 359-60
and underdeveloped countries, 237, 373 ff.
vs. commercial exports, 237
and World Food program, 379-80
Food and Agricultural Organization (FAO)
on Bangladesh, 368
Farm Mechanization Working Group, 176
Industry Cooperative Program, 74-75
Integrated Meat Development Working Group, 307
Pesticide Working Group, 74-75
Plant Protection Service, 61
Food Cooperatives, 496-97

Food Day, 7
Food deficit areas (see MSA's, Sahel, and Bangladesh)
Food First, meaning of, 90-91, 271-72
Food for Work programs, 414
Food Power, 55, 237-74
American consumer, 266-70
and "free market," 255-62
benefits to grain trading corporations, 255-60, 271
impact on small farmer, 261-66, 271
long-run ecological costs, 253-54
support for U.S. military presence, 271
Soviet grain deal, 55-56, 245 ff., 256-61
vs. Food First, 271-74
Food processing industry, 167, 313
acquisition strategy, 324 ff.
advertising, 324, 327 ff., 339
breakfast cereal industry, 326-27
cost of processed foods, 326-27
concentration of control in, 217, 218, 269-70, 302 ff.

convenience foods, 321-22

diversification into non-food products, 322

impact on nutrition, 270, 321, 326, 327, 329, 333-34

infant formula, 336 ff.

overseas expansion of, 322, 328

research and development costs, 326

share of retail food dollar, 269

soft drinks, 330-33

Food producing resources, control of (see also Self-reliance; Land; Landlords)

control of grain trade, 255

concentration of, 10, 14, 22, 41-43, 49, 58, 115-16, 138-40, 154-55, 174, 183 ff., 202 ff., 217-18, 220-21, 230 ff., 263, 266, 272-73, 391, 430, 439, 497-98

decision-making, 199

democratization of, 272, 442

misuse of, 15-17, 44-48, 166-67, 283

monopoly, 10, 217-18, 266, 269-70

redistribution of, 431

underutilization of, 14-15, 42-43, 391

Food redistribution, not the solution, 6-7

Food security, 154-65 (see also Self-reliance; Food)

Food Self-Reliance (see Self-Reliance)

Food stamps, 17, 270

Forbes, 251

Ford Foundation, 127

Foreign exchange (see trade)

Foreign investment (see also Agribusiness; Multinational corporations; Underdeveloped countries)

capital investment of U.S.-based multinational corporations, 241, 371, 389, 400, 404, 436

in land in U.S., 264

in South Korea, 371-74

Forests

comparison of North American and Amazon, 51-52

destruction of, 42, 50

Formula feeding, 336 ff.

Fossil fuels, 239-40, 242-43 (see also Fertilizers)

France, 18, 19, 103, 114, 284

Frank, André Gunder, 220-21

"Free market" (see Food Power)

Free trade (see Trade)
Freeman, Orville, 309, 372-73
Freire, Paulo, 448
Fungicides, 69-70 (see also Pesticides)

G

Galeano, Eduardo, 112-13
Galtung, Johan, 468, 471
Gambia, 102
Game Cropping, 47 (see also livestock)
General Foods, 4, 212, 325, 329, 336, 478
General Mills, 322, 326, 327
Genetic diversity, 132, 157-60 (see also Green Revolution)
George, Susan, 411
Georgia Pacific, 50
Gerber, 423
Germany, Federal Republic of, 237-38
Ghana, 18, 102-103, 213, 216, 217, 225-26
Global Farm, 278-80
Global Reach, 7
Global Supermarket, 167-68, 278-80, 350-51, 427, 429, 475, 501 (see also Agribusiness; Food; Food producing resources)

GNP, as social indicator, 146-47, 384
Goldberg, Ray, 282
Goldschmidt, Walter, 266
Goodyear, 50, 423
Gough, Kathleen, 481-84
W. R. Grace Co., 324
Grain
imports by industrial countries, 237-38
and poultry industry, 304
for livestock and poultry, 292-93, 371
reserves, U.S., 56, 246
Soviet grain purchases, 245 ff.
speculation, 20, 88, 94
trading corporations, 246, 255-60, 271, 365
world grain production, 13, 121-22, 154
Greece, 135-36
Green manuring, 157 (see also Fertilizers)
Green Revolution, 121-96 (see also Mechanization; Seeds; Fertilizers)
agriculture serving industry, 124-28
in Bangladesh, 139, 141, 146
benefits to large farmers, 128, 135-39
bought us time?, 147-48
in Colombia, 138, 139, 141
divorce of agriculture and nutrition, 145-48, 152-53

effects on small farmers,
128, 136-37, 145-46
and food security, 154-
65
genetic narrowing, 132,
157-60
in India, 29, 130-31, 132,
138-41
in Indonesia, 132, 141,
149, 156
increased production,
121, 134-48, 150
land concentration, 138-
40
landless laborers, 140-44,
145, 147
and mechanization, 172
in Mexico, 121, 122, 123-
27, 131, 142-43
monoculture, focus of,
151-52, 157-58, 164
in Morocco, 139
in Pakistan, 130, 141,
142
in Philippines, 146
in Sri Lanka, 149
taxes increased, 138
in Upper Volta, 130
vulnerability to disease,
131-34, 156-58
Griffin, Keith, 175, 187
Gross National Product
(GNP), 146, 384
Guadeloupe, 42
Guatemala,
child malnutrition, 221
coffee, 28
Del Monte in, 107, 300,
349

earthquake relief proj-
ects, 376-78
flowers, 295
food aid, 376-78
infant formula, 340, 343
LAAD loans, 425
mechanization and em-
ployment, 28
World Bank loans, 394
Guinea Bissau, 447, 449,
486
Gulf and Western, Inc.,
231, 251
Guyana (British Guyana),
108-109
Gyorgy, Paul, 338

H

Haiti, 19, 42, 368-69, 383,
415, 422, 440, 441
Hanbury-Tenison, Robin,
53
Hanlon, Joseph, 178-79
Hanover Brands, 425
Hardin, Garrett, 6, 360
Harkin Amendment, 400
Harrar, George, 148
Harrigan, Anthony, 5
Hartmann, Betsy, 366, 385,
387, 390
Hawaii, 348-49
Hawaiian Agronomics,
(C. Brewer and Co.),
314
Haynes, Eldridge, 370

Health care
  in Bangladesh, 451-53
  in China, 37-38
  decline in Chile, 429
Heinz, H. I., 302
High yielding varieties
    (HYV's) (see Seeds;
    Green Revolution)
Hightower, Jim, 261-62,
    304, 308, 326-27, 351
Hillman, Elizabeth, 347-48
Hoarding, 93 (see also
    Speculation)
Hodges, Tony, 349
Hoechst, 74, 75
Hoffman-LaRoche, 74
Honduras,
  Bananas, 218, 219
  pesticide use and malaria,
    63
  plantations abandoned,
    210
  United Brands bribery,
    219
Hoover, Herbert, 378
Hormel Meats, 426
*How Europe Underdevel-
    oped Africa,* 103, 105,
    113
How the Other Half Dies,
    411
HRV's (see Seeds; Green
    Revolution)
Human rights
  in Bangladesh, 384
  Center for International
    Policy Report, 437
  in Chile, 406, 428, 429,
    438

and Food Aid, 383-87
and Food First, 273, 380
in Nicaragua, 432-33
in South Africa, 435
in South Korea, 435
violators of, 384, 431
and the World Bank,
    406-409
Humphrey, Hubert, 379,
    387
Huston, Perdita, 32
Hybrid seeds (see Seeds)

I

Import quotas, 216 ff.
Import tariffs, 216 ff.
India
  birth control, 38
  biogas, 179, 483
  colonial effects on agri-
    culture, 79-80, 114-15
  compared to Thai Binh,
    Vietnam, 481-84
  divorce of agriculture
    and nutrition, 147
  Emergency Food Act,
    364
  farm productivity, 25
  famine in Bengal, 378
  fertilizer, 151, 483
  food imports, 238, 360
  food aid and domestic
    production, 376
  food processing industry,
    334

grain production, 457
Green Revolution, 29, 130-31, 132, 138-41
industrial decentralization attempts, 470-71
land concentration, 139
land reform and landless laborers, 459
land speculation, 137-38
landless laborers, 141, 147
mechanization, 29, 174, 176
nutritional well-being, 334, 338
population growth, 31-32, 34-35
sharecroppers, 136, 137, 186
small farm productivity, 183, 186
Indonesia (Java), 150
Dutch colonial policies, 104, 106, 110, 115
Green Revolution, 132, 141; 149, 156
landless laborers, 141
OPIC, 354
pesticide damage, 66
poverty and GNP, 146-47
and U.S. AID, 418, 420, 433, 437
World Bank loans, 398, 400, 407, 437
Industrial countries
as food importers, 237-39, 252, 279, 287, 360

Industrialization
and agriculture, 25-27, 168, 252, 270, 419, 469-71
and employment, 25-27, 469-71
Industry Cooperative Program (of the F.A.O.), 74-75
Inefficiency (see also Food producing resources, control of)
of giant food companies, 324
and inequality, 9, 183-96
land use, 14-15, 192, 209
of monopolies, 9, 23 217, 266, 269-70
Inequality (see Food producing resources, control of)
increasing in U.S., 438-39
and inefficiency, 9, 183-96
Infant Formula Action Coalition (INFACT), 346
Infant malnutrition
in Africa, 340, 345
Fanta babies, 333
in Guatemala, 340
infant formula controversy, 336-46
milk banks, 343
in Philippines, 345
Infant mortality
in Africa, 340

in Brazil, 49
in Chile, 427
infant formula feeding,
336-46
in India, 338
in U.S., 346
Infrastructure, 400, 403,
418-23
Insecticides (see Pesticides)
Institute for Food & De-
velopment Policy, 397,
495
Integrated Pest Manage-
ment (IPM)
alternative to pesticides,
70
and crop rotation, 71
success in U.S., 72-73
success in China, 73
Interamerican Develop-
ment Bank
loans to Chile, 428
loans to Nicaragua, 432
Interfaith Center for Corporate Responsibility
(ICCR), 346
International Flavors and
Fragrances, 336
International Harvester,
175
International Labor Or-
ganization (ILO), 145-
46
International Monetary
Fund, 435-37
lending criteria of, 436
loans to South Africa,
422

most powerful financial
institution, 435
no accountability, 435
U.S. veto power in, 435
International Rice Re-
search Institute (IRRI),
127-28, 131, 149, 169
International Telephone
and Telegraph Co.,
334, 335
Iowa, 162, 253
Iran
Khuzestan, 313-16
land reform, 175, 313-16
livestock, 315
locally improved seeds,
149
mechanization, 176
sugar consumption, 330
unemployment, 315-16
U.S. assistance to, 442
Iraq, 149
Irish potato blight, 157
Irrigation (see also Green
Revolution)
in Bangladesh, 21, 22,
390-93
center-pivot, 253
China, 82-83
India, 183, 482
Iran, 314-15
saline seepage, 254
Vietnam, 482
Zamora Valley, Mexico,
312
Israel, 434
Ivory Coast, 90, 222, 367

J

Jacobsen, Michael, 327
Jacoby, Charlotte and
    Erich, 187, 188-89
Jamaica, 110, 436-37
Japan
    food imported from U.S.,
        56, 237, 248
    labor-intensive farming,
        25
    and land reform, 459
    locally improved seeds,
        149
    mechanization, 169, 177
    pesticide standards, 67
    small farmers, 169
Jolly, Hugh, 338
Justice and Peace, 449

K

Kellogg's, 334
Kenya, 18, 223, 345, 349,
    353
Kerr, Warwick, 48
Kersten, Charles, 364-65
Khuzestan (Iran), 313-16
Kissinger, Henry, 53, 95
Kruitenbrouwer, J. B. W.,
    459, 472

L

Labor-intensive farming
    (see also small farms),
    25

Ladejinsky, Wolf, 137
La Leche League Interna-
    tional, 344
Land (see also Food Pro-
    ducing Resources,
    Control of; Cash
    Crops, Export Agri-
    culture)
    misuse of, 15, 209
    private ownership of, 15,
        21, 114-15
    reclamation, 85
    underutilization, 14 ff.,
        192
Land grant colleges
    and agribusiness, 74
Landless laborers
    in Asia, 195
    in Bangladesh, 20, 141
    in Brazil, 48
    in Chile, 429
    Green Revolution, 140-
        44, 145, 147
    in Guatemala, 394
    increased under colonial-
        ism, 116
    in Iran, 315-16
    and land reform, 458 ff.
    in Mexico, 285, 310-11
    as percentage of rural
        labor, 413
    in Philippines, 430
    and U.S. AID, 414
    wages, 226
    and World Bank, 395-
        96
Landlords, 115 (see also
    Colonialism)
    absentee, 21, 41

benefits to, 21, 136-37, 189-90, 391, 414
conspicuous consumption, 191-92
as moneylenders, 20, 114-15, 187, 395
risk-taking, 190-91
sabotaging irrigation, 452
traditional obligations, 136, 141, 414
Land reform, 187-98
in China, 197-98, 462, 465, 466-67
fake, 48 ff., 313-16, 458 ff.
in Mexico, 123-27
misconceptions, 200-202
Philippines, 227
and productivity, 197-200, 461
United States, 202-205
Vietnam, 197, 201, 462
Land speculation, 137-38, 264
Land-to-person ratios, 18-19, 25
Laos, 384
Latin America (see also individual countries)
agricultural mechanization, 142-43, 172, 177
colonial inheritance, 101-17
debt bondage, 187
LAAD, 423-26
landless, 195
as market for processed food, 322-23

nutrition and malnutrition, 19, 222
population density, 19
small-farm productivity, 184
U.S. AID loans, 417-18
World Bank livestock loans, 397
Latin American Agribusiness Development Corporation (LAAD), 423-26
Ledogar, Robert (*Hungry for Profits*), 329, 331
Legumes, 151, 153 (see also Fertilizers)
Lele, Uma, 223, 293
Leveen, Phillip, 204
Liberia, 103, 110, 421
"Lifeboat ethics," 6, 361 (see also Triage)
Lilienthal, David, 314
Liguigas, 50, 74
Livestock (see also beef; overgrazing)
cassava consumption, 16-17, 144
for export, 16, 19, 41, 289-92
grain consumption by, 13, 16, 58, 166, 167, 291-92
milk consumption, 58-59
mixed herds, 44-45
vs. game cropping, 47
World Bank, credit to, 397-98
Long, Ngo Vinh, 201
Los Angeles Times, 204

L.T.V., 291
Ludwig, D. K., 50, 51, 53
Luxury crops, 281-86, 294-96, 304 (see also cash crops; export agriculture; agribusiness)

M

MAESCO, 288
Malaria, 62-63
Malawi, 340
Malaysia, 62, 149
  export crops, 214
  increase in poverty, 146
  landlord-tenants, 136, 143-44
  pesticide damage, 66
Mali, 16, 46, 86-88, 221, 480
Mallory, Walter, 81
Man and Land, 187, 188-89
Marketing boards, 104, 222
Market system economy
  (see also Trade; inefficiency, inequality)
  divorce of agriculture and nutrition, 103-11, 145-47
  elimination in China, 469
  focus on production, 124-28, 134-48, 165-68
  market prices, 56-58

speculation, 20, 88, 93, 137-38, 212-13, 246-47, 264
Marschall, Fritz, 286
Martinique, 42
Massachusetts, 109
Massey, Ferguson, 52-53, 176
Mauritania, 92
McDonald's, 248, 290
McKee, James, 296
McNamara, Robert, 24, 393, 396, 410, 412
Meat, international trade (see livestock; beef exports; poultry)
Meat vs. non-meat diet, 293
Mechanization, 168-80
  and agribusiness, 174-77
  alternatives to, 173-74
  benefits to large landholders, 174-75
  and China, 176-77
  concentration of ownership, 174
  and Cuba, 177, 199
  and employment, 231-32
  forces behind, 174-77
  in Mexico, 142-43
  and sugar cane, 231
  and tenants, 175
  and U.S. AID, 175
  in U.S. cotton farming, 171
  in U.S. tobacco farming, 171
  and World Bank, 175

Mennonite Central Committee, 453

Mexico
agrarian reconstruction, 123-27
agribusiness in, 126-27, 155-56, 280-82, 284-86, 350, 352
commercial agriculture vs. subsistence, 152, 281-82
export crops to U.S., 65, 155, 156, 280 ff., 295
export platform, 241
government agricultural policies, 123-28, 155-56
Green Revolution, 124-28, 138-43
infant mortality in, 155
landless laborers, 202
land-to-people ratio, 19
large commercial growers, 126-27, 190-92, 280 ff.
livestock, 16
mechanization, 126, 142-43
multinational food processors, 281 ff., 323, 335
National Agricultural Credit Bank, 139
nutrition and well-being of people, 152, 155, 281, 335
peasant resistance, 152
pesticides, 62

price supports, 190
Puebla project, 152
strawberries in, 281-84, 310-12
traditional diet, 153, 282

Milk
banks, 343
consumption by cattle, 58-59
trade, 239, 290

Mill, John Stuart, 102
Minnesota, 497, 498
Mitsubishi, 50
Mixed cropping, 71, 151-53
and employment, 152, 312
Mixed herds, 44-45 (see also Livestock)
Moneylenders, 20, 114-15, 187 (see also Credit)
Monoculture (see also export agriculture; cash crops)
and colonialism, 108-10
effects on traditional diet, 152-53, 222-23
and employment, 28, 152, 231
encouraged by U.S. aid, 415
and environmental destruction, 43, 86
and increased pest damage, 72
and mechanization, 152
U.S. mixed cropping, 72, 151-52, 312

Monopoly, 9, 217, 266, 269-70 (see also Food Producing Resources, Control of)
Monsanto Chemical, 213
Montana, 254
Morgan, Dan, 260
Morley, David, 341
Morocco, 139
Morrell, James, 407 ff. 435
"Most seriously affected" nations (MSA's), 214-15
  and food aid, 382
  as food exporters, 237
Moynihan, Daniel P., 99
Mozambique, 108, 447, 473-74, 486
Mulching, 71-72
Multinational corporations (see also Agribusiness; Foreign Investment)
  in Brazil, 50
  and employment, 26
  in F.A.O., 74, 176
  foreign investment by, 241-42, 370, 476-80, 501-502
  government incentives to, 50
  infant formula, 337
  in LAAD, 423
  in pesticide business, 74 ff.
  in Sahel, 94
Multiple cropping, 158, 172, 390, 482
Mushrooms, 350-51

Myths
  of export agriculture, 226-27
  about fertilizer, 161
  of free trade, 209, 256, 261
  about hunger, 8, 9, 25-29
  of natural advantage, 209 ff.
  about small farmers, 183, 492-93
  of U.S. agricultural productivity, 277-78
  of U.S. oil dependency, 240, 242-43

N

Nabisco, 322-23, 334
National Farmers Organization, 303
National Land for People, 204
National Peach Council (U.S.), 76
National Science Foundation, 326
National Security Council, 359
Nation's Business, 55
Natural advantage, myth of, 209 ff.
Nebraska, 253-54
Nestlé, 50, 218, 334

infant formula campaign, 337-48

New Guinea, 345

New York Times, 4, 154, 180

Nicaragua, 62, 227, 409, 413, 417 ff., 422, 425, 432, 437, 438

Niger, 87-90, 94

Nigeria, 72, 89, 103, 152, 340, 341, 342-43

Nixon, Richard, 4, 244 ff. (see also Soviet Union)

Nomads, 44-47, 86

North Dakota, 498

Nutrition (and Malnutrition), 99-111, 145-47, 320-46
 in Africa, 18-19
 in China, 18, 81-82
 decline in, 333-34, 335
 in India, 334, 338, 379
 in Latin America, 19, 221
 in Mexico, 152, 155, 281, 335
 in U.S., 17-18, 270, 439

O

O'Brien, Patrick, 252

Olsen, Arthur J., 180

Omololu, Adewale, 340

Organization of Petroleum Exporting Countries (OPEC), 216, 239-40

Organizing for Change (see Appendix A)

Organophosphates, 67 (see also Pesticides)

Orsi, Robert, 332

Overgrazing, 44-48 (see also Sahel; Livestock)

Overseas Private Investment Corporation (OPIC), 251, 299, 325, 352-54
 relation to AID, 423, 435

Oxfam, 377-78, 450, 453

P

Paarlberg, Don, 252, 259-60, 387

Paddock, E. and W., 297-99

Pakistan, 451
 CPC International (Rafhan Maize Products), 166, 316-20
 commercialization and the landless, 318
 credit, selective government policies, 186
 food imports, 238
 Green Revolution, 130, 132, 142
 industrial agriculture, 173
 land reform in, 459

mechanization and un-
employment, 28, 142,
175-76
U.S. aid to, 362, 421-22
Palmby, Clarence, 257 ff.
Palmer, Ingrid, 129, 149,
150, 193, 223
Palm oil, 103, 211, 214,
217-18, 251, 404
Panama, 210, 252, 417,
424
Paraguay, 251
"Parity" ratio, 258-59
Parker, Daniel, 443
Pastoralism vs. ranching,
44-47
Payer, Cheryl, 226
Peanuts, 43, 87, 90, 91,
486-87
Peasants' resistance, 110-11,
354-55, 485-87
in Africa, 91, 104, 487
in Bangladesh, 449-50
in El Salvador, 449-50
to foreign aid, 440
in India, 423, 486
in Philippines, 313
in West Indies, 113
Pennsylvania, 350
Pepsi-Cola, 333
Per capita production, 146-
47
Peru, 61, 113, 340, 426,
436
Pesticides, 62-76 (see also
Individual Corpora-
tions; Green Revolu-
tion)
alternatives to, 70-71

basic facts about, 60-61
blind spraying, 72
chemical corporations,
67, 74
and cosmetic standards,
69-70
and crop rotation, 71
DDT, 67
entering food chain, 67
exported from U.S., 65
growing resistance to,
63 ff., 69
health hazard, 64 ff.,
311, 313
Integrated Pest Manage-
ment (IPM), 70-71
Pesticide Working Group
(FAO), 74-75
Phosvel, 65
use in UDC's, 61
Pfizer, Inc., 375
Philippines
banana industry, 218-19,
279
Del Monte, 65, 279, 313,
348
farm productivity, 25
Green Revolution in,
127-28, 132, 138, 156
infant formula, cost, 345
land reform, failure of,
227, 313, 459
mechanization, 175
moneylender usury, 186
OPIC, 353-54
pesticide damage, 66
poverty increase, despite
production gains, 146
rice exports, 457-58

suppression of peanuts, 437-38
U.S. AID program, 175, 413, 421, 422, 426, 430, 435, 437, 438, 442
U.S. military support, 442
World Bank loans to, 175, 395, 437-38
Phosvel, 65
Pillsbury, 304
Pimentel, David, 70
Pineapples, 334, 348-50
Planning, 471-74
Plantations, 103, 105-106, 107, 404 (see also Colonialism; Individual Commodities)
Pioneer Hy-Bred International, 160
Poland, 461
Population, 13-52 (see also Birth Control; Birth Rates)
  "bomb," 4-7
  growth, 30-32, 33-36
  growth of urban, 25-26
  rationale for large families, 30-33
Population Council, 33
Population-to-land ratios, 18-19, 25-28
Portugal
  land reform, 200
Potatoes, 167
  processed, 326
Potter, Gene, 303

Poultry industry, 292-93, 304-307, 371 ff.
Poverty of Power, 242
Price cycles, 56-58
Price Supports, 54, 190-91, 245-47, 267-68
Proctor and Gamble, 218
"Production strategy," 124-28, 134-48, 165-68
  "More Food Means More Hunger," 145-47
Productivity
  better farming, 150
  in China, 201
  in Japan, 25
  and land reform, 197-201
  and mechanization, 171-72
  per worker, 25
  of small farmers, 169, 183 ff.
Profitability
  as determinant of investment, 57, 155-56, 405
  in food processing, 166-67, 217, 269, 321-22, 324, 327-28, 333-34
  of growing vegetables in Mexico, 280-81
  and infant formula, 342, 348
  of soft drinks, 330-32
  stressed by AID, 426
Prosterman, Roy, 421
Protein-calorie deficiency, 18, 19-20 (see also Infant malnutrition)

Protein sources, 23, 47, 293
    (see also Meat vs.
    non-meat diet)
complementary, 152-53,
    320 ff.
and infant formula, 338,
    342
Public Law (P.L.), 480
    (see United States
    food aid)
Puddling, 157
Puebla project, 152
Pulse crops, 151, 293 (see
    also Fertilizer)

Q

Quaker Oats, 375

R

Rafhan, 166, 316-19 (see
    also CPC Interna-
    tional)
Raikes, P. L., 464-65
Ralston Purina, 155, 292-
    94, 297, 304, 307,
    353, 371, 375, 423
Raw materials
  U.S. need for, 242, 248
Rents (land), 136-37 (see
    also Green Revolu-
    tion; Landlords)

Repressive governments,
    383-86, 412-38
  in Bangladesh, 384-85
  in Chile, 406, 428, 429
  in South Korea, 435
  in Nicaragua, 432, 437-
    38
  in Philippines, 430, 437-
    38
  in South Africa, 435
  U.S. support for foreign
    police forces, 437-38
  World Bank loans to,
    406-409
Resnick, Idrian, 447 ff. (see
    also Economic Devel-
    opment Bureau)
Rice, 20-22, 51, 56, 66,
    102, 156
Rice virus, 156
Road building
  Indian resistance to, 423
  trans-Sahel, 91
  U.S. AID-financed, 421-
    22, 430
  who benefits most, 422
Road to Survival, 83
Rockefeller Foundation, 4,
    125, 148, 149
Rockefellers, 124, 307
Rodney, Walter, 103, 105,
    113
Rotary weeder, 173
Rubber, 103, 110, 179, 214,
    398-99, 421
Rudell, William, 377
Rural electrification, 418-
    20, 454

Rural elites, 440-41 (see
    also Landlords; Food-
    Producing Resources,
    control of)
    supported by World
    Bank, 390, 393
Rural industry, 26-27, 418-
    19
Rural unemployment (see
    Mechanization; Indus-
    trialization)
Rwanda, 210, 222

S

Safeway Stores, 204, 425
Sahel, 84-95
    agribusiness investment,
        94-95, 286-88
    cash crops in, 87-95
    colonialism in, 45
    drought in, 16, 46, 88
    exports from, 16, 87, 89-
        92, 94, 238, 286-88
    foreign exchange, mis-
        use, 91-92
    peasant resistance, 91
    population-to-land ratio,
        18
    speculation on food, 88,
        93
    U.S. aid, 46
Saline seepage, 254
Saudi Arabia, 435
Scarcity, myth of, 13-76
    caused by hoarding, 55

of food and land, 13
    as illusion, 54-56
    overproduction and sur-
        plus, 13, 54, 57-58,
        121-22, 154, 165-68,
        256 ff., 267-68, 283,
        365 ff., 457-58
    triage, 359-60
Scheduled spraying, 72 (see
    also Pesticides)
Science, 6
Seeds
    apomictic, 161
    banks, 160
    genetic loss, 132, 160
    HRV's, 129-34, 157-58,
        172
    HYV's, 129-34
    locally improved varie-
        ties, 149-52, 156-57
Seeds of Change, 175
Self-reliance (food), 457-
    87
    and agribusiness, 478-80
    basic education, 463,
        470-71
    in China, 462, 465-67,
        469, 471
    in Cuba, 461, 470
    and development funds,
        476-84
    equality, 465-67
    fundamentals of, 457-76
    and industrial countries,
        475-76
    and industrialization,
        469-71
    Mozambique, 472-73
    and nutrition, 468

participation, 463-65
not self-sufficiency, 457-58
and social planning, 471-74
in Tanzania, 465
and trade, 467-68, 472
in the U.S., 497-98
in Vietnam, 462, 472-73, 481-84
what is, 457-76
Senegal, 91-92, 221-22, 286-88, 486-87 (see also Sahel)
Sen, Sudhir, 186
Servbest Foods, 42
Sharecroppers (see also Small farms; Tenant farming; Colonialism)
affects of Green Revolution, 136
in Bangladesh, 21
in the U.S., 253
Shell Oil Co., 66, 176
Sidick, Abba, 91
Sierra Leone, 343, 345
Singapore, 241
Sisters of the Precious Blood, 346
Slash and burn, 50
Slater, Charles C., 336
Slavery, 18, 113
Small farms
AID, stated focus of, 413, 414-15
"demonstration effect," 193-94
excluded from loans and credits, 185-87, 394

and LAAD, 424
losing land, 22, 28
myth of, 492
productivity of, 169, 183-85
in U.S., going out of business, 439
vs. large farms, 183-96
World Bank, stated focus of, 394-95
Soft drinks, 330-33
Soil (see also Ecological destruction; Fertilizer)
bank, U.S., 55
depletion, 16-17, 40-43, 51-52, 162, 253-54, 285-86
improvement, 151, 157
Somalia, 210, 471
Somoza, Anastasio, 425 (see also Nicaragua)
South Africa, 384, 435
Southern Pacific Corporation, 203
South Korea, 350, 354, 371-73, 374, 382, 383, 407, 435, 437, 442
Southland Stores (Seven-Eleven), 425
Soviet Union, 342
and Cuba, 232-33
grain purchase from U.S,. 55-56
low agricultural productivity, 196
production stagnation on State farms, 461, 469
Sowing the Wind, 306

Soybeans, 16, 153, 223, 250-51
Speculation
in commodities, 212
in food, Bangladesh, 20
in food, Sahel, 89, 93
in grain trade, 246-47, 259-60
in land, 137-38, 264
Spitzer, Robert L., 364
Sri Lanka
better farming, 151
British colonial policies, 105-106
decline in consumption standards, 146
HRV's, replaced by local varieties, 149-51
tea plantations, working conditions, 221, 226-27
and World Bank, 410
Standard Fruit Co. (Dole), 210
Standard Oil Co., 204
State Farms, 461
Stavis, Benedict, 198
Strawberries, 281-82, 284-85, 309-11
Subsistence agriculture vs. commercial, 106-11, 144, 220-21, 228-29, 279-80, 289-99, 334-35, 396-99, 486-87
Sudan, 426
Sugar, 41, 42, 108, 199, 222, 230-31, 397, 398
and soft drinks, 330
Sugar Without Slaves, 108

Sunkist, Inc., 69
Sweden
imported food, 238
Swedish International Development Agency, 390-91, 447-48

T

Tachai, 198, 481
Taiwan
agribusiness in, 350-51
food imports, 372
Green Revolution, 133, 149
labor-intensive farming, 25
land reform, 464
small farm productivity, 25, 183-84
Tanzania, 446-47
export crop production, 213, 223, 228
food crops vs. cash crops, 102-104, 109-10
grain storage project, EDB, 447-48
infant formula control, 345
pesticides, 74-75
self-reliance, problems, 464-65
World Bank loans, 401-402
Ujamaa villages, 464-65

Taxation (see also Colonialism; Green Revolution)
  havens and concessions, 264, 280
  U.S. farmlands, 498
  for U.S. food-processing research, 327-28
Tea, 221, 397
Technology (see Appropriate technology)
Tenant farming, 174, 187-88, 392 (see also Small farms; Sharecroppers)
Ten Times More Beautiful, 481-84
Thailand, 16-17, 131, 252, 354, 413
  and small farmer, 183, 349
  U.S. aid, 429, 431, 437
  World Bank, 403
Third World (see Underdeveloped countries)
This Hungry World, 4, 188, 194, 309
Thornbrough, Albert A., 53
Thrips, 69
Tobacco, 91, 171, 397
Togo, 151
Tomatoes, 69-70
Tractors, 175 ff. (see also Mechanization)
Trade (see Speculation; Export Crops; Commodities)
  commodity substitutes (synthetic), 213

Food First policies and, 467-68
foreign exchange, 91-92, 210, 214-15, 220 ff., 226, 231
and the IMF, 435-37
international, declining terms of trade, 212, 215
myth of Free Trade, 244 ff., 261-63
natural advantage, myth of, 209 ff., 214-15
U.S. restrictions, 216
Triage, 359-60
Tubewells (see Irrigation)
Tunisia, 128, 149
Turkey, 150

U

Uganda, 103, 210
Underdeveloped countries (see also Colonialism; Development Models; Myths; Food Produc- in Resources; Export Agriculture; and individual countries, regions)
  advertising in, 321 ff.
  debt burden of, 361-62, 435-36
  declining birth rates in, 33-36

definitions, 99-101, 115-17

development assistance, 388-444

food aid, 237, 363-83

growth rates (GNP), 146-47, 384

as markets, 320-21, 334-35, 402-403, 426

as source for raw materials, 426, 431

Unemployment, 171, 231-32 (see Employment; Mechanization)

Unilever (United Africa Company), 104, 217-18, 226-27, 334, 404

Union of Banana Exporting Countries (UBEC), 219

Unitarian Universalist Service Committee in El Salvador, 449

United Brands (United Fruit), 210, 219, 290, 291, 295, 300

United Nations (see also Food and Agricultural Organization)

Food and Agricultural Organization, 61, 74-75, 176, 307, 368

Fund for Population Activities, 32

Protein Advisory Group, 342

Relief and Rehabilitation Administration (UNRRA), 378

Research Institute for Social Development, 129

World Food Program (WFP), 379-80

United States (see also individual states; food power; Americans, Responsibilities of)

agricultural legislation, 54, 498

AFL-CIO, 353

balance of payments, 240-45, 248, 252

capital exports, 241

consumer prices, 260, 268-69

corporate control of production and trade, 255-56

dollar devaluation, 245-46

as exporter of agricultural goods, 58-59, 237-74

farm costs, 268-69

farm debt, 263-64

farm inheritance taxes, 498

farmers' strike, 266-67

fertilizer use, 161-63

food aid, 237

food and energy, 272

as importer of agricultural goods, 16, 167, 238-73, 289

income inequality, 263

land ownership, 202, 264, 497

land reform, 202-205
military support, 244, 498-99
nutrition, 17-18, 270, 439
oil dependency, myth of, 239-40
poultry industry, 304-307
price supports (U.S.), 54, 244-47, 267-68
small farms, 261 ff.
soil depletion, 162-63
Soviet grain purchase, 55-66, 245, 256-61
surplus food, 57-58
tax laws, 352
trade restrictions, 216
as world's breadbasket, 237-39
United States Agency for International Development (see U.S. AID; Aid, foreign; World Bank; Voluntary Agencies)
United States Department of Agriculture (USDA), 252, 256-61, 265, 354
Commodity Credit Corporation, 245, 280-81, 371
Foreign Agricultural Service, 247-48
and Soviet grain purchase, 55, 245, 256-61
study of small farm communities, 265

United States Department of Commerce, 438-39
United States Environmental Protection Agency, 64-65, 67
United States Export-Import Bank, 428
loans to Chile, 382, 428
no congressional review, 434-35
United States Federal Tariff Commission, 351
United States Feed Grains Council, 370-71
United States Food and Drug Administration, 70
United States military support, 244, 437-38, 442
United States National Reclamation Act, 203-205
United States Overseas Private Investment Corporation, 352-54
United States Senate Select Committee on Nutrition and Human Needs, 270
Upper Volta, 88, 93, 108, 130, 151, 223, 367
Uruguay, 438
and World Bank, 406
U.S. AID, 412-44
alternatives to aid, 499
benefitting large farmers, 416

commercializing small
farmers, 415
congressional presenta-
tion on, 412, 418, 420
farm mechanization,
174-75, 414-15
and food-for-work, 414
and insecticides, 62
projects in,
Bangladesh, 419, 454
Bolivia, 417
Cameroon, 421
Colombia, 419
Costa Rica, 419
Haiti, 415
Indonesia, 418, 420-
21
Israel and Egypt, 434
Liberia, 421
Mexico, 152
Nicaragua, 62, 417,
422
Pakistan, 421-22
Peru, 426
Philippines, 421, 422
in Sahel, 46
Thailand, 429 ff.
Puebla project, 152
and Rafhan, 166, 317-
19
satellite projects, 421
and Security Supporting
Assistance, 374, 429,
434
support for repressive
regimes, 412, 421, 422,
429-30, 431-34
strengthening social
power structure, 433,
440
undercutting progressive
governments, 413,
429-30, 431-32
and unemployment, 418-
19
and U.S. corporations,
413, 423-26

V

Valdez, Abelardo L., 361-
62
Van Dam, André, 323
Vavilov, N. I., 159
Velsicol Chemical Corp.,
65
Venezuela, 113
Vicker, Ray, 4, 180, 188,
194, 309
Vietnam, 201
as colony, 103, 114
compared to Thanjaver,
India, 481-84
and fertilizer, 483
Green Revolution, 131
land reform, 196-97,
462-63
large farming units, 195-
96
and self-reliance, 482-
84, 486
U.S. war in, 241, 244,
379, 380, 381

Voelker, A. J., 101
Vogh, William, 83
Volkswagen, 50, 290
Voluntary agencies, 422-23, 444-54

W

Wall Street Journal, 309, 321, 398, 401
Ward, Barbara, 24
Ware, Helen, 31
War on Hunger, 415
War on Want, 337
Washington Post, 379
Washington (state), 72, 203
Waste (see also Inefficiency; Food surplus)
  when harvest unprofitable, 57-58
Weather
  effect on food supplies, 56
  not direct cause of famine, 79-80
  protection from in China, 82-83
  and Soviet grain purchase (1972), 245, 256
Wellford, Harrison, 306
Wells, 46 (see also Irrigation)
West Africa Cocoa Control Board, 105
West Indies, 109-10, 113

Wheat, 157-58, 372, 374-75
Wilkes, H. Garrison, 158, 159, 160
Williams Commission, 244-46
Winski, Joseph, 321-22
World Bank
  in Bangladesh, 389-93, 395-96
  and cash crops, 397
  commercialization of agriculture, 396-400
  credit to agribusiness, 288, 404
  credit to smallholders, 393-94
  export financing, 369, 400, 402-403
  farm mechanization loans, 175-76
  and human rights campaign, 406-409
  International Finance Corporation, 403-404
  and the landless, 395-96
  lending priorities, 399-400
  loans to Ethiopia, 288
  loans to repressive governments, 406-409
  loans for livestock, 290-91, 397
  and national economic planning, 405-406
  no accountability, 409-11, 434-35
  reckless lender, 400-402, 453-54

studies, 43, 184, 192, 366
support to Chile, 429
support for rural elites,
    390-93
U.S. veto power in, 428
World Council of
    Churches, 173
World Food Conference
    (1974), 7, 379
World Food Program, 379-
    80
World Health Organization
    (WHO), 337
*World Hunger, Causes and
    Remedies,* 7
World Neighbors, 377, 453
Women
    in Bangladesh, 450
    and breastfeeding, 341-
        45
    in China, 35
    exploited labor, 230, 310
    and Green Revolution,
        144
    in Guinea-Bissau, 449

powerlessness of, 32-33
in Sri Lanka, 221, 227
undernourishment of, 32
wages on plantations,
    221-22
Wrigley's chewing gum,
    477

Y

Yeutter, Clayton, 374
Yugoslavia, 461

Z

Zaire, 225, 404
    and World Bank, 408
Zambia, 156, 333, 345
Zwarthuis, Robert F., 288

THE INSTITUTE FOR FOOD AND DEVELOPMENT POLICY is an independent, not-for-profit research, documentation, and education center for issues that link together U.S. agriculture, hunger in America, world hunger, and underdevelopment.

The Institute publishes occasional pamphlets and articles, maintains a speakers' bureau, and has prepared a twenty-minute slide-tape show. All royalties and speaking honoraria go directly toward the support of the Institute's work.

To receive more information about the Institute, please fill out and send us this coupon.

Name ....
Street ....
City/State .... Zip ......
Comments   ....
....
....
....
....

Send to: Institute for Food and Development Policy
2588 Mission St.
San Francisco, Calif. 94110